MICHIEL HORN

Academic Freedom in Canada: A History

UNIVERSITY OF TORONTO PRESS
Toronto Buffalo London

© University of Toronto Press Incorporated 1999
Toronto Buffalo London
Printed in Canada

ISBN 0-8020-0726-0

Printed on acid-free paper

Canadian Cataloguing in Pulication Data

Horn, Michiel, 1939–
  Academic freedom in Canada : a history

  Includes bibliographical references and index.
  ISBN 0-8020-0726-0

  1. Academic freedom – Canada – History.   I. Title.

  LC72.5.C3H67 1999   378.1'21   C98-932443-5

This book has been published with the help of a grant from the Humanities and Social
Sciences Federation of Canada, using funds provided by the Social Sciences and
Humanities Research Council of Canada.

University of Toronto Press acknowledges the financial assistance to its publishing
program of the Canada Council for the Arts and the Ontario Arts Council.

For Cornelia

and in memory of
Leonard Marsh (1905–1982)
Ken McNaught (1918–1997)
and
Frank Scott (1899–1985)

Contents

Preface

My interest in academic freedom began more than thirty years ago, when I was a graduate student at the University of Toronto. Under Ramsay Cook's supervision, I wrote a doctoral dissertation on the League for Social Reconstruction, a Depression-era group of left-wing intellectuals. Their views were unpopular with the powerful. Three of the LSR's members, King Gordon, Leonard Marsh, and Eugene Forsey, lost their university teaching positions amidst suspicions that their social and economic heresies were at issue. Other LSR academics were silenced, and the most prominent among them, the University of Toronto historian Frank Underhill, was in 1940–1 at the centre of an unsuccessful attempt to force him to resign.

One of the chapters of my dissertation and of the book I later wrote dealt with 'professors in the public eye'; in it, issues of academic freedom loomed large. That no history of academic freedom in Canada existed struck me as regrettable, and from the late 1960s on I occasionally urged some colleague or other to write that history. Since no one volunteered for the task, I decided in 1984 to tackle it myself.

Early encouragement came from Donald C. Savage, a historian who was the executive secretary of the Canadian Association of University Teachers (CAUT) from 1972 to 1997. In the summer of 1984 we lunched at Toronto's Auberge Gavroche (now, alas, defunct) in the company of a mutual friend, Jeffrey Sack, in order to discuss the history of academic freedom, a subject that interested all three of us. Don wanted to write a book examining academic freedom in the recent past; I staked my claim to the period ending in the early 1960s. We were wise to divide the subject, for it turned out to be much larger than I, for one, had suspected. I have nevertheless written an extended postscript dealing with some of the major developments since 1965, and I hope that Don will forgive me and, where necessary, set me straight in *his* book.

At the outset I drew up an ambitious schedule that included visits to the archives of almost every Canadian university in existence before the mid-1960s. In time, ambition yielded to reality. At several universities, access to official records was unreasonably restricted, but at least as important was the fact that in almost every archive I needed more time than I had anticipated. I decided to restrict my in-depth research to a dozen universities – among them provincial, nonsectarian private, and Protestant institutions – and on the whole to exclude those that were Roman Catholic.

That the Catholic universities were mainly outside my ken was a view I had reached even before reading Charles E. Curran's assessment: 'Before the mid-1960s, Catholic higher education and its leaders in the United States were strongly opposed to the concept of academic freedom.'[1] This also applied to Canada's Catholic universities, whereas in Canada's Protestant colleges academic freedom was by the early twentieth century a recognized and even valued principle. The concept was not completely absent from the Catholic universities, but as late as 1964 Paul Lacoste of Laval University remarked on 'the most fundamental restraint' to which professors in Catholic institutions were still subject, 'namely ideological control.'[2] Tellingly, Laurence K. Shook's encyclopedic history of Catholic higher education in Canada has no index entry for academic freedom. One consequence of my decision largely to exclude the Catholic institutions has been that Canada's major French-language universities – Laval, Montreal, and Ottawa – appear only occasionally in this volume. In spite of this, I believe my book does justice to the complexities of the subject.

My interest in academic freedom has been practical as well as scholarly. I was elected to a three-year term on the CAUT's Academic Freedom and Tenure Committee in 1984 and again in 1987, and for six years I also served as the committee's liaison with the Comité de la liberté universitaire of the Fédération des associations de professeurs des universités du Québec. The many hours of discussion and debate in Ottawa and Montreal enriched my understanding of the subject.

A narrow definition of academic freedom limits it to the freedom of professors to teach their subjects, carry out research, and publish its results, subject to professionally sanctioned limits. Over the years, academic freedom has come to include the freedom to participate in public life and, perhaps still controversially, to criticize the institutions in which professors work. A freedom to do something implies a potential for offence. Over the decades, various people and groups have tried to restrict academic freedom because they disliked the intellectual or moral discomfort it is capable of producing, or because they believed that it got in the way of functions that universities can fulfil more successfully in its absence.

A current example is so-called political correctness. Some of this is no more than an expression of the dislike of hearing or reading things thought to be offensive, but some of it expresses the conviction that all knowledge is political and that what matters is to entrench one's own intellectual position. People who hold the latter view deprecate the disinterested search for knowledge and truth, which has been the chief justification of academic freedom for a century and more. Their influence, though, is limited.

Another challenge to academic freedom comes from the champions of 'economic correctness' and their insistence that universities become more business-like and be subject to market discipline. This often includes a characterization of teaching as a service to the student as consumer, whose satisfaction and success in finding employment become the tests of teacher performance.

I reject both forms of correctness. I believe that the disinterested search for knowledge, however difficult, is central to the purpose of the university, that professors should state their findings and opinions clearly, and that our students are not our customers, whatever else they may be. Scholarship, I have found, is similar in several ways to raising children. Each takes a lot of time and effort; each can be highly frustrating, and each is greatly rewarding. Neither can be validated by reference to 'the bottom line.' Whatever other uses children and scholarly projects may have, they must be valued for themselves. It is in the spirit of such perhaps old-fashioned convictions that I have written this book.

Acknowledgments

This book would not have been possible without a lot of help. The Social Sciences and Humanities Research Council of Canada funded much of my travel and some of my research assistance, the rest of it being supplied through York University's graduate program in history. The research grants committee of Glendon College awarded supplementary funding. My work in the University of Manitoba Archives was partly paid for by a Thomas Glendenning Hamilton Research Grant. A Glendon College Leave Fellowship allowed me to start writing, and a sabbatical enabled me to complete the first draft. This book has been published with the help of a grant from the Humanities and Social Sciences Federation of Canada, using funds provided by the Social Sciences and Humanities Research Council of Canada. Finally, I am grateful for my tenure, which enabled me to complete a project that proved to be far more time-consuming than I had anticipated when I began.

I owe a debt to many archivists, but the University of British Columbia's Laurenda Daniells and Chris Hives went so far beyond what I had any right to expect that I must thank them by name. Bennett McCardle gave me insight into the trials, tribulations, and occasional triumphs of archivists and commented sensibly on many other things as well. The staff of the Leslie Frost Library at Glendon College were always helpful. As president of the University of Winnipeg, Robin Farquhar gave me access to the minutes of the Board of Regents of United College for the years 1958–9. As president of the University of Alberta, Myer Horowitz allowed me to examine several closed files in that university's archives. Richard Allen, Maureen Aytenfisu, Olivia R. Barr, Susanne Borrmann, Terry Crowley, Geoffrey Ewen, Raymond Houde, Kenneth McLaughlin, David L. McQueen, Barry Moody, Norman Penner, Escott Reid, Henry Roper, Ronald Rudin, Albert V. Tucker, and P.B. Waite drew my attention to incidents or documents of which I might otherwise have remained ignorant.

Over the years I have spoken or corresponded about academic freedom with men and women far too numerous to list, but I do want to single out my brother Jack, an art historian at the University of Guelph, who listened to me often and with exemplary patience. Various draft chapters and segments were read by Irving Abella, Richard Allen, Harry W. Arthurs, Paul Axelrod, A.G. Bedford, Alwyn Berland, Jean Burnet, David M. Cameron, Douglas L. Cole, Ramsay Cook, Sandra Djwa, Judith Fingard, R. Douglas Francis, Stanley Brice Frost, John Furedy, John Grube, Michael Hayden, Tom Hull, Roger Hutchinson, William D. Irvine, Cornelius Jaenen, Charles Levi, Martin Loney, A.E. Malloch, Michael Marrus, Kenneth McNaught, Desmond Morton, David J. Mullan, William Packer, Alison Prentice, Donald C. Savage, Marlene Shore, Ernest Sirluck, J. Percy Smith, Daniel Soberman, Lalit Srivastava, Louise Starkman, Kenneth B. Strand, Jon Thompson, Chris Tollefson, P.B. Waite, Reg Whitaker, and Jerald Zaslove. Although I did not always heed their advice, I always appreciated their comments. I acknowledge the work of my research assistants, Jamie Glazov, Kristopher Churchill, and the incomparable Charles Levi, as well as the superb support provided by Marina Sakuta, secretary and factotum of the Glendon College history department. None of these people is responsible for whatever flaws my book may still contain.

At the University of Toronto Press, the book has benefited from the efforts of Gerry Hallowell, Emily Andrew, Darlene Zeleney, Frances Mundy, and my copy editor, Carlotta Lemieux. I am grateful to the two anonymous readers who assessed the manuscript and made a number of suggestions for improving it.

In addition to professional obligations, I owe debts of a more personal nature. As I worked in archives from Victoria to Halifax, friends offered me a drink or two, a meal, sometimes a bed, and always good conversation. If I mention by name Alayne and Rob Hamilton, Judy and Martin Bergbusch, Belle and Chris Meiklejohn, and Charlotte Glencross and Jon Thompson, it does not mean I am not grateful to the others.

My sons, Daniel and Patrick, deserve a special note. 'The academic book of freedom,' as Daniel titled it some years ago, would probably have been completed sooner had they not been born while I was working on it. But their lives have more than compensated for any delay they have caused, and the more measured pace that they imposed has helped to improve the book.

The contribution made by my wife, Cornelia Schuh, has been huge throughout. Although her own work is demanding, she put up with my absences as I left on one research trip after another, was always willing to listen to my findings when I returned, read my final draft with care, and commented judiciously on it. This book is dedicated to her, my best and dearest critic, and to the memory of three late friends who are part of the history of academic freedom in Canada and who taught me much about my adopted country.

Michiel Horn
Toronto, November 1998

ACADEMIC FREEDOM IN CANADA

1

Introduction: Not a Burning Question

'Academic freedom is not ... a burning question in Canadian universities.' President Carleton Stanley of Dalhousie University was writing to John Wesley Dafoe, the editor of the *Winnipeg Free Press*. 'Despite criticism I have heard, I think our record is pretty clean that way. But ... it's not a question that we can neglect.'[1]

Stanley was trying to organize a session on academic freedom for the 1937 annual meeting of the National Conference of Canadian Universities (NCCU), scheduled for the end of May. His efforts were meeting with scant success. Although he and the NCCU secretary, the Queen's University economist William A. Mackintosh, had begun to plan in January, one proposed speaker after another (Dafoe included) turned them down.

One of those who declined, Governor General Lord Tweedsmuir, wrote: 'I am very glad that your Conference is taking up the subject of academic freedom, for there is much need of plain speaking on that subject today.' Thus encouraged, Stanley soldiered on. But after President Walter C. Murray of Saskatchewan and Principal Robert C. Wallace of Queen's also begged off, an exasperated Stanley confided to Mackintosh, 'I have given up the subject of academic freedom.'[2]

In the end, he had to content himself with saying a few words about the topic in his presidential address. An interest in academic freedom, he asserted, was in the light of recent events in Europe 'nothing but the instinct for self-preservation. No freedom, no university.'[3] No doubt his listeners, university presidents and professors, applauded. But Stanley's failure to find a speaker suggests that interest in the subject was not intense.

In the two decades after that 1937 meeting, interest remained at a generally low level, not only among presidents but also among professors. The issue arose occasionally here and there, but when the Canadian Association of University Teachers (CAUT) got going in 1951, it at first paid little attention to academic freedom. For several years the two most pressing issues were salaries (which in real terms were lower around 1950 than at any other time in this century except for a brief period after the 1914–18 war) and benefits, especially medical plans and pensions. 'Academic freedom has become one of the central issues of our time,' the U.S. historians Richard Hofstadter and Walter P. Metzger wrote in 1955.[4] This may have been true in the United States, but it was certainly not the case in Canada. Brecht's *Three-Penny Opera* notes aptly, 'Erst kommt das Fressen; dann kommt die Moral' (first grub; then ethics).

Not until June 1958 did the CAUT national council authorize the drafting of a statement on academic freedom and tenure; three months later, a committee at the University of Western Ontario assumed the task. When it reported in November, interest in its mandate had risen markedly. The reason was the dismissal of the historian Harry S. Crowe from United College, Winnipeg, in the summer of 1958 and the CAUT-sponsored inquiry into it by the Saskatchewan economist Vernon C. Fowke and the Toronto law professor Bora Laskin. Since then, academic freedom has been a matter of continual concern to the Canadian professoriate. During the last few years, interest has been especially high, for this freedom has been under challenge from within the university and from without. The subject is likely to remain contentious for years to come.

Scholars have given two main meanings to academic freedom: the freedom of universities from external control, and the freedom of teachers and researchers to do their work. The former, university autonomy, is a fascinating subject in its own right, one with implications for academic freedom in the latter sense.[5] However, it is the second meaning that concerns us here.

'Academic freedom is a modern term for an ancient idea,' wrote Richard Hofstadter. 'Although the struggle for freedom in teaching can be traced at least as far back as Socrates' eloquent defense of himself against the charge of corrupting the youth of Athens, its continuous history is concurrent with the history of universities since the twelfth century.'[6] The desire for academic freedom has at various times involved an effort to secure freedom from control by church, state, lay governing boards, the parents of students, and even students themselves, and to validate a claim to the pursuit of knowledge no matter where it led. Professors have invoked academic freedom in order to free themselves from religious tests, to resist the authority of administrators and boards, to claim independence in their research, to control the content of their courses, to be judged by their peers and not by outsiders, and to be assessed on their achievements and not their beliefs.

Inherent in the modern concept of academic freedom is a scepticism about revealed or received truth and about authority founded on it. It is rooted in the Enlightenment as well as in the realization, earned in the course of two centuries of religious wars in Europe, that exclusive claims to truth are murderously disruptive not only of society but also of intellectual work. Professors have used the concept of academic freedom to justify their right to participate in public life and express opinions on matters of public interest. However, they have also invoked the idea in order to criticize the university's administrative officers or governors and as the basis for a claim to increased participation in the governance of their institutions.

Champions of academic freedom contend that disinterested inquiry and comment are essential if a society is not to become intellectually and ideologically hidebound. Most working people cannot afford to assume a stance of disinterest. Whether they are self-employed or employees, the need to earn a living usually takes precedence over the inclination to indulge their curiosity, to challenge authority or received wisdom, or to state the truth about some subject as they see it. Without academic freedom, only the independently wealthy or those unconcerned about their financial and professional prospects would be able to pursue research of unpredictable duration and expense and of uncertain payoff or to make public comments that might prove unwelcome.

'The itch to be intolerant of something is very deep indeed,' writes the historian Conrad Russell.[7] Almost all people fear or dislike the unhindered discussion of certain ideas or the implications of some lines of research. In consequence, they may try to control or eliminate sources of intellectual or emotional discomfort or to end the 'waste' of money implied by the subtly derogatory term 'idle curiosity.' They may seek to prevent manifestations of antireligious or antigovernment sentiment, of bias against business, and, more recently, of racism or sexism. Some presidents or governing boards will try to prevent the harm, real or imagined, that may befall a university if its professors express unpopular views or pursue troubling research.

Challenges to authority within the university present a different problem. Accustomed to a workplace in which open disagreement with one's superiors is dangerous and criticism of 'the organization' is all but unthinkable, many people have little sympathy for men and women who take issue with presidents or deans, or criticize the institutions within which they earn their bread. Why should professors be able to do something that is denied to other employees?

The defenders of academic freedom assert that its benefits are so important that its restriction is not in the public interest. The critical spirit that is at the core of academic freedom is or should be at the core of university work. To hobble that spirit when it touches on difficult subjects or when it requires seemingly endless resources for research that may lead nowhere, or even when it puts the university's administrators or governors in a bad light, is to threaten it everywhere, to the detriment of the university and society at large.

People who seek to restrict the range of discussion, to maintain existing power relationships, or to bend scholarly pursuits to nonscholarly ends have taken a dim view of academic freedom and especially of a broad definition of the concept. Politicians, religious leaders, business and professional people, newspaper owners and editors, university administrators, members of governing boards, parents, students, and all too often even professors themselves have at times found some exercise of academic freedom offensive, inconvenient, or excessively costly and have sought to curtail it.

The method has been predictable: there are demands for restrictions and sanctions, for the disciplining or even dismissal of professors who offend. Usually, such demands are accompanied by the claim either that academic freedom is not at issue or that something objected to is actually an abuse of that freedom. This reflects the general if unfocused belief that academic freedom is a Good Thing. As the sociologist and university president Lorna Marsden has pointed out, people tend to accept academic freedom in principle even though they often dislike it in practice.[8]

Legitimate restrictions on academic freedom do exist. Academic freedom does not imply that the campus must be host to any and all behaviour short of the actually illegal. It does not justify defamation or the counselling of insurrection, or doing as little work as possible. Nor does it confer the liberty to teach whatever catches one's fancy. Course content may depend on the choices made by individual professors, but the subjects to be taught must be authorized by academic bodies, departments, faculty councils, and senates, which also act as assessors of the qualifications and competence of professors. And civility, which is sometimes seen as an unacceptable limit on academic freedom, may in fact be one of its necessary conditions. The 'heckler's veto,' for example, is a negation of academic freedom, not an exercise of it.

It is an abuse of academic freedom to bully junior colleagues or students, to tailor one's work to nonacademic needs or purposes, and to use one's position in order to attach spurious weight to nonscholarly opinions. Pulling rank has no legitimate place in academic debate, and harassment is illegal. Professors who have obtained outside support for their research and then fudge or withhold their results for fear of losing future funding, and those who pull their punches lest they endanger their consulting fees, are subverting academic freedom. As for using one's academic title in the hope of getting an audience for views on issues unrelated to one's area of competence, the abuse may be trivial, but the practice is objectionable.

The modern Canadian concept of academic freedom has three main sources. One is German in origin though adapted by Americans; the second is essentially British, and the third is largely North American. German and U.S. ideas upholding a research-based professionalism were combined with British traditions of academic free speech and with claims to faculty autonomy and self-government.

Reformed in accordance with the ideas of the Prussian scientist, explorer, and public servant Alexander von Humboldt, the German universities, particularly those in the Protestant states, came in the nineteenth century to emphasize *Lehrfreiheit* – the freedom to teach and publish – and the essential role of research as their basis. *Lehrfreiheit* was held to be 'the distinctive prerogative of the academic profession, and the essential condition of all universities.' (Students enjoyed *Lernfreiheit*, the freedom to learn, the essence of which was freedom from administrative control in the learning process, and which largely governs student life in Germany to this day.)[9]

The Humboldtian ideal influenced the research-oriented universities that took form in the United States after the Civil War. Until that time, the issue of academic freedom had usually been bound up with sectarian conflict. Those who claimed an enlarged freedom for faculty members argued that their personal convictions should matter less than their intellectual achievements. This view was now joined by the assertions that professors should not be penalized if their research findings, honestly arrived at, challenged received wisdom and that the religious or philosophical views of professors were no concern of universities worthy of the name.

The first American university to incorporate the Humboldtian ideal was Johns Hopkins, founded in 1876. Most of its early professors had studied in Germany, and 'what it called the graduate school was the equivalent of the German faculty of philosophy – broad in its range of specialties, nonutilitarian in its objectives, devoted to the tasks of research.'[10] Johns Hopkins made the professor's needs and aspirations central to the academic enterprise.

By 1900 more than a dozen major graduate faculties had come into existence, adapting the German model to North American conditions by fusing graduate schools to undergraduate colleges. All asserted the freedom of professors to teach and carry out research. Yet even in the research universities, the professors did not get full *Lehrfreiheit*. German academics could, in the classroom, seek converts to their own philosophical views, but their American counterparts were expected to assume a neutral position with respect to the subjects they taught. 'It is not the function of the teacher to settle philosophical and political controversies for the pupil, or even to recommend to him any one set of opinions as better than any other,' Charles Eliot said as he assumed the presidency of Harvard University. 'The notion that education consists in the authoritative inculcation of what the teacher deems true may be logical and appropriate in a convent, or a seminary for priests, but it is intolerable in universities.'[11] This view enjoyed wide support.

The variation from the German model is explained in large part by the absence of *Lernfreiheit*, the German student's freedom to learn. American (and Canadian) students were a captive audience in a way that German students were not, and thus the perceived drawbacks of indoctrination were greater on this side of the Atlantic Ocean. If U.S. professors faced greater restrictions within the university, however, they were able to claim greater freedom than their German colleagues outside it, for the latter were under an implicit obligation to maintain political neutrality. Although some German professors were active in politics, a few in opposition to the government, 'it was not generally assumed that *Lehrfreiheit* condoned or protected such activities ... It was generally assumed that professors as civil servants were bound to be circumspect and loyal, and that participation in partisan politics spoiled the habits of scholarship.' The famous sociologist Max Weber commented acidly, '"Freedom of scholarship" exists in Germany within the limits of political and ecclesiastical acceptability. Outside these limits there is none.'[12]

In contrast with the state of affairs in imperial Germany, the right to free speech was protected in the U.S. constitution, and some professors took advantage of this to utter political or even partisan opinions. If they thereby displeased members of their governing boards or, in the case of public institutions, members of state legislatures, professors could and sometimes did get into trouble. 'To argue that the institutional position of professors should not be affected by what they said as citizens,' Walter P. Metzger comments, 'was to urge immunity for them from the economic penalties that may repay unpopular utterances – the dwindling of clients, the boycott of subscribers, the loss of a job.'[13] Board members and lawmakers wondered on occasion why professors who expressed objectionable views should escape institutional sanctions. Did no line exist to distinguish inappropriate from appropriate utterances?

Such a question was easier to answer in Great Britain than in the United States. Well into the twentieth century, the cult of research did not have the following in British universities that it had in Germany or in U.S. research universities. However, a tradition of academic free speech and political involvement existed that must have struck German and even some American academics as unusual. In discussing academic freedom in Great Britain, A.H. Halsey and M.A. Trow write, 'As regards freedom to follow and express political and social views in opposition to government or convention there has never been any serious question.'[14] 'Partly responsible were British habits of academic self-government, most clearly evident in Oxford and Cambridge. Also important was an atmosphere in which social and intellectual elites claimed a wide measure of freedom of expression. In the forefront of those who asserted the right of Canadian professors to state their opinions freely were a number of Canadians who had studied in Britain, as well as some British academic emigrants.

The British influence was particularly important in Canada because the research universities that grew up in the United States were almost without counterpart north of the border before the 1914–18 war. The earliest Canadian universities had two main purposes, 'the training of clergy and the general education of the future leaders of society.' Before 1900, professional training in medicine, law, engineering, agriculture, forestry, home economics, and the like were being added as a more practical orientation took hold, derived from Scotland and the United States. But this development affected the provincial and nonsectarian institutions to a greater degree than it did the many denominational institutions, Catholic and Protestant. Their objectives continued to be religious and moral well into the twentieth century, and research was no essential part of their mission.

For example, McMaster University's chancellor, A.L. McCrimmon, stated in 1920 that the mission of the Baptist institution over which he presided was 'to produce educated men and women for Christ ... so that their theoretical and practical life is organically related to the creative personality of the Saviour of the World' and so that they could 'bring the Kingdom of God to bear upon national and international affairs.' This did not mean that McCrimmon and the governors of McMaster thought the advancement of knowledge to be an unworthy goal. It did mean that other ends were more important.[15]

The provincial universities – by 1914 there were six (New Brunswick, Toronto, Manitoba, Saskatchewan, Alberta, and British Columbia) – stressed undergraduate liberal arts education as well as the practical applications of learning, particularly in agriculture and engineering. Applied research was part of their reason for existence. But in both the provincial and the three private nonsectarian institutions (Dalhousie, McGill, and Queen's) heavy teaching loads and scarce funds kept most professors from doing much research. This was true even where small graduate schools came into existence, notably at McGill and the University of Toronto.

In this environment, a concept of academic freedom rooted in the Humboldtian research ideal had limited relevance. More influential in Canada was the British tradition, which linked academic freedom to professorial self-government and academic free speech. Yet the Humboldtian ideal did have an impact. Some Canadians took advanced degrees in Germany before 1914; others attended the U.S. research universities. When Canadian university presidents sought faculty recruits, they often canvassed American institutions for men (rarely women) who had been born in Canada and could be induced to return to their native land. The intellectual baggage of such people might well include the idea of academic freedom American-style, centred on research and the status of the professoriate.

The third source of the concept of academic freedom in Canada owed something to the British tradition of academic self-government but was in large part indigenously North American. From the mid-nineteenth century on, in Canada as in the United States, some professors sought to assert their autonomy at the expense of the power of employers and administrators. Whereas German professors were civil servants, North American professors were employed by lay boards. (The Roman Catholic institutions also had boards, but were exceptional in that they were supervised by religious orders and bishops.) German professors elected their rectors and deans; but in North America, administrative hierarchies were headed by presidents who were appointed by boards consisting of business and professional people. The challenge facing professors who sought to safeguard their autonomy and freedom was clear.

Until 1915 there was no overarching organization charged with defending the interests of the American (or Canadian) professoriate. Discipline-based bodies did exist, but there were several barriers to a more inclusive association: first, 'the institutional and disciplinary barriers that cut across the professorial community'; second, 'a deep aversion among academic men to entering into an organization whose purposes smacked of trade unionism'; third, 'a fear of administrative reprisal'; and finally, 'a certain timidity which the academic mind had acquired through years of ivied isolation.'[16]

In the United States, the barriers collapsed in the second decade of the twentieth century in the wake of a controversial dismissal from Lafayette College in 1913. The American philosophical and psychological associations appointed a joint committee of inquiry to look into the matter, but when it asked Lafayette's president for a statement he answered them dismissively. This drew criticism in the committee's report: '[His] attitude ... does not seem to this committee one which can with propriety be maintained by the officers of any college or university towards the inquiries of .a representative national organization of college and university teachers and other scholars.'[17]

The rebuke may have made the committee members feel better, but it cannot have escaped their notice that learned societies lacked the power to force administrators or boards to cooperate with them. Two years later, in 1915, the American Association of University Professors (AAUP) was founded by some of the brightest stars in the U.S. academic firmament. In the early years, its membership was open only to university teachers 'of recognized scholarship or scientific productivity'[18] who had held a teaching or research position for ten years. This was meant to attract members whose prestige as individuals the AAUP hoped to share as an organization. A similar concern influenced the language of the AAUP's landmark 'General Report of the Committee on Academic Freedom and Tenure' (1915). It was the language of a profession seeking to assert and govern itself.

The report rejected the assumption that professors were mere employees of governing boards: 'The responsibility of the university teacher is primarily to the public itself, and to the judgment of his own profession; and while, with respect to certain external conditions of his vocation, he accepts a responsibility to the authorities of the institution in which he serves, in the essentials of his professional activity his duty is to the wider public to which the institution itself is morally amenable.'[19] In support of this claim, the report argued that it was in the ultimate interest of society that professors be autonomous and free. Associated with this claim was a disdainful attitude to proprietory institutions, such as denominational colleges, which tended to impose restrictions on teaching and to discourage research.

Of the report's thirteen signatories, eight had studied in Germany. Not surprisingly, they linked academic freedom to research and insisted that professors limit themselves to teaching subjects in which they were competent by virtue of their scholarly work. The committee accepted the norm of neutrality and counselled temperateness in setting forth the results of scholarship and research. Its members insisted, too, that classroom remarks by professors were privileged communications that should not be made public, in whole or in part, without their authorization.

The committee believed that professors had a role to play in public affairs and that the rules of neutrality and competence need not govern the manner in which they performed this role. But the committee also stated that 'academic teachers are under a peculiar obligation to avoid hasty or unverified or exaggerated statements, and to refrain from intemperate or sensational modes of expression.'[20] Having failed to reach agreement among themselves over whether professors should be able to work for a political party or run for office, the committee members left these issues open.

Academic freedom did not, the report stated, cover all professorial speech. 'Not the absolute freedom of utterance of the individual scholar, but the absolute freedom of thought, of inquiry, of discussion and of teaching ... is asserted by this declaration of principles.' However, if restraints were called for, they 'should be in the main ... self-imposed, or enforced by the public opinion of the profession.' Disciplinary action, if needed, should be taken by professors, not boards: 'In matters of opinion, and of the utterance of opinion ... boards can not intervene without destroying, to the extent of their intervention, the essential nature of a university.'[21]

Just as important as the guidelines for faculty behaviour were the procedures that were to govern tenure and dismissal. Academic tenure will be discussed in detail in chapter 11, but here it should be noted that tenure, in the form of a continuing or permanent appointment (known in the French-Canadian universities as *permanence*), was a familiar feature of the North American academic landscape well before 1900.[22] This gave most academics the economic security they desired. But because it was typically held not 'during good behaviour' but 'during pleasure,' i.e., at the discretion of governing boards, and because cause did not need to be shown to end a tenured appointment, it was unreliable as a safeguard of academic freedom – or, indeed, of nonconformity.

The 1915 report recommended that after a probationary period of ten years, academics should either be granted tenure or let go. While on probation they should receive adequate notice of nonrenewal; once they were tenured, if they faced dismissal, they should be given a fair hearing from a committee of their peers at which they could defend themselves against specific charges. Committee findings would presumably be binding on boards.[23]

The report was a conservative and communitarian statement. According to the historian Ellen W. Schrecker, it 'reveals how deeply enmeshed the notion of academic freedom was with the overall status, security and prestige of the academic profession.' 'Historically speaking,' the historian Thomas L. Haskell writes, 'the heart and soul of academic freedom lie not in free speech but in professional autonomy and collegial self-governance.' Seeking support from senior scholars and acceptance from university presidents and governing boards, the AAUP presented itself as a responsible association of professional men. (Women were virtually absent from the higher reaches of academe.) Accordingly, the AAUP's idea of academic freedom was rooted in the idea of discipline-based competence as defined by well-established professors.[24]

No analogous organization took shape in Canada until thirty-six years had passed (though some Canadian academics joined the AAUP). The barriers to faculty organization here were even greater than in the United States. There were far fewer Canadian professors, and they were divided by region and language. Moreover, the number of senior, established scholars was too small to serve as the basis of an association like the AAUP. When the Canadian Association of University Teachers (CAUT) was founded, it was the creation not of a group of eminent professors but of the faculty associations that were already established on various campuses. The elitism of the AAUP's early days was absent from the CAUT's origins. This helps explain the Canadian organization's initial focus on bread-and-butter issues and its lack of concern with academic freedom. When in time that freedom came to engage the CAUT, it was academic free speech and freedom of conscience that were at issue, rather than disciplinary competence.

The history of academic freedom is part of intellectual history. It is also part of the history of the professoriate and the universities in which they work. The concept was developed in Canada in the course of a series of incidents involving professors in their institutional settings. Before the 1914–18 war, the term 'academic freedom' was very little heard in Canada. However, it was at issue on a number of occasions. Several of those incidents involved a dismissal prompted by the exercise of academic free speech (one helped spark a student strike at the University of Toronto in 1895). In some denominational colleges, scientific and historical discoveries that called received views of the Bible into question produced bitter controversy. In other cases, the conflict was between claims to professorial autonomy and the authority of university heads or governing boards.

The incidents were few. Indeed, at no time in our history have there been many, for as a group Canadian academics have been uncontroversial. (This does not distinguish them greatly from professors of other nationality.) Academic freedom in Canada has long been subject to self-imposed limits that have been rooted in a sense of what was socially, politically, and – not least important – academically acceptable. And, of course, academics share in a general human reluctance to offend, make waves, give pain or cause discomfort to others, or court these for themselves. Nor are they eager to be separated from the herd at the cost of friendships or career. Drawn largely from the comfortable and contented middle classes, most professors in the early years were predisposed to acquiesce in the way things were and to avoid offending their colleagues, employers, and fellow Canadians. The financial dependence of the universities had the same effect. Few professors failed to understand that biting the hand that fed their institutions might have unhappy consequences.

Some academics had a further reason for avoiding controversy. Faculty women increased gradually in number in the course of the twentieth century, but before 1940 they were virtually excluded from many fields, and as late as 1960 they were less than 15 per cent of all university teachers. Jewish professors, few and far between before the Second World War, became more numerous after 1945, but not until the early 1960s did they cease to be uncommon. At that time, non-white professors were still exotic: it seems that the first anywhere in Canada was not appointed until 1959. Having cause to feel exposed and vulnerable, members of minority groups almost invariably tried to fit in and stay out of the limelight.

Complaisance and an understandable caution help explain the quietude of Canadian professors. Yet to this generalization there have always been exceptions. As well, some professors have got into trouble in spite of themselves. The resulting incidents and controversies have done much to define the idea of academic freedom in Canada. They also form a large part of its history.

The university, Cardinal Newman has told us, exists because knowledge is its own end.[25] Yet knowledge has its uses, and that is true also of a knowledge of history. 'It's in vain ... to recall the past,' Dickens's Betsey Trotwood says, 'unless it works some influence upon the present.' A knowledge of the history of academic freedom enhances our understanding of Canadian universities and Canadian society. It can also strengthen the resolve to defend the university's important cultural, intellectual, and social functions, and to preserve the freedom that is found within it.

2

A House Divided

In November 1860, Queen's College in Canada West welcomed a new principal. Drawn from a pastorate in Scotland, William Leitch was 'a man of solid attainments with, in addition to the usual classical and theological training, a wide knowledge of and a great enthusiasm for the natural sciences.'[1] The small institution at whose head he found himself seemed ready to expand. Instead, it became embroiled in conflict. Within four years, several professors had resigned or been dismissed, and Leitch himself was dead of heart failure.

The problems began in the College of Medicine. In 1862 the professor of anatomy, John Stewart, was dismissed 'for publishing "injurious and calumnious statements," treating his colleagues "in an ungentlemanly and insulting manner," and failing to attend faculty meetings.' (He had criticized the other members of the medical college, the board of trustees, and Leitch for allowing an allegedly unqualified person to share in a course of lectures.) Stewart did not try to reclaim his position, but it was otherwise with George Weir, the professor of classics. Dismissed from his position in 1864, he sued to be reinstated.

Weir had first come to the notice of the trustees when a quarrel arose in the late 1850s between him and the professor of philosophy, James George. The trustees admonished both men and urged them to patch up their differences. For two years peace prevailed. Then Weir's younger sister bore a child out of wedlock and identified George, a married man, as the father. Weir charged George with adultery and asked the board to investigate. George denied the accusation but resigned soon afterwards, claiming ill health. Doubtless relieved, the trustees accepted his resignation and decided to investigate no further; but Weir and his friends continued their campaign of denunciation against George while publicly decrying the board's failure to continue the inquiry. A trustee, John Paton, then charged Weir with conduct detrimental to good order in the college, adducing as evidence an attempt to enlist students in his cause. A majority of the trustees voted to admonish Weir for allowing 'personal feeling to prevail over concern for College discipline.'

By this time, Principal Leitch regarded Weir as a nuisance. This feeling grew when he learned upon his return from Scotland in the fall of 1862 that the senate, of which Weir was secretary, had drawn up a set of statutes deal- ing with the governance of the college and that the board had appointed a committee to consider them. Believing the document to impose undesirable restrictions on his power and on the prerogatives of the board, Leitch, assisted by Paton, drew up his own statutes and substituted these for the ones the sen- ate had proposed.

In January 1863 the trustees adopted Leitch's draft statutes. Their effect 'was to retain for the board and to grant to the principal very great powers of initia- tive and veto, even in purely academic matters.' Most obnoxious from the fac- ulty perspective were the statutes that translated 'into explicit terms the authority given by the charter to the trustees to hear complaints and to admon- ish, suspend, or dismiss anyone.' Henceforth, professors would be subject to dismissal if they made remarks 'injurious' to other professors or 'disrespectful' to the college authorities. The document gave offence, too, because it equated the university with the board and reduced professors to the status of employees serving 'during pleasure.' As well, although professors had hitherto been eligi- ble to serve as trustees, this would no longer be allowed.

At a meeting on 1 October 1863 the board heard protests from the faculty but took no action to amend the statutes. Two weeks later, George Lawson, profes- sor of chemistry and natural history, resigned to take an appointment at Dalhou- sie. Leitch's irritation – the notice was short – turned to anger when he heard that Lawson, in informing his students of his resignation, had criticized the new statutes. The executive committee of the board summoned Lawson, accused him of conduct tending to 'lower the respect of the students for the College authorities and for the statutes,' and entered their disapproval in the minutes. Lawson's colleagues, in turn, expressed their annoyance with the board at a farewell meeting for the departing chemist.

It was perhaps inevitable that Weir would be held largely responsible for the student unrest that broke out afterwards. In February 1864 the board, citing 'the present alarming state of the College,' dismissed him with six months' salary – and 'the trustees added a scarcely veiled threat to dismiss any other professor who might fail to take warning by Weir's fate.' One professor, John Dickson of the medical college, resigned in protest against both Weir's dismissal and the new statutes. The commotion subsided after Leitch's sudden death in May 1864, but the trustees still had to defend themselves against a lawsuit by Weir. Rejecting the severance payment offered him, he sued for reinstatement, claiming a life interest in his chair during good behaviour. He won his case in Court of Chancery but lost on appeal.

Hilda Neatby (the historian of Queen's in the nineteenth century) criticized Leitch mainly for his habit of spending half the year in Scotland, but she reserved most of her criticism for Weir. Conceding that he was 'able' and 'charming, capable of making and keeping friends who easily excused his faults as the foibles of a brilliant and sensitive person,' she regarded him as unreasonable and worse: 'In modern terms, no doubt it would be said that Weir had a paranoia with a persecution complex' (though she offers not a shred of evidence for this diagnosis). Weir's activities, argued Neatby, made it impossible for Leitch 'to claim the support and loyalty which undoubtedly were due him as principal.'

Combative in pressing his views, Weir was bound to prove troublesome to such an authoritarian person as Leitch seems to have been. Weir had a vision of the university that assigned a key role in its governance to the faculty. Not the trustees but the academic collectivity – the principal, professors, alumni, and students – were the university, Weir once said. The statutes he helped draft incorporated this vision, in which the principal was the first among equals in the management of academic affairs, and the trustees had supervision only over the management and augmentation of the endowment. Very different was the vision evident in Leitch's draft. It made the principal the chief executive officer and the trustees judges of all matters of importance; in this scheme, only the inoffensive were completely safe.

The dismissal of the classicist William E. Wilson from King's College, Nova Scotia, in 1884 resembled Weir's case in several ways, not least because Wilson also sued to be restored to his position. He had been a professor of classics at King's for eight years when he was drawn into a controversy described by the historian Henry Roper as 'not only a crucial episode in the history of the college, but ... perhaps the most dramatic episode in Nova Scotian higher education in the late nineteenth century.'[2] A major cause of the conflict was the unpopularity of the president, John Dart, who had incurred the hostility of several professors by founding a divinity school that had lower academic standards than the arts faculty. It did not help that his chief faculty ally was the roundly disliked professor of modern languages, Alfred de Fourmentin.

In June 1883 the alumni association passed motions claiming that modern languages were ill taught at King's and asking the board of governors for an inquiry. Some months later, the board ordered a test of the translation skills of the students in modern languages. This took place in June 1884 under Dart's supervision, and the students performed to satisfaction. But soon afterwards,

Wilson, who had been approached by an alumnus, warned Hibbert Binney, Anglican bishop of Nova Scotia and the Visitor of King's as well as chairman of its board of governors, that Dart might have helped the examinees in French. Then the alumnus who had approached Wilson, a clergyman named Henry How, informed the board of his belief that the exam had been fraudulent and that Dart was responsible.

Confronted with these claims, the board discussed not the exam but Wilson, and decided to fire a warning shot across his bow. 'We have learned from those best qualified to give the information,' Binney wrote to him, 'that you habitually speak disparagingly of the president and the other professors to the junior members of the college, which must tend to the subversion of discipline.' This would not do. 'A house divided against itself cannot stand' (the bishop was paraphrasing Mark 3:25). Wilson must work 'to promote peace and harmony, and support the president.' Unless he did so, Binnie informed him, 'I need not tell you what the result must be.'[3]

An outraged Wilson replied that his first impulse had been to resign, but he had decided instead to 'demand ... the regular public investigation of these very grave assertions' so that they might be 'openly proved or openly retracted.' He added, 'I am willing to stake my position at King's College on the result of a regular fair and public enquiry.' Meanwhile, he went even further. Angry because the governors were doing nothing about How's charge against Dart, Wilson distributed one hundred and fifty copies of a statement charging the president with being responsible for irregularities in the conduct of the examination in French. This forced the governors to investigate. They concluded that Dart's conduct had been 'in some respect injudicious' but that he had 'not intended any fraud' and that the help he had given the students had not affected the validity of the test results.[4]

Wilson thought this was a whitewash, and he soon found occasion to say so publicly, for in October Binney wrote to the *Halifax Herald*, denying neglect of his duty with respect to the charge against Dart and implying that it was ill-founded and malicious. Wilson now threw caution to the winds. On 20 October the *Herald* carried a letter from him accusing the governors of delay in dealing with How's charge; he accused them also of dishonesty in blaming him for the troubles at King's and of incompetence in conducting the inquiry. 'The resolution of the board of governors ... is not in accordance with the evidence,' Wilson concluded. 'That evidence is to a great extent before the public. The public must judge whether a charge of fraud has been substantiated. Can any mind that is not besotted by the worst type of ascetic theology, that is not warped by ecclesiastical tyranny, have any doubt?'[5]

Not only was Wilson questioning the board's competence, he came close to explicit criticism of Binney's Anglo-Catholic beliefs and autocratic habits. Binney, the wealthy scion of one of Nova Scotia's most prominent families, was not used to being criticized, and he was angered by Wilson's letter. His rage increased when on 23 and 24 October the students rioted, locking Dart out of the college and burning him in effigy.[6]

Dart and De Fourmentin resigned in 1885, but Wilson's days were even shorter. A special meeting of the board took place on 4 November 1884; by a majority of eight to two, the board dismissed him on the charge that he had disparaged Binney, the board, and the president 'in language ... unbecoming his position as a professor.' According to the college statutes, however, professors could only 'be removed for neglect of duty, inefficiency, or other just cause, if nine members of the Board vote for such removal.'[7] Since the motion had fallen one vote short of securing the necessary nine yeas, a further meeting took place on 5 December to confirm the resolution.

The board had neither notified Wilson of the two meetings nor given him an opportunity to defend himself. This led the Supreme Court of Nova Scotia to order Wilson's restoration, with the proviso that if the board could show that it had duly removed him for cause, the dismissal would stand.[8]

Apparently adopting the view that its grounds for dismissing Wilson had been justified, the board did not reinstate him. He therefore commenced a suit for damages, but it seems never to have gone to court. Henry Roper infers that Binney 'had no intention of being intimidated by a nobody like Wilson,' that the board must have had legal advice to the effect that the judgment was unenforceable and that the best course would be to await whatever Wilson might do.[9] Lacking the means to continue the battle, he quit the field.

John Clark Murray was for many years McGill's professor of logic and mental and moral philosophy. Educated in Scotland and Germany, he came to Canada in 1862 to take the chair of philosophy at Queen's, moving to McGill ten years later. He was an early champion of women's education. The historian Margaret Gillett writes that Murray defined Woman 'not as an adjunct of Man, but as a "person with the right of freedom of action which is the inalienable right of every person who does not forfeit it by intruding upon the rights of others."'[10] Murray denied that women were mentally less competent than men, and he deplored the fact that they were deprived of the higher education that would allow them to support themselves. During the 1870s he periodically advanced his views, but to no avail. Only in 1882 did the McGill Corporation pass on to a committee his motion that the Faculty of Arts admit women.

The committee report stated that most North American universities were by then admitting women, either by setting up a separate college or by allowing them to attend the same classes as men, and that the latter option, where adopted, seemed to have had no ill effects on students or institutions. Still divided, the corporation asked Principal William Dawson to look into the matter. Before he was due to report, however, McGill received a commitment from Donald Smith (later Lord Strathcona) of $50,000 for women's education on condition that the classes be conducted separately from those for men. Dawson favoured separate education, and he was in any case not disposed to look this gift horse in the mouth. He recommended to the board that it accept Smith's offer, and it agreed to do so.

Murray objected. The procedure originally adopted had been set aside, he protested, and a discussion on the respective merits of separate and co-education had been avoided. And why? Because a tycoon had donated a large sum of money! This demonstration of the power of wealth struck the moral philosopher as deplorable. The dispute between Murray and Dawson soon became public, and it exposed the latter to criticism. Stanley Brice Frost (McGill's official historian) writes that most students agreed with Murray: 'The male editors of the college paper openly questioned the wisdom of the "equal but separate" arrangements, and the women students were said to be unanimous in desiring non-segregation.'[11] Dawson sought to discourage discussion for fear of offending Smith; but Smith, apparently little offended, donated a further $70,000 for women's education in 1885.

The issue disappeared from view only to re-emerge in 1888, when Murray wrote to a Montreal newspaper arguing that the general experience with co-education showed it to have no undesirable results, and criticizing separate education because of the need to give some lectures twice, which increased already heavy teaching loads. Smith expressed regret to Dawson that Murray had publicly opposed the policy adopted by the board of governors. Dawson agreed with him. In any case, he could not ignore Murray's remarks at the annual university dinner on 30 April 1888 and at a meeting of the Donaldas (as the women students were known) on 1 May. On both occasions Murray praised co-education and urged the students to make their voices heard on the issue.

Dawson asked Murray for an explanation of his remarks, which he said would tend 'to influence the minds of students against the regulations of the University' and could therefore subvert good discipline and cause damage to 'the interests of the University.' So annoyed was he that he did not wait for a reply before placing the matter before the board. Consequently, soon after getting Dawson's letter, Murray received another, which conveyed to him the board's request for information. His reply to Dawson accused the principal of deliberately attempting to damage him socially and professionally by placing the matter before the board, and he asked Dawson to withdraw his letter. In his reply to the board, Murray claimed that he had always abided by university regulations. In response, the board asked two of its members to inform Murray in person that no charges would be laid but that he must conduct himself in accordance with board policy, support the principal, and 'abstain from public complaints or agitations before the students.'

By this time, the press had got hold of the story, and several letters to the editor appeared in support of Murray. Encouraged, he wrote to the board stating that if Dawson's charges were not withdrawn, he 'would seek vindication before another tribunal.' The governors trumped this 'by saying that if Murray would not conform to the decisions of the university, the board would with very great reluctance be forced to accept his resignation.'[12] This caused Murray to back off. Thenceforth, he limited himself to sending private letters to Dawson.

In the new century McGill became steadily more co-educational. 'Since World War II, co-education has simply been taken for granted as the unchallenged norm,' Gillett writes. 'Ultimately, then, the victory could be considered Murray's.' Was it also a victory for academic freedom? The board did not dismiss a man whom it clearly regarded as insubordinate and whom Dawson described as 'insolent and untruthful.' But the outcome fell far short of recognizing a professorial right to criticize a policy of the board.[13]

The dismissal of the classicist William Dale from the University of Toronto in 1895 helped spark a student strike, which in turn led the Ontario government to appoint a royal commission. It is the only dispute over academic free speech that has inspired a play, James Reaney's *The Dismissal*. The origins of the affair lay in the control which the provincial government exercised over the university and the short rations on which it kept the institution. The University Act of 1887 had established a university council, consisting of the president and professors, which was charged with the maintenance of discipline, the direction of university societies, and the control of occasional lectures and teaching. A senate with mixed academic and nonacademic membership controlled the curriculum, and a board of trustees supervised the budgets of University College and the university.[14] Ultimate authority remained with the government, which appointed the professors.

This prompted charges of political interference. There were complaints, too, that Sir Oliver Mowat's government habitually kept the institution in poverty. While the charges of interference were difficult to substantiate, those of niggardliness were not. One result was that junior faculty members, in particular, were chronically unhappy; another was that in the absence of a pension plan, the trustees' limited ability to pension off professors led some senior faculty members to stay on longer than they should have done.

By the 1890s the university was troubled for other reasons as well. There was tension between those who welcomed the emphasis on research associated with the German tradition and those who championed the older British-influenced humanism. There was also tension between Canadian nationalists and those who looked to Britain for academic talent. In 1892 James Loudon, a physicist, succeeded Sir Daniel Wilson in the presidency. Loudon adhered to the Humboldtian research ideal, and in recommending appointments he was a strong Canadian nationalist. On both counts he faced opposition.[15]

In 1894 the appointment of George Wrong to the professorship of history brought criticism. Controversy had surrounded Wrong since his appointment as lecturer in English history two years earlier. The starting salary for a lecturer was $800, but Wrong had received $1,500. This was less than he had earned at Wycliffe College, the evangelical Anglican divinity school, but the suspicious discerned another reason for his generous treatment. He was the son-in-law of Edward Blake, chancellor of the university and a former Liberal premier. Critics charged that Wrong owed both his appointment and his salary to patronage.[16]

Wrong's elevation to the chair, a foregone conclusion after his appointment as lecturer, prompted renewed rumour in the press, which the student newspaper, the *Varsity*, copied with an avidity that some of its readers regarded as unseemly. Of greater concern to the students, though, was the allegedly low quality of some of the teaching. Also an irritant was the decision of the university council to prohibit a debate, arranged by the Political Science Club, between Alfred Jury, a Liberal politician and well-known agnostic, and Phillips Thompson, a socialist author. (They debated off campus.)[17]

Attacks on the university council led in February 1895 to the suspension of the *Varsity*'s editor, James Tucker, but this was thin beer compared to what followed. On 9 February the *Globe* devoted part of its front page to a letter from William Dale. Claiming that he had 'no desire to add to the literature which has already arisen out of the difference between the students and the faculty of the University,' the classicist poured oil on the fire of controversy surrounding Wrong's appointment. The historian's recent career could be more easily explained by assuming Blake's influence than otherwise, Dale wrote, since neither Wrong's qualifications nor his performance since his appointment were stellar. However, the appointment in itself mattered little, Dale said. It was merely a symptom of the preference for mediocrity, which he claimed was damaging the university: 'If during the next ten years the character of professorial appointments continues to be what it has been during the last ten years, the professoriate of the University will have lost the respect both of students and public, and the results to learning will be most disastrous.' He urged the adoption of an independent system of appointment.[18]

Dale's letter aroused outrage among some of his colleagues and led Loudun to recommend his dismissal. The government acted on this advice within the week. This did not take Dale by surprise. 'I was ... aware that such an outcome was quite probable,' he told a *Mail and Empire* reporter, 'but I thought the letter should be written, and so I wrote it.' Soon afterwards a lecturer in his department, F.B.R. Hellems, resigned in sympathy with him.[19]

Several of Dale's colleagues, describing his conduct as 'subversive of all discipline and a violation of the amenities which should prevail between members of the same faculty,' publicly welcomed his dismissal. Both the *Globe* and the *Mail and Empire*, which did not usually agree, also approved of it, the latter asserting that Dale's letter had been 'tantamount to a declaration of war against the institution of which the writer was a member.'[20]

The *Star* saw the matter differently. A rowdy, muckraking journal, it took its stand on 15 February 1895 with the front-page headline 'The Ablest Lecturer Gone.' The editor followed this up the next day by questioning Dale's 'disloyalty': 'Was Prof. Dale any less loyal to the institution he served than his inefficient colleagues?' Two days later the *Star* added, 'The objection to Mr. Dale's action is not so much regarding what he said as that he spoke at all.'[21]

Dale's willingness to court dismissal suggests that he believed his criticisms to be justified. Most of the students agreed with him. He was well regarded as a teacher, and his dismissal, coming within days of Tucker's suspension, brought on a short-lived student strike. In time a royal commission issued a report exonerating the university authorities while mildly criticizing them for want of tact in dealing with the students. It said nothing about Dale's dismissal, which was outside its terms of reference.

Whether Dale's criticism was right or wrong was beside the point in the view of most commentators. Dale had criticized his colleagues and drawn unfavourable attention to his institution, and academic free speech did not extend to criticism of the university by its servants. Dale knew this and accepted its logic. The owner of a good property near St Marys, Ontario, he took up farming; but he retained his interest in the classics and later had sessional appointments at Queen's and McMaster universities.

The case raises questions that are difficult to answer – indeed, perhaps impossible to resolve. Is candid criticism of the teaching abilities or scholarly attainments of one's colleagues an exercise of academic freedom or is it an infringement of professional ethics? Which ranks higher – one's obligation to one's colleagues or to one's students? What protection does academic freedom offer to a whistle-blower or a critic of the university? The answer to the last of these questions has changed since 1895. For example, the response to *The Great Brain Robbery* (1984) and its reprise, *The Petrified Campus* (1997) – two book-length assaults, by three historians, on the customs and practices of universities, which are said to be on 'the road to ruin' – indicates that internal criticism, even when ill-informed and intemperate, is tolerated now. (If the authors had named names, of course, they might have got into trouble.) Answers to the other questions are less obvious. For example, in case of a faculty strike, what weight should professors give to their duty to colleagues on the one hand and their duty to their students on the other? Can faculty members who in this or some analogous way defy the majority of their colleagues claim that they are exercising their academic freedom? Such questions are still unanswered.

The removal of Michael Francis Fallon from the University of Ottawa in 1901 was, like Dale's dismissal, due to a difference of opinion between an individual and the administrative leaders of an institution. However, the Fallon case had consequences far greater than those of the other cases discussed so far. Fallon was a member of the Oblate order that ran the university; he was appointed professor of English literature in 1894 and became vice-rector two years later. His promotion did not sit well with the French-Canadian faction in the university: he was seen as hostile to them and their interests. In 1897 he allegedly predicted that English would replace French throughout the world and 'ridiculed the French language in the presence of his French-Canadian students.'[22]
  As long as Ottawa had a rector of Irish background, Fallon was safe, but in 1898 the university underwent a change. J.M. McGuckin having resigned because of ill health, the chancellor, Archbishop Joseph-Thomas Duhamel, appointed H.A. Constantineau to be the rector. Fallon, who had hoped to succeed McGuckin, did not hide his displeasure. Although he later assured Constantineau of his support, his first reaction had been noted. So, presumably, had his views about French. Within months he was removed from the vice-rectorship and given an Ottawa pastoral appointment. However, he continued to teach at Ottawa and to play a leading role among the city's Irish Roman Catholics.
  Under Constantineau, and with Duhamel's blessing, Ottawa rapidly changed from being a mainly English-language institution to one that was predominantly French. This dimmed Fallon's academic prospects, for at this new University of Ottawa he was unwelcome. He responded with criticism of the changes, thereby increasing his unpopularity. As long as he was at St Joseph's Church, it was difficult to exclude him, but there is proverbially more than one way to skin a cat, and the Oblates found it. In June 1901 they transferred Fallon to a parish in Buffalo in the State of New York. This had the desired effect of severing the priest's connection with the university, but it enraged Fallon and his supporters. He later claimed that his removal to Buffalo had been part of 'a deliberate conspiracy'

hatched by Duhamel and other French Canadians. The same conspiracy, he believed, kept him out of the rectorship in 1902 and again in 1903.[23]

If revenge is a dish best eaten cold, Fallon was to enjoy a gourmet meal. After 1909, as the bishop of London, Ontario, he initiated a campaign against the use of French as a language of instruction in Ontario's separate schools. He had significant influence on the passage in 1912 of Regulation 17, which greatly limited the use of French as a language of instruction in the schools.[24] If Duhamel and the Oblates had been able to see into the future, they might have chosen to leave Fallon at the University of Ottawa.

Fallon's case is not strictly comparable to those of Weir, Wilson, and Dale. There was no dismissal; Fallon was assigned to pastoral duties. As long as Roman Catholic institutions were controlled by bishops and staffed by priests, this device was useful in dealing with professors who had become 'difficult' in some way. It was used in 1922 to exile J.J. Tompkins from St Francis Xavier University to a Canso parish when his support for Nova Scotian university federation offended his bishop. (The university's historian, James D. Cameron, does not seem to see this as an academic freedom issue.) It was still available to Cardinal Emmett Carter in 1984 when three professors in the Toronto School of Theology roused his ire. Reassignment versus dismissal: from the vantage point of academic freedom, this is a distinction without a difference. It should be noted, however, that academic freedom was not until recently a value acknowledged by Roman Catholic universities.[25]

Although in the latter half of the nineteenth century the Darwinian debate engaged the minds of intellectuals throughout the Western world, in Canada it did not lead to significant conflict within the academy between evolutionists and anti-evolutionists. Religiously conservative and still suspicious of the claims of science except when tempered by religious faith, Canadians were largely hostile to Charles Darwin's thought. Many Canadian academics concurred in this – including the leading university scientists, McGill's William Dawson and Toronto's Daniel Wilson, who were champions of the *anti*-Darwinian cause. Darwin found his first followers in Canada outside the academy. Only late in the century did academic supporters of Darwin gradually emerge.[26]

According to Carl Berger, 'Aspects of evolution entered into the thinking and practice of Canadian naturalists in a pre-eminently Darwinian way – slowly and selectively.' References to creation or to God in nature 'steadily disappeared ... from the literature of science [with] the gradual acceptance that the parting between science and religion was no longer a temporary separation but a permanent divorce.'[27] Had any academic scientist said so in 1870 or 1880 – none did – he might have been asked to resign.

If the theories of Darwin did little to disturb academe, this was not true of modernizing trends in biblical scholarship. Anglicans and Presbyterians by and large managed to accommodate the 'higher criticism,' the examination and reinterpretation of the Bible using up-to-date historical and textual methods and techniques, but Methodists and Baptists had trouble with the new ideas – and with those who promulgated them. George Coulson Workman taught in the Faculty of Theology of the Methodists' Victoria University from 1882 until 1884, when he left leaving to study in Leipzig. There he drank deep from the spring of German biblical scholarship before returning to Victoria in 1889. C.B. Sissons (the historian of the university) comments, perhaps uncharitably, 'A bigger man could have held and taught German-made ideas in theology without causing himself and others the troubles of later years.'[28]

In May 1890 Workman stated publicly that the Bible should not be taken literally but should be read within its historical context. Invited to publish his remarks in the October 1890 issue of the *Canadian Methodist Quarterly*, he opened himself to attack by writing that a literal interpretation of the Bible was in conflict with the findings of science and historical scholarship and could not be sustained.[29]

Leading the attack was the editor of the *Christian Guardian*, E.H. Dewart; his main ally was Albert Carman, general superintendent of the church and chairman of Victoria's board of regents. At a board meeting in May 1891, Carman introduced a resolution requiring Workman to explain his views. Workman came and spoke; the board then resolved 'that ... Dr. Workman be transferred from the Faculty of Theology to the Faculty of Arts,' where he was to teach Hebrew and Semitic philology.[30]

Slow to understand the objections to modern biblical scholarship, Workman asked for a further opportunity to explain himself. Early in 1892 he again appeared before the board and said, 'If I cannot teach honestly and openly and unrestrainedly ... I cannot teach at all.' He had a champion in Nathanael Burwash, Victoria's chancellor. Nevertheless, the regents confirmed their action of the previous May by a narrow majority.[31]

One commentator, George A. Boyle, describes the board's action as 'tantamount to ... outright dismissal.' This is an exaggeration. The regents did not dismiss Workman; most of them probably did not want him to resign. Believing, though, that the board had shown lack of confidence in him, he did resign. The historian A.B. McKillop comments, 'At one level the Workman affair may be seen as the first controversy regarding academic freedom in an Ontario college or university.'[32]

Workman carried out pastoral duties until 1903, when he became professor of Old Testament exegesis and literature at Montreal's Wesleyan Theological College. His views had not changed; neither had those of the conservative faction.

In October 1907 Wesleyan's board resolved, by a vote of ten to seven, that Workman's doctrinal views were inconsistent with the standard of doctrine and articles of religion of the Methodist Church, and gave him notice of dismissal.[33]

Workman appealed this decision to the church courts, but without success. Principal William Shaw maintained steadfastly that the sole issue was the power of the board to dismiss and that what constituted cause was for the board alone to judge. He enjoyed the crucial support of Carman, who not only sat on Wesleyan's board but also headed the court that heard Workman's appeal. Several other board members also served on the court that ruled against Workman. Similarly, the 1910 Methodist General Conference dismissed Workman's appeal 'on the ground that the Board of Governors has jurisdiction to appoint Professors and to terminate their engagements on any grounds that may to them seem sufficient, provided their action is in harmony with the law of the land.' The conference ruled, though, that the board's views about Workman's theological soundness had 'no legal effect upon his ministerial standing, which can be affected only by proceedings taken as provided in the Discipline of this Church.'[34]

Perhaps fearing that the church courts would not give him satisfaction, Workman had already turned to the civil courts. In 1909 he had sued Wesleyan's board for wrongful dismissal and libel. The board responded that Workman's dismissal had been for cause, in that his teaching contravened Methodist doctrine. In 1911 Mr Justice William A. Weir of the Quebec Superior Court held that neither a board committee nor the board as a whole had the right to determine whether or not Workman's doctrinal views were sound, and he awarded Workman $3,500 damages. This award was overturned on appeal, however, the Court of King's Bench (Appeal Side) ruling that the board had correctly found Workman's beliefs to be heretical. Although the judgment is short and cryptic, it seems that the appeal court had erred.[35] But the case ended there, for Workman lacked the money to continue the action.

Whatever satisfaction conservative Methodists took from Workman's fate was soon spoiled by the defeat their cause sustained in the matter of George Jackson, an Englishman who had recently been appointed to the chair of English Bible at Victoria. On 26 February 1909 Albert Carman used the letters column of the Toronto *Globe* to attack Jackson's theological views. Jackson's reply the following day, asserting that the Bible was not a history or a science textbook but a revelation of spiritual truth, confirmed Carman's fears. Worse, the same issue of the *Globe* carried a letter in Jackson's defence from one of Toronto's leading Methodist laymen, Joseph W. Flavelle.[36]

Carman had another letter in the *Globe* on 1 March. 'A firm believer in the integrity, sufficiency and trustworthiness of Holy Scripture must in these days take his stand,' he wrote.[37] He knew that theological liberalism was making inroads everywhere. The *Christian Guardian* had passed into the hands of the liberals, and the church's ministers increasingly accepted the 'German' ideas. So did a growing number of their better-educated parishioners. A direct appeal to the laity, who by and large (though with important exceptions) were more conservative than their pastors, seemed to be the only way of applying pressure on Victoria's board of regents to get rid of Jackson.

That Carman's effort failed was a victory less for academic freedom than for the power of money. Methodists such as Flavelle, the industrialist Chester Massey, and the lawyer Newton Wesley Rowell were inclined to regard Jackson's views as unexceptionable and Carman's as outdated. Just before the general conference of the church, held in Victoria, British Columbia, in August 1910 – the same conference that heard Workman's appeal – Massey wrote to Rowell about the interest that rich Methodists had shown in the university in recent years: 'These men ... have succeeded because they have used up-to-date methods, and using a trade phrase, have adopted the "latest tools and machinery." Now they are not going to give liberally to a church whose institutions are not up-to-date, and who do not turn out up-to-date men, but to a church which ... [does] everything in a business-like manner to build up our institutions and [our] professors.'[38] (Anyone who has wondered whether Stephen Leacock was too broadly satirical in *Arcadian Adventures with the Idle Rich* need wonder no longer; he was not.) Against Massey's attitude, joined to Chancellor Burwash's defence of academic freedom, Carman's warnings about the improper influence exercised by rich men were of little avail. The conference defeated a motion censuring Jackson's views by a vote of 125 to 84, thereby confirming the earlier decision of Victoria's board of regents to maintain him.

The committee on education had already successfully introduced a proposal that in any future complaint about a professor's teaching, 'the Board of Education shall ... select five persons, being ministers of good repute for their knowledge of questions of doctrine, who shall constitute the Committee of Trial in the case, and name the presiding officer, who shall be one of the General Superintendents.' Because the clergy as a group were more liberal than the laity in their views, the proposal all but guaranteed that storms like those surrounding Workman and Jackson would not recur. 'Since 1910 no group has ever tried seriously to interfere with theological teaching at Victoria University,' C.B. Sissons noted in 1952, crediting this 'to the wisdom and firmness displayed by Burwash, the Faculty, and the Board in dealing with the Jackson controversy, and more especially to the strong blow that was struck for academic freedom in the realm of theology at the General Conference of 1910.'[39]

The conflicts within Methodism over the higher criticism were centred in Toronto and Montreal. The theology faculties at Mount Allison University in Sackville, New Brunswick, and at Winnipeg's Wesley College witnessed little of the controversy. At Mount Allison, Charles Stewart, the professor of theology until his death in 1910, 'was ... very desirous of defending the "young brethren" from the leaven of modern thought.'[40] His attitude restricted debate, John G. Reid (the university's historian) states, but by the second decade of the twentieth century the Faculty of Theology had become more liberal. The appointment in 1903 of William G. Watson as professor of Old Testament exegesis and systematic theology began the change. In 1912 his teaching led a prominent layman to charge that Watson's beliefs 'amounted to Unitarianism.' The matter was resolved without damage to Watson or Mount Allison, but it helped draw attention to the issue of academic freedom.

So did the fact that in 1912 President Byron C. Borden was looking for a recruit to the chair in psychology and logic. The man he sought to appoint, Winthrop Bell, was a Mount Allison graduate then studying in Germany. In offering him the job, Borden surmised that since Bell was familiar with 'the views that are held among our patrons and governors upon ... religious and philosophical questions,' he would know how to avoid giving offence through 'unguarded utterance or ventilation of doubts.' Bell rejected Borden's offer in no uncertain terms: 'To have any institution devoted to higher learning or scientific research under the control of a body with rigid dogmas or preconceived beliefs is enough of an anomaly. To try and prosecute philosophical investigations under such circumstances is almost farcical.'

Approached a second time, Bell accepted the appointment on condition that the board of regents understood 'that it was engaging one who regarded as open all the questions which the Church dogmas treat as settled.' As well, he insisted, 'No one outside the University should have the right or power of interfering with my position because any of my professional utterances disagreed with any belief of his or with any creed of any church.' Neglect or incompetence should be the only grounds for dismissal. Bell added that academic freedom would be more secure if the theological faculty were to be clearly distinguished from the other faculties; adherence to Methodist doctrine might reasonably be expected in the former, but not in the latter. In the end, Bell decided to join Harvard, but something like his proposal was part of a revision of Mount Allison's statutes in 1913. A clause was deleted which stated that 'nothing should be taught ... that contravened the doctrines of John Wesley.'

With respect to Wesley College, A.G. Bedford (the official historian of the University of Winnipeg) notes that the most prominent liberal before 1914, Salem Bland, met with opposition less for his doctrinal views than for his political activism. The other Methodist college in the West, Regina College, lacked a

Faculty of Theology and was from the outset for all practical purposes nondenominational. Disputes over biblical criticism were therefore unlikely.[41]

Baptists had more trouble than most with the higher criticism. A literal interpretation of the Bible commanded widespread assent well into the twentieth century, though less so in the Baptist colleges – Acadia, McMaster, and Brandon – than among the laity. By and large, liberal professors stayed out of the limelight, an exception being McMaster's Isaac Matthews, professor of Old Testament, who came under vigorous attack between 1908 and 1910. Matthews was one of two McMaster professors about whom conservatives entertained doubts, the other being the historian George Cross. However, Cross did not teach that most sensitive of subjects, the Bible. Matthews did.[42]

From the time of Matthews's appointment in 1901 the quality of his 'spirituality' troubled some leading Baptists. One of them, Elmore Harris, told the McMaster senate in 1908, 'I feel that the attitude to the Old Testament Scriptures in the Chair of Old Testament Literature in this institution is not the attitude of the Baptist denomination.' No man, Harris continued, 'ought to enter our institution and, without letting us know, teach things contrary to the views of the ministers of this denomination.' It was not only the content of Matthews's lectures that worried Harris, but also the books read by students: 'I think young men often get views from books that they do not get from a professor.'[43] The potential for harm was increased because Matthews asked students to work things out for themselves. Harris questioned the soundness of this method. Was it not better to tell future ministers what was right?

Harris's views carried weight. He was the pastor of Walmer Road Church in Toronto's well-to-do Annex; and as the son of a manufacturer of agricultural implements he enjoyed substantial means, which enabled him to be one of the university's benefactors. His was not the only view, however. The dean of theology, J.H. Farmer, noted that Baptists insisted on personal freedom and said he had never 'undertaken to correct what any other professor teaches.' Similarly, D.E. Thomson, a lawyer who was chairman of the board of governors, said he thought it unnecessary that 'all teachers in an institution have the same views.' It was better if teachers led young men to 'to look at subjects from different points of view.'[44]

Harris reiterated his view that the content and method of instruction should not be a matter of professorial discretion. This was implicit in three questions he posed. First, 'Can a teacher in the realm of theology teach what he likes?' Second, 'Can a teacher teach in any way that he likes?' Third, was Matthews's the kind of teaching that they would like to have in connection with their institution?[45]

In response, Thomson stated: 'It is a serious matter ... to have anyone in the institution whose teaching is of an unduly disturbing nature ... [but it is] a more serious thing still to plant ourselves ... in the position that we are committed to a cast iron view and that we exclude the right of enquiry and investigation with reference to what is going on in the world.' Roman Catholics were able to make the dogmatic method work, he noted, but 'wherever it is attempted without that ecclesiastical control it is absolutely certain to wreck and produce worse injury than a large measure of latitude would produce.' As for teaching methods: 'Preparing the thing ready-made and imposing it on a man is a good way to stuff turkeys. It is not a good way to educate people.' Several other senators agreed with Thomson. A small committee that included Harris was then charged with interviewing Matthews, and in due time it reported him to be 'sound on all the fundamentals of Baptist faith and practice.'[46]

In the spring of 1909 George Cross came under attack for allegedly advocating a syncretistic faith made up of Christianity and elements of other religions. He denied that he had advocated anything of the kind, and Chancellor A.C. McKay sided with him. But Cross found the experience unsettling and soon afterwards accepted appointment at the University of Chicago.[47]

The Cross incident helped focus attention on Matthews once again. It was probably no coincidence that Harris revived his attack at this time. Basing it on his reading of some transcripts of Matthews's lectures, he charged that Matthews's teaching was 'destructive of the historicity, truthfulness and integrity of the Word of God.' The missionary and evangelistic work of McMaster was in danger, Harris wrote: 'I feel quite sure that ... the usefulness of Professor Matthews to our University is gone.'[48]

The senate appointed a seven-man committee of investigation, which duly reported that 'after a careful weighing of the evidence,' it was convinced that Matthews's 'removal from the Chair of Old Testament would be an injustice to him, a grief to his colleagues, and an injury to the University, and that such an action would be resented by practically every member of the student body.' Accepted by the senate and the board, this report was received by the Regular Baptist Convention of Ontario and Quebec, held in Toronto in October 1910. At this meeting Matthews made it clear that although he accepted a good deal of the historical criticism of the Old Testament, he also believed in the divine inspiration of the Scriptures and 'in the Deity, Atonement and Supreme Lordship of Christ.' Although Harris continued to be sceptical, Matthews's speech, when added to the committee report, satisfied most of the delegates.[49]

McMaster had resisted an attempt to dislodge a professor. In the process, members of the Faculty of Theology had made a statement of their belief in 'the divine inspiration of the Scriptures ... as a complete and infallible rule of faith and practice.' They also agreed that although 'complete freedom' should prevail 'in the investigation and discussion of facts,' no theories should be taught which failed 'to give their proper place to supernatural revelation and inspiration, or which would impair in any way the supreme authority of the Lord Jesus Christ.' In accepting this statement, the senate noted that its action was not 'an endorsation of any particular critical views that [had] been challenged,' but was to be interpreted as being 'in the interest of that reasonable liberty which has always been cherished by our people as a sacred possession.'[50]

A 'reasonable liberty': academic freedom at McMaster was limited, in theology at any rate. But given the role of the theological faculty within the life of the Baptist community, the limitation made sense. And the scrutiny to which professors of theology were subject did not extend into the arts faculty. Leslie Armour has said of James Ten Broeke, professor of philosophy from 1895 to 1932, that he 'preached the universal validity of individual religious experience and espoused a kind of neo-Hegelian rationalism without being disturbed.'[51]

Armour adds that the views of George Blewett, who was appointed to teach philosophy at Victoria in 1906, 'seem more dangerous and revolutionary than anything preached by ... George Jackson and George Workman.' Yet conservatives failed to react to Blewett or to Ten Broeke. Philosophical speculation was not a threat to orthodoxy comparable to criticism of the Word of God. As well, 'there was a general respect for philosophy as a long-established part of the western intellectual tradition.'[52] The obscurity in which philosophers worked also played a part. Obscurity is not the surest safeguard of academic freedom, but it is a safeguard all the same. What other people don't know about your work can't hurt you.

The two main Presbyterian universities (until they were secularized), Dalhousie and Queen's, as well as Knox College in Toronto, avoided the disputes that agitated Victoria and McMaster. The intellectual leadership of George Monro Grant played a significant role in this. A Nova Scotia clergyman, Grant took an active interest in Dalhousie and later served as principal of Queen's. He believed that higher education should be nonsectarian and should accommodate new trends in scholarship. The Dalhousie Act of 1863 owed much to his vision: although Dalhousie would for some time to come remain a Presbyterian institution, its board of governors included Anglicans, Baptists, and Methodists.[53]

Dalhousie's willingness to live with doctrinal differences eased the acceptance of new scientific and biblical knowledge. The endowment of five well-paid chairs between 1879 and 1884 also played a part. Not only did this give new confidence to everyone associated with Dalhousie, but the men who filled the chairs were well-trained scholars, four of whom had done advanced work in Germany.[54]

In 1877 Grant answered a call from Queen's, whose head he would be for the next twenty-five years. 'The enemy of all narrowness and of every kind of parochialism,' he shaped and defined Queen's during the last decades of the nineteenth century. Like the philosopher John Watson, the most eminent member of the faculty, Grant 'acknowledged the power of Darwin, Huxley and Spencer' and insisted that there was no fundamental contradiction between science and religion. The sense of security he fostered – he told potential recruits that they would have life tenure during good behaviour, no matter what the statutes said – helped to draw outstanding professors to the institution, among them the literature scholar James Cappon and the political economist Adam Shortt.[55]

Grant's principalship was free of controversy involving academic freedom, but his successor, Daniel Miner Gordon, was less fortunate. A man of liberal outlook, Gordon arrived at a difficult time. Soon after he assumed his duties in 1902, the general assembly of the Presbyterian Church reversed an earlier decision to secularize Queen's. In the decade that followed, the trustees were divided. So were the faculty – until it emerged that the university's denominational ties prevented it from taking part in the pension scheme established in 1905 by the steel magnate and philanthropist Andrew Carnegie. In 1911 secularization gained approval at last.[56]

In the first decade of the century there were two incidents involving academic freedom. In 1905 Cappon contributed an article to *Queen's Quarterly* criticizing Sir Wilfrid Laurier's attempt to impose separate Roman Catholic schools on the new provinces of Saskatchewan and Alberta. The *Quarterly*'s business manager objected to the tone of the article and enlisted two of the trustees in a campaign to prevent its publication. Its partisanship, they argued, might harm the campaign to increase the endowment. Stating 'that the principle involved was not the merit of the article but the independence and authority of the editors,' Gordon supported their decision to publish it.[57]

The second incident involved a professor of English, John Marshall, who in his capacity as an editor of the *Quarterly* contributed an article in 1910 opposing the formation of a Canadian navy. This was very controversial, and the other editors relieved him of his duties – a step, comments the historian Hilda Neatby, 'not entirely consistent with the declared policy of the *Quarterly*.' Gordon defended the editors, and Marshall left Queen's without bothering formally to resign.[58]

Academic freedom figured in a different way in the Queen's University Act of 1912, which was intended to give legal form to the decision to secularize the university. The private member's bill that was introduced in the House of Commons contained a clause eliminating religious tests for any trustee or professor 'save the profession of Christianity.' This phrase, introduced at the insistence of a prominent member of the church's general assembly, caused some concern.

When moving the bill, W.F. Nickle, Conservative MP for Kingston (and Gordon's son-in-law), confessed that he believed the incorporation of the phrase was a mistake that would 'cut off the university from taking advantage of the intellect of certain of the Jewish people who display great aptitude in matters legal, literary, and scientific.' It might also prove 'a stumbling block in the way of the university' when application was made to the Government of Ontario for assistance. But Nickle did not believe that these drawbacks should stand in the way of the bill's passage, since 'to say that a university is National and to say that [it] is distinctively Christian, is practically saying legally one and the same thing, but in different terms.'[59]

The minister of justice, C.H. Doherty, stated that he had received complaints from the Jewish community; so had several other MPs. Robert Bickerdike (Liberal MP for Montreal–St Lawrence), who was a Presbyterian, thought that some phrasing could be found that would 'not be offensive or insulting to any of the minorities in this country' yet would express the wishes of the university: 'Why pass a law declaring that the great Queen's university shall be debarred from employing a Hebrew in any capacity?' To which George Foster, minister of trade and commerce, replied, 'If the university wants it that way, what is the objection?' Two MPs supported Bickerdike; three defended the right of Queen's to deny employment to whomever it chose. John H. Sinclair (Guysborough) argued, 'We are not excluding anybody, but we are providing for the education of people belonging to all the Christian churches in the country.' This, he added, was no insult to the Jews, who had 'put no money into Queen's.'[60]

There was enough unhappiness with the clause for the House of Commons to accept an amendment, pending agreement by the bill's sponsors, that the phrase 'save the profession of Christianity' be replaced by something less offensive to non-Christians. When the bill received its third reading, however, it stated that Queen's would 'continue distinctively Christian' and that the trustees should 'satisfy themselves of the Christian character of those appointed to the teaching staff.'[61]

Hilda Neatby writes that this may 'well have irritated any Jewish professor who troubled to read the statute.'[62] But in 1912 there were none. When a Jew was appointed to the faculty more than a quarter century later, the clause was ignored, as it had been from the outset where unbelieving Gentiles were concerned. What was in principle an infringement of academic freedom was in practice largely a dead letter.

How the clause offended against academic freedom – that is, by artifically limiting the range of discussion and debate – would hardly have been understood in an age when all institutions thought it fair to discriminate against Jews.

Although Jacob Maier Hirschfelder, a convert to Anglicanism, taught Hebrew and Oriental languages at King's College and then at University College, Toronto, from the 1840s to the 1880s, and although Abraham de Sola taught the same subjects at McGill after 1848, neither institution appointed another Jew until well into the twentieth century. (In 1911 the University of Toronto's Department of History had an opportunity to appoint Lewis Namier, a brilliant scholar of Polish birth who in time became one of this century's pre-eminent historians of Britain. Several board members baulked, and Gilbert Jackson got the job. Jackson had taken only second class honours, but he was British and a Gentile.) As the historian Irving Abella has pointed out, anti-Semitism increased in the second half of the nineteenth century and remained strong for decades.[63]

In 1908 the Orientalist Thomas Eakin at the University of Toronto was the centre of controversy. At issue were the content of a course and the right of the university to teach a subject with religious implications.[64] Late in 1907 a delegation appeared before President Robert Falconer and charged that his institution was in breach of the terms of the federation between the university and the denominational colleges. Although the university was not supposed to teach theology, the Department of Oriental Languages was allegedly examining the Bible from the perspective of the higher criticism. Leading the group of complainants were Albert Carman and Elmore Harris. Hovering in the wings was Samuel Hume Blake, an evangelical Anglican who was a prominent lawyer and a governor of the university.

Falconer, a Presbyterian minister, told the delegation that he could see no valid objection to the study of biblical literature and history at University College. This left his interviewers unhappy, and Harris undertook to try to get the board of governors to take up the case. One step he took was to interview Thomas Eakin, who turned out to be an uncompromising higher critic. Such a man had no business teaching biblical studies, Harris thought. Blake agreed, and in November 1908 he contacted John Hoskin, the chairman of the university's board of governors, to complain about Oriental languages in general and Eakin's teaching in particular. 'As far as I can discover,' Hoskin replied, 'there is no dogmatic teaching and no work of interpretation being carried on ... It would seem necessary that a properly equipped University should take some cognizance of Literature which is ranked with the most important any nation has given to man. This is all that is being done.'[65]

Unwilling to take no for an answer, Blake wrote again, this time sending a copy to Victoria's chancellor, Nathanael Burwash. Somewhat more responsive than Hoskin, Burwash acknowledged the existence of a constitutional cavil. But he added that the teaching of biblical knowledge in University College could be regularized by means of an amendment to the University Act.[66]

This prompted Blake, in an anguished ten-page letter to Burwash, to show exactly where the shoe pinched. It was not the constitutional issue that bothered him, but the fear that Eakin's teaching was undermining faith. 'I abhor the thought,' Blake wrote, 'that our Toronto University should aid in the work of shaking men's confidence in the Bible as being the Word of God.'[67]

The publicity Blake gave to this letter – he arranged to have it published as a pamphlet – forced the board of governors to deal with his complaint. After all, the University of Toronto might be secular, but it was not supposed to promote unbelief. The board established a committee of inquiry headed by D. Bruce Macdonald, a Presbyterian clergyman, which met late in February 1909. First it called on Eakin and the senior member of the department, J.F. McCurdy, to answer Blake's allegations. Eakin said he treated the Bible as a historical and literary document, and avoided theological discussion. McCurdy stated this to be the general rule in the department.

Elmore Harris appeared before the committee to attack the higher criticism and call for the abolition of the teaching of Oriental languages in the university. William Meredith, a former leader of the provincial Tories, asked, 'Isn't it our business as a Provincial University, if certain things give offence, to avoid teaching them unless it is necessary to do so?' To this, the banker Byron E. Walker replied that 'all proper criticism' should be available to students 'for the purpose of getting at the truth.' Falconer warned that free investigation would become difficult if the teaching in one department was subjected to censorship. 'To be consistent, I think you would have to go through the whole University and cut out probably fifty percent of the work, and use the blue pencil freely and say "You must not teach that because it is contrary to somebody's views."'[68]

The report the committee presented to the board in December characterized as 'unfounded' the charges against University College's Department of Oriental Languages, though the committee did urge that professors be warned against raising theological issues, since this was bound to create difficulties. Falconer had already taken note of this. Upon reading an early draft of the report, he had written to a committee member, Zebulon Lash: 'In the future all semblances of theology must as far as possible be avoided. I realise this will involve good judgment, but competent professors should be able to draw a distinction between theology, as understood in the Act, and literature or ethics.'[69]

The report was a victory of sorts for academic freedom. But the warning qualified the victory. Professors who read it were likely to feel constrained in their teaching whenever a religious issue arose. It goes almost without saying that professors at denominational institutions felt so constrained, the bold claim of a Winthrop Bell notwithstanding. Given the place that religion had in Canadian life, unfettered freedom in this sphere was inconceivable. Not until the second half of the twentieth century would this change.

A near-constant in the cases discussed so far – the Fallon incident is the sole exception – is the central role played by lay boards and the executive heads who reported to them. Lay control had its origins in the sixteenth-century Geneva Academy, from which it spread 'to all universities and colleges in Europe and the New World founded in the Calvinist Reformed tradition.' Other North American colleges followed suit. In the process, academics were usually excluded from boards. The main reason, John S. Brubacher and Willis Rudy write, was that 'in America the financing of higher education was an unremitting anxiety.' Where the raising of money and its frugal management were of central importance, it seemed to make sense to exclude those people who represented the major item of expenditure, the faculty.[70]

In 1852–4 McGill reformed its statutes, adopting the governing structure that soon became the rule in Canada. A lay board took control of business matters and became the final authority in the appointment and dismissal of faculty and staff. A body that did admit professors to its membership, the McGill Corporation (elsewhere this body was called the senate), took charge of academic affairs but was subservient to the board.[71] This was the dominant pattern also in the Atlantic provinces. The University of New Brunswick, as reformed in 1859, adopted a variant of the scheme in that it made do with a single governing body, the lay senate, which excluded professors. (Not until 1952 did UNB get an academic senate.)

McGill, Queen's, and Dalhousie, with their bicameral structures, shaped the pattern of governance in the newer Canadian universities. When reform of the University of Toronto came under consideration in 1905, the influence of McGill and Queen's dominated. The secretary of the royal commission headed by Joseph W. Flavelle was A.H.U. Colquhoun, the deputy minister of education, and it was to him that Frederick C. Hamilton wrote in October 1905. Hamilton was a biographer of Principal George Monro Grant of Queen's, and he thought that too much of that institution's success had been credited to Grant and not enough to its plan of administration.

The essence of Queen's success, Hamilton said, was the concentration of power and responsibility in one body, the board of trustees: 'Partly by design, partly as a result of special conditions, the Board of Trustees really is the University.' The senate, Hamilton noted, 'has no part in the management of university affairs in the administrative sense. Finances, appointments etc., all centre in the one body.' Other than the principal, no professor could serve on the board. 'This decision was arrived at many years ago, at a time when so thoroughly popular and amiable a man as Professor Williamson was a member of the Board.' (James Williamson, professor of natural philosophy and mathematics, had sought to succeed Principal Leitch in 1864, but the board had regarded him as insufficiently 'tough' and had passed him over for William Snodgrass.) For the University of Toronto, Hamilton suggested 'full control by a Board of Trustees (or some such title),' and 'the expulsion of the teaching staff from the Board.'[72]

The royal commission would very likely have recommended this in any case; lay boards that excluded the faculty were by this time the rule in North America. The commission reported early in 1906, and a month later the government introduced legislation incorporating most of the report's recommendations, among them the placing of the university's business affairs, including the appointment, promotion, and dismissal of all its employees, in the hands of a board of governors of which the president would be the only academic member.[73]

The Toronto model influenced the provincial universities in western Canada. The University of British Columbia offers a clear example. The original University Act of 1890, amended in 1891, was 'modelled on English and Scottish university procedure particularly as regards the preponderance of members of the teaching staff in governing the University.' The 1908 Act, however, imposed a lay board of governors with power over all business and employment matters. The act confined professors to the university senate and further limited their influence by means of amendments to the act in 1912. The first historian of UBC, F.H. Soward, saw in this the triumph of 'Eastern Canadian practice.'[74]

The University of Toronto Act served as a model, too, for the University Act passed in Saskatchewan in 1907, for amendments made to the University of Alberta Act in 1908, and for changes made in Manitoba's University Act nine years later. The Manitoba experience is particularly interesting. The Manitoba University Council, which had governed the institution since 1900, counted two representatives of the teaching staff among its twenty-one members. In 1917 the government replaced this body with a conventional board. Exercising wide-ranging power over the university's business affairs, including appointments and dismissals, it excluded all members 'of the regular and permanent teaching or executive staff of the University or of any affiliated college.'[75] By excluding even the president from voting membership on the board, Manitoba went a step further than other provincial universities.

Academic freedom in Canada had to develop within a framework in which power was very unequally distributed. As employees dependent on lay boards, professors were ill-positioned to assert themselves, particularly when confronting their own universities. There is no reason to suppose that this troubled large numbers of academics. Challenging authority did not come easily to people whose social origins were mostly in the professional, business, and well-to-do farming classes and who probably ranked loyalty higher than independence of mind. The 'disciplined intelligence' of the Victorian era made limited room for academic rebels.[76]

Historically, loyalty was highly valued in Canada. United Empire Loyalists had shaped the early intellectual environment of the colonies that came together in 1867, and if before the end of the nineteenth century the UEL influence had yielded to that of immigrants from the British Isles, the idea of loyalty did not thereby lose its potency. Loyalty was due to the Crown, the Empire, one's country, one's church. But it had other objects as well. Commenting on the Canadian imagination as exhibited in our literature, Northrop Frye noted the prevalence of a 'garrison mentality' that developed in 'isolated communities surrounded with a physical or psychological "frontier," separated from one another and from their American and British cultural sources ... In the earliest maps of the country the only inhabited centres are forts, and that remains true of the cultural maps for a much later time.'[77]

For Canada's universities, located among a population that often seemed indifferent or even hostile to higher education, loyalty had real value. With loyalty, however, came deference to authority and a strong concern for order. These sapped the critical spirit. Yet a handful of professors did assert themselves, refusing to remain silent when faced with what they regarded as errors of policy or abuses of power. Speaking up when it would have been prudent to say nothing, they were the early heroes and martyrs of academic freedom in Canada.

3

The Great War

The years from 1914 to 1920 sorely tested the universities. Faculty and students went overseas to fight; many did not return. The diversion of money to the war effort also hurt the institutions. Hardships did not end with the armistice in November 1918. A deadly influenza epidemic closed the universities for several weeks in the winter of 1918–19, and war-caused inflation raged into 1920. There was much social unrest, the best-known instance being the 1919 Winnipeg General Strike, but the universities remained quiet. During the war there had been virtually no professorial criticism of the war effort, and in the aftermath social criticism among the professoriate was almost as rare. But there were some exceptions. Wesley College's Salem Bland held capitalism to be contrary to the spirit of Jesus Christ, Robert M. MacIver of Toronto and O.D. Skelton of Queen's asked whether the capitalist system should not undergo at least a measure of reform, and McGill's Stephen Leacock posed 'the unsolved riddle of social justice.'

Although the academic self-image gives a prominent place to the lonely champion of unpopular ideas, most professors (like human beings generally) are herd animals. In war, the herd has a strong tendency to be patriotic and illiberal. But the analogy should not be pushed too far. It is human to want to belong; it is also human to resist going against one's conscience. Still, although not all academics supported every single aspect of the war effort, they were as one in their support of the Allied powers. The country's place in the British Empire was partly responsible for this; so were the abhorrence of the German invasion of Belgium and the belief that 'Prussianism' was a threat to civilization.

In the absence of academic opponents of the war, attacks on professors were few in Canada, even while the United States witnessed a frontal assault on academic freedom. The historian Carol Gruber writes that the war 'exposed the repressive underside of majority sentiment on the campus; it exposed a lack of commitment to academic freedom within the profession at large and a willing-ness even of its chief defenders to bend the principle to the pressures of the moment.'[1] Tolerance may not have been higher north of the border, but Cana-dian academics were readier to toe the line. Although a few professors did get into trouble for their opinions, those who lost their jobs owed their fate less to what they said than to what they were. At two institutions faculty members were forced out because of their national background.

At the outbreak of war, the University of Toronto employed three German nationals. They had little in common besides their ethnicity. Paul Mueller, who taught German, was a graduate of the university who had lived in Canada for twenty-one years. (The historian Arthur Lower later recalled him as the 'one exception' among the 'mediocrities' who made up University College's depart-ment of modern languages before the war.)[2] Mueller's three sons, all born in Canada, belonged to Harbord Collegiate's Cadet Corps; the oldest was drilling part time with the Queen's Own Rifles of Canada when the war began.

The other two Germans were more recent arrivals. Bonno Tapper was a jun-ior member of the German department who, having lived in North America for several years, needed no reminder that on the subject of the war, silence was golden. Immanuel Benzinger was less prudent. An expert on Semitic languages, he had been appointed to the university in the spring, and on reaching Toronto he had naïvely imparted to a *Globe* reporter the official German version of the outbreak of the war. The editor, J.A. Macdonald, was a governor of the univer-sity. Recognizing the trouble Benzinger's remarks might cause, he killed the interview but told the president, Sir Robert Falconer, about it. Falconer asked Benzinger for an explanation and, finding it sufficient, asked him in future to keep his own counsel. This Benzinger did. But rumours about the interview began to spread, and when it became known that Benzinger's son was serving in the German army, questions arose about the father's fitness to teach in Can-ada. There were also questions about Mueller. Soon after the war began, he objected to some blatantly anti-German remarks made by the principal of Har-bord Collegiate, and this brought him a certain notoriety.[3]

Propaganda about German atrocities, combined with signs that in its early stages the war was not going well for the British and French, helped make the three Germans targets for harassment – proxies for the German soldiers in Bel-gium and France. That the three taught in a provincial institution also affected them, for the argument lay to hand that a publicly financed university ought not to employ enemy aliens. Knowing that some of his backbenchers shared the growing public hostility against the three, Premier William Hearst privately urged Falconer to say something, and the latter wrote to the Toronto newspapers on 16 November, denying that grounds existed to dismiss the three. But this did not have the desired effect. Disappointed patriots attacked Falconer; he did not seem to grasp the gravity of the situation.[4]

Falconer could take comfort from the knowledge that most of the faculty and students supported him and that he also enjoyed the support of powerful members of the board, such as the chairman, Sir (Byron) Edmund Walker, the vice-chairman, Zebulon Lash, and Joseph W. Flavelle. Chief among their opponents was Sir Edmund Osler, stockbroker, bank president, Conservative MP for Toronto West, and a bigot where Germans were concerned. He wrote to Walker in November 1914: 'President Falconer does not seem to realise that one of these men has a son in the German Army, and that all of them are openly and avowedly sympathizers with Germany.'[5]

Walker countered by stating that the university should be above prejudice. If the board responded to opinion 'in an unusually excited city,' it seemed probable that in a few years' time, he said, 'we shall regret having acted in a spirit of rather petty retaliation.'[6]

Walker wished to keep the institution from surrendering to pressure; he also wished to maintain Falconer in the presidency. The board could not dismiss anyone without a recommendation from the president, and it was clear that Falconer was determined to keep the three Germans. An attempt to force their dismissal might therefore prompt his resignation. Similar concerns may have motivated Flavelle, who later commended Falconer's 'courage, wisdom, [and] firmness of purpose' in the matter of the German professors.[7]

The issue had its first full airing at a board meeting on 3 December 1914. Falconer outlined the qualifications of the three and the nature of their appointments; he pointed out that Mueller and Tapper had lived in Canada long enough to regard it as their home, he noted that all three were performing their duties satisfactorily, and he assured board members that none had been disloyal. There being no grounds for dismissing the three, he concluded, he could only recommend that 'their services be retained.'[8]

The meeting continued into the next day, and eventually Osler moved that Falconer ask the three to resign, 'and in the event of their not doing so that this Board recommend to the President that he recommend their dismissal.' An amendment that sought to replace the original motion with one effectively negating it failed by a vote of four to nine, with Falconer abstaining. The four voting for the amendment were Walker, Lash, Flavelle, and J.A. Macdonald. Chancellor Sir William Meredith then moved an amendment giving the three men leave of absence with pay until 30 June 1915. This passed by ten votes to four, with both Falconer and Osler, for different reasons, opposed.[9]

The board's minutes provide no details of the discussion that led to this compromise, but it is likely most board members hoped that the three would resign before the 1915–16 session began. Falconer stood firm. No professor, he argued, should be asked to resign without cause or for reasons irrelevant to the university's purpose. Also important, in his view, was that the university should resist current passions. Most board members disagreed. The implications for academic freedom were unhappy.

Because the board repudiated the course Falconer had recommended, he would have been justified in resigning. But this would not have helped the three Germans. Instead, he tried to arrange exchanges with American universities and even to place Benzinger and Mueller in the United States permanently (Tapper had returned to Chicago to complete his graduate work). These exertions bore no fruit.[10]

Benzinger resigned effective 31 December 1914 and found a job at a small U.S. college. The atmosphere in Toronto made his return to the university unthinkable at this time, he wrote; perhaps after the war? Falconer replied that the future was impossible to predict.[11]

Mueller became a British subject and arranged to pay the person hired to teach his courses during the winter term. Did Falconer intimate to him that his return was unacceptable to the board? In the fall of 1915 he was teaching at McMaster, where he stayed on even after the war came to an end.[12]

The compromise reached in December 1914 did not mollify those who thought that the three should be fired. 'If we cannot get university professors of British blood,' a Conservative MPP said, 'then let us close the universities.' On 15 December an all-party delegation saw Premier Hearst. One member accused Falconer of seeking 'to exercise an autocratic despotism with money that came from the public purse,' and several more demanded the imposition of tighter control over the university. Hearst promised to look into the matter and perhaps to appoint a committee of inquiry.[13] (He did not do so.)

Was academic freedom at issue in the cases of Benzinger, Mueller, and Tapper? It was deeply objectionable to harass the three because of their nationality and to force them to resign for no good academic reason. These practices did nothing to promote an atmosphere in which academic freedom might flourish. But probably nothing was further from the minds of Sir Edmund Osler and his fellow zealots than the cause of academic freedom.

Platon Reich, a sessional lecturer in German at Trinity College, was briefly at the centre of controversy in October 1914. A British subject of Moravian origin, he had studied in Germany, Belgium, and the Netherlands. As he had been in Europe when the war broke out, he must have seemed to the editor of the *Varsity* an ideal subject for an interview – as indeed he was. He stated, 'Though the

British cause seems to us perfectly just ... upon examination there arises a complete case for Germany, which the Germans uphold in all honesty and sincerity.' Reich went on to say that the conflict was rooted in mutual distrust between the German and British peoples, fostered by the press of both countries, and in the Germans' belief that both Russia and France had been preparing 'to crush their country.' Reich thought that Britain, France, and Russia would win, 'but at a terrible expense.' Germany would lose German Poland and Lorraine at the very least, and the German people might depose the Kaiser in order to establish 'a limited monarchy or a republic.' But under a more efficient form of government the Germans would 'work doubly hard for the attainment of Germany's greatness.' The end of the war, then, would begin a renewed struggle: 'Only one thing can save Europe and that is the abandonment of the practice of forming alliances for an economic federation of the whole continent, with a common coinage.'[14]

Today's reader will appreciate the clarity of Reich's view. But in 1914 many were unable to read beyond his assertion that Germans believed as strongly in their own cause as the British and French did in theirs. This offended the editor of the *Mail and Empire*: By what right did the heathen worship their false gods? Offensive, too, was Reich's prediction that the war would end in a compromise peace: 'No remark could show more clearly the propensity of a certain type of university professor to embrace views with which the Canadian people will have nothing to do ... It is a war to the death, and will not end until one side or other is put out of the combat.'[15]

While implying that Reich was disloyal, the *Mail and Empire* stopped short of saying so, but some of its readers were less inhibited. One of them wondered whether 'our universities are so pervaded with agnosticism and German "culture" that they cannot distinguish between right and wrong.' A member of the University of Toronto's board of governors, Colonel Reuben Wells Leonard, mistakenly believing Reich to be employed by this institution, urged Falconer to dismiss him.[16]

The editor of the *Varsity* defended Reich against the charges of disloyalty, writing that he had performed a public service in pointing out that the Germans believed in their cause, would fight tenaciously, and would be difficult to defeat. Reich in the meantime was Trinity's concern and needed to satisfy only its governors. Perhaps they read the *Varsity* interview more carefully than the editor of the *Mail and Empire* had, for at their meeting of 14 November they renewed Reich's contract without recorded comment.[17]

This did not mean that Trinity was a bastion of academic freedom. A German national who taught there, W.A. von Lubtow, was pushed into resigning in December 1914. Since 1908 Lubtow had been at Cambridge, whence he had come to join Trinity's German department in the fall of 1914. He was willing 'to take out naturalization papers if this were deemed desirable,' but was not required to do so. However, he undertook not to express sympathy with 'any country with which the British Empire is at war,' or to do anything that 'might embarrass the College.'[18]

Several weeks passed, weeks during which the tempest around Benzinger, Mueller, and Tapper gained in strength. On 11 December, Provost G.S. Macklem enjoined Lubtow neither to discuss the war nor to speak to the press: 'Any disregard of this injunction might quickly imperil your position on the staff.' In fact, that position was already in peril. The very next day Sir Edmund Osler tossed a poisoned dart. 'Talk is beginning very freely about the German Professor in Trinity College,' he told Macklem. 'I think it is unwise and unpatriotic to keep him and I believe that the voice of the country is almost a unit [sic] in that view.'[19]

The sound heard in reply was that of a backbone buckling. Macklem promised Osler that an early meeting of the governing body would discuss the matter: 'It is my desire ... to take whatever course is most consonant with true patriotism.' Macklem added that although Lubtow deplored Germany's violation of Belgian neutrality and hoped that the Germans would be defeated in the West, it might not be possible to keep him: 'The present state of public opinion should be given all due weight and consideration.'[20]

Some days later Macklem informed Lubtow that his position would be discussed at a special meeting of the Trinity Corporation on 29 December. Calls for his dismissal were not 'due to any fault or indiscretion of your own,' Macklem explained, but rather to the suspicion to which Germans were now subject, 'coupled with an unwillingness to allow them to remain in any position of influence in British communities.' Taking the hint, Lubtow resigned, asking only for $1,380 in compensation for salary due and for various expenses. Perhaps grateful that he was going quietly, the corporation met his request. Early in 1915 he left for the United States.[21]

There was yet another professor of German origin in Toronto, the dean of forestry at the University of Toronto, Bernhard Fernow. In January 1915 Falconer informed him that Osler had reported a conversation with a student who claimed that Fernow had failed to encourage students to volunteer for the armed forces. 'I told Sir Edmund that this was very different from everything that I had heard during the winter,' Falconer wrote, 'that on the contrary, you had encouraged your students to enter the Officers' Training Corps.'[22]

Fernow responded directly to Osler, asking him to call upon members of his faculty, upon 'the leading men' among the students, 'and especially upon Captain A.D. LePan ... now in command of a battalion in the O.T.C., who heard me address the students, urging them as a sacred duty to join the O.T.C. and prepare for the eventuality of joining a contingent.' Falconer was pleased: 'I felt confident that this was your attitude.' Several months later an alumnus expressed appreciation for 'the firm stand' Falconer had taken 'in opposing persecution of the German professors – and especially Dr. Fernow.' Fernow had been very discreet this winter, Falconer replied: 'I have not of late heard any remarks about his being a German.' Fernow's acquired British patriotism had served him well.[23]

The Queen's political economist O.D. Skelton might have become an exception to the rule that no Canadian academics lost their positions because they were thought to be unpatriotic. Early in 1918 Skelton learned from his friend G.Y. Chown, registrar and treasurer of Queen's, that a wealthy alumnus, James Richardson, had sought his dismissal because of his opposition to conscription for overseas military service. However, 'the Principal [Bruce Taylor] talked to him of the freedom that the University stood for and the necessity of presenting both sides.' Tayler had asked Richardson 'if he would like his son to be educated in his views only and after a few minutes talk to and fro Richardson frankly admitted that he was in the wrong.'[24]

'The position which the Principal took is the only one that could be expected from Dr. Taylor or from a Principal of Queen's,' Skelton replied, 'but I am glad to learn that he took it with such firmness and tact that he was able to make a man so narrow-minded as Richardson see the error of his ways.' Faculty members should 'abstain from one-sided or partisan discussion in the classroom,' Skelton continued, and should speak publicly 'only after giving careful & scholarly consideration to the subject and in a moderate & reasoned fashion.' In times of crisis, furthermore, professors should try to avoid criticism of the government. But within these limits, they should have the right to state their views, especially if their training and experience made them 'more familiar than the average man' with issues that came before the public. Skelton wondered whether he might not be freer to write 'as editor of a weekly than as professor in a university.' As he pointed out, the effort 'to keep one eye on truth ... and the other on the interests of the institution ... tends to make one intellectually cross-eyed.'[25] Never has the tension between academic freedom and the university's need for support been more graphically described.

Skelton's stand on conscription endangered a gift from Chancellor James Douglas. If Queen's could raise $500,000, the financier had promised to match it, but Skelton's views led Douglas to have second thoughts. He took a dim view of 'pacifism.' In January 1918 Douglas's son Walter conveyed his father's view 'that if a professor was out of touch with the prevailing sentiment on a great public & patriotic issue he ought to resign.' Taylor, who had become principal only a few weeks earlier, demurred: 'It would be a perilous thing to treat every great political issue as a determining factor in university life.' Did this comment persuade Douglas senior and junior? At all events, the son indicated that the gift would be made as promised.[26]

Taylor subsequently wrote to a friend at McGill: 'Influences inside ... [and] outside the University were trying to force the resignation of a Professor, whose views on the conscription question I thoroughly disagreed with.' But Taylor had resisted, he said, because 'liberty of utterance for every honest opinion' was essential: 'Queen's is going to be a place of freedom so long as I have anything to do with it.'[27] Would he have remained steadfast if Douglas had insisted on Skelton's dismissal as the price of financial support? We can only guess.

When the University of British Columbia historian Mack Eastman took leave at the end of 1916 to volunteer for military service, Walter C. Barnes, an American teaching at the University of California, was engaged to replace him. The appointment drew criticism from the *Vancouver Sun*, its editor asserting that 'only a Canadian, or a man of British stock, should be given the important work of teaching British history.' Eastman responded that Barnes's ancestry was British, that he had been a Rhodes Scholar, and that like most historians in the United States, he was pro-British: 'Yes, I daresay some Canadian slacker might have been found who would undertake to teach our youth to "understand our history and the great ideals to which it leads the student." But I did not vacate my chair for the convenience of caitiffs.'[28]

Eastman failed to persuade the *Sun*'s editor, who insisted, 'It is impossible for an American to appreciate our history or our national ideals.' A *Sun* staff writer added, 'Only a British subject is fit to teach British history to British boys in British universities.' But UBC did not reconsider Barnes's appointment, though President Frank F. Wesbrook did send a copy of Eastman's letter to Minister of Education John D. MacLean. In his covering letter, Wesbrook expressed the hope that the matter would 'be allowed to drop at this point.'[29]

Fifteen months later Barnes was squarely at the centre of another controversy. In April 1918 Wesbrook received a letter charging the historian with having said that 'the Germans are not to blame for this war,' that they accused the British of 'similar atrocities with which they are charged,' that the violation of Belgian neutrality had many precedents, and that 'the only reason why Britain won't accept the German peace terms is because they want to totally crush Germany & get all her boundless commercial wealth.' The letter writer was outraged: 'In the States a professor giving such teaching ... would be very promptly dealt with & it is a disgraceful thing that in a Canadian university ... such pro-German propaganda should be permitted.'[30]

The secretary of the board of governors, S.D. Scott, replied that it had been decided in January that Barnes's appointment would end on 31 May 1918, but there would be an inquiry all the same. It took place on 27 May. Four students, one of them a returned soldier, testified that Barnes's teaching was unexceptionable. Barnes himself said he believed 'that the war had been forced upon the Germans by their own rulers and not by the Allies,' and that 'while he thought it his duty as a scientific teacher to mention the German point of view, he undertook to show that the cause of the Allies was a just one.'[31]

After some discussion, the board 'agreed unanimously that ... the charges against Mr. Barnes were not proven.' He returned to the United States, his reputation cleansed of Germanophilia.[32]

Although President Wesbrook had in 1917 rejected a demand that he not appoint Barnes, his role in 1918 was ambiguous. He could not ignore the letter he had received, of course, but could he not simply have sent a reply conveying Barnes's explanation? Why launch an inquiry? After all, it had been decided months earlier that his appointment would end on 31 May 1918. Or had it? Eastman was not expected back (if at all) until the war had ended, whenever that might be. Neither the board minutes nor Wesbrook's presidential files contain any references to the issue of Barnes's appointment before the complaint about his teaching. The man who succeeded him, Walter Sage, was not appointed until the fall, months after Barnes had departed. Thus, it seems likely that the decision not to renew Barnes's contract was prompted by the unwelcome attention that came his way.

As for the inquiry, it probably took place only because Wesbrook knew MacLean was interested in the Barnes case. When the provincial Liberals entered office in 1916, they inherited in UBC an institution which some MLA's had not wanted and many thought too costly. The new government exerted relentless pressure on UBC.[33] By 1918, if MacLean had said 'jump,' Wesbrook's impulse might have been to ask, 'How high?' It was clearly prudent to demonstrate to MacLean that UBC did not harbour disloyal teachers.

In 1916 the University of Toronto political economist James Mavor used the pages of the *Financial Post* to attack the Ontario Hydro-Electric Power Commission (known today as Ontario Hydro). Mavor had friends among the entrepreneurs who were hostile to Hydro, but the historian H.V. Nelles does not believe that 'these connections [were] of any great significance as an explanation of Mavor's opposition to Hydro.'[34] More important were his faith in the benign workings of the free market and his fear of government-sponsored enterprise, especially one enjoying a monopoly.

The utility had been created by the Conservative government of James P.

Whitney – and Whitney's successor, William Hearst, did not appreciate
Mavor's criticisms. On 2 November 1916 the premier registered a complaint
with Sir Robert Falconer. Was it wise, he asked, 'to have in the very important
position Professor Mavor occupies, a man who is as reckless in his statements
and as illogical in his arguments as this gentleman shows by his writings?'
Mavor had also criticized the Workmen's Compensation Act, Hearst added, and
seemed 'anxious to injure the Government whenever he [could] and to attack
everything in the nature of progressive legislation for the benefit and comfort of
the people.' This had 'the result of bringing condemnation upon the University,'
and it undermined the government's efforts to support the institution. He suggested that the matter required 'attention by the proper authorities.'[35]

Falconer conveyed Hearst's letter to Mavor, who made six points in
response. The first three defended what he had written; the others were an affirmation of academic freedom and university autonomy. Introducing the university into the discussion as Hearst had done was wrong, Mavor concluded: 'A
University is fundamentally a group of scholars who meet for free discussion. If
the Members of the University are to be subjected to the dictation of the Government as to what they may or may not discuss, the University may as well at
once strike its name from the roll of Universities.'[36] This was as strong a
defence of academic freedom as anyone in Canada had made to this point.

Falconer copied Mavor's letter to Hearst, prudently omitting a sentence comparing the government's performance unfavourably with that of the university.
Hearst probably already realized that he had a tiger by the tail, for he must have
known that Mavor's friends included Sir Edmund Walker, Zebulon Lash, and
the utilities magnate Sir William Mackenzie.[37]

The premier declined to respond directly to Mavor. However, he sent Falconer
a rough draft of the letter he proposed later to send to the president officially,
inviting him to comment on it. We may assume, therefore, that Hearst's response
of 30 November 1916 commanded a measure of assent from Falconer. Hearst
denied that he had ever, 'directly or indirectly, by hint, insinuation or otherwise,'
intimated that the university might suffer as a result of Mavor's articles: 'I did,
however, point out the unwisdom ... of a Professor ... of the Provincial University
largely aided by public funds, carrying on a newspaper campaign of the kind in
which Professor Mavor has been engaged.' Enemies of the university were using
his articles 'to create distrust as to the ability and judgment of its Staff,' asserted
Hearst. Many who had not personally enjoyed the benefits of higher education
were uneager to fund the university, and it was this class of person who resented
Mavor's articles and inferred 'that the University is the friend and ally of the rich
and the corporations, as against the labouring man.'[38]

Hearst was hiding behind the common man. But Falconer had to take the premier's comments seriously. The lesson Falconer drew from the experience (a lesson he probably had already learned) was that University of Toronto professors were unwise to bite the hand that fed their institution, and that its autonomy and financial welfare required that limits be imposed on academic free speech.

The best-known wartime incident allegedly involving academic freedom was the dismissal in 1917 of Salem Bland from Winnipeg's Wesley College, where he had taught church history since 1903. Released as part of an effort to reduce costs, Bland took this to be evidence of hostility to his Social Gospel views, critical as they were of many aspects of capitalism. He and his supporters charged that the college's directors were ridding themselves of someone who had made a habit of afflicting the comfortable.[39]

Two facts are incontrovertible: first, Wesley College did face a budgetary crisis; second, Bland's preaching had annoyed some well-to-do Methodists. But the relative importance of these facts in explaining Bland's removal is open to debate. Early in 1917 Wesley's board learned that despite efforts to economize, the college was operating in the red for the third year in a row. By the end of the budgetary year there would be an accumulated deficit of $30,000, an amount close to the college's annual salary bill. Caused by inflation and reduced donations, the crisis led Principal Eber Crummy to inform the executive committee of the board that the only possible course was 'such a reduction of the teaching staff as might be effected with the least serious results to the efficiency of the college.'[40]

Crummy was asked to discuss this with the faculty. When he reported back, he proposed that an economist and two professors in the Faculty of Theology be asked to resign. A board committee found that one of the three, Bland, would not agree. His obstinacy seemed to stymie the committee. Confusion grew when board members disagreed among themselves about what should be done, and the situation grew even worse when a few faculty members, alleging that Crummy was a secret drinker, questioned his fitness to direct the college. He denied the charge but felt his moral authority to be so weakened that he resigned in late May.[41]

After accepting Crummy's resignation, the executive committee returned to the matter of retrenchment: 'It was felt that the new principal ... should have a fairly free hand ... It was therefore moved ... that the Executive recommend to the Board of Directors that all officers, teachers, professors and other employees of the College be notified that their term of service will expire on the 30th day of June next.' The full board met on 31 May, narrowly approved the executive committee's recommendation, and appointed a committee to find a new principal and to consider the reorganization of the staff.[42]

When Crummy's resignation became public, the faculty came to the view 'that all internal control [should] be placed in the hands of a committee of four, chosen from their own members.' This would save the salary of a principal and lessen the need for reductions. The suggestion had support among students and alumni, and 'for a time there was some hesitation on the part of the board itself.'[43] There was none on the part of the board's chairman, a businessman named James H. Ashdown. He wanted a strong leader who would restore Wesley's finances to their prewar health. Most board members shared his view.

The search committee met on 4 June and voted unanimously to offer the principalship to John H. Riddell, an Edmonton clergyman. Next on the agenda was 'the reconstruction of the faculty.' The committee decided not to reappoint an economist and a mathematician, and voted six to one to 'retire' Bland. Noting that Riddell could do most of the work being done by the New Testament professor, Arthur J. Irwin, the committee released him as well.[44]

Bland and Irwin chose to fight for their jobs. Their main battlefields were the Manitoba and Saskatchewan conferences of the Methodist Church, where they had considerable support. Bland's home conference of Saskatchewan held the nonrenewals to have been irregular and recommended that the college retain both men. The Manitoba conference appointed a committee of investigation, which found that although the grounds for nonrenewal were indeed financial, the men had been unfairly treated, and it recommended that the board reconsider its action.[45]

The Grain Growers' Guide asserted in June 1917 that Bland had 'aroused considerable hostility among the privileged rich and the "let-well-enough-alone" members of the clergy,' and that this had contributed to his dismissal. Was this true? The court of appeal of the Methodist Church did not answer the question, even as it awarded Bland and Irwin a year's salary in lieu of notice. Members of the Saskatchewan conference were dissatisfied and in 1918 ordered their own inquiry into the dismissals. Chaired by the chief justice of Saskatchewan, the commission of inquiry heard twenty-one witnesses and concluded that although some board members did oppose Bland's views, the reason for his removal was budgetary. His supporters remained unpersuaded.[46]

If they were right, Bland's dismissal offended against his academic freedom. The evidence is slight at best, however. All the same, the board can be faulted for high-handedness and secretiveness. The decisions to appoint Riddell and to remove some faculty members were taken without consultation. Even those who were reappointed resented the secrecy in which the directors had acted. They ran the college as if it were a business enterprise whose operations should be kept from the public as much as possible. This attitude, which was characteristic of the boards of Canadian universities for many years, bred mistrust and misunderstanding. Openness would have served the college better, as would consultation with the staff and with the Methodist conferences.

Criticizing the board for not adopting a policy of openness is less anachronistic than it may seem. We do not know whether any of the Wesley faculty had read James McKeen Cattell's *University Control* (1913), with its call for greatly increased involvement of professors in university governance – or, indeed, whether they were familiar with the American Association of University Professors' 1915 document on academic freedom and academic tenure. But ideas of faculty power were in the air by 1917; one example was the suggestion that the direction of Wesley college be entrusted to a committee of four professors. Finally, the board's decision in May 1917 to terminate the contracts of all faculty members and reappoint them selectively, though not illegal, caused unnecessary anxiety and made a mockery of the tenure that professors thought they enjoyed.

When Wesley's board of directors put all professors on notice in 1917, they thought they were taking a lead from the University of Manitoba. Earlier that year all of Manitoba's professors had been put on notice, but the purpose was to accommodate amendments to the University Act and the way the institution was governed. A series of measures over the years had led to the establishment of a complete arts course by 1914, and by 1917 the University of Manitoba had 616 students and a staff of 53, with the province providing some 60 per cent of total income. In February 1917 the minister of education, R.S. Thornton, introduced a bill to amend the University Act. 'It does not appear ...,' he stated, 'that such an expenditure of public money should be made any longer except by a body directly responsible to the Government and the Legislature and so to the people of the Province.'[47]

The university council, which to that point had had charge of the institution, comprised ten people chosen by the graduates of the university and by other universities in the British Empire, seven chosen by the cabinet, and two chosen by the teaching staff, while the minister of education and the university president were members *ex officio*. The government replaced this council with a nine-person board of governors appointed by the cabinet. The new board excluded all members of the permanent teaching or executive staff of the university and of the affiliated colleges. The university's historian, W.L. Morton, comments that thereby the 'perhaps not undesirable association of academic men and men of affairs which had obtained in the old council was ended.'[48]

The board was to appoint all employees of the university, to fix their salaries, 'and to define their duties and their tenure of office or employment which, unless otherwise provided,' was to be 'during the pleasure of the board.'

Because the university council was no longer the employer, the new board thought it advisable to terminate and reappoint everyone. Virtually all faculty members were in fact reappointed, though there were a few exceptions. An instructor in political economy, who was on military leave, was given 'no assurance of appointment on discharge,' and the professor of civil engineering's contract was not renewed. He appealed to the board for a hearing, which he was granted, but the board reaffirmed its decision; the reason cannot be inferred from the board minutes.[49]

More information is available about the nonrenewal of an assistant professor of French in 1919. In March the board appointed a committee to inquire into the complaint of W.F. Osborne, head of the French department, that his junior colleague, Charles Muller, was uncooperative. Upon hearing from the committee in April, the board informed Muller that he would not be reappointed 'unless, before the next meeting of the Board, he presents assurances satisfactory to the special committee and to President [James A.] MacLean that he will, in future, carry out the course of study as laid down by the Department and work in harmony with the head thereof.'[50]

Muller disclaimed responsibility for the difficulties in the department and expressed a willingness to work with Osborne, but he offered to resign rather than cause continuing friction. '[His] objections to the changes proposed by Professor Osborne are so fundamental and are supported by him so vigorously as matters of conviction,' MacLean reported, 'that it seems to me ... practically impossible for us to expect co-operation between Professor Osborne and him in administering the new curriculum.' The board voted not to reappoint Muller.[51]

Faced with a disagreement between a department head and a junior instructor, the president and board had sided with the senior man, one imagines almost instinctively. It cannot have helped Muller that the issue came to a head during the Winnipeg General Strike, when the board was peculiarly sensitive to challenges to authority. What aspect of academic freedom, if any, was at issue in this case is impossible to judge. It was generally the case, however, that junior professors were ill advised to cross their elders. Of course, even the most senior professors were in trouble if they fell foul of presidents and boards.

Few Canadian universities have ever been more racked by dissension than Saskatchewan in 1919. After several months of turmoil, the board of governors dismissed three senior professors and the director of university extension. The effects were felt for years afterwards. Michael Hayden (the university's official historian) identifies two underlying reasons for the blow-up: the inflation that accompanied the war and its aftermath, and the university's budgetary problems.[52] Government grants were frozen even as prices came close to doubling.

But these conditions were not unique to Saskatoon. From Halifax to Vancouver, university budgets became increasingly inadequate, while salaries lagged far behind the rising cost of living. Nowhere were professors easily reconciled to this, but only Saskatchewan witnessed a major conflict.

There was more to the incident than money. Still, money mattered. Academics do not live by bread alone, but they do need bread to live. The decade before 1914 had been something of a golden age for academic salaries. In Canada as in the United States, professors enjoyed incomes comparable to those of averagely successful lawyers and physicians.[53] Full professors in Canada earned from $2,000 to $5,000 annually, depending on the institution, seniority, and teaching subject. Junior faculty members were notably ill paid only in the denominational colleges. (Benefits were minimal by today's standards, however. Few institutions had pension plans as yet, and regular sabbaticals were hardly dreamed of.)

During the war academic salaries had increased hardly at all, sustaining a blow from which they took half a century to recover. The leader of a faculty delegation to Manitoba's board of governors stated in 1919 'that the increase in the cost of living had made it impossible for members of the Faculty to maintain their homes in the condition they should, and that it was necessary for their wives and even themselves [sic!] to perform all the menial domestic tasks.' Alberta's President Henry Marshall Tory reported complaints from the faculty that 'they were unable to buy houses and houses could not be rented.' The first faculty association in Canada took form at the University of British Columbia in 1920, and its objective was to secure higher salaries.[54]

University of Saskatchewan faculty submitted a petition in 1918 stating that 'while professors had once been able to afford domestic help, now a number were in danger of losing their houses.' They wanted an immediate one-third increase in their salaries and more in the future. The government undertook to increase the university's budget so that it could at least introduce the University of Toronto salary schedule, but the members of the board qualified this promise by resolving that if the condition of the university required it, they reserved 'the right to withhold any or all annual increments.' As well, the board wanted to be able to give extraordinary increases 'or to exceed the maximum fixed for a grade.' This would enable it to reward those whom President Walter C. Murray held to be particularly deserving.[55]

The trouble with rewarding deserving academics, an anonymous wit has said, is that 80 per cent of them believe themselves to be more meritorious than the other four-fifths (an attitude not limited to academics, of course). The discretion enjoyed by Murray increased the unhappiness of some faculty members. In fact, the president contributed to the feeling of malaise in other ways. Highly able, dedicated to the welfare of the university as he saw it, Murray liked to have things his own way, took advice from few, did not like to delegate, and deprecated opposition. To some he appeared as a stern but kindly father figure, to others as a power-hungry autocrat. 'In 1919–20 the basic issue was the power of the president,' Michael Hayden writes.[56]

The incident began when the director of extension, Samuel Greenway, went to Regina in March 1919 and informed the minister of agriculture, Charles Dunning, that six years earlier Murray had falsified a financial return for Greenway's department. He added that most of the faculty were disenchanted with Murray's leadership.[57] When informed of this by Dunning, Murray was shocked that Greenway had approached Dunning rather than simply asking for an explanation of the financial return (and in fact this might have saved a lot of grief, for the 'falsification' was a clerical error). Murray regarded Greenway's action not only as disloyal but also as being likely to invite intervention in university affairs. His linking of the issues of loyalty and institutional autonomy was to his advantage, for it led some to confuse the attack on him with a threat to the university.

It became known that before going to Regina, Greenway had conferred with three professors. One was John Hogg, the head of physics. A popular teacher and an able scientist, Hogg was concerned about the difficulties that faced scientific research. He had been unhappy with Murray's authoritarian style for some time, and he may have been casting covetous eyes on the president's job.[58]

(Michael Hayden quotes A.B. Macallum of the National Research Council as saying that Hogg had been a 'trouble-maker' at the University of Toronto, 'intriguing' against President James Loudun and the physicist John C. McLennan. This was a reference to an objection that Hogg and thirty-five other students had raised in 1900 to the awarding of a scholarship to a student who had neither applied nor submitted a thesis as required, but who had been nominated by McLennan, one of the judges. The university council had dismissed the complaint, but in 1905 a new government had appointed a committee of inquiry. Its report stated that McLennan should not have served as a judge and that 'the recommendation that the scholarship should be awarded to [the winner] was irregular, and should not have been made.' This criticism did not sit well with McLennan and his friends and associates, Macallum among them.)[59]

Another with whom Greenway had spoken was Robert MacLaurin, the head of chemistry. He, too, deplored Saskatchewan's low salaries and inadequate funding of research. The third man was Ira MacKay, professor of law and political science. He had come to Saskatoon as Murray's protégé, but although he liked and respected his mentor, he had grown critical of the university's autocratic form of government. He seems also to have thought that an investigation of Greenway's charges would clear the air.[60]

The charges help explain why Saskatchewan rather than any other university became the battlefield. Alberta's Henry Marshall Tory, for example, was at least as autocratic as Murray and probably less popular,[61] but Tory's enemies lacked a point of attack, whereas Murray's critics thought they had found one. They were mistaken. Murray counterattacked vigorously, with most of the faculty in support. Dissatisfied though they were with their salaries, they either had confidence in the president or were afraid to show they lacked it. Some disliked Hogg and his allies. Others may have feared political intervention.

The university council, consisting of faculty with the rank of assistant professor or higher (Greenway was not a member), met on 7 April. Murray explained the situation, intimated that he wanted a vote of confidence, and left. Notice of motion was then given that 'this University Council wishes to go on record as affirming its confidence [in] and loyalty to the President and resents any imputation of disloyalty or lack of confidence in the President or his conduct of the University.' Two days later, thirty of the thirty-one faculty members voted on the motion, twenty-six of them in favour and four abstaining: Hogg, MacKay, MacLaurin, and the physicist J.M. Adams. (The absent member, when contacted, cast his vote in favour of the motion). A further motion encouraged the four abstainers to give their reasons.[62] None did.

Murray took the abstentions to signify disloyalty. Informed of what had happened, several of his friends urged him to take a hard line. 'These people ... poison academic life and they ought to be driven out of it,' A.B. Macallum wrote, while Sir Robert Falconer commented, 'It is now a case of either you or them. One University cannot hold both.' Similarly, Dalhousie's President Stanley MacKenzie encouraged Murray to 'unload ... the undesirables' who had caused all the troubles: 'You owe it to the University and you owe it to yourself.'[63]

On 21 April Murray reported to the board, which then instructed the secretary to ask each faculty member whether he was dissatisfied with the administration and, if so, to appear before the board. During the next few weeks all but Adams, Hogg, and MacKay asserted their loyalty in writing. Although MacLaurin made a statement and duly expressed no dissatisfaction with the president, he failed to clear himself of disloyalty in Murray's eyes. 'In ordinary circumstances the proper thing would be to utter a word of warning and pass on,' Murray wrote to the chancellor of the university, Sir Frederick Haultain, '[but] I do not think in the case of one or two the warning would be any use.'[64]

In June Murray issued an ultimatum: he would resign unless the board interrogated those whose loyalty to him was in doubt and took whatever action seemed justified. Faced with a choice between the president and his critics, the governors interviewed Hogg, MacKay, MacLaurin, and Greenway on 10 July (Adams had resigned to take a position in California), then stated their unanimous view 'that it is in the best interest of the University and of all concerned that certain persons retire.'[65]

Greenway, along with MacLaurin, whom Murray had charged with neglect of his teaching and with improperly obtaining university research support for a private business enterprise, were to be paid until 31 October 1919. Hogg and MacKay, whose main offence was their alleged disloyalty to Murray, were to be paid until 31 March 1920. Then they, too, would be 'retired' unless they resigned first.[66]

Hogg had antagonized the board of governors by implying in writing on 23 June that not all its members had 'a deep and intelligent interest' in the university. As well, he had not endeared himself by insisting on being heard by an independent tribunal.[67]

MacKay had offended the board by stating that the president had too much power and the faculty too little. MacKay may have been influenced by James McKeen Cattell's proposals for greater faculty participation in university government. 'It would be strange,' the biologist John S. Dexter told the board, 'if in a University there were not at least a few men influenced by Cattell's anarchism.' Michael Hayden suggests that Cattell's ideas may in fact have enjoyed fairly wide acceptance among the faculty. 'But the proponents of change did not dare to speak up. Their jobs had been put on the line and that ended that. Too bad for MacKay.' His association with the other three offenders doomed him. Murray could not save his protégé without seeming to be partial. He did, however, secure a position for MacKay at McGill, whereas neither Hogg nor MacLaurin taught in a university again.[68]

All four men asked to be informed of the grounds for their dismissal, and to be given copies of Murray's recommendation that they be let go. (The University Act stated that a staff member could be dismissed only if the president recommended it.) The issue being one of disloyalty to him, Murray had so far declined to recommend dismissal. Not until 25 July did he advise the course of action that the board had adopted a fortnight earlier. He added a letter stating that since 'the accused' might be seen to be 'passing judgment upon his accusers,' he was placing his own resignation at the board's disposal.[69]

A memorandum earlier prepared by Murray for the board, outlining the meaning of tenure and possible grounds for dismissal, had included as cause the sort of 'intrigue' of which he held Hogg, MacKay, and MacLaurin to have been guilty.[70] But whether their offence was that they had believed Greenway or had given him bad advice or had criticized Murray or had declined to affirm confidence in him, Murray was exacting vengeance in getting rid of them, and he knew it. By offering his resignation, he hoped to remove the blot on his self-image.

The governors, accustomed to the harsher ways of the business world, took a simpler view of the matter. 'The Four' (as they had come to be known) had been disloyal to the president – so fire them! The board may have been all the more inclined to take a hard line because in 1919, in the aftermath of the Winnipeg General Strike (which had taken place in May and June), people in authority were peculiarly apt to discern subversive plots. Premier William Martin wrote that the Four had 'shown their disregard for properly constituted authority,' and Charles Dunning referred to them as 'the Bolsheviki.'[71]

The board saw no reason to accept Murray's resignation, but he continued to have doubts about the propriety of his action. As well, the stress had sapped his strength. In August, while on vacation, he suffered a depression and took a leave of absence; not until January did he return to the university.[72]

In his absence, the board on 11 August asked the secretary to inform the Four 'that the best interests of the University demanded that they should retire from the teaching staff.' In response, Hogg, MacLaurin, and MacKay finally gave their reasons for abstaining in the April vote. They had not wanted to support a motion that effectively attacked Greenway in his absence; they had doubted that the university council was an appropriate place to lay charges against him; and they had believed that his claim that most of the faculty lacked confidence in Murray could not be established by an open vote. The board rejected this explanation and made the dismissals public.[73]

For the next several months Saskatchewan newspapers were full of the story. Although the four men had no open support from their colleagues, they did have student support, and outside the university they had many allies, among them a young lawyer and future prime minister, John Diefenbaker. Most of these people hoped that a meeting of the university convocation would authorize an inquiry into the dispute. Convocation, consisting of the members of the board, the senate, and the university council as well as all graduates, met on 20 November, with Chancellor Sir Frederick Haultain in the chair. A resolution asking for a royal commission failed; so did a motion asking the university senate to investigate. A resolution deprecating the manner in which the four men had been dismissed did pass, as did motions expressing appreciation for their work and regretting 'that circumstances have arisen which have led the Board of Governors to dispense with their services.' But these resolutions were anodyne. '[Arthur] Moxon is delighted with the Chancellor's part in the proceedings,' the president's secretary, Jean Bayer, wrote to Murray's wife. 'He certainly made an ideal chairman, and while we knew he was with us, he was clever enough to hide it.'[74]

The cause of the Four gained unexpected support in December. K.G. MacKay of the Department of Dairy Husbandry resigned, stating that his vote of confidence in Murray had been misused and that he wished to withdraw it. He also deplored the board's dismissal of professors without stating cause, thereby undermining security of tenure.[75] This led to renewed pressure on the government to order an investigation of the dismissals.

Premier Martin resisted for a time, writing to one inquirer that since the object of the University Act was 'to keep the University away at all times from political discussion, he thought it would not be wise to interfere.'[76] But the pressure continued to mount, and the government introduced a bill assigning the role of visitor, which belonged to the lieutenant-governor, to the Court of King's Bench, which was asked to adjudicate the dismissals.

From 23 March 1920 until 9 April three judges inquired into the case. Hogg and company had their say; so did their opponents. The chairman of the board, James Clinkshill, at last provided the grounds for dismissing the three faculty members:

Dr. MacLaurin – disturbing influence in the university; refusal to appear before the Board when repeatedly requested so to do.
Prof. Hogg – disturbing influence. Refusal to discuss the question at issue when appearing before the Board.
Prof. McKay [sic] – lack of discipline. Refusal to appear before the Board ... unless under conditions he himself laid down.

Clinkshill barely hinted at the issue of disloyalty, though it had been central to the dismissals. But board members did not think they should have to explain themselves at all.[77]

On concluding their deliberations, the judges found against the Four in every particular. Greenway's action in speaking to Dunning was held to justify his dismissal, while the dismissal of Hogg, MacKay, and MacLaurin, was justified by their abstention on 9 April 1919. If they had believed that Murray might have falsified the return, their continued employment was impossible once he had been cleared of wrongdoing. The judges added that Hogg and his colleagues had shown 'a spirit of contumacy to the Board and a disrespect for its authority,' but they did not say whether this or other lesser offences warranted dismissal.[78]

From this judgment there was no appeal. More than a year after Greenway's journey to Regina, the struggle had ended leaving Murray in unquestioned control. His biographers comment that his 'view of tenure and reasons for dismissal would not stand up in today's university world,' while Michael Hayden opines,

'There is no doubt that matters would turn out differently today.' However, Hayden justifies the dismissals as being in the university's best interest. The alternative, a divided institution, would have been worse, he writes: 'Four malcontents among thirty, especially given the pressure of war, sickness and salaries, was very serious. Because of what Murray did, the university was able to grow peacefully through the 1920's and to weather the drought and depression of the 1930's.'[79]

Yet although peace and solidarity are valuable, they may not describe the optimum conditions for academic freedom. It was not just Greenway's misunderstanding of a clerical error, or personal ambition on the part of Hogg and MacLaurin, or the stresses of wartime and illness, or the university's penury that were to blame for the blow-up. The university's form of government was also responsible. The University Act enabled Murray to run the university with a firm hand, an acquiescent board supporting him. This offered the advantage of clear direction, but it excluded professors from taking part in decisions that affected them, and it made even constructive criticism difficult.

Murray's model for university government was analogous to an eight, its crew loyally pulling together under his watchful eye. An analogy for the model favoured by his critics might be a municipal council, its members uniting on some issues and dividing on others. The events of 1919 preserved Murray's model, but the university paid a price in its institutional health. 'By 1937, when Murray retired,' Hayden writes, 'there was pent-up ambition, frustration, and idealism among the faculty, almost all of whom had grown up afraid of or reluctant to challenge Murray, and among the members of the board of governors.'[80] Fear is conducive neither to academic freedom nor to sound university development.

The events in Saskatoon reminded Canadian professors how vulnerable they were if they fell foul of a strong president. The visitorial judgment left no room for doubt about this; the board had quite properly dismissed Hogg and the others for their disloyalty to Murray. This reverberated through Canada's ivied halls for years, though one example will suffice. In the spring of 1931, the University of British Columbia's President Leonard S. Klinck, facing opposition to proposals he had made for cuts in academic programs, warned the dean of arts and science, Daniel Buchanan, of the possible consequences of opposing him. Referring to criticism that department heads had directed against his proposals, Klinck said that he was 'much disturbed at the findings of the Heads since [he] feared that they had, though quite unwittingly, set the stage for a close parallel to the Saskatoon incident.'[81] Klinck did not elaborate, but by recalling that crisis he was putting his senior faculty on notice that the board might have to choose between them and him. And everyone knew who had left the University of Saskatchewan and who had stayed.

In 1932, after the government again slashed the university grant, UBC entered a period of unprecedented turmoil. In response, the government appointed Judge Peter Lampman to inquire into university affairs. Mindful of what Klinck had said to Buchanan the year before, faculty members were wary of testifying. Buchanan addressed a memorandum to Lampman stating that he and his colleagues 'desire to be assured that what we may say ... shall not in any way be made the ground for action to our detriment on the part of the President and Board of Governors.' Lampman gave no such assurance. The economist Henry F. Angus some months later reported to a friend that after careful thought, he and others had decided to testify and that although they had been critical of Klinck, no disciplinary action had so far been taken.[82]

The man to whom he wrote was the historian Frank Underhill, who had been on military leave from the University of Saskatchewan during the spring and summer of 1919. He may have thought that Angus and his colleagues were luckier than Hogg and his associates had been. The dissidents in Saskatoon had been expelled, to the applause of everyone who valued authority over liberty. Among those applauding were other university heads, perhaps concerned for the autonomy of their institutions, certainly convinced of the legitimacy of the power they exercised. People at the top usually have difficulty in seeing the merits of forms of governance that would reduce their power and control.

The conflict in Saskatchewan demonstrates a truth easily overlooked – that the autonomy of universities does not equate with the freedom of those working in them. There has generally been a positive correlation between institutional independence and academic freedom, but some autonomous universities kept their professors on quite as short a leash as institutions working under government or church auspices. Much depended on how presidents and boards interpreted professorial freedom in practice. Before 1919 even the principle of academic freedom had not been enunciated in Canadian terms. The American Association of University Professor's 1915 statement on academic freedom and tenure had little immediate effect even in U.S. universities. It found an echo of sorts in James Mavor's letter to President Falconer in 1916, but as a private communication this had no influence on the behaviour of professors at the University of Toronto, let alone anywhere else. The war and its revolution-troubled aftermath were hostile to freedom of many kinds. Among the wealthy and the middle classes, a wholehearted patriotism was the order of the day, while the principle of loyalty ranked higher than ever. Amidst the clash of arms and the conflict of ideas, academic freedom was a losing cause.

4

The Most Treasured Privilege

'It is one of the most sacred privileges of a university that its professors shall enjoy academic freedom.' Sir Robert Falconer, addressing alumni of the University of Toronto on 14 February 1922, was in full oratorical flight: 'A university in which professors are overawed by political, social, or sectarian influence cannot aspire to an honourable position in the Commonwealth of Learning ... We can measure the rank and stability of a university by the security given to a professor to pursue and expound his investigations without being compelled to justify himself to those who differ from him.'[1] Bold as these words may have seemed to some of his listeners, they were actually conservative. While claiming full freedom for professors in their teaching and research, Falconer seriously restricted their freedom to discuss matters of public concern.

Before the Great War, controversies involving academic freedom had usually centred on issues of religion or institutional governance. These issues were still present in the 1920s, as were occasional concerns about what happened in the classroom; but it was conflicts over the political and public role of professors and over academic free speech that came to the fore. Not that this involved many professors. Electoral politics never attracted more than a few of them, even where they were not required to resign when they sought to enter public life, and other partisan activity was scarcely more common than the electoral kind.

Those who ran for office were the exception, then. Richard Weldon, while dean of law at Dalhousie, was also from 1887 to 1896 the Conservative MP for Albert County, New Brunswick. 'The Dalhousie Law School was in consequence peculiar,' the historian P.B. Waite writes. 'It began two weeks before the regular arts and science classes, but it ended early in February, two months before the others. This allowed the dean of law to go to Ottawa for the session of the House of Commons!'[2] Howard P. Whidden, president of Brandon College, was elected to the House of Commons as a Unionist in 1917 and served both his constituents and his institution until he left active politics in 1921.

The political scientist Norman McL. Rogers had his introduction to electoral politics in the mid-1920s while teaching at Acadia University. Defeated at that time, he succeeded in his second try, in 1935, when he was at Queen's. He resigned his university position upon entering William Lyon Mackenzie King's cabinet as minister of labour. Similarly, Cyrus Macmillan of McGill's English department took leave early in 1930 to become King's minister of fisheries, apparently on the understanding that he would resign from McGill if he were elected to the House of Commons. He failed to get elected, and as the government also went down to defeat he was back in the classroom in the fall.[3]

Among the private institutions, only Wesley College seems to have adopted (in 1910) a regulation barring faculty from running for office. By contrast, the provincial institutions all held it to be inconsistent with academic employment. This was because of the fear that governments might punish universities for partisan activity engaged in by their professors. In 1909 the University of Saskatchewan adopted a regulation stating that 'no Professor ... shall become a candidate for a seat in the Provincial Legislature or Dominion House of Commons.' At the other provincial universities the prohibition was implicit but no less real.[4]

Indeed, not just running for office, but all activities that could be regarded as partisan met with varying degrees of disfavour in the provincial and sometimes also the private universities. At the University of Montreal, for example, the historian Lionel Groulx found in 1926 that his critical view of Canada and its constitution stood in the way of a salary increase. As he recalled the incident in his memoirs, the board of governors (commission d'administration) refused his request, then made an increase conditional on his signing an undertaking, first, 'à prêcher à mes étudiants la loyauté à la constitution du Canada,' and, second, 'à ne rien dire ni écrire qui puisse blesser les légitimes susceptibilités de nos compatriotes anglo-canadiens.'[5]

Groulx would not agree, saying he would rather resign. His friend and fellow nationalist Antonio Perrault then went to bat for him in a fashion that came close to challenging academic freedom in general even while claiming it for Groulx. As Perrault told the story to Groulx, he had charged the rector, Mgr Vincent-Joseph Piette, with harbouring infidels while asking a priest for a promise of good conduct. Perrault had added that the rector was delivering the university into the hands of 'la plus dangereuse école: les héritiers de la vieille garde rouge de 1850,' and had threatened to take the story to Le Devoir, where in any case Groulx's friend Omer Héroux was waiting for a signal. At this point, according to Groulx, 'le pauvre recteur lève les bras au ciel; il ne sait plus quel saint invoquer.' The university did not enjoy a good press: 'Une nouvelle polémique, et sur un sujet aussi délicat que celui de la "liberté académique" des professeurs, n'avait rien de fort souhaitable.' Perhaps the reference to infidels on the faculty touched a nerve; or perhaps Piette sensed that Groulx's anti-Ottawa opinions were less offensive to the Quebec public than to the federalist Liberals who dominated the board. At all events, the rector caved in and undertook to look after Groulx's interests. For months nothing happened, though, and only after Perrault acquainted the university's chancellor, Archbishop Georges Gauthier, with the problem did Groulx get his raise.[6]

Groulx managed not only to get his way but also to write about history and politics as he chose. Not all academics had a well-positioned friend like Perrault, however (in this respect Groulx's case was similar to James Mavor's). Most academics, whether in public or private institutions, were unwilling to risk opposing their presidents and governing boards. As part of this reluctance, they avoided political involvement in any form. Where running for public office is concerned, academic freedom may seem only tangentially involved, but should it not include the freedom, even the right, to exercise one's freedom as a citizen and 'put one's money where one's mouth is?' To put barriers in the way of political activity does not constitute an infringement of academic freedom as serious as interfering with teaching, research, or publication, but it is arguably an infringement all the same. Few academics saw it as such. Most were content to shun politics – indeed, to avoid controversy in any form. The reasons for this included the background of those who sought academic careers, the process by which they obtained appointment and promotion, and, not least important, the financial dependency of the institutions that employed them.

A.B. McKillop writes of mid-nineteenth-century hiring practices in Ontario that 'careful attention was paid ... to the academic pedigrees, social backgrounds, and personal connections of professors ... in order to assure that no heretical views issued from the lectern. Family ties and letters of recommendation by scholarly acquaintances ... dominated academic hiring at the time.' Since a central part of the purpose of higher education well into the twentieth century was to build character and good deportment in students, those who taught them had to be sound themselves.[7]

In the 1920s Canadian academics were still overwhelmingly male, Protestant or Catholic, of British or French stock, and from professional, business, or prosperous farming families. Academic job seekers depended on the good offices of senior academics willing to put them forward. In institutions that were tiny by today's standards, presidents, principals, and rectors retained close control over hiring. They tried to make sure that those they selected had 'the right stuff' as teachers and as guides for the young and were the sort of people who would not get themselves and the university into trouble.

In 1914 President Frank F. Wesbrook of the University of British Columbia described one candidate as 'a large, upstanding, athletic, manly fellow of thirty to thirty-five, with very wholesome views, with seemingly a very charming wife, who appears to be a good house-keeper.' Nine years later, McMaster's Humfrey Michell described Harold Adams Innis to Sherwood Fox of Western University (later the University of Western Ontario) as 'a very nice fellow in every way and one likely to be an agreeable colleague, a consideration which is an important one.' He added, 'I have never met Mrs. Innis, but am told she is a very charming girl. All these things count ... in choosing a man for a permanent post.' Fox agreed: 'What you say regarding his personality, his acceptability as a colleague and his wife are very pertinent to a proper consideration of him as a candidate.'[8]

In 1923 W.T. Jackman of the University of Toronto said of a candidate that although he was very able and promising, there was one thing that militated against him as a teacher – 'his shortness of stature.' 'One could not help noticing it on meeting him,' Fox replied, 'but any objection that one might hold to it is largely overcome by the fact that his voice, manner and looks are very masculine. If he had a squeaky little voice it would certainly be a prohibitive combination.'[9]

That same year McGill's principal, Sir Arthur Currie, received a letter describing a candidate as having 'a pleasant personality and good manners,' and as being someone who liked sports, 'especially tennis and boxing.'[10] Academic achievement mattered, but the emphasis was on 'soundness' and 'the whole man.'

Hiring practices affected academic freedom not only by excluding candidates who were regarded as 'difficult' or 'radical' but also by discriminating against those who were of the wrong sex or ethnicity. By 1921 roughly one in every fourteen Canadian academics was female, but the women were largely confined to modern languages, home economics, nursing, and the biological and botanical sciences. Often expected to remain single, they typically earned lower salaries than their male colleagues and had to wait longer before promotion. Many never got beyond the lower ranks, nor did they get tenure. Rarely did they protest against this situation. As members of a minority, they had reason to be cautious.[11]

Jews had even greater difficulty than Gentile women in obtaining university jobs. The denominational colleges did not appoint Jews until well into the twentieth century, but even the nonsectarian and provincial universities tended to exclude them. Anti-Semitism was potent. The Jews holding university positions in Canada in the 1920s could probably have been counted on the fingers of one hand. Professors of African, Asian, or aboriginal background did not exist.

To exclude qualified candidates on the basis of sex, appearance, or ethnic background not only restricts the range of discussion and debate but also creates an environment in which members of minority groups who do gain appointment are isolated and likely to feel vulnerable. As a result, they may be even less disposed than other academics to assert themselves or court controversy. Freedom does not flourish in an atmosphere of insecurity.

In an important sense, of course, insecurity was part of the experience of all Canadian professors. Not only did they serve during pleasure rather than, like the judiciary, during good behaviour, but the universities they worked for were mostly impecunious. Endowments provided only a few of the private institutions with significant income. In 1921 the total endowments of universities were a mere $28.3 million, with McGill easily the richest. The six provincial universities depended heavily on annual government grants, tuition fees being their other major source of income – though the University of Toronto could have had a more secure source of revenue and a larger one as well, because the reform of 1906 had accorded it half of the succession duties collected in Ontario. In 1914 the government of William Hearst replaced this with an annual grant, however, and in 1921 a new government, led by E.C. Drury of the United Farmers of Ontario, ignored a royal commission's recommendation that the university once again get half the succession duties.[12]

Tuition fees loomed particularly large in the budgets of the denominational colleges. Almost all institutions relied on regular donations from friends and alumni. Since challenges to conventional wisdom or partisanship might discourage donations or imperil provincial grants, presidents and governing boards tried to control and limit academic free speech and political activity, extending that control into the classroom if the needs of the university seemed to require it. With rare exceptions, Canadian academics acquiesced. They had been selected to do so, and they believed it to be in their interest. It made no sense to draw attention to oneself; better to keep quiet. One consequence of this situation was that when academic freedom came to be discussed in the late 1910s and early 1920s, professors took virtually no part in the discussion.

The first Canadian to speak publicly about academic freedom seems to have been Principal Bruce Taylor of Queen's. Addressing the graduating class of the University of Manitoba in May 1919, he discussed the effects that financial dependence had on academic freedom. Predicting that the state would take an ever-increasing part in financing higher education, Taylor asked whether this entitled it to control the type of teaching in the University. 'Will the administration of a University ... depend upon the whims of the Legislature?' he asked. 'Will men of independence accept positions when the tenure may be insecure?' And what if 'large interests' hinted to a government 'that the removal of a certain professor might be advisable, that his maintenance is closing the money bags?' Would the university be pressured, and how would it react?

The freedom most highly valued by Taylor was that of professors to teach, do research, and publish as they pleased. He feared that administrators might discourage the expression of 'inconvenient and original' ideas in order to please those who provided the money: 'It is the business of the University teacher to stimulate thought and set forth ... the new point of view ... If the right temper is in a University the sympathy of the administration will be with the thinker and the intellectual adventurer. Far better the crank with brains than the unexceptionable nobody.' But there were limits to academic freedom, he pointed out. The need to live within a community and to 'play fair' with students meant that professors could not do or say whatever they wanted. They had to use common sense. All the same, the university's main task was 'not to give instruction but to awaken and to inspire.' A university, said Taylor, 'is not a superior kind of technical school; it is not in the first place a device for preparing a man to make a living. It is a challenge to the mind.'[13]

Taylor's silence about the threat that wealthy benefactors might pose to professors of whom they disapproved is surprising, since at the end of 1917 he had faced down an attempt to dislodge O.D. Skelton. It was left to another president to discuss this topic. Speaking at the spring convocation of his own institution in June 1919, E.E. Braithwaite of Western University stated that wealthy men had put 'undue pressure' on professors in the United States and that similar pressure was not unknown in Canada. This undermined 'the spirit of independence in ... which alone the best work can be accomplished.' Scientists should not be judged by the financial benefit of their research to the college or the community, continued Braithwaite, nor should teachers be judged by the number of students their courses attracted. 'If the Professor of Political Economy must make his conclusions conform to the ideas of the capitalists who may occupy a seat on his governing board, the usefulness of the institution is seriously impaired.'

Braithwaite was in favour of free inquiry and discussion, and he said that governing boards should foster it, remembering that 'it is the faculty that make the institution, and not the trustees. In inquiring about the worth of an educational institution nobody cares who constitutes the latter body.' But he saw problems with faculty self-government, pointing out that many professors shirked their duty to think independently and to challenge their students to do likewise; they would not oppose infringements of academic freedom if those who applied pressure were powerful enough. 'We must retain the ideal freedom to think independently,' Braithwaite concluded, sounding somewhat less than sanguine.[14]

Taylor and Braithwaite presided over small private institutions. As president of the largest university in the country, Sir Robert Falconer was the leading figure in Canadian higher education, but his address on academic freedom was shaped largely by local events: the pressure put on the university over the German professors in 1914; Premier Hearst's reaction to Mavor's articles on Ontario Hydro two years later; and, more recently, evidence that the government of E.C. Drury did not appreciate what the 1906 University Act had accomplished in freeing the institution from political interference.[15]

In addition to these problems, a member of the board, Reuben Wells Leonard, had been complaining about the political economist Robert M. MacIver. In 1919 MacIver had published *Labour and the New Social Order*, which supported industrial workers in their efforts to organize. Leonard was hostile to anything that smacked of unionization. He also believed that higher education should not foster ideas that subverted the economic order. When he got wind of MacIver's book in early 1921, he complained to the board chairman, Sir Edmund Walker, about the Scot's 'ultra-socialistic teachings.' Walker expressed mild concern but added, 'Nothing would seem more dangerous than to restrain a free expression of opinion by a professor short of almost anything but treason.'[16]

Having received copies of this correspondence, Falconer felt compelled to add his voice to Walker's. It would be 'extremely injurious were the Board of Governors to attempt to restrain the expression of views on economic subjects which were different from their own,' he wrote to Leonard. That was not the British way. Besides, 'The most treasured privilege of the University is freedom of thought.' In the end, free discussion would do less harm than repression, Falconer observed, 'unless the views were ... so extreme as to cause some injurious action.' Barring this, 'unrestrained discussion results in ... the stability of the people.'[17]

Leonard was unpersuaded: 'If we are to encourage ... the teaching of one line of extreme, unusual or dangerous doctrine, why not encourage many others, such as anti-vaccination etc., or now that Mrs. Besant has played out in India we might bring her over here; or Lenine [*sic*] when Russia should get tired of him.' (Annie Besant was an English theosophist who had become a champion of India's independence.) No, insisted Leonard, the board should prevent 'any teaching tending to upset a civilization which has been the result of some thousands of years of struggle.'[18]

Falconer replied that Canada had nothing to fear from 'the thoughtful, earnest man, who is endeavouring to arrive at principles that will stabilize the country.' However, he called MacIver into his office for a chat. Subsequently, MacIver sent Falconer a statement of his views, adding that it should not be regarded as 'in any way' a defence of them: 'To offer a "defence" would be to imply an economic orthodoxy and a correspondent tribunal whose very existence would render economic science nugatory. It would also be contrary, not only to the dignity of a University teacher, but also to the idea of the University.' MacIver added that he would feel his integrity as a teacher so threatened that he would have no choice but to look for another position.[19]

Falconer did not share this letter with Leonard. That was wise. Later in the year the millionaire stated that if MacIver was allowed to teach his views, 'we should be honest with ourselves and true to the trust imposed upon us by the people of Ontario, and establish a Chair of Political Anarchy and Social Chaos, so that the people of Ontario, who pay for the University, and the students who take the courses, will know what is being taught under its proper name.' Falconer replied that MacIver's views were not outlandish, that repressing freedom of expression was wrong, and that social progress came through discussion. Was he growing tired of making these points? According to James G. Greenlee, his biographer, Falconer thought the time had come for a statement that would make it awkward for Leonard to continue attacking MacIver.[20]

Speaking to the alumni in Convocation Hall on 14 February 1922, Falconer began by praising 'the freedom which gives its distinction to the ancient English academic life.' Academic freedom, he explained, 'is best understood as a phase of the general course of people's development in liberty of thought.' Having studied in Berlin and Marburg, he might have mentioned *Lehrfreiheit*, but little more than three years after the end of the war, that would have been impolitic. Instead, Falconer cited British thinkers and writers: John Milton, Jeremy Taylor, John Locke, John Stuart Mill, Edward Caird, and T.H. Green.

The nineteenth century had been one of bitter scientific, religious and social controversy, he noted, and universities had become 'centres of fierce discussion.' The new knowledge had triumphed, however, and with it academic freedom. Universities existed for teaching 'ascertained knowledge and truth,' for training professionals, and for the investigation and extension of new truth. The freedom to investigate and evaluate new truth was of the essence of university life.

The academic freedom enjoyed by professors was 'one of the most sacred privileges of a university,' continued Falconer. However, professors should not be merely destructive; they should also be constructive, providing information that 'will be intelligible to [students] and will equip them to fulfil their duties as citizens and as searchers for the truth.' Academic freedom involved other restraints too. The professor was 'not fixed for life in an easy place' in which he was 'free to do as he will and say whatever he pleases.' He was 'the servant of the nation' in matters of the intellect. Like judges and civil servants, he was not free to do as ordinary citizens did. Perhaps thinking of Mavor, Falconer stated, 'It is ... expedient that a professor in a State University should take no active share in party-politics' whether running for office or engaging in partisan debate. Any discussion of 'burning political questions' might harm his institution. 'A government might well without giving any reason easily show its displeasure in such a way as to affect adversely the fortunes of the institution and the financial position of many guiltless and wiser colleages.'

Finally, in a few remarks that were clearly directed to Leonard, Falconer discussed the role of governing boards. One of their duties, he said, was to secure 'the best possible persons available for the professorial office.' The views of such people might differ from those held by the governors, but the latter would be unwise either to challenge a professor's competence or to deny 'that there is a place in the University for his type of thought.' It was better 'to tolerate an erratic or even provocative teacher' than to disturb the normal functioning of the university. In any case, students would not long be taken in by 'the spurious afflatus of a false prophet.'[21]

What Mavor thought of this speech is unknown, but Leonard stuck to his guns: 'The inference I would draw from your Paper is the necessity for exercising extreme caution in the selection of Professors.' In 1923, when Falconer recommended that MacIver succeed Mavor in the chair of political economy, Leonard dissented. 'If I had not made this nomination,' Falconer wrote, 'there would have gone abroad a feeling that a man was not at liberty to express views which are widely held in the economics departments of the leading English Universities.' This would have harmed the University of Toronto more than 'any subversive doctrines that MacIver would ever promulgate.'[22] MacIver received the promotion and served as head of the department until 1927, when he resigned to go to Columbia University. (In the 1950s he headed the project that gave birth to studies of academic freedom by Richard Hofstadter, Walter P. Metzger, and MacIver himself.)

Newspaper coverage of Falconer's address focused not on academic freedom but on the limits he had imposed. 'No Party Politics for the Professor,' stated a headline in the *Mail and Empire*. 'Says Professor Must Keep Out of Politics,' noted the *Toronto Star*. The *Telegram* sent a reporter to ask whether a complaint from the government had prompted Falconer's comments (he denied that it had). The *Globe* was alone in commenting editorially. Surely, Falconer did not mean that professors 'should keep silence on public questions such as the tariff, the railways, immigration, or public policy in regard to education?' Referring to O.D. Skelton, identifiably a Liberal, and to the discussion of public affairs in the *Queen's Quarterly*, the *Globe*'s editor asserted, 'It is a decided advantage to university students to have even party politics presented in this reasonable way.'[23]

James G. Greenlee states that 'the views outlined were widely shared and not only, one suspects, by administrators and politicians.' Falconer might nevertheless have done well to emulate Harvard's President A. Lawrence Lowell, who a few years earlier had declined to discipline a professor for making pro-German statements even though Harvard stood to lose a large bequest as a result. Lowell had said, 'A university that takes responsibility for deciding what professors may not say thereby assumes responsibility for everything professors do say, and a wise university would refuse the first responsibility in order to relieve itself of the second.' This statement had been well-publicized, and Falconer must have been aware of it. But he may have thought that the dangers his university faced from the Ontario government exceeded those that Harvard faced from its donors.[24]

One thing was clear: another James Mavor would be in trouble unless his friends, like Mavor's, were powerful. Falconer's speech was intended to discourage professors from discussing even subjects in which they were expert if these subjects were controversial. For example, an economist might believe that a system of free trade found support in economic science. However, if he publicly counselled free trade, he might be regarded as 'an exponent of party views.' In 1931 British Columbia's Conservative minister of education, Joshua Hinchliffe, took UBC's President Leonard S. Klinck to task about the Liberal partisanship of some of his staff. As partial proof, Hinchliffe cited a social scientist, C.W. Topping, who had opposed protective tariffs![25] It is unlikely that Falconer would have been surprised.

The Conservatives returned to office in Ontario in 1923 under Howard Ferguson. Like Hearst before him, he believed that the University of Toronto's professors should stay out of politics. In June 1924 he complained to Falconer about the use in class of the *Communist Manifesto*. The document should be 'exterminated,' the premier opined: 'If it is true that members of the staff either encourage or condone this kind of doctrine, they should be summarily dismissed.' Falconer pointed out that the professor using the document was the staunchly anticommunist Gilbert Jackson, who in his course on economic history could not very well ignore Marx's ideas.[26]

When the *Financial Post* charged in 1925 that the political economist C.R. Fay sympathized with communism, Ferguson wrote to Henry J. Cody, who had succeeded Walker as board chairman: 'If it is true that he holds these views and gives expression to them, I do not think he is the sort of man that should be on the staff.' Similarly, in 1928, when MacIver's successor as head of political economy, E.J. Urwick, using data gathered by his colleague H.A. Innis, said that gambling and alcohol abuse were rife in Ontario mining towns, Ferguson called it 'a gross exaggeration,' adding, 'My understanding of the duty of the staff of the university is to teach, not to interfere with matters that are in a sense political.'[27]

Not long afterwards he complained about the historian Frank Underhill, who had been back at the University of Toronto since 1927 and had allegedly said in a public lecture 'that the British were as much if not more to blame for the war than the Germans.' This was wrong, Ferguson told Cody, and besides, professors had no business conveying their views about the war's causes to their students.[28]

Cody passed this letter on to Falconer, who questioned Underhill. The historian replied that he had not in fact made such a statement, though he had said that Anglo-German imperial rivalries had contributed more to the coming of war than Belgian neutrality had: 'This I thought to be a commonplace among informed persons, but it may have so surprised some one in the audience that he became suspicious of my loyalty.' Falconer urged Underhill 'to be careful in his casual remarks.'[29]

When informed of all this, the premier seemed satisfied. He told Falconer that he had wondered how 'one who had taken such an active part in the war' could have said such a thing: 'It indicates ... how careful those occupying teaching positions should be in discussing this subject.'[30]

In April 1929 Underhill again got Ferguson's dander up with a column in the *Canadian Forum* about Canada–United States relations in general and bootlegging in particular. 'These articles are purely political,' Ferguson wrote to Cody. 'Some day when the estimates are brought over here I will be tempted to tick off a number of salaries of some men who seem to take more interest in interfering in matters of public policy than they do in the work for which they are paid.'[31]

Did Cody inform Falconer of this? Perhaps not. If anyone knew how to assess Ferguson's bluster it was Harry Cody, who thirty-five years earlier had been his college roommate. But if Falconer heard of the threat it must have confirmed his belief that academic free speech was dangerous to the university's health. Ferguson's view, his biographer Peter Oliver claims, was 'not out of line with the views expressed by Falconer in 1922.'[32] Their motives differed, however. Ferguson wanted to suppress what he did not like to hear; Falconer sought to safeguard the university's autonomy against the likes of Ferguson.

The head of history at the University of British Columbia, Mack Eastman, was involved in more than one controversy in the 1920s. One involved a student organization of which he was honorary president, the Socialist Club. Late in 1920 an angry citizen bent President Klinck's ear about socialism in general and the club in particular. Having earlier been assured by Eastman that 'so far as he knew, there was not one Marxian socialist at the University,' Klinck did not take his caller very seriously. However, when the prominent socialist J.S. Woodsworth was invited to address the club in 1921, Klinck had a chat with Eastman: 'I told Dr. Eastman that their [*sic*] were some who a few years ago were of the opinion that he was rather radical.' Eastman protested, pointing out that some of the labour organizations had come to the conclusion that ... he had become a reactionary.'[33]

If Eastman had ceased to be radical, he had not become uncontroversial. In late 1922 he locked horns with Joshua Hinchliffe, MLA, about the textbook used in the survey course in European history. Hinchliffe charged that *The History of Europe* by J.H. Robinson and Charles Beard should not be used because it was 'written by Americans for American students' and said too little about the British and Canadian contributions to the war effort.[34]

In defending UBC, Minister of Education John D. MacLean noted, less than relevantly, that Eastman and his colleague Walter Sage had volunteered for wartime military service. But Hinchliffe kept up the attack. 'I see by this evening's paper that the Canon has exploded again,' Eastman wrote to MacLean (Hinchliffe was an Anglican clergyman): 'This time he lauds Hazen's *Modern European History* ... It will amuse you to learn that it was the object of attack on exactly the same ground of Americanism and anti-Britishism. The attack was as silly as the present attack on Robinson and Beard.'[35]

In reply, MacLean thanked Eastman for a copy of his paper on 'Textbooks in European History,' which soon afterwards appeared in the *Vancouver Province* and from which MacLean quoted while replying to Hinchliffe in the legislative assembly. The war, Eastman wrote, had stimulated popular interest in history. One result was that 'the enlightened, scientific and truthful historian has been oppressed by ambitious autocrats and badgered by ignorant democrats,' among them 'honest fanatics' and 'vote-catching politicians,' none of whom liked a balanced treatment of the past. If UBC's historians were incompetent, he continued, 'the remedy is dismissal.' If they were competent, this should be taken as 'presumptive evidence that the history courses will be scholarly, truthful and beneficial; and that the choice of textbooks will be at least defensible.'[36]

President Klinck stood by Eastman, and the book by Robinson and Beard continued to be used. But in the long run the incident may have damaged UBC. Hinchliffe became minister of education in 1929, and during his tenure in office he showed a high degree of animus towards the university. Its budget, reduced by more than 60 per cent, would have been cut even further had Hinchliffe had his way.[37] If, as seems possible, the tussle with Eastman was partly responsible for the minister's attitude, it suggests that apprehensions about the ill effects of academic free speech were grounded in reality. Yet should professors fail to defend professional standards just because in doing so they may offend influential people?

Eastman was at the centre of another curriculum-related controversy in April 1923. At a meeting of the UBC faculty association he told his colleagues that his course on the Renaissance and Reformation had come under attack from Principal W.H. Vance of the Anglican Theological College. 'One of the topics treated in it was the Higher Criticism – a subject which, it was alleged, it was contrary to the University Act and otherwise inappropriate to treat in a University course, inasmuch as it involved the discussion of religious questions.' Eastman had agreed to drop the topic in 1923–4 but wanted the association to discuss the matter because 'he thought that criticism of this nature raised the whole question of academic freedom.' The discussion was inconclusive, and Eastman was asked to report to the council of the Faculty of Arts and to the senate.[38]

The *Calendar* described the course as follows: 'A brief outline of the rise of the Christian Church; a close study of the Renaissance, the Reformation and the Counter-Reformation, and, in conclusion, a short account of the subsequent history of religious thought down to our own times, with special reference to the English Deists, the French Philosophes, Wesleyanism, Pietism, Catholic Modernism and the Higher Criticism.' After consulting with the university senate, Eastman deleted everything that followed the words 'to our own times.' He also asked Klinck for 'a ruling as to whether there be any ground for Principal Vance's doubt concerning the propriety and legality of treating such topics as the Higher Criticism.' His treatment of the subject had always been 'purely objective and historical,' he said, and he saw no grounds 'for opposition to the ... impartial summary of an historical development.' Still, a legal opinion seemed desirable: 'I believe that, if I had not voluntarily promised last spring to omit the Higher Criticism this year, the Anglican Synod would have taken up the matter ... in a manner very harmful to the cause of education.'[39]

According to section 95 of the University Act, UBC was 'strictly non-sectarian in principle and no religious creed and dogma shall be taught.' This did not bar 'all reference to religious disputes or differences, where they are part and parcel of an epoch,' explained the university's solicitor, R.L. Reid. 'To do so would make it impossible to properly teach the history of the time.' However, he added, 'the treatment of any such subjects ... may easily become the subject of complaint by those who have strong feelings on these matters.' Such questions should therefore be treated 'with impartiality and only to such extent as may be necessary to give the student a proper idea as to their effect on historical events'; the historian should avoid taking sides in assessing 'motives having origin in religious feelings.'[40]

On reading Reid's letter, Eastman told Klinck that no one had ever challenged his treatment of contentious subjects, but he pointed out that Vance had 'raised the question as to whether the subjects themselves were not forbidden by the Act. Obviously an affirmative answer to his question would have crippled the teaching of History in the University.'[41] Despite this statement, the course description that Eastman submitted for inclusion in the 1924–5 *Calendar* contained no reference to currents of thought of any kind. Neither he nor the senate wanted to present potential critics with a target.

Such caution was understandable. One of Eastman's colleagues, Garnet Sedgewick of the English deparment, had been asked in October 1923 to appear before the board of governors to explain some unspecified remarks that were held to be 'offensive to English people.'[42] Sedgewick managed to clear himself, but in view of the incident, Eastman may have thought it unwise to go looking for trouble. The university senate and Klinck seem to have agreed.

Few issues in the 1920s were more contentious than prohibition. When the Alberta government scheduled a plebiscite on the sale of beverage alcohol in 1923, the Moderation League campaigned to replace prohibition with provincial control. One of its more prominent members was the University of Alberta classicist William Hardy Alexander; this brought objections from temperance advocates. President Henry Marshall Tory reported to the board in October 1923 that Alexander's activities were causing offence. Having asked the classicist to comment, the members of board briefly discussed his statement (unhappily not preserved) at their November meeting before dropping the matter. Since Albertans had recently voted to sanction the government sale of beverage alcohol as well as the sale of beer in licensed premises, it seemed pointless to pursue the issue further.[43]

The events of 1923 cast a shadow, however. Five years later, in explaining to a new president why he was turning down an invitation to address the students in the university hall on Sunday morning, Alexander cited his Unitarianism as one obstacle. 'But my offence does not end there. In the campaign of 1923 I stumped the province against prohibition.' This made him objectionable to vocal churchgoers, he said, and made it 'inexpedient' to include him in the list of speakers.[44]

President Robert C. Wallace expressed regret: 'Sincerity in viewpoint and courage to express it coupled with reverence in matters that are of deepest importance mean much more than a uniformity of point of view.'[45] This was handsomely said. But Wallace probably appreciated Alexander's scruples, for they saved the university possible embarrassment.

The participation of professors in public life was an issue mainly in the provincial universities. However, Louis A. Wood of Western University may have lost his position at least partly because of his political views. In 1923 he told the Progressive MP W.C. Good that he was being forced to resign because of his support for the United Farmers of Ontario: 'I was offered a labor-progressive nomination in London at the [1921] federal election, and they are very anxious to eject me from the city before another election draws around.' He surmised that his successor would be no critic of 'the present condition of things in the country.'[46]

Pressed for details, Wood offered an account in which Sherwood Fox, since 1919 Western's dean of arts (and later president), loomed large. Wood alleged that Fox resented him for having refused to join the campaign to unseat President E.E. Braithwaite. (Western's official historian, John Gwynne-Timothy, does not solve the mystery that surrounds this incident.) 'He is reactionary in his views,' said Wood, 'and has fanned the sentiment of the Board against me.' Wood believed that his stillborn political candidacy in opposition to a member of the board also counted against him: 'In January I received a note saying that my services would end at the close of the academic year. No reasons were given. My father talked to one of the board. All he could draw from him was that I was not "a big enough man for the position."' Fighting was useless; better to go quietly. A newspaper clipping of a banquet held in his honour stated, 'Attention was ... drawn to the fact that Dr. Wood is leaving the university because of ill health.' That was a white lie.[47]

In his memoirs, Fox recalled an unnamed professor whose 'peculiar behaviour' during Fox's term as dean 'demonstrated either a refusal to work with [Fox] and his colleagues or a congenital inability to collaborate with anybody.' A board member demanded 'that the man be summarily dismissed at the end of the term' because he had publicly supported 'the United Farmers of Ontario, and had offered himself as a candidate at the impending election.' But Fox did it his own way. When the man was let go, 'the communication contained not a single word about a teacher's political views or party, but did contain ample assurance that the University's policy regarding the engagement of professors and their tenure of office was just and in conformity with the practices of modern universities.'[48] The outcome was fortunate, Fox concluded, in that it established policies 'of vital importance in the direction of a university.' One, presumably, was that professors should not be dismissed for their political views or their political activity.

Wood was a full professor who had been at Western since 1914, and he had a continuing appointment, but since there was no requirement that cause be shown for dismissal and since in any case no copy of the letter informing Wood of his dismissal has survived, we cannot say why he was dismissed. Furthermore, a potential source of information, the minutes of the board of governors, is closed to researchers. (In 1992 President George Pedersen denied a request for access to the minute book for the years 1918–23 because of 'the confidentiality of University records which deal directly and specifically with personnel matters' and because the board by-laws 'restrict access to the Official Minute Book to ... current Board members.' Pedersen added that the university secretary had reviewed the minutes and had reported that the references to Wood were 'so circumspect as to provide no context or evidence concerning this particular case.')[49] The mystery remains.

The only difference of opinion between Fox and Wood for which there is any evidence concerned a new registrar's request that faculty members supply a record of student absences. Fox and Wood exchanged letters about this in December 1919 and January 1920, but eventually Wood complied in order 'to save continued dispute.' Other documents on file indicate a high level of satisfaction with Wood into 1920, when he became head of economics and chaired the committee that drafted a program for the Department of Business Administration.[50]

Early in 1921, however, Fox decided for some reason that it had been a mistake to put Wood, who had earlier been head of history, in charge of economics. In March 1921 Fox told an acquaintance, 'Confidentially, we are contemplating making a change in the Headship of our Department of Economics.' The greater part of Western's income, Fox explained to another person at the same time, now came from the province. As a result, the institution had a greater duty than before 'to interest itself in a practical way in the various activities of its constituency,' which Fox identified as 'the very large and important commercial and industrial interests of the western parts of the province.' The university needed 'to have on its staff a strong and constructive economist' who could 'cooperate with the businessmen of the community in solving their problems and the problems of Canadian business in general.'[51]

In April 1921 Fox informed Wood: 'An effort will be made to appoint a second man in the Department of Economics who would become its head or acting head.'[52] Did Wood object to being displaced, and were his objections the reason Fox and the board soured on him? Or did something else bring this about, such as his brush with political candidacy? We can only guess. Fox's recollections are not credible, and Wood's account cannot be substantiated. Norman Penner's claim that Wood was fired for his 'radical views' outruns the evidence. James J. Talman, a student at Western in the early 1920s who later wrote a history of the university, commented in 1993 that 'Wood resented losing the history post [in

1920], was a nasty person not much liked and quit with no encouragement to stay.' But Talman's friendship with Fox may have affected his judgment.[53]

What is clear is that Fox wanted an economist who would be useful to business. Late in 1922 he asked the University of Toronto's Robert M. MacIver to recommend some young economists with 'a clear and practical knowledge' of industry and commerce, since businessmen were 'looking to the University for guidance in their search of solutions of many of the problems that confront them.' To a businessman Fox wrote, 'One of the most important desidorata [sic] in an economist is ... that he be practical; personally, I am very fearful of these theoretical economists.' Obviously, 'practical' meant 'useful to the business community.' Other groups – farmers, employees, consumers – mattered less, if at all. Fox, in fact, was looking for the sort of 'intellectual garage mechanic of Canadian capitalism' at whom Frank Underhill would in 1935 poke fun.[54]

By adopting a policy designed to make the economics department serve business, Fox undermined Western's intellectual autonomy while offending against Wood's academic freedom. The offence was not evident, however, for Wood's removal caused no commotion. While living in Toronto in 1923–4, he wrote the *History of Farmers' Movements in Canada* (1924). In July 1924 he reported to Good that he had not yet found a new position, but soon afterwards he took one at the University of Oregon. There he taught for twenty-five years before retiring, and it is interesting to note that in 1946 he ran unsuccessfully for the House of Representatives as a Democrat. At Western, his brush with electoral politics in 1921 remained the only such incident for many years. Not until after the Second World War, when the classicist R.E.K. Pemberton contested London in the 1953 federal election, did any professor run for office.[55]

Sherwood Fox's search for a business-minded economist was characteristic of the decade. During the 1920s, materialism and a mood of self-indulgence – roots of the consumerism to which Canadians were becoming habituated – gained strength at the expense of religion and such reform causes as prohibition. At the same time, the Protestant colleges became increasingly secularized. Still, the old verities had continuing influence, and religion mattered to Canadians to a degree difficult to recall today.[56]

One consequence was that conflicts over biblical criticism continued to disturb the dovecotes of academe from time to time. It was central to a controversy that surrounded William Irwin of University College, Toronto, in 1928. In April the *Toronto Daily Star* reported him as saying 'that the God of the early books of the Old Testament not only was an unscrupulous liar himself and an encourager of liars' but was also in other ways immoral. The 'God of Truth, who came into His own with the great prophets, Isaiah, Jeremiah and Ezekiel' was a very different being. When asked to comment, Rabbi Ferdinand Isserman explained that Irwin's point of view was far from revolutionary among biblical scholars. But he could understand its capacity to shock, and he hoped it would not get Irwin into trouble: 'He is too good a man.' Nevertheless, several clergymen and some letters to the editor accused Irwin of blasphemy. He responded that newspaper reports had misrepresented his paper.[57]

Possibly. One examination question he set that year asked to what extent the stories of Noah, Abraham, and Moses might be accepted as dependable history; another invited examinees to decide whether the book of Jonah was history, allegory, or 'something else.' The head of Irwin's department, W.R. Taylor, wrote to Sir Robert Falconer that these two questions were 'unfortunate' though the purpose was 'constructive.' He added, 'The other questions are, I think, above suspicion.' Falconer disagreed. No fewer than three questions contained 'dangerous explosives,' he replied: 'It is unfortunate that in a subject that has to be handled with such great care he did not show more discretion.'[58]

Falconer did not comment publicly on the controversy, but he may have warned Irwin to be more prudent. Irwin, for his part, thought the university had not done enough to defend him. In January 1930 he resigned to take a position at the University of Chicago. Two days later the *Varsity* carried a letter from him claiming that the University of Toronto did not adequately protect the academic freedom of its professors because it was afraid of the government. The institution, he said, was 'mildewed with discretion.'[59]

Irwin cited as evidence the university's failure to defend his colleague T.J. Meek after he had been manhandled by police as they were breaking up a communist demonstration in Queen's Park in the summer of 1929; he also cited the lack of support he himself had received. The *Varsity* deplored the fact that 'whenever a professor makes any statement that some voters object to, there is an immediate shout of "quiet, quiet,"' and it demanded that the extent of political control over the university be investigated.[60]

A former principal of University College, Maurice Hutton, described the claims as 'rather absurd.' Meek said he had felt confident of the unspoken support of Falconer, of Arts and Science dean A.T. DeLury, and of University College Principal Malcolm Wallace, adding, 'It is an open question as to what official action should have been taken.' Premier Howard Ferguson suggested that the university might be able to limp along without Irwin. The *Telegram* and *Mail and Empire* deprecated his charges, while the *Star*'s 'Observer,' Salem Bland, supported him; but the press soon dropped the matter. In that first Depression winter, there were stories with greater human interest.[61]

To deal with a 'problem' quietly has ever been the preference of presidents and governing boards. To paraphrase a remark by the historian Charles Lightbody, university administrators fear bad publicity the way wild animals fear fire.[62] And controversy usually means bad publicity.

In the Methodist colleges there was no repetition in the 1920s of the Workman and Jackson controversies early in the century. When the Old Testament scholar Samuel Hooke was eased out of Victoria University in 1924 because of 'the extreme radicalism of his views of scriptural exegesis,' it was done so discreetly that hardly anyone noticed.[63]

In 1922, however, a conflict not over biblical scholarship but over governance attracted unwanted attention to Wesley College. Desirous of making changes in the organization and curriculum of the college, Principal John H. Riddell and the board of directors had the previous year obtained the services of the University of Toronto psychologist (and Methodist clergyman) W.G. Smith, who was expected to lend new lustre to Wesley.[64]

Aware that Smith was a theological liberal attracted to the Social Gospel, Riddell responded skittishly when Smith mentioned sociology as a possible subject of instruction at the college. Describing it as 'a very important field,' the principal also saw it as potentially hazardous: 'The recent strike ... coupled with the vigorous propaganda carried on ... in favour of what is generally regarded as an extreme social and industrial programme, make for us a very sensitive people.' He added in warning, 'Any unwise advocacy of radical measures would at this juncture here be fatal to us and to the larger cause we seek to advance in this new land.'[65]

Smith replied that the causes of the Winnipeg General Strike had not been removed 'by the unfortunate direction that strike took,' and he regretted that the church was 'not yet sufficiently unified and informed as to have contributed largely toward making such a strike impossible.' Yet all would work for the best, he said, 'if only we ... strive for a square deal "for the least and the last."'[66]

Riddell must have felt reassured. In April 1921 the board met Smith's salary request – $4,500 to start, with $100 increments for the next five years to $5,000, a handsome emolument at any Canadian university and at Wesley nothing short of princely. On Riddell's proposal, Smith became vice-principal and ex officio chairman of a committee of heads of departments that was to supervise and direct Wesley's academic work. He arrived in Winnipeg believing he had a mandate to reshape the curriculum, expand the influence of the college, and 'direct Wesley's contribution to the new order in Canada.'[67]

As Smith began to reform parts of the academic program, however, he offended some faculty members both at Wesley and at the University of Manitoba, with which the college was affiliated. He also frightened Riddell. Smith seemed to be undermining his authority![68]

By the 1922 winter term, the faculty were dividing into factions. Concerned by what was happening, the board's chairman, James H. Ashdown, tried to effect a reconciliation between Riddell and Smith. 'The one difficulty has been that there was not ... a proper understanding as to your duties and intention of the Board when you were first employed,' Ashdown wrote to Smith. But such an understanding was still possible. A board committee, he told Smith, would 'go into the matter with yourself, and define your duties.'[69]

On 20 April the executive committee of the board adopted a statement outlining the duties of the principal and vice-principal. Its wording made unequivocally clear who was in charge: 'The vice-principal shall perform such duties and have such powers as the principal may from time to time assign to him. The principal shall have power to vary or revoke any duties or powers he may have so assigned to the vice-principal.' Two weeks later, the committee added that the vice-principal was to act for the principal in his absence, but 'in so doing shall always be guided by and follow the plans, programmes and policies of the Principal.'[70]

This was a far cry from the duties Smith thought he had assumed, and he did not wait long to challenge the board. Before he did so, however, he himself came under attack. On 6 June 1922, five men charged that in the course of some lectures given to a young men's club at a local church, Smith had denied the miraculous conception and virgin birth of Jesus, his resurrection, the significance of his atonement, and the historicity of the Gospel of John. Thirty-three others supported the complaint and asked the board to obtain Smith's resignation or dismiss him.[71]

These charges were grave; but to the board, Smith's actions a few days later may have seemed graver. On 12 June, speaking to the Saskatchewan Conference of the Methodist Church, he criticized the administration of the college. Five days later, he told the Manitoba conference that the collegiate division was an unnecessary financial drain on Wesley, and he showed 'in detail' what he would do, 'if his leadership were recognized,' to enable the college 'to carry forward a programme worthy of her history and achievements in former years.'[72]

Ashdown had heard enough. He invited the executive committee of the board to a meeting in his office, and they agreed with him that a special board meeting should be held to consider whether Smith should stay in the employ of the college and how the complaint against his lectures should be dealt with. This meeting, which began on 29 June and continued on the thirtieth, heard Smith claim that he was responsible to the board 'only in regard to such matters as might be included in [his] contract,' that the board had no power to change that contract, 'that he was really sent ... by leading laymen and ministers of the Methodist

Church in Toronto with a view to remodelling the policy and programme of Wesley College,' and that 'he had with him the support of every member of the Faculty save two.' He added that he neither trusted Riddell nor liked him, but denied that he could not work harmoniously with him.[73]

Smith's alleged heresy seems to have had no place in the discussion that followed; it was his insubordination and disloyalty to Riddell that dominated. Some board members thought that Riddell had shown himself to be incompetent, but a resolution asking for his resignation found little support, not least because he had Ashdown in his corner. A resolution to dismiss Smith with a year's salary in lieu of notice then passed by a vote of thirteen to six.[74]

Smith used the appeal court of the Methodist Church to challenge the board's right to dismiss him. When this court ruled that it lacked jurisdiction, Smith turned to the civil courts, claiming $30,000 damages for wrongful dismissal. But to no avail. Mr Justice A.K. Dysart ruled that Smith's employment was terminable on a year's notice if 'in the honest opinion of the board, the best interests of the college so demanded.' The dismissal met this test, Dysart wrote, for in challenging Riddell's authority and criticizing his administration, Smith had disrupted Wesley and damaged its interests.[75]

Was academic freedom at stake? Not even Smith himself used the phrase. The dispute was perhaps essentially administrative in nature. Yet some undercurrents give us pause. The complaints in June 1922 about his alleged heresy raised the issue of academic freedom at least potentially, while the charge of insubordination and disloyalty raised the issue of academic freedom in a familiar form. However, the fact that Smith was vice-principal complicated the matter. It is doubtful even today whether administrators share in a freedom now claimed for other academics – the freedom to criticize the administration of the institution in which they work.

George Rawlyk wrote in 1988 that during the 1920s, McMaster University, the chief Baptist university in the country, helped 'precipitate a furious denominational civil war, from which the Convention has still not yet fully recovered.'[76] The appointment in 1925 of the English theologian Laurance Henry Marshall was the *casus belli*; the main antagonists were Chancellor Howard P. Whidden and the pastor of Toronto's Jarvis Street Church, T.T. Shields. At issue was the university's claim to orthodoxy.

The struggle had been years in the making, for its underlying cause was secularization. Even as Whidden's predecessor, A.L. McCrimmon, was glorying in the denominational mission of McMaster, the institution 'was being transformed by the forces of change unleashed by the war into an increasingly secular institution of higher learning.' Whidden, who came to McMaster in 1923 after eleven years as president of Brandon College, was well qualified to supervise McMaster's secularization. At Brandon he had shown superior administrative skill, combining his presidential duties with those of a member of Parliament from 1917 to 1921. He was less noted for his spiritual gifts. Nevertheless, 'closely associated with the Ontario business elite, an active Mason and a committed Conservative, Whidden was perceived by many members of McMaster's Board of Governors ... as just the man to lead the university ... into the mainstream of North American bourgeois success and respectability.'[77]

Shields lacked any university education or seminary training, but in 1910 his very considerable gifts as a preacher had secured him a call to Jarvis Street Church, the largest Baptist congregation in the country. For more than forty years he used its pulpit to attack liberalism and modernism in all their guises. In the early 1920s Shields veered between the hope that McMaster might yet serve fundamentalist Baptism and the fear that the university was already sunk too deep in modernism to be saved. He opposed Whidden's appointment, and his apprehensions increased when Whidden's installation was used to grant an honorary degree to the president of Brown University, William H.P. Faunce, a religious liberal. Shields denounced this provocation, and at the 1924 convention of Ontario and Quebec Baptists he was vindicated. It was none other than Whidden who seconded his successful motion that 'this Convention relies upon the Senate to exercise care that honourary degrees be not conferred upon religious leaders whose theological views are known to be out of harmony with the cardinal principles of evangelical Christianity.'[78]

Shields took this as evidence that McMaster might yet become a bastion of the faith. His disillusionment was great, therefore, when the board appointed Marshall to the chair of pastoral theology. Having heard from English acquaintances that Marshall was a liberal, Shields resumed his attacks on McMaster. In November 1925 he charged in the *Gospel Witness* 'that a group of men in the Denomination are determined to force upon us a moderate Modernism – and that, of course, means, ultimately, Modernism in its extreme form. Who wants a mild case of smallpox, or of leprosy?'[79]

The battle raged on for the better part of two years, as some congregations supported Whidden's McMaster and others its critics. The students also were divided. Some of them publicly attacked Marshall for his statement that the book of Jonah was 'a Divinely inspired prophetic sermon in the form of a parable or an allegory.' To many fundamentalists, the literal accuracy of this book, including its account of Jonah's sojourn inside a large fish, constituted an acid test of orthodoxy. Shields avidly seized on this issue; friends of McMaster feared that he was hoping to use the controversy to gain control of the university. However, at the October 1926 meeting of the convention, a motion endorsing the work of McMaster's officers and faculty passed by a wide margin.[80]

Shields had probably already lost interest in McMaster. Stating that he was 'at war' with both the university and the convention, he had established the Toronto Baptist Seminary in the spring of 1926. The next year, Jarvis Street Church having been expelled from the convention, Shields founded the Union of Regular Baptist Churches of Ontario and Quebec. The split in Canadian Baptism was complete.

Whidden defended Marshall against attack, and the latter also defended himself. At an educational session of the Baptist convention in May 1926, he declared that he stood for the 'historical method' in studying the Old Testament, and he went on to say, 'We must not fear science ... Is this Christian religion of ours such a flimsy thing that it cannot bear examination? I think it can bear the most relentless scrutiny.' At the 1927 convention he asserted, 'If scholarship and sound methods of study ... are to be ... held up to shame and execration, exposed to abuse and persecution, then the Baptists of Ontario and Quebec cannot have a university at all, for as soon as a university shuts its door on learning it ceases to be a university.' McMaster, he said, must stand 'for sound scholarship, for the love of truth, for reasonable liberty, with the McMaster motto as our watchword: "In Christ all things consist."'[81] The phraseology indicates that the denominational connection imposed curbs on the freedom to teach, do research, and speak publicly. McMaster would in time become a secular university, but it was not one yet. No openly avowed atheist or agnostic could expect to be employed there.

Marshall returned to England in 1930, the very year that McMaster moved from Toronto to Hamilton. He might have become dean of theology, but he confessed to feeling that he did not enjoy the 'full confidence' of many Baptists. Doubtless he was right. Nevertheless, his freedom to teach and publish, though attacked, had also been vigorously defended.[82]

In 1923 King's College moved from Windsor, Nova Scotia, to the campus of Dalhousie University. The two institutions established a joint Faculty of Arts and Science, roughly a quarter of whose professors were employed by King's. Among them was the psychologist Norman Symons, who resigned in 1929 under circumstances that clearly involved academic freedom. 'The case of Norman J. Symons,' Henry Roper and James W. Clark write, 'provides an insight into the stresses generated by the conflict between prevailing religious and social attitudes and the secular, even anti-religious, ideas which threatened them.' Symons was one of two members of the joint Department of Philosophy and Psychology. By 1924 he was a convert to Freudianism, a doctrine virtually absent from Canadian intellectual life before the 1920s, and from 1925 to 1929 he published five papers on the interpretation of dreams in the *International Journal of Psycho-Analysis*. Based on accounts provided by his students, these papers 'showed both great inventiveness in interpreting symbols and an overriding preoccupation with sexuality.'[83]

In 1924 a new president took office. A.H. Moore, a clergyman and journalist, was an energetic and practical man who managed to raise $400,000 for the erection of buildings on the Dalhousie campus. In the process, he had to deal with an Anglican community that was divided between evangelicals and high churchmen. Himself neither an intellectual nor a scholar, and being uninterested in 'reconciling freedom of thought with denominational interest,' Moore came to see Symons 'as a threat to his hard-won success in putting the future of King's on a secure footing,' and he was eager to be rid of him.

Roper and Clark believe that an item that appeared in the Dalhousie student newspaper, the *Gazette*, early in 1929 provides the key to Symons's abrupt departure:

At a recent meeting of Psychology 3 Prof. Symons asked one of the ladies for a definition of necking (a touching subject one must admit). She said that a few days previously she had asked another girl (imagine that!) and received the answer that 'it' was from the *neck up*. Well this is food for thought but we are still unconvinced about the direction pursued after leaving the neck. Somehow we feel that co-eds do not have to be necked by 'degrees.'[84]

Symons could hardly be held responsible for this comment, a risqué one by the standards of the time. But Moore may have faulted him for posing a question likely to cause embarrassment. In mid-April Symons wrote a letter of resignation in which he acknowledged, without being specific, 'the seriousness of the position which arose out of an error of judgment on my part.' The executive committee of the board accepted the resignation and awarded Symons two months' extra salary. The promise of a glowing letter of reference may have induced him to leave quietly instead of fighting for his job. (He did not, in fact, ever teach in a university again.)

The incident might have led to no more than a reprimand if Moore had not already had strong misgivings about Symons. 'We have had a pronounced Freudian on the staff,' he confided to a professor at Duke University: 'I found him here when I became President in 1924 and have feared that his dogmatism along his espoused line might terminate his usefulness to us and it has now done so.' In future, no 'propagandist of Freudianism, Behaviourism or any other modern cult' would be welcome, he stressed: 'We cannot have a man who has made a shipwreck of his religious faith or who teaches modern theories regardless of the way in which he may shock the religious convictions or the sense of delicacy of his students.' To someone else Moore wrote, 'We have no religious tests for either staff or students, but we must have a man who accepts the Christian religion and works from that as his background.' He rejected one candidate because he was Jewish and another because she was pregnant (though married), and finally appointed a United Church clergyman to succeed Symons.

Symons's fate and the issues it raised about academic freedom and due process attracted little notice. His friends held a farewell dinner for him at Halifax's Lord Nelson Hotel and then got on with their lives. Much juicier was the scandal that soon surrounded the Dalhousie zoologist James N. Gowanloch. The Gowanloch scandal merits description mainly for the light it sheds on attitudes that also affected Symons, but it is of interest as well because of the high-handed way in which the board dealt with it.

An able teacher with wide-ranging interests, Gowanloch 'was an atheist, and did not hide his views.'[85] During most of his stay at Dalhousie, his wife was studying medicine in New York, but in the summer of 1929 Louise Ross Gowanloch joined her husband, and that fall she began teaching in the biology department on a one-year contract. On 17 March 1930 she filed a petition for divorce, naming an undergraduate student as her husband's co-respondent. She thereby set in motion a process that led to his dismissal and her own suspension.

Both Henry Roper, who has brought to the case the skills of a detective as well as a historian, and P.B. Waite (Dalhousie's official historian) cast doubt on the stories told by James Gowanloch, his wife, and the student named as co-respondent, leaving it unclear whether adultery did in fact occur. Only one thing seems clear: Louise Gowanloch, having apparently decided to sue for divorce well before rejoining her husband, was willing to go to great lengths to secure the evidence she needed. (Adultery was the main ground for divorce in Canada at the time.)

On 20 March the board suspended both Gowanlochs, and the next day James Gowanloch submitted his resignation. His wife did not give in so easily. Believing herself to be the aggrieved party, she asked the board's chairman, G. Fred Pearson – President Stanley MacKenzie was out of town – why *she* had been suspended. He informed her 'that in all the circumstances the Board thought it wise that she should not be around students.' Her lawyer then informed the board that his client was willing to resign at any time, provided her suspension was expunged from the record and this action was given the same publicity her suspension had received.

The board considered her proposal, along with her husband's resignation, at a meeting on 2 May which neither was permitted to attend. The board members refused to accept the zoologist's letter of resignation and insisted on dismissing him instead. As for his wife, noting that her appointment was for one year and that the teaching term had ended, the board saw no need to hear her appeal and left her suspension in force. Both this action and the board's treatment of James Gowanloch offended against due process. However serious his offence was held to be, he should have been allowed either to resign or to be heard by the board. Worse still was the treatment of Louise Gowanloch, which lacked any justification. James Gowanloch did not find other university employment and died in Louisiana not long afterwards. His former wife, who returned to New York, became a hospital physician there.

Historians of Canada have devoted less study to the 1920s than to any other decade in the twentieth century. Both the cause and the consequence of this has been that those years have an image of relative tranquillity. The image affects our view of Canadian universities too, yet during the decade several significant controversies took place, involving governance, religion, and academic free speech. As well, Sir Robert Falconer's 1922 speech gave the idea of academic freedom a certain amount of public exposure. However, it was in the Depression-bound 1930s that conflicts over academic free speech assumed centre stage and a few academics began openly to claim academic freedom as a professorial right.

5

The Great Depression

The worst economic slump of the twentieth century began in 1929 and continued into 1933. In Canada the recovery, interrupted by a new downturn in 1937–8, was incomplete when the Second World War began. Canadian universities shared this experience as total university income, which had been $22 million in 1930, fell to $15.4 million in 1935 and rose to only $17.5 million by 1940.[1] Tuition fees increased everywhere by as much as 50 per cent as other kinds of income declined. Library purchases dropped, construction and maintenance were interrupted or postponed, salaries were cut, and some academics lost their jobs.

The Depression prompted sharp attacks on capitalism; it also contributed to the growth of illiberal and antidemocratic movements, both in Canada and abroad. Among these the most menacing was German national socialism, not least because it espoused a revanchism that rekindled fears of another European war. This led to debate about the nature of Canada's relations with the British Empire. Canadian membership in the League of Nations, too, raised questions about the country's commitments abroad in the event of war.

When criticism of the capitalist system, the political order, the imperial connection, or British foreign policy emerged from Canadian universities, it prompted charges that the barrier separating appropriate from inappropriate professorial comment had been crossed. Could professors who criticized received wisdom be trusted to teach Canada's future leaders? Ought they to be silenced? Such questions and their answers had grave implications for academic freedom.

On 15 and 16 January 1931 the Toronto newspapers carried a letter criticizing the city's police commission. Asserting that 'the right of free speech and free assembly' was in danger and that its arbitrary restriction was 'short-sighted, inexpedient, and intolerable,' the sixty-eight signatories claimed it was their duty to protest: 'In doing so, we wish to affirm our belief in the free public expression of opinions, however unpopular or erroneous.'[2] Police interference with 'radical' meetings had begun two years earlier, but until 1931 only one or two professors had commented on it. The free-speech rights of communists and other left-wing radicals were not an academic concern. The letter of the sixty-eight appeared only after a 'respectable' organization had been targeted by the police commission.

The Fellowship of Reconciliation (FOR) had been founded in 1914 'to create international, inter-racial, inter-class fellowship.' In 1930 a Toronto branch took form under the presidency of Rabbi Maurice Eisendrath; the executive included Henri Lasserre, a member of the Victoria College French department, and Salem Bland. These were not men likely to fall foul of the police. Nevertheless, the FOR failed to obtain a hall for a meeting in October. (Hall owners risked losing their licences if they rented to groups found to be communist, and this prompted caution.)

The members of the FOR objected to what they believed to be police interference, and some weeks later the organization announced an 'Open Forum' series, somewhat provocatively scheduling for the first meeting a debate on the resolution 'that the Toronto Police Commission is justified in its attitude in regard to free speech.' Police Chief D.C. Draper and the senior police magistrate, Judge Emerson Coatsworth, were invited to argue the affirmative – but they denounced the debate as 'a communistic meeting under a thin disguise,' and the FOR's booking of the Empire Theatre was abruptly cancelled. The FOR then demanded an investigation of the police commission.

Soon afterwards the letter of the sixty-eight appeared. It had been drafted by Frank Underhill and the Victoria College classicist Eric A. Havelock. Those who signed it must have known that they would quickly be identified as members of the staff of the university and its federated colleges. Among them were Principal Malcolm Wallace of University College, the heads of philosophy (G.S. Brett), history (Chester Martin), and political economy (E.J. Urwick) in the Faculty of Arts and Science, the supervisor of commerce and finance (Gilbert Jackson), and the Victoria College classicist C.B. Sissons.

The response to the letter was not what many of the sixty-eight had expected. Their critics far outnumbered their supporters. The *Globe* called it 'a ridiculous document'; the *Telegram* asserted that not even the signatories believed free speech was in danger; and the *Mail and Empire* quoted with approval Sir John Aird, president of the Canadian Bank of Commerce, who suggested that the sixty-eight should 'stick to their knitting.' By what right, the editor asked, did professors meddle in a dispute between the police commission and its enemies?[3]

Asked to comment, Sir Robert Falconer told reporters, 'As a citizen I am in favour of the British habit and practice of free speech.' Writing to Coatsworth, he affirmed his 'profound conviction that in the long run there is greater safety to a community in allowing freedom of speech than in repressing it,' but he asked not to be quoted. To an engineering graduate who urged him to dismiss the signatories, he replied, 'If the Governors were to adopt the method you propose ... they would find that the University would have been so injured that it would be long recovering from the blow.' He took the same line with a professor of medicine who wrote that if he was in Falconer's place, he would have reprimanded the signatories and even fired them. (But in this reply, Falconer did express some annoyance with the sixty-eight: 'As to the expediency of these gentlemen writing as they did, that is another matter.')[4]

More pointedly critical than Falconer was a prominent member of the board, Sir Joseph Flavelle. Writing to George Wrong, Flavelle faulted the sixty-eight for endangering their main source of support: 'The University must ... carry public opinion whereby it can be adequately housed and maintained. Every teacher ... is a trustee for the institution, that no act of his resulting from hasty and unreflective impulse shall jeopardize the progress and development of the University.' Flavelle added that 'a very, very influential member of the Legislature' had asked him what the governors were 'going to do about "this damn nonsense." '[5]

What the governors did was to establish an ad hoc committee. Its members, who included Chairman Henry J. Cody and Chancellor Sir William Mulock, decided not to censure the sixty-eight but asked Falconer to speak to some of them. A few days later, Falconer informed Cody that he had met six of the signatories to apprise them of the board's fears for institutional autonomy, and he had warned them that if they did not use their privileges wisely, 'the time might come when the university would again be subjected to partisan politics.' The six, he reported, had undertaken 'to use their influence with the members of their staff to refrain from further discussions on this or other political matters.'[6]

On 11 February the board passed a resolution dissociating the university from the letter of the sixty-eight. 'Undoubtedly the public received an erroneous impression from the publication of the letter,' Premier George S. Henry wrote upon receiving the board resolution. 'I trust, however, that the speech delivered by Sir William Mulock ... has largely cleared the air and relieved the public mind of the misunderstanding that had apparently developed.'[7]

Henry was referring to a speech the chancellor had made at a banquet on 4 February, during which he had called on the authorities to stamp out communism. According to a newspaper report, Leopold Macaulay, the Ontario minister of labour, had 'jokingly remarked that ... Sir William's speech was more agreeable than other unofficial messages from the University,' whereupon

Mulock and Cody had 'laughed and slapped each other's knees at this intimation that the professors were being answered unofficially by the University authorities.' Some people assumed that the board resolution likewise masked a rebuke to the sixty-eight.[8]

Falconer had in fact come close to rebuking them. Theirs was precisely the sort of activity against which he had warned in 1922. Addressing the students in September 1931, he used phrases he may have meant also for the ears and eyes of the faculty: 'When gales are carrying destruction over sea and land, it behooves all except those whose duty calls them to face danger, to shun foolhardy adventures which may imperil themselves or others. Now, more than ever, skylarking on the edge of folly enrages onlookers.'[9]

Not everyone at the university agreed that prudence was the watchword of the hour. Falconer was disagreeably surprised when the *Mail and Empire* demanded in June that Underhill 'be called upon the carpet' for criticizing Prime Minister R.B. Bennett in the pages of the *New Statesman and Nation*. Falconer wrote to the historian warning him that journalism of this kind endangered institutional autonomy.[10]

Falconer's letter took two months to reach Underhill, who had taken his family to Muskoka for the summer. By then Underhill, who read the Toronto newspapers, knew that the *Globe* had come to his defence, and he referred Falconer to this fact. 'If professors at Toronto must keep their mouths shut in order to preserve the autonomy of the University,' he concluded, 'then that autonomy is already lost. A freedom that cannot be exercised without danger of disastrous consequences is not a real freedom at all.'[11]

'Your letter leaves me still of the same opinion as to the inexpediency of professors in the University of Toronto taking part in political journalism,' Falconer replied. Professors had the right 'to teach their subjects with complete freedom,' he said, 'and that freedom I hope will always be maintained,' but to meddle in politics was 'dangerous to the well-being of the University.' As for the *Globe*, Falconer commented that since it had earlier attacked the sixty-eight, it showed 'no manner of consistency.'[12]

Seeing institutional autonomy as the chief good, Falconer sought to restrict academic freedom in a manner perhaps suggested to him by the tradition of *Lehrfreiheit* and its disdain for political activity. Underhill, on the other hand, favoured a broad definition of academic freedom rooted in the British tradition of academic free speech. The conflict between these points of view affected more than one university in the 1930s.

The sixty-eight were not the only University of Toronto professors to court controversy in the early 1930s. Another was Willis N. Millar of the Faculty of

Forestry. Except during his wartime service with the U.S. Army, he had taught at Toronto since 1914. At one point there seems to have been a difference of opinion between Millar and a colleague on a matter of administrative practice, but there was no other sign of trouble until the annual newsletter of the Foresters' Club appeared in April 1931. In it Millar criticized the forestry profession in Canada for its intellectual apathy, and forestry education for its emphasis on silviculture.[13]

One who took this ill was the dean of forestry, Clifton D. Howe, who prepared a memorandum for Falconer listing eight points of disagreement with Millar's paper. Soon afterwards Millar asked Falconer for 'an hour or so to discuss with you my position.' Howe was seeking his resignation, he claimed, because of the animosity towards him of one of his colleagues and because of 'the unorthodox and schismatic views in matters of forest policy' that had made him unpopular 'with certain influential employers of foresters.' He charged that Howe was using him to deflect attention from troubles in the faculty and from the failure of many forestry graduates to find jobs: 'If I am to be ejected from the University ... it seems to me only common decency that I be convicted of something other than merely independence of thought and expression in ... my profession.'[14]

No copy of a reply exists in Falconer's files, but there is a memorandum, based on a letter from Howe in the spring of 1932, asking for Millar's resignation. He was charged with three 'offences': a 'lack of co-operation in the educational policy of the Faculty,' including 'attacks upon the teaching of the fundamentals of silviculture at variance with the convictions of the majority of the staff'; a 'lack of tact and violence of his criticism [by which] he antagonises his employers and other people with whom he makes contact ...'; and 'public discussions of policies [that] contain so many irresponsible or exaggerated or unsubstantiated statements or distortions of fact as to disclose of [sic] type of mind unfitted to carry on the work of a professorship.' The third and most damaging charge was based on the 1931 newsletter and on a letter Millar had sent to the *Globe* in March 1932 criticizing the reforestation policy of the provincial government.[15]

Quite possibly, Falconer held this letter to be an inappropriate comment on a political question. If so, he might have reprimanded Millar in the same way he had reprimanded Underhill the year before. Instead, he gave in to Howe's demand that Millar be removed. 'Uncharacteristically, Falconer seems to have made little effort to investigate the case personally,' Falconer's biographer writes. 'Perhaps, with his mandate very near its close, he felt constrained to act on Howe's pointed advice.' But he could have delayed, leaving his successor to deal with the matter; or he could have launched an independent inquiry. Instead, he called Millar into his office, gave him the memorandum to read, and asked him to resign. Probably believing that he had no choice, Millar complied. He left Toronto and Canada in 1933, dying prematurely soon afterwards.[16]

Acting on Howe's recommendation was the path of least resistance for Falconer, but he was not obliged to take this path. In 1932 the University of British Columbia's president, L.S. Klinck, foiled an attempt by the dean of arts and science, Daniel Buchanan, to use a budgetary crisis as a pretext for dismissing a 'difficult' member of the mathematics department.[17] In failing to establish whether Howe's demand was rooted in a professional or personal disagreement between him and Millar, or whether there were more substantial reasons for asking the latter to resign, Falconer ignored due process. This undermined the guarantee of academic freedom that he had given to the faculty in 1922.

Something like the League for Social Reconstruction (LSR) might well have emerged in any case, but its birth was hastened by a serendipitous meeting at Williams College in Williamstown, Massachusetts, in August 1931 between Frank Underhill and Frank Scott of McGill's Faculty of Law. The two men undertook to organize a sort of Fabian society, and with the help of a few others that fall and winter they founded 'an association ... working for the establishment in Canada of a social order in which the basic principle regulating production, distribution and service will be the common good rather than private profit.'[18]

Most of the founders were academics, but they were never more than 10 to 15 per cent of its membership, and only in Toronto did the LSR have as many as a dozen academic members. Elsewhere they were rare even before the LSR came to be linked to the new social democratic party, the Co-operative Commonwealth Federation (CCF). That link never became official, or Falconer's successor, H.J. Cody, might have objected more strenuously to Underhill's presidency of the LSR. Cody objected to the historian's close association with the CCF. The University of Toronto had no formal policy on political activity, but Falconer's 1922 address on academic freedom had signalled that such activity was unwelcome. When, late in 1932, Underhill joined the executive of the Ontario CCF Clubs, Cody ordered him to withdraw. The historian gathered data about American and British academics who were active in politics, but to no avail. He had to submit.[19]

The following year Underhill, assisted by Harry Cassidy of the University of Toronto's Department of Social Science (forerunner of the Faculty of Social Work), by Joseph Parkinson of political economy and Escott Reid, national secretary of the Canadian Institute of International Affairs, provided the new party with a draft of what became the Regina Manifesto. None of the four attended the CCF's convention in Regina that summer, but Frank Scott and Eugene Forsey (also from McGill) did, as did King Gordon of Montreal's United Theological College. This led the Winnipeg journalist George Ferguson, who knew some of them personally, to describe the LSR's leading figures as the 'C.C.F. "Brain Trust."'[20]

The publicity was not wholly welcome, particularly to one of the Toronto men. 'I think that I can, for the present at least, be more useful if I am free of connection with a political party,' Cassidy wrote in resigning from the St Paul's CCF Club in October 1933. He also asked the secretary of the CCF Clubs to remove his name from the speakers' list: 'It would be easier for me to meet criticisms if my name did not appear.' His prudence had an unexpected payoff when George M. Weir, provincial secretary of British Columbia, recommended him to Premier Thomas D. Pattullo for appointment as supervisor of social welfare in 1934. Although Cassidy was 'inclined to be radical in [his] economic views,' Weir wrote, he was not a member of the CCF.[21]

Cassidy's cautiousness may have been due to President Cody's attitude. Conservative in every sense, Cody not only believed that professors should avoid controversy, but he had a low tolerance for left-wing views. In his first annual report as president of the University of Toronto, he stated: 'While academic freedom is rightly held to be essential to true university teaching, academic responsibility accompanies it, and is equally imperative. The teacher to whom freedom is gladly given must realize and practise the responsibility which its possession imposes within and without the academic walls.' In the same vein, he told a Montreal audience late in 1933 that professors were better employed as teachers and scholars than as aspiring politicians: 'I do not believe that ... universities will do their best work if they leap into the arena of practical politics or active economic and industrial questions.'[22]

Yet Cody sanctioned some forms of political involvement. In 1933 and 1934 he was openly enthusiastic about some aspects of Italian fascism. More benignly, he approved the participation of members of the faculty, among them Cassidy, H.A. Innis, and a professor of international relations, N.A.M. (Larry) MacKenzie, in two political summer schools in 1933 – Conservative at Newmarket and Liberal at Port Hope. This, Cody wrote, was 'a duty that members of the university staff really owe to the public.' When Cassidy was leaving the university's employ in 1934, he wrote to Cody: 'I can assure you that I appreciate very much your tolerance of faculty members such as myself expressing unorthodox ideas and of our being given genuine freedom in the University of Toronto to discover and express the truth as we see it – even if we may be wrong.' (Cassidy's praise might have been less fulsome had he not hoped to return to Toronto.)[23]

In his 1935 report, Cody said that professors enjoyed 'a full measure of academic freedom' but owed a duty to the university to use that freedom with wisdom and good taste: 'Academic freedom lays on the University the responsibility to allow freedom of research and of teaching ..., but it also lays on the instructor the responsibility to approach his work not as a propagandist or partisan, but as a seeker for the whole truth, with open mind, fair judgment, and regard for all the facts.' As well, because the public often mistakenly assumed that statements by faculty members implicated the university, professors should realize that the legal right to express their views did not imply a moral right to do so.[24]

The argument resembled Falconer's in 1922, but one highly interested observer found Cody's message more permissive. 'Our president ... has come out with quite a strong statement for academic freedom,' Underhill wrote to Alberta's W.H. Alexander, 'though of course everything depends on what his interpretation of this may be in a particular case.' There seemed, noted Underhill, to be 'a loosening up,' either as a reaction against U.S. excesses – 'Toronto hates everything American, even their bad points' – or because the recent election had revealed that the CCF represented no real danger.[25] (In October 1935 the Liberals had replaced the Conservatives in Ottawa, and the CCF had taken a mere seven House of Commons seats.)

The CCF nevertheless continued to be under a cloud. Invited by its leader, J.S. Woodsworth, to join a committee formed to interpret the party's financial policies in simple language, Joseph Parkinson declined: 'I have refrained from becoming an official of the CCF ... in view of ... the fact that this step would put a weapon in the hands of opponents who take different views from ourselves as to the rights of a professor in a state university.'[26] Parkinson offered informal help instead. We may infer that he believed that the LSR was less open to objection than the CCF, for the LSR's book, *Social Planning for Canada*, had appeared some weeks earlier with Parkinson listed as one of its seven authors. (The others were Eugene Forsey, Leonard Marsh, and Frank Scott of McGill, King Gordon, by this time a travelling lecturer for the United Church of Canada and the Fellowship for a Christian Social Order, the journalist and political organizer Graham Spry, and Underhill.)

No Canadian academic was more visible in the 1930s than Frank Hawkins Underhill. His notoriety was due partly to his discussions of politics and foreign policy, partly to his style. Like Robertson Davies's schoolmaster Dunstable Ramsay, the historian could not resist getting off 'good ones' – sarcastic barbs that wounded. Late in 1933 a friend praised his 'integrity, candor, prophetic spirit and courage' but also told him, 'Sometimes you put a little more sting into your remarks than a judicially-minded professor should find necessary.'[27]

A similar comment came from George Wrong. Worried that his sometime protégé was bringing harm to the university, he tried to set him straight. 'You and every one in the University should be free to express the opinion you hold on questions proper for discussion in the University,' he told Underhill, but he said one should not introduce the partisan spirit or give needless offence: 'You attack leaders by name in terms not gentle nor courteous. I do not regard your opinions as "deplorable" though I should have such a word in mind, I fear, if I were discussing your mode of expressing them.'[28]

In fact, it was not just the style of Underhill's remarks that offended. The content was also at issue, particularly when he criticized the British connection. He had fought on the Western front, which coloured his outlook. 'The stupidity of G.H.Q. and the terrible sacrifice of so many of the best men among my contemporaries sickened me for good of a society, national or international, run by the British governing classes,' he wrote much later.[29] After Adolf Hitler seized power in Germany in early 1933, Underhill gave public voice to his view that Canada should emancipate itself from British foreign policy in order to avoid participation in another European war. This exposed him to attack. For many Canadians, patriotism was not merely national but imperial. To those who regarded Britain and the Empire with a mixture of affection, loyalty, and pride, criticism of the British connection and British policy seemed almost treasonable.

In the fall of 1933 Underhill lectured in Orillia under the auspices of the university's Department of Extension, speaking about issues of Canadian domestic and foreign policy. In attendance was C.H. Hale of the *Orillia Packet and Times*. What he heard angered him. 'Certain professors [are] deliberately instilling into the youth of Canada a feeling of lukewarmness, if not of hostility, towards the mother country and the British Empire,' he wrote. Uttered from a soap box, Underhill's words might matter little: 'But when he affords us evidence that he is using the university extension lectures to spread his anti-British views, and gives reason to suspect that he is doing the same thing among the students in the university ..., the matter takes on a serious aspect.' Canada could not afford 'to pay university professors to undermine the foundations of her political and economic systems, vilify her public men, and loosen the bonds that bind her to the Empire.'[30]

Following suit, the *Mail and Empire* charged that Underhill was abusing his position at a university 'supported by the taxpayers of Ontario, in a manner which will not be approved by a great majority of those taxpayers.' A 'vociferous minority among the professors should [not] be allowed to poison the minds of young men and women whose fathers help pay the professors' salaries,' announced the editor. The university should silence the historian.[31]

The controversy spilled over into the political sphere when someone wrote to

Prime Minister R.B. Bennett asking why Underhill was drawing a salary 'provided by the citizens of Canada.' Bennett's secretary forwarded the letter to Premier George Henry's office for 'whatever action is deemed necessary.' Henry's secretary replied, 'As you are aware, the University is a self-governing unit,' but he added, 'I understand those in authority are not unaware of these activities.'[32]

Certainly, Cody was aware of them. Asked why the people of Ontario should 'be taxed to pay the salary of a man and keep him in a sheltered position from which to spread his pernicious propaganda,' Cody replied, 'The only lecturing he will do in the future ... is his undergraduate teaching in his own department.'[33] Underhill was to give no more extension lectures. Cody also asked him to tone down his speeches.

For the better part of a year Underhill complied. At the 1934 Couchiching Conference, however, he launched an attack on Canada's links with the Empire and the League of Nations. And in October, speaking in London, Ontario, he predicted (accurately) that a future world war would spell the end of the British Empire. His most eye-catching remark was historical, however: 'We went into war blindly because we swallowed the British propaganda about democracy.'[34]

Called on the carpet once again, Underhill agreed to Cody's demand that he make no public speeches for a year. In fact, he avoided speaking about Canada's place in the Empire for longer than that. When he wrote about foreign policy (mostly in the *Canadian Forum*), he usually did so anonymously. In writing for a wider audience, as in *Maclean's* in 1937, he acknowledged the importance of British ideals and traditions for Canada even as he questioned the direction of British foreign policy. Although this article generated a few letters of protest to Cody, it did not create a major stir.[35]

Underhill did not cease to give offence, however. When Sir Edward Beatty, president of the Canadian Pacific Railway, criticized socialist academics in 1935, Underhill wrote in the *Canadian Forum* that Beatty's comments constituted 'an invitation for some Canadian would-be Hitler to work up a demagogic agitation against our ... universities and, when the opportunity comes, to discipline them in the customary fascist manner.' A pained Beatty thought that the article offered 'adequate evidence as to the correctness of [his] present pessimism concerning some phases of Canadian university education.'[36]

Underhill also offended Harold Adams Innis. The economic historian had signed the letter of the sixty-eight and had shown an early interest in the LSR, but when it aligned itself with the CCF he withdrew, for he saw in this party a threat to the disinterestedness of social scientists. It was unsurprising, therefore, that he objected to the paper that Underhill read to the 1935 meeting of the Canadian Political Science Association. So far, social scientists had for the most part tacitly justified the policies of Canada's elites, Underhill said, but in future they must either openly accept the social objectives of the present economic system or decide what those objectives should be and publish their conclusions for the criticism of their fellows. An attempt to avoid this choice was 'a retirement to the ivory tower.'[37]

Innis responded in a review of the LSR's *Social Planning for Canada*: 'Footloose adventurers in universities turn in some cases to business and its profits during booms, and in others to political activity and popular acclaim during depressions,' he wrote: 'Elections in a depression are not conducive to high standards in the discussion of complex problems in volumes written for political purposes.' Stung by this, Underhill looked for an ulterior motive. The entry of professors into politics was not new, he wrote, but recently some had become active on the radical side. Was this what had prompted Innis's disapproval? Underhill then went on the attack: 'All Canadian economists are divided into two classes, those who have already served on Royal Commissions and ... those who are still hoping to do so.' A reputation for respectability was essential, he added. 'But for any reader who is familiar with the inside of our Canadian universities there is no need to develop this point further.' This was *ad hominem*, of course, but Innis's comments were little better.[38]

In 1937 Underhill was in the news again. Speaking on CBC radio, he argued that the concentration of ownership in the newspaper industry was compromising freedom of the press. The recent merger of the *Globe* and the *Mail and Empire* was an example. The mining magnate William H. Wright owned the new *Globe and Mail*; George McCullagh, a wealthy bond salesman and stockbroker, was its publisher. As a result, Underhill quipped, 'I have no alternative to reading at my breakfast table ... whatever a couple of gold-mining millionaires may think is good for the people of Ontario.'[39]

In response, the *Globe and Mail* thundered that if the CBC could find no one better qualified than Underhill to discuss press freedom, it should close down: 'The same thing could be said of the University of Toronto, and especially Victoria College, where socialism is seething.' Underhill had expressed the suspicion that Canada's educational systems turned out 'masses of sheep' who were 'just literate enough to become the victims of newspaper propaganda.' It was time, said the *Globe and Mail*, that 'certain professors, like Mr. Underhill, were turned out en masse and the public purse was relieved of supporting the kind of "education" they promote.'[40]

Since McCullagh was known to be close to Premier Mitchell Hepburn, Cody again spoke to Underhill. 'The President is very anxious that I don't cause any more trouble in the near future,' he reported to a friend, 'and since he has treated me pretty decently I don't want to make trouble for him.' Of the fifty-four articles and editorials that Underhill contributed to the *Canadian Forum* during the next two years, only three appeared under his name. One result, as Underhill told his fellow historian Arthur Lower in 1938, was that things were 'fairly quiet in Ontario and around the University' and he was 'enjoying an unaccustomed peace.'[41]

Peace ended when, during a radio broadcast about U.S. politics in November 1938, Underhill quipped that 'Britain did not seem able, at the present time, to do anything beyond giving away the territory of other nations.' If some listeners thought this fair comment on the Munich Agreement and its appeasement of Hitler by forcing Czechoslovakia to cede the Sudetenland to Germany, the editor of the Toronto *Telegram* was not among them. He faulted Underhill for his inability to grasp the wisdom of British foreign policy and added, 'Is it any part of the essential liberty of expression which should belong to a University that its underlings ... should promulgate false charges against a partner in the British Commonwealth of Nations?'[42]

There was the predictable repercussion. 'Would you please call to see me on Tuesday morning at eleven o'clock, if that is convenient to you?' Cody asked Underhill. The timing turned out to be good. When the two men met, Underhill was able to quote from a *Saturday Night* editorial making much the same point about British policy that he had made. There, for the time being, the matter ended.[43]

The presidents of most other universities welcomed political controversy no more than Falconer and Cody did. But the issue loomed larger at the provincial institutions because of their dependence on governments and legislatures. The University of Alberta's President Robert C. Wallace, for example, believed most forms of political activity by professors to be unwise, and in 1930 the board expressed its agreement with him in a resolution to that effect.[44]

When a faculty member, W.H. Alexander, undertook to speak in Calgary late in 1932 in support of a CCF candidate in a provincial by-election, Wallace asked him not to. Alexander complied. A government backbencher, Fred White, then complained to Premier John Brownlee about Alexander's withdrawal. (The province was governed at this time by the CCF-affiliated United Farmers of Alberta [UFA].) Brownlee relayed White's complaint to Wallace, who defended his decision. Professors, he informed White, were 'free to express their points of view at any time in whatever method they desire,' but they should not take part in provincial elections: 'There is no doubt whatever that if this were done the University ... would be dragged into provincial politics, and there is no doubt in my judgment that the University would inevitably suffer.'[45]

In 1934 Alexander expressed his intention to seek the CCF nomination in a federal constituency in Edmonton. Wallace was unhappy, and in December he gave Alexander a copy of a memorandum that was to be discussed by the board of governors in early January. 'On the one hand, the best interests of the University have to be safeguarded,' Wallace had written. 'On the other hand, there are rights of citizenship which must be protected and maintained.' The interests of the university required that professors should not involve themselves in provincial politics, he stated. Federal politics were not similarly sensitive, and in that area professors should be free to express their views, but running for office was another matter: 'A member of the staff cannot serve as a member of the House of Commons and carry on his duties in the University ... He should not ... offer himself as a candidate without first resigning his university position.'[46]

Alexander declined Wallace's invitation to address the board: 'I do not feel called on as yet to take up the old fight on behalf of the liberty of the subject in my own person.' But he identified the illogicality in Wallace's argument that faculty members must resign before running for office because membership in the House of Commons was inconsistent with their university duties. Running was one thing, winning another. 'If the position you are suggesting ... is to be defended on the ground that it is logical and not simply authoritarian,' he wrote to Wallace, 'it becomes very necessary to be sure that the logic will stand ... searching examination.' Of course, if Wallace's position *was* 'purely authoritarian, that was 'a less important consideration.' But in that case, observed Alexander, 'others arise which are rather more alarming still.'[47]

At the meeting of the board of governors on 4 January 1935, one of the governors, Elmer Roper, who was a member of the CCF, immediately identified the flaw in Wallace's argument: 'This seems completely to overlook the fact that a candidate may be defeated as well as elected.' Candidacy as such need not interfere with a professor's duties, Roper said, so why should he resign before offering himself as a candidate? Indeed, were rules governing political activity necessary at all? Most of his fellow governors obviously believed that they were, for only two board members opposed Wallace's proposal.[48]

Alexander told Underhill that he had not expected the board to deny him, though he had been worried about the legislature. Now only that body could offer him a remedy. He hoped it would: 'My political ambitions are few – getting too old for one thing, and for another rather like being a professor – but I had hoped to give radicals a chance to vote for a half-sensible candidate in a bourgeois constituency, where I should certainly have been trimmed handsomely.' Alexander could not understand why the board had saved him the experience, 'but of course, like all such bodies as at present constituted in Canada, they are incurably dull and stupid, even in safeguarding their own interests.' The ruling was 'ridiculous,' said Alexander, but, given a choice between political candidacy and his job, he preferred the latter.[49]

When the board resolution became known, the reaction in some circles was hostile. Meeting in Lethbridge, the Alberta Federation of Labor passed a motion that called on 'the Alberta Legislature to amend the University Act to prohibit the board of governors from putting into effect any ruling which would restrict the citizenship rights of members of the University staff.' Delegates to the annual convention of the United Farmers of Alberta also wanted an amendment to the University Act to prevent the board from restricting any member of the staff who wished to run for office, as long as this did not 'interfere with the efficient performance of his duties as a member of the staff.'[50]

Several weeks passed. Then Fred White introduced a private member's bill that replicated the wording of the UFA motion almost verbatim. When it came to be discussed in committee, Wallace appeared to register his objections. Referring to two unnamed 'men of long experience and great wisdom in the administration of Canadian provincial universities,' he said that they were 'very firmly of the opinion that the only wise course' was 'to keep the university free from political activity' and that they had 'consistently administered accordingly.' He denied that the board's ruling was unreasonable, saying 'that no recommendation would go to the board for the permanent filling of a vacancy caused by a candidature until after the election.' This would enable the board to rehire someone who had failed to win a seat. He denied, too, that the board's action had been directed against Alexander personally or against the CCF. Alexander contradicted this: 'The board's order was directed against himself and no one else, as he was the only person who was within striking distance of a nomination.'[51]

Aware that the classicist had support in UFA circles, yet unwilling to interfere with the university's autonomy, the government was eager to neutralize the issue. To this end, Premier R.G. Reid and the man he had succeeded, John Brownlee, met with the board on 10 April. The policy, Reid said, 'had become to some extent a political issue which could not be settled in the best interests of the University in the heat of a political contest.' Could the matter be 'removed from the political arena?' he asked. After Reid and Brownlee left, the governors agreed to suspend the policy 'for the present year.' (Alexander did not seek another nomination: 'I should thank our Bd of Govs for having saved me $200,' he later wrote to Underhill.) No doubt as a result, Reid opposed White's bill on final reading and it went down to defeat: fifteen for, thirty-three against.[52] The policy came into effect in 1936 and remained in place until 1942.

At the University of British Columbia the involvement of academics in political issues occasionally led to controversy. The economist Henry F. Angus ruffled feathers in the mid-1930s when he began to advocate the extension of the franchise to Canadians of Asian origin. The historian Peter Ward writes that 'nativists condemned Angus when he began to speak in public, and at least one of his critics demanded his dismissal from the University.' The board ignored this demand. A letter of complaint from the Native Sons of Canada was tabled when President Leonard S. Klinck said that Angus would meet with the group in person. What the outcome of this meeting was is not recorded.[53]

In 1935 some UBC professors openly supported a health insurance bill introduced by the provincial government. Many physicians objected to the bill as a threat to their autonomy and incomes; much of the business community also opposed it. Early in 1936 the board of governors received a complaint from the Vancouver Medical Association about the activities of some professors in connection with the bill. Asked for information, Klinck gave the board 'an outline of the addresses given by Dr. C.W. Topping, and a letter from Dr. G.G. Sedgewick, and a number of other communications.' A board committee was formed 'to study the question,' but before it could report, the government announced a delay before the legislation would take effect. This turned out to be the bill's death knell. With interest in the subject subsiding, the board dropped the matter.[54]

More dramatic than these incidents was the process whereby UBC professors gained the right to run for office. In May 1933 Klinck recommended J. Allen Harris for employment as an instructor in the summer session. Harris had been an assistant professor of chemistry before losing his position in a budgetary crisis in 1932, and he had been promised preferential consideration when UBC resumed hiring. While he was waiting, he had accepted the Liberal nomination in a provincial constituency. Upon discussion, the board passed a motion opposing the appointment of 'any person who is entering public life.' At the next board meeting Klinck, having consulted with Dean Daniel Buchanan, again proposed Harris for appointment, but when the board persisted in its opposition to Harris's political candidacy, Klinck withdrew the recommendation.[55]

In August the board received a request that forced on it a different course of action. George M. Weir, head of UBC's Department of Education, asked permission to accept the Liberal nomination in a Vancouver constituency. This required careful handling. Years of economic hardship had discredited the governing Conservatives. Few doubted that the Liberals would enter office, and Weir was rumoured to be Liberal leader Thomas D. Pattullo's choice for the Education portfolio. Buying time, the governors passed a motion stating that they had 'taken no action nor do they intend to take any action which will in any way curtail the civil rights of any member of the staff, but should any person on the staff be elected as a representative of the people then the Governors will consider the situation thereby created.'[56]

On 2 November 1933 the Liberals (and Weir) triumphed, and that December the board had to consider his request for leave of absence without pay while he served as provincial secretary and minister of education. Klinck reported that he had told the premier that he 'expected Dr. Weir to resign,' but Pattullo had disagreed: 'It would not be fair to Dr. Weir to ask him to resign unless the Board should decide to appoint a Head to the Department of Education.' When Klinck expressed doubt that the board would do so 'at present,' Pattullo asked him 'to re-open the case ... as soon as the Governors felt they were in a position to appoint a man to the post.' The board then resolved, with two members dissenting, 'that Dr. Weir be given leave of absence, without salary, from the time he became Minister until such time as the Board shall decide to appoint a permanent Head in the Department of Education.'[57]

In 1935 one of the dissenters, Judge J.N. Ellis, left the board. When Pattullo wrote to thank him for his service, Ellis replied with bitterness and reproach: 'I would have thought more of the thanks had you carried out your promise made to me in the Vancouver Hotel when we both agreed that Dr. Weir's conduct, in remaining on the Faculty, while a responsible minister of the Crown, was to say the least in bad taste and reprehensible.' Having stayed on the board at Pattullo's express request, Ellis said he had waited 'patiently' for him to implement his promise that after the first session of the legislature he would induce Weir to resign; in vain. Ellis regretted that he had not in 1933 obeyed his first impulse to leave the board.[58]

Pattullo replied that he could not recall the promise Ellis referred to, and he added that he saw nothing reprehensible in Weir's conduct. He urged Ellis to take a wider view: 'Political life is very uncertain and I think it would be an unfortunate thing for the country if capable men must be excluded unless they are prepared to give up their businesses or professions.'[59]

This, of course, had implications that went beyond Weir's case. Allen Harris was appointed to the 1934 summer school even though he had become an MLA (the legislature did not sit during the summer), and in the fall of 1935 Klinck informed the board of a telephone conversation with Weir. Apparently, Harris wished to return to full-time employment. The board undertook to accept Klinck's recommendation to appoint Harris, but 'on condition that [he] resign his seat in the Provincial Legislature' and that money be made available to pay him. The first condition did not suit Pattullo, who asked that Harris be appointed while retaining his seat in the assembly. A board committee discussed the matter with the premier; the result was that Harris became a research assistant, his salary and the costs of his research funded by a special $10,000 provincial grant, on the understanding that he would take leave without pay during the legislative session.[60]

In 1937 Harris did not seek re-election. That fall, on Weir's request, the chemist was appointed assistant professor for a term ending on 15 May 1938, half of his salary to be charged to the research grant. The final step in Harris's reintegration took place in the spring of 1938, when he rejoined UBC on a full-time basis at his old salary, the special grant being added to UBC's regular income. The board's willingness to see things the government's way was in part due to the circumstances under which Harris had lost his position in 1932. It also helped that money was made available for his re-employment. As well, the board's acquiescence in Weir's long-term leave of absence made it hard to insist that university employment and politics were incompatible. Finally, the governors were unwilling to resist Pattullo. As for Weir, he resigned from politics in 1941 when he obtained leave from UBC to do war-related work in Ottawa. In 1944 he returned, only to request renewed political leave the following year. This time, though, upon assuming the Education portfolio in the cabinet headed by John Hart, he resigned from UBC at last.

The policy reluctantly adopted by UBC's board embodied Premier Pattullo's wish that academic employment and political service should not exclude each other, especially where his choice of cabinet ministers was concerned. Did this infringement of the university's autonomy harm UBC? It would be difficult to make that case. Weir did make his influence felt within the institution, notably with respect to admissions policy, but his predecessors John D. MacLean and Joshua Hinchliffe had both been more interventionist than he.[61]

At the University of Saskatchewan in the 1930s, Carlyle King stood out. He was active in the CCF and became a vocal critic of the British connection. In March 1938 he told listeners at a meeting sponsored by the Young Communist League that they should oppose Canadian rearmament. The British government 'would go to war for only two purposes,' he said, 'to maintain the British Empire or to prevent the spread of Socialism in Europe.' Neither was worth fighting for.[62]

Letters addressed to President James S. Thomson carried a clear message: fire King. 'This man ... should not be engaged to render services to the youth of our country,' one man wrote. Thomson downplayed King's remarks, describing the English literature professor as 'exceedingly foolish.' But he defended 'the liberty of Professors to express their views publicly.' It was best to let the storm blow over, he advised board chairman P.E. MacKenzie. The student body had been 'loud in protestation for free speech, so that if anything were attempted in the way of interference we should have more trouble than ever on our hands.'[63]

In early August 1938 the minister of education, J.W. Estey, alerted Thomson to a meeting at which King had addressed a group of Doukhobors 'in an anti-

British sense.' Then, in September, King opposed Canada's participation in the war between Britain and Germany that loomed because of Hitler's claim to the Czech Sudetenland. 'Mr. King in his speeches holds up the British Empire to contempt and ridicule,' a Regina lawyer wrote to Thomson. 'The sooner you call for his resignation, the better it will be for the prestige of the University of Saskatchewan.' Similarly, a letter sent to the Regina *Leader-Post* stated, 'We do not pay our taxes to provide a living for traitors.'[64]

Thomson upheld academic free speech publicly but undermined it privately. He spoke to King, who thereupon cancelled an undertaking to speak at an antiwar meeting. When this prompted charges that he had silenced King, Thomson denied it. King had agreed, Thomson wrote to the Saskatoon *Star-Phoenix*, 'that it would be regrettable if the University should become involved in public controversy through speeches made by members of the Faculty.' Thomson said he had suggested that King express himself less provocatively; and that, unwilling to accept the 'compromise of principle' this might involve, King had decided to make no more speeches: 'I made it very clear to Mr. King ... that this decision was being made entirely by himself and was not being forced upon him by the University ... At no time by threat of dismissal or otherwise, has the University of Saskatchewan attempted to induce Mr. Carlyle King from speaking in public.'[65]

Whatever Thomson meant, King took from the meeting the conviction that his job was on the line. Thomson had said 'that another offence of the kind would bring a demand from the Board for my dismissal,' he wrote to Underhill, 'whereupon I announced that I should not speak again in public upon international affairs.' Having received no support – even the provincial CCF had been 'silent as a clam' – he was giving up.[66]

Of all provincial universities, the one at which professors were least likely to meddle in politics was the University of New Brunswick. This was because of its close links to the government. UNB was governed by a senate that was the equivalent of a board of governors but included as *ex officio* members the minister and deputy minister of education. Moreover, in 1938 Attorney-General John B. McNair, soon to be premier, joined the senate.

In spite of the close relations between the university and the government, faculty enjoyed a measure of academic freedom. A member of the chemistry department, F.J. Toole, recalled in 1973 that he and his colleague Robert Wright had tried in the 1930s 'to let people know that something horrible was happening to the world, and that we were sort of mixed up in it ... That's when we began to get the reputation of being Communists.' However, the university put no pressure on them to stop speaking. Later in the decade, Toole said, Chief Justice J.H. Barry asked the head of philosophy and education, W.C. Keirstead, whether 'he had noticed any growth of communism in the university – because, if so, it should be stamped out.' Keirstead had replied that he had noticed no such growth, 'and if I had,' he said, 'I would not agree that it should be stamped out.' Barry's reaction goes unmentioned.[67]

The close relationship between university and government was evident in the appointment of the historian Alfred G. Bailey. In 1935 Bailey returned to the province to become the assistant director of the New Brunswick Museum in Saint John. As history was only intermittently taught at UNB, he offered to teach a course free of cost to the university except for his rail fare. President C.C. Jones agreed, and in 1937–8 Bailey made a weekly trip to Fredericton to lecture to third- and fourth-year students.

When Bailey proposed that he be appointed to a new history department, Jones did not hold out much hope – the university was desperately poor – but encouraged him to take up the matter with the government. Bailey went to see McNair, who liked the proposal and put it before the cabinet. There it ran into flak. Minister of Education A.P. Patterson wanted to appoint an extension lecturer in his own department who would lecture in the university. As a civil servant, such a person could be instructed to promote the Compact theory of Confederation, the notion that the federation was the creature of the provinces and could be changed only by them. Patterson was much attached to this idea.

Bailey thought it wrong that the minister should dictate what was taught. He maintained that the university should have its own historian, and that person 'should be free to give what courses he thought desirable, and from the point of view that he thought desirable.' Besides, he said, 'I didn't want to be coerced into putting forward a theory which I didn't agree with.'[68]

He had a strong ally in McNair, who carried cabinet opinion on the issue. At a senate meeting in February 1938, Jones reported that the government had approved the establishment of a chair of history. The senate then appointed Bailey, his academic freedom unimpaired.[69]

The experience of Escott Reid illustrates the difficulties faced by 'radicals' who sought university appointments. A Rhodes Scholar, he returned to Canada in 1930 to study the growth of Canada's political parties, a project funded by the Rockefeller Foundation. In 1982 the historian J.L. Granatstein described the six essays Reid wrote, on the basis of his research, as 'brilliant examples of political analysis to which students, half a century later, are still referred.'[70]

In 1932 Reid passed up an offer of employment from Harvard in order to become national secretary of the Canadian Institute of International Affairs. A member of the League for Social Reconstruction (LSR), he was a neutralist in foreign policy. When the political scientist R.A. MacKay took a year's leave from Dalhousie in 1937 and President Carleton Stanley chose Reid to replace him, eyebrows went up. 'Mr. R. has something of a reputation for indiscretion in the matter of urging Canadian nationalism, and for radicalism generally,' Stanley wrote to President Thomson of Saskatchewan. 'I was well aware of this when I engaged Mr. R., and heard, as I expected to hear, some rumblings about the appointment, even though it was known that he was here just temporarily.'[71]

Stanley was replying to an inquiry from Thomson, to whom Reid had been recommended for appointment. 'They say he is somewhat radical in his outlook,' Thomson had written, 'but probably he is none the worse for that.' He had gone on to outline his view of academic freedom in a state university: 'I am all for liberty of thought and expression and would be the first to step in and defend any one who was attacked because he had spoken his mind. At the same time, there is a wisdom and a discretion in all things and, particularly, in a chair of Political Science.' Thomson did not contact Reid.[72]

That winter Reid's name came up also at Manitoba. President Sidney E. Smith, who was soliciting suggestions for filling an associate professorship in political science, learned from an acquaintance that 'Escott Reid is knocking around loose.' He was better qualified than anyone else he could recommend, Smith's informant continued, but 'his politics may not please you.' Was this the kiss of death? Smith had no love of radicals. Looking for an economist in 1935, he had written, 'I have been told that [Robert] McQueen is a radical in his economic thinking and if this is the case I would rule him out.' Only after J.W. Dafoe of the *Winnipeg Free Press* had assured Smith that rumours of 'any undue political activity etc. on his part are groundless' had Smith recommended McQueen for appointment. He did not recommend Reid, who wrote to a friend in March 1938, 'Still haven't got a university job ... Looks as if I shall be with the Institute till June 1939 and then go on the bread line.' As things turned out, Reid did not have to go on relief. In early 1939 he joined External Affairs – Under-Secretary O.D. Skelton was unworried by his reputation – and he had a distinguished career in the public service before becoming the first principal of York University's Glendon College in 1965.[73]

Since the private universities were little or not at all dependent on government grants, involvement in politics even of a 'radical' kind was of less concern than at the provincial institutions. The most problematic case was that of McGill, which will be the subject of the next chapter. During the long presidency of Sherwood Fox, Western Ontario allowed considerable latitude to professors. The classicist R.E.K. Pemberton, active in the CCF in the 1930s, 1940s, and 1950s, reported that he had felt no restriction on his activities and writings. Neither does McMaster seem to have interfered with the political free speech of its faculty.[74]

Queen's presents a more complicated picture. The university was tradition-ally tolerant of political activism, and by the later 1930s the philosophy depart-ment harboured two committed socialists, Gregory Vlastos and H. Martyn Estall. Vlastos later said that 'the administration maintained a correct attitude'; he felt no pressure to quit working in the LSR, CCF, or Fellowship for a Chris-tian Social Order (FCSO), and no one hinted that he was endangering the uni-versity's finances. 'I served under six principals,' Estall wrote in 1977, 'and had no cause to feel constrained politically by any of them.'[75]

Yet Principal William Hamilton Fyfe did set a limit on academic freedom. If a professor ventured into the larger world, he wrote in his report for 1933–4, 'it behoves him to remember what astonishing weight that world attaches to a pro-fessorial pronouncement.' This dictated prudence: 'A University teacher should certainly be clever; he needs also to be wise; and of the factors of wisdom not the least are self-restraint and kindliness and patience.'[76] Fyfe was trying to head off the sort of controversy that occasionally embroiled the University of Toronto. The man who succeeded Fyfe in 1936, Robert C. Wallace, had shown at Alberta that he opposed political activity by professors. And certainly there were no incidents at Queen's in the 1930s. Although neither Vlastos nor Estall felt constrained, both may have exercised a measure of self-censorship of which they were unconscious.

Still, Queen's was freer than Toronto, for it was not under the same close scrutiny as the provincial university. This probably shaped the attitude of James M. Macdonnell, chairman of the Queen's board of trustees from 1930 to 1957. A businessman and a Conservative, he nevertheless believed that professors should enjoy a wide measure of freedom. In 1931 he took issue with Sir Joseph Flavelle's criticism of the Toronto sixty-eight, and six years later he objected to an attack on socialist academics by Sir Edward Beatty. Macdonnell's attitude helped maintain an intellectual climate at Queen's that was amenable to a broad definition of academic freedom.[77]

At Dalhousie, academic freedom was strongly influenced by the positive view taken of it by Carleton Stanley, who assumed his presidential duties in 1931. In October of that year R.A. (Bert) MacKay, the Eric Dennis Professor of Political Science, contributed an article to *Maclean's* with the title 'After Beau-harnois – What?' A House of Commons inquiry into the Beauharnois hydro-electric development had uncovered a scandal that stained several leading Liberals, but MacKay concluded that the Conservatives as well as the Liberals were beholden to corporate interests.[78]

His article enraged R.B. Bennett. The Liberals had received $700,000 from the Beauharnois Syndicate while his own party had refused an offer of money; yet MacKay seemed to implicate both parties. Bennett's term on Dalhousie's board of governors was up for renewal late in 1932, and he made it known that he would not serve a further term unless MacKay was removed.[79]

Although Bennett's demand had some support among board members, Stanley thought dismissal both unwarranted and unwise. Board Chairman Fred Pearson agreed with him and tried to change the prime minister's mind by making light of MacKay – 'an idealist without much contact with the everyday affairs of life, a sort of Don Quixote.' Bennett replied, 'A man who ignorantly or recklessly makes statements such as those contained in his article is not the kind of man whom I ... would hold out to the people of this country as being the proper person to give instruction to youthful students.' He informed the secretary of the board that he wished to resign: 'There is no excuse for any responsible teacher ... making statements such as those to which I refer.'[80]

The affair was complicated by a quarrel in late 1932 between Pearson and Stanley over the governance of Dalhousie. Pearson sought the president's dismissal and, when unsuccessful, resigned. Pearson's successor as chairman, Hector McInnes, implored Bennett to stand by his alma mater: 'We ask you not to visit on your old College the indiscretions of a member of the Staff, for which the Board is in no wise responsible.' To this McInnes joined a personal appeal: 'I think you will not consider it out of place if in these trying times I ask for the support ... of my old friends.' Bennett relented.[81]

Those who knew of the attempt to force MacKay's dismissal kept it quiet. 'Just think,' Stanley wrote to Bennett's brother-in-law W.D. Herridge, 'of the damage done to himself if someone like J[ohn] S[tevenson] in Ottawa got hold of this.' (Stevenson was a journalist.) But in time a rumour did leak out. Late in 1933 an External Affairs officer, Hugh L. Keenleyside, conveyed it to Underhill. MacKay himself did not hear of the matter until several years had passed, and then only unofficially.[82]

In 1935 MacKay gave a speech to the Halifax Board of Trade about 'Canada and the European Crisis.' It is probable that he called for collective security in a reformed League of Nations and a clarification of Canada's status so that Ottawa might pursue the country's interests unhindered by lingering colonial ties. (*Canada Looks Abroad*, a book co-written by MacKay and published in 1938, made proposals of this kind.) Whatever he said, someone complained to Stanley, who asked to see MacKay. Afterwards the political scientist wrote that he knew Stanley had intended neither to warn nor to censure him: 'I am free to say or write (whether within or without the University) what I wish on any subject.' He had no wish to seem provocative, he said: 'When I do speak or write on controversial issues ..., I measure my words carefully ... in order to keep myself and the University out of unnecessary difficulties.' But he did not think that his position obliged him to avoid such issues: 'In the matter of academic freedom I feel that Dalhousie will compare most favorably with any university in Canada ... I have tried not to abuse that freedom.'[83]

A year later, MacKay began work on a manifesto asserting Canada's right to neutrality in case of a war involving Britain. Late in 1936 Arthur Lower, a historian at Wesley College, asked whether MacKay had got anywhere with it: 'I suppose you did not ... We are all cowards, no doubt, horribly afraid of injuring our own interests. One more speech here from me and no doubt I would be nailed.' MacKay replied that he had done 'nothing in any practical way' but thought 'that we should before long take the plunge and get the manifesto ... published.' There would, he knew, be unpleasantness: 'It might mean the jobs of some of us. I have some reason to expect that I would at least have a fight on my hands here. And I have a wife and four kids to think about.'[84]

'I don't think I'd put my job in jeopardy just yet,' Lower responded: 'You are more useful alive than dead. Anyway, an extreme statement at the moment would carry its own repudiation for we've all become "British" again.' At one time, he said, he had thought that an appeal for independence would get a response, 'but I do not believe it would now.'[85]

If Lower thought it wise to keep silent, it was time for discretion indeed. He had first come to public notice in 1934 by saying 'that the price of our remaining in the Empire would be our participation in the next private European squabble on much the same terms as the last.' There had been 'quite a row,' he wrote to a friend. The *Winnipeg Tribune* had criticized him; letters to the editor and to Principal John H. Riddell had asked that he be silenced or dismissed. 'Things more or less culminated ... with the chief publishing a letter in the "Free Press" stating in most emphatic terms that he stood for complete freedom of discussion and people were free to criticize ..., but not to silence. It was an excellent and valuable performance.'[86]

Riddell's attitude encouraged Lower to continue to state his views openly. Although some responses were highly unfavourable, Lower was unrepentant. 'For an academic to get involved in a current issue is always dangerous,' he wrote in April 1936, 'but ... the historian stultifies himself if he refuses to pursue the issues his study of the past forces on him.' Still, by December he was evidently beginning to feel pressure, and a year later he was censoring himself. He wanted a transfer to the University of Manitoba and had heard that a board member there was objecting to him as 'unsafe.'[87]

In March 1938 he signed a pseudonym to an article on British foreign policy that he had written for the *Canadian Forum*. When the editor, George Grube, wondered whether the pseudonym was necessary, Lower replied that he did not wish 'to get into further hot water.' In June 1938 he told W.H. Alexander: 'Wesley College is a fairly safe haven for free speech. At least the state cannot get at it, and so far the Principal has stood like a rock.' But soon there would be a new man in the job, and who knew what he might think or do?[88]

More than any other educational institution in Canada, Victoria University had to cope with the hostility aroused by Christian socialism. The Depression had rekindled the 'social passion' in the United Church of Canada. Its clergy and laity were at the centre of the Fellowship for a Christian Social Order (FCSO), whose members pledged themselves 'to the task of building a new society in which all exploitation of man by man and all barriers to the abundant life which are created by the private ownership of property shall be done away.' These objectives dismayed church members who took the parable of the talents literally or who, saving religion for Sundays, practised a robust social Darwinism during the working week. When the FCSO published its book *Towards the Christian Revolution* (1937), the Canadian Pacific Railway's Sir Edward Beatty wrote, 'I have heard it described by those who understand Christian Doctrine as a "grotesque blasphemy."'[89]

The two most active Christian socialists on the Victoria University faculty were the Victoria College classicist Eric Havelock and a divinity professor in Emmanuel College (the divinity school), John Line. Himself a United Church-man, Ontario's Premier George Henry complained repeatedly about them. In 1932 he suggested to a member of Victoria's governing board that Line 'might better be sticking to his living than leading a meeting of what might reasonably be styled socialists.' When Havelock was quoted as saying that governments were 'the puppets of capitalism' and that Canadian tariffs were the result of the influence that businessmen had on politicians, Henry was again unhappy. 'Freedom of speech does not mean license to carry on such as Professor Havelock apparently was doing the other evening,' he wrote to President Edward W. Wallace. 'Those in control of colleges will need to assert some authority and discipline these wild tirades.'[90]

Three months later Henry criticized Havelock for his membership in the LSR, an organization the premier correctly linked to the CCF. Wallace replied that he could 'not see on what ground the college [could] interfere with the freedom of a member of its staff in his political relationships.' Besides, it seemed to Wallace 'all to the good' that a democratic road was open to those who sought change: 'Our British tradition of open discussion is infinitely safer in the long run than the Italian or the Russian suppression of opposition to the governmental policies.'[91]

Henry's response bordered on the intemperate. 'I have always felt that Professors should be men of character and ability and with some capacity for leadership,' he fumed, 'and I doubt very much whether a Professor in ... Victoria should be actively engaged with an organization ... which is definitely affiliating itself with ... the CCF.' Linking that party in turn to 'the Communism and Despotism of Russia,' Henry warned: 'There is a definite feeling in the Province that Victoria College is the seat of ... extreme radicalism and many people are seriously considering leaving the United Church if the College ... cannot give better leadership than it appears to be giving now.'[92]

After discussing Henry's letter with the board, Wallace wrote that he abhorred 'violence and the threat of force in achieving political or social ends,' and for that reason he believed in freedom of expression. To draw a line between wise and unwise use of that freedom was not always easy: 'There are bound to be sincere differences of attitude among men who are united in their desire to see progress made by sane and ordered development.' That, he concluded, was the heart of the problem in the university context.[93]

At this point Henry seems to have given up on Wallace. When he read in January 1934 that Line was scheduled to address a CCF Club in the Toronto area, Henry complained to the principal of Victoria College, Walter Brown: 'I cannot see why a man styling himself a professor ... should be allowed to sow seeds of discord and disunion.' In his reply to Henry, Brown could have pointed out that Line, being on the staff of Emmanuel College, was not really his responsibility. Instead, Brown defended academic freedom and concluded, 'I have discussed the particular address with Professor Line and from his account I am sure that he could not be charged with "sowing seeds of discord and disunion."' Indeed, said Brown, he thought Henry 'would personally agree with the larger part of it.' The premier must have read this with scepticism.[94]

Henry left office in July 1934 but continued to fret about academic radicals. In March 1936 he asked the minister of education what he intended to do about an unnamed academic 'who goes around the province making radical speeches and styling himself as a professor of the University of Toronto.' Liberal MPPs asked for specifics and wondered if the Conservatives were trying to limit free speech. Not so, responded the former minister of labour, Leopold Macaulay. He stated that he could not 'get excited at what some professor says,' but added 'I object only when they plaster it all over the Province, when they are making these speeches, that they are professors of this and that.' Identifying himself as a member of Victoria University's board of regents, he opined that a professor was 'just the same as [a] coal-heaver at the University' – as long as he did not identify himself as a professor, he had the right to speak his mind.[95] Macaulay did not address a related issue: What if professors did not mention their affiliations but the press did? Still, he was clearly less concerned about academic radicals than the leader of his party was. Perhaps taking his colleague's point, Henry dropped the matter.

His successor, Premier Mitchell Hepburn, seems to have been generally unworried by what professors said. However, in April 1937 he featured in an incident that added a sheaf of documents to Victoria's files. In the strike that began in Oshawa on 8 April, Local 222 of the recently formed United Auto Workers (UAW) confronted General Motors of Canada (GMC). Six days later, Havelock and another classicist, George Grube of Trinity College, addressed the strikers. Carried away by the 'mood of defiance' which Havelock sensed in his audience, he asked rhetorically whether Hepburn and his cabinet had a pecuniary interest in GMC. No reporters were present, so the story the *Globe and Mail* carried on 17 April was second-hand: 'Professor Havelock is alleged to have suggested that the Government's backing of General Motors in the present strike possibly had been influenced by the shares of stock which the Prime Minister and members of his Cabinet held in the Motor Company.' Hepburn 'indignantly denied the suggestion,' and Provincial Secretary Harry Nixon said that Havelock's remarks were being brought immediately to the attention of 'whatever governing body is responsible for paying the man's salary.'[96]

At Victoria, Havelock's remarks caused dismay. The bursar, J.W. Little, told President Wallace that he had no idea whether Havelock was right, but he noted, 'This form of publicity is most undesirable ... I have grave fears regarding the effects of this publicity upon anticipated support for Victoria University.' Members of the staff had 'freedom of thought, speech and the exercise of the franchise,' said Little, but did they not also have 'a responsibility to the institution?'[97]

When Wallace learned from Harry Nixon that George McCullagh had a verbatim report of the address, he asked for a copy. McCullagh replied that he had destroyed the report but added, 'I might say that the statements Professor Havelock made in this speech, in my opinion, were disgraceful, and I do hope that you in your wisdom will find it convenient to make an example of him.'[98]

Havelock recalled in 1967 that in the course of 'a long and unpleasant conversation,' Wallace had charged him with harming Victoria – there were rumours that the promise of a large gift had been withdrawn – and ordered him not to do so again. He was also instructed to apologize to Hepburn. Havelock did so. On 1 May he also wrote to Wallace to express regret that he had 'embarrassed the college community' and promised that for 'at least a year' he would 'abstain altogether from any platform discussions concerning controversial issues.' Because Wallace had not requested this, it was 'all the easier ... to propose it without raising any issues involving freedom of expression.' A day later, Havelock added a note indicating that he expected his withdrawal from public life 'to last longer than a year.'[99]

In conveying their own regrets to Hepburn, the members of the executive committee of the board stated that Havelock had 'over-stepped the limit which good judgment should set to the exercise of the traditional freedom of speech of a university professor.' President Wallace took a similar line with Gregory Vlastos of Queen's University, who had written in support of Havelock. Conceding that 'the witness of the Christian in the world today' was necessary and that 'no one can question the right of the individual to determine when that witness must be uttered,' Wallace asked Vlastos to recognize 'the realities of the present situation.' Havelock had spoken as a member of the FCSO, he conceded, but people were bound to associate him with Victoria. By his 'unwise' remarks he had injured the institution and 'increased the difficulty of maintaining that freedom of discussion and expression for which a university should stand.'[100]

Wallace's argument resembled Flavelle's in 1931: because the university might suffer by what its professors said, they must choose their words carefully. What Havelock had said had indeed been improper; he lacked evidence of what the interest of the government was – and in fact Hepburn was less worried about GMC than about the inroads of unionization into the gold mines of Ontario, which a UAW success at Oshawa might encourage.[101] The accuracy or otherwise of Havelock's innuendo was almost beside the point, however. His offence had little to do with the factual basis of what he said and much to do with its possible effects. If Havelock had said that Hepburn's concerns about the Oshawa strike were due to his solicitousness for the interests of leading mine owners, he would have been correct. Would President Wallace have approved such a comment? Hardly. Where the interests of potential benefactors are at risk, academic free speech is unwelcome even (and perhaps especially) when true.

In any discussion of academic freedom in the 1930s, the dismissal of J. King Gordon demands close attention. Appointed by Montreal's United Theological College (UTC) in 1931 to teach Christian ethics, Gordon was not there for long. In 1933 his chair was abolished. The stated reason was the financial crisis of the college, but some people thought there was more to it than that. There had been hostile reaction to the Montreal-based Social and Economic Research Committee, in which Gordon was active, and to his rose-tinted account of the Soviet Union, which he had visited in 1932.[102]

The budget crisis was genuine. In 1931 the college had 121 students; a year later enrolment had dropped by half. Losses on ancillary services were mounting as a result. As well, income from investments was declining as some of the mortgages held by UTC fell into arrears. The audited deficit for 1931 was $4,658; by 1933 it was $8,113. In the context of an annual budget of less than

$50,000, these amounts were huge. In 1932 the General Council of the United Church instructed the board to reduce the number of professors from five to four within two years.[103]

This made financial sense – salaries were the largest item of expenditure. Whether it made pedagogical sense is doubtful. Principal James Smyth said that the directive 'would handicap the College in the work it was trying to do,' but this did not alter the instructions the board had received. W.M. Birks, chairman of the joint board of the federated theological colleges, wrote to McGill's Principal Sir Arthur Currie in March 1933: 'I understand that the Board of the United Theological College, which is forced to economize, is compelled to drop its youngest professor and has already decided ... to drop ... King Gordon from its staff.'[104]

That Gordon lost his position and not the Old Testament scholar R.B.Y. Scott, who had joined the UTC faculty at the same time as Gordon, reflected prevailing attitudes: Scott was married, Gordon was not. Like Gordon, Scott was an outspoken Christian socialist (he later co-edited the FCSO's book, *Towards the Christian Revolution*). This did not keep *Saturday Night* from hinting at an ulterior motive for Gordon's dismissal: 'It is of course explained that the suppression of his chair has nothing to do with his social and economic views, but is entirely a matter of economy. Christian Ethics ... has become a luxury that the authorities ... can no longer afford themselves. They can still afford Hebrew, Pastoral Homiletics, and the History of Early Christian Dogma.'[105]

Upon hearing that Gordon's chair was to be abolished, some of his friends undertook to raise a salary for him. He was willing to teach for the $1,500 they managed to get together, and in late April the UTC senate noted 'that through the generosity of friends it has not been necessary ... to declare vacant the chair of Christian Ethics and Religious Education.' In 1934, however, the board would not consider an extension of the arrangement. Frank Pedley, who headed the committee that had come up with the $1,500 in 1933, expressed surprise that the board had not asked for renewed support. The chairman responded that this possibility had not been discussed, and he added later that without a signal from Pedley's group, the board had assumed that its support would end. He denied that disapproval of Gordon's views explained the board's action: 'Prof. Gordon is going because he is the latest comer and his chair can most easily be vacated.' Backing up this statement, W.D. Lighthall, a board member acquainted with Gordon, assured him, 'The decision of the Governors was not influenced by any hostility to yourself or your work. That was a very minority attitude & was dropped.' The issues, said Lighthall, were the budgetary crisis and the instructions from the church council.[106]

Gordon may have wanted to believe Lighthall. However, several of his friends – Gregory Vlastos, J.S. Woodsworth, George Ferguson of the *Winnipeg Free Press*, Terry MacDermot of the League of Nations Society, and Harry Ward of Union Theological Seminary in New York – encouraged him to be sceptical. Meanwhile, *Saturday Night* asked that Gordon be reinstated. So did the United Church weekly, the *New Outlook*.[107]

In September 1934 the general council of the church ratified the board's action but added that 'the question ... has become for many identified with the rights of freedom of thought and speech' and asked that Gordon be reappointed for a two-year period. But the board, noting that the general council had not suggested where the money might be found, turned down its request. Commenting in the newspaper of the Ontario CCF, Gordon's friend Graham Spry charged that the board's action resulted from 'a deliberate and determined effort on the part of reactionary members of the Board.'[108]

A subsequent report to the general council simultaneously defended academic freedom and the board's autonomy. 'The mind of the Church on the question of liberty of speech and of academic freedom is in no wise affected by the action of the Montreal College Board,' the statement concluded. 'Liberty of thought and teaching was characteristic of all the traditions ... of the United Church of Canada.' The *New Outlook* commented, 'That this statement will comfort or reassure many by its claims we do not believe.' Not a few people continued to believe that Gordon had been removed for his opinions.[109]

In 1972 Gordon himself seemed unsure: 'I doubt if you will be able to get "proof" that the elimination of the chair of Christian Ethics was on account of the political views of its occupant.'[110] He added, though, that the board seemed curiously unwilling 'to explore other methods of economizing to meet the crisis' – by cutting salaries, for instance – or to accept for a second year the outside funding that was available to maintain him.

Were it not for the board's reluctance to renew the 1933–4 arrangement, we might safely conclude that Gordon's views were not at issue. Salary reductions of about 20 per cent would have been needed to match the effect of eliminating Gordon's chair. In salaries that were none too generous to begin with, cuts this deep might have seemed too severe. However, the board's failure to accept continued outside funding gives grounds for suspicion. Some board members, at least, may have been happy to drop a man whose views they found uncongenial. But there is no hard evidence that Gordon was let go for his opinions or activities, and there is a good deal of evidence that the college deficit provided the grounds for the abolition of his chair. All the same, his well-publicized fate and the rumours that surrounded it can only have reinforced the general habit of professorial caution.

Gordon landed on his feet. In 1934–5 he was a travelling lecturer for the

FCSO, and the following year the executive of the United Church general council appointed him a roving lecturer in Christian ethics. In 1937 he left Canada to work in New York. Not until 1962 did he return, to teach political science at the University of Alberta.

The Munich Agreement of 29 September 1938, forcing Czechoslovakia to cede the Sudetenland to Germany, postponed war in Europe. Fearing that a new crisis might soon arise, some academics redoubled their efforts to make the case for an independent Canadian policy. Late in the year, Percy Corbett of McGill's Faculty of Law and Larry MacKenzie of Toronto's Department of Law reportedly urged during a radio broadcast 'that Canada should take steps to obtain the right of neutrality in the event of another war involving Great Britain.' Corbett was quoted in the *Quebec Chronicle-Telegraph* as saying that Canada's long-range interests were in the New World rather than the Old.[111]

The broadcast passed largely unnoticed in Toronto; when interviewed, MacKenzie claimed to have been misquoted. But in Montreal, J.W. McConnell, publisher of the *Montreal Star* and a member of the McGill board, asked Principal Lewis Douglas whether something could be done. 'I do not agree with Corbett,' Douglas replied. 'However, precisely what it is I should do in this instance I don't know, except that it is pretty wise to follow that old rule, "When in doubt, do nothing." To do something, he added, might prove 'fatal' to academic freedom.[112]

The *Chronicle-Telegraph* having asked whether McGill approved of Corbett's statement, Sir Edward Beatty told Douglas that the newspaper was known to be 'very close to the Government and is generally thought to reflect, in many instances, the views which Mr. Duplessis and his colleagues do not care to express publicly.' Could no effort be made 'to ensure wise and fitting observations by the members of staff?' he asked. In a further letter, Beatty worried that men such as Corbett were 'accepted in the public mind as speaking for ... professors as a whole.' Confidence in McGill might be more easily maintained if professors who disagreed with Corbett, such as Cyrus Macmillan of English, could be persuaded to 'to participate more actively ... in the discussion of public affairs of this sort.'[113]

That was for Douglas's eyes only. Writing to Arthur G. Penny of the *Chronicle-Telegraph*, Beatty defended Corbett's right to free speech. But Penny disagreed with Beatty. 'It is an abuse of his position for a university professor to ... give public expression to his personal views on political issues of current controversy,' he replied. Universities had the right to restrict their employees' freedom of expression and were wise to do so, he added in an editorial; if a university 'approved or tolerated' academic free speech, its professors could remain 'comfortably indifferent to outside criticism.' However, because the institution might be adversely affected by the utterances of its employees, even those 'purely personal in nature,' a professor who wished to speak his mind really ought to resign in order to save his employer from harm.[114]

In fact, Penny sought to restrict professors to the expression of politically correct opinions. He would not have attacked Corbett for arguing in favour of aligning Canada with Britain, but he wanted to ban challenges to the British connection. This went too far for Beatty, who promptly told Penny that it offended against 'the right of every citizen to complete freedom of speech ... on points of importance to the public at large.' Beatty acknowledged that professors ought to show 'greater discretion and a greater sense of responsibility' than others, but he insisted, 'It is most important to avoid any implication that liberty of thought or speech in our universities is in danger of being curtailed.'[115]

'Excellent,' Douglas commented. '[This] states what seems to me to be the only tenable position the University can take.' Although Penny was far less sure, he reluctantly granted that 'if there is to be any error ... it is far better that it should be on the side of protecting freedom of speech.' But this did not negate his earlier advice that universities would do well to limit the free speech of their professors.[116]

Better known than Corbett for criticizing the British connection was his colleague Frank Scott. After one such criticism in April 1939, an alumnus charged in a letter to Beatty that Scott's opinions were designed to 'weaken the loyalty of others to the Empire and their willingness to fight for it if necessary.' Another wrote to Douglas that Scott should be deported to Italy or Germany: 'He might adorn the classrooms of the University of Montreal or Laval University, where they manufacture mongrels, but surely does not belong to the atmosphere of McGill.'[117]

As long as such demands did not come from major benefactors, Beatty and Douglas paid little heed to them. In far greater danger than Scott were two of his Toronto friends. At the very same time that he was making *his* offending comments, George Grube and Frank Underhill were in hot water for their views about the British connection. The controversy began with something Grube said at the Ontario CCF convention on 7 April. The *Globe and Mail*, identifying him (mistakenly) as a 'U. of T. Professor,' quoted him as saying 'that any war that would come in Europe at the present time would "have nothing to do with democracy."' Grube had made the remark in speaking to a motion that described the Canadian defence budget as 'a waste of public funds in the interests of British imperialism.'[118] When some MPPs put the text of the motion into

Grube's mouth and attacked him for it, they unloosed a storm that threatened to blow away not only him but also Underhill.

Liberal and Conservative MPPs unanimously deplored Grube's remarks. Premier Hepburn implied that Grube was a communist; others suggested that the University of Toronto should set him straight. Contacted by the press, President Cody pointed out that Grube was employed by Trinity College, not by the University of Toronto. When he was informed of this, Hepburn said that either Trinity should discipline 'this foreigner' (a naturalized British subject, Grube had been born in Belgium) or its link with the university might be adjusted in some way harmful to the college – might even be revoked.[119]

At this point attention shifted to the more familiar figure of Underhill. The architect of this shift was the leader of the opposition, George Drew, who raised the matter in the legislature. Grube was not the only professor whose loyalty was in doubt, he said. Underhill was another. Drew quoted from a book he was holding: 'We must therefore make it clear to the world, and especially to Great Britain, that the poppies blooming in Flanders fields have no further interest for us.'[120] 'Shame, shame!' Hepburn cried. Drew read a while longer, then looked up: 'The time has come to stop ... permanently statements of that kind by a man who either in or out of the educational institution is speaking to the public as a member of that institution.' He added that much depended on universities to teach youths to value and defend 'British democracy' and not to 'do anything to assist subversive elements which are seeking to destroy these ideals in which we believe.'

Agreeing with Drew, Colonel Fraser Hunter (Liberal) described Grube and Underhill as 'rats who are trying to scuttle our ship of state,' and he introduced a motion to have them dismissed for 'hurling insults at the British Empire.' However, the minister of education, L.J. Simpson, wanted to consult the university authorities: 'I would hesitate to support any measure that would take power away from those who are in control of our educational institutions.' Drew concurred. So did Hepburn, but not without promising that the government would act if the two offenders were not dealt with. (Commenting some weeks later in the *Canadian Forum*, the architect Humphrey Carver noted that not one MPP had defended free speech. He asked, 'Are [they] ... so intimidated by their infernal party machines that they cannot recognize a fundamental issue when they see one?')[121]

For a time the University of Toronto was embattled as it had not been since the letter of the sixty-eight. Not only were Hepburn and Drew in agreement, but they enjoyed a good deal of press support. The *Globe and Mail* criticized Grube and Underhill; so did the *Telegram*, which supported Hepburn in his threat to act if the university did not. In the opinion of the Montreal *Gazette*, 'An intellectual and political house-cleaning seems necessary in more than one of this country's larger educational centres and there appear to be some excellent reasons for commencing the process in Toronto.'[122]

The *Toronto Star*, which was often a champion of free speech, said nothing; but *Saturday Night* defended academic freedom and university autonomy, and it was not alone. The writer and broadcaster Alan Plaunt reported to Frank Scott in late April that 'adverse comment on the Drew-Hepburn gag racket' had also appeared in the *Winnipeg Free Press*, the *London Free Press*, the *Windsor Star*, the *Ottawa Citizen*, the *Ottawa Journal*, and *Le Devoir*.[123]

The editorial in the *Ottawa Journal* was particularly interesting. While describing the comments by Grube and Underhill as 'foolish, demonstrably false, [and] mischievous,' it said that free speech should not be set aside simply because one disliked what was said: 'There is no law in Canada ... denying to a university professor or to any other man the right to ... express his conscience and beliefs, short of advocating them by violence.' Denying professors the right to speak freely outside the classroom, like requiring them to teach approved ideas within it, would be to copy the dictatorships, argued the *Journal*: 'Freedom of speech, if it is to mean anything, must ... mean freedom to speak error; or what the majority deems to be error. Otherwise, it is not freedom at all.'[124]

Having been forewarned of Drew's intentions, the board of governors met on 13 April and asked President Cody to determine whether Underhill had been accurately quoted, whether the passage had been used with his permission, and whether he still held the views expressed in it. Cody first spoke with the head of history, Chester Martin, who described Underhill as a loyal member of the department and the university, but one whose behaviour outside the institution was open to question. The passage Drew had quoted was 'indefensible and unworthy of a scholar in Mr. Underhill's position,' he said.[125]

Cody saw Underhill before the latter appeared before the board. They had been thinking of firing him, Underhill wrote to George Ferguson: 'Cody was terribly worked up ... and abused me as a trouble-maker who was costing the University untold sums of money (this trouble came just in the midst of troubles about our estimates) and told me it would all depend on how I behaved before the Governors whether I came out of the business safely.' When Underhiull appeared before the governors, he found that Dean Samuel Beatty, Principal Malcolm Wallace of University College, and Harold Adams Innis had interceded on his behalf, and the board at least listened to him. He thought he would get off with a reprimand but was still worried: 'A few days ago I was preparing to drop my golf club so as to economise before going on relief. This is the worst business I've been through yet, and it ruined both my sleep and my appetite for a while.' To Arthur Lower he wrote ten days later, 'This trouble has been so extreme that we pretty well have to keep quiet for a time.' He was almost fifty and could not afford to lose his job. 'I think the only effective protection that professors will ever have in a society like ours is to form a trade union of their own and affiliate with one of the American bodies,' Underhill told Lower. But none of his colleagues agreed with him.[126]

The letter Underhill sent to Cody was contrite in tone, explaining that the sentences Drew had quoted were part of a private document written for the Canadian Institute of International Affairs in 1935. The document had appeared in print without his knowledge, said Underhill; he had not meant disrespect for those who had fought in Flanders (after all, he was one himself), and he regretted that his choice of words had offended. He had very largely lived up to his promise in 1937 to 'try to avoid undesirable publicity,' he continued, and although he could not guarantee that he would never offend anyone in the future, he would endeavour to do so: 'I think you might take the fact that I have behaved myself reasonably well in these recent years as a guarantee that I can be trusted when I say that I shall do my best in future to behave as reasonable men would expect a professor to behave.'[127]

Who these men were and how they expected professors to behave were questions neither asked nor answered. Was Drew a reasonable man? Or Hepburn or Fraser Hunter? Or the University of New Brunswick economist Burton S. Keirstead? 'Now that [Hepburn] has raised the issue of academic freedom,' wrote Keirstead in a letter to Underhill, 'I hope that the University of Toronto will stand behind you and fight the issue out with him.' Bert MacKay, another staunch supporter, described Drew's action as 'a damnably dirty trick.' And Escott Reid, from his diplomatic post in Washington, DC, wrote: 'I had no idea that the stupidities of the Ontario Legislature were to be taken seriously. Now I am no longer amused. I am ashamed and frightened. I had expected that sort of thing in war-time but not in these pre-war days. If the patriots are so hysterical now what will they be like when the bombs begin to drop on London?'[128]

Underhill was fortunate in the support he enjoyed. On 19 April a petition in defence of him and Grube, signed by 1,014 students, was brought to Cody's office. In addition, the Board of Evangelism and Social Service of the United Church passed a resolution in defence of academic freedom, and the Christian Social Council of Canada adopted a statement on 'Academic Freedom and the Rights of the Citizen,' which defended Underhill and Grube. A number of alumni also wrote in support, including one who opined: 'In the classroom, any teacher should confine himself to the subject he is hired to expound & lecture on, but outside, he [has] a perfect right to his own opinion, and unless we want a state of affairs such as exists under Hitler & Mussolini, he should not be penalized for expressing his views.'[129]

Even more important than his widespread support may have been the fact that interest in the affair waned quickly. The legislature was about to rise, and Hepburn and Drew had other things to think about than Underhill. As well, Peter Oliver writes, a former premier who was a member of the board, Howard Ferguson, smoothed ruffled feathers in order 'to help Harry Cody out of a tight spot.'[130]

Yet some people tried to keep the issue alive. One board member, the mining engineer Balmer Neilly, argued in a letter to the board secretary that Underhill should be fired. If he stayed, 'and he or others like him transgress again, we may find our grant again reduced and the whole future of the University put in jeopardy,' argued Neilly. But Cody, in a statement to the board in June 1939, wrote that Underhill had promised to mend his ways. As well, stated Cody, some 'senior men' in Arts and University College were setting up 'a small committee which would ... assume the task of investigating public statements made by members of the staff which prove to be irritating to a section of the public to the detriment of the University.' This group 'would not only ensure thorough investigation' but would help prevent 'unwise and and unwarranted public statements on the part of members of the staff.' Pleased by the prospect of professorial self-censorship, Cody recommended 'that the Board take no further action at present.'[131]

The committee does not seem to have got off the ground, and the proposal may have been no more than an attempt to take the heat off Underhill. Still, it spoke to issues of interest to academics. One was the wish to be more like a self-governing profession; another was the belief that professors were better qualified than presidents or boards to investigate incidents and recommend remedial action. There was also the understandable wish to see the university's support maintained.

Unlike their colleagues at the University of Toronto, the Trinity College authorities did not need to fear a cut in the government grant, for they did not receive one. However, Hepburn's threat of changing the college's relationship to the university was unwelcome. So was the attention that Grube had attracted. Aware of this, the classicist expressed regret to Provost Frederick H. Cosgrave for 'the unfortunate publicity' he had caused, and though he claimed the right to participate in public discussion, he undertook to be more careful in the future.[132]

On 17 April 1939 Grube wrote at greater length. He had been misquoted, he said, and he defended his right 'as a free Canadian citizen' to criticize government policy and to state his view that 'non-intervention in any European war was the best policy for Canada.' But if the country declared war, he would abide by its decision, he announced. 'I was a soldier in the last war and, if necessary, will be a soldier in the next. But, until that day comes, and indeed beyond it, I shall fight for democracy, freedom of speech and civil liberties every step of the way. Which is more than can be said for most of my opponents.'[133] This hit the wrong note. The board had been looking for contrition; what it got was very close to defiance.

In response, the board reminded Grube who was boss. The statement that the college executive committee sent him began ominously: 'We believe that the issue in this case is not one of Freedom of Speech.' Rather, it was one of responsibility. Professors should speak only when they were sure that their words would not harm those with whom they worked. Offensive speech put the college authorities in the position where they 'must either limit the freedom of an individual or suffer in silence the consequences of his actions,' and it was surely 'grossly unfair that they should be placed on the horns of such a dilemma.' Someone who spoke or acted 'in a way that outrages the feelings of many of his fellow-citizens' ought to think of resigning. In short, 'Trustees should see that teachers have reasonable freedom and teachers should be mindful of the main interest which it is the purpose of their profession to promote.'[134] Taken in its entirety, this statement significantly curtailed academic free speech, though it is unlikely that this bothered the executive committee. The sense of British loyalty was no weaker among Anglicans than among Ontarians as a whole, and it may well have been stronger. Moreover, Trinity was bound to be solicitous of the opinions of its financial supporters.

In his reply to the provost, Grube granted 'that one has a loyalty to the institution with which one is connected' and that adverse publicity should be avoided whenever possible. He pointed out that until this incident he had written about current events without incurring attack; but he realized that he would 'have to be even more careful in the future,' and he undertook to try not to associate his name 'with statements so construed that they are likely to give rise to the kind of emotional outburst which is regrettable from every point of view.'[135] This seemed to satisfy the Trinity authorities.

The *Canadian Forum*, on whose editorial board Grube and Underhill both served, decided – oddly, given the circumstances – that it was too early to say whether the incident was a victory for academic freedom or not: 'Although professors are always told that they have the full right of free speech, it has often been made plain to them that they should exercise that right in silence. How far this usual procedure has been followed in Toronto, and with what success, only time can tell.' An observation by a foreign service officer, Gerald Riddell, showed better insight. 'The war ... or at least the battle, is over,' he wrote to Arthur Lower, 'but no one has got any further forward on the question regarding the right of university people to express themselves – & we'll have the whole show over again soon.'[136]

Lower, for his part, ridiculed Hepburn but reserved his harshest words for Drew: 'Potentially the most dangerous man in Canadian public life ... because clever, plausible, more or less cultured. But completely reactionary.' Another of Underhill's friends tackled Drew directly. Alan Plaunt charged that the politician was trying to abrogate 'academic freedom' – which was 'cherished by all genuine democrats as one of the pillars of democracy' – and to negate freedom of expression. Worse, he seemed to be proposing 'that no educational institution receiving funds from the provincial government should harbour opinions dissimilar from those of the majority of the legislature.' Describing this as 'unadulterated fascism,' Plaunt said that it would bring about 'the destruction of intellectual freedom and the drying up of the sources of a university's vitality.'[137]

Drew replied that free speech was not at issue: 'Those of us who believe that Canada should remain British have a right to say that in our great institutions of learning anti-British doctrines shall not be taught. It is the duty of those charged with the education of our young people to play their part in making sure that Canada will remain British.' This, in Drew's view, was like a congregation telling its minister 'that if he wished to continue to occupy the pulpit he would not express opinions outside of the church ridiculing the religion upon which the church was founded.' Drew quarrelled also with Plaunt's remarks about democracy, which the politician thought 'much more likely to survive on a simple acceptance of the fact that we are British than if our youth are instructed by parlour pinks who preach Empire disunity from the cloistered protection of jobs which give them all too much free time.' As for academic freedom, it must yield to 'the duty of teachers to make sure that Canada remained British.'[138]

Two key questions arise from all this, namely, 'What are the functions of a university?' and 'How does it best serve society?' Plaunt saw the institution mainly as a forum for free inquiry; Drew saw it primarily as a servant of the state. Plaunt believed that freedom of expression was basic to democracy and that, in fostering this freedom, a university served the country. Drew's comments suggest that he believed the university to exist primarily to inculcate loyalty to King and country.

Drew's view was of greater antiquity than Plaunt's. Indeed, the University of Toronto had its origins in an Anglican foundation, King's College, that had been charged with a duty to shore up church and state. Another concept emerged later in the nineteenth century, one that saw the university as a bulwark of the conservation and advancement of knowledge, but in 1939 this view did not yet command universal assent. While Plaunt's remarks were loaded with the rhetoric of democracy, Drew's reply unconsciously partook of something far more odious. By 1939 not a few universities in Europe had been charged with inculcating patriotism and the values of the state. The consequences for academic freedom and for scholarship were dismal.

The 1930s feature prominently in a history of academic freedom in Canada. The country's economic problems and the threat of renewed war created a climate in which that freedom was notably at risk. Defenders of capitalism and of Canada's ties with Britain resented criticism, and when the criticism came from academics, it prompted questions about what was wrong with the universities and suggestions that they might be set right by silencing those who gave offence. In some circles, Canadian universities came to be seen as institutions filled with detractors of the established order. Yet the reality was different. Academics who overtly opposed the capitalist system or the British connection were in fact few and far between. The 'radicals' (and some were radical only in the eyes of the more fevered kind of Tory) were a small fraction of the faculty. The outspoken ones were rarer still. That this small handful loomed so large in the eyes of defenders of the status quo is a fruitful subject of inquiry for a social pathologist.[139]

The total number of socialist university teachers, most of them members of the LSR or CCF, was probably not much more than thirty among a total of some three thousand. Communists were fewer still. The historian Stanley B. Ryerson identified several professors who might have been philosophical Marxists, but he doubted that any of them belonged to the Communist Party of Canada (CPC). Academics were in fact discouraged from joining the party, because it was feared that they would be dismissed if their membership became known. Ryerson himself had joined the CPC before taking a position at Sir George Williams College. He kept his membership a secret, but when the principal learned in 1937 that Ryerson had written some CPC pamphlets under an assumed name, his contract was not renewed. (He did not teach at a university again until the mid-1960s.) A Trotskyist, Earle Birney also used a *nom de plume* when writing about politics. Unlike Ryerson, he escaped detection.[140]

In necessarily focusing on a small minority of professors and on controversy and conflict, a history of academic freedom distorts the reality of academic life. In the midst of depression and budgetary distress, Canadian universities were mostly tranquil. The great majority of professors steered clear of trouble. Ensconced in the culture of contentment – the phrase is John Kenneth Galbraith's – most academics shared in the dominant capitalist and imperialist systems of belief. The economic order might not be perfect, and some adjustments in the imperial relationship might be desirable, but by and large the world seemed satisfactory enough. Like middle-class Canadians generally, most professors worshipped in the church of things-as-they-are.

In 1934 Alberta's W.H. Alexander asked the question, 'Will radical leader-ship emerge from our Canadian universities?' He thought not. 'The "success-ful" way of life in our universities may be equated with the life of conformity both to doctrine and authority.'[141]

Five years later, by then teaching at the University of California in Berkeley, he wrote that there was an agreeable future in academe for those who censored themselves, but not for those who were openly critical. Addressing himself to a 'young man contemplating an academic career,' he noted that capitalism sanc-tioned 'a most painfully unbalanced distribution of the satisfactions and oppor-tunities of life, to say nothing of the bare necessities.' But it was dangerous for academics to admit this, he added, for in a state university it was 'invariably described as Bolshevism,' and in a privately endowed institution the situation was 'worse still, because an unflinching examination of the defeat sustained by the "good life" in modern capitalistic conditions is regarded as a personal criti-cism of the benevolent persons who have established the academic foundation.' Most professors sensibly did not challenge the status quo, he continued; they were easily replaced, and academic freedom offered them little protection. If such freedom had ever existed in the past, 'and personally,' added Alexander, 'I do not think [it ever did] in things deemed by the ruling powers to be essential to the preservation of their power,' it was in decline. 'We affect to shudder at the fate of the German universities without quite realizing the tendency of our own to move towards ... the same silence on "essentials" accompanied by loud mouthings about inconsequentials.' *Noli episcopari*, do not join the clerisy, Alexander concluded, for the universities 'are too respectable either to fight or to tolerate within themselves a fighter.'[142]

The letter was partly a parody, but it was rooted in Alexander's own experi-ences. Repeated attacks on his views and activities had disillusioned him. 'Despite a hundred and one petty narrownesses of Canadian life,' he wrote in 1938 to Arthur Lower, 'there has always been heretofore a very deep basic respect for ... the "fundamental liberties," but it doesn't seem to bother people much ... that ... these things are being flagrantly invaded or even wholly denied. I can't help thinking that the majority of my colleagues – the finest chaps in the world in all else – would function quite cheerfully under a fascist regime.'[143] He may have been right about his colleagues. But did his disillusionment allow him to assess the state of academic freedom accurately?

Perhaps not. Alexander's comments do help explain, though, why critics of capitalism aroused so much hostility in the early 1930s, whereas a few years later hostility was directed primarily against those who questioned the British connection. In 1932 and 1933 capitalism seemed to be in peril, prompting demands that socialist professors be silenced lest they help bring about its ultimate collapse. By mid-decade the economy was recovering, and the federal election of 1935 showed the CCF to have limited appeal. The attack on capitalism largely lost its capacity to frighten *bien pensant* Canadians; the attack on the Empire took its place. In the later 1930s the mounting threat of war brought increased intolerance of those who questioned the value of the British connection or counselled neutrality in the next European conflict.

Alexander saw in this intolerance a serious threat to academic freedom. Others saw no danger. In 1937, as we have seen, Carleton Stanley was unable to find anyone to speak on academic freedom to the annual meeting of the National Conference of Canadian Universities. He at least thought the subject worth discussing. His fellow presidents were more complacent.[144] Were they afraid of opening a Pandora's box? Or did they think that the flaws of Canadian universities did not merit mention alongside the offences against academic freedom in the dictatorships of Europe? Either way, a discussion of the subject would not have been out of place.

Academic freedom was unsafe in the Depression. A small handful of professors tested the limits of academic free speech by stating unpopular views on matters of public interest. Their comments were not well received. Some 'radicals' were tolerated, if grudgingly; others lapsed into silence. A few were expelled from their universities for their political beliefs, among them Eugene Forsey and Leonard Marsh by McGill. To this university's history in the 1930s we must devote closer attention.

6

Socialism and Academic Freedom at McGill

'I do not think anybody need be alarmed about socialism in this University ...'[1] Principal Sir Arthur Currie was dictating to his secretary on 26 October 1933. Enjoying the support of English-speaking Montreal, still the wealthiest community in the country, McGill was far from being a hotbed of left-wing activity. If some people nevertheless believed the institution to have fallen prey to socialism, two men were mainly responsible for the misapprehension – Frank Scott and Eugene Forsey.

By five years the older of the two, Francis Reginald Scott belonged to a prominent Anglo-Quebec family. Appointed in the Faculty of Law in 1928, he reached a turning point in his life on 3 February 1931, the day the *Gazette* published his letter of protest against the actions of the Montreal police in breaking up meetings of the unemployed. 'Whether or not these meetings are attended by communists or merely by unemployed labourers makes not a particle of difference,' Scott wrote, 'for communism is no more criminal than liberalism or socialism.' The actions of the police, if reported accurately, were 'clearly high-handed and apparently illegal' and violated 'the rights to freedom of assembly and freedom of speech.'[2]

Montreal's police chief denied the charges of high-handedness and illegality, and the *Gazette* commented, 'There is nothing to be gained by a microscopic examination of abstract principles or attempts to refashion those principles through the nice refinements of academic discussion.' Within a week the newspaper carried two more editorials denying free speech where communists were concerned. At McGill, Currie did no more than warn Scott against linking his opinions to the university – he had signed himself 'Associate Professor of Constitutional and Federal Law, McGill University.'[3]

During the months that followed, Scott became an outspoken advocate of economic, social, and political change, as did Forsey. Towards the end of 1932

Currie told a board member that he was gathering 'quite a file of things said by Professors Scott and Forsey.' More than one person, he added, had asked him 'to bridle the tongues of these young men.'[4]

Eugene Alfred Forsey, a sessional lecturer in political economy first appointed in 1929, had become highly critical of capitalism. When he first came to public attention, however, it was for another reason. In 1932 he and his friend King Gordon visited the Soviet Union and returned as admirers of its supposed accomplishments. 'I have no doubt that we were kept well away from anything that might have created an unfavourable impression,' Forsey wrote in his memoirs.[5]

Forsey's rosy-hued account of Soviet life drew hostile comment. Fairly typical was a letter from the stockbroker A.J. Nesbitt, who hoped that Currie would dismiss Forsey or at least stop him 'from commending the Russian government and its policies.' Forsey's reportage also prompted a suggestion from RCMP Commissioner J.H. MacBrien that Currie chase the communists from McGill. 'Perhaps you might just mention to him,' MacBrien wrote to Currie's assistant, Wilfrid Bovey, 'that such action would be strong support to those who are trying to stamp out Communistic activities in Canada.'[6]

Bovey replied that three men had caused misunderstanding, but no one need worry about them. King Gordon was not McGill's responsibility, and in any case he believed in change by peaceful means. So did Scott. As for Forsey, he 'could have no possible influence over anyone who knew him, least of all over the students,' who regarded him 'as a young idiot.' Bovey added, 'We are not satisfied with him and he is not likely to be here long.' Meanwhile, Currie told Nesbitt that Forsey had 'never written anything of value, does not adopt ... the proper professorial attitude in his lectures, and certainly brings a good deal of criticism upon the University for the things he says in his public addresses.' But he had no intention of getting rid of Forsey for his political views, Currie told a board member: 'When we dismiss him we shall do so because he has been a failure as a teaching professor.'[7]

In writing to Currie, MacBrien said that he had been concerned about Scott and Forsey but that Bovey's reply had satisfied him that Currie was 'doing all that is possible at McGill to assist in the control of Communism.' Currie sent a copy of this letter to Herbert Molson (a board member who had queried him about communists on campus) with the comment: 'I keep a very close watch over such activities and I am quite convinced that no one need lose any sleep over Communism here.'[8]

Currie reappointed Forsey in 1933 after receiving a letter from his department head, Stephen Leacock. Having been asked whether Forsey should be let go, Leacock replied that it would not be 'in the permanent interest of the college.' Leacock said that Forsey was 'not a good teacher' and that his opinions were 'mistaken and silly,' but if his contract was not renewed, people would think it was because of his opinions: 'They will be wrong but that is what they will think and say.' Leacock added that he would be willing to live with this criticism if Forsey was 'an open agitating Communist' or used his classes 'for propaganda instead of for instruction,' but he was unaware that Forsey was the one or did the other.[9]

Leacock's letter all but forced Currie's hand, causing him to recommend reappointment. Yet he remained unhappy about Forsey – and also about Forsey's critics. Concerning the latter, Currie wrote in July 1933, 'Much of the criticism directed at Universities to-day arises from the fact the capitalistic class feel that many university professors are sympathetic with Communism.' This was not the case, said Currie, though 'certainly a number are with the socialists.' This had its dangers, yet 'equally dangerous' was the dominance in educated circles of the main political parties, which had done 'little or nothing' to accommodate the changes that had taken place during the previous two decades or 'to bring their policies into line with what people are thinking about today.'[10]

Currie's scepticism concerning Forsey's critics did not mean that he was coming to approve of the young economist. When a letter arrived in October 1933 from William Lawson Grant, principal of Upper Canada College, praising Forsey's 'unselfishness and enthusiasm and also his powers as a lecturer,' Currie responded that Forsey was 'very dogmatic' in his teaching and had been known to mark down students who disagreed with him. 'You will be doing the University a kindness if you will recommend Mr. Forsey to someone else,' he told Grant.[11] Currie's dislike of dogmatism was in the tradition of the American Association of University Professors' 1915 statement: professors were not supposed to be propagandists for their political opinions in the classroom.

Within days of writing to Grant, Currie had new reason to deplore Forsey's activities. Addressing the St James Literary Society on 17 October, Forsey allegedly described capitalists as 'greedy' and predicted the demise of capitalism. Complaints predictably followed. The Conservative *Quebec Chronicle-Telegraph* asserted that Canada's English-language universities had been infiltrated by teachers who were spreading socialist ideas: 'If nothing can be done to check it, an acute problem will shortly be created, not merely for higher education but for the established order in this country.' According to the Toronto *Globe*, socialist professors were 'becoming increasingly vocal' throughout Canada, 'with impressive effect on undergraduates.' Worried about this, the *Globe*'s editor asked why these professors were 'being paid out of public funds to carry on their propaganda' and take up time 'that should be given to worthwhile studies.'[12]

There were other views, however. The *Toronto Star* thought that worry about the spread of socialist ideas among students was misplaced, and the *Ottawa Citizen* stated, 'As for infecting students with radical ideas, it might be argued that it is not a bad thing at all. Do we want them all to grow up as chips off the old block? Think how disastrous that might be.' Meanwhile, several people, some of whom had been at the St James Literary Society meeting, wrote to Currie in defence of Forsey's right to speak.[13]

The problem for Currie was that Forsey's defenders were not among McGill's benefactors. One of the latter tribe was Arthur B. Purvis, president of Canadian Industries Limited. He did not object to professors holding views different from his own, he told Currie, but as someone whose support McGill had solicited, 'it seems to me that it is a little bit too much to ask a "greedy capitalist" to subscribe to his own downfall!' Furthermore, he thought that 'a man who denies to the other camp qualities of character which he regards as inherent in the followers of his own philosophy [was] a poor type to prepare the young for their positions in the world.'[14]

Asked by Currie to explain his remarks, Forsey said that the press had distorted them and that he was sending a letter to the *Montreal Star* to that effect. Currie still thought the economist had been unwise. It was difficult enough to administer McGill's affairs, he informed one correspondent, 'without having members of the staff alienating from the University the sympathy ... [of] those members of the community who constitute the field from which the main resources for McGill have come and must continue to come, i.e., "those who have."' In answering another of Forsey's defenders, Currie wrote, 'I don't see how we can get away from the fact that the "greedy capitalist" pays Mr. Forsey's salary.'[15]

Purvis, on the other hand, was told that Forsey had been misquoted and that 'the press pays altogether too much attention to what this young man says.' To Premier Louis-Alexandre Taschereau, Currie explained that for two years he had been trying to shed Forsey without creating a *cause célèbre*, and he hoped to do so yet, though it would not be easy. Noting the 'great importance' which professors attached 'to what they are pleased to call "academic freedom,"' Currie wrote, 'I am between the devil and the deep sea. If I dismiss Mr. Forsey ... it will be heralded from one end of Canada to the other that McGill dismisses its professors because of their political views, that we are a ... university ... in which freedom of speech is not tolerated.'[16]

It was 'ridiculous' to take Forsey's remarks as evidence that McGill was socialist, Currie wrote to Senator Lorne Webster, who was president of Holt, Renfrew and Co. as well as Imperial Trust; of McGill's 450 full- and part-time faculty members, only Forsey and Scott were socialists. It was 'intolerable,' moreover, that some newspaper editors sought to deny free speech to academics. He might 'be forced to make a public statement' defending 'the right of free speech,' Currie continued: 'To our university men we should look for the greatest enlightenment on these public questions and the most honest presentation of all that is involved.' But he also wanted to make clear his view that 'no man should get his living from holding a position as a teacher in a university, and yet devote his time and effort to planning for and speaking on behalf of a particular political party.'[17]

Two days after writing to Webster, Currie dictated a long memorandum to his secretary, Dorothy McMurray. It recorded a solution to the Forsey problem, for he had reportedly undertaken to 'refrain absolutely from any comment on political matters for at least six months to come [and to] devote himself wholeheartedly to ... his own subject and to research in his own field.' But the document is more important for its discussion of what might be behind the attack on socialism in the universities and what could be done about it.

No one need be alarmed about socialism at McGill, Currie thought: 'And I am not sure that Mr. Forsey's critics are greatly alarmed about it. I am not sure but that behind it all there is a desire on the part of those who pay the great bulk of the taxes to be free from any obligation which adds greatly to those taxes. This agitation may be one directed not against socialism in particular but against higher education in general.' Currie had asked one of Forsey's critics why he gave money to McGill. Did he want to control 'the thinking of the students and the teaching of professors,' or did he believe in higher education? 'His answer was rambling and meant nothing,' noted Currie.

Did the critics, he asked, want 'to live amongst people who have been trained to think for themselves and are capable of forming correct judgments,' or did they prefer 'a population whom they can dominate or control?' Currie feared the worst: 'We may be called upon to fight a battle ... for the existence and development of universities themselves. An institution which tries to stimulate a respect for truth and sincerity, for honesty and honour, for justice and fair play, may not be one that selfish interests like ... It would seem sometimes as if higher education were tolerated only because those who have it can thus become hired men.'

Currie reported a telephone conversation with H.J. Cody of the University of Toronto, who claimed to have told the editor of the *Chronicle-Telegraph* 'that there was no reason to be anxious about the question of socialism in universities' and that if he was anxious at all it should be about socialism in the United Church – 'to my mind,' commented Currie, 'a rather impolitic reply for an Anglican President to send to a Roman Catholic editor.'[18] On this impish note he ended his memorandum. Within days he fell ill, and five weeks later he was dead.

That Currie did not have the time to make a public statement on socialism in the universities is something we can only regret. It does seem, though, that his suspicion that higher education and not socialism was the target had some basis in fact. His comment that people did not wish to pay more taxes suggests that he was thinking of universities in general and not primarily of McGill, which did not receive public funds. In British Columbia, for example, a committee of businessmen headed by the Vancouver stockbroker George Kidd (appointed in 1932 by the provincial government to investigate the fiscal and financial problems facing the province) proposed deep cuts in the public sector, among them the elimination of the grant to the University of British Columbia.[19]

Although this would almost certainly have had the effect of closing the university, the proposal had some support. A few commentators said that the costs of higher education should be paid by those receiving it, and at least one person argued that it would save taxpayers' money if scholarships were awarded to meritorious students for use outside the province. Neither view was widely shared: the social benefits of higher education seemed obvious and sending money out of the province seemed wasteful. Outside the business community, the Kidd committee's report gained little support. Its purpose – 'to steal from the poor and give to the rich,' in the historian Robin Fisher's phrase – was too crass and harsh for even a cash-starved Conservative government to adopt.[20]

During the Depression years, every provincial university saw its public grant decline steeply. UBC's fell by a huge 60 per cent from 1929–30 to 1932–3. Private universities did not go unscathed either. McGill's endowment income was 44 per cent lower in 1934 than it had been in 1927. (However, the declines were mitigated to some extent by a 23 per cent drop in the consumer price index from 1929 to 1933.)[21] Currie was right, too, in surmising that some powerful Canadians had no use for critical thought. Such people expected of universities no more (and no less) than that they supply Canada with well-trained managerial and professional workers. Beyond that, universities and their professors should uphold the law and the social and economic order, and not in any way challenge them.

Sir Arthur Currie's successor, Arthur E. Morgan, did not take office until well into 1935. For two years executive authority rested with the chancellor, Edward (after 1934 Sir Edward) W. Beatty. President of the Canadian Pacific Railway, he supported higher education generously, but he also feared the influence of socialist professors on students, and occasionally he warned against it. One such occasion was his receipt of an honorary degree from Western Ontario in 1935. Socialism, Beatty told his audience, was 'based partly on a lack of adequate knowledge of the structure of the existing economic society, and partly on an emotional desire for correction of admitted defects in our society, which outruns the slower but safer processes of logical reasoning.' Much of the discussion among the younger economists was uninformed and ill-considered, said Beatty: 'I view with alarm the possibility that our universities, unquestionably competent to instruct our young men and women in arts and science, may not be as safe sources of instruction in the field of economics.' This was dangerous. If Canadians came to believe that the educational system did not produce 'men and women ... qualified to deal with the harsh realities of life, no theory of the sanctity of education [would] save its institutions from such criticism and such destruction as the people at large believe they deserve.'[22]

Beatty's dislike of socialists was not personal. In 1936 he told Morgan that, having met Frank Scott, he liked his 'frankness, obvious mental honesty and his sense of humour. Scott 'debates a question good naturedly and without animus,' said Beatty, though he thought the man 'woefully deficient in practical knowledge of affairs.' On related grounds, he criticized McGill's Social Science Research Series, which was under the direction of Leonard Marsh: it did not do the sort of work that businessmen were looking for. Moreover, some of the academics associated with the project were uninformed propagandists: 'We will have no hope of business-university cooperation, unless confidence in the mental honesty of the professors is established.' McGill, stated Beatty, needed to build up an economics department 'of men of the calibre, ability and appreciation of business affairs which is so essential.'[23]

Morgan agreed: 'We need here in McGill an economist of pre-eminent standing and quality of mind and personality who will be the pivot of all this kind of work.' But although Morgan shared Beatty's opinion on this point, he differed with him on the issue of the professor as propagandist. Late in 1936, responding to a complaint by Beatty about academic socialists in general and Scott in particular, Morgan said that he hoped the problem would not disappear, 'because as I see it the only condition of its solution is the establishment of an authoritarian state, which God forbid!' Beatty and he, continued Morgan, 'must hope that heaven will endow our teachers with the blessed gifts of wisdom, tact and a sense of responsibility. All that we can actually do is to impress on them ... that rights imply responsibilities.'[24]

Morgan underestimated the danger, Beatty rejoined: 'Socialism and communism ... are definitely attempts to break down the existing structure of society.' Professors who held these views could 'exercise a most disturbing effect on the minds of their students.' They claimed that 'academic liberty' required them to discuss any subject with their students, but 'every socialist professor,' said Beatty, was 'at all times a definite propagandist for his faith,' and propaganda did not belong in the university. Beatty added that he doubted whether he or Morgan would permit a Jesuit to teach the history of the Reformation at

McGill – 'academic liberty or no academic liberty' – even though they might, 'very improperly of course,' be less careful to prevent 'a violent Protestant propagandist' from teaching the subject: 'After all, we are only human and subject to prejudice in favour of those things in which we believe.'

What was Beatty's point? On the one hand, he did 'not wish to suggest for one moment that Scott should be disciplined or penalized.' On the other hand, he said that Scott was 'definitely a socialist propagandist and not a mere dispassionate examiner of political and economic principles.' And he asserted that since McGill 'should avoid any colourable assertion' that it was 'a hotbed of teaching for or against socialism,' the faculty should be informed that 'academic liberty is not an adequate excuse for propaganda of any sort which is based on blind faith.'[25]

Two lines from Scott's poem 'W.L.M.K.' come to mind. On the issue of academic freedom, Beatty 'never let his on the one hand / Know what his on the other hand was doing.' At a February 1937 banquet of the McGill Union, Beatty said, 'We allow and insist on the greatest measure of academic freedom, because we desire that our youth shall be brought up in an atmosphere of absolute freedom.' But he warned that this freedom could 'degenerate into license' and lead the government to reduce free speech. This was undesirable, 'and he therefore called for safeguards,' one of the most important being a duty to be 'accurate.'[26]

The inaccuracies that worried Beatty were those of the critics of capitalism, not those of its defenders. In the course of a 1937 convocation address at Queen's, he asserted that socialist academics tended to mislead their students as well as the public: 'A sense of responsibility must be brought into play even if it prevents the turning of a striking phrase or the gaining of a little passing and useless publicity.'[27] That pro-business academics might likewise mislead students seems not to have occurred to Beatty – or if it did, it struck him as a venial sin at worst.

Beatty's view of socialist academics was fairly moderate compared with the views of some other critics. In August 1938 the Montreal *Gazette*, noting that Scott was on the national council of the CCF, argued that this was 'out of line with the functions and responsibilities of a university professor, and especially of a teacher of civil law.' Could he and other professors who were active in the CCF, 'holding political views, economic opinions, perhaps even legal conceptions, that [were] not acceptable to the great majority of Canadian parents, confine their teaching to the principles in which these parents believe?' Should professors, in fact, be actively involved with political parties at all? The editor thought not: 'Surely there is a line to be drawn somewhere, and surely the time has come to draw it?'[28]

The industrialist Francis Clergue agreed. Describing Scott's views as 'subversive of all the doctrines which are the foundation of the British race,' he suggested to Beatty that 'at a suitable time, Dr. [sic] Scott should be ... given his last salary cheque.'[29]

Beatty's reply to Clergue distinguished between public and classroom speech. It would be 'highly improper' for Scott to indoctrinate his students, he stated, but as long as he did not do that, his politics were his own concern. To the new principal, Lewis Douglas, Beatty wrote: 'This question of academic freedom ... is about as old as democracy, and to interfere with it, except in cases of flagrant abuse, is a very dangerous thing. I have no objection to Scott, Forsey, Marsh and other alleged intellectuals indulging their penchant for publicity – which is what it amounts to in many instances – provided it does not taint the quality of their lectures or otherwise adversely affect the University.' Yet he continued to fear that professors who held a political or economic theory 'quite unconsciously' became partisans of it in the classroom. What could be done about this situation? 'It seems we must rely, in the main, on the honesty and wisdom of the members of our own staff.' Beatty conceded academic freedom, but grudgingly.[30]

Not all opinions that might today be described as 'radical' were so regarded at the time. On 2 December 1935, E.W.R. Steacie, an assistant professor of physical chemistry at McGill, told the Montreal branch of the Canadian Engineering Institute that having recently spent a year at a German university, he 'resented criticism of Germany on the part of people who had never been there.' The press was muzzled there, he said, 'but he asked if it was any better off in Canada. He preferred the control of Goebbels [the Nazi propaganda chief] to that of the advertising manager of a large store.' This may have been a reference to the gingerly manner in which the press in 1934–5 had treated the damaging evidence presented before the Parliamentary Committee and the Royal Commission on Price Spreads concerning the employment and buying practices of the department stores (which, of course, were major advertisers in the newspaper).

Steacie then turned to a subject that had attracted international attention since Germany's passage of the Nuremberg Laws in September 1935, the persecution of the Jews. He conceded that Jews in the Reich 'had some cause for complaint. He could not condone the way they had been treated, but politically the discrimination against them was justified,' for the Jews had been 'the large mortgage-holders and ... had gone to extremes in evictions.' As well, claimed Steacie, they had been overrepresented in the professions, where they had discriminated against non-Jews: 'Every other country had taken a similar anti-Semitic attitude when it was found suitable. The only reason there was no outward anti-Jewish movement here was because discrimination existed underneath.'

To those who worried about the fate of democracy in Germany Steacie offered food for thought. The Montreal *Gazette* reported him as telling his audience that

80 to 90 per cent of the people were persuaded that Hitler's regime was the best thing for the country. The Germans liked to be regimented. 'If virtually everyone in Germany does not want freedom, why should we worry?' The Nazi programme held the nation to be more important than the individual, but there was more freedom than was popularly realized ... The speaker contended that, good or bad, stable government was preferable to uncertainty, and Hitler had brought stability. He had restored the national self-respect.

Steacie went on the deprecate fears of German rearmament: 'Germany's increased army was a point of honor.' Besides, Hitler had dealt more efficiently with unemployment than any other country had: 'He had drafted the men into labor camps, put them into uniform, and their morale was as good as that of the regular troops ... Hitler had brought action while other governments had done nothing but talk.'[31]

Steacie, who later became president of the National Research Council, must in time have repented of this claptrap. But more interesting than remarks that strike today's reader as wrong-headed and offensive was the response to them. The *Gazette* printed two letters, one mildly critical and one (from H.M. Caiserman of the Canadian Jewish Congress) strongly critical of Steacie's speech, but the speech itself elicited no editorial comment – something all the more astonishing in view of Steacie's disdainful assessment of the Canadian press. Neither politicians nor anyone associated with McGill discussed the speech publicly. If Principal Morgan said anything to Steacie, he did it off the record.

Sherlock Holmes's remark in the story 'Silver Blaze' comes to mind. Told that 'the dog did nothing in the night-time,' Holmes said, 'That was the curious incident.' In 1935 Hitler still had a good many admirers outside Germany – not only fascists and their fellow travellers but also many people who saw in him a man of action who got things done. Steacie's remarks expressed, in part, an impatience with 'do-nothing democracy.' During the 1930s, such a reaction was all too depressingly common in the Western world. As well, anti-Semitism was widespread in 1930s Canada, including at McGill. 'A rough-and-ready quota system' limited the number of Jewish students in medicine and law, while the Faculty of Arts required higher grades from Jews seeking admission. These practices did not end until after the war had begun. In 1940 Principal F. Cyril James thought it fair comment to say of a man that 'although of Jewish descent, [he] has a very pleasant personality.'[32]

Anti-Semitism helps explain why McGill did not appoint a refugee from

Nazi-occupied Europe (Karl Stern, a Jewish convert to Catholicism) until 1940. Asked by Sir Arthur Currie in 1933 to comment on a Carnegie Foundation document concerning refugee professors, Dean Ira MacKay had written, 'The simple, obvious truth is that the Jewish people are no use to us in this country.' Most went into trade, money lending, medicine, and law, he explained, and Canada already had too many people in these fields. 'I have the highest regard for the better class of Jews,' continued MacKay, 'but as a race ... their traditions and practices do not fit in ... a very new country. What we need ... is men who will explore and work and make the very best of our natural providences.'[33]

In believing that neither Canada nor McGill needed Jews, Ira MacKay was not alone. In July 1938 Terry MacDermot, who had taught history at McGill earlier in the 1930s, offered the opinion that weaknesses in the Faculty of Arts and Science might be corrected with the aid of a few refugees.[34] Since Principal Lewis Douglas was opposed, this suggestion went nowhere.

Douglas's attitude to refugees – or, more accurately, to their potential for controversy – emerges from a memorandum in January 1939. The registrar, T.H. Matthews, had asked him whether McGill should adopt a policy to deal with German Jewish students and whether the issue should be raised at the next meeting of the National Conference of Canadian Universities in the hope that the universities might make 'a really good Samaritan gesture across the Atlantic.' His suggestion was not well received. 'This is a controversial, even dangerous subject,' Douglas replied, 'on which much embarrassment might develop from public discussion.' Matthews retreated quickly: 'On second and more mature thought I thoroughly agree with your opinion on this matter.' If assistance to refugee students was this contentious, it is hardly surprising that McGill did next to nothing to help refugee faculty.[35]

From 1935 to 1940, McGill had three principals. The first, Arthur E. Morgan, who came from England where leftist dons were common, worried little about McGill's socialists. This may be one reason why Sir Edward Beatty soured on him. More important, however, was that board members came to regard Morgan as impractical and kept him largely in the dark about financial matters. In the spring of 1937 he resigned, citing irreconcilable differences between himself and the board over McGill's management.[36]

On 1 January 1938, McGill got a different kind of principal. Lewis Douglas was an American industrialist who had served in Franklin D. Roosevelt's cabinet in 1933–4 as budget chief. He took a dim view of deficits, and at McGill he made balancing the budget his first task. He took a dim view, too, of the prominence that a few radicals had in the social sciences at McGill, more particularly in the social science research group.[37]

The historian Marlene Shore writes that 'the Social Science Research Project ... evolved into something quite different from what the university's officials had envisaged.' Established in 1931 with a five-year $110,000 grant from the Rockefeller Foundation, its original purpose had been to examine the relationship between industry, the community, and employment in the Montreal region. By the time research got under way, however, the Depression had overwhelmed industries and workers alike. As Leonard Marsh explained in 1935, the focus of research had shifted to 'problems of employment and unemployment [with] special reference to Canadian conditions.'[38]

Born and educated in England, Marsh had gained appointment in the economics department in 1930 and became director of social research later that year. (At $3,500, his salary was out of line with his rank as sessional lecturer, and in 1931 Stephen Leacock recommended that he be promoted to assistant or even associate professor and get a continuing appointment. The recommendation failed, and Marsh never did have tenure.) Marsh reported to a council and an executive committee, but to a considerable extent the research was shaped by his Fabian-style socialism. He served as national president of the League for Social Reconstruction from 1937 to 1939, and was co-author of its two books. He was the author of two volumes in the Social Research Series, one of which, *Canadians In and Out of Work* (1940), was the first scholarly study of social class in Canada. As well, he was co-author of two other books in the series and editor of Lloyd G. Reynolds's *The British Immigrant* (1935). (Its criticism of Canadian immigration policy greatly irritated Beatty.)[39]

Douglas soon reached the view that much of the work done under the heading of social research was political and economic propaganda. This impression gained support from a memorandum prepared by the formidable Dorothy McMurray, the secretary he had inherited from Morgan and Currie. Marsh, 'the driving power' in the research project, came in for severe criticism. He had been chosen not by Currie but by Acting Principal C.F. Martin, McMurray wrote. After attending a few meetings, Currie had 'worried' about the project. 'Meanwhile Dean Ira MacKay withdrew and washed his hands of Marsh, Leacock was ... refusing to be drawn in, and so the socialist-sociologist-psychologist group on the staff were left to their own devices.'[40]

Douglas stated his own views on research in the course of the Founder's Day dinner in October 1938. The university was 'an institution in which the inquiring mind can roam untrammeled and unrestricted by conventions,' he said, but it must insist 'on intellectual competence, on intellectual balance, on mental integrity ... Its one and only goal ... is the determination of the truth.' Unfortunately, he continued, some people claimed that the university should be an instrument to indoctrinate students with 'an economic or political philosophy agreeable to the personnel occupying places of public power'; others wanted the university to serve certain social or economic interest groups. Both attitudes must be resisted.[41] Douglas's view of research was rooted in the tradition of the U.S. research university, which was ostensibly neutral with respect to ideology, and in the American Association of University Professors' idea of communities of competence as the basis of academic freedom.

In February 1939 Douglas wrote to Beatty, 'There is not a single man on the staff ... competent to present and to support with evidence so plentifully available the alternative point of view to that of the collectivists.' Yet it was important that 'the collectivist philosophy' be examined critically, with full attention to its flaws and failures: 'I feel ... that, given a little patience and a well-considered programme, the necessary correctives can be applied here.' There should be 'a definite, precise policy with respect to tenure,' stated Douglas, as well as selective salary increases and promotions. Having changed the university's policy on the granting of tenure, 'we will be able to calculate on a fairly rapid turnover of younger men, selecting here and there, as they pass through, those whom we think to be competent to carry on as the older men retire.' As a result, competence could be 'slowly but steadily ... improved.'

Douglas also proposed the establishment of visiting professorships in political economy and history. These should be generously remunerated, at up to $10,000 annually, he said, and supported with $3,000 annually for research. (The $10,000 would have easily doubled the normal salary of a full professor in Canada at that time.) Douglas believed this might attract someone of high calibre and sound ideas, such as the English economist Lionel Robbins. (Believing the Depression to be a natural and salutory cure for the speculative excesses of the 1920s, Robbins argued that it must be allowed to run its course without government intervention.) Douglas added, 'The same type of competence in the field of History would reinforce the beneficial effects which I am sure will flow from the presence of an excellent man in Political Economy.'[42]

Douglas evidently was for change. He began to plan amendments to McGill's rules concerning tenure and promotion soon after arriving in Montreal, and by February 1939 his plans were complete. Their realization he left to others. Convinced by the spring of 1939 that war in Europe was imminent and that Canada would be a belligerent while the United States would remain neutral, Douglas judged that McGill would be better served by having a British subject at its head. In May he announced his resignation, effective 31 December 1939. Some months later the English-born F. Cyril James, recently recruited to McGill from a professorship of finance in the Wharton School of Business, University of Pennsylvania, was appointed to replace Douglas.[43]

Five weeks before the expiry of his term, Douglas outlined for Beatty 'the major moves that the University has taken, and is now contemplating, aimed at minimizing the influence on the student population of certain members of the University staff and at [improving] the quality of the scholarship and teaching of its staff members.' Tenure had been redefined, he explained, so that 'those who do not hold permanent appointment and who do not measure up to the standard of teaching and scholarship which the University cherishes, will not be reappointed.' As well, a revision of McGill's statutes had facilitated 'a modification of the curriculum, changes in the courses of study, and better selection of personnel.' The appointment of a senior economist had been foiled by 'the imminence of hostilities,' noted Douglas, but he hoped that a scheme that had brought distinguished scholars to McGill during the 1938–9 session would be expanded. The full plan was to be carried out by his successor.[44]

The 'major casualties' of Douglas's plan, writes Stanley Brice Frost (McGill's official historian), were Eugene Forsey and Leonard Marsh. Marsh went first. In the fall of 1937 he had sought clarification of his status, and the acting principal, W.H. Brittain, had told him that a decision would have to await Douglas's arrival. When Douglas reviewed the matter, he had before him Dorothy McMurray's memorandum criticizing Marsh's direction of the Social Science Research Project as well as her assessment that no injustice would be done if he were let go: 'He knew when he came that the project was for 5 years only ... He has had more than that out of it already.'[45]

Late in 1938 Douglas informed Marsh that 'all concerned ought to be warned that the research project will terminate upon the expiration of the Rockefeller grant' in 1940. A proposal to carry on with a reduced budget was rejected as too costly for the university. Douglas told the board in November 1939 'that under the regulations governing Tenure of Appointment it was necessary to give notice before December 15th to Mr. L.C. Marsh ... whose term of appointment ends on August 31, 1940, and who will not be re-appointed.'[46]

The board agreed, but on 30 November Douglas dictated a memorandum stating that the incoming principal and the dean of arts and science, C.S. Hendel, should 'decide ... whether they wish action on the Marsh case.' If they decided that he should not be reappointed, McMurray was to inform Marsh that the responsibility was Douglas's: 'I don't want them to take the onus of it.'[47]

The next day Cyril James discussed the matter with Hendel and J.C. Hemmeon, the head of political economy. Hemmeon had said in 1937 that the Department of Political Economy did not need a research professor 'however well qualified,' and he now stated that 'he was not willing to recommend the appointment of Mr. Marsh on any basis other than the present situation' (namely, as a part-time sessional lecturer). 'In view of the fact that Mr. Marsh would certainly not be willing to stay ... on such a basis,' James commented, 'it would seem to me wise to announce that fact to him.'[48]

Marsh did not get a choice. The secretary of the board informed him in a brief letter, devoid of a word of thanks for his work, that his appointment would end on 31 August 1940. He did not protest. The termination of the Rockefeller grant was reason enough for ending his contract, he said in 1967, his understanding being that his director's salary was paid from the grant. In fact, the Rockefeller Foundation did not permit its funds to be used for that purpose, and McGill had paid his salary all along. Had Marsh known this, would he have fought his nonrenewal? We cannot know. And if his work had been tinged by *right*-wing bias, would he have lost his job? The question answers itself.[49]

Shedding Forsey was more difficult than getting rid of Marsh. Forsey's had always been a teaching appointment, and his nonrenewal was bound to prompt charges that McGill had fired a radical. Although he had toned down his language after his speech to the St James Literary Society in October 1933, he remained conspicuous. He was a co-author of the LSR's book *Social Planning for Canada*, had written three booklets for the LSR and contributed two chapters to *Towards the Christian Revolution*, the book issued by the Fellowship for a Christian Social Order. He was also active – a good deal more so than Marsh – in the controversial campaign for the disallowance of the Padlock Act that had been passed in 1937 by the government of Maurice Duplessis in order to harass people thought to be communists. Neither Douglas nor James would have wanted it believed that such activities were the reason for Forsey's nonrenewal. Other grounds had to be found.

In June 1940 James informed Forsey that he was being reappointed for 1940–1 but added, 'It is my understanding that your success in obtaining the Doctor of Philosophy degree this spring was to have been the criterion for deciding your future career in the University.' Since Forsey had failed to get this degree, and James, 'I must therefore assume that [your] appointment as Lecturer will not be renewed next year, i.e. for the session 1941–42.'[50]

Forsey wrote in his memoirs that no such agreement existed. This is borne out by a letter that his department head, J.C. Hemmeon, wrote to him in July 1940. Reporting 'a long and heated conversation' with James, Hemmeon told Forsey: 'There was no understanding that the rejection of your thesis by the outside examiner should be the test. [James] sent me a copy of his letter to you and I replied at once, protesting strongly against his decision and denying the existence of any understanding such as he refers to. We shall see what we shall see.'[51]

What they saw was a letter from James to Forsey in December, stating that it had been agreed in 1939 to postpone a final decision on Forsey's position until the summer of 1940, 'in order that your doctoral dissertation might provide the evidence which the then Dean and Principal required.' He regretted that Forsey had failed but said 'that this criterion must still be the determining factor' and that he would not recommend him for reappointment. Forsey's reply controverted the principal's letter in every particular, but James did not intend to debate the issue. 'Thank you very much for your letter of December 18th, acknowledging my previous communication,' he wrote in early January 1941. Forsey was through.[52]

Having won a Guggenheim Fellowship, Forsey left in triumph. Any inclination to resist was sapped by an awareness that he would have few allies among his colleagues. 'Rabbits,' he called them in a letter to Frank Underhill: 'Hemmeon fought hard till he found the Principal had on file recommendations for my dismissal from Leacock and three former Deans ... and found also that he would have almost no support from anyone here if it came to a showdown.' Forsey predicted that Hemmeon or Scott might soon need help: 'There you'd have a clear case, unaccompanied by any recommendations for dismissal, or thèses manquées!'[53]

Did Forsey know that C.H. Cahan, a Forsey family friend who had been secretary of state in R.B. Bennett's cabinet, had written to Sir Edward Beatty urging that Forsey be retained even though his views were unorthodox? 'I can assure you that Mr. Forsey's personal opinions on political and social questions have no influence on the action which the University authorities contemplate taking,' Beatty replied; it was Forsey's poor teaching and his failure to complete his thesis that were the reasons for his nonrenewal. If Forsey knew of this exchange, he would have had even less desire to challenge his dismissal. As for Forsey's surmise that James would soon move against Hemmeon or Scott, this was almost certainly groundless. Both had tenure. To dismiss them would not have been impossible, but it certainly would have been messy, exposing McGill to a storm of criticism.[54]

Were there any grounds for the statement that Leacock and three deans had recommended that Forsey be let go? The files that are open to researchers do not bear this out. McGill has closed a file marked 'Economics and Political Science: Forsey Dismissal,' but I have been informed by Helen Forsey, who has been allowed to examine this file, that it contains no letters from Leacock or any arts dean recommending that her father be dismissed.[55] And what of the alleged agreement linking Forsey's reappointment to the completion of his thesis? Douglas may have misinformed James, or Hemmeon and Forsey may have chosen to forget an agreement that had become inconvenient, or James may simply have invented it. The last of these is perhaps most likely, for the 'agreement' served nicely to get rid of Forsey while neutralizing the issue of his politics.

Writing in 1969, James accepted full responsibility for the decision to expel Forsey: 'It is now more than a quarter of a century since I had to face Hemmeon ... and tell him I would not recommend to the Board of Governors the re-appointment of Eugene Forsey who, troublesome as he was, constituted less of a menace to the university than [Stanley] Gray does now. It was not a pleasant task and a lot of very unpleasant things were said about me ... I still think however that this kind of decisive action is the only way to deal with a problem of this kind.'[56] Forsey's politics, it seems, was the issue after all.

Expelling Marsh and Forsey may have damaged McGill more than it did either of the two men themselves. Marsh became research adviser to the Ottawa-based Committee on Postwar Reconstruction, headed by none other than James, and in 1943 he wrote its *Report on Social Security for Canada*, which has been described by the historian Michael Bliss as 'the most important single document in the history of the development of the welfare state in Canada.'[57] After the war, Marsh worked for the United Nations before joining the University of British Columbia in 1950 and teaching there until his retirement twenty years later. Forsey also landed on his feet. He returned to Canada from a year's study and writing at Harvard to become director of research for the Canadian Congress of Labour, a post he held until he retired in 1969. Appointed to the Senate in 1970, he was for a decade one of the Red Chamber's brightest ornaments. His book *The Royal Power of Dissolution of Parliament in the British Commonwealth* (1943) has become a classic.

Commenting on 'the Douglas-Beatty strategy' of terminating the Social Science Research Project and expelling Marsh and Forsey, Stanley Brice Frost writes, 'The thrust of social science research in the university was dissipated, and never again achieved the same sense of a unified purpose.' The effects of the strategy reinforced the ill effects of the resignation in 1938 of a promising young sociologist, Everett C. Hughes. He had begun his important book *French Canada in Transition* (1943) under the aegis of the Social Science Research Project.[58]

As faculty members on annual appointment, Forsey and Marsh were highly vulnerable. Given Douglas's negative view of socialist academics, a view apparently shared by James, their eventual expulsion was almost a foregone conclusion. But the expulsions were handled so skilfully that no one, Marsh and Forsey included, grasped what precisely had taken place. Academic freedom was infringed in the nonrenewals of the two social scientists, but little in the way of controversy resulted. James and probably also Beatty (and Douglas) must have been pleased. In 1939 there had been three socialists on the faculty of McGill. Two years later only Frank Scott was left.

7

The Second World War

War began on 1 September 1939 with Germany's invasion of Poland. Pressured by a public opinion that had turned against further appeasement of Adolf Hitler, Britain and France declared war on Germany two days later. Most Canadians regarded Canada's entry into the conflict as a foregone conclusion. The War Measures Act came into effect on the first day of September; the Defence of Canada Regulations followed on the third. The country did not formally declare war until another week had passed, but emotionally Canadians (apart from most Québécois) entered the conflict the moment Britain did. And once at war, many Canadians saw solidarity in the face of the enemy as essential. Academic freedom was immediately at risk.

The first wartime incident involving academic freedom centred on the McGill historian Edward R. Adair. He was no stranger to controversy. In 1937 he had caused offence in Roman Catholic circles by criticizing the church in Spain, where a civil war was raging, and in Quebec; in 1938 he had attacked British policy at Munich. But these incidents were small change compared with the commotion caused by his assessment of recent Polish history in November 1939. Speaking to the Rotary Club of Montreal, Adair sought to put Poland's collapse in historical context. After identifying the country's mainly domestic weaknesses, he said; 'There is one last weakness I cannot ignore – the trust that Poland appears to have reposed in the guarantee given them by ... Mr. [Neville] Chamberlain.' This 'was a desperate attempt on his part to save his face and to save the prestige of his foreign policy and that of the Conservative Party.' Men like Winston Churchill and Lloyd George had warned Chamberlain that Poland could be helped only if Britain formed an alliance with the Soviet Union. 'This warning,' said Adair, 'Mr. Chamberlain was stupid enough to ignore and the inevitable happened. Russia made her own arrangements with Germany and Poland fell.'[1]

Adair's unflattering comment on Chamberlain's foreign policy caused a furore. The *Montreal Star*'s editor charged that Adair had given aid and comfort to the enemy: 'We yield to nobody in our defence of freedom of speech, but we are equally insistent that such freedom, when it is allowed to degenerate into license, ceases to be either a virtue or a right.' Some time later the editor quoted approvingly a point made by F.H. Wilkinson, rector of the Church of St James the Apostle, in a recent sermon: 'Anything that tends to offend [against] good taste and good judgment, and work against the best interest of the majority, is a violation of free speech.' Adair had offended grievously.[2]

The *Gazette* took a similar line, its editor denying that he sought to curtail either academic freedom or free speech: 'Nobody has ever suggested that Mr. Adair's opinions would be bad for Canadians to hear, or that the loyalty of Montreal would be shaken by the discovery that this eminent thinker does not approve of the Republic of Poland or of the Prime Minister of Britain.' But there was another dimension: 'This is a war of morale. We have reason to believe that already the unity of the German nation is cracking under Nazi tyranny.' Adair's remarks would 'encourage the German people to support Hitler.'[3]

Adair was not without defenders. Among them was the Law Undergraduate Society, which sent an official letter to the *McGill Daily*: 'We are ostensibly fighting a war for the preservation of freedom; if in order to be successful in that effort, it has become necessary to suspend the ordinary democratic rights of free speech, free press, and academic freedom, then ... the war is not a just one, and should be stopped at once. Satan cannot cast out Satan.'[4] But this was a minority view. Those who wrote letters to newspaper editors were mostly of the view that McGill should 'deal with' Adair, preferably by dismissing him.

While the debate raged in the press, McGill's administrative officers said nothing. Lewis Douglas, whose principalship was about to end, did not believe that academic freedom was at stake – 'for him the issue was responsibility during time of war'[5] – but he did not comment publicly. His successor, F. Cyril James, was principal-in-waiting, and public statements were not yet his responsibility.

Nor did Sir Edward Beatty say anything, though as chancellor he was a likely spokesman at a time when one principal was passing the baton to another. To Dalhousie's Carleton Stanley, who had urged him not to heed demands for Adair's dismissal, Beatty wrote: 'You may be assured that nobody is excited up here about Professor Adair's indiscreet speech ... It was an unwise speech to make, is harmful to the University and has created further anxiety as to the quality of teaching at McGill'; but no one proposed to silence or dismiss him.[6]

Stanley's response captured the ambivalence of a university president concerned to protect academic free speech while knowing the problems this could cause. 'Believe me, I have my troubles too about these things ...,' he wrote. 'It is hard enough not to be caught off-balance on some occasions.' He went on to express disappointment with the attitude of the *Gazette*, which he read regularly: 'All I ask ... is that the journalists allow the academic folk the same freedom which the journalists demand for themselves.'[7]

Stanley knew how difficult this could be. In late 1938, speaking on the national network of the CBC, he had debated academic freedom with C.O. Knowles, editor of the Toronto *Telegram*, who had argued that academic freedom was undesirable if it allowed professors to speak publicly on issues of current interest. The prestige they enjoyed meant that when they got things wrong they did real harm, stated Knowles. They should stick to timeless truths and leave current events to journalists and politicians. 'If our universities are to become hotbeds of propaganda, melting pots of half truths, and homes for the propagation of idle political theories, then Time must pass the university by and Truth must settle in other halls unmarked by this taint. The way to keep the standards of our universities high ... is to regard truth as more desirable than unlimited academic freedom.'[8] Stanley had had no difficulty in exposing the flaws in Knowles's position on academic free speech as well as on the existence of some great Truth which it was the duty of professors to shield from harm. But he had not changed Knowles's mind, and he must have remembered the debate when he was writing to Beatty.

A curious aspect of the history of academic freedom is the limited tolerance that academic free speech received from segments of the press. In the 1930s and 1940s some newspapers, notably the *Ottawa Citizen*, *Toronto Star*, and *Winnipeg Free Press*, generally upheld it, but more of them, including the Toronto *Telegram*, *Winnipeg Tribune*, *Montreal Star*, *Gazette*, and *Quebec Chronicle-Telegraph*, usually attacked it. In part this may have been a turf war. Journalists claimed the advantage when current events were at issue, for this was terrain on which professors, impractical by definition and ostensibly obliged to shun partisanship, appeared as interlopers. More important was a reluctance to accommodate views that were likely to offend readers and advertisers. By the 1920s most of the costs of newspapers were being met from the sale of advertising space. An advertising executive, Carlton McNaught, wrote in 1940 that the result of this growing dependence on advertising had been, 'on the one hand, an effort to please as many and offend as few readers as possible, and on the other hand, a certain tenderness of conscience where the interests of advertisers are concerned.' As well, the industrialization of the press had made it seem natural 'that a publisher should be first and foremost a business man' with 'a point of view which is that of the business groups in a community rather than that of other ... groups.' A publisher's point of view, McNaught added, was 'more likely than not to be reflected in his paper's treatment of news' and to influence editorial policy.[9]

The business point of view, committed to capitalism and often also to the British connection, was widespread in the newspaper industry when the war began. In any case, the coming of war made the views of dissidents particularly unwelcome. When seas are rough, has anyone the right to rock the boat?

The storm set off by Adair's speech had subsided by the time Stanley and Beatty exchanged letters in late November. Although Adair remained in his position, he may have learned his lesson. He did not make trouble again. More generally, the incident probably reinforced habits of discretion that suited most academics well enough.

As in 1914, civil liberties were at risk from the outset of the war, but nonconformists who had not yet got the point surely got it on 6 June 1940 when, under the Defence of Canada Regulations, Ottawa proscribed the Communist Party of Canada (CPC) and fifteen other organizations. In July 1940 the Jehovah's Witnesses were added to the list.[10]

Only two academics seem to have been tried under the Defence of Canada Regulations. One was a Dalhousie law professor, Allan Findlay, who was charged because in October 1939 he included a crude sketch of Halifax harbour in a letter to his fiancée in Denmark. Intercepted by the censors, the sketch was held to be potentially useful to the Germans, with whom the young woman was believed to be in contact. The board chairman J. McGregor Stewart thought Findlay should be fired, but Carleton Stanley, who believed the letter to be innocuous, resisted. A magistrate found Findlay 'technically guilty' but fined him one dollar plus costs of six dollars – an acquittal in all but name. He kept his job.[11]

The other trial had a different outcome. Samuel Levine, a research fellow in geophysics at the University of Toronto, was charged in September 1940 with two counts of possessing communist pamphlets. He claimed that they belonged to a boarder and that he had not known of their existence, but the magistrate trying the case believed neither his testimony nor that of the boarder and sentenced Levine to six months' imprisonment. His appeal was denied in December.[12]

Upon Levine's arrest, President H.J. Cody suspended him pending the outcome of his trial and later his appeal. Only after the latter was denied did Cody recommend dismissal. He doubted Levine's guilt and argued for his early discharge on the grounds that he would be doing more for his country in a laboratory than in prison. 'Personally,' Cody added, 'I have never thought that the man had any interest whatever in politics.' After the RCMP transferred Levine to an internment camp upon completion of his sentence, Cody helped secure his release, which was accomplished in October 1941.[13]

A note in the American journal *Science* suggested that Levine's reinstatement was appropriate, and several people wrote to Cody to urge him to effect it. In replying, he denied that anti-Semitism had played a part in the university's treatment of Levine, explained that the research fellow had been paid from outside funds, and stated that Toronto lacked the money to employ him. By April 1942 Levine had given up trying to find work in Canada and was soliciting Cody's help to enable him to enter the United States.[14]

Levine's story is doubly sad because it unfolded in the context of a war fought to defend human freedom. The abuse of his civil liberties was the work of a government all too willing to meet the wishes of the RCMP and the Catholic hierarchy in Quebec for a repressive policy towards real and imagined communists. By the time Levine regained his freedom, of course, public attitudes to communists were shifting. After Germany attacked the Soviet Union on 22 June 1941, the CPC's policy changed from opposition to the war to unstinting support, and by the second half of 1942 all interned communists were released. In the summer of 1943, the Labor-Progressive Party (LPP) was established as a legal entity. It was the CPC in all but name, but that party, paradoxically, was still banned.[15]

Few academics were more suspicious of the LPP and the Soviet Union than Watson Kirkconnell, a professor of literature at McMaster and a polyglot who served Ottawa by monitoring the ethnic press for subversion. Cooperation between countries with conflicting ideologies was 'necessary for the political equilibrium of the world,' he wrote in 1944, but our view of the Soviet Union should be clear-eyed and 'not based on sentiment and illusion.' Communism was no greater friend of freedom than Nazism.[16]

Criticism of the Soviet Union was unfashionable in 1944: for three years, Canadians had been propagandized to see the Soviets as gallant heroes and allies in the war against Nazi Germany. Kirkconnell came under attack, especially after he wrote a series of articles critical of Soviet imperialism and domestic policy that appeared in the Toronto *Telegram* in April and May of 1945. According to Kirkonnell's memoirs, Albert Matthews, chairman of McMaster's board of governors, told him in mid-May 1945 'that he had been waited on by Joe Atkinson, proprietor of the *Toronto Daily Star*, and a lady member of his editorial staff.' And 'this precious pair,' wrote Kirkconnell, 'had urged him to dismiss me from my professorship because of my articles in the *Telegram*.'[17]

There is no corroborating evidence for this story and no reference to it in Ross Harkness's biography of Atkinson, but the *Star*'s hostility to Kirkconnell is on record. On 29 May 1945 a *Star* editorial charged that 'those who stir up hostility toward the Soviet Union, who try to weaken the bonds between the

Allied Nations, are doing what the Nazis want done. Such people are carrying on Goebbels's work now that his printing presses have been stopped.' Two weeks later the *Star*, taking its lead from *Saturday Night*, contradicted Kirkconnell's claim that the Soviets were abusing the Jews and claimed that he had 'revealed his intention to arouse hatred toward Russia.'[18]

It seems less than likely that Atkinson sought Kirkconnell's dismissal, however. The *Toronto Star* favoured academic free speech more consistently than almost any other Canadian journal of the time. Kirkconnell may not have remembered clearly what was said two decades before he wrote his memoirs; or Matthews may have misrepresented Atkinson's views. In either case, neither Kirkconnell's academic freedom nor his job was in any danger. When he left McMaster in 1948 it was to become president of Acadia University.

The University of Alberta biochemist George Hunter first came under RCMP surveillance in 1939. Scottish born and educated, he taught at the University of Toronto before becoming professor and head of biochemistry in the Faculty of Medicine at Alberta in 1929. Independent of mind, he showed a healthy scepticism in the face of authority. As well, he took a broad view of science and the scientist's social role. A researcher with a particular interest in nutrition, he became a fellow of the Royal Society of Canada in 1933.[19]

The Depression radicalized Hunter. He became conversant with the writings of Marx, Engels, and Lenin, and took an interest in 'the experiment going on in the USSR.' In 1939 he and his wife met veterans of the Mackenzie-Papineau Battalion, recently returned from the Spanish Civil War, and supported other communist-sponsored causes. This brought them to the attention of the RCMP.[20]

Anticommunist surveillance on campus reached a peak by the late 1930s and early war years. The RCMP *Intelligence Bulletin* claimed in 1940 that 'the virus of Communism, long coursing ... in our social blood-stream, has now reached the heart of our educational system as represented by undergraduates and even college professors.' Noting that the RCMP's own surveillance reports contradicted this claim, Paul Axelrod comments, 'Though communists were surely to be found in some university-based organizations, they were a tiny minority.' Hunter, it seems, was regarded as part of that small group.[21]

In April 1940 an RCMP informer who was enrolled in Hunter's introductory course wrote a report on the last lecture of the session. President W.A.R. Kerr received a copy; it stated that Hunter had given 'a philosophical discourse upon the relationship of Science and Religion and Modern Concepts of Living' whose 'general trend ... was anti-Christian and pro-Marxism.' A short list of comments critical of capitalism, disdainful of the Bible, and admiring of the

Soviet Union followed. The report concluded: 'On various occasions during the past year, Dr. HUNTER has spoken along these lines, but today more than previously he distrubed [*sic*] his students, raiding [*sic*] the ire of many, but still receiving an interested and attentive listening from others.'[22]

Kerr could have ignored a report from someone he did not know and whose veracity he could not test. In view of the remarks Hunter was alleged to have made, however, and because the document emanated from the RCMP, he probably rejected this option out of hand. He could have asked the biochemist to comment, of course, but instead he apprised the board of governors' executive committee of the document. The committee then asked him to get a statement from Hunter.[23]

Kerr saw the biochemist on 19 April, showed him the informer's report, and requested a written response for discussion by the board at its May meeting. Three days later Hunter sent Kerr a letter that criticized the report in detail and offered his own recollections of what he had said. He disowned much of what the informer had ascribed to him. His lecture had been 'along broad philosophical lines,' Hunter wrote. He denied that it had been anti-Christian and doubted that it could be described as pro-Marxian. He denied, too, that he regularly digressed from teaching to discuss unrelated subjects. 'It has been my practice in previous years to give a concluding ... lecture along philosophical lines,' he explained. 'This year, perhaps unwisely, I continued as usual to exercise the academic freedom which we have hitherto enjoyed. If in your opinion, Mr. President, such lectures [should] be not given in future, I shall, of course, discontinue them.'[24]

The board met on 14 May. The minutes indicate that most members did not believe Hunter's account of what he had said, and all agreed that he 'should not have presented ... his so-called philosophical ideas to his students.' Several wanted to dismiss him, but 'it was finally decided to have Dr. Hunter appear before the Board.' The chairman, Chief Justice Horace Harvey, informed Hunter 'that the Board were in possession of evidence through the R.C.M.P. that he had made certain statements in his final lecture to his class which were of a political nature with a Communistic bias.' (It was a sign of the times, perhaps, the war having taken a sudden turn for the worse, that an anonymous police spy should seem more credible than a distinguished scientist.) Hunter claimed that his lecture had been misquoted and wrongly interpreted, but he 'expressed regret that objection had been taken to his philosophical ideas ... and stated that in future he would refrain from giving this type of lecture.' Some board members still wanted to fire him; others wanted him placed on probation 'while the R.C.M.P. continue their investigations.' Eventually Kerr 'was instructed to write to Dr. Hunter to the effect that any further complaints or criticism would place him in a very difficult position and endanger his retention of his post.'[25]

Kerr's letter informed Hunter that the board objected to his use of class time to discuss 'subjects in which you possess no professional authority.' This was all the more censurable because he had dealt 'with questions of political theory, sociology and religion, all of them matters of grave difference in the community.' Canada was at war, Kerr reminded Hunter, and 'tempers and nerves [were] strung to the breaking point. One incautious word might put the University into an extremely difficult position.' If 'the present offence' should recur, Hunter's position would be in grave danger.[26]

However, Hunter never actually received this warning. Acting on Chief Justice Harvey's advice, Kerr did not send him the letter. Harvey believed that the CPC would soon be proscribed, that Hunter would be interned, 'and in that case we would have nothing to do but dispense with his services.'[27] In June 1940 the party was indeed outlawed, but Hunter remained at liberty. The belief that he was a communist lingered, though, and would later serve him ill.

The Hunter affair was handled in deep secrecy. Outside the board of governors, hardly anyone knew what had happened. This was a complete contrast to the highly public scandal that embroiled the University of Alberta in 1941, one result of which was the rescinding of the policy on political candidacy that had come into effect five years earlier.

In May 1941 the senate committee on honorary degrees unanimously recommended that a doctorate be conferred on William Aberhart, premier of the province and minister of education since 1935. The senate baulked. In spite of President Kerr's assertion that 'ever since his accession to power, [Aberhart had] shown himself a warm friend of higher education and of the ... University of Alberta,' the motion to grant the degree was narrowly defeated in a secret ballot.[28] (Whether the senate's academic or nonacademic members were mainly responsible cannot therefore be known.)

This was gravely embarrassing, for Kerr and the board's chairman H.H. Parlee had already invited Aberhart to accept the degree of Doctor of Laws and to deliver the convocation address. This, Kerr later explained, was the usual procedure. It had not occurred to him that the senate would disregard 'its invariable custom and practice' of adopting the committee's recommendation, especially since every previous premier who owed his position to election had been given an honorary degree. 'It is clear that for reasons of personal grudge or grievance, politics have been introduced into this institution,' Kerr wrote to Lieutenant-Governor J.H. Blackmore in a letter that accompanied his resignation.[29] (Until 1967 the president of the University of Alberta was appointed by the cabinet.)

Aberhart must have resented the snub he had received, and in August 1941 he took a revenge of sorts. The government appointed a 'Survey Committee' to carry out a detailed examination of the university. Among the issues to be examined were 'the use now being made of the monies available and probable financial needs in the near future,' the relationship between the courses offered and the need for them, 'the ability of the Province to finance them, and the number of students served by each,' the qualifications and teaching loads of faculty members, and the university's research performance.[30]

Fortunately for the university, the committee members included Parlee and the acting president, Robert Newton. When the committee reported, it was at pains to show how useful the institution was while also stating 'that an independent University, free from outside control, is one that is most satisfactory and best serves the state.'[31] With the hullabaloo over his honorary degree receding in memory, Aberhart acquiesced in the principle of autonomy.

One of the committee's recommendations sanctioned political activity by professors. This owed much to Newton. Having served in the federal public service, he had noticed 'that the need for caution in public utterance to avoid statements at variance with government policy tended to cramp and restrain expression, and in the long run to discourage constructive thinking about public questions.' Newton thought this unfortunate; Aberhart agreed that the public responsibilities of professors should be widened.[32]

The survey committee report stated that the university had a duty to give leadership 'with regard to social and economic problems' and that professors 'ought to be encouraged rather than restrained from exercising their full rights of citizenship.' They should be free to participate in politics 'unless it appeared, in particular instances, that the activities of any member of the staff were prejudicial to the University.' The board ought not 'to pass general regulations restricting the political activities of members of the staff' but should deal with each case 'on its merits and as the occasion arises.' All committee members supported this, with a minority arguing that the legislature should give it statutory force.[33]

When the board of governors came to consider the matter in June 1942, it learned that the government also favoured the rescinding of the policy proscribing political candidacy. Some board members were unhappy about this, but Newton, recently confirmed in the presidency, argued in favour of change. As the minutes record, 'The ruling in 1935 had created controversy and made enemies for the university. He thought it safe in general to trust the discretion of the staff and deal with any unusual case on its merits.' Some months passed while a board committee studied the matter. In December 1942 Newton moved that the policy on participation in active politics be rescinded. The motion passed.[34]

Thenceforth Alberta permitted professors to run for federal and provincial office (though until the 1960s no professor seems to have taken advantage of this). Like UBC's board of governors a decade earlier, Alberta's board felt government pressure to loosen the restraints on professors. In these two cases, at least, academic freedom benefited from interference with institutional autonomy.

In the history and mythology of academic freedom in Canada, only the Harry Crowe case at United College in 1958 looms larger than the attempt in 1940–1 to dismiss Frank Underhill. The affair began innocently. On 23 August 1940 Underhill was a member of a Couchiching Conference panel discussing 'A United American Front.' There was much to discuss. The war in Europe was going badly. Denmark, Norway, and the Low Countries had fallen to the Germans in April and May; France had followed in June. The Royal Air Force and the Luftwaffe were locked in combat over England. An early invasion of the island kingdom seemed possible.

In response to what was happening overseas, President Franklin D. Roosevelt and Prime Minister William Lyon Mackenzie King met at Ogdensburg, New York, on 17 and 18 August to establish a Permanent Joint Board on Defence. That Roosevelt was prepared to sign 'what amounted to a joint defence pact with a belligerent ... had to count as a gain for the hard-pressed Allies,' J.L. Granatstein writes. With Britain in danger, King thought it 'prudent and wise to safeguard the Dominion by accepting the protection of the United States. No Canadian government could have done otherwise.'[35]

Speaking at Geneva Park five days later, Underhill outlined the likely results of the Ogdensburg agreement. It would help the Canadian war effort; it also introduced a new phase in Canada's relations with the United States. Canadians now had 'two loyalties, the old one to the British connection involving our backing up of Britain, and the new one to North America involving common action with the United States.'[36] Both would persist, observed Underhill, but over time our ties with Britain would weaken while those with our American neighbour would strengthen.

Underhill's remarks seemed unexceptionable to many of his listeners. But not to all. Henry Marshall Tory of the National Research Council objected: 'I say to you [that] it is the duty of every one of us to see that the thing that is likely to happen doesn't happen.' C.H. Hale of the *Orillia Packet and Times* asked whether the university ought to be giving Underhill 'the opportunity to inoculate the coming generation of Canadian citizens with views subversive of the accepted traditions and established political status of the Dominion.' Some weeks later the *Toronto Telegram* stated that the historian's predictions might warrant internment. Former Prime Minister Arthur Meighen privately urged Minister of Justice Ernest Lapointe to intern Underhill.[37]

President Cody received several letters urging that the historian be fired. One man called him 'a menace to truth and patriotism,' fit to be 'a teacher of German youth but not ... a guide to Britons.' A past president of the alumni federation asked whether Underhill could not be transferred 'to the staff of some Institution of some English-speaking country where his philosophy ... would be less offensive to graduates and public alike.' If today Underhill's remarks seem to have foretold the almost inevitable, in 1940 they struck some people as treasonable.[38]

Underhill was taken aback by the criticism. Most surprising to him was an editorial in the *Toronto Star*, usually a defender of academic free speech, stating that if Underhill had been quoted accurately he had chosen 'a most inopportune time' to make such remarks. 'With the Empire at war for the preservation of democracy and Canada herself wholeheartedly in that war with all the resources she can command,' he should have kept his own counsel.[39]

It was to the *Star* that Underhill replied, complaining that reports of his speech had been inaccurate. Aware that the press coverage would trouble President Cody, Underhill sent him a copy of this letter with the comment, 'If you wish ..., I can refer you to plenty of well known citizens of Toronto and elsewhere who heard what I said and did not find in my remarks the undesirable qualities which the Toronto editors have so characteristically uncovered.'[40]

When Cody received this letter he already had before him one from Chancellor Sir William Mulock, calling for an 'immediate investigation,' and one from a board member, Balmer Neilly, urging that Underhill be dismissed. Cody asked the historian for the text of his remarks, which Underhill then sent him, together with a covering letter explaining that his speech had been made from 'fairly brief notes' but that 'the line of argument was certainly exactly in this way.' Underhill added, 'I haven't consciously watered down in my typescript anything that I may have said.'[41]

A police investigation, set in train by Ontario's attorney general, concluded that no action was required under the Defence of Canada Regulations, there being no evidence that Underhill had said anything to warrant it. But this mattered little to the board, which on 12 September agreed unanimously with Mulock and Neilly that Underhill should be dismissed, in part because of the recent incident, in part because of his record over the preceding thirteen years. Pending a report from Cody and an opinion from the university's solicitor, though, the board postponed the matter to the next meeting.[42]

Cody's attitude was crucial, for the University Act required the president to recommend dismissal – and Cody was under pressure from two sides. Letters in support of Underhill were reaching him in number. C.E. Silcox, a Toronto clergyman who had been on the panel with Underhill, saw a 'conspiracy to "get"

Frank' and warned that his dismissal would give ammunition to the 'die-hard isolationists' in the United States. E.J. Tarr, the president of Monarch Life, who had been in the audience, said that 'there was nothing in the address that could reasonably be interpreted as an undermining of Canada's war effort' or of its ties with Britain. B.K. Sandwell of *Saturday Night* wrote that if Underhill was fired, the result would be a discussion on 'the broad subject of academic freedom which might have most undesirable consequences ... in the United States.'[43]

Principal Malcolm Wallace of University College predicted that a dismissal would split the university, with 'the more liberal-minded' professors tending 'to denounce the action taken by the Board, and to declare that the University has ceased to be a centre of genuine scholarly discussion and investigation.' As well, Underhill was defended in person by James S. McLean, the president of Canada Packers, and by James M. Macdonnell of the National Trust Company. These two had been 'magnificent,' he wrote to Carleton Stanley. 'Malcolm Wallace also worked nobly and a great many other friends.'[44]

When the governors met on 16 September they had before them a letter from the university's solicitor, Hamilton Cassels. Without a verbatim account of the address, he wrote, 'it would be unwise to discharge Professor Underhill basing the action on the ground that he had made the statements recently attributed to him.' Furthermore, 'I do not think ... earlier statements could now be considered as constituting grounds for dismissal.' But if the board thought it 'undesirable' to maintain Underhill because 'the interests of the University and perhaps the welfare of the students might suffer,' advised Cassels, it could give him notice effective 30 June 1941 or pay him his salary to that date in lieu of notice.[45]

Cody then stated, 'There is no stenographic report of [Underhill's] speech and of the subsequent discussions, nor is there other satisfactory evidence to support the published account of what he said. I therefore recommend that no action be taken in respect thereof.' The board reluctantly agreed, and the chairman, D. Bruce Macdonald, told the press that 'the incident was closed.'[46]

Underhill heaved a sigh of relief. To his friend Larry MacKenzie, recently appointed president of the University of New Brunswick, he wrote: 'This was the nastiest business I've ever gone through ... What saved me was chiefly the argument that it would look terrible in the U.S. just now for a professor to be fired for his pro-American sentiments ... Take a drink with your professors now and then, and they'll never get you into trouble.'[47] Whether the thought of having an occasional drink with Cody really appealed to Underhill must remain an open question.

Was the incident closed? A worried Carleton Stanley told Underhill that at a meeting in Ottawa, Cody had said he thought some people were trying to 'ambush' Underhill. Cody had 'complained wearily,' said Stanley, 'of what he had to go through on your account, and thought that if you knew his weariness you would say nothing until the war is over.'[48]

The chief source of overt pressure was the Toronto *Telegram*, which on 18 September denounced the board of governors for failing to discipline Underhill and hoped that the government and people of Ontario might yet have something to say about the matter. In response, the *Globe and Mail* argued that it was not the board's job to censure Underhill's utterances as a private citizen, however foolish his remarks might be. This argument did not convince a businessman who urged Cody to read *Social Planning for Canada* and *Towards the Christian Revolution*, and asked whether their authors were fit to teach history, economics, politics, and religion to young people: 'It is difficult to understand why university authorities should allow themselves to be blocked by "the magic circle of academic freedom" which unbalanced teachers draw around their sacred forms.'[49]

If the *Telegram* was Underhill's most vocal enemy, he was in greater danger from Balmer Neilly. At a board meeting on 26 September, the engineer gave notice of motion 'that the President be instructed to advise Professor F.H. Underhill that this Board will not continue to pay [him] a salary equivalent to that which he is now receiving.' Neilly's purpose became clear at the next meeting. Quoting Underhill's 1939 promise to do his best 'to behave as reasonable men would expect a professor to behave,' Neilly commented that: 'few honorable men would stoop to couching a voluntary promise in such slimy terms' – and that Underhill always seemed to have his fingers crossed behind his back. 'That we are today discussing his conduct for the eighth time in less than two years proves ... that he has lost our confidence and become a common nuisance to the University,' concluded Neilly. Whatever Underhill's worth had been when first appointed in 1927, it was surely less now.[50]

Chief Justice Hugh Rose then pointed out that Underhill had a continuing appointment and therefore could not be *re*-engaged. This kept a majority of the board from voting for the motion, whereupon Neilly withdrew it, 'pending a Report from the President.' Anticipating that Cody would again counsel inaction, Neilly then proposed an alternate motion: 'That the President be instructed to advise Prof. Underhill that this Board will not authorize, in next year's estimates, the payment to him of a salary exceeding the sum of One Dollar per year.'[51]

This colourable device proved unnecessary. Having decided that Underhill was more trouble than he was worth, President Cody was at last prepared to recommend dismissal.[52] At a special board meeting on 19 December, he noted that

Underhill had repeatedly been asked to explain his public utterances and had been told that a faculty member of a provincial university 'must, in the substance, manner and opportuneness of his public statements, impose upon himself ... restraints demanded by the grave responsibility which inheres in the teaching office and by the recognition of his responsibility for the welfare of the institution in which he teaches.' Underhill had been unable to apply such restraints, noted Cody, and his public statements had 'aroused widespread misunderstanding of and indeed hostility to this institution.'

The president went on to say that the university had 'during the course of its history enjoyed a full measure of academic freedom in research and in teaching,' but professors who used the language of the partisan aroused the fear that their university teaching might be 'so marked by bias as to interfere with its truth and fairness.' Besides, professors could not 'divest themselves of their obligation to the institution to which they belong.' Furthermore, Underhill had more than once offended against the spirit of promises not to involve the university in controversy. The board had so far shown 'great patience,' but it no longer had 'confidence in his willingness or his ability to carry out his promises of silence or amendment.'

The university suffered financially for keeping him, concluded Cody: 'Whether he goes or stays there will be trouble of some kind. We have had recurrent trouble over him ... ever since he became a member of the staff; we shall probably have trouble over him from some members of our staff, of our student body, and of our graduates, if he has to leave. Which trouble is it better to face?' To this question, Cody gave his own answer: 'Without reference to specific details of the writings or utterances of Professor Frank H. Underhill and viewing the record as a whole, I believe it is in the best interests of the University that his services be dispensed with; and I so recommend.'[53]

Nowhere did Cody discuss whether Underhill's comments, in August 1940 or at any other time, had been true or false. What mattered was not the accuracy or otherwise of the historian's utterances or whether he had made them in good faith, but the public response to them and the feared consequences for the institution. For Cody, as for many another university president, the autonomy and financial health of the university took precedence over academic free speech – and, indeed, over academic freedom itself except in forms that did not offend. By a delicious irony, however, Cody's recommendation to dismiss Underhill, though intended to protect the university, exposed it to an attack quite as strong as any it had incurred as a result of anything Underhill had ever said.

A majority of the board wanted to ascertain the government's attitude before acting, and the issue was deferred so that a delegation could meet the minister of education, Duncan McArthur. He proved agreeable to the proposal to dismiss Underhill, but when this was reported to the board, action was deferred once more until the next regular meeting, which was scheduled for early January. It was decided that before that meeting, Cody, Bruce Macdonald, and Leighton McCarthy would try to induce Underhill to resign quietly. 'Later, it was decided to replace the president by the chancellor, since Underhill's president, who had final say, had to appear impartial in the affair.' (Harry Crowe's 'Vishinsky corollary' comes to mind: 'It is important not only that justice be done but that it be seen to be done, especially when it is not being done.')[54]

More than four months had passed since his speech at Geneva Park by the time he received a summons to meet a committee of the board at 3:30 PM on Thursday, 2 January 1941, in Simcoe Hall. According to notes that Underhill made soon afterwards, Sir William Mulock spoke for about fifteen minutes. 'He explained that "public opinion as expressed in the newspapers and elsewhere" made it necessary that I should leave the University ..., that the Board considered that my continued presence on the staff was doing harm to the University,' and that Cody had recommended dismissal. The board had no wish to ruin Underhill's career, he was told, and it hoped he might find another post. In order to prevent 'a great fuss,' therefore, and in his own interest, the board proposed that he resign. Were he to do so, he would be allowed to keep the university's contributions to his pension plan and would probably also get a year's salary. Mulock asked Underhill to let the committee know before the board meeting on 9 January what his decision was, and 'Mr. McCarthy said that it was a case of mutual incompatibility ... and that the simple, sensible solution was separation.'

Underhill objected. Everyone would know why he was leaving, he said, and 'since universities do not take men on their staff who have been in trouble elsewhere ..., the proposition of this committee really meant that they were giving me a week's notice of a death sentence.' He pointed out what the others should have remembered from Cassels's letter of 16 September: the board's contributions to the Teachers Insurance and Annuity Association, the pension fund to which Toronto professors belonged, were Underhill's already. As well, he disputed the strength of the public demand for his dismissal. Macdonald then assured him that the board 'felt nothing but the greatest good will' towards him and that it was not threatening him. Underhill responded 'that it was useless to quarrel about forms of words when the situation that faced me was the end of my academic career. With this we parted. The interview lasted for about forty minutes.'[55]

Underhill quickly acquainted friends and colleagues with his predicament.

He also asked his lawyer for an opinion concerning his rights. These were few, Leopold Macaulay told him; he held his tenure during the board's pleasure, so if Cody recommended his dismissal, he was gone. Urgently, Underhill wrote to Frank Scott: 'This is an appeal for help to find me another job.'[56]

Another friend to whom he appealed, President Herbert Davis of Smith College, replied: 'I did not think that we should have the problem of refugee scholars from Canada quite so soon as this ... I can't help hoping that [Malcolm] Wallace and the rest will make it too hot for the Trustees to carry out this threat.' The heat, in fact, was on Cody. An anguished letter from Underhill's department head set the tone. 'I cannot find words to say how much I deplore this outcome,' Chester Martin wrote. 'Whenever you have asked my opinion I have given it consistently in favour of what appeared to me, and still appears to me, the less of two evils. I cannot help thinking that this outcome will only invite them both.' Deep division threatened the university, warned Martin, who felt 'despair.'[57]

Cody was the key. 'No appointments or promotions or dismissals can be made without his recommendation,' Underhill told Scott. That Cody had recommended dismissal, Underhill inferred from the meeting at Simcoe Hall, but he later wrote, 'I have since been told by members of the staff who have seen the President that [he] declares that I misunderstood this point.'[58]

Cody was probably already wondering whether he had done the right thing. Protests from faculty, students, alumni, and outsiders began reaching him almost immediately after the meeting on 2 January. All made one or more of the following points: academic freedom was in peril; Underhill was a good teacher whom the institution could ill afford to lose; the university's reputation would suffer if he were fired; and dismissing him would damage Canadian-American relations.[59]

On 7 January Cody met a deputation of senior faculty, led by Dean Samuel Beatty. The brief notes taken by Cody indicate that unhappiness ran deep. Several men wondered whether outside pressure was responsible for the board's action; others asked whether hostility to Underhill's pro-Americanism played a part. Harold Adams Innis cited the historian's war service as 'a cause of his delinquencies' and added that if he was dismissed there would be 'little hope of getting in good touch with labour.' Malcolm Wallace stressed once again that a dismissal would divide the university. Only W.P.M. Kennedy of the Department of Law, who said that the 'basis of academic freedom was common sense,' seemed to support Cody's stand.[60]

Cody attached a précis of his own remarks. The 'supreme question' was the 'welfare of university,' he wrote. 'The issue of freedom of speech – academic freedom – [is] not really involved ... Is there any method of getting rid of an unsatisfactory member of staff?' Another note read: 'Disregard of pol'l & financial considerations – the staff wd. be affected by these considerations.' And finally: 'The nuisance gets the sympathy.'[61]

The 'nuisance' was exerting himself on his own behalf. On 8 January he informed Macdonald of his refusal to resign and asked 'that if the Board at its meeting to-morrow decides to go further in this matter, you give me in writing a statement of the case against me, and that I then be afforded an opportunity of defending myself before the Board or a committee of the Board.' To Cody he wrote that he wished to be told in person why his dismissal was being contemplated. As well, 'I assume that I am also going to be allowed to present my defence to you before you finally make up your mind.'[62] This was shrewdly put. It reminded Cody that he had failed to observe due process. By assuming that the president was still weighing the matter, moreover, Underhill showed Cody an escape: he could withdraw his recommendation with little public loss of face.

The pressure on Cody was mounting. Two petitions, one signed by third- and fourth-year students in modern history, the other by 258 former students of Underhill, affirmed his integrity as a teacher. (The signatories included Claude Bissell, Gerald M. Craig, Bertrand Gerstein, Douglas LePan, Harold I. Nelson, Saul Rae, Albert Rose, and Gordon Skilling.) A Toronto lawyer, Evan Gray, asked Cody to make an 'uncompromising defence of academic freedom'; the Ottawa lawyer O.M. Biggar did the same. Clifford Sifton, newspaper owner and financier, stated that without academic freedom it would be hard to attract 'first class men' to the university, nor would they stay for long.[63]

A telegram from Hugh L. Keenleyside, the Canadian secretary of the recently formed Permanent Joint Board on Defence, asked that nothing be done until the 'present international crisis is ended.' To dismiss 'a man widely known in [the] United States as [an] exponent of [the] idea of continental cooperation might have [the] most serious repercussions.' He urged that a controversy be avoided 'which would create dissension at home and add to our difficulties abroad at a time when every effort should be concentrated on ... winning the war.'[64]

As Cody was mulling this over, Innis gave him a letter from J. Bartlet Brebner, a Canadian historian at Columbia University, who wondered 'whether there is much general recognition in Toronto of how serious an effect [a dismissal] would have down here.' Restraints on freedom of expresssion in Canada had already prompted negative comment, advised Brebner, and this was not the time to fire a professor for speaking his mind. 'Above all, can Canada risk widespread dissemination of extracts from the Canadian press charging Underhill with the sin of being pro-American?'[65]

Having decided that it was more trouble to keep Underhill than to let him go,

Cody found that he had miscalculated. Not only was the university under attack, but informed people were telling him that a dismissal would damage Canadian-American relations. The replies he dictated were querulous. 'I do not feel that ... academic freedom is involved,' he told Gray. To Biggar he wrote: 'A professor of History should be a historian and not merely an advocate. For the last thirteen years my predecessor and myself have had reason to reprove Professor Underhill because of ill-advised methods of speech.'[66]

That Underhill's style was the reason for the board's displeasure was an argument Cody pushed furthest in his reply to Clifford Sifton: 'There are 938 members of the teaching staff of the University and University College and the only one ... who has ever caused difficulty has been Professor Underhill and that not because of the substance of what he says but the manner in which he says it.'[67] This was untrue, but Cody, sensitive to charges that he was violating academic freedom, may have wanted to believe it.

To Hugh Keenleyside he wrote: 'I thought it wise to give the substance of it to the Board of Governors, although we had about the same time received a message from Mr. Hepburn stating that high authority in your Department had asked us to delay any action in regard to Professor Underhill.' Then irritation broke through. Cody was keen to foster cooperation between the Empire and the United States, he said, but 'I am really puzzled to see how the success of that co-operation can in any way be involved in the character and conduct of Professor Underhill.'[68]

Keenleyside assured Cody that British-American relations did not sink or swim with the board's treatment of Underhill. It would nevertheless be a mistake to dismiss him. Isolationists would depict the dismissal 'as a flagrant violation of academic freedom which could be compared with the purging of the universities of Germany and other totalitarian countries ... The liberal forces in the United States ... would be disappointed; all our enemies would be encouraged.' As well, observed Keenleyside, dismissing Underhill would do Canada no good in Britain, where the action 'would be looked upon as an indication that Canada has still a long way to go before reaching intellectual maturity. British universities do not fire their nonconformist professors.'[69]

Keenleyside had personal experience of the difficulties Underhill was facing. After assisting the 1924 presidential campaign of Senator Robert La Follette, he had lost his position at Syracuse University. He believed that academics were 'fully entitled to the free public expression of their political and other views.' But as he explains in his memoirs, rather than making this argument to Cody, it seemed expedient to make the case 'on the basis of its possible international repercussions.'[70]

Keenleyside claimed to be unaware that anyone in External Affairs had communicated with Mitchell Hepburn and said that he had written 'without prior reference to either the Prime Minister or the Under Secretary.' This was untrue. In fact, Keenleyside had shown O.D. Skelton a memorandum that he proposed to send to Mackenzie King signalling the ill effects of a dismissal on U.S. public opinion. Skelton, who must have remembered the attempt made in 1917 to force him out of Queen's, had endorsed Keenleyside's action, adding that not one member of the Toronto board seemed to have 'the faintest appreciation of the meaning of the liberty about which they yap so loudly when it is a question of Europe and not of Canada,' and that he could think of 'nothing more stupid or unnecessary than this action at the present time.'[71]

Rumours that Hepburn was behind the affair kept King from doing anything; his relations with the Ontario premier were far from cordial. Less constrained was one of King's secretaries, J.W. (Jack) Pickersgill, a former academic who, like Keenleyside, knew Underhill personally. Pickersgill discussed the case with Brooke Claxton, MP, another Underhill acquaintance, and on his advice approached Charles G. Power, minister of national defence for air, who was on good terms with Hepburn. Pickersgill explained the problems a dismissal might cause and asked whether Power could discreetly draw these to Hepburn's attention.

Power, it seems, told Hepburn that he was phoning at Pickersgill's request to say that King was concerned about the effect Underhill's dismissal might have on U.S. opinion. Unhappy that King's name and his own had been dragged in, Pickersgill tried to explain the foul-up to his boss. The prime minister's only comment was, 'Pickersgill, it just shows you can never be too careful.' But Pickersgill had the impression that King 'was not displeased that Power's telephone call ... had probably saved Underhill's job.'[72]

At a board meeting on 9 January, Cody read the telegram from Keenleyside and told the board of Hepburn's worries, which had been conveyed to him by Provincial Secretary Harry Nixon. Most of the governors still favoured dismissal and resented the pressure from Queen's Park as an infringement of institutional autonomy. After the meeting, Bruce Macdonald told the press that the board would resist outside influence, while Cody informed more than one person that 'if and when the Board of Governors take any action, they will do so freely, according to their own judgment and not under pressure ... from without.'[73]

At their 9 January meeting the members of the board deferred a decision on the Underhill affair, and two weeks later they passed a motion to postpone it until June. On 26 June Howard Ferguson moved that 'without any reference to specific details of the writings or utterances of Professor Frank H. Underhill and viewing his record as a whole, it is in the best interests of the University that his services be dispensed with.' Cody then announced that he was with-drawing the recommendation he had made in December concerning Underhill and recommended 'that no action be ... taken to dismiss him.' Sir William Mulock pointed out that nothing could be done without Cody's approval. The board nevertheless passed the motion by a vote of seven to four.[74]

Three months later, Balmer Neilly asked why the board's wishes had not been carried out. 'The chancellor recommended letting matters rest,' Douglas Francis writes. 'The majority of the members consented. So, finally, ended the Underhill case.'[75]

At least one fascinating question remains: Did Hepburn authorize the dis-missal and then reverse himself? It is unlikely that his education minister would have approved the dismissal without letting his chief know. Yet Hepburn told the advertising executive Carlton McNaught (who later told Underhill) that he had neither sought the dismissal nor known of it. As soon as he had got wind of it, he added, he had let the university authorities know that he feared its possible ill effect on Canadian-American relations.[76]

Reporting to John W. Dafoe a telephone call he had received from Hepburn, Clifford Sifton wrote that the premier claimed to have been 'improperly' asso-ciated with the case 'by an interested person,' and that he believed it to be a mistake 'to fire Underhill at the present time' because it would offend the Americans and damage the province's tourist industry. 'Mitch was obviously eager to dissociate himself,' Sifton added.[77] He thought the tale unconvincing. The full story will probably never be known.

The resolution of the affair was a victory for Underhill and his friends, but was it also a victory for academic freedom? The triumphalist answer is Jack Pickersgill's: 'The ... case was the decisive victory for academic freedom not just in Toronto but elsewhere in Canada ... Academic freedom has never been seriously challenged in Canada since 1941.' (If only this were true!) The histo-rian Donald Creighton, for many years Underhill's colleague, takes a more sceptical view, in which the infringement of university autonomy assumes a major role. He points out that the denouement was prompted 'by the very man who had made a practice of ... denouncing political intervention in university affairs.' The victory, Creighton implies, was too dearly bought. It is worth reit-erating that university autonomy may be a necessary but is not a sufficient con-dition for academic freedom. The boards and executive heads of autonomous institutions have at various times undermined or stifled that freedom far more effectively than any outside agency has been capable of doing.[78]

If the outcome of the affair was a victory for academic freedom, it was a qualified victory at best. Had it been 'the decisive victory' celebrated by Pick-ersgill, it would have encouraged the exercise of academic free speech. It failed to do so. Underhill told a friend in August 1941 that he wanted henceforth to keep out of trouble: 'This is unheroic but I am now past fifty years of age.' He was aware that he had kept his job only through the influence of well-positioned friends. The comment made by Louise Parkin, a recent president of the League for Social Reconstruction, was accurate: 'It is lucky that F.H.U. is "news" – otherwise he would have been disposed of quietly.'[79]

There was more to Underhill's reaction than the wish for a quiet life. His biographer argues that he had already begun to move from the left bank into the political mainstream.[80] His wit remained waspish, but his opinions became acceptable.

A few short weeks after Underhill's speech at the Couchiching Conference, W.P.M. Kennedy addressed a letter to Cody recommending Bora Laskin for appointment. Kennedy wrote that Laskin had been asked 'to declare unequivocally that he has no connexion – public or private, expressly or implicitly – with organized or unorganized Communism, Fascism or any subversive movement.' Added Kennedy, 'I have told him – as indeed I tell *all* those whom I recommend to you for appointment – that his duties are to teach law, not to make any public statements ... on political or public questions.' Cody could rely on Kennedy not to recommend anyone who was disloyal or indeed, as Kennedy phrased it, anyone who was not endowed with practical common sense. 'If I fail, such a man will *go*,' he asserted, adding that the law staff wanted only 'to be left alone to do our university work ... undisturbed by being condemned ... due to either disloyalty or loquacity – or both.'[81]

The reference in Kennedy's letter to Underhill's Couchiching speech, though oblique, is unmistakable. Kennedy clearly wanted to stress his opposition to 'loquacity' of the Underhillian kind and to indicate that it offended against common sense. Cody doubtless approved Kennedy's attitude. Something else was also at work, however. Kennedy did not refer to Laskin's Jewishness, but no other faculty recruit of that time had to submit to the sort of loyalty test that Kennedy was imposing on Laskin. Whether Cody required it or Kennedy acted on his own is not known. What is known is that the University of Toronto shared in the widespread anti-Semitism that had kept Laskin from obtaining a position at Manitoba in 1939 and that made it very difficult for even the most promising Jewish scholars to find university positions in Canada.[82]

A Toronto graduate, Marvin Gelber, had written to Underhill in 1936: 'The Canadian universities ... are full of anti-Semites who would furiously reject the application [of the term to them], but who are consistently conscious of Jewish inroads into the cultural life of our country.' Gelber's brother Lionel, a brilliant scholar, taught briefly at Toronto during the war but was given no permanent appointment. When Leon Edel, who had a BA degree from McGill, returned from his graduate studies already at work on the Henry James project that later gained him international renown, he could find no university post in Canada. Jews who wanted academic careers usually left for the United States.[83]

Anti-Semitism helps explain the poor record of Canadian universities in accommodating refugees from Nazism. By September 1939 only sixteen refugee academics, fourteen men and two women, had been appointed, in most cases with funds supplied by the Carnegie Foundation. Toronto took six, Dalhousie three, and Saskatchewan two, one of whom, the chemist and future Nobel Prize winner Gerhard Herzberg, soon moved to the University of Toronto. Five of the sixteen were Jewish, one was a 'baptized non-Aryan,' and six were not Jewish. (Whether the remaining four were Jewish is unclear.) A few refugees gained positions during the war, but the total number appointed between 1933 and 1945 barely exceeded twenty. The universities' budgetary woes contributed to this niggardly record, of course. As well, the federal government placed major obstacles in the way of refugees. High unemployment seemed to argue against the admission of people who might do work that could be done by Canadians.[84]

Growing public support for the Co-operative Commonwealth Federation (CCF) after 1941 was evident on Canadian campuses, where students flocked to the party in unprecedented numbers. Professors who were active in the party continued to be few, but some of them were prominent, notably Frank Scott, George Grube, and J. Stanley Allen, a professor of science at Sir George Williams College in Montreal. Scott and Grube served on the CCF's national executive, Allen on the national council. Scott, indeed, was national chairman from 1942 to 1950. Grube was also active in the Ontario CCF, while Scott and Allen were mainstays of the small Quebec wing of the party.

Scott's election to the chairmanship of the CCF did not please the McGill board. Soon afterwards Principal Cyril James asked Dean C.S. LeMesurier to have 'a frank talk' with Scott and 'find out the exact demands of his political duties upon his time in order that we might be able to arrive at a satisfactory solution of the problem.' LeMesurier passed this letter on to Scott and, with it, James's order that he was not to use the secretarial and telephone facilities of the faculty for his political work.[85]

Scott was left free to serve his party, though he experienced some minor harassment. Having been asked to offer an extension course on 'Constitutional Issues of Today,' he learned in July 1943 that the extension committee had resolved 'that as long as any member of the University carries as an outside responsibility a prominent position in a political party ... this member should not offer courses on political problems under the auspices of the Committee.' Scott protested, and a further meeting of the committee decided to approve his course after all, 'the question of principle being left open for further discussion.'[86]

It was not only Scott's chairmanship of the CCF that was an irritant. So also was an article he contributed to the *Canadian Forum* in June 1942. Commenting on a nationwide referendum held on 27 April, Scott purported to explain the large majority of Quebec votes cast against releasing the federal government from a pledge not to introduce conscription for overseas military service. He adopted an understanding tone: 'All that Quebec means by the "no" vote is that she does not wish her children to die for any country other than their own. This is nothing very startling.' Until English Canadians made up their minds whether Canada was 'fighting this war as a British colony or as one of the United Nations,' said Scott, the gulf between Quebec and the other provinces would be likely to persist.[87]

Several French Canadians wrote to Scott in appreciation, but most English Canadians reacted negatively. Even liberal-minded people attacked him. Eugene Forsey wrote a critical letter to the *Canadian Forum*, and the *Winnipeg Free Press* claimed that the article was actually 'advocacy, subtle and skilful, of the case for a limited contribution to the war.' In the course of three articles in the late summer and fall of 1942, *Saturday Night*'s B.K. Sandwell accused Scott of failing to recognize that the war was a 'struggle between democracy and tyranny' from which only one side could emerge victorious.[88]

The incident led Principal James to ponder the meaning of academic freedom and the need for a 'clear statement of university policy' on this subject. In notes penned for possible inclusion in his 1942–3 report, he wrote that it was 'vitally important' to maintain 'academic freedom of speech' while recognizing that the federal government had 'necessarily restricted ... the limits of legality' for the duration of the war. As well, 'all things that are lawful are not expedient'; faculty should 'use wisdom and judgment above average.' To express 'mere hypotheses' or opinions that disturbed public morale was 'highly undesirable.'[89]

This did not go far enough for James's secretary, Dorothy McMurray. She advised him against saying anything on academic freedom unless he could say something 'really convincing enough to silence our critics.' James should 'look facts squarely in the face,' she urged. Scott had been advancing the cause of the CCF to the detriment of his university work and should be stopped: 'This is [*sic*] nothing whatever to do with the vexed question of academic freedom'; no civil servant was permitted to be active in politics, and 'no teacher on a university staff should be allowed to do so.'

McMurray knew that muzzling Scott would not be easy. Reducing his salary would be pointless – the CCF would make up the difference and he would become a martyr. If he were dismissed, he might sue and win. In any case, the board might simply not want 'to force a Frank Scott issue.' But they ought to do something. 'They could summon him before the full Board,' McMurray suggested: 'Nothing much has been heard from Underhill ... since the Board of Governors there at least scared him. He hasn't published a controversial statement since, has he?'[90] In the event, James did not discuss academic freedom in his report. And the board did not meet to discuss Frank Scott. He was left free to be national chairman of the CCF.

In 1940 George Grube asked permission to run as a CCF candidate in the federal election that year. The executive committee of Trinity College offered no objection to his candidature, 'provided that the campaign will not interfere with his duties to the College or with the progress of the students under instruction in the Department of Classics.' However, if he was elected, he would be expected to resign his academic post.[91] Grube ran in Toronto-Broadview and finished a distant third. He ran again in that constituency in the general elections of 1945 and 1949, and in a 1950 by-election, each time coming third. He did not run in 1953, but in 1957 and 1958 he was the CCF standard bearer in Toronto-Eglinton. Victory again eluded him, and he did not run again.

Why did Grube not give up earlier? An answer may be found in a speech he gave in 1944. Seeking to justify the participation of intellectuals in politics, he said that life was not easy for candidates who held unorthodox views. Their statements were twisted, their views misrepresented, their characters smeared: 'In the course of a campaign I acquire the most varied racial origins according as to which is the most unpopular at the moment, and half a dozen curious religions. These things are hard to bear, and ... such tactics are often successful.' So why did he bother? Because somebody had to: 'Few university professors even ... can or dare to take part in political activities if their opinions be unorthodox ... But freedom of speech cannot survive in cold storage, and even the air in the ivory tower is vitiated when the air outside is poisoned.'[92]

Grube's political activities gave rise to criticism at Trinity. In June 1943 Provost Frederick H. Cosgrave mentioned 'certain difficulties' that had arisen out of Grube's role in public affairs. 'The objection was not that [he] was taking part in public life, but the character of some of these activities and utterances.' Six months later, a report of remarks Grube had made to the University of Toronto CCF Club led Cosgrave to complain that the classicist was breaking the promise he had made in 1939 not to comment provocatively on current events. Trinity might 'suffer severely' if this sort of thing continued.[93]

Grube replied that he had been misquoted. He had been reported as urging that the CCF, once in office, should act 'quickly and ruthlessly' against its enemies; but what he had actually said was 'that a CCF government would have to use its power "quickly, legally and democratically, but firmly and even ruthlessly" to put into effect its mandate.' Grube assured Cosgrave that he had 'never advocated anything but democratic processes, both in achieving power and in exercising it.'[94] This explanation seems to have have been sufficient.

Among the more visible CCF members in Quebec was the chemist J. Stanley Allen, since 1932 a professor at Sir George Williams College. A member of both the League for Social Reconstruction and the Fellowship for a Christian Social Order, Allen ran as a CCF candidate in Mount Royal constituency in the 1940 federal election. He finished a very distant third but had greater success in seeking local office, serving during the war years as a member of the Montreal City Council and the Protestant School Board.[95]

Allen's Christian socialism, his work in the CCF, and his staunch opposition to the limits imposed on the number of Jewish students at Sir George Williams irritated some members of the college's governing board. They also annoyed prominent Montrealers, among them the president of the Aluminium Company of Canada, R.E. Powell. In November 1943 Powell complained to a board member, the lawyer W.H. Howard, about Allen and about the college, a YMCA-owned institution which Powell characterized as a breeding ground of supporters for the CCF.

Howard rejected the charge and went on to write that although the board members did not like their association with Allen, 'we do not know what to do about it. McGill University cannot solve the problem of Prof. Scott. So, no discredit attaches to us in respect of Dr. Allen.' He added that he thought discharging Allen because of his work with the CCF would be 'the worst thing that we could do.' It would draw attention to Allen 'and increase his influence.'

Summing up, Howard said that Sir George Williams was not financially self-supporting, that it included a CCFer among its teachers, and that 'it is unlikely that anything will be done to stifle or strangle or eliminate Dr. Allen so long as he does his teaching job and does not use our class-rooms as places for preaching C.C.F doctrines or deliberately create the impression that, when he speaks, he speaks for the college or the Y.M.C.A.' Howard urged Powell to continue to support the YMCA, arguing that it was in the interest of his company and other business organizations to do so. Failure to support the YMCA might cause it to fall into 'bad hands,' he suggested, and to become 'a source of great danger to all of us who are opposed to "red" or "pink" doctrines.'[96]

Given a copy of Howard's letter by W.M. Birks, who at various times served on the boards of both Sir George Williams and McGill, Cyril James was impressed: 'Few letters that I have seen express the whole matter so cogently and tersely.'[97] But were all members of the Sir George Williams board of a similar opinion as Howard? It seems not. Six months later, Principal Kenneth Norris asked for Allen's resignation, stating as the grounds that his public life encroached on his teaching and on his service to the college. A board member, D. Prescott Mowry, told Allen some days later that his socialist activities constituted the real reason. The issue remains somewhat obscure, however; the historian Richard Allen has found that the board's minutes contain no record of a discussion of the case.

Norris must have informed Stanley Allen that an appeal would be useless and that a dismissal might prompt a scandal that would harm both him and the college. After leaving Norris's office, Allen immediately conferred with Frank Scott and David Lewis, the national secretary of the CCF. They decided that a resignation would be best, and they created a job for Allen as assistant treasurer of the national CCF and fundraiser for its Quebec wing. (Neither Scott's biography nor Lewis's memoirs mentions the incident.) He ran as a CCF candidate provincially in 1944 and federally in 1945, before moving in 1947 to Hamilton, Ontario, where the CCF's prospects looked brighter. He never taught at a university again.

Allen had, it seems, sometimes mentioned politics in the classroom, and his work as a municipal politician had occasionally interfered with his work at Sir George Williams. Whether these offences were serious enough to constitute grounds for dismissal neither Norris nor the board undertook to show. They did not need to do so, of course. Allen's tenure was during the board's pleasure. The notice given was short, but quite possibly Sir George Williams shared with some other colleges the practice of paying its faculty from 1 September to 31 August. One thing seems clear: the circumstances of Allen's resignation touch directly on academic freedom.

Although Howard's letter stated that the board would probably not act against Allen because of his politics, it also signalled that his association with the CCF was unwelcome. It implied, too, that Allen was an impediment to fundraising. It is entirely possible that in the course of late 1943 and early 1944 as the CCF showed unprecedented strength and came under harsh attack from business sources,[98] a majority of board members reached the view that Allen must go. If this was indeed the case, the offence against academic freedom would be unmistakable. In the absence of hard evidence, however, a definitive judgment is elusive.

Victoria University's President Walter Brown reported to the board of regents in April 1945 that he had been 'approached by a representative of one of the political parties with the request that a certain member of our staff be allowed to run in the forth-coming election.' He had discussed the matter with a group of board members, without identifying either the individual or the party, he said, and the group had expressed the view that electoral politics 'was not a type of life that develops scholastic interests.' As well, it might antagonize donors as well as parents of prospective students. Some thought this enough to ban running for office, but 'the majority ... took the view that it was not advisable ... to deny members this right, and therefore no absolute prohibition was made.' It was decided that anyone seeking election 'should be given leave of absence with the privilege of protecting his pension rights, and the college would assure that man, as far as possible, a position when he returns.'[99]

In early May, Eric Havelock applied for leave of absence from 9 May to 4 June in order 'to contest the Provincial Riding of Wellington North in the CCF interest.' Having obtained leave, the classicist left for the politically stony fields north of Guelph. Neither he nor the party leader, E.B. Jolliffe, thought the riding to be winnable for the CCF, he recalled in 1967. But in the election of 1943 the CCF had become the opposition in the province, and in 1945 the party hoped to form the next government. Havelock's understanding with Jolliffe was that if the CCF was victorious, he would get the Education portfolio, and an urban seat would be vacated for him.[100]

Havelock lost as expected and returned to the college, the CCF having sustained a major defeat. Brown welcomed him back and expressed the hope that he would 'henceforth eschew politics.' Havelock said he thought Victoria 'a bit cheap' in withholding three weeks' pay from him even though the teaching term had ended and he had marked all his examinations. More important, he sensed that his incursion into politics had reinforced his reputation as a 'marked man.' When Harvard offered him a position in 1947 he accepted with few misgivings. He later capped a distinguished career by becoming the Sterling Professor of Classics at Yale.[101]

The most startling evidence of the CCF's wartime strength was the party's victory in the Saskatchewan provincial election in June 1944. As a consequence, the 1909 regulation of the University of Saskatchewan which declared political candidacy to be incompatible with academic employment was called into question. In December 1944 the new minister of education, Woodrow S. Lloyd, asked President J.S. Thomson about his views on political candidacy. Thomson cited the 1909 regulation and noted that Rupert Ramsay had resigned from the university after accepting the provincial Conservative leadership in February 1944. Lloyd did not follow up on his inquiry.[102]

In January 1945 the board of governors appointed a committee to study the

University Act, institutional government, and administrative practices. This body received the name Survey Committee in a reference to the committee appointed in Alberta a few years earlier. Probably the government felt reassured that the university was contemplating necessary changes. However, there is no record of any reply from Premier T.C. Douglas when a former member of the law faculty, Raphael Tuck, wrote to him in March 1945 arguing that 'this very unjust rule at the University ... should be abolished,' and that professors should not have to resign 'for the privilege of being nominated as a candidate.'[103] Perhaps the issue did not strike the premier as particularly urgent.

Not the least important point that Lloyd made in his submission to the survey committee was: 'It is essential that academic freedom be preserved. Consequently it is highly undesirable that any government interfere with or dominate the work of the University.' He said not a word about political candidacy.[104]

The survey committee reported in December 1945. It had examined the acts governing many Canadian and several American universities and had paid particular attention both to the report of Alberta's survey committee and to the revised University of Alberta Act of 1942: 'In view of the special interest in the operation of this new Act, the Secretary visited Edmonton for several days and prepared an account of the more significant features of the present organization of the University of Alberta.'

In the absence of a strong signal from Douglas's government that it wanted a change in the policy on political candidacy, the Saskatchewan committee saw no need to copy Alberta's permissive policy, which had been prompted by the report of its survey committee. None of the recommendations of the Saskatchewan committee addressed the issue of candidacy, so that the board of governors simply maintained the 1909 regulation.[105]

The board finally rescinded the regulation in 1950, though its reasons for doing so remain obscure. Michael Hayden thinks 'that the change came as a result of pressure from the CCF government,' but he lacks direct evidence for this belief. Whatever the reasons for the change, until the 1960s no professors seem to have taken advantage of their new freedom.[106]

Less dramatic than attacks on professors for their opinions or political activities – but no less menacing to academic freedom – were wartime attitudes to research on the one hand and to the relative worth of academic disciplines on the other. At the larger universities, as at the National Research Council, research took place whose objective was to aid the war effort. Much of it was done in deepest secrecy. There were occasional questions about the threat this posed to academic freedom, but the needs of the war effort trumped such scruples. (A journalist, John Bryden, found in the 1980s that the Departments of

National Defence and External Affairs were still blocking access to many files, believing that secrecy should continue to envelop the 'very sensitive' work done in the war years.)[107]

One result of the movement into military research, which continued into the postwar years, was described by President Robert Newton of the University of Alberta. During the war it proved difficult to interest scientists in pure research, and this had a detrimental effect on science, he wrote. 'Universities are the traditional seat of research in pure science. Our stock of theoretical knowledge must be constantly replenished, else technological progress would peter out for this lack of raw material.' In the same vein, President Sidney Smith of the University of Toronto stated in 1957 that 'there could be no question where the research scholar's duty lay in those years when national survival was in the balance,' but a continuing preference for applied research had serious implications: 'Practical, applied research is an important public service which universities should not refuse to perform, but at the same time they must remember their more important duty to the lonely scholar whose inexplicable interest in a seemingly trivial question may lead to real advances on the frontiers of knowledge.' Smith regretted that neither government nor business seemed much interested in subsidizing such research. Nor were all scientists drawn to it. As the historian Donald Avery notes, not a few of them appreciated the reliable availability of research funds for military and quasi-military purposes.[108]

The view that research findings should be held back if their publication might conceivably harm the war effort had wide application. For example, in April 1940 John D. Ketchum of Toronto's psychology department polled a group of 180 arts students about their attitude to the war. Asked whether it was 'in Canada's best interests to put everything she has into this war, and to continue the fight, whatever it may cost, until Germany is defeated,' some 23.2 per cent responded that they were 'not convinced at all' and 25.8 per cent were 'not quite convinced.' Eight months later these figures were down to 9.4 and 16.7 per cent; by November 1941 those who were unconvinced or not quite convinced were together only 10 per cent.

Arts students were unrepresentative of the population, Ketchum wrote to President Cody, but '*changes* in opinion occurring among them are probably indicative of factors which are also operating in the wider situation.' Cheered by the 'trend of change from the uncertainty of the first winter,' he asked Cody's permission 'to continue work of this kind.'[109]

Cody was shocked that one in ten was still unconvinced: 'I should doubt the wisdom of the government providing two-thirds of the cost of their education.' He authorized Ketchum to continue his research but asked that he not make his findings public without clearing this first. Ketchum agreed 'that it would be most undesirable to have the press get hold of material such as this.'[110]

Two months later he asked permission 'to show half a dozen slides' during a talk on 'Morale' to be given to the Royal Canadian Institute. 'The results on "Conviction about the war" would appear only in a composite graph, as a single line, rapidly sloping upwards,' he explained, and the audience would have no figures to carry home. 'But in view of your letter to me I would like to be sure that my own sense of discretion corresponds with yours.'[111] Cody approved.

Without making too much of this one case, it confirms the notion that professors clung to their general belief that discretion was the better part of valour. The University of Saskatchewan economist George Britnell confessed to Frank Underhill in early 1941, 'I expect it is lack of moral fibre but all last year from September 3rd, 1939, I refused to make any speeches on International Affairs as I had a conviction I should get into trouble and serve no useful purpose.'[112] He was not alone. In silence there was safety.

Some professors were nevertheless in danger from an unexpected source – the low priority accorded to subjects that were of no demonstrable use in the service of Mars. The value of science, engineering, agriculture, and the health professions was beyond question; each had a direct contribution to make to the war effort. The humanities and social sciences, on the other hand, as well as education, law, and commerce, made no such contribution. Some Canadians came to see them as expendable.

During a war in which science and technology loomed large, these fields would have grown in any case, but they benefited from policies that favoured their students over those in subjects deemed to be less important. In 1944 faculty members at the University of New Brunswick complained about the policy of allowing physically fit male students in the arts and other 'non-essential areas' to carry on with their studies only if they were in the upper half of their class. The professors said it had 'artificially inflated the enrolments in science and applied science and made it difficult for students in other faculties to concentrate on their studies.'[113] Doubtless this was true elsewhere too.

In September 1940 Alberta's President W.A.R. Kerr told the executive committee of the board that there were 140 applicants for 80 places in the first year of applied science. He added 'that as war conditions had created a demand for trained engineers, the available supply of whom were being rapidly drained, the University should be prepared to meet this national war-time emergency by admitting a larger number of students than the quota now fixed.' The board accepted this recommendation, though there was no evidence that the senate had approved it. Two years later Kerr's successor, Robert Newton, obtained executive committee approval for a policy that would allow deans to admit less than fully qualified students into programs, 'such as engineering,' that were judged to be 'essential to the war effort.' Again, there was no sign that the senate had approved the action.[114]

By 1942 Principal R.C. Wallace of Queen's pointed to the gap that had opened up between the liberal arts, a majority of whose students were now women, and more practical fields: 'The trend today is to science, applied science and medicine, and our best students follow that path. The humanities are in eclipse.' At the meeting of the National Conference of Canadian Universities (NCCU), he announced the end of the liberal arts college 'devoted to the humanities and to culture, splendid in its own isolation,' claiming that it was incompatible with 'our modern ways.'

This, of course, reflected what had been happening in universities since before the 1914–18 war. Even more than the scientific disciplines, vocationally oriented fields such as law, commerce, medicine, and engineering had been growing at a fast pace. The liberal arts, meanwhile, were becoming increasingly feminized. This made it easy for Wallace to propose that arts students who were not in the honours program be given an Associate in Arts certificate after the end of their second year instead of the Bachelor of Arts degree, thereby releasing the men among them more rapidly into the armed forces. Although not in principle hostile to the arts of peace, Wallace saw the disciplines that might help defeat the enemy as more important. He came from Britain, where wartime restrictions on the study of the liberal arts were severe. He also knew that, since the American entry into the war in 1941, arts enrolments had been curtailed in that country.[115]

The debate over conscription in 1942 raised questions about the role that the universities were playing in keeping students out of military service or war-related work. The *Financial Post* asked its readers whether Canada should close all courses except those that trained war specialists, and it reported a positive response. In December the *Globe and Mail* editorialized: 'Those thousands of young men taking non-essential courses are not making any immediate contribution to the winning of the war.' Some university people made similar noises. Walter P. Thompson, dean of arts and science at the University of Saskatchewan (and later its president), wrote to the secretary of the NCCU: 'We can no longer defend encouraging students who are of military age and physically fit to take courses in the Humanities and Social Sciences subjects.'[116]

By the end of 1942 Wallace and McGill's Cyril James were ready to propose the curtailment and acceleration of instruction in 'non-essential' fields for male – and presumably also female – students. There was no mention of the latter, though by this time well over half of arts students were women. Assuming that Wallace and James had considered this fact, they probably wanted to put more women into aircraft factories or munitions plants. But it was all too easy to overlook women students. First admitted in the 1870s, seventy years later they were still on the metaphorical periphery of universities largely staffed with and almost exclusively managed by men.[117]

When Wallace and James tried to solicit support for their ideas, humanists and social scientists got the wind up. Rumours flew that Ottawa wanted to close faculties of arts and education as well as commerce and law, and that a special meeting of the NCCU in January 1943 was intended to get that body to agree. In November 1942, Harold Adams Innis and the Queen's historian Reginald G. Trotter drafted a petition on behalf of the social scientists, urging the government to resist proposals that the arts faculties be closed down. Innis also encouraged the humanists to organize. Watson Kirkconnell took charge of a small committee that managed to get a petition signed by forty-one senior humanists into the hands of Prime Minister Mackenzie King by the end of December 1942. Canada, it stated, needed people who had been taught to think and reflect as well as to be practical.[118]

The defences built by Innis, Kirkconnell, and company may have been unnecessary. The ideas of Wallace and James owed more to their own than to Ottawa's assessment of the country's needs. At the special NCCU meeting, Arthur MacNamara, deputy minister of labour and director of the National Selective Service, said that the government had no wish to discontinue instruction in subjects not directly related to the war effort, and that even if it should in future be thought necessary to ration such instruction, 'he hoped that the student population would be held at a level "sufficient to permit the maintenance of staffs and educational standards."' If the universities would 'ruthlessly' weed out the incompetent and marginal students, he said, and would continue to enforce military instruction on all students, 'no immediate further restriction would be necessary.'[119]

Far from wanting to raid the universities for recruits, Mackenzie King wanted to leave them alone. The debate over conscription had divided Canada and the Liberal Party. The last thing he wanted was a resolution urging his government to meddle in higher education – political poison, especially in Quebec.[120]

The Wallace-James proposal threatened academic freedom, and MacNamara's attitude threatened the integrity of grading. The first threat is obvious and not without relevance today: people who are told that what they are teaching is unimportant or even unnecessary may justifiably infer that their freedom to teach or do research does not much matter either. The threat to the integrity of grading was more subtle, but any instructor giving a poor grade knew that the student might as a consequence be forced to withdraw and, if male, be drafted into military service. Harsh grading could be justified by the needs of the war effort, soft grading by a reluctance to force someone into the armed forces. The potential for abuse should have prompted a debate.

Not all liberal arts departments survived the war. A few days before the war began, McMaster's financial advisor told Chancellor Howard P. Whidden that it might be necessary 'to drop some of our cultural, but not essential educational courses.' As a result, fine arts became vulnerable, for although the department maintained its prewar enrolment levels, its extension work declined. In April 1942 Whidden's successor, George P. Gilmour, informed Stanley Hart, an art historian who had been at the university since 1936 and held the rank of associate professor, that his department would be closed down in the course of the next year and his position terminated on 31 August 1943.[121]

The board of governors – it is unclear what role the senate played – took this step with some reluctance. The Carnegie Corporation had supported the department since its founding in 1930, and suspending it might endanger the success of future appeals. However, Gilmour anticipated a decline in McMaster's enrolment in 1942–3 and believed that 'the withdrawal of all work in this department would not seriously upset the curriculum, and would recognize that in wartime student interest may well be diverted into other channels.' He also gave it as his opinion that Hart was 'probably not the best man for permanent work here.'[122]

This assessment of Hart seems to have had two grounds. A popular and apparently effective lecturer, he was less successful as an administrator. As well, his grading practices were deemed to be excessively indulgent. In early 1940 the associate dean of arts, W.B. Hurd, reported to Whidden the remark by Dean A.B. McLay that Hart's Christmas grades had been high, but that they could do nothing about it because 'an instructor, if competent, must be considered competent to set and mark his own examinations, irrespective of standards maintained elsewhere in the institution.' Hurd disagreed with this view and scorned Hart's explanation that his grades reflected superior teaching.[123]

Whidden gently reproved Hart for making such a claim: 'I prefer to believe that you made this statement humorously.'[124] Whether he did so or not, asking him to change his grades had implications for academic freedom. McLay was surely right: if you trust people to teach, you must trust them to grade responsibly. Hart's file does not indicate whether a repetition of the grading incident occurred. It is possible that concern about his grades contributed to the decision to close down fine arts; though a more likely explanation is that the subject seemed expendable, not least because it appealed mainly to women students.

No university president in the 1930s and 1940s took a livelier interest in academic freedom than Carleton Stanley. In 1931–2 he helped shield R.A. MacKay from the wrath of R.B. Bennett. In 1936 he defended the right of a member of the French department, René Gautheron, to state his views on the place of the French language in Canada and even to use Dalhousie stationery in doing so. In 1937 he tried to put academic freedom on the agenda of the NCCU, in 1939 he wrote to Beatty in support of E.R. Adair, and in 1941 he told Cody that he would publicly resign his University of Toronto degrees – one earned and one honorary – if the board of governors continued to harass Underhill. It is ironic, therefore, that in 1945 he was forced out of office in circumstances which, in his own eyes and those of some of his supporters, raised the issue of academic freedom.[125]

Stanley had left McGill's department of classics in 1931 to assume the presidency of Dalhousie. Independent-minded and stubborn, he was soon in conflict with the board's chairman, G. Fred Pearson. The quarrel ended with Pearson's resignation, since other board members believed that their new president should have a chance to do things his own way. Over the next decade Stanley's influence grew, and after J. McGregor Stewart vacated the chair in 1943 in favour of K.C. Laurie, Stanley's power increased further. Stewart, who was still a governor, came to believe that the president was trying to turn the board and senate into rubber stamps for his own projects.[126]

Stewart was also annoyed because Stanley opposed his proposal that the premier of Nova Scotia be asked to sit on the board *ex officio*. Stewart hoped that this might lead the provincial government to provide financial support; but Stanley, having asked President Sherwood Fox of Western Ontario and Vice-Principal W.E. McNeill of Queen's for their views (both advised against), remained sceptical. Whatever the reason, by the fall of 1944 Stewart was Stanley's enemy.[127]

The president had other enemies too. P.B. Waite (Dalhousie's official historian) writes that senate opposition to him began in the 1930s: 'By 1944 it's almost certain that Stanley could not have mustered a vote in Senate in his support in his quarrel with the Board, and it may be significant that he seems to have made no attempt to do so.' When an ally of Stanley's, the geologist G. Vibert Douglas, tried to rally support, he 'got nowhere.'[128]

In the fall of 1944, Dalhousie's board was about to embark on a fundraising drive. A special meeting on 15 September produced agreement that the greatest need was for an arts building but that a campaign for such a project would get a weak response. Stanley objected: 'The Arts and Science Faculty was the heart and core of the university,' he said, 'but the maintenance of the professional schools ... has resulted in the neglect of that faculty. $3,500,000, if the cost of a new building for the faculty is included, would be required to bring that faculty even.' This, he thought, should be the campaign's objective.[129]

The board charged a committee consisting of Laurie and four others to examine the problems facing a campaign. When the committee met on 29 September, its members concluded that a successful campaign was impossible in view of 'the antagonism which – rightly or wrongly – exists ... to the present President.' Two members of the committee were asked to speak with Stanley, 'so that any suggestions that he might wish to make [might be] carefully considered' by the board at its November meeting.[130]

Laurie and Stewart saw the president on 24 October. Saying that the criticism was too vague, Stanley refused to respond to it. Instead, he visited the vice-chairman of the board, Dr J.C. Webster, who in two letters charged Laurie and Stewart with animus against Stanley arising from differences over administrative matters. 'The President's ability, scholarship, devotion to duty, or success in advancing the fortunes of Dalhousie,' were not at issue, stated Webster, and neither was his moral character. The committee had objected to Stanley's 'dictatorial manner, obstinacy, egotism, self-glorification,' all of which Webster rejected. He could see 'no justification' for asking Stanley to resign, and he threatened to resign from the board himself and make his reasons known widely if the attack on the president succeeded.[131]

A rump meeting of the board on 10 November indicated that at least ten members (of a total of thirty-five) wanted Stanley to resign. The provincial archivist, D.C. Harvey (an alumni representative on the board), was then asked to try to persuade Stanley to resign quietly. Harvey failed in this mission. At the board meeting on 28 November, Stewart, in moving concurrence in the committee report, disclaimed 'criticism of the great qualities of President Stanley' but asserted 'that as a public relations officer [Stanley] has not been successful.' He had aroused hostility within and outside the university, argued Stewart, and this 'precluded a successful campaign.' Asked whether voting for the motion implied a call for Stanley's resignation, Stewart said it did not: 'No indication of that sort. Concurrence in report only.'

This was clearly untrue. However, Stanley did himself no good with the speech he gave. The only way in which the board could help the president, he said, was 'to find the money to maintain the institution,' it being 'obvious that while he is President, the Board will approve his recommendations about appointments and promotions.' Denying that he was a hindrance to fundraising, he noted that the endowment had risen from roughly $2.3 million in 1931 to almost $4 million on 31 December 1943 (at least half the increase came from R.B. Bennett). He then talked about his meeting with Laurie and Stewart, suggesting that they had lied. Worse, holding up two letters of Laurie's, he ridiculed his spelling and grammar.[132]

The meeting degenerated into a succession of charges, countercharges, denials, and counterdenials, ranging over the years from the present back to 1931. Aware that they were in the minority, Stanley's supporters hoped to postpone a vote on Stewart's motion until a later meeting, but a motion to postpone failed narrowly. The motion to concur in the committee report then passed, sixteen for and six against.

At this point, a less principled or less obstinate man would have begun to negotiate the terms of his resignation, but Stanley believed that the attempt to force his resignation was the result of his refusal 'to promote ..., appoint or dismiss professors on improper grounds' and that his academic freedom was at issue. He chose to fight. In December 1944, when he was in New York to speak with officials of the Rockefeller Foundation and Carnegie Corporation, one of them urged him to contact the American Association of University Professors (AAUP). The organization's associate secretary, Robert P. Ludlum, asked Stanley for documentation and, after reading it, thought he had a case. He thereupon wrote to Laurie in order to offer 'the good offices of this Association to the end that [the] differences between Dr. Stanley and members of the Board of Governors may be adjusted amicably,' and asked that a decision about Stanley's presidency be postponed until an AAUP representative could visit Halifax.[133]

This accomplished nothing. If the governors would not yield to the wishes of so important a benefactor as R.B. Bennett (by this time Viscount Bennett of Mickleham, Calgary, and Hopewell), they were not likely to be moved by an organization of American academics. A telegram from Bennett was read to the board on 23 January 1945, at a meeting called to discuss Stanley's tenure. 'It is almost incredible,' Bennett wrote, 'that sixteen adult Maritimers could deliberately place on record a resolution declaring they were unable [to] discharge their duties to [the] institution of which they are Governors because of [the] alleged antagonism of unnamed persons to perhaps the most scholarly President of any Canadian University.' Controverting the claim that Dalhousie could not raise money because of Stanley, Bennett added that the board had never given the president the support he deserved. He warned that Dalhousie would suffer seriously if the board persisted in its attempt to dismiss Stanley: 'No really competent man will accept [the] Presidency of [a] university where his official life depends upon [the] attitude of [the] governing body or gossip and alleged antagonisms.'[134]

Bennett's words stung, but Stewart neutralized their effect. Although admirable in every way, he said, Bennett was 'at too great a distance to enable him to be a competent judge of the relations between the President and the Board or of the correctness of the Resolution that has been proposed tonight.' Seven other communications were then read, all opposing the proposed action. A member of the committee of five dismissed them as having been written by people who were misinformed. In any case it was clear that 'either the President or the Board has to go.' Webster was not allowed to vote by proxy; had he attended the meeting, the vote would have been eighteen for asking Stanley to resign and six against.[135]

'The matter is simple,' Stanley said, 'I am not resigning.' This made no sense. Whatever the rights and wrongs of the dispute, he could not carry on with a board most of whose members lacked confidence in him. Two weeks passed before Stanley accepted his fate. 'I do not recede at any point from the position I took in the Board meetings of November 28 and January 23,' he wrote, 'but I cannot see how the interests of the institution can be adequately served with the present impasse between myself and eighteen members of the Board.' He resigned as of 30 June 1945. To a friend he wrote, 'Further contention on my part ... would be perverted into a charge that I am willing to have damage done to the institution in order to assert my own claims.'[136]

Stanley's resignation saved the board the embarrassment and bad publicity that would have attended a dismissal. The financial settlement was appropriately generous, and on 13 February 1945 Stanley and Laurie issued a joint statement which cited a 'fundamental divergence between the President and the Board as to their respective functions in University government.' Stanley served out his term without further controversy and took a position teaching English at United College, Winnipeg, where he became a favourite with students.[137]

The affair did not escape notice, however. The *Winnipeg Free Press* raised the question of academic freedom and hoped that an inquiry would take place. *Saturday Night* took the same line, stating that 'an independent investigation' would clear the air. The *Globe and Mail* carried an article surmising that Stanley's criticism in his 1944 convocation address of the existence of slums in Halifax had made some influential people unhappy and had 'probably cost Dr. Stanley his job.'[138]

Writing in the *Nation*, the journalist Judith Robinson ventured another suggestion: 'What, besides personal dislike, has inspired the successful vendetta against him can best be guessed by glancing at one of the current examples of his lack of tact, the Dalhousie Labor Institute.' Inaugurated by Stanley in 1944 with the help of a Rockefeller grant, the institute's declared intention was 'to equip union officials with better knowledge of social and economic trends so that they might better serve organized labor.' The biggest employer in Nova Scotia was the Dominion Steel and Coal Company (Dosco), which was currently arguing that miners' wages must be cut. Robinson pointed out that the union representatives opposing this measure included men who had 'already made good use' of the institute, and she went on to say, 'Among the leading citizens of Halifax who have and still hope to have pleasant and profitable relations with Dosco, its subsidiaries and affiliates, is J. McGregor Stewart, ex-chairman of the Board of Governors of Dalhousie University.'[139]

This introduced the issue of academic freedom at least tangentially. However, there is no hard evidence for Robinson's hypothesis. If dislike of the institute was a source of Stewart's hostility to Stanley, he took care to hide his tracks. Moreover, neither the university's records nor Stanley's own files provide signs of the opposition to the institute that Robinson implies. Indeed, if board members had been hostile, the institute would hardly have come into being. Robinson's article was the last to appear on the subject of Stanley's resignation. As neither he nor the board would talk about their differences, the incident soon faded from public awareness, and life at Dalhousie went on under a new president.

Was academic freedom in fact at issue in Stanley's dismissal? What does that freedom encompass where university presidents are concerned? The board majority's wish to be rid of Stanley was rooted in its judgment that working with him had become unacceptably difficult. A member of the committee of five, Mr Justice John Doull, wrote to R.B. Bennett in January 1945 that the president had forgotten his place. Citing Stanley's November statement to the board as evidence, Doull commented, 'I am of the opinion that any President who would address the Board of Governors in these terms is unfit to hold the office.' Four months later, Laurie wrote to Bennett in greater detail but much the same vein. What he held to be decisive in disqualifying Stanley was 'his opinion – and practice – of considering he was the University and the Board merely there to approve his recommendations and find the funds.' Laurie did not repeat the claim that as long as Stanley served as president, no campaign for funds could succeed. That had been no more than a pretext for encouraging him to resign.[140]

Rejecting the suggestion that he was an obstacle to fundraising, Stanley had initially resisted the attempt to oust him. But when he recognized that by continuing to resist he would harm the university, he had come to terms. It is hard to see what academic freedom had to do with this. Stanley mentioned attempts by board members to influence decisions concerning appointments and promotions, and he suggested to the AAUP that his resistance to these efforts had led to the demand for his resignation. This can be discounted. There are indications that board members occasionally spoke to Stanley on such matters, but there is no evidence that he felt pressure to act in a certain way or that the board wanted to get rid of him because he would not yield to its wishes. Did Stanley's criticism of the existence of slums in Halifax perhaps prompt board members 'to ask themselves privately about the suitability of Stanley for his role'?[141] They may have done so, but there is no evidence that it contributed to their decision to jettison the president. Nor is there evidence that his unfashionable views about the importance of the liberal arts were at issue.

Finally, of what does the academic freedom of presidents consist? Insofar as they are teachers and scholars, presidents are entitled to the same freedom in teaching and research enjoyed by other academics. They cannot, however, presume to exercise the same academic free speech of ordinary professors. It is essential that presidents enjoy the confidence of their boards. After all, they are jointly engaged in overseeing their universities and representing them to the larger world. In this enterprise a high degree of unity seems essential.

Such considerations played no part in the condolences that Stanley received from friends. They sympathized with him and deplored the implications of his resignation for Canadian intellectual life. From Mount Allison the biologist Roy Fraser wrote: 'This is a major loss, not only to Canadian education, but also in the battle to save those ideals of scholarship and of true culture without which all other university activities are without meaning.' Similarly, W.H. Alexander reported from Berkeley, California, where he had taught since 1938, that news of the affair left him 'nauseated.'[142]

A letter that may have touched Stanley more than most came from an old friend and classmate. 'I've always been rather proud that we had at least one University president in Canada with genuine intellectual ideals,' Frank Underhill wrote, 'and it would be hard to think of any of [the others] ... who would ever get into trouble with his board because of the stand he took on education. Would you want us [the *Canadian Forum*] to do a note on the subject or would you rather that we kept quiet?'[143]

'My dear Frankus,' Stanley replied, 'as your connection and mine is as well known as anything, I should say that it is mere wisdom for you to avoid any reference just now.'[144] Did he reflect on his own effort to defend Underhill in 1941? It seems more than likely.

What were the effects of the Second World War on academic freedom? There is very little evidence that professors felt that they were inhibited in the classroom, and here academic freedom may have been reasonably secure. George Hunter's experience seems to have been the exception. When it came to research and publication, however, the picture was less clear. Research findings might be censored or suppressed altogether. Meanwhile, academic free speech in the form of comment on public events, even by those who could claim professional expertise, could be dangerous.

The war reinforced the well-established preference of Canadian academics for keeping their heads down, although the swift response to rumours that

Ottawa sought to restrict work in the liberal arts showed that they could organize in self-defence when the issue seemed important. The attacks on Adair,
Grube, Scott, and above all Underhill evidently struck few academics as important enough to lead them to take a stand. Perhaps many were afraid to do so.
After all, the controversies were reminders that those who stuck their necks out
risked decapitation and that Canadians attached little value to professorial outspokenness. Neither, with some exceptions, did Canadian professors.

8

The Coming of the Cold War

The Cold War came (some would say 'returned') to Canada with the defection of Igor Gouzenko, a cipher clerk in the Soviet embassy in Ottawa, in September 1945. Early the following year the federal government established a royal commission to inquire into his disclosures. Consisting of Justices Lindsay Kellock and Robert Taschereau, the commission implicated several people in acts of espionage, among them two professors. Both were tried. Raymond Boyer, a chemist at McGill, was convicted of passing classified information to an agent of a foreign power and was sentenced to two years in prison. The charges against Israel Halperin, a mathematician at Queen's, were dismissed.

In March 1946 McGill announced that Boyer had been suspended pending the outcome of his trial, which took place later that year. By the time he was sentenced, in January 1948, he was no longer in McGill's employ. His contract had ended on 31 August 1947; renewing it had been out of the question. His connection with McGill had not gone unnoticed, however. Indeed, of the scientists implicated by the Kellock-Taschereau Commission, six had graduated from McGill. Solon Low, leader of the federal Social Credit Party, referred to this in describing the institution as a 'hot-bed of communism.'[1]

Editors defended McGill, as did one of its alumni, Minister of National Health and Welfare Brooke Claxton – and with reason. McGill, like Canada's universities generally, was staunchly anticommunist. Avowed 'reds' did not get academic positions. However, the very few who, upon appointment, came under suspicion of being communists or fellow travellers were often ignored. The Gouzenko hearings did not change this.[2]

Concerns within McGill focused not on communism but on something altogether different. As Stanley Brice Frost comments, 'These incidents raised again a question which had been vigorously debated in the early days of the war' – the propriety of doing secret research on behalf of any agency, public or private. 'The thrust of university research, it was agreed, was the discovery and dissemination of new knowledge; research findings which could not be published were inimical to the idea of the university.'[3] Alas, in the postwar world the practice did not always live up to this ideal.

Israel Halperin was charged in April 1946 with conspiracy and a breach of the Official Secrets Act. The Crown's case collapsed when the sole witness against him refused to testify, and he was acquitted on both charges. His troubles with the law ended at this point, but his troubles at Queen's had just begun.[4]

A trustee, D.A. Gillies, took the view that the dismissal of the charges did not invalidate the findings of the Kellock-Taschereau Commission and 'that Halperin's record as a Communist fellow traveller indicates that he is not the type of individual who should be teaching in a Canadian university.' Principal Robert C. Wallace doubted the wisdom of any attempt to act on the report of the royal commission – 'a very strong repercussion would be felt in university circles across the land' – but sought legal advice. 'While it may be improper to conclude that where there was so much smoke there must have been fire,' Francis King (the university's lawyer) wrote, 'this same smoke has in itself brought about a situation in which the Trustees ... may find it best to exercise their authority and clear the air by removing the cause.' Citing the case law on tenure, he thought the trustees 'would be quite within their rights in terminating [Halperin's] employment by any reasonable notice.'[5]

When the board met in the fall, Gillies moved that Halperin be asked to resign. The discussion revealed a serious difference of opinion among board members, and the matter was deferred until May 1948. The board executive interviewed Halperin a fortnight before the May meeting and found that he would not answer questions arising out of the findings of the Kellogg-Taschereau Report. (To this day, he declines to discuss the affair.) He did appear briefly at the board meeting on 15 May, but added nothing to what he had said earlier.

Several trustees argued that Halperin should be asked to resign, but Chancellor Charles Dunning argued that it would be wrong to dismiss 'a professor who had been acquitted by the courts of the only charges brought against him.' To do so, he said, 'would place a black mark beside the name of Queen's, a mark which would remain there for many a long day.' His speech was decisive: 'After lengthy discussion it was agreed ... that no action be taken.' But if no trustee with Dunning's prestige had spoken in defence of due process, Halperin might have been dismissed, and since his wartime associations as well as his presumed political views were at least partly at issue, his dismissal would certainly have touched on academic freedom.[6]

Academic freedom was central to the case of Halperin's colleague, Glen Shortliffe. A scholar of nineteenth-century French literature and history, to whose study he brought a left-wing perspective (he was a member of the CCF), Short-liffe was also interested in current French politics. In 1945 he began to contribute talks on this subject to the CBC program *Midweek Review.* His point of view emerges from a letter written in 1947. Communism did not have a chance of wrecking 'a healthy social organism,' he wrote, and it was 'childish' to think that one-third of French voters had cast their ballots for the Communist Party 'because Joseph Stalin [had] hypnotized them.' Their votes expressed 'disillusionment' with official excuses for the existence of grinding poverty alongside abundance. As for the Cold War, Shortliffe refused to submerge his reason 'in an hysterical hate-fest directed against one particular dictatorship by those whose real complaint is not her assault on human liberty, but her attack on certain concepts of private property.'[7]

Neither Shortliffe's attacks on anticommunist dictatorships nor his efforts to explain the appeal of communism in France commanded universal admiration. But he got far more praise than criticism. He was 'not inclined to attach too much importance to this sort of work,' he told Wallace in 1948. 'At the same time it is an educational endeavour, I believe, in the best sense, and is not without benefit to my own reputation and that of Queen's.'[8]

That fall he agreed to share with his colleague Martyn Estall the political commentary on another CBC program, *Weekend Review.* Instead of the 270 seconds of airtime that he was used to having, he would have fifteen minutes, allowing him to deal with subjects in greater depth. He was apprehensive. 'I feel nervous as a bride,' he informed his producer, Marjorie McEnaney, in October, 'mainly, I suppose, because the world situation has just about reached the point where all public discussion of it will be drowned in bugle calls.'[9]

Speaking more regularly than in the past, Shortliffe had to inform himself about areas other than his beloved France. One of these areas was China, where Chiang Kai-shek and his Nationalist forces were losing a war to Mao Tse-tung and the Chinese Communist Party. By November 1948 Shortliffe was at odds with the *Kingston Whig-Standard*, challenging its claim that China 'had been left virtually unaided in its fight against the Communists there.' His criticism brought a charge that the tenor of his letter was characteristic of 'Communist apologists.'[10]

A broadcast on getting along with the Soviets so annoyed the editor of the Montreal *Gazette* that he charged Shortliffe with deliberately downplaying the USSR's record of tyranny. Among those who sent a copy of this editorial to Wallace was a trustee, J.B. Stirling: 'Dr. Glen Shortliffe's address made a poor impression in these parts!' After a publication called the *Radio Broadcasting Report* identified Shortliffe as 'either a communist or a fellow-traveller,' two other trustees forwarded copies to Wallace. One carried the annotation: 'Are there any advantages to our university in retaining a Communist or a sympathizer of the Stalin fraternity?'[11]

In February 1949 Shortliffe spoke about the trial of Cardinal Mindszenty and the conflict between church and state in Hungary, comparing that country's experiences with those of late-nineteenth-century France. A provincial civil servant in Toronto would have none of it. 'Claptrap,' he called the talk, saying that its purpose was evidently to defend 'the gangsters' who had seized the government of Hungary. Wallace passed this letter to Shortliffe during a conversation that shattered the latter's composure. It was not the only letter of its kind he had received, Wallace told him. Criticism had also come from people close to the university. This was a problem, for a campaign for funds was about to begin, and Shortliffe's views were unpopular with the very people from whom large sums were expected.[12]

Shortliffe appealed to the principle of academic freedom but wrote within hours to express regret that he had unwittingly embarrassed Queen's: 'I do not consider my own views on freedom ... to be sufficient justification for continuing to bring opprobrium upon my colleagues.' The broadcasts would cease, he promised. 'I had no thought that you might discontinue the broadcasts,' Wallace replied. 'I felt simply that you should be aware of the type of communication that has come to me from time to time.' Yet a feeling of relief surfaced: 'I appreciate greatly the attitude that you have indicated in your letter.'[13]

The historian of Queen's, Frederick W. Gibson, writes that Wallace, while believing in academic freedom, 'unfortunately' gave more weight to his university's need for money, and that this caused 'an uncharacteristic lapse in judgment.' Wallace probably hoped only that Shortliffe 'would tone down his comments and be more prudent and discreet.' But that sort of prudence and discretion were not part of Shortliffe's character. After reading the copies of the *Radio Broadcasting Report* that Wallace had lent him, he informed the principal that he had 'contempt [for] the motives of those who choose to attack the University because of their disagreement with the view of one member of its staff.' It was apparent, he said, 'that so long as prominent citizens do not consider such action beneath them, universities are bound to be placed in an almost impossible situation,' and since he had 'no desire whatever' to make an issue of his broadcasts or 'to become the centre of a *cause célèbre* which could only harm both myself and the University,' his decision to end the broadcasts stood.[14]

This decision did not end the story. A radio talk in October 1948 had brought a request from the editor of the *International Journal* for an article on politics in France. The article Shortliffe wrote analysed class conflict from 1789 into the mid-twentieth century and the legislation it had prompted, with parenthetical comments on U.S. foreign policy since 1945. Read with the benefit of hindsight, the article seems at times shrewd, at times naïve. It drew criticism from Frank Scott and the journalist George Ferguson but did not deserve the following smear by an employee of the Canadian Chamber of Commerce: 'Mr. Shortliffe's professorial gobbledygook often obscures just what he is driving at, but there is little doubt about where his sympathies lie in the great ideological battle between Communism and the Democracies.'[15]

An annotated – 'Yes, Queen's has 'em!' – copy of the Chamber of Commerce newsletter landed on Wallace's desk in May, courtesy of J.B. Stirling. 'I am sorry to say,' Stirling wrote, 'that several of my prospects on Special Names drew my attention to the article, with a smile of course, but at the same time deploring such activity.'[16] (The reference was to a group of potential donors from whom large gifts were expected.) Shortliffe had written a serious article for a scholarly journal, but a biased reading of the article, joined to the suggestion that its author was a communist or fellow traveller, seemed to be affecting the university's campaign for funds.

Whether Stirling was reporting his own attitude or that of potential donors, his comment struck at the very heart of academic freedom. Even in the restrictive version enunciated by Sir Robert Falconer in 1922, it included the freedom to do research and publish its findings. But what should a president and governing board do when the scholarly work of a professor threatened to harm the university financially? Maintain academic freedom and suffer the consequences? Or redefine that freedom to exclude anything that might weaken support from donors? There is no sign that Wallace did anything about Stirling's note. No executive head would have been eager to try to answer the questions it posed. Such questions rarely needed to be confronted, however, for the spreading miasma of Cold War fear and suspicion fostered much the same kind of self-censorship that had prevailed during the Second World War.

Shortliffe's failure, later in 1949, to gain admission to the United States after he had accepted an offer from George Washington University in St Louis may have been the result of the attention his broadcasts had drawn. (In October, when the U.S. attorney general said that he was admissible after all, he no longer wished to go.) Another disturbing incident took place in 1954. Invited in the spring to teach French to subalterns in the summer school of the Royal Military College, Shortliffe was relieved of his duties on 8 June, just as the course was about to begin. His efforts to get an explanation from the Department of National Defence were for some months unsuccessful. Not until December did he receive a letter from the minister, Ralph Campney. Technical competence was not the sole criterion in selecting teachers, Campney explained: 'Active participation in public controversy on the part of ... officers is naturally viewed with disfavour and the Armed Forces are inclined to regard those with an established tendency in this direction as somewhat unsuited for the task of instructing junior officers.'[17]

A CBC writer, gathering information in 1961 for a program on security screenings, asked Shortliffe how the incident had affected him. He answered that, coupled with his experiences in 1949, it had undermined his scholarship. Aware that he would tend to censor himself 'in an effort to demonstrate ... his own "reliability,"' he preferred 'not to write at all on any subject which might have social significance to our thought police.' This ruled out large areas of research, he said. For instance, he had found 'some unknown sources in the French National Archives dealing with the impact of the Revolution of 1871 upon certain French writers, had published an article in this area, and was working on a book,' but he had 'found it psychologically impossible to continue.' Instead, he had begun to work on language laboratory techniques, which were uncontroversial and eminently safe (a textbook of which he was co-author appeared in 1954): 'In other words I think I have voluntarily blown my own brains out.'[18]

Henry S. Ferns, a graduate of Manitoba and Cambridge, was apparently a victim of mistaken transliteration. It seemed as though his name had appeared in the notebook of a Soviet intelligence officer, part of the Gouzenko disclosures.[19] It did not help that he had become a Marxist while at Cambridge in the later 1930s and was a friend of Herbert Norman, a diplomat who was at one time under suspicion of disloyalty. (Hounded by U.S. red baiters, Norman committed suicide in 1957.)

Ferns was in the Department of External Affairs until 1944, when he resigned to embark upon an academic career. He taught history at United College from 1945 to 1947, but his contract was not renewed when he refused to sever his connection with a cooperatively run Winnipeg newspaper. After two years at the University of Manitoba, he applied for an associate professorship in economics and history at the Canadian Services College at Royal Roads, near Victoria, B.C. The salary and the area were attractive, but he was also concerned to clear himself from the suspicion of disloyalty that clung to him after the Gouzenko affair. If the Government of Canada would employ him to teach future officers, he reasoned, 'who then could say I was a red?'[20]

Ferns was offered the Royal Roads job in April 1949, but in August he received a letter from the Civil Service Commission informing him, 'The Department of National Defence has now indicated that your services are not acceptable.'[21] He tried to obtain a reason, but without success. Ferns's impression was that no civil servant was willing to tell the truth lest it be used to embarrass a cabinet minister.

While Ferns was making inquiries, he and his wife sensed that they were under surveillance. 'There was no government-induced terror in Canada,' he later wrote, 'but the press had created an atmosphere of fear and suspicion about reds. When I saw what this did to me and to friends I began to realize, not in theory but in practice, how useful real terror must be to tyrants.' In the end, he signed a form releasing the government from all claims and received $2,000, close to half a year's salary – 'a sweet little example of the Canadian art of compromise.' He later emigrated to England, where he had a distinguished academic career.[22]

In 1947 C.S. LeMesurier announced his retirement as McGill's dean of law. Although next in line, Frank Scott was passed over. In explanation, Principal Cyril James told LeMesurier that the position required full-time attention. For this reason 'the Board [had] unanimously adopted a resolution providing that no individual who is a Cabinet member or an executive officer of a political party can be considered as eligible for a Deanship.' James continued, 'Quite frankly, I would be very doubtful, if I may judge the sentiment of the Board of Governors, whether [Scott] would be considered a desirable candidate even if he were to resign from executive office in the party to which he belongs.'[23]

LeMesurier passed this information on to Scott. Angered by this evidence of anti-CCF bias, he asked the assistance of the American Association of University Professors, of which he was a member. The associate secretary, George Pope Shannon, pointed out that the refusal of an administrative appointment did not ordinarily justify an inquiry. However, if Scott could supply evidence of discrimination on political grounds, Committee A would be able to determine whether there were grounds to proceed. Scott sent Shannon a copy of James's letter to LeMesurier, saying he was sure the charge of discrimination would stick. But realizing that his case was 'border line,' he had second thoughts and deemed it wise not to file a grievance.[24]

Not satisfied with keeping Scott out of the deanship, the board in January 1948 adopted a resolution on political service, which made the following three points. First, 'The duties of the Dean of a Faculty are such that they cannot adequately be performed by anyone who is a member of the Federal Parliament or any Provincial Legislature.' Second, service as a cabinet minister or parliamentary secretary is incompatible with the duties of a full-time member of the faculty. Third, 'The Board has no desire to interfere with the political views or activities of any member of the teaching or administrative staff, but considers it adversely affects the interests of the University for members of the staff to hold positions on the principal executive body of any political party.' This resolution was not to apply retroactively but was intended as a guide for the future.[25]

Determined to undo this policy if he could, Scott asked his friend Harold

Laski, a political scientist at the London School of Economics, what the rule was at LSE and the University of London. Professors were allowed to hold executive offices in political parties, Laski replied: 'I have myself been a member of the executive of the British Labour Party since 1936; its Vice Chairman in 1944–45, and its Chairman in 1945–46.' Armed with this information, Scott prepared a memorandum arguing that the board's resolution was inappropriate: 'The only limitation on the extra-mural activities of a professor should be based on the time spent outside the university ... Politics is only one of many possible activities which may cut into the professor's time. It should not be singled out for special restriction.' Vulnerable to the charge of harassing one member of the faculty, the board backed off. A new resolution adopted in March 1948 deleted all mention of executive office in a political party.[26]

'Actually the situation suited me admirably,' Scott wrote in 1968 about his exclusion from the deanship. 'No one in his right senses wants to be Dean, but he certainly wants even less to belong to a university which discriminates against its staff for political reasons.' In fact, he did become dean in 1961 and served three conflict-ridden years that he did not much enjoy.[27]

The board's refusal to appoint Scott to the deanship in 1947 had the unintended effect of enhancing his reputation as a constitutional lawyer. His biographer Sandra Djwa points out that his failure to gain promotion freed him to act as counsel in *Roncarelli v. Duplessis*. This case made Scott a hero to Quebec's Jehovah's Witnesses, who were under significant civil disabilities in the province, but it angered Premier Maurice Duplessis. Scott's involvement in another case, *Switzman v. Elbling*, which led to the invalidation of Quebec's Padlock Act, also annoyed the premier.[28]

Scott's work on the *Roncarelli* and *Switzman* cases may have had disagreeable consequences for McGill when Duplessis's government began to fund all of the province's universities in the 1950s. In the course of an essay on McGill's Faculty of Law, Roderick A. Macdonald claims that, partly because of Duplessis's animus against Scott, the provincial government treated McGill less generously than other Quebec universities. Stanley Brice Frost (McGill's historian as well as James's biographer) neither confirms nor denies this claim.[29]

In time, Scott came to appreciate the measure of academic freedom he did enjoy at McGill. In the preface to his last book he wrote: 'I never at any time felt my position as teacher and writer was threatened, and while my behaviour was under close scrutiny and doubtless constrained in consequence, I owed the university my freedom from the much more inhibiting restraints imposed by the active practice of law in which I was first engaged. A group of law partners can be even more repressive than a Board of Governors, as I was eventually to learn in the Padlock Act and Roncarelli cases.'[30] Scott did not enjoy unrestricted academic freedom. Nevertheless, McGill did *nolens volens* provide him with a platform from which he was able to challenge and, on two occasions, defeat one of the most autocratic provincial governments ever.

Premier Duplessis's influence extended into the French-language universities of Quebec, for he joined the bishops in guarding against communism and other 'dangerous' ideas. Father Georges-Henri Lévesque took great care to protect Laval's Faculty of Social Sciences against charges of anticlericalism and irreligion – and with reason. When Paul-Émile Borduas of the École du meuble took the lead in issuing *Refus global*, the 1948 manifesto of the *automatiste* group of artists, its anticlericalism led the government to order his suspension. Soon afterwards Borduas was dismissed, Principal J.-M. Gauvreau explained that the artist's 'writings ... as well as his state of mind make him unsuitable for the kind of teaching we wish for our students.'[31]

Political heterodoxy was no more welcome than the religious kind. Pierre Elliott Trudeau, a known dissident, 'was denied the teaching job he wanted at the Université de Montréal, where the government controlled academic appointments through the church hierarchy.'[32]

The universities began to change even before the Quiet Revolution of the 1960s. In the aftermath of the 1956 provincial election, two Laval academics discussed the corruption of Quebec elections, the role played in them by clerics, and the pervasive use of the 'red smear' in linking social legislation to socialism and communism, with the aim of discrediting it in the eyes of the electorate. Since they did not single out any particular political party, both major Quebec parties, the Liberals as well as the governing Union nationale, were implicated.[33]

'Lendemain d'élections' was published in a low-circulation periodical, *Ad usum sacerdotum*, which was intended exclusively for members of the clergy. On 7 August 1956, though, Montreal's *Le Devoir* published the article in its entirety, while the *Globe and Mail* quoted liberally from a translation.[34]

The next day the authors were identified as Gérard Dion, head of the Department of Industrial Relations in the Faculty of Social Sciences, and Louis O'Neill, a chaplain at the university and professor of ethics in the Seminary of Quebec. They expressed surprise at the sensation their document had caused. As they pointed out, what they had written was hardly news: 'En somme, qu'y avons-nous dit de plus que ce que tout le monde savait déjà? N'est-il pas troublant de constater que dans notre province, la vérité pure et simple ne puisse apparaître au grand jour sans provoquer ce qu'on pourrait appeler le scandale des faibles?'[34] The really astonishing development, they implied, was the response (most of it favourable) to what they had written.[35]

Within a few days, several other newspapers in Quebec, among them *Le*

Soleil (Quebec), the *Quebec Chronicle-Telegraph*, and *La Réforme* (Montreal), reproduced the document, and articles on the issue appeared in a large number of Canadian newspapers as well as in the *New York Times* and the *Manchester Guardian*. That fall, 'Lendemain d'élections' appeared in full in periodicals in France and Belgium.[36]

What lent the document a good deal of its sting was the use to which the press put it, particularly *Le Devoir*. Although newspaper editors pointed out that the Liberals were not averse to using dirty tricks – Liberal leader Georges Lapalme declined to comment – they suggested that the Union nationale was the primary target of the two academics. On 11 August, noting that Premier Duplessis had skipped his usual Friday press conference, *Le Devoir* speculated editorially that he was afraid of questions about the Dion-O'Neill article. When the premier cancelled his press conference for the second week running, the editor suggested that 'before stepping on such ultra-slippery ground,' Duplessis was waiting to see whether the church authorities would reprimand the two clerics.[37]

The interest of these authorities manifested itself early. On 9 August the rector of Laval, Mgr Alphonse-Marie Parent, wrote to Dion: 'Mgr L'Archevêque m'a demandé s'il y an un censeur à la disposition de "Ad Usum Sacerdotum."' If there was a censor, who was he? asked the rector. If there was not, it was the wish of the archbishop (who was also the university's chancellor) that one be appointed.[38]

Dion replied that all issues of the periodical were submitted to ecclesiastical censorship before they appeared, and he named his censor: 'Le censeur qui m'a été désigné par l'autorité diocésaine est l'ancien doyen de la Faculté de théologie ..., Monseigneur Ernest Lemieux.' This evidently settled the matter from Parent's point of view. If the archbishop was unhappy with the document, he may have expressed his irritation to Lemieux. But having observed ecclesiastical due process, Dion and O'Neill were covered. When the director of the social action department of the Diocese of Brooklyn expressed the hope that they had 'not unduly suffered' from their 'forthright, courageous expression,' Dion replied, 'Until now I didn't get any trouble from the Bishop or the Rector of Laval.' He added that the politicians were 'very mad,' but speculated that public opinion seemed to be so strongly behind him and O'Neill that it was difficult for the government 'to do anything.'[39]

Duplessis never did respond to Dion and O'Neill, but more than one newspaper editor perceived an indirect reply in a speech he gave in early September, when he said, 'Il n'y pas ailleurs au monde de population plus honnête que celle de notre province. Et il n'y a pas un clergé plus noble que celui de la province de Québec.' Duplessis asked his listeners to pay no attention to tales that suggested otherwise.[40]

Several journals associated with the Union nationale (prominent among them *Le Bien public* from Duplessis's hometown of Trois-Rivières) had attacked Dion and O'Neill when their article appeared, linking them to *Le Devoir*'s editor, Gérard Filion. Some time later the Union nationale propagandist Robert Rumilly wrote a pamphlet that denounced the two priests as leftists who enjoyed communist approbation, condemned their article as 'un mémoire anti-québécois,' and labelled *Le Devoir* 'le quartier général du mouvement gauchiste dans la province de Québec.' But the premier himself said in October that he had not read the article by Dion and O'Neill and that it seemed to interest mainly people living outside the province.[41]

Duplessis may have cared little about what Dion and O'Neill wrote, but someone in the premier's office, the government, or Union nationale headquarters cared enough about it to hire detectives to monitor Dion's activities. A report, which seems to have been one of several (there is reference to an earlier report), made available to Dion by the provincial Liberals after they gained office in 1960, gave details of his comings and goings over a period of several days in September 1956 and added, 'Avons l'intention de travailler avec microphone ultrasensible et enrégistrer sur fil conversation intérieure. Nous avons la machine pour enrégistrer.'[42]

It is not known whether this unlawful proposal to record Dion's conversations was acted on, nor is it known to whom the detectives were reporting. In a note covering the report, Dion surmised that it was Duplessis.[43] But that was a guess. Still, we may safely assume that any dirt dug up by the detectives would have been used against Dion.

If political pressure was put on Laval to silence the two men, this did not become public. In October, several newspapers reported a rumour that Parent had instructed O'Neill, the younger of the two, to desist from discussing politics, but they added that Parent had denied the rumour. In writing about this subject, Gérard Filion cited a strong defence of academic freedom – 'sans laquelle nul travail intellectuel n'est possible' – made by Mgr Irénée Lussier, rector of the University of Montreal.[44]

In November 1956, Blair Fraser asked in *Maclean's* whether 'two humble priests could make such charges against the all-powerful Duplessis regime and get away with it.' The answer, apparently, was yes. Dion and O'Neill remained at Laval undisturbed. It is possible, therefore, using the words of Raymond Houde of the Université du Québec à Trois-Rivières, to see the incident as 'the dawn of academic freedom in the Roman Catholic universities of Quebec.'[45]

Sometime after 1945 the University of Alberta biochemist George Hunter resumed the practice of using his last lecture of term to link his subject to the larger world. As in 1940, this landed him in trouble. On 8 April 1949 the assistant to President Robert Newton, Walter Johns, received a telephone call from an *Edmonton Journal* reporter. In class the day before, Hunter had allegedly made 'remarks which seemed to support views more commonly associated with the Soviet Union and members of the Communist Party.' Johns made inquiries and learned from a student that Hunter had discussed the negative effects of war on nutrition, had denounced the decision to drop the atomic bomb on Japan in 1945, had criticized the recently announced North Atlantic Treaty Organization (NATO) as likely to lead to war, and had urged students to work for peace.[46]

A protest against Hunter's remarks and his use of class time to make them, signed by 17 of the 257 students in his course, reached Newton on 25 April. (Nothing indicates that anyone had solicited the protest, but someone of unknown identity did promise the seventeen that their names would not become public.) A month later, Newton brought it to a meeting of the board's executive. He then informed Hunter that a complaint had been made against him, that the board would discuss it on 29 June, and that he might wish to appear.

Hunter asked to be informed of the nature of the complaint, but only on 25 June did he receive a copy of the protest, without the names of the signatories. In response, he denied that he had propagated his political views. He had ended the final class, he said, with a farewell message in which he had tried to link issues of nutrition to the world situation: 'Throughout this farewell message I was ... not teaching them. I was confronting them with problems faced by all responsible citizens, and kept asking my students "what are you going to do about that and that." As my lectures were concluded I did not feel that I was improperly using lecture time.' But he said he recognized that some students might disagree, and he would cease the practice if the board objected to it.[47]

Hunter appeared before the board in the early afternoon of 29 June, read his statement, answered a few questions, and withdrew. His appearance was a formality. In the morning Newton had discussed his file and given notice of motion to dismiss him, 'the latest incident being simply one in a series which had caused dissatisfactions accumulating over a period of years.' The motion passed unanimously that afternoon. The board then passed another motion 'that the date of termination of Dr. Hunter's appointment be June 30, 1949, and that he be given the sum of $2,000 in lieu of notice.' (his salary was $5,100). Thus ended his academic career. He found a laboratory position in England but never taught in a university again.[48]

The board's right to dismiss Hunter was beyond challenge. He held his tenure during pleasure, though the president's recommendation was needed to dismiss him. As well, the board was under no obligation to give a reason for its action, and it declined to do so. Hunter let it be known that he had lost his position because of unpopular views expressed during class, but Newton denied this. To a friend he wrote of 'a long career of trouble and making trouble.' Publicly he spoke of 'dissatisfaction over a period of years' and of Hunter's 'whole unsatisfactory history in this university,' but he would say nothing more on the grounds that this might injure both Hunter and the university.[49]

Vagueness served Newton, for it obscured the fact that the dismissal made a travesty of due process. The procedure used conformed neither to the board's statement on dismissals, adopted in 1943, nor to common standards of fairness. Most important was the fact that Hunter did not get a proper chance to defend himself. When he met the board, he believed that his lecture of 7 April was at issue, and it was to the protest against it that he responded. Unknown to him, it was his whole record during the preceding nine years that the board had been reviewing.

Newton's vagueness made it difficult, too, for observers to judge whether the case involved an offence against academic freedom. A committee appointed by the Association of the Teaching Staff of the University of Alberta (ATSUA) spoke with Newton and decided that the dismissal 'was based on grounds other than those of academic or professional deficiency,' but also that 'the Board's action ... in no way involves any infringement of academic freedom or civil liberties.' Worried about the suddenness with which Hunter had been removed, however, the committee questioned the procedure used.[50]

In August 1949 ATSUA carried a motion regretting the board's procedure and asking for more information. It did not get any. Thus stymied, a general meeting of ATSUA in October resolved 'that in the view of the absence of further information, this body feels it can take no further action.' In truth, there was little wish to do so. One of Hunter's allies, the zoologist William Rowan, wrote to a friend, 'It is most unfortunate that Hunter was the unpopular individual he was,' for this made many of his colleagues insensitive to the issue of academic freedom which Rowan believed was involved.[51]

During the 1940s Hunter had become a difficult colleague. A dispute in 1941 over his salary seems to have embittered him. Five years later a nasty row took place between Hunter and Newton over the university's regulations governing travel to scholarly conferences. Believing that Hunter had tried to claim a small sum of money which he had not actually spent, Newton asked the secretary of the Faculty Relations Committee (FRC), Ralph Shaner, to convene an ad hoc group of three in order to determine whether grounds existed to dismiss the biochemist. This group agreed with Newton that Hunter's expense claim, added to the 1940 classroom incident, justified his demotion as well as dismissal with a year's notice. No one seems to have thought it necessary to hear what Hunter might have to say in explanation or defence – an abuse of due process that compounded Newton's failure to observe FRC regulations for dealing with matters of this kind.[52]

From the file that President W.A.R. Kerr had opened on Hunter in 1940, Newton knew that the biochemist was thought to be a communist or fellow traveller. Moreover, in addition to his 1946 challenge to the university's policy on travel expenses, Hunter had twice, in 1943 and 1945, attacked the policy requiring members of his department to invigilate exams in courses other than their own. Newton almost certainly resented the implicit criticism of himself in these attacks. An able autocrat, he owed his appointment in part to a promise made to Premier William Aberhart that he would 'handle staff problems firmly,' and he was true to his word. Even his admirers could be critical of his approach. One of them wrote in 1950, 'As a young president he was somewhat dictatorial, impatient of old regulations, rather ruthless, and even contemptuous of the views of others.' Rowan, who was far from being an admirer, was more outspoken. He told a Calgary journalist, 'He has hurt members of the staff, over-ruled the wishes of heads of departments and introduced needless and unforgivable unpleasantness and grief among those whom he personally doesn't like, and that's quite a number.'[53]

The dispute over Hunter's travel claim had brought him before the board, and he had not made a good impression. The board had unanimously condemned his remarks as 'offensive and truculent,' his attitude to the regulations as 'entirely wrong,' and his 'disrespect for constituted authority' as something that would in future not be tolerated. Left to a later date was a discussion of his future with the university.[54]

Since meetings of the full board were infrequent and the agendas long, the matter was twice postponed, and Newton said he saw no reason for keeping it on the agenda. A brief discussion followed. Several board members wondered whether 'avowed Communists' should be teaching at the university at all, given that they were 'working for the downfall of our Canadian constitution and way of life.' Newton said 'that the attitude of mind that makes men Communists might also explain their general antagonism to all other forms of Government, including university government ..., but he thought it preferable that any action taken by the Board should be based on the satisfactoriness or otherwise of their contributions to the life and work of the University.' The board voted to drop the matter.[55]

Newton's refusal to indulge board members who wanted to fire Hunter may have been the result of letters he had received from two fellow university heads. 'Have you any avowed Communists on your academic staff and, if so, what is your attitude towards them?' Newton had asked. McGill's Cyril James had replied, 'I should be inclined to pay no attention to the fact that a member of the teaching staff was a theoretical communist, provided that his political beliefs did not interfere with the efficiency of his teaching and his general cooperation in the work of the University.' It was not a man's beliefs 'but his efficiency and loyalty as a member of the University community' that were the important thing.[56]

Toronto's Sidney Smith said he knew of 'only two avowed communists' on his staff – he did not name them – and 'to date' they had been 'very discreet.' To act openly against them would be a mistake, he observed, for they would thrive on persecution: 'Of course, if any member of the staff participates in activities which would carry the disapproval of his colleagues, one would be on good ground for tough treatment.'[57]

At that time Newton was already gathering evidence of Hunter's poor relations with some of his colleagues. Late in 1946 the dean of agriculture called him 'a difficult and dangerous man [who] had a capacity for stirring up trouble in very wicked ways, putting people at odds with one another.' A note dated 2 April 1947 states: 'Dean Ower said Dr. Rawlinson at meeting of Med. Res. group in Winnipeg overheard Dr. Hunter ... make disloyal statements to Dr. Trueman concerning the President of U. of A.' Five days after that, Newton heard from Shaner that Hunter was constantly complaining about the university administration: 'He had become like the Ancient Mariner.'[58]

Nothing in Hunter's file suggests that he could not get along with his students or the members of his small department; but a good many others, Newton among them, found him to be a nuisance. This seems to have been an important reason for his dismissal, his 'last lecture' of 1949 serving chiefly as a means of persuading board members that he really was a communist.

The Alberta dailies reported the dismissal and speculated on the reasons for it. The Canadian Press filed a story that referred to Hunter's political radicalism and quoted Newton as saying that although the biochemist's 'political views were not directly responsible for his dismissal ..., the Board of Governors had to take note of repeated [sic] complaints from university students that Dr. Hunter was using his classroom to propagate his political views.' This allowed readers to infer that the lecture of 7 April was the proverbial straw that broke the camel's back, thereby justifying Hunter's dismissal. A brief report in Time permitted the same inference.[59]

A Saturday Night editorial, on the other hand, claimed that Hunter's academic freedom was at issue, and an article in the Canadian Forum put academic freedom front and centre, charging that Hunter had been the victim of an anticommunist witch-hunt in which the provincial government was implicated.[60]

Upon reading this, Arthur Lower asked Frank Scott, 'Can you tell me anything about this man Hunter in Alberta who was dismissed last summer?' If the Forum article was correct, he continued, the matter was 'pretty shocking.'[61]

Scott in turn asked two friends in Edmonton for information. W.F. Bowker, Alberta's dean of law, wrote that Hunter had been 'quarrelsome and obstinate and disaffected' and had deserved dismissal. His alleged communism had not been at issue, so 'academic freedom was not involved.' Scott's other contact was Elmer Roper, a CCF member of the legislature. He reported that, as far as he could determine, Hunter was 'a communist or a very rabid fellow traveller' who had been indiscreet in expressing his opinions in class and outside, and that this, presumably, was the cause of his dismissal.[62]

Bowker and Roper had offered contradictory assessments, but Scott ignored this fact when informing Lower that Hunter seemed to be 'an impossible fellow to represent because he insisted in filling his lectures full of political propaganda.' Scott added, though, that the incident once again raised 'the question whether we should not have some professional organization in Canada which could take up cases of this sort and make an independent investigation.'[63]

An organization that did attempt such an investigation was the Association for Civil Liberties (ACL) in Toronto. Its executive included several University of Toronto professors, among them Leopold Infeld (applied mathematics), C. Brough Macpherson (political science), and Albert Rose (social work), and the editor of *Saturday Night*, B.K. Sandwell. Supplied with information by William Rowan and, upon request, by Hunter himself, the ACL executive authorized an investigation by the University of Toronto biochemist Hardolph Wasteneys. Since Wasteneys was on good terms with both Hunter and Newton, he might have done a better job as mediator. Having read Hunter's brief, he sought to balance it by soliciting Newton's account. He then wrote a report, which he offered for comment to Newton and Shaner but not to Hunter. The report recommended that 'the matter be dropped.'[64] It was.

While Wasteneys was carrying out his inquiry, Hunter wrote to the president of the First International Congress on Biochemistry, A.C. Chibnall, complaining that he had been 'dismissed with a day's notice ... without stated cause,' and charging Newton with having 'a personal animus' against him. When approached by Chibnall, Newton denied the charge. Chibnall suggested that the university would appear 'in a better light' if the board were to state that Hunter's political views were irrelevant to his dismissal: 'Nevertheless ... I know very little of the whole background, and I have no doubt that you and your colleagues have taken the steps that you think best.' Hunter also wrote fruitlessly to the Royal Society of Canada (of which he was a fellow), the National Research Council, and the American Society of Biological Chemists. If he had approached the American Association of University Professors, he might have got some action. Why he did not do so is unknown.[65]

Was academic freedom at issue in the Hunter case? The answer depends in part on how we define the concept but even more on what we believe to have been the grounds for the biochemist's dismissal. If Hunter lost his position because he was believed to be a communist or a fellow traveller, the offence against academic freedom would be clear. (The argument that communists are not entitled to academic freedom because their ideology leaves them unfree in their thinking, an argument heard in the United States during the Cold War years, begs the question.) The issue is less clear if Hunter was dismissed for using his classroom to advance political views. There was probably broad agreement at the time that professors should not air their political opinions in class, except perhaps as *obiter dicta* – a lectern was not a soapbox. (In fact, it was argued in Frank Underhill's defence that he did not use his classes as a platform for politics.)[66]

Yet the line between professional and personal opinion, between pedagogy and propaganda, is fine and hard to draw. Central to academic freedom is the freedom to teach. Who can say exactly where this freedom ends? Besides, Hunter's 'offence' is one that many professors commit but for which few are ever called to account. 'If there was a single offence, or even a few offences,' *Saturday Night* observed cogently, 'the use of them to justify dismissal is simply silly.'[67]

There was no policy at Alberta prohibiting what Hunter did. No Canadian university had such a policy. Presidents and boards, if they thought about it at all, probably realized that devising one would be difficult. It was easier to deal with incidents as they occurred, objecting to the expression of some views while ignoring others. If Hunter had praised NATO and the bombing of Hiroshima and Nagasaki rather than criticizing them, his remarks would have had no more connection to biochemistry than what he did in fact say, but no one in authority would have taken a student protest seriously. No professor, it is safe to say, has ever been disciplined for asserting what is politically correct or anodyne, no matter how distant from the subject of instruction.

Although Newton denied that Hunter's classroom expression of his political views had prompted his dismissal, the board minutes indicate that his alleged communism weighed against him and that the use of class time to state his opinions compounded his 'offence.' But Newton's assertion is correct insofar as his recommendation to dismiss Hunter was based on his assessment of the biochemist as dishonest, fractious, and disloyal. Very likely it was because they agreed with this assessment that the ATSUA committee and Dean Bowker asserted that academic freedom had not been at issue in Hunter's dismissal.

Were they right? This requires us to ask another question: Can criticizing or annoying a university president, or being generally 'difficult,' be protected by an appeal to academic freedom? The answer at Alberta in 1949 was no. Even William Rowan noted, 'If [Hunter] had been fired on the grounds of being a thorn in the flesh of the management, I don't believe much would have been said for we would all have believed it and considered it, at least from some angle, justified.' Unfortunately, the available documents do not indicate how Hunter's prickliness manifested itself, other than in his criticism of the university's invigilation and travel policies, and of Newton personally. Bowker wrote to Scott of 'pin-pricks' which, though individually insignificant, were cumulatively intolerable, but he offered no details.[68]

Today's concept of academic freedom includes candid criticism of administrators, even though these may regard it as carping, self-serving, or just plain wrong. Professors must be free to challenge not only their peers but also the authority of executive heads or governing boards. Without this freedom, no aspect of academic freedom is really safe. On the other hand, an appeal to academic freedom cannot be used to justify behaviour that interferes in a major way with the work of others – students, colleagues, or administrative staff. Someone's actions may become so disruptive that they warrant disciplinary action against that person, up to and including dismissal. This would typically have to be established by an independent committee appointed to arbitrate the case.

No evidence has survived to prove that Hunter's behaviour was of this kind, nor was he ever charged with it. We do know that Hunter annoyed his president and many of his colleagues. His 'last lecture' was a godsend to Newton, for it gave board members a sufficient reason to dismiss him. But Hunter's espousal of an unpopular point of view in class, though not irrelevant to his dismissal, was not the main reason for it. Newton's enmity was a more important consideration.

Hunter was soon forgotten. He had not been a 'good' colleague; his acerbity had isolated him. Unlike Underhill, for example, he was not well connected, either locally or nationally, and after his departure for Great Britain, where he died in 1978, he faded quickly out of mind. Newton retired in 1950 and left Edmonton. Both men had been disliked, and with both gone it was easy for others to forget the incident that linked them. When Walter Johns, who had been a supporting actor in 1949, came to write a history of the university, his reference to the affair was brief and misleading. (Newton's own account, in his unpublished memoirs, is little.less brief and no less misleading.)[69]

Was Hunter a Cold War casualty? Yes and no. Certainly, his alleged communism troubled members of the board and contributed to his dismissal. But contrary to what some observers inferred in 1949, there was no witch-hunt at the university and no evidence of pressure from Alberta's Social Credit government to get rid of him.

A limited insight into government attitudes emerges from a minor incident in the late fall of 1952. After the U.S. presidential election, some forty Alberta professors sent a telegram of condolence to the defeated Democratic candidate, Adlai Stevenson. This prompted criticism of a presumably improper intervention in Canada's conduct of foreign relations and led Premier Ernest Manning to ask for a meeting with President Andrew Stewart.

Afterwards, Stewart put the substance of his remarks on record. The telegram had 'no political significance,' he wrote. 'The embarrassment which has arisen from the malicious manner in which the Edmonton Journal forced the action of the professors to the attention of the public is regretted by all.' Stewart added his 'considered opinion' that the university did not 'at this time have on its staff anyone connected with the Communist Party, or who could be described as an active Communist or accused of propagating Communist ideas.'[70] Stewart's remark implies that Manning was interested in the possible presence of communists on campus, but we cannot be certain of the nature of his interest. We can, however, be certain that no tears were shed in government offices over the dismissal of George Hunter.

The Cold War had a major effect on the career of the theoretical physicist Leopold Infeld. He had left his native Poland for the United States in 1936 and two years later was appointed in the Department of Applied Mathematics at the University of Toronto. As he was the co-author with Albert Einstein of *The Evolution of Physics* (1938), his appointment was regarded as a coup. A year later, with President H.J. Cody's support, he obtained landed immigrant status.[71]

Infeld made his mark not only in his discipline but also as a prize-winning novelist and biographer. His memoir *Quest*, published in 1941, is notable both for its command of English (his fourth language) and for the insight it offers into the making of the scientific mind. It also contains these lines, memorializing a city now almost forgotten: 'It must be good to die in Toronto. The transition between life and death would be continuous, painless and scarcely noticeable in this silent town. I dreaded the Sundays and prayed to God that if he chose for me to die in Toronto he would let it be on a Saturday afternoon to save me from one more Toronto Sunday.'[72]

As a Jew and a man of the democratic left, Infeld loathed Nazism. After Germany attacked the Soviet Union in 1941, the year he became a British subject, he helped Barker Fairley of the University College German department found the Canada-Soviet Friendship Society. The support this society enjoyed during the war ended with the Gouzenko disclosures; Fairley and Infeld then sought to raise funds for the legal defence of such men as Israel Halperin. They 'were both at once dubbed "fellow-travellers,"' Infeld later recalled.[73]

Perhaps so. There is reason to be sceptical of the memoir of Infeld's Toronto days that appears in *Why I Left Canada* (1978). He wrote it well after the events took place and, living in Poland as he then did, he may have wanted to present himself as having been more radical in the 1940s than he really was. His extra-curricular activities at that time troubled neither President Cody nor his successor, Sidney Smith. On the contrary, he was something of a favourite. In informing Infeld of his promotion to full professor in 1948, Smith praised his 'splendid work for the University.' And when the physicist was invited to lecture at Warsaw University in the summer of 1949, Dean Samuel Beatty commented, 'It is a great tribute to him and a just recognition of his place in the world of scholarship.'[74]

In the fall of 1949 Infeld received an invitation to take up a visiting professorship at Princeton in the 1950 spring term. Beatty noted that this would create difficulties for graduate instruction and that it would be easier if he took a leave of absence for part or all of 1950–1. This gave Infeld an idea. Having taught without a break since 1938, on 7 November he asked Smith for sabbatical leave, and a few days later Beatty applied for it on Infeld's behalf.[75]

'While I can assure you that I will recommend to the Board of Governors that such leave be granted,' Smith informed Beatty on 19 November, 'I do not feel disposed to take this matter to the Board at the present time ... We should learn more about the details of his programme before we make a definite recommendation.' Beatty reported that Infeld was weighing two plans. The first would see him work on a book in Toronto, with visits to Harvard, Princeton, and the University of Chicago. The second would take him to Denmark and Switzerland before he went on to Poland, where he would work 'with several young mathematicians' on the theory of quantum electrodynamics. Infeld preferred the latter plan, for he thought that the Polish government would pay his passage and his expenses in Poland. Beatty asked Smith whether 'some blanket assurance could be given him that he will be allowed to go away on leave, leaving the details of time and payment over until the future, when the situation becomes clearer.' Smith saw Beatty and annotated the letter: 'S.B. Dec 1st. Yes. Leave at least ½ salary.'[76]

With a wife and two young children to support, Infeld had to augment his half pay or make it stretch. He found a way of doing both when, in March 1950, Warsaw University invited him to give a series of lectures. His transatlantic travel and his expenses while in Poland would be paid by the Polish government. Soon after Infeld received confirmation of this offer, Jack Thompson, a journalist working for a Roman Catholic weekly called the *Ensign*, asked him for an interview. Infeld spoke with him, gave him offprints of three articles from the *Scientific American*, including one about his 1949 visit to Poland, and mentioned that he would be there again soon. Having somehow formed the impression that Infeld was politically unsound, Thompson asked Smith to comment on the proposed visit. Smith turned to Infeld, who sent a telegram, approved by Smith, to the editor of the *Ensign*: 'The President has informed me of Mr. Thompson's telegram ... Some statements contained in it are false, others misleading.' Nevertheless, the article that appeared in mid-March asked why a man familiar with the theory and much of the practical application of atomic energy was going behind the Iron Curtain.[77]

This caught the eye of someone in the office of the leader of the opposition in Ottawa. On 16 March 1950 George Drew used the House of Commons question period to claim that Infeld intended to go to Poland 'armed with certain atomic knowledge that he gained during two years' association with Dr. Einstein in the United States, and from several years' activity in the fields of mathematics and physics at the University of Toronto.' He asked what the government proposed to do about it.[78]

As Infeld was not a nuclear physicist, the government proposed to do nothing. Smith took fright, however. When a reporter asked him to comment on Drew's question, he distanced himself from Infeld's plans. He knew 'nothing' about them, he said: the board would deal with Infeld's application for leave when it came before them.[79] Memory can be conveniently selective. It suited Smith to forget that he had approved Infeld's sabbatical plan in principle. He may suddenly have sensed that a scientific sojourn in Poland would look suspicious to some; and, himself a Conservative, he may have been unwilling to correct Drew publicly or privately, possibly embarrassing or offending him.

Infeld told reporters that Drew was misinformed about his knowledge of atomic matters. But he did intend to give some graduate lectures and work with people who were interested in the field of research that interested him: 'It never entered my mind that this could be regarded by anyone as something wrong.' Having visited Poland in 1949, he thought that his going again might do good: 'Meetings among scientists of different countries, when there is no question of secrecy involved, are very beneficial.' Besides, he wished to show his American-born wife and Canadian-born children the place where he was born.[80]

In response, Drew descended to innuendo. He was surprised to learn that Infeld had been in Poland in 1949 and wondered why he had been invited for a second visit: 'Anyone who is opposed to communism would not be permitted to teach in a Polish university today. Dr. Infeld's statement alone is sufficient reason to inquire why he is so acceptable to the Communist educational authorities in Poland.'[81]

Smith was torn. He had good reason to want to accommodate Infeld, whose value to the university was considerable. If a reminder was needed it came on

21 March in the form of a report from the institution's director of publicity, K.S. Edey, who was happy to report that Infeld had addressed the Toronto Men's Press Club on the subject of atomic energy control: 'Professor Infeld declines many invitations to address groups large and small. He made an exception in this case (and set a fine example for his colleagues) because he felt it was an opportunity to do a job of public relations for the University.' The journalists, Edey added, had been 'delighted and grateful.'[82] Infeld was indeed an asset, Smith must have thought, but his proposed visit to Poland was a public relations headache. If only he could be persuaded not to go!

On 4 April Beatty formally asked that Infeld be granted leave. It was 'unfortunate' that he should have become 'an object of suspicion in some quarters,' Beatty wrote, but 'there is no chance whatever that he would attempt to pass over scientific secrets to the Soviet masters of Poland. His thought is entirely against the form of mass tyranny practised by the Soviets. On the contrary, his respect for individual freedom is one of the most characteristic things about him.' From the beginning Infeld had been candid about his plans, added Beatty. He needed and deserved a change and a rest; his leave would benefit both him and the university.[83]

Perhaps. But in a meeting with Infeld and Beatty, Smith said that he did not know whether he would recommend leave. When Infeld pointed out that his application had been made in November, Smith first denied it, then said that 'it had nothing to do with this particular leave.' He claimed that Ottawa regarded 'the company that Professor Infeld keeps in Poland as questionable and indeed dangerous.' Infeld responded that going to Poland was 'a matter of honour'; he did not wish it to be said 'that he was swerved from his purpose by those who had maligned him and that thereby he admitted the truth of their allegations.' Asked what he would do if he was denied a leave, 'he declared that perhaps it would not be possible for him then to go to Poland because he would not like to give up his University post.' Moreover, if a directive or even 'an unofficial hint' were to come from Ottawa that the government did not wish him to go, 'then he would not go ..., provided he could get to the United States where he could carry on his research.'[84]

After the two men left him, Smith sent a letter to George Glazebrook, a member of the history department on loan to External Affairs. If Ottawa asked Infeld not to go, Smith wrote, his 'honour would be satisfied and he would seek to take his leave of absence in the United States.' Could Glazebrook speak to his chief 'with a view perhaps to you or someone else in the Department having a talk with Infeld?'[85]

Six days later, Smith and Glazebrook spoke by telephone. According to Smith's notes, Glazebrook reported that Mike (the secretary of state for external affairs, Lester B. Pearson) had said that the government would not prohibit Infeld from going. But either Pearson or Glazebrook – it is unclear who – was willing to be quoted as saying that a Canadian 'should not mix up with that crowd at this period' and that going to Poland would be a black mark against Infeld with the U.S. security agencies.[86]

When Smith saw Infeld and Beatty again, he tried several different tacks: Infeld's leave had not been approved; another member of his department, A.F.C. Stevenson, was expected to ask for leave and they could not both go; if Infeld went to Poland he might in future be barred from the United States; he might even have to resign from the university.[87]

Infeld asked for time to think. A month later he left for England, having promised to let Beatty know by the end of May what he proposed to do. 'In the meantime,' Beatty told Smith, 'I have told Stevenson that if Infeld is away for the year ... it will not be possible to give him leave.'[88]

Stevenson then resigned. This gave Smith an idea. When Beatty wrote that he had received a letter from Infeld asking for leave 'on the original basis, namely at half salary and to be free to go to Poland if he wished,' Smith was ready with an answer. 'Now that Stevenson has resigned,' he replied, 'there will be no possibility of my recommending to the Board any type of leave of absence for Professor Infeld during the session of 1950–51.' This reflected existing policy: 'We cannot establish any precedent in this regard. Otherwise, we will have difficulty in explaining our action to colleagues such as Professor [Donald] Creighton.'[89]

In fact, Creighton's case was markedly different from Infeld's. After two other members of his department had yielded to a third in the matter of leave, Creighton had also applied for leave – and this while Frank Underhill was expected to be absent because of illness. The department head, Chester Martin, had told Smith that it would be unfair to ask others to stand aside so that Creighton, who had had two leaves during the preceding ten years, could go for a third time.[90]

Smith had a better argument where the effects of Stevenson's resignation were concerned. Yet if Infeld's leave had been approved earlier, Smith could hardly have insisted in May that he give it up. Furthermore, although Smith would not recommend a leave for Infeld because of its effect on the department, he was quite willing to risk his resignation. Smith's objection, of course, was not to Infeld's leave but to where he wished to spend it.

Beatty informed Infeld of Stevenson's resignation and asked him to postpone his leave for a year. In mid-June, having received no answer, Beatty told Smith that Infeld was budgeted at half salary for 1950–1 but that money was available in the budget of the arts faculty to pay him his full salary. If he resigned, 'it would be quite a loss to us, but we should get along some way,' he added. Some days later, Smith decided to treat Infeld's absence overseas as a vacation: 'If he does not resign during summer & does not come back by Sept 20 then retire. So pay two months salary July & August.'[91]

During these two months, Beatty tried to persuade Infeld to return, while the latter sought to justify his decision to stay away. 'I cannot change my plans now,' he wrote to Beatty on 10 August: 'I'm also to be in Paris in the late fall. I shall *not* be in Toronto ... While I am very sorry that Professor Stevenson has resigned, and that the department is in such a bad way, I cannot feel any responsibility in the matter since I talked to you and the president about just this danger, and made several suggestions, none of which were accepted.' Given a copy of this letter, Smith told Beatty that he would wait until 15 September before giving instructions not to pay Infeld that month. 'That ... will mean that he will be retired from the staff as from August 31st. I do not like the tone of his letter and his comment about Applied Mathematics.'[92]

Smith was working himself into a state of righteous indignation. So was Infeld. The letter Beatty received from him in mid-September reviewed the history of discussion about his leave as he saw it. He had made it clear from an early point that his plans included a visit to Poland, he stated. Beatty had told him that Smith approved, and he had therefore proceeded to make commitments. 'Then the entire situation changed because I was publicly attacked in a newspaper and by Mr. Drew in Parliament.' The university had failed to support him effectively during the resulting furore, noted Infeld, and this had made his choice easier: he would help his native country restore its scientific institutions. Although he felt grateful to Canada and the University of Toronto, he was resigning so that he could contribute to the research being done in his field in Poland, and to work for peace throughout the world: 'In so doing, I am convinced that I likewise continue to serve the people of Canada.'[93]

Smith's relief was almost palpable in the letter he sent to the chairman of the board of governors, Eric Phillips. He had resolved to recommend ending Infeld's employment, he wrote, but 'in order to avoid questions among the staff with respect to a forced retirement ... I was praying that we would receive a final refusal to return.' Smith denied that he had ever approved a leave of absence for Infeld, especially one that would take him to Poland. When Beatty had finally made application for Infeld's leave, Smith continued, Stevenson had resigned, so Smith had refused to take the matter to the board: 'The news of Infeld's staying in Poland has shaken those on the staff who might have been ready to support him. His resignation has, however, prevented any speculation on their part. We are well rid of him!'[94]

A brief announcement of Infeld's resignation appeared in the Toronto dailies and in the *Varsity*, and was picked up by the Canadian Press. A few days later the *Globe and Mail* dismissed Infeld as no great loss: 'Canadian principles of academic freedom include the right to choose the sort of freedom open to intellectuals in Soviet-controlled areas. They also include the concept that the more intellectuals who think like Dr. Infeld and follow his example, the more room there will be left in Canada for the development of the kind of academic freedom we like to keep here.' What this kind of freedom was the editorial writer did not say.[95]

Infeld's departure was the result of mutual incomprehension. Smith and Infeld seemed to speak different languages, and Beatty failed in the role of interpreter. As a result, Toronto lost an eminent scientist. What issue of academic freedom can be discerned in this?

Infeld's application for leave was made on academic grounds, but his decision to spend part of his leave in Poland had personal significance as well. When he returned to his native country in 1949, he was appalled to hear at first hand what his compatriots and fellow Jews had suffered during the German occupation. Having spent the war in safety, did he feel guilty? His son Eric doubts it.[96] Still, Infeld believed that he should play a part in Poland's reconstruction.

We should not underestimate the strength of the expatriate's feelings for the country in which he was born and reached maturity, feelings to which Smith seemed oblivious. Beatty understood Infeld at least in part, and in his letter to Smith of 29 May 1950 he tried to clarify Infeld's point of view. Smith did not get the point. He respected Infeld and appreciated the lustre he brought to the university, but during that spring and summer of 1950 he increasingly saw Infeld as a troublesome employee who was refusing to put the university's interests first.

What were these interests as Smith saw them? Simply put, they were the avoidance of controversy and of the harm that controversy might bring. He shared this outlook with his two predecessors, but either Falconer or Cody might have seen what Smith did not see – that in Infeld's case the controversy was spurious. It is understandable that Smith was unwilling to set Drew straight publicly, but he could have informed the politician privately that Infeld had no atomic secrets, that he, Smith, had approved the proposed visit to Poland, and that it would be helpful all around if Drew would to correct the record. Why did Smith not do this? Perhaps Thompson's questions had aroused doubt in his own mind about Infeld's political sympathies. Perhaps Eric Phillips (who was personally close to the former Ontario premier, Drew) had suggested to Smith that Infeld's visit to Poland would be a mistake. (Claude Bissell, Smith's assistant in 1949–50, surmises that Smith would have heeded Phillips's comments.)[97]

The most likely explanation may be that the Cold War climate discouraged Smith from meeting the issue of Infeld's research interests head-on when Drew first raised it, that he felt progressively less able to meet it as time passed, and that he became utterly unwilling to do so once the Korean War began in June 1950. Doubtless Smith did not want to take the chance that someone might accuse him of being 'soft' on communism. The affair demonstrates some of the effect that the Cold War had on academic life. Ignorance, fear and innuendo influenced the assessment of a matter that should have been assessed on academic grounds alone. Smith had used nonacademic grounds to deny Infeld's proposal for leave, Stevenson's resignation being no more than a pretext. In fact, Smith had played fast and loose with the facts and had subverted academic freedom.

Infeld flourished in Poland, where until his death in 1968 he encouraged the development of theoretical physics. He was active in the international campaign for peace and nuclear arms control, and in 1955 he was one of eleven signatories (two others being Albert Einstein and Bertrand Russell) of the manifesto against nuclear weapons that led the industrialist Cyrus Eaton to establish the Pugwash conferences. In 1995 the sole surviving signatory, Joseph Rotblat, won the Nobel Prize for Peace.[98]

Infeld lost his Canadian citizenship, a fate to which all naturalized Canadians were subject when they ceased to reside in the country. When his Canadian-born son Eric, aged seventeen, approached the Canadian legation in Warsaw in December 1957 to determine his own status, he was told that an inquiry would be made on his behalf. He waited a year before learning that an order-in-council had been passed on 22 December 1958 rescinding his citizenship and that of his younger sister Joanna.[99] The relevant files being closed to researchers, it cannot be known what part, if any, Smith played in this. He was at that time secretary of state for external affairs.

Time, which is said to heal all wounds, may have done so in this case. Both the Infeld children have regained their Canadian citizenship, and one now lives in Canada. Infeld himself gained a vindication of sorts when the University of Toronto on 17 May 1995 posthumously made him a professor emeritus. Time's healing work was assisted by Louise (Rappaport) Starkman, the daughter of neighbours of the Infelds and in childhood a close friend of Eric's. She began the process in 1993 by speaking to Rose Wolfe, chancellor of the university. Wolfe spoke to Jack Dimond, secretary of its governing council; he and the historian Michael Marrus, a member of the council, did the necessary research and recommended that amends were in order; the council accepted his recommendation, and the ceremony in 1995 was the result. The Cold War having ended some years earlier, it had become possible to see Infeld clearly at long last.[100]

Finally, there is an aspect of the Infeld case that is worth special notice – the fact that anti-Semitism seems to have played no part in it. One reason may have been that Infeld was not an observant Jew. The Milton scholar Ernest Sirluck – who in 1970 became the first Jewish president of a Canadian university (Manitoba) – recalls that Jews continued to face prejudice of a more or less genteel variety in the immediate postwar years but that hostility was stronger towards Judaism, which was resented as a challenge to Christianity. Albert Rose, who joined Toronto's Faculty of Social Work in 1948, concurred in this assessment and its corollary: observant Jews had a harder time in the university than those who were not conspicuously devout.[101]

In 1946, when Sirluck became a lecturer at University College, he was the first Jewish faculty member in a department of English in a Canadian university. (He had offers also from Queen's and Western Ontario but was told by Fulton Anderson of Toronto's Department of Philosophy that 'a Jew would not be happy at either institution.') Rose recalled that Jacob Finkelman of the Department of Law asked him in 1949 to canvass among the faculty for the United Jewish Appeal. The list he was given comprised seven or eight names, among them that of Infeld, who gave money but said it should not be used for religious purposes![102]

In the aftermath of the Second World War, with veterans flooding the classrooms and laboratories, Canadian universities offered expanded opportunities for women. The environment they entered, though, was often unwelcoming. We know more about the experiences of faculty women at Dalhousie than at most other universities. The historian Judith Fingard writes that President Alexander E. Kerr (1945–63) was 'very hostile' to female faculty. His attitude emerges from an exchange with R.A. MacKay, the head of political science, in September 1946. MacKay mentioned as a possible candidate for appointment Elisabeth Wallace, who at the time was teaching at the University of Toronto. 'I have not ... raised the question with Miss Wallace, since I thought it desirable to clear with you whether there would be any objection to taking on a woman.' Kerr replied, 'Your suspicion is correct that I do not wish to have too large a percentage of women on the staff. When we are choosing teachers with the date of registration within a couple of weeks, however, we are obliged to take what we can get and hope for the best.'[103]

Wallace did not join Dalhousie. She was wise not to. Unfriendly as Toronto may have been to faculty women, it was less so than Dalhousie under Kerr. During his presidency, three policies were introduced that discriminated against women. The first was a rule, passed in 1946, forcing women to retire at sixty rather than, like men, at sixty-five, a policy that remained in effect for a decade.

(The University of Alberta, too, discriminated against women in this way, and other universities may have done so as well.)

A second policy change took place in 1950. The biologist Dixie Pelluet, married to another faculty member, unwittingly prompted it when she protested against being paid less than the floor of her rank. (She was not alone in being short-changed: in 1953 the salary of Johanna Richter, a widow, was $600 below the floor for her rank.) The outcome of Pelluet's protest was that Dalhousie adopted an antinepotism policy, not uncommon at that time: the wife of a permanent member of the faculty could only be employed on an annual contract. Fortunately for Pelluet, the policy was not made retroactive.[104]

In 1955 the board adopted another antifemale policy: 'Marriage by a woman faculty member is deemed to terminate her appointment, but the University is free to propose an appointment under a special contract.' This change was the result of the refusal of Louise Thompson Welch, professor of clinical psychology, to resign when she became pregnant. She had joined Dalhousie as a professor in the Faculty of Graduate Studies in 1950, her position funded by a grant from the federal Department of Health and Welfare. Two years later she obtained Kerr's approval of her marriage to a Halifax businessman, and in 1953 she announced that she was pregnant. A nonplussed Kerr solicited advice from the dean of arts and sciences, George Wilson. 'Under ordinary circumstances I think the answer is easy,' he replied. 'Having a baby ends a woman's appointment. She can't have her cake and eat it too.' Mindful that Ottawa was paying her salary, though, he urged caution.[105]

His own conviction, Kerr told K.C. Laurie, the chairman of the board, was that the psychologist should relieve 'the University of the embarrassment of suggesting to her what she should do.' Instead, she was proposing to work part time for a year. Kerr did not like this, but since Dalhousie had no policy on pregnancy he was loath to take action against her. To prevent a recurrence of 'the problem,' it seemed to him desirable that Dalhousie should adopt a rule 'that marriage terminates the appointment of a woman member of the academic or administrative staff.'[106]

The upshot was the policy introduced in 1955. It did not affect Thompson Welch, who 'continued to teach on terms satisfactory to herself, producing a second child before she resigned in 1957 to pursue part-time work at the children's hospital.'[107] The policy remained in force until 1966. The antinepotism policy was not abolished until 1970.

The contrasting experiences of two University of British Columbia historians, Sylvia Thrupp and Margaret Ormsby, are illuminating. Thrupp joined the faculty of her alma mater in 1936. Although it was customary for holders of the doctorate to have at least the rank of assistant professor, she was annually reappointed as an instructor until 1945, when at long last she was promoted. She was on leave on a Guggenheim Fellowship at the time and did not return, joining the University of Chicago instead.[108]

Ormsby, who also was a UBC graduate, returned to Point Grey in 1943 as a replacement for F.H. Soward, who was on loan to the Department of External Affairs. When he returned, she stayed on because the classes were swollen by veterans. Promoted to the rank of assistant professor in 1946, she became a full professor in 1955 and head of the department in 1964.[109]

What explains the difference between the experiences of the two? Someone who knew Thrupp explained her treatment this way: 'Walter Sage didn't care for her.' The head's attitude was less personal than professional, it seems. He was willing to hire women but did not think they should be encouraged. Ormsby, too, would have suffered from Sage's attitude except for one thing: she caught the eye of President Larry MacKenzie (1944–62), who fancied himself a judge of merit. 'Larry used a free hand with promotions and salary increases, not always bothering with any formal channel of communication,' P.B. Waite (his biographer) comments. 'Margaret Ormsby ... heard of her promotion to assistant professor, not from her department head ... nor from the dean of Arts, but from Larry MacKenzie ... Her increases and promotions all seemed to come from this same source. Larry liked to reward talent.' By this token, of course, if he did not recognize it, it was not talent.[110]

Patchy information from other universities suggests that Thrupp's experiences were more typical than Ormsby's. In the 1950s appointments, promotions, salary increases, and tenure continued to be more readily available to men than women. Jean Burnet, who taught sociology at the University of Toronto in the 1950s and 1960s, writes: 'Women who aspired to academic careers were told straightforwardly that they should not set their sights too high: that, for example, many years of service and high scholarly productivity might possibly lead as far as an associate professorship. Nor should they hope for many women colleagues.'[111]

This state of affairs had implications for academic freedom. The awareness that they were marginal, and that they might be held to be superfluous, did not encourage faculty women to be assertive or outspoken (Pelluet seems to have been exceptional) or, indeed, to draw attention to themselves. It is unsurprising, therefore, that well into the 1960s no woman was at the centre of an issue involving academic freedom or free speech.

The universities were male-dominated, but men did not always have the advantage, as the fate of Marcel de Merten demonstrates. Belgian born, he came to the University of New Brunswick from St Mary's University in 1939 to teach

French, German, and Spanish. (Continental Europeans, though relatively rare in Canadian universities, were common in language departments.) De Merten was an eccentric. Jean Burnet, who taught at UNB in 1948–9, recalls that he 'drove the goats he raised around in his car.'[112]

De Merten was alone in the department of modern languages until 1945, when the coming of the veterans prompted an expansion of his department and he was joined by Mary Louise Whimster, a teacher of French. In April 1946 the dean of arts and science, F.J. Toole, had to deal with De Merten's complaint that Whimster was undermining his authority as head.

Deans did not usually side with junior against senior faculty, but Toole, who may have had doubts about De Merten's competence, took Whimster's part. It was UNB's 'excellent tradition' to give heads a generally free hand in selecting their staff, 'arranging the courses offered, and conducting the "external affairs" of the Department vis-à-vis the rest of the University,' he wrote to President Milton Gregg, but De Merten was in danger of abusing this freedom. It was his 'obvious intention ... to make things unpleasant for Miss Whimster.' In order to prevent this, Toole recommended that Whimster be put in charge of first-year French courses and 'have full authority within these courses in arrangement, prescription of books, etc.' As well, someone should be appointed to assist De Merten in upper-year French, and a committee should be formed to examine 'possible inadequacies' in the modern languages department.[113]

Gregg decided instead that De Merten should vacate the headship and should no longer teach French but could continue to teach German and Spanish. Did Gregg's successor, Albert W. Trueman, think it anomalous that modern languages did not have a head? Or did Allan G. McAndrew, professor of French since 1946, see an opportunity and seize it? In April 1950 he proposed several changes in language teaching. A month later Trueman recommended to the university's governing body, the senate, that McAndrew be appointed head of modern languages, that De Merten be released from teaching German in order to teach French, and that a new professor of German be engaged.[114]

In late May, Trueman informed De Merten that the senate had appointed McAndrew to the headship of the new department of modern languages and that De Merten should discuss his new teaching assignments with McAndrew. De Merten was deeply offended. To the former UNB president Larry MacKenzie, he complained that his seniority and military record had been ignored. To Trueman he wrote a rambling three-page letter whose gist was that he refused to report to McAndrew. He no longer felt wanted: 'It is therefore very reasonable for me to leave.'[115]

Had Trueman anticipated this? Five days after receiving De Merten's letter, the president informed him, 'The Senate of the University has given consideration to your letter to me' and has decided 'that your further association with the University has become an impossibility.' If de Merten did not resign within ten days, he was to take Trueman's letter as a dismissal. But 'all things considered' said Trueman, 'the Senate would prefer to bring your long association with the University to an end by accepting your resignation.' De Merten's salary would continue until 31 December, he added.[116]

The senate had not, in fact, considered the matter, though Trueman may have telephoned some of its members. His letter had the desired effect, however. De Merten resigned on 23 June 1950. As he ruefully told MacKenzie, 'as a gentleman' it was the only thing he could do.[117]

In May Trueman had recommended that a new professor of German be hired; De Merten's resignation made this easier. The president had a candidate in mind. An old friend, Jean Hamilton Hubener, was at Mount Allison, where Trueman had taught in the 1930s. The Australian-born Hubener had come to Canada in the company of her husband, Gustav Hübener (in UNB's records spelled Hubener), an anti-Nazi professor of English at Bonn University who had joined Mount Allison's English department in 1937. Upon his death in 1940, his widow had been given a full-time position in modern languages; a decade later, Trueman wanted her for UNB.[118]

Because she was not available in 1950, Trueman offered a sessional appointment to an Austrian refugee, Franz Stoessl. 'I wished to leave the post open for you in the event that you developed any interest in it,' Trueman wrote to Hubener a few months later. 'You suggested ... that it might be advisable to create a separate department [of German]. This is not possible at the present time ... I have only just succeeded in getting the Department of Modern Languages created, and it would be impossible tactics for me to go back to the Senate ... and suggest ... setting up a different arrangement.' It might be possible to do so in the future, he added, and he assured Hubener that, for the present, McAndrew had agreed that she would 'be given a very free hand and ... would ... be quite independent.'[119]

After Hubener accepted his offer and joined UNB in 1951, Trueman tooks steps to secure her a department of her own. McAndrew's 1951 report on modern languages cast doubt on the future of German and Spanish at UNB, enrolment in both having dropped. Nevertheless, in the fall of 1952 Trueman recommended to the senate that 'German be removed from the Department of Modern Languages and created as a separate department with Dr. Hubener at its head.' The senate approved. When Trueman left in 1953 to preside over the National Film Board, he must have looked back with satisfaction on his recruitment of Hubener and on her elevation to the headship.[120]

The tale illustrates once again the key role played by presidents in appointments, promotions, and dismissals. The manner in which Trueman eased out De Merten is particularly striking. It is hard to discern a concrete issue of academic freedom here, but Trueman clearly rode roughshod over academic due process. The solicitousness shown for two faculty women was unusual. Dean Toole and President Gregg protected Whimster from De Merten, while President Trueman went out of his way to favour Hubener. The manner in which he advanced her interests would, of course, be unacceptable today. Had it been known, it might have troubled some people even then. But favouritism was common in an age when the 'old boys' network' served to fill positions and when promotion was subject to administrative discretion. Much less common was that a woman benefited from it.

The right of professors to run for office made little headway during the early Cold War years. In 1950 the University of Saskatchewan adopted a policy permitting leave of absence for political purposes, thereby joining the Universities of British Columbia and Alberta. The governing board of the University of Manitoba, on the other hand, continued to resist. In March 1951 Manitoba's dean of agriculture, Grant MacEwan, received an invitation from the federal Liberal party to contest the Brandon constituency in a by-election. The editor of MacEwan's journals, Max Foran, comments: 'This challenge, plus his growing disenchantment with university work, led him to contest a seat that was presumably his for the taking.'[121]

In early April the board chairman asked what the board's policy should be if MacEwan accepted the nomination. A 'full discussion' ensued – the details are not on record – resulting in this resolution: 'That if and when the present Dean of Agriculture accepts nomination as a candidate at an election for a seat in the House of Commons ... he shall immediately submit his resignation.'[122] MacEwan did resign, but his political career did not unfold as anticipated. On 25 June 1951 he lost to the Progressive Conservative candidate. MacEwan then moved to Calgary, where he became active in local and provincial politics. A prolific popular historian, he was appointed lieutenant-governor of Alberta in 1965.

MacEwan's resignation attracted the attention of the recently founded faculty association. Its secretary, W.G. Stobie, informed the board in 1952 that he had been asked 'to enquire ... what limitations if any the Board considers should be imposed upon the participation of members of the staff of the University in local, provincial and federal politics.' Would the board consider a proposed by-law, to be drafted by the association, 'defining the rights of staff members to participate in politics?'[123]

The board did not reply, and in early 1953 the association renewed its approach. After stating that the executive committee was 'deeply concerned' by the board's action in forcing MacEwan to resign, Stobie added, 'The Committee is given to understand that there is no by-law of the Board governing the exercise of political rights by members of staff.' This seemed unsatisfactory, he said, and the faculty association executive had therefore drafted a proposed by-law for discussion by and with the Board.[124]

The document claimed for faculty, 'while continuing as members of the University,' the freedom 'to exercise their right as citizens to participate fully in civic, provincial, and municipal politics, as members of a political party, as candidates for office, or as elected representatives.' No one was to be asked to resign upon becoming a candidate; instead, there was to be a leave of absence. The document did not anticipate that professors who became rank-and-file MLAs would require extended leave, but it did state that administrators as well as anyone who became a cabinet minister or parliamentary secretary, as well as those who became MPs, would need such leave.[125]

The minutes of the board of governors offer no evidence that the document was ever discussed. The faculty association did not press the issue, moreover, its members being more concerned about salaries and benefits. The report that the chairman of the association made to the members in 1954 said not one word about the fate of the proposed by-law on political activity.[126] The issue does not seem to have re-emerged until well into the 1960s.

The University of Toronto's governing board also continued to take a dim view of political candidacy. In 1950 Harry M. Cassidy, who had returned to the university to become the dean of social work, wanted to contest the provincial Liberal leadership. President Sidney Smith told the board that if Cassidy was elected leader, he would have to 'resign from the staff of the University within a reasonable time thereafter ... and in no event later than December 31st, 1950'; but if he was unsuccessful, he could continue as a faculty member.[127] Without discussing the possibility of a leave of absence for Cassidy, the board approved what Smith had proposed. Cassidy was unsuccessful and remained at the university. Smith himself resigned in 1957 to run for federal office.

A view of the Canadian universities during the Cold War pales in the glow of the McCarthyite blaze south of the border. This may foster the comforting belief that academic freedom was safer here than in the United States. Such a belief is almost certainly mistaken. To be sure, no witch-hunts by legislative committees took place in Canada, but smugness on this score is out of place. The absence of witch-hunts is evidence not of a higher degree of tolerance for communism in Canada and its universities, but of differences between the two North American societies.[128]

By the late 1940s many Americans were unhappy with the increased state intervention in the economy which they associated with the New Deal and the war. They disliked the growth of 'big government,' identifying it with collectivism and communism. Most Canadians did not react to the changed role of government in the same way. Many welcomed the modest federally sponsored expansion of the welfare state that occurred in the 1940s and early 1950s. Indeed, this helped re-elect the federal Liberals in 1945, 1949 and 1953.

Secondly, Americans tended to resent their country's vastly enlarged involvement in international affairs – a result of the Second World War and the Cold War. The exercise of world leadership brought heavy expenditures for defence and foreign aid, which were often felt as an unwelcome burden. Canada, on the other hand, had no opportunity to exercise world leadership and Canadians had no occasion to resent its costs. Although Canada had greater involvement and representation abroad than before 1939, many people saw this as welcome evidence of the country's enhanced stature.

Third, Canadians were less concerned than Americans about the 'loss of China' and had no need to find scapegoats for it. Canada sent troops to Korea in 1950 as part of the United Nations action there, but the war was not really a Canadian show, and Canadians did not feel its frustrations, setbacks, and human losses as Americans experienced them.

Fourth, the Canadian government carried on a quiet campaign to expel real or imagined communists and their sympathizers from the public service and the National Film Board but did not expand this campaign to the campuses.[129] Education, after all, was a provincial responsibility. Not only that, but into the 1950s most Canadian universities were private.

Finally, the most important reason for the absence of an anticommunist witch-hunt in Canadian universities was a lack of real or apprehended witches to be hunted. With rare exceptions, the CCF was as far left as Canadian professors (and not many of them) had ever been inclined to stray. In 1944–5 the party became the butt of scurrilous attacks financed by business.[130] However, in the postwar years few if any Canadian opinion makers said the CCF should be off limits to academics. After all, it was solidly in the anticommunist and anti-Soviet camp, and it supported the formation of NATO as well as the United Nations action in Korea.

There were no witch-hunts, and some Canadian universities became havens for U.S. academics who had become politically *non grata* in their own country.[131] However, the Cold War did have an effect all the same. The Canadian attitude to civil liberties had always been ambiguous, and academic freedom had usually been valued only as long as its exercise did not disturb influential people. The Cold War restricted the free expression of personal and professional opinions.

In the universities this was old news. The long-established culture of the institutions discouraged outspokenness on controversial subjects. A telling comment comes from the pen of P.B. Waite, who began teaching history at Dalhousie in 1951: 'We were "brought up" by older staff, like G.E. Wilson and others, to keep our conversations on current life and politics for our friends' dinner tables, or as occasional *obiter dicta* in class. A strong public position on a contemporary issue compromised academic integrity, for not all the data was in on which one could make a proper judgment. One did have colleagues who got their exercise jumping to conclusions, but they were usually marked down as eccentrics ... whose judgments one learned to mistrust.'[132]

Doubtless, other young scholars had similar experiences. In this way, of course, the early probationary years of a professorial career reinforced the tendency to appoint people who were or seemed to be sound in every way. Still, the Cold War very probably was partly responsible for the virtual absence of academic free speech controversies during the 1950s. Once the Cold War had settled in, moreover, professors seem to have been less willing than ever to risk open association with 'radical' causes.

The German literature scholar Barker Fairley was banned from entering the United States in the fall of 1949, and although no reason was given, his wife Margaret's membership in the Labor Progressive Party was probably the reason.[133] Fairley himself is unlikely to have given cause, for although he supported some of the causes embraced more enthusiastically and conspicuously by his wife, he drew little attention to himself other than as a distinguished Goethe expert. The political scientist C.B. Macpherson applied Marxist theory to the political culture of the foothills province in his book *Democracy in Alberta* (1953), but he, too, avoided public controversy. As a consequence, perhaps, the presidential files in the University of Toronto Archives yield no evidence of attacks on Fairley or Macpherson similar to the ones earlier made on Frank Underhill.

Canadian professors had always been a cautious crew. At no time had more than a handful of them openly championed political or social causes, let alone those that were unorthodox. During the 1950s, though, the identifiably heretical were probably fewer in number than at any time since the First World War.

9

The Crowe Caws

'Giving advice to university heads is not exactly in my line, but I feel rather worked up about the Harry Crowe case in United College.' Frank Underhill was writing in December 1958 to an old friend, Principal W.A. Mackintosh of Queen's. Crowe had been dismissed in the summer, and two other historians, Kenneth W. McNaught and J.H. Stewart Reid, had resigned in protest. Could anything be done for them? asked Underhill: 'No sensible University head is likely to feel like experimenting with men who have been in trouble at other academic institutions, but the treatment of Crowe seems to me so outrageous that liberal universities should feel some obligation to help him and his friends.'[1]

'Of course I find the action of the United College Board to be, on the information I have received, completely outrageous,' Mackintosh replied. But it was too early to think of other jobs for Crowe and his colleagues: 'The pressure on United College is still building up and I am not without hope that there may be some drastic changes there.' He ended on a jocular note: 'This whole miserable affair has produced one lighter comment which came from the most unlikely of places, the St. James's Club. The club punster summed it up by saying: "You cannot dismiss a Crowe without caws!"'[2]

The Crowe case stirred up the academic community in Canada to an unprecedented degree. It was also a pivotal point in the history of the Canadian Association of University Teachers (CAUT). Founded early in the decade, the CAUT was still weak in 1958. Crowe's dismissal led to its first-ever committee of inquiry and hastened the establishment of a permanent national office. Most important, the case significantly affected the self-image of the professoriate and the idea of academic freedom in Canada. For these reasons as well as for its intrinsic interest, the affair merits treatment in depth.

The Canadian universities have usually been treated like proverbial step-children. This was certainly the case in the years right after the Second World War. Provincial governments were slow to increase their funding, and neither the federal subsidy in support of military veterans nor private giving could make up for more than fifteen years of neglect. Even as professors extended themselves to teach classes bulging with veterans, their salaries, already low, continued to deteriorate. By 1950–1 the crest of the veterans' wave had passed, and tuition income was beginning to decline. There was a steady drain of academics to the United States, where salaries and research opportunities (in institutions of the first and second rank) were better than in Canada. Other faculty members, it seemed, might have to be dismissed for lack of money.

Relief came from an unexpected quarter. In response to lobbying by the National Conference of Canadian Universities (NCCU) and to a recommendation by the Royal Commission on National Development in the Arts, Letters and Sciences (the Massey Commission), Prime Minister Louis St Laurent announced on 19 June 1951 that Ottawa would pay fifty cents per head of provincial population in aid of higher education in 1951–2. Within each province the money would be divided among universities and colleges on the basis of enrolment and would be paid directly to the institutions, to be spent as they might choose.[3]

The CAUT was launched at almost exactly the time that St Laurent made his announcement. In November 1949 the Association of the Teaching Staff of the University of Alberta had authorized a country-wide poll of selected professors to see whether interest existed in an association that would deal with 'salaries and pensions, sabbatical leave and academic freedom,' as well as student and faculty exchanges, federal aid to universities, and related issues. Five months later the political scientist Henry B. Mayo reported that the proposal enjoyed widespread support. An organizing committee took form during the 1950 meetings of the Learned Societies, and the CAUT was founded a year later.[4]

Some university presidents were less than thrilled. 'One thinks of all the existing organizations of an academic character and wonders whether any real purpose would be served by adding to their number,' New Brunswick's Albert W. Trueman wrote. The University of British Columbia's Larry MacKenzie thought that professors and presidents should work together in the NCCU: 'Universities ... can only perform the functions for which they were designed, if they continue to be communities of scholars and not associations of employers and employees.' Conscious of their subordinate status, however, professors wanted an organization of their own.[5]

Academic freedom was not the first issue to concern the CAUT's founders. Its revenue minimal, its national office shifting from university to university, the association was stretched to serve as a clearing house for information about salaries and benefits. Bread-and-butter issues were front and centre; behind them hovered hopes for respect and recognition. It was mainly as the result of a growing interest in university government that the CAUT took up the issue of academic freedom. The first of several reports and articles on governance appeared in the *CAUT Bulletin* in 1955, and in 1958 the executive council formed a committee to examine the subject. Partly because some delegates argued that the issues of governance and academic freedom were inextricably linked, and partly because of indications that trouble was brewing at United College, Winnipeg, the council decided also to solicit a report on the CAUT's role 'in protecting individuals in matters of academic freedom and tenure.'[6]

In late July 1958 the president of the CAUT, the University of Manitoba economist Clarence Barber, wrote to Robert W. Torrens of Western Ontario's French department: 'In a brief conversation in Edmonton I asked you if you would take up with your local association the question of forming a Committee on Academic Freedom and Tenure.' Torrens replied on 12 September that his faculty association had formed a committee to respond to the request. The undertaking came none too soon. Eight days earlier the *Winnipeg Free Press* and Toronto *Telegram* had featured a story about the dismissal of a historian from United College in circumstances that seemed to contravene both academic freedom and academic tenure.[7]

Two men were central in the crisis at United College, an associate professor of history, Harry Sherman Crowe, and Principal Wilfred Cornett Lockhart. Key supporting roles were taken by the chairman of the board of regents, Allan Watson, Crowe's colleagues Stewart Reid and Kenneth McNaught, and the economist and (after October 1958) dean of arts and science, Gordon Blake.

A student at United in the early 1940s, Crowe had interrupted his studies to join the army, reaching the rank of captain and winning the Military Cross in Europe. After graduate studies he returned to the college in 1950, joining a small department whose two other members were Reid (department head) and McNaught. The three saw the world in much the same way, from a generally left-of-centre perspective. As well, along with some friends in other departments, they enjoyed the occasional drink, which made them unusual in a United Church institution. The classicist Edwin D. Eagle said in 1987 that their colleagues knew them as 'the cocktail circuit.'[8]

Lockhart was a liberal-minded clergyman who had come to the college in 1955 after spending two decades in pastorates in the Toronto area. Succeeding the widely respected William C. Graham, he had some early difficulty in asserting his leadership. However, he enjoyed the full support of the board of regents, which was chaired from January 1958 by Watson, a retired bank manager of conservative views and decisive habits.

United College was consciously Protestant. When asking Harold Adams Innis about recruits for the Department of Political Economy in 1949, Graham had written, 'It would be desirable if these men were members of the United Church of Canada, or failing that, of some Protestant Church. We would not ... care to consider any man who had an unsympathetic attitude toward the Christian Church and in particular had no sense of the importance of the Christian values in our civilization.' Although the faculty enjoyed 'a maximum of academic freedom,' said Graham, 'we do want people who besides being able to appraise the problems of their field objectively have ... sound basic convictions about the meaning of life.' He was not rigid on the issue, however. Kenneth McNaught recalled that when he was hired, Graham telephoned to ask about his religious affiliation. 'I replied: "Anglican, but I only use it to fill in forms." He said nothing and didn't mention the subject again.'[9]

Dissatisfaction with low salaries and meagre benefits led in 1953 to the founding of the United College Association (UCA). Some of its members emerged as critics of the administration after Graham's retirement, the chief 'dissident' being Stewart Reid. Shortly after Lockhart's selection, Reid wrote to Underhill that having been mentioned as a possible successor to Graham, he had been promised 'something in its place,' but it had not materialized. He complained also that Lockhart did not seem to share his enthusiasm for the honours program; and he had misgivings about the selection of yet another clergyman as principal.[10]

Among Reid's main allies were his two colleagues in the history department and the political scientist Michael Oliver. Opposing them were the 'loyalists' or 'Old Guard,' led by Dean of Theology Edwin G.D. Freeman and Victor Leathers of the French department. But William Packer, who joined the German department in 1954, recalled four decades later that many faculty members were not strongly committed to either side.[11]

In 1957 the college was divided over the use to which the federal grant should be put. Ottawa having increased the per capita amount from fifty cents to a dollar, the UCA argued that the entire increase should be devoted to faculty salaries, since several politicians had said that this was its purpose. The board of regents nevertheless decided to use one-quarter of the money for improvements to the college building. This left many faculty members unhappy. Their failure to secure a greater role in college government also bothered some. Not everybody, therefore, was eager to take part in a fundraising campaign that began late in 1957.[12]

At that time Crowe was teaching at Queen's on a year's leave from United. He found the proverb to be true that a change was as good as a rest. 'Queen's is a good place to work,' he told McNaught in October.[13] He was in touch also with others at United, among them Packer, his successor as secretary of the UCA. It was to him that Crowe on 14 March 1958 addressed the most famous (or notorious) letter in Canadian university history.

Most of it dealt with the federal election scheduled for 31 March. 'I have an irrational foreboding of a Conservative sweep of unprecedented proportions,' Crowe wrote: He also thought the CCF would sustain losses. (He was right on both counts.) The letter did not reach Packer, however. Instead, on 10 April it landed on Principal Lockhart's desk in a blue envelope, together with an anonymous typed note: 'Found in College Hall. We think you should read it. Some staff loyalty???' The letter's first two paragraphs read:

I am most anxious to hear what the UCA is going to do with the freeloaders.* This whole business of Swayze and Taylor is most distressing. I can't understand faculty members going out to collect money when the Board told us so emphatically that administration was none of our business. I hope that few people answer that impertinent questionnaire. How did it pass?

Ken [McNaught] wrote a long sad letter. He seems most unhappy. I distrust all preachers and think we have abundant evidence that religion is a corrosive force – Graham, Lockhart, Freeman, Taylor, the two Hal[l]steads. People don't seem to have principles unless they are prepared to go to hell.[14]

Lockhart recalled in 1985 that as he read and reread these paragraphs, he became angry and worried – angry because he was offended by the references to himself, his colleagues, and religion, and worried because of the mysterious manner in which the letter had reached him. It covered both sides of a half-sheet of paper bearing the crest of Queen's University. When he turned the page and saw the signature, was 'Harry,' he knew it had been written by Crowe. But who were the 'we' who thought he should read it? How many were they? 'Dear Viljo,' the letter began. Who was Viljo?

It did not take long to discover that Viljo was the name by which Packer was known to his friends. It took Lockhart longer to give the letter to him – and before he did so, he had a photocopy made. It seemed 'the right thing to do,' he told me years later, during an interview. It was a precautionary measure to pro-

---

*'Freeloaders' referred to faculty members who had not joined the UCA. William Packer told me in an interview that Walter Swayze (English) and George Taylor (theology) had circulated a questionnaire asking their colleagues whether they had contributed to the college building fund or intended to do so, and whether they intended to canvass for the fund. Graham and Lockhart were the past and present principals, Robert N. Hallstead taught English, Edwin Freeman was the dean of theology, and Carl Halstead had recently retired as dean of the collegiate division.

tect the college and himself. But if he had known what would happen, he added, he would have destroyed the letter or buried it at the back of a file drawer. Had anybody asked, he would have denied receiving it.[15]

Who stole and redirected the letter is unknown. Apparently, someone took it out of the basket that contained faculty mail, and either that person or someone else sent it to Lockhart. Did the principal show it to or discuss it with anyone before he saw Packer? In May 1958 Dean Freeman claimed to have read the letter, but when and how remains a mystery. (Lockhart was vague on this point when I spoke with him in 1985.)[16]

On 16 April Lockhart asked Packer to come to his office, gave him the letter, told him he had made a copy of it, and said that he did not see how anyone holding Crowe's views could stay at United. Fearing that his own job as well as Crowe's was on the line, Packer said as little as possible, either that day or the next, when Lockhart asked him to come to his house for a renewed discussion. In conversation with me, Packer could not recall whether Lockhart said he had shown the letter to anyone else, but he said he inferred at the time that the principal had discussed it with Watson.[17]

A week later Lockhart wrote to Crowe: 'Your letter is a profoundly disturbing document. After reading it I have had to regretfully come to the conclusion that personally you have no sympathy with the avowed purposes of the College, and that you have no respect for or loyalty to the administration.' Crowe later described Lockhart's conclusion as 'grotesque' and 'incorrect,' saying that his remarks about preachers and religion had been largely facetious. Yet Lockhart's inference seems not unreasonable. The trouble was that he had formed it as the consequence of the illegal interception of a private letter.[18]

Lockhart left up in the air what he meant to do and later denied that he had intended a threat to Crowe's employment. Crowe's friends, however, suspected that Lockhart would try to get rid of him. 'I think he will try and make it impossible for you to stay, by some other means than direct firing,' McNaught wrote, 'and he will probably extend the offensive to me, Oliver, Reid and Packer.' Believing everyone's academic freedom to be at issue, he urged Crowe to resist.[19]

Crowe needed no urging. From the moment Packer telephoned, the historian was in a fighting mood, even playing with the idea of suing Lockhart for infringement of copyright. Upon receiving Lockhart's letter, he engaged a lawyer in Winnipeg, James Wilson, who advised him to wait before replying while he, Wilson, tried to obtain the photocopy and to get a sense of what Lockhart intended to do.[20]

If Crowe was determined to defend his rights, he was also getting ready to say farewell. On 23 May he authorized Wilson to tell three board members who had approached the lawyer unofficially that 'of course' he would 'get a job else-where.' However, since it was too late to find a position for 1958–9 he would return to United in the fall. 'I trust that my parting with United College will be pleasant, but if I should be dismissed ... I shall have to defend my interests, and this I am fully prepared to do.'[21]

Crowe had allies outside as well as within the college. Friends such as the Manitoba historian W.L. (Bill) Morton, the Saskatchewan political scientist Norman Ward, and the MP for Port Arthur, Douglas Fisher all urged him to defend himself. At Queen's a small support group took form, which included Vice-Principal J.A. Corry, the historians Frederick W. Gibson and Sydney Wise, Malcolm Ross of English, and Glen Shortliffe of French. One of Crowe's former teachers, Harry Ferns, advised him to place the case before the CAUT: 'Why worry about United College? A shakeup will do the joint a great deal of good.'[22]

In fact, United had already been shaken up. Packer had shared the story of the purloined letter with the members of the history department, Reid, McNaught, and Crowe's 1957–8 replacement, Margaret Prang, as well as with a fellow member of the UCA executive, Richard Stingle of English. Aware that rumours were swirling through the college and beyond, Lockhart had called a meeting of the General Faculty Council on 7 May to give his side of the story. At this gath-ering, did he express his intention to share the letter with the board of regents at their meeting the next day? Some said he did; others denied it. Events in the case have been described and interpreted very differently, depending on who was relating them. The journalist Pierre Berton wrote in 1959, 'This is an extremely complicated issue ... and I doubt that anybody outside the College is capable of unravelling it completely.' (Or inside, for that matter.) Nor is it pos-sible for an outsider to express fully the anger and anguish felt by the partici-pants in the struggle as trust was shattered and long-standing friendships foundered.[23]

On 8 May the chairman of the board, Allan Watson, informed his fellow regents 'of certain ugly rumours concerning the Principal and the College which are circulating in several quarters of the city.' He then read a telegram from Crowe, which stated that Lockhart had improperly come into possession of one of his letters and was using it to his discredit, and that if action was taken against him, 'full publicity will inevitably be given to all the facts in this inci-dent.' Lockhart then told his tale, whereupon the board unanimously passed a motion that it was 'unnecessary at this time to request production of the con-tents of the letter in question.' The mystery of the undelivered letters – Crowe had in fact sent three to United College on 14 March; the other two never did turn up – was referred to the post office. Its investigation was inconclusive.[24]

When Crowe apprised Lockhart later in May of his intention to return in the fall, he added a request that any photocopies of his letter to Packer be sent to him. At a board meeting on 27 May, Lockhart sought 'advice and authority for any further action.' After debate, the regents resolved 'that any further correspondence with Professor Crowe, or decisions relative to his association to the College, be referred to the Executive Committee.' Lockhart conveyed this motion to Crowe, adding that his future with the college would be decided by the board.[25]

Crowe then turned to Watson for the copies. His request was ignored. 'You have been advised that the question of your future relationship with the College is being considered by the Board,' Watson wrote, adding that 'a decision finalizing the matter' would be made at a meeting scheduled for 2 July: 'If you wish to make any further representations prior to the meeting please feel free to do so.'[26]

Crowe's reply quivered with outrage: 'The question of my relationship to the College has arisen as a result of the unauthorized reading, retention, photostating and employment by the Principal of a private letter.' His loyalty to the college, Crowe continued, and his confidence that the board would 'protect the interests and rights of faculty members' had so far kept him from taking the advice of friends and laying the matter before the CAUT. But if necessary, he would 'defend by every available means' his interests 'as a member of the academic profession and of the faculty of United College.' He would do so, he concluded, 'in the clear conviction ... that the well-being of the College would depend upon the success of my action.'[27]

At the 2 July board meeting, Reid appeared as department head but also as Crowe's representative. The minutes do not record his remarks, but in 1985 Lockhart recalled him as saying that Crowe knew he had 'no future with the college' and intended to look for a job elsewhere in 1959. After Reid left, the regents decided unanimously that Lockhart had 'acted in a responsible manner' with respect to Crowe's letter. They then considered 'the several phases of Mr. Crowe's recent actions, his relationship with the College and with the Principal.' A motion passed with the support of a 'substantial' majority: 'Notwithstanding that ... Mr. Crowe's conduct has been such that would enable the Board to dismiss him for cause and without notice,' he would be allowed to resume his duties for one year 'at the same salary and on the same conditions' as those he had enjoyed in 1956–7, provided he accepted these conditions by 25 July and returned to the campus by 1 September.[28]

The regents did not ask Lockhart for a recommendation and he did not make one: 'On 27 May they had taken the matter out of my hands.' It was Watson, not Lockhart, who conveyed the board's decision to Crowe and expressed the hope that he would find work 'in some other institution of higher learning' that would be 'more congenial' to him.[29]

The historian of the college writes that the board 'somewhat naively thought it had acted in the best interests of all concerned.' 'Somewhat naive' seems inadequate. 'Astonishingly inept' comes easily to mind. By giving Crowe notice, the regents brought wholly preventable trouble on the college. They had been told he intended to resign; they had been warned he would fight dismissal. They should have realized that a man who had won the Military Cross in combat against the Wehrmacht would not knuckle under to the lawyers, parsons, and businessmen who largely made up the board. 'Harry was a fighter,' Ken McNaught recalled with a half-grim smile. Jean Crowe, his widow, agreed: 'Harry didn't care about his job. He just wanted to beat United.'[30]

What explains the board's blunder? The board minutes offer no enlightenment. In writing to Crowe, Reid surmised that some regents had misunderstood the significance of what he had told them and thought they were merely registering the fact that Crowe would leave in 1959.[31] But some may have wanted to make sure he did not outstay the year, and others may have wished to punish him, either because they knew or guessed the contents of the letter or because they considered him insubordinate and disloyal.

A punitive attitude may be inferred from a memorandum written in December 1958 by a Winnipeg lawyer, Ralph Maybank, reporting a conversation with the board member Mildred McMurray. Crowe had been regarded as a troublemaker when he was a student, McMurray told Maybank, and some of the regents had opposed his appointment in 1950. 'I gathered from Mildred,' Maybank wrote, 'that in the years between that hiring and the present climax, Crowe and a group, such as McNaught and Reid, have always been a thorn in the side of the Administration. Of course, McNaught and Crowe have been strong CCFers and have preached that sort of thing in season and out of season to students and have been contemptuous of all others.'[32] A good many board members may have wanted to teach Crowe a lesson he would not forget.

As news of the dismissal spread, Crowe received letters of support from all sides. 'This is damnable, Harry,' Malcolm Ross exploded, 'but you have all people of conscience with you. In the long run you can't lose and we can't *let* you lose.' Bill Morton wrote, 'I should let you know how distressed I am that you should be treated in so appalling a fashion and with such complete lack of scruple.' Michael Oliver, who had very recently taken a position at McGill, reported conversations with the law professor Gerald LeDain – 'He is completely sympathetic and anxious to help in any way' – and with Frank Scott, who had also promised his support.[33]

Crowe wanted to challenge his dismissal as well as clarify what his salary would be. In reply to his inquiry, Watson wrote that his salary could be discussed when he reported for duty. Crowe objected. On 25 July he sent a telegram denying the board's right to dismiss or punish him 'for non-existent misconduct,' and objecting to being offered his 1956–7 salary. When Watson inquired whether Crowe was returning in September, the historian asked that his 1958–9 salary be set at $6,000, the floor for associate professors. Watson did not reply. There matters stood as Labour Day approached.[34]

From an early stage, some of Crowe's friends had urged him to ask the CAUT for help. As president of the United College Association (UCA) in 1958–9, McNaught attended the CAUT executive council meeting in Edmonton in June 1958. Afterwards he told Crowe that there was a lot of sympathy for him: 'There is not the slightest doubt of how the CAUT would respond to your being fired.' Writing in early July from his cottage near Kingston, Ontario, McNaught told Clarence Barber, 'Everybody from the east to whom I have talked agreed that this is *the* test case for CAUT and that lack of action would cripple it – this is the opinion of people like Corry, Fred Gibson, Jim Conacher, Donald Creighton, Dick Preston, Mac Ross, Lower, to name only a few.'[35]

The CAUT lacked guidelines for an inquiry, to say nothing of a budget. The executive nevertheless stood ready to intervene. Lockhart's action seemed egregiously improper, and the time seemed ripe to move the CAUT from the sphere of salaries and pensions to the more elevated plane of academic freedom. As well, Barber took a close interest in what was happening at a college that was affiliated with his own University of Manitoba.

In mid-July a request for an inquiry reached the CAUT from the Queen's faculty association, to which Crowe belonged at the time. Within days, the CAUT executive had appointed a committee consisting of two economists – Vernon Fowke of Saskatchewan and David Slater of Queen's – and the McMaster physicist Martin Johns. The terms of reference were 'to investigate carefully all relevant circumstances surrounding Professor Crowe's dismissal and attempt to determine to what extent issues of academic freedom and tenure are involved,' to make any recommendations they thought appropriate, and to report to the November 1958 meeting of the CAUT council.[36]

Should the request have come from the UCA? A former CAUT president, the historian H.W. McCready, thought it made sense to have the request come from Queen's but saw a problem. 'We ought to beware of getting ourselves into the position where the United Administration may take the line that this is an effort by outsiders to pry into their internal matters,' he wrote to Barber. 'They will probably take that line in any case but I would try to cover it by getting the United College Faculty Assoc. executive (& membership if possible) to pass some kind of resolution on the projected investigation.'[37] The difficulty was that UCA members were at sixes and sevens over the affair. Before the dismissal, most of them had probably hoped that the dispute would be settled quietly; but once the board had given Crowe notice and the CAUT had moved to intervene, battle lines hardened. It did not help that Barber was at the University of Manitoba; relations between the college and the university were not always easy.

In a struggle that became steadily more acrimonious, Crowe's supporters were led by Stewart Reid. Leadership of the anti-Crowe forces passed somewhat unexpectedly to the head of economics, Gordon Blake. If anything, he had been a dissident; he had actively backed the 1957 demand that the entire increase in Ottawa's grant be used for salaries. Packer had written to Crowe in January 1958 that he and McNaught believed Blake's views about education and religion to be sound, and they wanted him to be the next dean of arts and science. Until August, McNaught considered him a friend.[38]

Upon learning that the CAUT was launching an investigation, Blake became concerned about a threat to the college which, in his view, dwarfed the injury done to Crowe. Writing to Crowe in mid-July, Blake told him that in pressing Lockhart, he had 'taken the worst kind [of advice] available.' He added, 'I intend to take all means within my competence to oppose any action which you might pursue, which in my opinion would serve to bring discredit upon the institution of which I have the honour to be a member.' He next wrote a letter to the UCA executive claiming that it would be 'entirely improper and grossly unconstitutional' for the executive to support any CAUT action 'without first having been directed to do so by a properly constituted meeting of the entire United College Association in full session.'[39]

This letter came to an executive whose composition mirrored the divisions in the UCA. McNaught was president and Packer secretary, the other members being Victor Leathers, Alfred Longman (dean of the collegiate division), Richard Stingle, and George Taylor. McNaught, Packer, and Stingle were dissidents, while Leathers, Longman, and Taylor were loyalists. On the issue of a CAUT inquiry, however, Packer sided with the loyalists, arguing that the executive should do nothing until the membership had met. The loyalists regarded the inquiry as an unjustified intrusion into college affairs; Packer thought the CAUT, lacking investigative procedures of its own, should adopt those in use by the American Association of University Professors before acting. McNaught discerned a third motive. Some members of the executive opposed an investigation, he told CAUT secretary George Boyes, because they feared that 'an authoritarian administration' might fire them. 'The whole thing proves, if it ever needed proving, the desperate need for a strong national organization.'[40]

Yet another motive comes to mind – the wish to avoid adding to the commo-

tion. Without approving of Lockhart's action, some faculty members nevertheless disapproved of Crowe's effort to gain redress because it caused problems
for the college and seemed to be aimed against its administration. 'One of the
most distressing aspects of this controversy,' Longman wrote, 'has been the disproportionate emphasis placed upon an unfortunate incident to the disregard of
a regrettable attitude.'[41] He deplored what he saw as the dissidents' intransi-
gence where Lockhart was concerned.

Blake, too, saw Lockhart as more sinned against than sinning. 'We appear to
be in fundamental disagreement concerning the real reasons for this unfortunate
matter of Professor Crowe's relationship with the College having reached the
proportions that it has,' he wrote to McNaught, arguing that what his friend
regarded as 'infringements on academic liberty' might well 'turn out to be, in
reality, abuses of academic liberty.' Blake took a different line when writing to
Barber: 'It seems to me to be quite possible that the matter ... should be thoroughly investigated ... [but in] the absence of a definition of the terms "academic liberty" and "tenure" within the CAUT (a regrettable absence, I think) I
frankly do not see how the Association can act.'[42]

Blake's attitude took some of his friends by surprise. 'I have gathered from
several people that you blame this whole affair on Harry,' Stingle wrote. 'That,
to me, is simply incomprehensible. I am doubly distressed since your attitude ...
seems to be so inconsistent with what, in the past, your ideas of the academic
community have appeared to be.' McNaught, too, was astonished: 'You have
apparently misunderstood the reason why so many academics have been
shocked by the Crowe case. The reason is that they *did* hear of the essential facts
of that case – facts which have not changed since they were first announced by
Principal Lockhart.' He regretted that Blake opposed 'the only kind of impartial
investigation by which our College can now make its position known and
attempt to regain its reputation before academic and public opinion.'[43]

Barber thought Blake's objections might be explained by a rumour that Lockhart wanted him to be the next dean of arts. Still, it seemed advisable to ask faculty associations across Canada to comment on the inquiry. Although their
replies were not all uncritical, they were generally supportive. Fowke, who was
heading the committee, asked the AAUP for information and learned that it initiated its investigations at the discretion of the general secretary. Approval by a
local association was therefore not needed.[44]

On 20 August the regents decided to give Crowe one last ultimatum. He must
report by 2 September, the Tuesday after Labour Day, or he would be deemed to
have resigned. The board also decided to explain to the faculty why Crowe had
been given notice. A letter signed by Watson and sent to all faculty members

denied that Crowe's letter to Packer had prompted the board's decision. The issue was his subsequent behaviour: his attempts to intimidate Lockhart and the board by threats of legal action, his imputing of 'improper and false motives to the Principal,' and his 'aggressive belligerency that appears to make any long-term relationship between himself and the College impossible.' Academic freedom and tenure were not in danger, though the board would welcome a discussion 'for the purpose of more clearly defining these academic rights and of securing the best ways and means of effectively safeguarding them.' Finally, the board would cooperate in an investigation by 'any properly constituted committee.'[45]

Because it ignored Lockhart's actions while admitting that Crowe's protests against them had led to his dismissal, Watson's letter was useless in warding off the gale of publicity that soon broke over the college. On 4 September the *Winnipeg Free Press* carried a front page headline: 'United College Rocked by Row.' That same day the Toronto *Telegram* told its readers, '"Stolen" Letter Row Rocks 'Peg College.' The case was now food for gossip not only in academe but throughout English-speaking Canada.

The editor of the *Free Press*, Tom Kent, had been nursing the story for weeks. His reason for breaking it when he did emerges from a letter that Crowe (who had returned to Winnipeg on Labour Day), wrote to Fowke. Reid had told him that the Toronto *Telegram* was breaking the story, Crowe wrote, and that the *Free Press* was therefore going to publish what it had: 'I have declined to make any comments, and trust that is the right course for the present at least.' 'I hope the timing did not injure you,' Sydney Wise wrote to Crowe some days later, 'I feel some indirect responsibility, since it was Doug Fisher who briefed Simpson of the *Tely*.' (Wise had been feeding Fisher with information since May.)[46]

The newspaper stories led officials of the United Church to act. In June Crowe had given a copy of his Packer letter to E.E. Long, general secretary of the church, along with an undertaking to resign before the fall of 1959. Long had shared this information with other church officials, and on 5 September they decided that the United College board should have a copy of the letter. Four days later, Watson read the letter to a special meeting of the board. A long discussion followed before they 'unanimously' passed a motion that Crowe 'be dismissed forthwith on the grounds that his actions in recent months are incompatible with his continued employment on the teaching staff of United College.' A second motion stated that since Crowe had been dismissed for cause, the college had no further obligation to him. 'Mindful that such termination may result in some temporary hardship to Professor Crowe and his family,' however, the board authorized the *ex gratia* payment of a year's salary. (Crowe's lawyer proposed the sum of $6,000. Watson agreed, provided Crowe signed a general release. He declined.)[47]

In July the board had avoided public comment on Crowe's dismissal, but in September a statement was unavoidable. Watson told the media that Crowe's views about religion, as revealed in his letter to Packer, were inconsistent with continued service in the college. To this, Crowe replied that his letter had been one 'which neither the Principal nor the Board had any right to read, let alone to judge.' It had been photocopied and used against him 'all without the prior knowledge or consent of either myself,' he stated, 'or my colleague to whom it was addressed. This, and this alone, is the issue, and to this assault upon my personal liberty I cannot and will not submit.' The letters columns of the Winnipeg newspapers were soon dominated by attacks on the board; a new wave of support reached Crowe. Among those who wrote was Herta Hartmanshenn, formerly of United's German department, whose telegram spoke for all: 'Am right behind you in this. Justice will prevail.' What had begun as a dispute in a small college was turning into a national controversy.[48]

The CAUT inquiry did not begin smoothly. A provisional statement of facts, issued on 31 July, contained several errors of fact and seemed to assume (as Watson pointed out) that academic freedom had indeed been infringed. Objections to the presence on the committee of someone from Queen's led David Slater to step down, and it took several weeks for Barber and Fowke to find a replacement. In mid-September they got one in the University of Toronto law professor (and later chief justice of Canada) Bora Laskin, but then Martin Johns resigned. At a United Church general council meeting he had put his impartiality in doubt.[49]

With an eye on the calendar, Barber informed Watson that the CAUT executive had decided not to replace Johns. Watson objected, stating that the resignation raised 'a very serious question as to whether the Committee ... is properly constituted.' Instead of asking that Johns be replaced, though, Watson proposed that the committee be made up of two people appointed by the CAUT, two by the regents, and a chairman chosen by the other four. 'We consider that our position ... provides to all interested parties a fair and reasonable basis upon which an objective and impartial consideration of all the circumstances ... can be made,' Watson wrote. He added that if the board was not represented on the committee, it would not cooperate. But Barber rejected Watson's proposal. After all, the board was a party to the dispute whereas the CAUT was not, or at least not yet.[50]

Although the board's decision not to cooperate was a signal to Lockhart and loyalists such as Blake not to do so either, Fowke and Laskin decided to go ahead. The ten men and women who appeared as witnesses were all friendly to Crowe. Loyalists who suspected Fowke and Laskin of pro-Crowe bias found their suspicions further confirmed when the committee allowed Crowe as well as McNaught, in his role as UCA president, to attend the entire hearing. All this opened Fowke and Laskin to the charge of one-sidedness – a charge they evidently believed they could withstand.[51]

The Fowke-Laskin Report, supported by fifty documents affecting the case and another twenty on the formation and functioning of the committee, reached the CAUT executive on 21 November. One document not included was the now-famous letter. Fowke and Laskin had wanted to publish it, but Crowe was undecided and had sought the advice of his friends at Queen's. 'Without exception, every person whom I consulted believes that you should *not* accede to the request,' Frederick Gibson replied. Publication 'would divert attention from the central issue of what was done with your letter ... to the ... essentially irrelevant question of [its] substance.' Stuart Ryan, a law professor, raised a second objection: 'If a court should consider these remarks defamatory, then any action by you authorizing publication of the letter would constitute a far more serious defamation than anything which has occurred to date.' Because it seemed inexpedient to cite either objection, Gibson urged Crowe simply to say that since he had so far insisted on the private nature of the letter, he would be inconsistent if he now allowed its publication.[52]

Crowe found these arguments persuasive. In introducing the documents appended to their report, Fowke and Laskin did not comment on the absence of the document that had set things going. Was this evidence of a bias that affected the report more generally? It was perhaps as good as it could be in the circumstances, but it did not offer a complete or balanced account. There was bias, and there were errors and dubious assertions. For example, Fowke and Laskin assumed that Lockhart had shared the contents of the letter with the board in April or early May, a surmise based on an inference drawn by Crowe's lawyer but unsupported by evidence.[53] But the report's flaws were only partly the committee's fault. If Fowke and Laskin registered the views of one side only, it was because the other side refused to speak to them.

The report reinforced the loyalists' belief that Fowke and Laskin had been *parti pris* from the outset. Crowe and his allies went scot-free while Lockhart, Watson, and the board were castigated, complained the loyalists. Would not a balanced account have found fault on both sides? Indeed, it would. An impartial history of the college would have distributed blame more widely. The hostility and suspicion with which the dissidents regarded Lockhart and the board undoubtedly influenced what happened. But it was not the intention of Fowke and Laskin to write a college history, and even had they done so, they could hardly have reached a conclusion on the central issue other than the one they did reach: 'That Principal Lockhart and the Board of Regents were respectively tactless and arbitrary in their handling of a situation which they themselves had created' and that neither 'had any tenable ground for the severe treatment of Professor Crowe.'[54]

Fowke and Laskin found that Crowe's first dismissal had been due to his 'audacity in protesting an invasion of privacy and violation of what he conceived to be his legal rights, as well as protesting possible adverse use of the contents of the letter based on conclusions which he declared were unfounded.' His second dismissal, 'again without previous notice and without reasons given him at the time, was ... justified ... as based on the contents of his private letter.' Crowe was discharged 'for a private expression of opinion which he was given no opportunity to explain and which should not have been before the Board of Regents at all, or certainly not without a previous conference between Dr. Lockhart and Professor Crowe.'[55]

The board, though acting on the 1938 United College Act by which professors held their tenure during the board's pleasure, had nevertheless infringed on tenure as Canadian professors had come to understand it, wrote Fowke and Laskin, adding, 'Security of tenure is prerequisite to academic freedom.' Did Crowe's dismissal have any relation to that freedom? Fowke and Laskin concluded that it did.[56] Were they right? and by whose definition?

Although academic freedom had been discussed in Canada since the 1910s, the CAUT had barely begun to formulate a definition. What Fowke and Laskin referred to was the 'Statement of Principles on Academic Freedom and Tenure' that had been adopted by the AAUP and the Association of American Colleges in 1940. But this document offered little guidance.[57]

Two former professors at United College, A.G. Bedford and J.E.G. Dixon, have argued that although the regents offended against Crowe's right to privacy and against his tenure, they did not infringe his academic freedom. The geographer John Warkentin, who resigned from the college in sympathy with Crowe, agrees. 'Academic freedom had nothing to do with it,' he said recently. In seeking to make the affair into 'a *cause célèbre* in the annals of violations of academic freedom,' Dixon writes, the CAUT 'did so ... either because it did not know the distinction between academic freedom and civil or legal rights, or because "academic freedom" is a much weightier club to belabour a university administration with.' The argument is, in effect, that the writing of a private letter is not an exercise of academic freedom and cannot be regarded as such. Whatever one makes of this, it was irrelevant to Crowe's dismissal in July. The board gave him notice because they held his demeanour to be unacceptable.[58]

This raises the question whether the concept of academic freedom covers actions that boards may regard as insubordinate. The 1915 and 1940 AAUP statements do not discuss this, and it may be that to this day some academics do not see an issue of academic freedom here. Fowke and Laskin, however, judged that Crowe, in protesting against an invasion of his privacy, was 'neither intemperate nor vigorous beyond the point of reasonable firmness.'[59] In the board's use of his protests to justify his dismissal they saw an attack on his academic freedom.

They were even more concerned about an implicit attack on the dignity and autonomy of the professoriate. At United College – and not only there – faculty were expected to defer to the authority of executive heads and lay boards. In challenging this, Fowke and Laskin signalled a change in the self-perception of the Canadian professoriate. Commenting on the photocopying of Crowe's letter, they wrote, 'Canadian scholars are not commonly or properly held in such low esteem that they must abstain from protest in such circumstances.'[60]

The attitude to which they objected was well stated in the fall of 1959 by T.B. McDormand, executive vice-president of Acadia University. Crowe, he wrote, 'was dismissed not in violation of the principle of academic freedom, but in recognition of the principle that individuals in influential positions are responsible for what they do, what they write, and what they are. Irresponsibility in these fundamental matters disqualifies any man for the privilege of exercising academic freedom.' Who was to judge what was responsible behaviour and what was not? The governing board, of course:

A college has some rights as well as its faculty members. It has, among other things, a right to determine what kind of people shall be on its faculty, and what kind of behaviour shall be considered unacceptable in the light of standards which the college prizes and seeks to maintain ... No one has the right to deny a group of responsible men the right to discipline an individual whom they consider unacceptable in terms of the group standard.

To deny this 'could lead by a short route to social anarchy and a chaotic fragmentation of society as we know it,' concluded McDormand.[61]

His assumption that the board was synonymous with the college had legal support, but it was increasingly being questioned by professors. By 1958 a growing number were asking why members of lay boards, who did none of the institution's essential work of teaching and research, and often seemed to lack interest in or sympathy for this work, should be able to dispose of professors' careers. Fowke and Laskin took a logical leap in linking this issue to the idea of academic freedom. That academics across Canada were willing to join them in making the leap implied a rocky future for McDormand's college. It also signalled a significant development. Henceforth professors were likely to appeal to the principle of academic freedom when they criticized administrators or governing boards.

Of Crowe's second dismissal, in September 1958, Fowke and Laskin wrote: 'For a man to be discharged on the basis of an interpretation of his remarks ... would create a situation fraught with peril for academic freedom. To find a discharge made in the face of a remonstrance by the teacher that he has been misunderstood, and without being afforded an opportunity of explanation, makes the offence against academic freedom grave indeed.'[62] This assessment seems unassailable. If people can be fired on these grounds, neither teaching nor research is safe.

But was not Crowe, by virtue of teaching in a church college, subject to restrictions in stating his views about religion? The 1940 AAUP document said that 'limitations of academic freedom because of religious or other aims of the institution should be clearly stated in writing at the time of the appointment.' Crowe's letter of appointment did not refer to limitations of any kind, but common sense kept professors at United College from publicly criticizing religion. However, Crowe's letter to Packer was a private communication.[63]

With the appearance of the Fowke-Laskin Report on 24 November, the Crowe affair entered a new phase. Academics showered the report with praise. 'A very fine job indeed,' David Slater wrote. Dalhousie's George P. Grant judged it 'a model of clarity, fairness and firmness.' Also from Dalhousie, James Aitchison gushed, 'It was a crucial task and it was superbly done.' 'You did a grand job,' the University of Toronto's Vincent Bladen asserted. 'A masterly piece of work,' was Frank Underhill's assessment. Perhaps most gratifying was a letter from the AAUP's Bertram Davis: 'This is a splendid report ... I have no doubt that it will serve as a model for any future reports which the CAUT is called upon to publish.'[64]

United's board saw the report very differently, describing it as 'a prejudiced document by an improperly constituted body which was not in possession of all the facts,' and discounting its conclusions as 'unsound and incorrect.' The Board of Colleges and Secondary Schools of the United Church was also unimpressed, saying that nothing in the report shook the church's confidence in 'the integrity of Dr. Lockhart and the board of the college.' The *United Church Observer*'s editor, A.C. Forrest, commented, 'There was no issue of academic freedom for Professor Crowe. There was no issue of religious narrowness in United College. No issue of Principal Lockhart interfering with the mails.' In Forrest's view, there were only two issues: Crowe had been 'difficult' at a time when Lockhart 'needed the co-operation of every member of his staff'; and church colleges needed proper procedures to deal with professors whom boards wanted to dismiss.[65]

Two weeks later, Forrest expressed the hope 'that the CAUT will not look upon this incident as a model for future procedure, but as an experience from which lessons should be learned.'[66] (In 1958–9, as a first-year student in Victoria, British Columbia, and a member of the United Church, I remember agreeing with Forrest's editorials.)

Faculty loyalists were especially critical. One of them, Robert N. Hallstead, had already written to Barber that academic freedom was in no danger at United and that the CAUT and its committee seemed unconcerned about the damage being done to the college. In April 1959 the UCA majority voted to issue a 'Statement of Events Connected with United College, 1958–59,' whose purpose was to correct the errors and biases in the Fowke-Laskin account and to set the record straight. Acting on the same motive, an alumnus, D.S. Barber, wrote *In Defence of a College* (1959). Both publications made valid points, but neither seems to have had much influence outside the circle of those already converted. By and large, outside observers tended to blame Lockhart and the board for the troubles at United.[67]

Newspaper response to the report was restrained. The *Winnipeg Free Press* noted its one-sidedness but agreed with its major finding that Crowe had been improperly dismissed and said that the report offered an opportunity for settling the conflict. This was more easily said than done, the conflict having sharpened since early September. Primarily responsible for this development was Blake's appointment to the deanship of arts and science in late October 1958, O.T. Anderson having died in an automobile accident. The board had thought it prudent to solicit the views of the faculty and had found that a majority of respondents – no numbers were given – named Blake as their top choice.[68]

From the point of view of Crowe's supporters, Blake's selection was bad news. Even worse, Reid, McNaught, and Crowe learned from a seemingly unimpeachable source that since the summer, Blake had been working with Watson – Lockhart was kept in ignorance – to find grounds for the dismissal of Reid and McNaught, as well as Crowe. Lacking hard evidence, Reid and McNaught pondered for some weeks what they should do, and on 20 November they resigned. They linked their resignations not only to Crowe's dismissal but also to Blake's appointment, which, Reid wrote to Lockhart, 'seems deliberately designed to emphasize your decision, and that of the Board, not to reconsider your policy in the matter of Prof. Crowe.' McNaught stated that he would not return in the fall of 1959 'unless the decisions with respect to the deanship and ... the dismissal of Prof. Crowe are revoked.'[69]

Six days later the board accepted the two resignations and what they chose to regard as a resignation from Richard Stingle (who, in a letter critizing Blake's appointment, had added, 'If the lamentable injustice against Prof. Crowe is to remain as it is now, I shall be obliged to seek another position for the next year'). The regents were digging in their heels: 'The letters of Professors Reid and McNaught make it clear why the reinstatement of Professor Crowe ... is not a possible or proper solution.' Lockhart's position as well as Blake's would be untenable, they claimed. Administrative authority 'would in effect become vested in the three members of the history department, and the authority vested in the Board of Regents to conduct the affairs of the college would be destroyed.'[70]

During the next two weeks, twelve more people resigned or asked not to be considered for reappointment. Among them were two tenured faculty members, Packer and John Warkentin, as well as the college librarian Michael Jaremko and the dean of women Elizabeth Morrison. Embarrassing as these resignations were, they were almost welcome compared with Lockhart's. Troubled by charges that he had behaved unethically, chagrined not to have received the support in church circles he had expected, and believing that his usefulness at the college had come to an end, he informed the board on 6 December of his intention to leave at the end of August 1959.[71]

The board was under growing pressure from all directions. On 1 December the regents heard that Premier Duff Roblin had offered to mediate the dispute. Watson now declared himself in favour of conciliation 'as a proper course for a Church College to follow in any dispute,' and suggested that this course should have been pursued earlier. Two days later, with the president of the Manitoba conference of the church, S.R. McLeod, serving as mediator, the board agreed to reinstate Crowe as well as Reid, McNaught, and Stingle, and to exchange expressions of regret with Crowe. He rejected the deal, reportedly because he had been asked to permit publication of the letter to Packer and to apologize publicly to Lockhart. McLeod denied that these had been conditions of the agreement, and the board changed course once again, asking for a judicial inquiry whose findings it undertook to accept. The Winnipeg newspapers called for provincial arbitration. If the dispute continued, the *Winnipeg Tribune* stated on 11 December, 'the very existence of the college as an institution of higher learning could be threatened.'[72]

Among those most worried by this prospect were the faculty. On 13 December a score of them met with several board members, urging them to reinstate Crowe without conditions of any kind. More productive was Gordon Churchill's attempt to forge an agreement between the board and Crowe. A graduate of the college and a member of its board, Churchill was minister of trade and commerce in John Diefenbaker's cabinet. Three hours spent with Crowe produced a statement in which the historian said he had not anticipated that 'the very existence of United College ... would be brought into question,' yet that was now the case. As an alumnus and a faculty member he was proud of United, he continued: 'For this reason and in the interests of the students I am most anxious to effect the termination of the public debate of the affairs of the College, to resume my duties in the classroom, to begin within the walls of the College the process of reconstruction and the restoration of academic confidence in the college.'[73]

Upon presenting this statement to his fellow regents on 14 December, Churchill moved that they withdraw the letters of dismissal 'and affirm that Professor Crowe is a member of the staff of United College in the position of Associate Professor of History with all the rights and privileges thereto pertaining.' This was capitulation. Of the twenty-five men and women in attendance, thirteen voted in favour. The rest abstained.[74]

If the settlement was a defeat for the board, was it a victory for Crowe and his supporters? Neither the motion drafted by Churchill and approved by Crowe nor the board's press release mentioned the men and women who had resigned in sympathy with him. The press release expressed the hope 'that all concerned will now unite in an effort to enable United College to continue its rightful place in the academic world.' It remained to be seen how inclusive that phrase 'all concerned' would be.

Observers by and large hailed the settlement as a sensible resolution of the affair. 'Some will say that the rebels have won,' the *Toronto Daily Star* stated, but this was not so; 'the principle of academic liberty' had been the victor. Ramsay Cook, a former United College student who was teaching at the University of Toronto, was of the same view. 'Whatever else happens,' he wrote to Crowe, 'this must seem an important day for academic freedom in Canada.'[75]

Others were not celebrating. Senator Thomas A. Crerar, the elder statesman of Manitoba politics, wrote to Alfred Longman, 'I cannot understand why Crowe and the others insist on remaining on the Faculty when they are so much out of harmony with the administration.' Watson Kirkconnell wrote from Wolfville, Nova Scotia, 'I have the impression that Crowe and the Professors' Union had access to all the media of propaganda and made a shocking abuse of them.'[76]

The subexecutive of the General Council of the United Church approved the agreement forged by Churchill and issued a press statement reaffirming the church's commitment to academic freedom. This statemen expressed confidence in Lockhart, describing his copying of the letter as 'a mistake in judgment, without malicious intent, for which he [had] made a public apology'; but Crowe was 'justified,' it said, 'in protesting the use to his detriment of his private letter.' It added, 'We are glad that the Board of Regents has rectified the situation ... by reinstating Professor Crowe.'[77] These comments were not well received everywhere, and Moderator Angus J. MacQueen had to respond to complaints that the subexecutive had 'stabbed [Lockhart] in the back' and exonerated Crowe. He denied that the subexecutive had done either, adding that it had been necessary 'to make a statement because the issue had become one of national importance. Numerous requests had been received from academic circles, theological professors, church sessions, and individuals from Halifax to Vancouver.'[78]

That not a few church members believed Lockhart to be right and Crowe to be wrong may have influenced the board of regents as they considered what to do about the resignations they had received. In late December they referred them to a committee consisting of Lockhart, the two deans, and two professors to be chosen by the principal. A month later Lockhart reported that Deans Blake and Longman had agreed that 'it was inopportune to work through such a committee at this time.' Instead, and after consulting with the board executive, they recommended that the board ignore most of the resignations while maintaining those of Reid, McNaught, and Stingle. The principal offered no reasons for this recommendation, which the board accepted.[79]

McNaught had written to Fowke in early December: 'Almost my worst fear is that we might, in an outside possibility, be reinstated!' Distressed by the rancourous divisions among the faculty and resenting the time lost in fighting the principal and board, he was eager to leave the college. But after Crowe got his job back, reinstatement of his allies became a symbol of total victory. The board resisted. The names of Reid, McNaught, and Stingle had not been mentioned in the negotations leading to the Churchill settlement, Watson told the board in April, and that took care of that![80]

By this time Crowe had resigned, citing the board's failure to give assurances of academic freedom and tenure, its refusal to reinstate his friends, and the absence of 'any interest in the possibilities of Christian reconciliation within the College.' Conditions had become 'intolerable,' he told Churchill. McNaught comments in his memoirs: 'On March 22 Harry resigned. Of course, he had to. From the moment of his December 15 "reinstatement" it had been clear to Stewart, myself and Dick that hell would freeze over before Watson, Blake or Lockhart would see us return to old United.' Crowe, he writes, had 'in a characteristic fit of wishful thinking' seized on his own 'unconditional reinstatement' as the 'symbol of vindication' he had been looking for. Inasmuch as he had failed to obtain a guarantee that his friends would also be reinstated, he had been outsmarted. (If so, it is not clear who outsmarted him, Churchill or Watson.)[81]

On 30 March the board accepted Crowe's resignation as well as that of five others, including Packer's. In the end, sixteen men and women left United in support of Crowe, thirteen in arts and the collegiate division, and three members of the administrative staff.[82]

Crowe became research director of the Canadian Brotherhood of Railway, Transport, and General Workers, and did not re-enter academe until 1966, when he was appointed in York University's Atkinson College. Where Reid might have found another university position became moot when he was chosen to be the first permanent national secretary of the CAUT. McNaught joined the University of Toronto's history department. Stingle went to the University of Saskatchewan, moved on to a teaching job in Sudbury, then settled down at the University of Western Ontario. Packer taught German in a secondary school for several years before joining the faculty of University College, Toronto.

One resignation the regents declined to accept was Lockhart's. For several months he insisted that he would leave in August 1959. However, the board did not begin a search for his successor, and that winter and spring he received many indications of support from both within and outside the college. He decided to stay.[83]

Late in 1958 Pierre Berton wrote in the *Toronto Daily Star* that the regents had gone 'blithely along accepting resignations, convinced of their absolute Right, and generally bungling matters nicely without any real understanding of the moral or the human issues involved.'[84] It is possible, however, paraphrasing Polonius, that 'though this be bungling, yet there is method in't.' If Watson had come to the view that United College would be better off without Reid, McNaught, and Crowe, what better way to get rid of them than to sack Crowe and hope the other two would resign in sympathy? Watson changed course when he realized he had steered the college into peril, but a willingness to reinstate Crowe was not accompanied by a similar attitude to his main allies. It is possible to see method in this, too. The failure to restore them guaranteed that Crowe would go.

Whether this was Watson's conscious strategy or not, he got what he very probably wanted. And the disappearance of so many of the dissidents had a pacifying effect, one reinforced by the departure of most of the senior students in history for the main campus of the University of Manitoba. 'This evening all members of the faculty and their wives or husbands are attending a reception at the principal's residence,' Longman reported to Watson Kirkconnell late in 1959. 'One could hardly conceive of such happening a year ago.' Cornelius Jaenen, who joined the history department in 1959, recalls, 'There was a certain new esprit de corps, a new degree of cooperation among the faculty, as the college tried to rebuild its reputation.'[85]

One reason for the new mood was the fact that the new UCA executive was not divided as its predecessor had been, and consequently its relations with the board improved. By late May 1959 the regents were weighing an agreement dealing with salaries, benefits, and the terms and conditions of employment.

Two separate documents dealt with tenure and academic freedom. With minor amendments, the board approved the agreement and its appendices.[86]

Even among those faculty members who did not believe that academic freedom had been at issue in Crowe's dismissal, some had worried about its implications for tenure. The agreement fed a sense of well-being.[87] So, quite probably, did not having to listen any longer to negative opinions about Lockhart and the board, which had caused some faculty to feel resentful and others to feel ill at ease. Organisms are said to strive towards a state of equilibrium. United College had achieved this state, if only for a time.

The appearance of the Fowke-Laskin Report, followed by Crowe's reinstatement, put the CAUT executive in a celebratory mood. The euphoria dissipated as it became clear that the board of regents did not intend to restore Reid, McNaught, and Stingle. After United College placed advertisements for appointments in history and English in the *Times Literary Supplement* in December 1958, the CAUT placed notices asking prospective applicants to contact the association's secretary. When Watson complained, Barber denied that the CAUT was trying to 'blacklist' the college. In fact, the notices were intended to encourage United's board to restore the status quo. In this they failed, and in April 1959 the executive appointed a committee to examine developments in the dispute.[88]

This committee, chaired by Frank Scott, reported in June. Expressing 'deep regret' that the Churchill settlement had broken down, it recommended that Barber and the executive be commended for their handling of the affair; that the findings of Fowke and Laskin be reaffirmed; that a synopsis of the Scott Report be published; and 'that the CAUT take no further action with respect to the situation at United College.' The UCA delegate, John Clake, objected to the report's tone but supported its fourth recommendation: 'Enough bitterness had now been engendered and ... it would be in the best interests of everyone concerned to drop the matter.' Although this sat badly with some delegates, the council voted, eighteen to six, to accept the report. When Scott asked for 'a standing ovation' for those who had resigned in defence of the principle of academic freedom, 'there was a very vigorous response from the overwhelming majority of those present.' Clarence Barber and Percy Smith (then at the University of Saskatchewan) recall that only Clake did not join in.[89]

The published synopsis of the Scott Report stated that Crowe had reasonably believed everyone would be restored, and that when the board indicated that its idea of a 'general reconciliation' did not include Reid, McNaught, and Stingle, Crowe saw this as a breach of faith: 'He concluded that as a man of honour he had no alternative but to resign. In this latter conclusion we concur.'[90]

In April 1960 the *CAUT Bulletin* contained thirty-eight pages of documents that had appeared since the appearance of the Fowke-Laskin Report. Some would deplore 'this opening of an old wound,' the editor wrote. 'We do so only because we are profoundly convinced that truth suffers more from confusion than from error ... We are grateful for this further opportunity to serve the cause of academic freedom.'[91]

'Now tell us all about the war, / And what they fought each other for.' The question asked in Southey's 'Battle of Blenheim' is appropriate. What *did* they fight for? Seen from the perspective of many Canadian professors, the battle was fought for Crowe's job, for academic freedom, and for respect. Seen from the perspective of the board of regents and a number of faculty members at United, it was fought to maintain Lockhart and to resist the efforts by dissident members to gain control of the college. Neither view was entirely right or entirely wrong.

Crowe received widespread support among academics because Lockhart's handling of the letter seemed morally wrong, because academic free speech seemed to be involved, and perhaps above all because he opposed the powers that were set over professors. To repeat, the Crowe case was in part about respect. It is impossible to mistake the sense of outrage that coloured both the Fowke-Laskin Report and much of the commentary on the case. To think that Crowe had been dismissed as though he were a servant or a hired hand! Was a professor of so little account?

In his farewell address as CAUT president, Barber cited the Crowe case as evidence of 'the vast gulf in understanding that often exists between University faculty on the one hand and members of the governing boards of Canadian Universities, on the other.' Too many of the latter seemed to have 'little genuine understanding of the basic importance of academic freedom in our society,' he said. A code of principles and procedures governing academic freedom and tenure might do good; better still 'would be a reform in the composition of governing boards.' Whatever happened, the equation of university and board must be challenged.[92]

'But what good came of it at last? / Quoth little Peterkin.' The improved contract between the faculty and board of United College was one result. Another was the maintenance of Lockhart as principal and the continuation of the board's control over the college, though whether this was a good thing depended on one's point of view.

The establishment of a permanent CAUT office in Ottawa had been decided on in June 1958, but the demands made by the Crowe case on the executive committee's time (and money) demonstrated the need for such an office with stark clarity. In June 1959 Barber announced that the office would open in the fall, with Stewart Reid as its first secretary. Reid's appointment reinforced the influence exercised by the Fowke-Laskin Report. Among other things, the report demonstrated the conditionality of academic freedom so long as professors held their jobs during the pleasure of lay boards and so long as these boards possessed the supreme power in university government. Reid was determined that the CAUT would give priority to the drafting of statements on governance, on academic freedom, and on tenure.[93]

The CAUT, then, got a needed shot in the arm. That it had lost the struggle with United's board of regents was an awkward fact that was increasingly ignored as the case became a symbol of triumph for academic freedom and professorial dignity. In the 1960s the CAUT built on the 'famous victory' in Winnipeg, strengthening the position of professors vis-à-vis executive heads and governing boards, and gaining a measure of protection for academic freedom that it had not previously enjoyed. Victories often are what we make of them.

10

A Place of Liberty

As the century and millennium lurch towards a close, many people who work in Canadian universities have come to regard the 1960s as a golden age. 'Age and forgetfulness sweeten memory,' T.S. Eliot reminds us. Nostalgia deceives. A clear-eyed view of the decade reveals many flaws, not the least obvious being some of the regrettable buildings that went up as prestressed concrete came to surround the older brick and fieldstone. The period was pre-eminently one of growth and optimism, though, and this is what people remember.

Not everyone welcomed the rapid growth or the secularization of the academy that took place as more and more universities severed their denominational ties. Some people asked whether Canadians could adequately support the greatly enlarged universities that were taking shape, whether too many ill-prepared students were entering them, and whether education that was not rooted in a religious world view could serve students well. But one cannot read the memoirs of Claude Bissell, president of the University of Toronto from 1958 to 1971, or Murray G. Ross, York University's founding president, without sensing the excitement of that time.[1]

Student numbers began to grow even before the very first 'baby boomers' showed up in 1964. Postwar prosperity and an awareness of the expanding opportunities for educated people led to a rise in the proportion of university-age Canadians who registered. In 1955 E.F. Sheffield of the Dominion Bureau of Statistics predicted that enrolments would double in ten years. 'In fact,' he wrote in 1970, 'they more than doubled in eight.'[2]

Money was available in unprecedented amounts. Public demand, the Cold War, and the needs of the economy all encouraged greater spending on higher education. The launching in 1957 of the Soviet satellites Sputnik I and II seemed to signal defects in scientific and technological education in the West that cried out to be fixed. Eight years later, the second annual review issued by the Economic Council of Canada, *Towards Sustained and Balanced Growth* (1965), stated that 'the potential future economic benefits ... from increased educational attainments [were] very large' and called for the further expansion of higher education.[3] Politicians, provincial as well as federal, were already responding to the call for cash, though they were rarely as generous as university people hoped they would be.

Federal funding of universities began in 1951 at a rate of 50¢ per head of provincial population. The grant rose to $1.00 in 1956–7, $1.50 in 1958–9, $2.00 in 1962–3, and $5.00 in 1966–7. (The federal government also became the major direct funder of research, establishing several research councils to distribute money to researchers.) From $7.1 million in the first year, direct federal grants increased to $99 million fifteen years later. The total rise in university income was so steep, however, that federal grants, which had been 12 per cent of all university operating income in 1951–2, were just 17 per cent in 1966–7.[4]

Along with the Crowe affair and the work of the Canadian Association of University Teachers (CAUT), the rise in university income and research funding helps explain what happened to the professoriate in the 1960s. Even more influential was a historical anomaly – a growing continentwide shortage of qualified academics. This strengthened the hand of professors as they sought to improve their condition and gain respect. Salaries, pension plans, and other benefits improved, teaching loads declined, and teaching duties and research interests were brought into closer alignment. Faculty also looked for an expanded role in university government, greater security of tenure, and a larger measure of protection for academic freedom.

In September 1958 the University of Western Ontario faculty association agreed to draft a statement on academic freedom and tenure for consideration by the CAUT council. Headed by the psychologist Gordon H. Turner, the committee at Western proposed to copy the 1940 document of the American Association of University Professors (AAUP) in all important details, but it also stated that it would be 'desirable' to make a survey of Canadian universities 'in order to discover what principles and practices concerning academic freedom and tenure are currently being followed.'[5]

Delegates to the CAUT council meeting in November 1958 asked Turner to do this survey and report to the next council meeting, to be held in Saskatoon in June 1959. Before that date the National Conference of Canadian Universities (NCCU) entered the picture. Its secretary, T.H. Matthews, informed the CAUT president Clarence Barber early in 1959 that the 'unfortunate dispute' at United College had led the NCCU board of directors to appoint a committee on academic freedom and tenure. Consisting of Claude Bissell (Toronto), Larry

MacKenzie (UBC), W.A. Mackintosh (Queen's), and Matthews himself, the committee had been asked to consider 'whether, if such a problem arose in the future, the NCCU might offer its services in helping to settle the dispute quickly and quietly, and if so, the procedures that should be followed to enable the Conference to do this.'[6]

Matthews attached a list of four 'preliminary suggestions.' First, the National Conference of Canadian Universities and Colleges (NCCUC) should 'offer its services in cases where Professors felt that they had a real grievance against their administration, or vice-versa.'* Second, a procedure to resolve conflicts seemed more useful than 'an elaborate code of Academic Freedom.' Third, grievances should be mediated by a committee of three, one nominated by the CAUT or local faculty association, one by the administration, and one, the chairman, by the NCCUC executive. Finally, when a grievance came to the attention of the NCCUC, 'it should offer its services ... but should proceed further only if both parties in the dispute accepted its offer.' In conveying this proposal to local faculty associations, Barber added that the committee had asked for a joint CAUT-NCCU meeting to discuss academic freedom and tenure in June.[7]

Only six associations responded. Alberta's thought the NCCU scheme 'well worth a trial' because 'a decision reached by a mediation committee such as that proposed would carry much more weight with the administration against which the grievance existed than one reached by a committee consisting of teaching staff alone.' A similar consideration weighed heavily with the Carleton University faculty association. But McGill's Keith Callard said his association could not accept the view 'that the CAUT is a kind of "prisoner's friend" while the NCCUC adequately represents the teaching staff as well as the university administration'; and R.J. Douglas of the Ontario Agricultural College in Guelph thought the way the committee was put together 'might well have the opinion of CAUT checkmated from the outset.' Saskatchewan's K.A.H. Buckley and the University of British Columbia's A.W.R. Carrothers were even more critical.[8]

Turner's own committee termed the proposals 'unacceptable' and recommended that the CAUT adopt a statement of principles and then 'negotiate with the NCCUC concerning the possibility of mutual adoption and joint publication of this Statement.' This done, the two organizations could collaborate in formu-

---

*The NCCU was surrendering its charter to clear the way for the Canadian Universities Foundation, consisting of the executive heads, and the NCCUC, which would admit to membership colleges that were ineligible to join the NCCU. In 1965 the two merged into the Association of Universities and Colleges of Canada.

lating dismissal procedures and 'institutional regulations consistent with the previously established principles of academic freedom and tenure.' These comments did not exactly encourage further discussion, and neither organization seems to have pursued the matter.[9]

The final report of the Turner committee stated, 'Canadian university teachers feel that there is virtually no restriction on their freedom to conduct and to publish the results of research of their own choosing, or on their freedom to conduct their classes as they see fit,' but that many lacked confidence 'that they could make utterances unpopular with their administrative officers and governing boards without fear of incurring discrimination or censure.' Uncertainty surrounded appointment, tenure, promotion, and dismissal, the report stated: 'Very few institutions have any regular practices or written rules of procedure for dealing with cases of termination, for cause, of a permanent appointment.' Few such cases even became known: 'Exerting pressure on unwanted faculty members to resign has apparently been very effective.' The committee presented four documents for discussion – a statement of principles and three sets of procedures, one for use by a committee that CAUT would establish in investigating alleged violations of academic freedom and tenure, one for use by local associations in dealing with disputes, and one for use by universities in dismissing faculty.[10]

The CAUT council authorized a six-person committee on academic freedom and tenure (AF & T), with the CAUT executive secretary as an *ex officio* member. Recently appointed to this position, Stewart Reid explained to a recruit that the committee was expected to resemble the AAUP's Committee A, 'but this was not spelled out, since it was felt that determining its own procedures ... should be the first task of the committee.' Turner became chairman, and four others soon joined him. After Bora Laskin declined – 'It would be inadvisable to have me on the Committee so long as the last echoes of the Crowe case have not died away' – Reid approached another Toronto law professor, James B. Milner, as the sixth committee member. Milner accepted. 'Although it is not likely to be a popular body with the governing authorities of the Universities,' he wrote, 'its work could be very important for all of us.'[11]

No one hastened to get the committee together. 'I see no need for tremendous hurry,' Reid wrote to Turner late in 1959, 'since in fact no case has come to us yet.' This was not quite true. The CAUT president Harold Good had heard from someone who sought 'an impartial and just investigation' of his grievance against the University of Ottawa. But he did not write again.[12]

In 1960 Reid and the McMaster historian H.W. McCready paid an exploratory visit to Waterloo Lutheran University. Two years passed before an appeal from a faculty member at Mount Allison prompted another such visit from the committee. Only in 1964 did it go public, Turner informing the CAUT's members that the committee was engaged in clarifying its procedures and in discussing the problems faced by academics before they filed a formal complaint. There had been four since 1959, he added, and for each complaint there had been roughly seven requests for advice and help. That so many cases had been resolved without formal complaint Turner attributed 'in no small measure to the consummate skill and wisdom of the late Dr. J.H.S. Reid.' (He had died in December 1963.) But the number of cases seemed likely to increase, since few universities had 'procedures mutually acceptable to faculty and administration for dealing with claims of unjust dismissal.' The AF & T committee could therefore expect more appeals against arbitrary decisions.[13]

Turner's first report was his last. He left the committee in 1964. His successor as chairman, James B. Milner, supervised its passage to a more active role. 'It was apparent that a good deal of injustice arose from unsatisfactory regulations respecting probationary appointments,' Milner wrote in 1965. The old committee had been charged only with alleged violations of academic freedom and tenure, but the terms of reference now included 'grievance procedures, problems of appointments, tenure, promotions, harassment and whatever other matters related to academic freedom or administrative procedures the Committee may see fit to consider.' He added that having received a report on the law of tenure prepared by Daniel Soberman of Queen's (it had already appeared in the *CAUT Bulletin*), the committee was 'preparing statements on policy on the purpose of tenure and how it may be established and protected.'[14] Milner and his committee were bracing themselves for an increased workload.

The three sets of procedures drafted by the Turner committee were adopted with minor amendments at the November 1959 council meeting. The statement of principles proved more controversial. Some delegates wanted a precise definition of 'the conditions which CAUT considers to be acceptable guarantees of freedom and security'; one delegate, fearing excessive legalism in its application, opposed any statement of principles at all. Adopted was the middle way: while 'precise definitions and detailed descriptions ... should be avoided, a very general statement would be of value.' The council voted to delete sections dealing with academic freedom at denominational colleges, with the freedom of professors as researchers, teachers, and citizens, and with appointments, probation, and dismissal for cause.[15]

The revised document stated that universities were conducted 'for the common good, and the common good depends upon the free search for truth and its free exposition.' To these ends academic freedom in teaching and research was essential. Tenure, justified as a means of safeguarding academic freedom and of providing professors with economic security, was to be granted at the end of a period of probation, after which removal might occur only for cause or at the age of retirement.[16]

A committee of the University of British Columbia faculty association commented that the statement contained 'little of substance.' Turner was even more scathing. Because the amended document was so vague, he complained, the AF & T committee's procedures made little sense: 'How can we determine if there was a "proper hearing" when the CAUT will not commit itself to the proposition that there should, in dismissal cases, be any obligation to provide a hearing, let alone a "proper" one?'[17]

In spite of such objections, the statement of principles adopted in June 1960 was essentially the stripped-down version of the statement of the previous November. In appraising it, Donald Savage and Christopher Holmes comment: 'The CAUT Executive and Council rejected the then AAUP view that there could be justifiable limitations on academic freedom notably in religious institutions, and that an academic had to dissociate himself from his institution when making public statements.' The recorded discussion does not, in fact, suggest that delegates made deliberate choices on these issues. Most seem to have thought that a detailed statement was a mistake and voted accordingly. All the same, Canadian professors would be less subject than their U.S. colleagues to self-imposed limits on academic freedom.[18]

'Due process' was (and still is) a concept often poorly understood. Professors and administrators shared a tendency to assume that the end justified the means. Even at institutions that had adopted procedures for dealing with tenure, promotions, and dismissals, untenured faculty members might have scant procedural protection. In 1960 the governing council of Victoria College in Victoria, British Columbia, adopted a document on appointments, promotions, and tenure. If tenured appointments were to be ended or term appointments ended before their expiry, the document stated, the faculty members should be informed in writing of the charges against them and should have the opportunity to be heard in their own defence by the college council. They were allowed to have with them an adviser of their own choosing who might act as counsel. A full record of the hearing would be made available to all parties. On the other hand, lecturers and instructors, appointed for one-year terms, were without protection.[19]

In early 1962 the head of English, Roger J. Bishop, wrote to Principal W.H. Hickman about a junior faculty member: 'I have now made up my mind that [he] is not of the calibre we wish in this institution ... I cannot, therefore, recommend his reappointment.' Of another instructor Bishop wrote, 'I have observed [him] teach and I have not been impressed. When I tried to talk over his methods with him he repelled my suggestions ... In addition I have had innumerable complaints from students in his classes. I do not think he should be reappointed.[20] Neither man was back in the fall of 1962.

Similarly, the following January the head of mathematics, F.E. Deloume, wrote of a lecturer in his department, '[He] is a brilliant scholar but as a teacher of undergraduate mathematics students he has not been very successful.' He had ignored all advice aimed at improving his teaching, stated Deloume. 'I cannot recommend [him] for reappointment.'[21]

These assessments may have been fully justified, but they were made in confidence. No one was obliged to give reasons to unsuccessful candidates for reappointment, who therefore had no opportunity to defend themselves. Moreover, the process was open to abuse. If a recommendation purportedly made on academic grounds was really due to a conflict of personalities, how was the principal to sort this out?

Still, Victoria's procedures offered protection to more senior people. Some institutions lacked the most basic safeguards even for the tenured. The dismissal of a music teacher from Mount Allison University made this starkly clear. In January 1962 President W.T. Ross Flemington informed Dorothy Allen that the board of regents, intent on making economies, had decided to 'retire' her on 30 June with a year's salary as a separation allowance. Fifty years old, Allen had taught at Mount Allison since 1937. She was neither the youngest member of the conservatory staff nor the most recently appointed, nor was she the least qualified. She did not know 'the official regulations at Mount Allison regarding tenure of position, freedom of speech, or dismissal of faculty members,' she wrote to Flemington, but she believed herself entitled to more consideration than she had received and that she had the right to defend herself against any charges that might have made against her.[22]

Allen got no satisfaction from Flemington and little more from the president of the faculty association, Alex Colville. 'In the case of choosing between two faculty members,' she wrote to Stewart Reid, 'the one receiving the higher salary would be considered of higher rank, and thus would remain in office. It was the understanding of Mr. Colville that my rank was lower.' In this way Allen learned that a colleague who had been at the conservatory only since 1956, a woman she believed to have fewer qualifications than herself, earned more and as a consequence ranked higher than she did.[23]

John G. Reid (Mount Allison's official historian) has sketched the background of the case.[24] Questions had arisen about Mount Allison's role in fine arts and music – fields originating in the girls' secondary school that had once been associated with the university. Service to the community had to be balanced against the need for academic standards consistent with university status.

There was also the fact that the School of Applied and Fine Arts and the Conservatory of Music had been incurring deficits since the mid-1950s. In 1959 a board committee recommended a cut in conservatory faculty numbers from seven to four. In response, the faculty proposed ways of raising income, and for two years the issue hung fire. Then a committee consisting of Flemington, the dean of arts, and the director of the conservatory, recommended that one faculty member be let go. The executive committee of the board chose Allen; how and why remains a mystery.[25]

Allen having appealed to the CAUT, Stewart Reid and Gordon Turner visited Sackville in June 1962 and spoke with Flemington about CAUT policies and how these might be used at Mount Allison. This availed nothing. On 26 June Flemington thanked Allen for twenty-five years' service, told her she would get a year's salary as well as the university's contributions to her pension plan to age sixty-five, offered her help in finding another position, and wished her well.[26]

'The official position is that her dismissal is necessary in order to put into effect the required reorganization of the Conservatory of Music,' Turner reported to the members of the AF & T committee. Reid added that the Mount Allison faculty association was 'not prepared to support Miss Allen for a complex of reasons, most of which, I take it, are personal.' He wondered whether the AF & T committee could proceed at all if, as seemed likely, Allen accepted the board's action.[27]

After consulting with a member of Western's Faculty of Law, Turner himself advised Allen to 'accept whatever the University sees fit to offer.' She would thereby undercut any action the CAUT might undertake on her behalf, but if she rejected the offer she might get even less. Allen pondered this for some weeks, then asked the AF & T committee to drop the matter.[28]

Early in 1963 Turner informed the chairman of the Mount Allison board that the AF & T committee would take no action. 'The Committee has, however, instructed me to express to you its view that there was ... a disturbing absence of due process in the failure to provide formal notice of dismissal or a statement of reason for dismissal or a procedure for appeal and hearing or even of adequate records.'[29] The CAUT would be willing to assist the faculty association and administration in drafting appropriate agreements, Turner added. The CAUT's files contain no reply.

By the end of the 1950s a growing number of faculty members believed that academic freedom would be safe only if university government was reformed. Typical of this point of view was a comment on the Allen case made by J. Percy Smith, a Saskatchewan English professor and a member of the AF & T committee. It seemed, he wrote, 'to underline once more the argument for greatly increased faculty participation in university government.' Until faculty members shared in making decisions about policy and administration, 'cases of this kind which imply the master-servant relationship' would continue to occur.[30]

Smith was not the first to express this attitude. Inquiring in 1951 about the embryonic CAUT, Dalhousie's George P. Grant had written: 'I would hope such an association would in no sense admit the employee-employer relationship that the Board here seems to lay down.' In their report on the Crowe case, Vernon Fowke and Bora Laskin did not hide their disdain for top-down management. The solicitor for United College, D.C. McGavin, seemed 'determined to treat the investigation as if it arose out of a labour relations dispute ...,' they observed 'The concept of a University as a community of scholars, as an integrated body of civilized men and women (composed of administrative heads, teaching faculty and students) dedicated to pursuit of knowledge and development of wisdom, was completely absent from his presentation.' Fowke and Laskin professed themselves unable to credit 'that Mr. McGavin's philosophy of a University' was that of the board of regents: 'The degradation involved is the very antithesis of higher education.'[31]

Fowke and Laskin were well aware, of course, that boards were the employers and professors their employees. Academic senates dealt with curriculum, grading, student discipline, and similar matters but yielded to boards when their decisions had financial implications. Boards, in turn, tended to follow the lead given by executive heads, the only persons with a comprehensive view of their institutions.

By no means all professors were unhappy with this kind of university government. The political scientist Norman Ward, teaching at Queen's in 1958–9 while on leave from Saskatchewan, wrote to Fowke:

The administration is paternalistic to a striking degree. The faculty association does not negotiate; it is informed. The president [sic] ... of the university gives an annual state-of-the-union message which is well-attended by the association members, most of whom think it is a normal sort of thing for the head man to dominate a meeting of the faculty association ... One session on pensions really turned largely on the fact that while theoretically the members ought to have some say in the matter, in cold fact a leading member of the Board was also a leading member of a large insurance company. As I understand it, the administration unilaterally announced changes in the pension plan while the association were still talking about it!

Ward added that the faculty had confidence in Principal W.A. Mackintosh and Vice-Principal J.A. Corry, and did not seem to mind their paternalism.[32]

Universities were usually benevolent autocracies. The potential for tyranny was there, however, affecting behaviour on both sides of the divide. Authoritarianism came easily to presidents and boards, just as deference came easily to the professoriate. As the institutions expanded and bureaucracies grew, the informal influence exercised by senior faculty tended to decline. Some of them resented this. One effect of the Crowe case was to strengthen the hand of those who sought to gain an enhanced role for professors in university government. The CAUT's first executive secretary played a key role in this development. At United College, Stewart Reid had argued that faculty should participate more fully in college government. By the fall of 1959, he had a national platform for such views.

He was not alone. Vernon Fowke, influenced by the inquiry he and Laskin had made into the dismissal of Harry Crowe, argued in 1959 that academics had a good deal of *de facto* control over academic policy but little or none over the allocation of funds or the selection of administrators. As a first step towards change, he recommended faculty representation on governing boards. In February 1960 Percy Smith made a plea that universities no longer be modelled on business corporations but be reorganized as communities governed by those who belonged to them: 'If a university is to function at its best, its members must be as free as possible from the threat of possible interference; and for this reason they must be able to determine the objectives and policies of the institution that they serve.'[33]

Later in 1960 the report of the CAUT's committee on university government, headed by the Carleton University political scientist Donald C. Rowat, took a similar line. It stated that many people had known that something was seriously wrong with Canada's system of university government but that the Crowe case 'was nevertheless a dramatic demonstration of the disastrous results that such a system can bring about, and awakened us to the fact that something must be done.' Rowat had no doubt where the problem lay: 'The essential function of university scholars is to pursue and propagate the truth as they see it, freely and without fear or favour; yet in Canada they are hired, paid, governed and controlled by an outside body whose members may have particular interests to protect or promote.' And the solution to this problem? – 'The scholars themselves must be given the predominant voice in governing their own university.' The academic staff should be a majority on the board and should choose the administrators.[34]

While approving 'the principle of greater faculty participation in university government,' the CAUT council voted only to 'receive' the report 'as a basis of discussion.' But the issue was now front and centre. Late in 1960, Reid told the Dalhousie faculty association, 'Within the last year, several associations have made recommendations to their Boards of Governors and to their Provincial Governments calling for extensive reorganization of university government.'[35]

This did not mean that change was taking place. Neither governing boards nor the bodies that appointed them eagerly embraced change. Board members had become accustomed to hearing faculty representatives argue for higher salaries and improved benefits, but sharing power was something else again. Inappropriate as the business model might seem to some professors, it looked good to the businessmen and lawyers who dominated the boards. Although they did not raise any large part of the money needed to run the universities, they saw themselves as eminently qualified to supervise the spending of that money. That those who worked in the university might serve as governors seemed fanciful, and that they might become a majority of board members was unthinkable.

The resistance that met calls for change was evident in Walter P. Thompson's response to Percy Smith. The recently retired president of the University of Saskatchewan declared the business analogy to be misleading. 'True in theory' but 'false in practice,' it pictured things not as they were, 'but as they might be' *if* the boards were to exercise their legal power – which Thompson thought unlikely. In practice, he said, faculty members had more, and board members less, influence than Smith allowed. Consequently, there was no need for professors to be represented on governing boards.[36]

Thompson did not persuade the champions of reform. One was W.L. Morton, a member of Rowat's committee who, as the official historian of the University of Manitoba, knew that professors had served on its governing body until 1917. Conceding that boards rarely used their power to oppress the faculty and that many board members gave selflessly of their time, Morton nevertheless dismissed as 'simply specious' Thompson's claim that boards shared effective power with senates. The vesting of legal authority in lay boards had several ill effects, he asserted, one of them being the growing gulf between administrators and professors. But worse was the subordination of 'the free activities of teaching and research to an external and alien control.'

An occasional arbitrary action such as Crowe's dismissal was one result of this situation. Another was the undermining of the effectiveness of professors. 'The scholar cannot properly be treated as a worker under contract ... Because no one but himself can direct his work, he can only be treated as a responsible member of a community, engaged in pursuits which, in the long run and overall, are necessary for the society in which that community lives.' Morton credited the intimacy of university life for the large measure of academic freedom that did exist. With explosive growth, however, the mutual alienation of administration and faculty was 'becoming a serious threat to the integrity of Canadian universities.' The pressing need was for 'a system of university government in which the faculty are responsible in every respect for the functioning of the university, and in which governments and the public may have confidence.'[37]

The next issue of the *Bulletin* contained an upbeat piece by the University of British Columbia's president, Larry MacKenzie, emphasizing academic involvement in decision making and downplaying the influence of board members. Alongside this appeared an editorial urging the CAUT and the Canadian Universities Foundation to join in a study of university government.[38] This proposal gained the approval of both bodies in June 1962. Funded by the Ford Foundation, the study got underway in 1964, with Sir James Duff (University of Durham, England) and Robert Berdahl (San Francisco State College) as the commissioners.

Well before Duff and Berdahl began their work, some academics tried to widen the debate. 'I don't know if you have heard that a number of us – Frank Scott, Frank Underhill, Bill Morton, Percy Smith, Don Rowat ... – are considering the possibility of a book of essays on various aspects of the government and administration of universities in Canada,' Reid wrote to George Whalley of the Queen's Department of English in 1961. 'As you will guess, none of us so far committed is a supporter of the status quo! We're going to try to talk you into agreeing to help us in the project.'[39]

Whalley became editor of the volume. One of the book's purposes, he told potential contributors, would be 'to destroy the widespread charge that academic persons are too "unworldly" or too lacking in administrative acumen to be allowed any active part in the secular and worldly side of university administration.' In July 1962 Whalley, Reid, Scott, Smith, and Underhill met in Ottawa to discuss the book. Afterwards Whalley reported agreement among them 'that a university is a community of scholars,' a body 'of a unique kind for which there is no parallel or close analogy in other forms of society; ... and that its life depends upon freedom of thought, freedom of action, and complete freedom from the orthodoxies and platforms of establishments and special interests.' Rejected 'without qualification' were the notions that the university was 'a business corporation, a civil service, or a mere teaching institution.'[40]

A Place of Liberty, subtitled *Essays on the Government of Canadian Universities*, appeared in 1964. The contributors shared four opinions, Whalley's preface stated: (1) the judgment of the academic staff should influence all university decisions; (2) governing boards enjoyed inordinate and inappropriate power; (3) the split between scholars and administrators should be ended 'as far as possible'; (4) all positive changes must be given legal status in order to entrench them.

The fourth item was deemed to be necessary so that the governments that were paying for expansion would find it more difficult to interfere. After all,

'when it comes to paying for pipers, the accident of having money to commission music was never any proof of musical knowledge or guarantee of good
taste.' Academic survival required 'responsible self-government ... by the university communities, a relation of intelligent goodwill between the universities
and the various representatives of "society,"' and, on the part of outsiders, 'a
genuine respect for the integrity of the academic world.'[41]

The contributors were Fowke, Laskin, Morton, Reid, Rowat, Scott, Smith,
Underhill, Maxwell Cohen (McGill, law), Pierre Dansereau (Montreal, botany)
Murray Donnelly (Manitoba, political science), Paul Lacoste (Laval, philosophy), and Whalley himself. Their essays repay reading to this day, most notably
those about the university and society (Smith), the functions of the scholar
(Morton), and the relations between French-Canadian universities and the
church (Lacoste). The best one-liner is Scott's: 'Better have scholars running
banks than bankers governing scholars.'[42]

Frank Underhill wrote about academic freedom. Using *A Man for All Sea-
sons* (1960), Robert Bolt's play about Sir Thomas More, as his point of departure, Underhill identified its theme: 'How can a man of penetrating intellect and
clear faith maintain his personal integrity in an age of revolutionary change in
which all the pressures from government, from his friends and from the public,
are to adjust himself, to conform to whatever orthodoxy is proclaimed by the
established authorities?' Bolt's Common Man avoided making trouble, noted
Underhill, but the committed university teacher could not help doing so: '[He]
is up against the Common Man. Directly or indirectly, he is requiring the
Common Man and his children to stretch their imaginations, to refine their
sensibilities, to discipline their intellects to a degree that they are apt to find
uncomfortable and disturbing.'

Why should professors be allowed to do things that those who paid for their
services might not want done? asked Underhill. In reply, he quoted from the
article on academic freedom which Arthur O. Lovejoy, first secretary of the
AAUP, had contributed to the *Encyclopedia of the Social Sciences* in the 1930s.
The paradox inherent in academic freedom was 'that those who buy a certain
service may not prescribe the nature of the service to be rendered.' Why was
this so? 'There are certain professional functions generally recognised to be
indispensable in the life of a civilized community which cannot be performed if
the specific manner of their performance is dictated by those who pay for them,
and ... the profession of the scholar and teacher in higher institutions of learning
is one of these.' Lovejoy, Underhill said, claimed for professors the role of a
collective Socrates.

The historian did not remind his readers of the fate of Socrates. Instead, he wrote about the gulf that existed in North America between the standards of university life and the 'collective mediocrity' of a society shaped by plutocracy and egalitarian democracy: 'Academic freedom will only be securely established through the growth in the community at large of a genuine belief in the supreme value of intellectual activity.' But since it could be damned as elitist, this belief was unlikely to triumph soon.

'Academic freedom,' Underhill continued, 'is the collective freedom of a profession and the individual freedom of the members of that profession.' But it was not absolute, for freedom entailed responsibility. The CAUT would be more persuasive if it were seen to worry less about salaries and benefits and more about professional standards: 'Members of the public learn from their sons and daughters at the university more than we suspect about how much dead wood is scattered among the academic departments.'

If academics needed self-criticism, they also needed to forge alliances with others who sought freedom of expression. 'In the meantime,' noted Underhill, 'the university today is being subjected to fresh pressures from outside which raise problems of academic freedom in new forms.' The demand for higher education created pressures to drop standards; growing enrolment led universities to rely on governments whose objectives differed from those of scholars.

Because its services were so essential to the powerful, continued Underhill, 'the contemporary university tends to be absorbed into the Establishment, and the ... administrative bureaucracy, which expands in accordance with Parkinson's Law, tends to become more and more Establishment-minded.' (Parkinson's Law – that 'work expands so as to fill the time available for its completion' – grew out of a study of the British Admiralty which led the historian C. Northcote Parkinson to claim, only partly in jest, that the annual rate of growth in the size of a bureaucracy would 'invariably prove to be between 5.17 per cent and 6.56 percent, irrespective of any variation in the amount of work [if any] to be done.' The Establishment was the term Underhill used to describe the leaders of business, government, and the media.) More than McCarthyite anti-communist witch-hunts, said Underhill, the tendency to give in to the power of the Establishment would threaten academic freedom in the future. He did not presume to specify a defence, simply stating, 'The price of liberty is, however, the same in universities as elsewhere.'[43]

Underhill's words were embedded in a book whose general tone was cheerful. In 1964, changes that were enhancing the position of the professoriate and of academic freedom were already in train. Thirty-five years later, though, his sceptical warnings seem more perceptive than the optimism of some of the book's other authors.

Absent from *A Place of Liberty* was any discussion of the place of faculty women, the discrimination from which they (and various ethnic minority groups) had long suffered, and the implications that this might have for university governance and academic freedom. All the contributors to the book were men. Moreover, it was still the custom to use only the male pronoun and the words 'man' and 'men' when discussing the professoriate. The title of Underhill's essay was 'The Scholar: Man Thinking.'

By the early 1960s, roughly one in seven Canadian academics was female. During the decade women found it gradually easier to gain appointment. So did Jews and members of visible minorities. When the biologist Howard McCurdy joined Assumption University in Windsor as a lecturer in 1959, he was the first Canadian of African ancestry to be appointed by a university in this country. No one of aboriginal or Asian origin seems to have been appointed before 1960, but in the 1960s that, too, began to change.

One reason was the shortage of qualified faculty during the decade; another was the increased availability of candidates who were neither male nor Caucasian. Although prejudice and discrimination were by no means dead, to discriminate overtly against people was becoming socially unacceptable and legally challengeable. The long-standing bias against women in particular came under attack. With this came an insistence that policies be introduced that would ensure fair treatment.

Before the 1960s, even where women worked under no disadvantage, it was less a matter of policy than of the practices of presidents and boards. The rule of men [*sic!*] and not of law prevailed. A benevolent autocracy is preferable to one less benign, but it is still an autocracy. In any case, one could not rely on its benevolence. Boards and presidents changed. Who knew what the future might bring? All academics were aware of this uncertainty, but the most vulnerable were most disposed to heed it. Keeping a low profile, staying close to the ground, not sticking one's neck out – the metaphors capture the behaviour of women (and members of ethnic minorities) even more than that of academics generally.

The founding of the CAUT's status of women committee in 1965 was evidence of the new attitude. But even those critical of the *status quo* were sometimes reluctant to push hard against it. The University of Saskatchewan historian Hilda Neatby, for example, joined the status of women committee at the outset and helped write its interim report on discrimination against female professors, issued in 1966.[44] But although the period was one in which department heads still enjoyed a relatively free hand in recommending appointments,

Neatby added only one woman to her department while she was head (1958–69). Her biographer, Michael Hayden, comments, 'There were not that many [women] around to appoint and Hilda was worried about male backlash because the History Department had three women, more than any [other] on campus.'[45]

In the 1960s a female department head was still uncommon; at the higher administrative levels, women were very rare. Not until 1974 did a woman, Pauline Jewett, become president of a co-educational university (Simon Fraser). Meanwhile, not a few women and, one supposes, minority faculty members continued to feel less than welcome in academe. This affected not only academic freedom but also university government. No women were in the forefront of those who in the early 1960s sought to secure a greater faculty role in university government, and the only Jews were Bora Laskin and Maxwell Cohen. Both were by this time academic elder statesmen. To challenge the citadels of power, a sense of belonging may not be essential, but it helps.

One of the issues taken up by the CAUT in the early 1960s was political candidacy. In 1962 the national council adopted a policy statement recommending that professors who wished to run for office should be given leave to do so. At many institutions they already enjoyed this right. In the June 1962 federal election eighteen academics ran for office. Four won their seats; no fewer than three were from St Francis Xavier University in Antigonish, Nova Scotia. One of them was the economist Allan J. MacEachen, who had first entered the House in 1953 but had been defeated five years later. (In 1963 he would join Lester B. Pearson's cabinet.)[46]

At Dalhousie, candidacy became a contentious issue in 1962. When the political scientist James Aitchison asked for leave of absence in order to run for the House of Commons, the board of governors objected. The objection was less to Aitchison's candidacy than to his political party. Having early in 1962 accepted a New Democratic Party (NDP) nomination, Aitchison reported to Stewart Reid in April, 'I have received unofficial word that the attitude of the Executive Committee of the Board of Governors toward my candidacy could not be more negative.' His dean, Henry Hicks, was 'holding up a formal communication' to him 'in the hopes of persuading the Board to change its mind.' If the board did not do so, said Aitchison, 'I shall vigorously and openly criticize it.'[47] He asked Reid for assistance.

Four weeks later, Aitchison wrote to report success: 'It was a famous victory, thanks, mainly, to the information you were able to provide.'[48] This was the only victory Aitchison enjoyed. In the general election that June he did not come close to saving his deposit. He did not run in 1963 but accepted an NDP nomination in 1965. Once again he finished last.

Even in the provincial universities the institutional barriers against political candidacy had largely disappeared by the time of the 1962 and 1963 elections. When Reid polled various candidates in the latter year, most reported having had no difficulty in obtaining leave to run. Fairly typical was the response of Carleton University's Pauline Jewett. It had been easy to get a leave of absence until such time as she might wish to return to academic life, she wrote.[49]

The University of Toronto was still a holdout. Change in this area, when it came, was a by-product of other changes. The historian William H. Nelson writes that around 1960 'the senior professors from the natural sciences who had dominated the faculty association since the War began to fade from the scene.' Social scientists such as Laskin, C.B. Macpherson, the historian James Conacher, and the political scientist James Eayrs took charge of the Association of the Teaching Staff.[50]

Responding to faculty criticism of the university's structure of government, President Bissell in 1964 set up an advisory committee, chaired by the physiologist R.E. Haist, to study and report on this and related issues, such as the granting of tenure and the appointment of academic administrators. One perhaps unexpected result was a resolution, adopted by the board in 1966, that outlined the conditions under which professors might run for office.

'Members of the academic profession,' the resolution began, 'ought to be as free as the members of any other profession to choose to enter public life. There is an obligation upon the University ... to see to it that no impediments are placed in the way of a member of the academic staff with a desire to enter public life.' However, the administrators were excluded: 'No Chairman or Dean, while such, should become a candidate for public office.' Candidates for election could get leave at full pay for up to one month, and successful candidates could get leave without pay or at reduced pay for up to five years. Those who became cabinet ministers would be expected to resign their university positions, as would those who wished to exceed five years of leave. Those who did return would not suffer loss of rank or academic entitlement.[51]

A sign of the times was that the *Globe and Mail* criticized the new rules as too restrictive. Not only Bissell but also two members of the faculty, Macpherson and K.G. McNeill, wrote to defend the policy. The first person to take advantage of it was the political scientist Robert Fenn, who obtained the NDP nomination in Toronto–St Paul's in the 1968 federal election. He finished far back.[52]

Occasional visits to Canadian campuses by the RCMP to carry out security checks and undercover intelligence work had begun in the 1920s, reached a peak around 1940, and continued after the war. The practice seems not to have worried the CAUT in its early years, but by 1960 some members had come to see the RCMP's activities, to use a phrase used in a CAUT document, as 'a threat to academic freedom.' At the conclusion of a debate at the November 1961 council meeting, Stewart Reid was instructed to ask for a meeting with the minister of justice, E. Davie Fulton, and to obtain more information.[53]

Reid's request brought a reply asserting the need for national security. Reid wrote again, saying the CAUT sought information about the policy of the Justice Department concerning security in the universities and about the techniques employed by the RCMP 'in investigating members of the university communities of Canada.' He enclosed a list of questions – some of them implicitly critical of RCMP activities – to which the executive council wanted answers.[54]

In May 1962 Reid received a telephone call from someone in Fulton's office. 'The Minister quite clearly was annoyed,' Reid reported to members of the executive. Although Fulton was apparently willing to admit that the RCMP had made mistakes, he 'would probably be unwilling to say that any particular technique of investigation is *per se* a mistake.' He was unable to grant an early meeting but would try to meet with a CAUT delegation sometime after the general election, scheduled for 18 June.[55]

In the election, the Progressive Conservatives were returned to office, though with a minority of seats, and on 21 August Reid and the CAUT president A.W.R. Carrothers at last met Fulton. The interview was unsatisfactory, partly because Fulton was about to leave the department and partly because he rejected all criticism of the RCMP's campus operations. 'Our impression,' Reid and Carrothers reported, 'is that the Government ... would be unwilling to agree that it should not ask questions about the political beliefs of students and faculty.'[56]

At the November 1962 council meeting a resolution was introduced asking the CAUT to 'express its disapproval of questions concerning the political or religious beliefs, activities or associations of students or colleagues,' and to advise members 'not to answer such questions, even when they are part of the security investigation of persons seeking government employment.' The choice of language was as controversial as the issue. 'The resolution provoked much discussion,' Reid reported: 'In fact, at one time there were no fewer than six alternative or amended resolutions before Council.' Finally the council charged a committee with drafting 'two or three possible resolutions for circulation to associations and for vote at the June [1963] meeting.'[57]

By that time, the Conservatives were out of office, the Liberals having formed a minority government after a general election in April 1963. Possibly sensing that the Grits were more flexible than the Tories, the CAUT council passed a relatively mild resolution; it asserted that the RCMP's investigations and procedures 'have serious implications for academic freedom,' urged 'a full review of RCMP security and intelligence investigation procedures,' and advised members that they need not answer questions about 'the political or religious beliefs, activities, and associations of colleagues and students.' If they did answer, they should do so in writing.[58]

At the end of July 1963, Reid and the CAUT's vice-president, Bora Laskin, met Prime Minister Lester B. Pearson, Justice Minister Lionel Chevrier, Pauline Jewett (recently elected to Parliament), and the clerk of the privy council, Gordon Robertson. A second meeting took place in November 1963. Chevrier was absent, but in attendance were Pearson, Jewett, Robertson, Reid, and Laskin, as well as the undersecretary of state for external affairs, Norman Robertson, the commissioner of the RCMP, George B. McClellan, and the president of the National Federation of Canadian University Students, David Jenkins. McClellan stated that 'since mid-1961, there has been an official policy of no general surveillance at university campuses,' but he conceded that counterespionage still occasionally took place and that officers sometimes interviewed professors while carrying out security checks on applicants for government employment. These policies and procedures, he said, were under examination.[59]

After Pearson had approved Laskin's draft report of the meetings, the text appeared in the *CAUT Bulletin* in April 1964. Laskin and Reid added a report stating that they 'were satisfied with the answers of both the Prime Minister and the Minister of Justice, that the Government appreciates the special position of the universities, and the absolute necessity of maintaining in them a climate conducive to freedom of thought and discussion.' Suspicion of the RCMP lingered in some academic circles, but from the CAUT executive's point of view the matter had been resolved to satisfaction. If any member of the AF & T committee thought differently, no record of his misgivings survives.[60]

By the 1960s the influence of religion had been declining for several decades. However, the process of secularization had not occurred everywhere with equal speed, and it was far from complete. In 1966 a visiting French historian, Marc Ferro, said after spending some weeks at the University of Calgary that secular values dominated in France but not in Alberta: 'You have freedom of religion here, but not freedom *from* religion.'[61]

Most Roman Catholic universities remained under episcopal control into the 1960s. The death of Premier Maurice Duplessis in 1959, followed by the defeat of the Union nationale in 1960 and its replacement by a Liberal government led by Jean Lesage helped clear the way for a new dispensation in Quebec, where the early 1960s became known as the Quiet Revolution. A sign of the times was the stand taken in 1961 when a group of professors at the University of Montreal signed a public protest against a Jesuit plan to open two new universities in the city. Among the signatories of *L'université dit non aux Jesuites* were Pierre

Dansereau (a member of the AF & T committee), the historian Michel Brunet, and the demographer Jacques Henripin. It is hard to imagine a similar protest occurring ten years earlier. What is more, the project was eventually abandoned. Paul Lacoste commented, 'It is obvious even to a layman in such matters that something has happened in French-speaking Quebec.'[62]

Lacoste's own university, Laval, had already entered on the process of secularization. The appointment in 1960 of a new rector, Mgr Louis-Albert Vachon, had been greeted with satisfaction by the clerics teaching in the Seminary of Quebec (of which he became the general superior) and with disquiet by the lay people who by this time largely staffed the university. 'Tous furent trompés,' Paul-André Laberge comments, 'les uns dans leurs espoirs, les autres dans leurs appréhensions.'[63] Vachon soon came to the conclusion that the university could not continue under the jurisdiction of the seminary. For practical purposes the two institutions were separated in 1963, and legal separation was complete by 1969. The following year Laval received a new charter from the provincial legislature, and with the adoption of new statutes a nonsectarian Laval came into existence in 1971. The University of Montreal had become secular four years earlier.

In Ontario secularization had taken place earlier, chiefly because, in contrast with the situation in Quebec, sectarian universities and colleges could not receive provincial funds. McMaster had been the first to move. Realizing that the university's traditional sources of income could no longer fund all its programs, President George P. Gilmour moved in the 1940s to hive the sciences off to the nonsectarian Hamilton College, which qualified for provincial support. In 1957 the Faculty of Arts severed its ties with the Baptist Convention of Ontario and Quebec, leaving only the divinity school under Baptist control.

Assumption University, a Roman Catholic institution, adopted the same course, establishing Essex College in 1954 and becoming the secularized University of Windsor in 1962. The Catholic Collège du Sacré Coeur became the University of Sudbury in 1957, then gave way to the nondenominational Laurentian University in 1960. The largest Catholic university outside Quebec, Ottawa, became nonsectarian in 1965. The denominational institutions federated with the University of Toronto (Victoria, Trinity, and St Michael's) managed to maintain themselves, but only because in most subjects their students were being educated by the university.

At Waterloo College two presidents swam against the tide. A small institution under the aegis of the Evangelical Lutheran Synod of Canada, Waterloo consisted of a seminary and a liberal arts college affiliated with the University of Western Ontario. In 1959 a new president, H.M. Axford, 'an economy-minded businessman and a strong Lutheran,' seemed eager to put an explicitly

Christian stamp on Waterloo College. He had succeeded J. Gerald Hagey, who had been trying to reshape the college so that most of its work would be eligible for provincial support. This involved the creation of a nonsectarian university, responsible for most instruction, with which the college would federate. As the new university took form under the temporary name of Waterloo College and the Associate Faculties, with Hagey as president, friction arose between a group of convinced Lutherans among the faculty and a larger number who had little attachment to Waterloo's religious roots. The former wanted the college to remain under church control while it became, in effect, the university's arts faculty; the latter thought the arts faculty should share instruction with the college and the university, after the college was freed from church control.[64]

The Waterloo College board of governors approved the federation project in January 1960 and confirmed the decision four months later. The faculty minority then made public its fear, one shared by Axford, that Waterloo would lose its Lutheran soul. A special meeting of the synod heard Axford's plea for an independent Waterloo Lutheran University, whereupon the delegates rejected the board's recommendation to federate, choosing independence instead. (In 1973 the institution severed its denominational ties in order to qualify for provincial funding and renamed itself Wilfrid Laurier University.)[65]

The debate over the future of the college complicated a concurrent conflict about the principles that ought to govern tenure, promotion, and academic freedom. In November 1959 the Waterloo College faculty association had submitted a position paper whose clause on academic freedom made three claims: (1) 'subject to the adequate performance of his duties, the teacher must be free to carry out research and to publish the results'; (2) 'the teacher is entitled to freedom of discussion in the classroom'; (3) 'when the teacher speaks, writes or acts as a private citizen, he must be free from institutional censorship or discipline.'[66]

A month later another document, signed by twenty-three of the thirty-one members of the faculty, had urged federation, a change in the board to make it nonsectarian, improved salaries and economic benefits, and 'conditions of academic freedom and tenure as outlined in the Faculty Association brief,' as well as faculty representation in policy making, 'including representation on the board.'[67] 'The battle lines are drawn,' the faculty association's president, James Stone, wrote to Stewart Reid: the eight nonsigners had presented a counter-brief. 'To judge by the tenor of their accusations, I presume it upholds them as defenders of the faith and condemns us ... as traitors and heretics,' commented Stone.[68]

In January 1960 Stone reported to Reid an assertion by Axford 'that "dedicated" teachers at a Christian liberal arts college should accept low salaries.' The president had also insisted 'that anyone who does not teach his subject with Christian emphasis – he used mathematics as an example – does not belong in a church-sponsored college; indeed, he suggested that one professor (who questioned the feasibility of teaching maths and science according to his formula) should resign.' Two weeks later Stone wrote that the dean of arts and science, Lloyd H. Schaus, had told J. Michael Sandison of the English department that his contract would not be renewed because 'his beliefs as expressed in class were not consonant with the aims (presumably religious aims) of this institution.'[69]

When the faculty association executive spoke to Axford about this, he expressed displeasure that they seemed to be acting 'as a "union" attempting to ensure the security of an individual.' Axford added that a board committee was preparing a document on academic freedom and tenure, and 'that no one at this time has tenure; nor will anyone have it until the Board decides what the conditions of tenure are.'[70]

A few days later, Sandison told his colleagues that Axford had asked him whether he was a communicant of any church and whether he knew 'that the constitution of Waterloo College has a clause requiring all its faculty members to be Protestant communicants.' When Sandison answered in the negative to both questions, Axford told him 'that only yesterday a Jew had been refused a position on our faculty because of this clause.' This prompted fears that Axford and the board intended to impose religious tests, and it led twenty-two faculty members to sign a petition predicting a 'flight from the college of both faculty and students' unless the board guaranteed academic freedom, adopted a hiring policy blind to 'race, colour and creed,' and committed itself to an expansion of the teaching staff and library.[71]

Two months passed. In early May, days before the synod rejected federation with the university, Dean Schaus recommended Sandison's nonrenewal, alleging incompetence. Immediately afterwards all faculty members received a copy of the board committee's report on academic freedom and tenure. A covering letter from Axford said it would become policy in September. Its preamble stated that academic freedom and tenure, though 'sound' in principle, should be subject to limits. Teachers were 'entitled to full freedom in research and in the publication of results' as long as this did not interfere with teaching, but 'freedom in the classroom is not to be used as liberty to attack or in any way to disparage the Christian religion.' Rather, it should 'be used as an opportunity for teachers to bring the light of the divinely inspired truth of the Holy Scriptures into the compass of their students.' Teachers should avoid 'controversial topics' as well as 'provocative discussions' of subjects outside their fields of study. Outside the college, teachers were 'entitled to precisely the same freedom and ... subject to the same responsibility as ... all other citizens,' and should make clear, when they spoke, that they were 'expressing only their personal opinion.' Tenure could be granted after a probationary period of seven years. Thereafter, employment was terminable for cause, 'interpreted as gross immorality, treason, professional incompetence, ...' (These ellipsis points must have been especially unnerving.)[72]

When Stone and the faculty association's vice-president, Donald Savage, met Axford, they found him unreceptive to arguments that the board should not have adopted the report without consulting the faculty or without including dismissal procedures. The next day, 17 May, Schaus informed faculty members that the college would soon be independent and that they must decide within ten days whether they wished to return in the fall. This put many in a quandary. It was very late to be looking for employment elsewhere, but the synod's rejection of university federation was bad news and the board's report on academic freedom and tenure was worse.[73]

Two days later seven people, including Stone and Savage, resigned, citing the failure of federation as their reason. Since five others had resigned earlier to take positions elsewhere or to return to graduate school, only nine faculty 'liberals' remained. Earlier, Stone had appealed to Reid for help, but he now wrote that those who remained did not want the CAUT to act. It seemed unlikely to improve the situation, and if it led to controversy, that might make it harder for them to find other jobs. Nevertheless, Stone asked if the CAUT executive could 'suggest any course of action that would be in the interests of the unemployed teachers ... and of those left captive at Waterloo College.'[74]

In July 1960 Reid and McMaster's H.W. McCready visited what had become Waterloo Lutheran University (WLU). They had the impression that neither Axford nor the chairman of the board was eager to incur the CAUT's displeasure and that both were willing to discuss the new policy and perhaps amend it. Nothing seems to have come of this, however, not least because the faculty association – Reid described its members as 'a very naive crowd' – was weak.[75]

Axford resigned in 1961; his successor, William J. Villaume, was no less determined to uphold WLU's religious mission. By the late winter of 1962, renewed cries of anguish reached Reid. Faculty association president Ralph Krueger wrote that the board had imposed a 'statement of university philosophy,' which called for 'a faculty that as a whole openly and unapologetically avows the Christian perspective in and out of the classroom.' Not every professor needed to be a Lutheran or even a Christian – exceptions might be made for a 'distinctly superior' person – but everyone had to respect Christianity, 'honour the Christian character of this institution, and co-operate in its programme of Christian nurture.'[76]

The board had also imposed a revised statement of academic freedom and tenure. 'Academic freedom in a church university,' it asserted, 'means full freedom in research and teaching and in expression within the limits of responsible action,' but criticizing the Christian religion or the Lutheran Church lay beyond these limits. Tenure, normally granted after seven years' probation, could be ended at any time for cause, such as 'an act of gross immorality, conduct discrediting the academic profession or this institution, professional incompetence or failure to perform satisfactorily the duties or practices of the position, abuse of the privileges of academic freedom, inability of the university to continue the appointment through lack of available funds, or by elimination of the position on reasonable grounds.' An appeal would go to the president (who would have made the decision in the first place) and beyond him to a board appeals committee, the final decision to be made by the board.[77]

'Five of us have resigned and found employment elsewhere,' Krueger reported. 'Two have decided that this would be an excellent time to shove off to do more graduate work. At least a half dozen would leave if they could.' For fear of reprisals, though, none of those was staying would complain.[78]

Reid asked the AF & T chairman Gordon Turner what they should do about the situation, adding that the documents were 'so widely contrary to good university practice' that they were 'almost ludicrous.' Should the CAUT council raise a complaint? Turner thought not. While agreeing that the state of affairs was 'unsatisfactory,' he advised, 'No matter how much you or the Council may know about a bad situation, the CAUT should not *formally* act or speak unless an individual or association complains formally of a situation in which he or it is involved.'[79]

Not to intervene was also the advice received from Hugh G. Thorburn, president of the Queen's faculty association. He wrote that a colleague had received a letter from a friend at WLU complaining about 'an invasion of academic freedom,' but that since this person did not want to 'stand up and be counted,' Thorburn's executive had refused to become involved. Reid replied to Thorburn that the WLU faculty association might yet ask the CAUT for help, but so far no request had come. None did come.[80]

The academic job market was increasingly lively in the early 1960s, allowing most academics to escape from situations they found disagreeable. Those who stayed at WLU accepted its limitations on their freedom either because they shared the institution's philosophy or because they were unable to get jobs elsewhere. The former did not suffer. The latter suffered in silence – with one exception. In 1967 a political scientist, George Haggar, complained to the AF & T committee that his one-year contract had not been renewed because he did not share the institution's religious orientation. Responding for the committee, the CAUT's executive secretary, Percy Smith, pointed out that WLU's statement of academic freedom and tenure had been part of the contract Haggar had signed. The committee was 'considerably disturbed' that he had received no reason for his nonrenewal, but even if he had been let go because of his lack of sympathy for the institution's objectives he could not, given his acceptance of the document, claim an infringement of his academic freedom. The AF & T committee believed the statement to be flawed, Smith added, but that was another issue.[81]

Secularization and resistance to it had dramatic consequences at Acadia University. In 1964 the board of governors selected a non-Baptist, J.M.R. Beveridge, to succeed Watson Kirkconnell. An Acadia graduate who had been teaching biochemistry at Queen's, Beveridge was a member of the United Church. Some Baptists found this disturbing, but more irritating was the fact that the board of governors had not consulted with the United Baptist Convention of the Atlantic Provinces before announcing the appointment. This perceived slight led the convention to appoint a committee to examine both its relationship with Acadia and the convention's 'philosophy with regard to the Christian orientation of higher education as well as its policy in educational matters.' Also to be examined was the case for an enlarged Acadia and its implications for the spiritual life of the institution. 'Is there a "Christian" way to teach, even at the University level?' the convention executive asked. 'Or are the dreams of the fathers passé in 1964?'[82]

The only academic member of the committee was Ronald S. Longley, Acadia's dean of arts and science, who became vice-chairman. The committee established three subcommittees, one to study Acadia's educational philosophy, another to study 'trends regarding the strengthening or loosening of denominational ties' at other church-related universities, and a third to seek information from Acadia and the United Baptist Bible Training School about their appointment policies and their control of student activities.[83]

Taking a keen interest in the committee's work was the editor of the *Atlantic Baptist*, Fred Gordon. Writing in November to the committee secretary, H.A. Renfree, Gordon expressed his fear that an expanded Acadia would lose all sense of Christian mission. He quoted approvingly WLU's President William J. Villaume: 'If in the organization and curriculum of a University, God is officially relegated to the optional, you teach with a tremendous force that ... religion is to be considered among the luxuries rather than the necessities if one is interested in the pursuit of truth.' Gordon said that an effort should be made to keep enrolment at 1,200 or 1,300 until the committee had reported and the convention had had an opportunity 'to make final decisions in the matter.'[84]

If Gordon needed evidence that Acadia's sense of mission was in danger, he could have found it in the *Athenaeum*, the student newspaper, on the very day he wrote to Renfree. *Irma la Douce* was to be produced on campus. Although this musical seems innocuous today, its tale of a golden-hearted hooker and the man who wants her exclusive attentions was still capable of raising eyebrows in 1964. More disturbing yet was a debate, sponsored by the Student Christian Movement, on the 'Necessity of Religion.' 'Religion Questioned,' screamed a headline in the *Athenaeum*. Two faculty members had reportedly said that religion in its present form did more harm than good.[85]

Within days, the members of the higher education committee received a report of the debate. When the committee met in February 1965, its members also had before them an unsigned statement attacking the 'cultural fare' offered at Acadia and the 'anti-Christian teachers' on its staff. If the board of governors did not clean house and insist that 'Christian men only' were appointed, the statement warned, 'the Convention paper reserves the right to present the whole story to its readers.'[86]

In a steady stream of editorials that winter and spring, Gordon upheld Acadia's Baptist mission. Criticized for opposing the university's growth, he made clear his reason for doing so – that suitable faculty might be impossible to find. 'We believe in every freedom of enquiry on the part of professor and student in the finest tradition of a liberal arts university,' he wrote in February, 'but we also believe in a Christian philosophy of education.' There was a Christian way of teaching, and the teacher was the key: 'One can only teach with a Christian mission if one is a Christian.' Asked what test should be applied, Gordon replied that 'the burden of responsibility of determining whether an applicant was or was not a Christian could be left with the individual himself.' A simple affirmation of faith was enough. It seemed not too much to ask.[87]

In April, Gordon yielded his column to a 'Baptist Layman,' who made a plea for a Christians-only policy in appointments:

'A teacher teaches himself first of all. When he teaches history or chemistry, mathematics or philosophy, he cannot keep from transmitting to his pupils his attitudes, principles, prejudices, enthusiasms, and his faith ... It takes Christian professors to perpetuate the faith of the fathers. Jews can't do it. Mohammedans can't do it. Atheists can't do it. Cynics can't do it ... The professors at Acadia must be Christians or Acadia will be cut off from her inspiration, her tradition and her people.'

Baptists, this layman concluded, must prevent such a tragedy from happening.[88]

In May 1965 Gordon took aim at a motion, introduced at a meeting of the Associated Alumni of Acadia University (AAAU), proposing an end to the requirement that their nominees to the board be approved by the United Baptist Convention. As the AAAU nominated fourteen of the board's thirty members, the proposal struck Gordon as revolutionary: 'No longer would the Board be wholly responsible to the Convention – it would be responsible to two bodies.' When the alumni accepted the motion, Gordon urged the convention to reject it.[89]

The implications of Gordon's views for academic freedom did not go unnoticed at Acadia. In July the *Atlantic Baptist* carried an article by the historian A.H. MacLean upholding academic freedom, which he defined 'as the uninhibited right of free examination and discussion of controversial issues.' Scholars had both the right and the duty 'to follow the search for truth wherever it may lead,' stated MacLean. In another article, Evan M. Whidden, professor of church history, argued that academic freedom was safe even in an explicitly Christian university because the untrammeled pursuit of truth must inevitably reaffirm the tenets of the faith.[90]

When the higher education committee met with representatives of the board, it learned that the board did not insist that faculty members be Christian. The committee's report to the convention stressed this issue. But it noted that although a philosophy of higher education at Acadia was nowhere explicitly stated, the historical record pointed to the belief 'that the Christian faith is basic to true education.' The report went on to say that it had been intended that all courses should be 'taught by teachers who themselves ... found in Jesus Christ the point of integration of the whole of learning' and who could 'lead their students to a Christ-centred life.' These goals had not been superseded: 'Never was there a greater need for having the highly developed mind and body girded with Christian faith and character.'[91]

Five recommendations followed. Two were anodyne; a third, proposing 'that academic and campus activities and publications be consistent with the Christian orientation of the University,' the convention referred back to the committee. The remaining two recommendations, both adopted, were 'that the Faculty members be Christian' and that board members, hitherto appointed for renewable nine-year terms, be limited to single terms of six years.[92]

The recommendation that all faculty be Christians caused a furore, something the committee members should have anticipated. Kirkconnell had warned them that the desire to appoint none but Christians was unrealistic, given Acadia's low salaries and the shortage of qualified recruits, and that an attempted purge of non-Christians would be calamitous. Canadian professors had become 'a militant professional union, ready to fight ... on behalf of any professor dismissed from any university staff for any cause short of gross criminal turpitude,' he wrote, and the Crowe case 'would be turbulently duplicated at Acadia if there were any attempt to drop any professor who had tenure.' Not only would the CAUT 'make Acadia's name stink'; it would be able to compel the reinstatement of any tenured professor dismissed 'for any cause short of a criminal act.'[93]

In spite of similar warnings from some delegates, the convention accepted the committee's main recommendations in late August 1965. On 8 September the Acadia University faculty association passed a resolution deploring 'the crisis that has arisen in the affairs of Acadia University' and called on all parties to find a compromise. Less inclined than faculty members to mince words, the AAAU executive denounced the proposed changes as 'unacceptable ... by reason of their manifest incompatibility with accepted principles of academic freedom and religious toleration.' The *Athenaeum* reported the results of an informal survey, which indicated that most students appeared 'to condemn restrictive moves taken this summer by the Baptist convention.' The editor added, 'Acadia University has reached that stage in her evolution when she and the United Baptist Convention ... must part company.' For his part, President Beveridge criticized the resolution concerning faculty members as well as the resolution governing the terms of board members and its effect of increasing convention control over the board.[94]

The convention's executive informed members that one of the proposals had been misunderstood: 'There was no suggestion that the position of any faculty member was at all in jeopardy.' Addressing the alumni directly, the executive explained that the recommendation did no more than restate 'that Christian responsibility requires sympathetic leadership.' Unhappily, 'the ideal of Christian leadership ... was seen as a threat to academic freedom,' even though Baptists had historically defended this freedom.[95]

On 16 November board members joined representatives of the AAAU and the convention in an effort to find a compromise (the faculty association was not represented). To use Kirkconnell's words, after 'the Convention group refused to budge an inch,' the board expressed its opposition to the two recommendations. Beveridge commented, 'The Board of Governors reaffirmed its stand on academic freedom and religious liberty. I am confident that its action will reassure the Faculty.' It did.[96]

The convention initiative had a result that few could have foreseen. Within days of the November meeting, the board of governors, adopting a proposal that came from the AAAU, set out to reduce convention influence at Acadia.[97] By February 1966, the legislature of Nova Scotia was considering a bill, introduced by the government of Robert Stanfield, to remove the institution from convention control.

One of the bill's strongest champions was Kirkconnell. Aware that pressure was being brought to bear on MLAs to oppose it, he wrote to all of them in its support. As president, he had 'preferred to hire a practising Protestant if a competent one were available,' he explained, 'so as to have as many men as possible who were congenial by faith and temperament to the traditions of the institution.' But to insist on this in the current labour market made no sense. 'The problem presently will be to secure any staff at all.' Furthermore, 'What of the five Jews who now serve on the Acadia faculty? They are now told ... that they are serving Acadia in breach of its new basic principles and that no Jew must ever again be appointed to the staff ... This is discrimination with a vengeance.' To Kirkconnell, the choice was clear: the draft bill must be passed.[98]

In a letter to a cabinet minister, G.I. Smith, Kirkconnell indicated where he thought the shoe really pinched. In the call for 'Christian teaching' he saw a desire 'for adulterating subjects like biology and geology with anti-evolutionary propaganda.' And in the convention executive's call for negotiation and delay he saw sly tactics: 'A confrontation at the August 1966 Convention would ... witness an emotional landslide in favour of Fundamentalist control. A progressive purge of all independent members of the Board has already been provided for, and another year would see academic freedom gone forever.' At risk, he said, were principles 'of freedom of thought and instruction that are essential to a true university.' Because of this, the board was appealing to the government 'to intervene and save the University from disaster.'[99]

The bill received royal assent in April 1966. The new board consisted of fourteen members chosen by the convention, fourteen by the AAAU, six by the provincial government, and two by the board. All would serve for six-year renewable terms, with the president as an *ex officio* voting member.[100]

Among the pleased spectators at this dénouement were the CAUT's executive committee and AF&T committee. In October 1965 the CAUT had condemned the recommendation that faculty members be Christian as 'a violation of the intellectual integrity and academic freedom essential to the well-being of the university community.'[101] It is unknown whether this had any effect on the fight over Acadia's future, but the CAUT's leadership certainly approved the outcome of that struggle.

Even at nonsectarian universities, religious issues continued to have the power to shock. In November 1962, Peter Remnant of the University of British Columbia's philosophy department addressed more than a thousand students on the subject of the Bible. He described it as 'the sacred writings of a primitive people: Tribal history, somewhat arrogant, pseudo-science, moral exhortation, folk wisdom ... liberally spiced with miracles and marvels.' There was no proof in it of the existence of God, he said, adding that he was an atheist. 'Gasps repeatedly rippled through the audience,' a reporter wrote in a *Vancouver Sun* front-page story. 'Said one student under his breath: "I can't believe it."'[102]

For a long week, letters to the editors of the *Sun* and the *Province* kept the controversy alive. In time the *Sun* commented editorially that, on the whole, the debate had been 'moderate and well thought out.' Those who wanted to punish Remnant or to shield students from his opinions seemed to be in the minority. Still, the storm suggested 'that we are dangerously unaccustomed to people striking out against the current of comfortable opinion.'[103]

The *Sun*'s editor regretted this. UBC's board of governors probably did so too, but for a different reason. At a board meeting on 27 November, Chancellor Phyllis Ross expressed 'concern' over the lecture, while Leon Ladner said 'that he believed in freedom of speech, but this in some cases developed into licence injurious to all concerned.'[104] The fear was that the government would object. Not only did the cabinet of Premier W.A.C. Bennett include several born-again Christians – one of them, P.A. Gaglardi, a Pentecostalist minister – but Social Credit enjoyed strong support among evangelical Protestants. If UBC seemed to condone atheism, its funding might suffer.

The budget was an annual source of worry. To this was added the likelihood that the government would soon found one or two new degree-granting institutions, potential competitors for public funds (and in fact the Universities Act, introduced in 1963, established full-faculty universities in Victoria and Burnaby). This was no time to make waves. President John B. Macdonald's response appealed to the concept of academic freedom: 'The University must uphold the right of every scholar to analyze any issue in a sober, careful and scholarly way.'[105] He was satisfied that Remnant had met this requirement. Some of the governors may have had their doubts, but happily at this point the media turmoil died down and, with it, the board's interest in the matter.

Into the 1960s, the discussion of sexual behaviour in the university remained what it had been for decades – a taboo that virtually everyone observed. When a University of Western Ontario sociologist, W.E. Mann, in 1964 began his study of sexual activity among undergraduates at Western, York University, and the Calgary campus of the University of Alberta, some of his colleagues disapproved. Mann was an Anglican clergyman, and his research was funded by the Anglican Church of Canada, but these marks of respectability did not sanctify the study in everybody's eyes. Neither President Edward Hall nor Mann's department head, Grant Reuber, ever criticized him openly, Mann says, but Reuber caused him to be moved to an office well away from other members of the department.

Annoyed by this and by having to do without a telephone for several months, Mann alerted a journalist friend. This led to a satirical skit on a CBC radio program, Max Ferguson's *Rawhide*. No one took him openly to task for his part in drawing attention to the university, Mann recalls, but the atmosphere in his department became chillier: 'Western was a very conservative campus and London a very conservative town.' Someone, possibly the academic vice-president, suggested he might prefer to teach at a university in a larger city.[106]

In 1965 academic positions were easy to find. Mann accepted the best of three offers, from York University's Atkinson College, where Dean D. McCormack Smyth was an old friend. Mann left London with little resentment: 'I didn't suffer.' Besides, he had been through this before. In 1960–1, while teaching at the Ontario Agricultural College, he had offended some people by working with inmates of the Guelph Reformatory, and it had been suggested to him that he might be happier elsewhere. 'I should have gone to York right away,' he said with a chuckle.[107]

Some fifteen months after Mann left Western, Maclean's carried an article about him and his study. 'I was encouraged to resign,' he was quoted as saying. 'I was told that I didn't have to go, but would I please go.' Possibly the UWO administration had considered the survey 'indiscreet,' Mann said, but he thought he might have been an embarrassment on other grounds. An extension course on parapsychology had 'raised academic eyebrows,' and some people had disapproved of two ex-convicts, research subjects for a book he was writing about the Guelph Reformatory, who had visited him in his campus office. A lecture to the Student Christian Movement on the subject 'Is There a Sexual Revolution on Campus?' had not helped. As well, sociology was 'still suspect at Western, still associated with socialism and radical change.'[108]

President Hall declined to comment on the Maclean's article. Reuber said Mann's resignation had not been 'explicitly' asked for, adding that he had not known about the sex survey until after Mann had left. This left the reason for his departure somewhat up in the air. But because Mann had no trouble finding another job, what might ten years earlier have become a controversy over academic freedom remained a subject for jokes at faculty cocktail parties.

Mann's experiences underline the function of the 1960s academic sellers' market in preventing major conflict. There was another example at the university to which Mann moved. In 1963 York had witnessed a quarrel over its future which had set some of the faculty against President Murray Ross and the board. But the controversy had faded quickly when the sociologist John Seelye and his chief supporters resigned to take positions elsewhere.[109]

A few years earlier, it had not been quite so easy to find a new berth, as the philosopher George P. Grant learned upon resigning from York even before he had begun to teach there. Having left Dalhousie in order to accept Ross's offer of the founding chair of philosophy, he found that, at least initially, he would

A Place of Liberty   277

have to report to the head of philosophy at the University of Toronto, Fulton Anderson. In the early 1950s, the two men had crossed swords over the report on philosophy that Grant had prepared for the Royal Commission on National Development in the Arts, Letters and Sciences (the Massey Commission). Grant had criticized the tendency of philosophy departments to foster religious scepticism and to neglect the actual practice of philosophy in favour of studying its history. His conclusion – that 'the practice of philosophy (and for that matter, all the arts of civilization) will depend on ... the intensity and concentration of our faith in God' – offended Anderson, and not only him.[110]

Unfortunately for Grant, York's first steps were to be taken under the aegis of the University of Toronto, and he found that he would have to teach the introductory course under Anderson's supervision. Furthermore, Grant would have to use as his text a book by Marcus Long, *The Spirit of Philosophy*, of which he disapproved. He complained to Ross about the lack of freedom he would have, but Ross replied that the tie to Toronto brought advantages that more than made up for the drawbacks. Disagreeing, Grant resigned from York in April 1960.[111]

Outside the academy for a year, Grant thought hard about academic life. To a Winnipeg friend he wrote, 'Educated Christians have a traditional respect for universities because they founded them and it is therefore hard for them to recognise that universities can be sources of evil as well as good.' Speaking at St John's College, University of Manitoba, he warned of the dangers of secularization. Largely divorced from religious faith and unequipped to think clearly about philosophy or theology, university graduates were a prey to 'listless and increasingly perverted pleasures,' or worse, he said.[112]

Yet for all his misgivings about secularization, it was at a recently secularized institution that Grant got his next position. Worried that religion would become peripheral at McMaster after it cut its ties with the Baptists, President George P. Gilmour had supervised the creation of a department of religion in the Faculty of Arts and Science. Grant joined this department in 1961, staying there until he returned to Dalhousie in 1980.[113]

As a practising Christian, Grant was far from alone in the university of the 1950s and 1960s, but in insisting on the centrality of Christianity in university life he was unusual. As well, the conservative nationalism of his best-known book, *Lament for a Nation* (1965), struck some academics as quixotic. He was conscious of the scepticism with which colleagues regarded his beliefs and the department of which he was a part. This did not much trouble him, though. 'He considered the religion department a sort of fifth column in the university.'[114]

In any discipline or department, several schools of thought and interpretation can coexist more or less peaceably. But scholars who belong to no school may quite understandably feel unsafe. In its German and American origins, academic freedom was rooted in the idea of communities of competence, implying both professional autonomy and collegial self-governance. When the great majority of scholars or scientists regard a school of thought or line of research as unproductive or mistaken, those who adhere to the one or pursue the other will often receive a grudging tolerance at best.

By 1960, Grant's views about the relationship between philosophy and religion were well outside the mainstream. If he suffered little as a consequence, it was because he was personally lovable – and also well connected. His grandfathers were Principal George Monro Grant of Queen's and Sir George Parkin, director of the Rhodes Trust, and his father was William Lawson Grant, principal of Upper Canada College, while Vincent Massey (governor general from 1952 to 1959) was an uncle by marriage. Nevertheless, for the last twenty-five years of his career, Grant did not teach in a department of philosophy. After 1971, when a sellers' market in academic employment abruptly became a buyers' market, another person holding his views might have had difficulty finding (or keeping) any university position.

By 1965 the mounting costs of higher education indicated the shape of the future for virtually all universities. Endowment income and financial aid from the private sector continued at relatively low levels; federal support, though welcome, was inadequate. The private universities enjoyed neither the academic nor the social prestige that would have allowed them, without loss of enrolment, to charge higher tuition fees than the provincial institutions. Full access to provincial funds seemed essential.

With the acceptance of unrestricted provincial support, which in most provinces involved the severing of denominational ties, came increased secularization. Was this a victory for academic freedom? We should not answer too hastily in the affirmative. Except for those institutions in which church bodies maintained close control over staffing and parts of the curriculum – as was typically the case in Catholic universities – faculty members in denominational colleges were generally no more constrained in their academic freedom than those who taught in secular institutions. Threats to academic freedom did on occasion emanate from churches or from factions (usually fundamentalist) within them. But far more often the threats came from business people, newspaper editors, politicians, various pressure groups, governing boards, administrators, and even professors themselves.

Overshadowing the secularization of university life was the growing dependence of virtually all universities on provincial governments. This cast provincial politicians collectively in the role of the most obvious threat to academic freedom. Since they were providing much of the money for construction and were paying an increasing share of operating costs, it seemed likely that they would try to influence how the dollars were spent, interfering with academic freedom in the process.

Other traditional enemies were lurking nearby, and a new one in the form of student radicalism was appearing on the horizon. The 'place of liberty' claimed by George Whalley and his associates was a fragile habitation, something the Crowe case and the Fowke-Laskin Report had made clear. Conscious of their basic vulnerability and aware of the opportunities provided by the 1960s academic labour market, some professors sought to bolster both their academic freedom and their economic security. As we have seen, one means of doing so was to try to increase faculty participation in university government. Another was to try to strengthen academic tenure. This term has appeared frequently in the preceding pages, and to its close examination we now turn.

11

Freedom and Security:
The Matter of Tenure

No other aspect of university life is as misunderstood as tenure. Even the usually clear-eyed John Ralston Saul gets it wrong. Defining it as 'a system of academic job security which has the effect of rating intellectual leadership on the basis of seniority,' he asserts that its 'initial justification ... was the need to protect freedom of speech, due to the justifiable fear that controversial professors might suffer at the hands of disapproving financial and governmental interests.'[1] This is not so. Tenure long antedates the modern concern with academic free speech. It is rooted in three ancient academic desires: for intellectual independence, collective autonomy, and the time and financial security needed to carry on scholarly and scientific work.

Not only is tenure misunderstood, but it is under heavy attack. When I bought my copy of Matthew W. Finkin's *The Case for Tenure* (1996), the bookstore clerk read the title and said with obvious surprise, 'The case *for* tenure? I thought everybody was *against* it.' The purpose of this chapter is to trace the origins of tenure, to examine and explain its legal and institutional development, and to indicate its continuing function in academic life.

In the medieval university, Walter P. Metzger writes, scholars 'sought immunity from the reach of power and a corporate autonomy that would empower them to assist and defend themselves.'[2] They incorporated themselves, made rules for their self-government, and claimed exemption from the jurisdiction of temporal and ecclesiastical tribunals. Tenure was 'an attribute of admission to a *corpus*, possessed of a legal personality.' The masters controlled admission and dismissal, the latter commonly being imposed for failure to adhere to collegial comities. Sanctions were not imposed arbitrarily: medieval scholars knew more about due process than the governing boards of some twentieth-century universities, not to mention some of their professors. Nevertheless, collegial tyranny (not unknown today) was part of medieval university life.

The Protestant Reformation wrought basic changes, almost obliterating 'the distinction between inside and outside, the old line of tenurial defense.' Having become subject to the will of local rulers, universities and their professors were charged with the promulgation and defence of whatever orthodoxy was locally in favour. On the European continent, it was only in the late eighteenth and early nineteenth centuries that 'a certain measure of the old autonomy and even a semblance of the old immunity regain[ed] institutional form.'

In the English universities, royal power and patronage were much in evidence from the reign of Henry VIII on. Still, 'the teachers of Oxford and Cambridge held to their corporate traditions more successfully than did their continental counterparts,' mainly because the colleges were allowed to keep their lands, the chief source of their income. The masters became fellows, members of self-governing corporations charged with the tutoring of students who lived in the college. The terms of fellowships imposed limits. After the Stuart Restoration, they were available only to those who subscribed to the thirty-nine Articles of the Church of England; and they were usually open only to bachelors. However, 'assuming good behaviour (that is, the continuing tolerance of peers), and no doctrinal misadventure or royal disfavour,' fellowships were for life.

Life tenure during good behaviour also became policy in the Scottish universities, but their professors, being salaried, were subject to closer scrutiny than those who dwelt along the Cam and Isis. Some of the latter took undue advantage of their security. 'The fellows ... of my time were decent easy men, who supinely enjoyed the gifts of the founder,' Edward Gibbon wrote, perhaps with pardonable exaggeration. 'Their days were filled by a series of uniform employments; the chapel and the hall, the coffee-house and the common-room, till they retired, weary and well satisfied, to a long slumber. From the toil of reading, or thinking, or writing, they had absolved their conscience.' What was sauce for the college fellows was, apparently, sauce also for the professors, those who held chairs. 'In the university of Oxford,' Adam Smith observed, 'the greater part of the professors have, for these many years, given up altogether even the pretence of teaching.' Not until the reforms of the mid-nineteenth century did Oxbridge habits of work improve.[3]

By that time, tenure was a familiar feature of the North American academic landscape. The oldest British college in the New World, Harvard, emulated the English model in not imposing any duration on fellowships. By 1760, Harvard also had several endowed professorial chairs, held by scholars who were permitted to marry and live outside the college. 'Though the bequests relating to professorships did not specifically prohibit term appointments,' Metzger writes, 'it appears that all who were appointed to these offices served without limit of time.' The dignity of the office and the eminence of those occupying it seemed to require that professors not be subject to periodic reappraisal. Term appointments 'were as likely to repel the worthy candidate as to eject the weak incumbent.'

The practice of appointing chairholders for life came to include professors who were paid out of general revenue; it also spread to other universities. But into the twentieth century, tenure was by no means universal. The most common alternative was the annual appointment of all professors. Although renewals were often routine, this system allowed presidents both to prune 'dead wood' and to get rid of troublemakers with ease. At the same time it encouraged faculty members to look for greener pastures in the form of universities that offered permanence.

Since institutions were loath to lose good faculty, tenure continued to spread. By 1910 most U.S. universities appointed junior faculty members to terms ranging from one to three years and, after probationary periods of varying length, gave many of them appointments without term. By and large, though, this did not mean tenure during good behaviour, with cause having to be shown before someone could be dismissed. Indeed, the awareness of professors that virtually all of them served during the pleasure of lay boards and that the courts offered little or no redress in cases of dismissal, contributed to the founding of the American Association of University Professors (AAUP) in 1915.

Those who signed the AAUP's statement on academic freedom and tenure acknowledged tenure's role in providing professors with economic security. They also thought tenure should be a shield for academic freedom, and they outlined the conditions under which it might be so. Upon completion of a probationary period, the AAUP's founders said, academics should get tenure or be let go. Once tenured, they should be dismissed only for cause and should receive a fair hearing from a committee of their peers, whose recommendation would be binding on a governing board.[4]

The AAUP wished to end the practice of retaining faculty on annual contracts, indefinitely or for long periods of probation. The organization's founders also wanted to end the practice of granting tenure too soon, for they thought this cheapened the profession. They did not discuss the role probation might play in 'house training' young faculty and producing safe and solid members of the academic community.

The AAUP's interest in dismissals had another source. Governing boards generally dismissed faculty without giving reasons or offering an opportunity for defence, and the courts sanctioned this. Tenure, then, was rarely helpful to the minority who ceased to please their masters. But if the power to determine cause and recommend dismissal was in the hands of senior professors, the

AAUP's founders thought that egregious abuses would end and professors and their freedom would enjoy the protection they deserved.

Tenure in Canadian universities has been mainly influenced by the usages of Great Britain and the United States (French influence was minimal). The first institution of higher education established in what is now Canada was King's College in Windsor, Nova Scotia, where into the 1880s professors had tenure for life during good behaviour.[5] However, most universities made no reference to tenure or dismissal in their charters or early statutes, creating a presumption that professors held their offices for life. Judicial interpretation after 1860 did not sustain this presumption.

The first British North American court case involving tenure took place in New Brunswick. Edwin Jacob was professor of divinity of King's College in Fredericton. Upon its transformation into the University of New Brunswick in 1859 he was appointed professor of classical and modern literature, but he soon fell foul of the new president, Joseph R. Hea, and of the university's governing body, the senate. In March 1861, having decided that Jacob was not only insubordinate but also too frail to carry on, the senate removed him from his professorship and granted him a $600 annual pension.[6]

Although this was not ungenerous, Jacob refused to 'go gentle into that good night.' He rejected the pension and asked the Court of Queen's Bench for *certiorari*, a judicial review, charging that the senate was not legally constituted, that it could not remove someone it had not appointed, and that an appeal to the visitor, the lieutenant-governor, was inappropriate because he had effectively approved Jacob's retirement.

The court found no merit in Jacob's claims, ruling that 'the offices of the Professors ... are not held for any fixed time, nor by any permanent tenure; but ... are held at the pleasure of the governing bodies of the University, i.e., the Senate in the first place, subject to the approval of the Crown.' Assuming such approval, it stated, 'the Senate may ... remove any of the officers, without any formal proceeding in the nature of a trial, in the same way that a private individual may dispense with the services of a clerk or other servant.' No formalities need be observed or notice given. Whether the grounds on which the senate acted, or the method it pursued, 'are strictly consonant with the principles of justice ... would not make it a matter of judicial cognizance, or give this Court jurisdiction.'[7]

Judicial process took a different course in George Weir's suit against the board of trustees of Queen's, but the outcome was similar. After being dismissed in 1864, Weir claimed that Queen's had been modelled on the University of Edinburgh, where 'the tenure of the office of a professor is *ad vitam aut*

culpam, that is, during the life of the incumbent, unless removed for impropriety of conduct'; he claimed that this therefore governed tenure at Queen's and
that it was the condition under which he had accepted appointment. Charging
that the trustees had acted improperly in dismissing him without notice and
without an opportunity to defend himself, he asked 'that the resolution might be
declared illegal and void, as having been passed at a meeting not duly held;
when no complaint was made against the plaintiff; and no impropriety of conduct on his part proved.'[8]

Weir's suit received its initial hearing in the Court of Chancery, a court of
equity used by those who sought to recover property rather than secure damages. The court ruled unanimously that Weir had a freehold in his chair and
enjoyed life tenure during good behaviour or as long as his chair existed, that
the board had abused its trust, and that 'the act of removal, done as it was done,
is *ultra vires*, and therefore a nullity.' The court ordered his restoration, with
payment of the entire salary due to him since his removal.[9]

In appealing the case, counsel for the trustees argued that the court lacked
jurisdiction; that any appeal from a decision of the trustees was to the visitor;
that Weir served during pleasure; that the court, in ordering his reinstatement,
had given relief by way of specific performance in a case in which the remedy
was not mutual 'inasmuch as the Court of Chancery does not possess jurisdiction to compel the plaintiff to perform the duties of the office of the professor';
that the board was empowered under the Queen's charter to dismiss Weir; and
that 'if such dismissal was wrongful, plaintiff's remedy was by action at law
only' (i.e., by means of a suit for damages).[10]

Victory on appeal went to the trustees, Mr Justice John H. Hagarty ruling that
since no specific endowment or trust was attached to Weir's chair, the Court of
Chancery lacked jurisdiction. Hagerty did not find that professors at Queen's
held their tenure during pleasure, but he saw no grounds for finding that they
had life tenure: 'We see nothing in the evidence of any contract for any engagement of plaintiff beyond a general hiring, which the law would probably hold to
be a yearly hiring.' Hagarty faulted the board's failure to hold an inquiry,
observing that if Weir were to sue in a court of law, he might win damages for
wrongful dismissal. Nevertheless, the court would not interfere with the action
of the trustees in ending Weir's employment, the case being one 'in which neither a court of equity nor law should interfere, except on the very clearest and
most conclusive pressure of authority and precedent.'[11]

Did Weir receive advice that a further appeal was unlikely to succeed? Or did
he lack the money to carry the proceeding further? The record is silent. However, a determination of the case by the Judicial Committee of the Privy Council
would have been useful, at least to the historian. In its absence, two questions

remain. First, if Weir had occupied an endowed chair, would he have had life tenure? Second, if tenure at Queen's was neither for life nor during pleasure, what was it? Hagarty had suggested that the courts would 'probably' find that tenure equated to a annual hiring, terminable with notice, but this was *obiter dictum*. Presumably, another court case would be needed to resolve this matter.

The judgment and the uncertainty it caused handicapped Principals William Snodgrass and George Monro Grant when they sought to hire faculty in Scotland. How Snodgrass coped with this is unclear, but Grant, in defiance of the ruling in the Weir case and of the university statutes, assured recruits that they would hold their positions for life during good behaviour. Asked in 1920 to define tenure at Queen's, Principal Bruce Taylor cited the Weir case but added, 'While the situation is thus definite in law the practice has been to regard appointments as permanent after the first two years.'[12]

The judgment that arose out of the 1884 dismissal of William E. Wilson from King's College, Nova Scotia, is unusual. By college statute, professors held their offices 'during good behaviour, but they [were] liable to be removed for neglect of duty, inefficiency, or other just cause' if nine members of the board voted for removal. Dismissed without a hearing, Wilson took action to recover his position. In April 1885 the Supreme Court of Nova Scotia ruled, three to two, that he had been improperly removed, and it made absolute a writ of *mandamus* to the governors to restore him.

The majority opinion was written by Mr Justice John Thompson (later prime minister of Canada). The failure to give notice to Wilson was the key to the case, he stated: 'On the sufficiency of his offence to justify removal, I think the Governors were the judges ... Notice, however, of those proceedings by which one's property or rights of any kind may be affected is ... "of the very essence of justice."' If the governors had observed due process, Thompson added, they would have had their way.[13]

They had their way in any case. Meeting soon after the ruling of the court, they apparently thought the judgment against them of so little weight that no discussion of it found its way into the minutes. Neither at that time nor later did they reinstate Wilson or even pay him damages. Moreover, in July 1885 the board of governors revoked the college statute which stated that professors held their offices 'during good behaviour.' Henceforth they would serve during pleasure.[14]

At the University of Saskatchewan in 1919, the board of governors also had its way. John Hogg, Ira MacKay, and Robert MacLaurin, having been dismissed, exercised their right to appeal to the visitor, the lieutenant-governor of the province. After the legislative assembly delegated the visitorial power to three judges of the Court of King's Bench, twelve days of hearings took place early in 1920.

The judges reported on 30 April. Noting that under the University Act all employees served 'during the pleasure of the board,' subject to the proviso that a recommendation by the president was required for appointment, promotion, and dismissal, they ruled that 'where the appointment is during pleasure no notice is required, nor need any hearing be given.' Citing the Weir case, the three judges said that the courts could interfere only if 'the professor was in the position of a *cestui que trust* having an interest in a particular fund or a freehold interest in property.' Unless professors were suing for breach of contract, they could appeal only to the visitor, and he could do no more than determine whether the act and the university's by-laws had been observed. This being the case, noted the judges, 'we have, in our opinion, no power to interfere with what has been done, unless the president or the governors exercised their discretion of removal in an oppressive manner or from a corrupt or indirect motive.' This they had not done; in light of the disloyalty that Hogg, MacKay, and McLaurin had shown to President Walter C. Murray, the board's action had been 'regular and proper, and necessary in the best interests of the university.' In consequence of this, the judges confirmed the board's decision.[15]

Writing in 1965, the Queen's law professor Daniel Soberman declared himself troubled by the emphasis on loyalty: 'It is doubtful whether loyalty to an institution should be a requisite of tenure at all; certainly to require loyalty to its officers is completely unjustified ... Indeed, the issue of loyalty is irrelevant if a teacher is carrying out his duties properly.'[16] Today few would disagree with this. In 1920 it was otherwise.

The case of *Smith v. Wesley College* was not about tenure, but Mr Justice A.K. Dysart's judgment did address that issue. Dismissed in 1922 with a year's salary in lieu of notice, W.G. Smith sued for damages, arguing that his contract had been for six years. Giving judgment in the Supreme Court of Manitoba, Dysart dismissed both the defendant's claim that Smith served during pleasure and Smith's claim to have been appointed for six years. Instead, he held that the psychologist's contract was for renewable terms of one year. Whether or not the board of regents would have been justified in dismissing Smith 'under any other tenure,' he observed, 'it seems beyond doubt that they were justified in terminating the employment under this, and that they acted *bona fide* in the interests of the college in doing so.'

Dysart went on to controvert the idea, expressed in the judgment in the Jacob case, that professors served at will: 'This language seems to me to treat alto-

gether too lightly the dismissal of college professors.' They were specially
trained for work of a special kind: 'Their opportunities for suitable employment
are rare, and if lost are not easily substituted by other congenial employment.
Their special training unfits them for general service. In their chosen field, the
material rewards are relatively small. In order ... that this noble profession may
still attract recruits, it is wisely acknowledged both in theory and practice that
the employment of professors by colleges should be characterized by stability
approaching to permanence.' How permanent? Dysart equated the security that
professors ought to have with that enjoyed by bank officers, whose jobs (in
those days!) were in normal circumstances safe until retirement.[17]

Daniel Soberman, writing when academic jobs were plentiful, described
Dysart's attitude as 'patronizing.' But it reflected the reality of the early 1920s.
Traces of Dysart's language may be found in the 1915 AAUP report, and more
than traces of it appeared in the justification of tenure offered by Ira MacKay in
1919. Only the tenure of the judiciary was more secure, he told a Saskatoon
reporter: 'The reasons for this security are apparent. University appointments
are made after a period of long probationary training ..., the remuneration is
small and the offices are few ... A university professor once removed from his
chair has very little chance of obtaining similar employment elsewhere.'
MacKay was fortunate – President Murray's intervention on his behalf secured
him a position at McGill – but in describing the general rule, his comment was
correct.[18]

The comments by Dysart and MacKay strike a modern note. 'University
employment is rather like membership of some profession,' the University of
Alberta law professor G.H.L. Fridman wrote in 1973, 'because dismissal is like
loss of professional status: the dismissed party is deprived of the means of
obtaining a livelihood by the exercise of that skill and expertise for which he
has prepared himself by years of training.'[19] This implies that the dismissal of
professors should be subject to the same high standards with respect to due process and demonstration of cause as those used in debarring lawyers or revoking
licences to practise medicine.

In 1993 Conrad Russell defended tenure partly on the grounds that the specialized nature of the knowledge acquired by academics made them unfit for
jobs outside their fields. Since no real labour market exists in many subjects, he
observed, it is likely 'that those dismissed from jobs in such subjects will be
deprived not only of their jobs, but of their professions.' In the same vein, two
U.S. labour economists, Michael S. McPherson and Gordon C. Winston, have
recently asserted that 'the system of rigorous probation followed by tenure is a
reasonable way of solving the peculiar personnel problems that arise in employing expensively trained and narrowly specialized people to spend their lifetimes

at well-defined and narrowly specialized tasks.' Except for those who enter administration, academics have little or no internal mobility in universities. This makes a high degree of security essential. To quote Lord Russell once more, 'It is unwise to enter into so risky an employment without being guaranteed some economic security in return.' Dysart was of the same mind.[20]

The suit that sprang out of the retirement of James A. Craig by the University of Toronto reinforced the established pattern of judicial interpretation. Canadian born but for years a professor at the University of Michigan, Craig returned to Canada for personal rather than professional reasons, in late middle age, to fill a vacancy in Semitic languages that had been created by the 1915 departure of Immanuel Benzinger, one of the three German professors. 'We can offer a position for one year as Associate Professor ...,' Sir Robert Falconer wrote to him, 'the permanence of the appointment to be considered a year from now.'[21]

In 1916 Craig was appointed at the rank of professor. His letter of appointment made no mention of the term, and he took this to mean that he had tenure for life. Was this a reasonable inference? In 1919 Falconer answered a query from British Columbia's minister of education by stating that professors and associate professors 'are not engaged under contract, but it is usually supposed that it is a life appointment unless the President has some adequate reason ... to recommend that the appointment terminate.'[22]

A life appointment – that was Craig's understanding. He was surprised, therefore, to receive a letter from Falconer in June 1920 informing him that a board regulation put the age of retirement at sixty-five and that he must retire a year hence. Craig replied that he had never been apprised of the regulation, could not admit its validity, and expected to occupy his chair for as long as he could 'discharge the duties of the position acceptably.' Falconer responded that a rule was a rule, that Craig had presumably qualified for a pension while at Michigan, and that it was time to make way for someone younger.[23]

Craig's rejoinder was a compelling critique of compulsory retirement. Claiming excellent health, he was 'quite unconscious of any "struggle against advancing years."' He added that retirement would not only hurt him financially, but it was 'a serious ... violation of the professor's rights which have been established by the historic traditions of centuries of university custom.' Moreover, it made no sense economically to waste the abilities of men who could still make a contribution. To retire him, he argued, would be both inexpedient and unjust.[24]

Craig's objections to compulsory retirement sound modern, but their context was different from today's. Well into the twentieth century, most universities had no pension plans. When, in Peter Cook's words (from *Beyond the Fringe*), professors got 'too old and sick and stupid' to carry on, they might get an *ex gratia* annual payment out of current revenue. This lent a certain piquancy to the term 'life tenure.' Not a few academics died in harness.

Humane considerations as well as a commitment to the improvement of teaching had led the U.S. steel magnate Andrew Carnegie to establish the Carnegie Foundation for the Advancement of Teaching in 1905. It offered, without charge, pensions at age seventy to professors employed by North American universities that were free from sectarian control, and it encouraged institutions to introduce pension plans that in time would make retirement at age sixty-five possible. By 1918 the Carnegie Foundation had enrolled seventy-eight institutional members on the continent – three of them, Dalhousie, McGill, and Toronto, being in Canada.[25]

In response to Craig's objections, Falconer referred him to a circular, sent to all faculty members in 1919, stating that the age of retirement was sixty-five. Craig then asked 'for at least another year' so that he might put his affairs in order. Falconer recommended this to the board, which allowed Craig to 'act for one year more, but one only, as Professor in the Department of Oriental Languages of University College.'[26]

Some months later, Craig informed Falconer that he questioned the board's right to retire him. Several of its members were working well beyond the age of sixty-five, he noted. 'Why should you and some of these men decree that professors in physique and mental vigour their equals, must lay down their life-work at their behest while they continue at their own?' (One of them, Sir William Mulock, became chief justice of Ontario at the age of seventy-nine and held that office until 1936, when he was ninety-two!) Falconer referred Craig's letter to the board, along with a petition 'signed by a number of students' asking that Craig be kept on. But the board declined to reopen the question. After Craig unsuccessfully proposed arbitration 'by a competent third party acceptable to both sides,' he filed suit against the university and its president, seeking $50,000 damages for wrongful dismissal.[27]

The board's statement of defence held that the tenure of professors was during pleasure and terminable without notice, that retirement at age sixty-five was a rule it was empowered to make and enforce, and that Craig's service had been ended in accordance with the University of Toronto Act. The trial took place without jury before Mr Justice John Orde of the Supreme Court of Ontario. He took little time in finding for the defendants. No definite term had been fixed at Craig's appointment, he noted, 'and the ordinary rule, that such a contract of employment could be terminated upon reasonable notice by either party, would apply, unless the particular nature of a contract of employment of this kind, or the circumstances in which it was made, override that rule.' Neither was the case.

Craig's contention that 'the appointment to a professorship ... without any limitation is an appointment for life, subject only to the appointee's good behaviour and his ability to perform his duties efficiently,' met with Orde's disbelief: 'If this contention were correct, the contract for a life-appointment must necessarily be mutual. It could not be binding on the University without at the same time binding the professor ... It should only be necessary to state this contention to show its absurdity.' (The doctrine of mutuality as an argument against life tenure also featured in U.S. jurisprudence, notably in an 1898 New York case to which, however, Orde did not refer.) Even if the board had always treated appointments as though they were for life, Orde stated, this could not affect its power to dismiss someone whose tenure was during pleasure. He did not adjudicate the contention by the defendants that the University of Toronto Act gave them 'power to dismiss at pleasure without any notice whatever,' saying it was unnecessary to do so in order to find for the board on the larger issue.[28]

The judgment in the Craig case defined the legal meaning of tenure at Toronto for several decades. In 1941, when Frank Underhill sought clarification of his status, his lawyer cited the Craig judgment and added, 'All professors at the University of Toronto, unless otherwise provided, hold office during the pleasure of the Board of Governors,' subject only to the requirement of a presidential recommendation for dismissal.[29]

This was the case also at the provincial universities of the western provinces, whose acts were derived from the University of Toronto Act of 1906. Professors could normally expect to serve for life or until a specified age of retirement, but they had no recourse if it pleased a governing board to dispense with their services earlier, provided only that the president had so recommended (though at the University of Manitoba the president's recommendation was not required).

Was notice required to end an appointment without term? The Jacob and Saskatchewan judgments answered this question in the negative; the judgments in the Weir and Smith cases implied otherwise. In 1932 the University of British Columbia's solicitor attempted an answer. Faced with a deep cut in the provincial grant, the board of governors wanted to know how to go about dismissing professors. 'Where the terms of the contract do not provide for its termination,' R.L. Reid opined, 'the law imposes the condition that it may be terminated provided reasonable notice is given.' No court had laid down 'a hard and fast rule' as to what constituted such notice, but it ranged from three months to a year: 'If it were possible in all cases to give six months' notice, we would advise that length.' Otherwise, each case would have to be considered separately in order to estimate whether three months' notice would prevent a judgment of wrongful dismissal.

The law was clearer in the case of those engaged for fixed terms, Reid continued: 'The employee can be dismissed before the end of such period, but such dismissal is *ex hypothesi* wrongful and is a basis for a claim to damages.' The damages that would be awarded would depend on actual loss suffered 'after diligent effort to secure other employment.' Therefore such employees should get 'as long notice as possible.'[30]

In the spring of 1932 a number of UBC faculty members were put on notice that their appointments might not be renewed, and late in July seven associate and four assistant professors received letters stating that their employment would end on 31 August 1932. Four had contracts ending in August 1933; one had a contract until 31 August 1934. The board obtained consent by means of severance pay and promises of re-employment when circumstances might permit (and some were eventually reappointed.) None sued, and only one even registered a reproach.[31]

None of the eleven was tenured. This prompts the question: Why were tenured professors exempted from dismissal, even though, being senior, they earned more than untenured faculty, and though Reid had advised that it was easier to dismiss tenured faculty than faculty with valid contracts? Neither the minutes of the board nor the files of the president's office offer a clue, and we are left to guess the answer.

It seems likely that President Leonard S. Klinck feared the effects on future recruitment of faculty if the board infringed on tenure. Did Premier Simon Fraser Tolmie convey to him the contents of a letter he had received from a UBC graduate then teaching at the University of Toronto? 'Dismissals of staff and drastic salary reductions ... lower British Columbia tremendously in the eyes of competent men who may be wanted for service there in the future,' Harry Cassidy had written. 'When the present depression is over and an offer is made to a Toronto or McGill professor to go to British Columbia he will very probably hesitate seriously, thinking that ... British Columbia will not be able to offer that security of tenure and position which is usually considered the chief economical advantage of academic life.'[32] We may assume that Cassidy's views were shared by those charged with UBC's affairs. Custom gave tenured faculty a measure of security even during a budgetary crisis.

The crisis reinforced a tendency to withhold tenure from faculty members for a decade or longer, something that set UBC apart from most other Canadian universities. The first board of governors had adopted a policy of appointing assistant professors for terms of up to three years and of granting appointments without term to associate and full professors. Within a few years, however, some associate professors were getting renewable three-year terms. The majority of these contracts were routinely renewed, but exceptions did occur. In 1940 an associate professor with ten years' service found he was no longer wanted, though no one would tell him why. The board refused to hear his appeal, leaving him without recourse. 'That was the point,' a long-time UBC professor, Robert Clark, commented. 'They didn't have to give a reason for not renewing a contract.'[33]

The UBC faculty association, formed in 1920 but for many years ineffectual, was by the mid-1940s showing interest in academic freedom and tenure as well as salaries and benefits. In response, President Larry MacKenzie established a faculty affairs committee in 1948. Its role was to advise him 'on matters pertaining to the general terms of faculty employment, salary schedules, basis for promotions and retirements, pensions, medical and other insurance, and related matters.' Some months later he reported to the board that this committee wished the board and senate to endorse the 1940 AAUP 'Statement of Principles on Academic Freedom and Tenure,' and suggested 'that the phrase "appointment without term," used in connection with contracts at this University, be defined to mean "tenure" as outlined in the 1940 statement.' The committee also wanted the board to award tenure to long-serving faculty members who were still on probation.[34]

In February 1949 the board approved this document in principle, though it doubted that the AAUP's version of tenure, which allowed for dismissal only 'for cause,' could be reconciled with the statutory fact that UBC professors served during pleasure. In the year that followed, an understanding took shape that fell well short of the AAUP document but did 'permit a considerable degree of Faculty participation' in the granting of tenure and gave permanent appointments to some of those who had served long periods of probation. In every way, however, the statutory powers of the board and president were maintained.[35]

In an occasionally amended form, the rules remained in effect for another decade. Late in 1960 President MacKenzie informed the board that the deans, faculty association, and senate had been discussing a document dealing with 'appointments, reappointments, promotion and tenure.' Approved in principle by the board in early 1961, this document appeared in a revised version of the *Faculty Handbook* in 1962. It reproduced in unaltered form the clauses governing the powers of board and president, but it contained a new clause on tenure, which was said to have been approved 'in principle' by the faculty association. The probationary period was to be seven years. Starting in year eight, it stated, those who had gained promotion to the rank of assistant professor or senior instructor 'shall have tenure in the sense that [their] services shall be terminated thereafter only for adequate cause, except in the case of retirement for age, total disability or under extraordinary circumstances because of financial exigencies.'

The process of granting promotion and tenure required the involvement of senior faculty in an advisory role. Although department heads were not bound by this advice, they were obliged to convey it to deans if it differed from their own view. In the case of dismissal 'for adequate cause' (left undefined), the faculty affairs committee had to hear the matter and render advice before the case went to the board. Clearly stated were the right to be informed of charges, to make a defence, and to have an adviser present at a hearing. No provision existed for appeals.[36]

The old dispensation survived in the 1963 Universities Act, which gave the boards of the University of British Columbia, Simon Fraser University, and the University of Victoria the power to appoint all employees, 'to fix their salaries or remuneration, and to define their duties and their tenure of office or employment, which, unless otherwise provided, shall be during the pleasure of the Board.'[37] The only legal check was the presidential prerogative to recommend appointments, promotions, and dismissals. The wording of the new act was essentially that of the University of British Columbia Act of 1908 and the University of Toronto Act on which it was based. The security enjoyed by tenured faculty in the three British Columbia universities ultimately depended on the extent to which their governing boards were willing to tie their own hands. In practice, though, tenured faculty members served during good behaviour until the age of retirement.

During the Depression some tenured academics did lose their jobs for financial reasons, three of them at Acadia University alone. King Gordon lost his tenured position at United Theological College primarily on budgetary grounds. But nowhere were tenured faculty more endangered than at the University of Manitoba. A cut in the government grant of almost 50 per cent from 1931–2 to 1933–4 was difficult to accommodate (though increases in tuition fees covered part of the shortfall). Even more devastating was the revelation in August 1932 that the chairman of the board of governors, J.A. Machray, had embezzled almost the entire endowment. Within days the board decided to notify all members of the faculty that they had a job only until 31 August 1933 and would be informed 'as early in the new calendar year as possible as to their future tenure.' Most of those who were let go were junior, but the dean of Manitoba Agricultural College was not. 'It is not possible, under existing economic conditions, for the University to have a Dean other than a teaching Dean,' a board committee stated in recommending his removal.[38]

The crisis led the board to assume an increased measure of control over the staff. Section 12 of the University Amendment Act (1917) stated that the tenure of the university's officers and employees, 'unless otherwise provided, shall be during the pleasure of the board.' The board sharpened this in early 1934, stating that every appointment and contract 'shall be terminable at the will of the board.'[39] Faculty anxiety, which had waned when the great majority of teachers were re-engaged in 1933, grew again upon publication of this by-law, which also lowered the age of retirement from sixty-eight to sixty-five and implied that professors might have to teach in the summer school without additional pay.

The board agreed to meet the faculty on 15 March. After one dean and several professors had complained about the insecurity in which they now worked, the board secretary summarized the faculty view thus: 'That there should be greater security of tenure, and that staff members should not be required to hold office at the pleasure of the Board of Governors.' A board member, H.A. Bergman, pointed out that tenure during pleasure was also the rule in Alberta and Saskatchewan. Because grants fluctuated annually, 'the governing body of a state University could ... not safely make commitments except from year to year,' but the board intended 'to retain its staff with as great a degree of permanency as the circumstances warranted.' Bergman added that he hoped that the spirit in which the by-law would be administered would 'soon allay any apprehension that may now be felt ... There was no intention to be harsh or unfair with any University employee, but ... it was necessary that the Board should exercise a proper measure of control.'

The board realized 'that the heart and soul of the University are to found in an efficient teaching staff,' the board's chairman, Mr Justice A.K. Dysart, said, 'and that the equipment and administration staffs were designed merely to support and give opportunities to teachers to instruct, inspire and direct the youth of the land.' Nevertheless, although the board wished to give professors peace of mind concerning their tenure, there was a 'still greater duty upon it, and that [was] to build up and maintain efficiency in the staff.' The board must be able to weed out those who, for whatever reason, had 'become incapable of rendering the requisite service.'[40]

The meeting may have had some result. In September 1934 the board adopted a by-law stating that henceforth three months' notice would be given. The board rejected a motion requiring a recommendation from the president before staff members could be appointed, promoted, or dismissed (the president, Sidney Smith, prudently sided with the majority). By 1936, though, Smith was able to secure approval of a motion that under most conditions his concurrence in a dismissal was necessary.[41]

As the financial crisis faded in memory, the faculty began to feel more secure. At a meeting of the board's staff committee in 1952, President A.H.S. Gillson said that professors seemed to think 'their appointments were permanent.' He considered this undesirable. Agreeing with him, the committee confirmed the by-law of September 1934.[42]

Writing in the immediate aftermath of Harry Crowe's reinstatement at United College, Gillson's successor took a very different line. President Hugh H. Saunderson explained to the Manitoba board in January 1959 that a tenured appointment was one without a terminal date other than retirement at sixty-five. Its purpose was 'to protect the community and its universities by maintaining places where scholars can seek to find the truth and to express their views, even although their individual views may currently be unpopular with a very large fraction of the community.'

Tenure was not 'a life appointment regardless of ... competence,' stated Saunderson, as he outlined 'the usual procedure for dealing with unsatisfactory staff members.' Normally, it resulted in improved performance or in a resignation; rarely was it necessary to dismiss someone. But what if a professor disputed a negative assessment? 'We haven't had such a situation in my time,' he said, but other universities dealt with it by setting up an independent committee before which the faculty member could appear. After all, 'presidents are human, and can make errors of judgmen.'[43]

The statement is striking for several reasons. First, the practice of tenure as Saunderson described it contradicted both the 1917 University Amendment Act and the board's 1934 by-law. Second, he failed to cite economic security as a justification of tenure. Above all, he gave a central place to the concept of academic freedom. The influence of the Fowke-Laskin Report is unmistakable. Saunderson's document is noteworthy, too, because he indicated a course of action for dealing with tenured professors whose performance seemed inadequate. His comments suggest that failure to clear out dead wood owed more to the circumspection, tolerance, reluctance to give pain, or even ordinary laziness of department heads, deans, and presidents, and less to the existence of tenure than was (and is) often thought.

That tenure offered no security to allegedly unsatisfactory professors was demonstrated at the University of Alberta in 1942. Premier William Aberhart had made an increase in the government grant conditional on President Robert Newton's 'cleaning house' – by which Aberhart meant ridding the institution of 'inefficient' professors. On Newton's recommendation, the executive committee of the board agreed in January to inform the heads of chemistry and pharmacy, as well as a professor of mechanical engineering, that they would be 'retired' on 31 August. There had been no hearing of any kind. One of the three dismissed faculty members had been on sick leave and died soon afterwards. Of the other two, one was allegedly an ineffectual teacher, but it is not known why the third was thought to be inadequate.[44]

If other presidents were less forceful than Newton, it was because they lacked the stomach for action, feared the consequences in the form of bad publicity, or worked within an institutional culture unfavourable to ruthlessness. The courts had indicated that in the absence of provision otherwise, a professorial contract was terminable upon notice. But institutional usage might dictate something else.

McGill's original charter did not provide for the removal of members of the faculty. In 1854, however, the statutes came to provide that professors should hold office 'for and during the pleasure of the Governors and no longer.' A later amendment turned this into 'subject to the provisions of the Charter,' an apparent reversion to the state of affairs before 1852, which left the nature of professorial tenure in doubt.[45]

In the spring of 1920, Vice-Principal Frank Adams gathered information from several North American universities about the nature of the tenure enjoyed by their faculty. Easily the most interesting reply came from Principal Bruce Taylor of Queen's, who offered comments that have relevance beyond their place and time. 'It is not possible to run a University as if it were a business concern solely and simply,' Taylor wrote. 'There is not likely to be much of a university spirit if men ... feel that they are at the mercy of a Principal, or of a cabal in a body of trustees.' Every university tended to gather a certain amount of dead wood, but Taylor believed in prevention rather than cure. Recruits should be monitored closely, and men whose work was undistinguished should be let go at once. 'Our difficulty arises from the fact that the man who comes on in a subordinate position is allowed to drift along till the question of his promotion or his dismissal becomes acute.'[46]

Having weighed the information obtained from other institutions, McGill's board adopted a few simple statutes. Demonstrators and lecturers would be appointed annually, assistant professors for terms not exceeding three years, and associate professors and professors 'as at present, that is, subject to the provisions of the Charter.' Finally, 'the University assumes the right to retire any member of the teaching staff at the age of sixty-five years.'[47]

Tenure and the age of retirement both figured in a messy conflict between two McGill faculty members that began in 1921. In August, the professor of modern languages, Hermann Walter, accused Joseph L. Morin, professor of French, of poisoning his well in the rural community where both men spent their summers. This led to a charge of attempted murder against Morin, who in turn sued Walter for defamation. Discussing the matter at a board meeting in

October, Principal Sir Arthur Currie said 'that the University's good name would suffer.' The board approved his suggestion that 'pending a settlement of their differences, these two Professors should be suspended,' and it authorized him to take any further steps that seemed necessary.[48]

Morin was acquitted in March 1922, whereupon Currie reinstated him and requested Walter's resignation. After the latter refused, Currie drafted a memorandum for the board stating that the Department of Modern Languages should be reorganized, and that he could see no place for either man in that development. By his charges against Morin, Walter had 'disclosed a lack of appreciation ... regarding his duty towards the University.' As well, although he was an excellent teacher, he was 'not so well known in the Scholastic World as the head of the Modern Languages Department should be known.' He should be asked to resign. As for Morin, since he was sixty-seven years old, he should retire. However, it was unwise 'for the impression to get out that he [was] being let go on account of any connection with this trial.' He should be given a year's salary and then pensioned off.[49]

The board continued Walter's suspension and reappointed Morin for one more year. When, late in 1922, Morin's action against Walter was dismissed, a nonplussed Currie wrote, 'After the judgment in both cases it is very hard to come to any clear conclusion regarding these two men. It is a most unfortunate case and has added unnecessarily to the troubles of McGill.' Still, he lifted Walter's suspension, and the latter taught until he was retired in 1936 at seventy-two years of age.[50]

His retirement was the result of a change in policy. Until 1935, professorial appointments were 'generally regarded as being for life on good behaviour' (the words are Currie's, written in 1933), but the statutes enabled the board to retire professors 'at any time' for what were 'considered good and sufficient reasons,' among them immorality, inefficiency, or anything which in the board's view 'affects adversely, or is likely to affect adversely, the general well-being of the University.' Moreover, anyone could be retired upon attaining the age of sixty-five, but most were 'permitted to run along from year to year.' Should it be thought necessary to dismiss someone, the professor concerned would be notified that the principal intended to make such a recommendation to the board of governors. 'If he were unwilling to accept the decision ... he would of course have the opportunity of appealing to the Visitor, who in our case is the Governor General of Canada.'[51]

By 1933, Currie had become critical of tenure as it existed at McGill. Writing to President Joseph S. Ames of Johns Hopkins University in April 1933, he complained that McGill was 'subject to the constant pressure for higher rank and higher pay which the chairmen of all departments feel they must exert annually on behalf of the subordinates.' As a result, he said, 'there is no money available to add new men of genius to the staff.' As well, 'there are too many men in our universities called Professor who do not merit that distinction.' As a cure, Currie envisaged a much higher turnover of junior faculty.[52]

Someone who disagreed with this was the head of political economy, Stephen Leacock, who wrote to Currie in May 1933: 'The tenure of a college teacher should not be on a mere basis of success. What has been called the "hire-and-fire" system makes every man tremble for his job. In the long run it kills a college at the root.' Once appointed, argued Leacock, faculty members should be kept on unless they did something egregiously wrong (he mentioned spreading communist propaganda).[53]

A different view was Dorothy McMurray's. Currie's secretary explained in 1934 to Chancellor Sir Edward Beatty that her late chief's remarks had been 'a preliminary to what he felt was the next step in the reduction of the deficit, the retirement of some assistant professors and lecturers.' He had come to believe 'that younger men should not be encouraged to settle down but should move from one university to another, needing the stimulation more than security of office to bring forth the best work.'[54]

McMurray did not venture to guess which university they were to move on to in those Depression years. In any case, the question became irrelevant when the board decided in 1935 that an easier way of reducing the deficit was to enforce the rule of retirement at sixty-five. As a result, fourteen professors who were beyond that age were retired on 31 May 1936, among them Leacock and Walter. As the *Montreal Herald* surmised, 'The ... scheme, no doubt, justifies itself on the idea of giving youth a chance.'[55]

Leacock 'was retired much against his will,' acccording to Robertson Davies. He loved teaching and, in his sixty-seventh year, felt more than able to carry on. Unlike Edwin Jacob and James Craig, Leacock did not sue his university, but his unhappiness was evident in the half-facetious, half-serious article he wrote for *Maclean's*. After discussing what he held to be the meaning of academic freedom in the case of students and faculty, Leacock turned to the 'academic freedom of the trustees or governors of a university.' This, he observed, consisted of their right to say that their money should not be used to teach what they did not want taught: 'Now we may say that if the trustees were farsighted men they would not impose such restrictions. But that is quite another matter. Suppose they do. There is no answer to it. They needn't give unless they want to. The truth is that any college which falls into the unhappy position of living on the current bounty of rich men, finds itself in chains.' In this situation, which existed at McGill for much of the 1930s as board members balanced the budget out of their own pockets, the idea of academic freedom 'must be put aside,' and professors such as himself, said Leacock, could suddenly be told to go, 'a piece of academic playfulness of which the joke is all on me.'[56]

Tenure re-emerged as an issue at McGill during the principalship of Lewis Douglas. In April 1938 he introduced some proposed changes for consideration by the deans; ten months later he recommended to the board a proposal that confirmed life appointments until retirement, or removal for cause, for all professors and for those who were currently associate professors and assistant professors with long service. Future appointments of associate and assistant professors would be for limited terms, up to five years for associates and three for assistants, with reappointment 'being exclusively within the prerogative of the Board of Governors.' Other appointments were to be for one year or less. The purpose, Douglas told Beatty, was to weed out unsatisfactory men before they could take root. In November 1939 the proposal was enshrined in the statutes of the university. It remained in effect well into the postwar years.[57]

In the absence of any reference in Dalhousie's charter to the term of appointment, writes P.B. Waite, 'tenure was understood as a contract subsisting on good behaviour ... You could indeed continue until you were ready to stop.'[58] That changed after faculty members became eligible for pensions under the Carnegie Foundation scheme, but the presumption remained that tenure was for life. James Gowanloch's dismissal in 1930 did not contradict this: his adulterous affair with a student constituted cause.

The minutes of the board of governors and the president's papers shed occasional light on prevailing practices. These were loose. Some of those appointed at the rank of assistant professor were on probation for one year, others for longer periods, while promotion to the rank of associate professor did not necessarily imply tenure.[59]

In 1951 the board executive appointed a committee to consider several faculty-related questions. This group reached the view that, given the high degree of security associated with tenure, greater care should be exercised before persons were added to the permanent staff. 'Whenever possible' initial appointments should be 'for a period of one to three years, to be renewable for from three to five years if service is satisfactory.' Initial appointments in upper ranks should be 'for a term of years before the University commits itself to indefinite tenure,' though exceptions might be made 'in order to secure outstanding men, or men in fields where candidates are few.' In April 1952 the board unanimously adopted this report.[60]

No one had bothered to consult the faculty association, which had been formed in November 1951; and a series of resolutions that it had submitted for consideration had been ignored. There was no need to consider them, the board pointed out, because the association lacked official standing. The only formal link between the board and the faculty was a joint board-senate committee, established in 1935, whose role was strictly advisory.[61]

Persistent faculty unhappiness about the way in which the board had proceeded led the senate to establish a committee 'to study the questions of faculty appointments, promotion and tenure.' This committee reported in March 1954. 'Academic freedom is of the very essence of a university,' its report stated. 'If there is to be academic freedom there must be some reasonable security of tenure for scholars.' The committee recommended that appointments should be terminable only 'with due notice by the man or with sufficient reason by the University.' For new appointees there should be 'a reasonable period of probation.' If this period was excessively prolonged, 'the probationer with no promise of security' would not be able to 'devote his whole mind to the purpose of the University,' which was to advance the work of 'the teacher, the scholar and the researcher.' The committee recommended that procedures be adopted that would safeguard this purpose.[62]

The senate adopted the report even though the board members of the joint board-senate committee proclaimed themselves 'averse to the compilation and publication of a systematic body or code of regulations.' The board executive, too, was unenthusiastic: 'To codify these procedures would not tend to simplicity, but rather the reverse, and would also tend to fetter the freedom of the Board.' The arguments of the senators on the joint committee were not without effect, however. In February 1956 the board adopted a set of 'Regulations Concerning Academic Appointments and Tenure' whose preamble asserted the importance of academic freedom and the role of tenure in safeguarding it. Probationary appointments should be made for an initial term of two years, it stated, and in total they would not normally exceed four years. Tenured appointments would not be ended 'except by resignation with due notice ... or with sufficient reason by the University' ('sufficient reason' was not defined). Finally, 'a permanent appointment does not preclude periodical appraisal of the service of the appointee, and adjustment accordingly of status or salary if required by the best interests of the University.'[63]

A senate motion expressing regret 'that the Board did not see fit to embody more fully ... the principles in the draft regulations' failed with only four votes in favour. Although the document left much to be desired from the faculty point of view, the board's acknowledgement of the central importance of academic freedom and of the role of tenure in protecting it was clearly a significant advance.[64]

The Crowe case was a defining event not only in the history of the Canadian professoriate but also in the history of tenure. In their report on the dismissal,

Vernon Fowke and Bora Laskin held the following postulates to be 'basic': 'That academic freedom and security of tenure are neither ends in themselves nor the exactions of special privilege but merely conditions for the performance of the purposes of higher education; that the search for truth which is the central purpose of institutions of higher learning cannot prosper without freedom of inquiry and expression; and finally, that security of tenure is prerequisite to academic freedom.' Harry Crowe, they stated, had been entitled to assume 'that no ground for dismissal which violated academic freedom could constitute just cause' and 'to expect that no adverse modification of his status would be effected without prior notice of the alleged cause and the opportunity to appear to answer to charges specified against him.' In both respects the board of regents had failed him.[65]

What Fowke and Laskin claimed for Crowe were 'moral' rights which they believed to be inherent in tenure as it was understood in Canada in 1958. They wisely did not argue that these rights would find support in a court of law. Under the 1938 United College Act, Crowe served during pleasure. Had he sued to get his job back, he would have lost. A suit for damages would also have failed, the board having given him more than a year's notice in July and a year's salary in lieu of notice in September.

The Crowe case heightened awareness of the difference between tenure as custom and tenure in law. It also hastened the CAUT's adoption of a statement on academic freedom and tenure. The document approved by the CAUT's national council in 1959 described tenure as 'a means to certain ends,' one of these being the professor's 'freedom as a teacher, as an investigator, and as a private citizen'; the other being the provision of 'sufficient economic security to make the profession attractive to men and women of ability.' These two ends were held to be 'indispensable' to a university's success 'in fulfilling its obligations to its students and to society.'[66]

Faculty members should get tenure at the end of a specified probationary period, the CAUT statement continued. Once granted tenure, they should be dismissed 'only for adequate cause, except in the case of retirement for age.' No optimum length for the probationary period was stated, nor was 'adequate cause' defined.

The adoption of a statement was only the end of the beginning of the attempt to make tenure more secure. A tenure practices committee went to work to find out what variations existed in Canada. More important yet was the fact that governing boards had to be brought to accept the CAUT's view of tenure and to codify it in the university statutes or, at the least, in an agreement with a faculty association.

A book about the uncommonly lurid dismissal of S.S. Orr from the University of Tasmania in 1956, reviewed by Wilfred D. Smith in the *CAUT Bulletin* in 1962, led the editor, the historian Stanley R. Mealing, to warn his readers that they were fooling themselves if they thought a similar thing could not happen in Canada. 'The legal basis for tenure, even where specific rules have been accepted, is uncertain,' Mealing wrote: 'We really depend on a vague convention that such a thing as tenure exists and on the ability of the CAUT to protest if the convention is ignored.'[67]

Bora Laskin's contribution to *A Place of Liberty* (1964) offered synopses of the judgments in the Jacob, Weir, Wilson, Craig, and Smith cases and the visitorial ruling in Saskatchewan, as well as giving a brief account of the Crowe case. The principles of tenure laid down by the courts, Laskin wrote, 'do not comport with the views generally held by the academic community.'[68]

The report on tenure that Daniel Soberman prepared for the CAUT made the same point in much greater detail. This document, which in the annals of the Canadian professoriate ranks second only to the one by Fowke and Laskin, appeared in the March 1965 issue of the *CAUT Bulletin*. Two editorials preceded it. One, by Laskin, called for 'a sensible policy on tenure' as part of the rules 'for the most effective deployment of the human resources which give a University or College its on-going life.' The other by the executive secretary, Percy Smith, sounded more urgent. In a period in which professors were able 'to bargain effectively for better salaries, pensions, insurance plans, and so on,' stated Smith, it was important that academic freedom should continue to be seen as a necessary condition for professorial work, and tenure as a means of defending that freedom.

Subsidies from government brought danger, Smith continued: 'Where government money goes, politicians' fingers follow,' and political meddling would largely nullify the positive effects of higher education. Professors must seek to understand the functions of universities and of academic freedom, must educate governments about them and organize to defend them. 'The most important means of protecting academic freedom is exercising it, continually and courageously. The second most important is the device of tenure.'[69]

After these exhortations, Soberman's report seemed almost anticlimactic. Quoting from *Tenure in American Higher Education* (1959), by Clark Byse and Louis Joughin, Soberman held 'the essential feature of tenure' to be 'continuity of service, in that the institution in which the teacher serves has in some manner – either as a legal obligation or as a moral commitment – relinquished the freedom or power it otherwise would possess to terminate the teacher's service.'[70]

Soberman found the prime justification of tenure in the protection it gave to academic freedom. Opposition to this view he dismissed as uninformed and trivial. More substantial seemed to be the criticism that 'scholars of questionable quality do obtain sinecures in our universities.' This, he thought, would diminish in importance if the automatic grant of tenure were to yield to a process in which applications for tenure were to be assessed by senior professors: 'University teachers should want not only to protect themselves from arbitrary dismissal, but also to protect their universities from becoming refuges for mediocrity.'

By itself tenure offered limited protection for academic freedom, argued Soberman. Faculty members must 'share substantially in university government' for that freedom to be secure. Yet tenure 'would remain important to the freedom of the individual teacher even at institutions where academic staff did participate in university government. And effective tenure regulations [formed] an important part of the whole scheme of academic freedom.' It would be best to combine the legal protection of tenure with an institutional effort to protect academic freedom.

The jurisprudence of tenure in Canada was on the whole 'not helpful,' Soberman continued, though the one case in which a court had ordered reinstatement, that of Wilson at King's College, was encouraging. 'There may be some doubt,' he added, 'but on balance I believe that in Canada a university teacher who has express tenure and is wrongfully dismissed from his institution, whether public or private, could obtain an order for reinstatement ... [Yet] the picture of our legal rights is an unhappy one. Indeed, if the legal picture were the whole story, the state of academic freedom in Canada would be intolerable.' Fortunately, noted Soberman, in most institutions 'a permanent appointment is considered by both staff and administration to give a security in practice that is absent in law,' but he thought that this was not good enough. The growing danger of outside interference in university life made reform essential.

Soberman counselled the creation of tenure during good behaviour by agreement between board and faculty, and the adoption of procedures dealing with dismissals, including hearings and appeals. Of these, a full and fair hearing seemed to him the most important, Finally, he found the procedures existing at nine universities to be unsatisfactory: 'The confusion of the roles of the university administrators and the boards of governors – acting as both prosecutors and judges – suggests a certain timidity in facing up to an open contest between teacher and university authorities. In some way this attitude is admirable, for it suggests a basic unity of purpose and trust.' But it was also unrealistic. Once a president sought to dismiss a professor, a battle was joined in which the resources of the combatants were highly unequal. Only a fair hearing could correct for this.[71]

Soberman's report spent little time discussing how tenure affected those who did not (yet) have it and how their academic freedom might be protected. While it detailed the procedures that universities should follow in dismissing the tenured, it said little about the procedures to be used in granting tenure, and nothing about removing the untenured. But then he had not been asked to address this matter.[72]

Missing, too, was a justification of tenure as a guarantee of economic security, which the 1960 CAUT statement had claimed was necessary to attract able men and women into the profession. The shortage of qualified faculty that had developed in the 1960s made the issue of economic security less pressing. It was absent not only from Soberman's report but also from the comments on it that appeared in the *Bulletin*.

Of the commentators, Harry W. Arthurs of Osgoode Hall Law School was most critical. He argued that Soberman's concern for due process had led him to propose machinery that was better designed to protect nonacademic values than academic freedom: 'While procedural safeguards are desirable, even essential, they are meaningless without firmly established standards against which to measure the facts found. These ... standards must affirmatively announce two distinct principles: (a) the right to freedom of opinion and expression in matters academic, administrative and political, and (b) immunity from dismissal for any reason save proven personal or professional misconduct.' Arthurs considered that Soberman's procedures were likely to work best in the large universities that needed them least, and to work badly in the small, sectarian, or new institutions that needed them most. 'Perhaps a useful device would be a joint CAUT-NCCUC declaration on the protection of academic freedom, and establishment of a joint commission to give effect to such declaration through adjudication, as well as investigation and mediation.'[73]

The chairman of the AF & T committee, James B. Milner, noted that the court cases cited by Soberman had mostly been decided by trial judges at a time when these judges may not have been familiar with universities and their traditions: 'One is entitled to ask, today, what the Supreme Court of Canada would decide.' If a permanent appointment was in most universities believed 'to give a security in practice that is absent in law,' then the Supreme Court might well establish it in law. (David J. Mullan of the Queen's law faculty has recently written: 'My sense is that the Supreme Court of Canada would not have entertained such an argument in a month of Sundays and, indeed, the same may hold true today! That, of course, does not mean that it is not a "good" argument.') Still, Milner hoped the occasion would not arise and that, instead, faculty associations and boards would establish mutually acceptable procedures for securing tenure during good behaviour.[74]

A study of tenure in Quebec, Canada's only civil law jurisdiction, prepared by René Hurtubise of the University of Montreal, appeared in 1966. The only

Quebec court case to arise from the dismissal of a professor, that of George Workman from Montreal's Wesleyan Theological College in 1907, had not pronounced on tenure but had implied that it was held during the board's pleasure. In the absence of jurisprudence, Hurtubise was forced back on general principles governing salaried employees: 'Bref, leur engagement, à moins de stipulations précises, serait pour une durée indéterminée ..., mais ils auraient droit à un avis de trois mois au cas où l'employeur désirait mettre fin au contrat puisque leur engagement est normalement de tant par année.'[75] The suggestion that professorial appointments, even those without term, might be interpreted as being on an annual basis was not reassuring. Indeed, the state of affairs in Quebec was no better than the one existing in the other nine provinces. Nowhere was tenure safe.

Even as the Soberman and Hurtubise reports were being prepared, tenure was in the process of becoming more secure. The main cause was a sellers' market in academic employment, which led professors to look for better terms and conditions of employment and led governing boards to concede them. The trend was becoming clear by the time the report on university government prepared by Sir James Duff and Robert Berdahl appeared in 1966. In addressing tenure, the report urged that care be exercised in granting it so that 'sub-standard' teachers might not receive this 'precious' good: 'The shortage of qualified faculty over the next decade will undoubtedly result in a pool of marginally qualified teachers, and these will require careful evaluation,' not least because those who were granted tenure were likely to remain in their positions for a long time.[76]

Many universities were either amending their procedures concerning promotion and tenure or adopting procedures for the first time. At the University of Toronto, for example, a presidential committee, appointed in 1964 and chaired by the physiologist R.E. Haist, authored the 'Haist rules' dealing with appointments, promotion, and tenure, which included a requirement to show cause in cases of dismissal. The board of governors adopted these rules in 1967.[77] Other governing boards were doing the same kind of thing.

By the late 1960s many university people, including presidents and board members, were of the view that tenure, a permanent appointment terminable only for cause, should be enjoyed by all professors who had passed a period of probation. The protection that academic freedom derived from tenure had become its chief justification, while its role in providing professors with economic security was scarcely mentioned any more. In the 1960s, of course, many salaried employees in both the public and private sectors had secure jobs. Not since the 1930s, in fact, had middle-class Canadians worried much about unemployment.

This was notably true of those who entered university teaching between 1962 and 1971, when almost anyone with a master's degree and an expressed willingness to get a doctorate could get an academic job. To these people tenure was not a central concern, at least initially. Salaries, benefits, teaching loads, the congeniality of colleagues, the quality of students, and the availability of research funds all figured more prominently. Tenure was mainly a concern of older professors with memories of a time when teaching positions were scarce and when the travails of a King Gordon, a Frank Underhill, a George Hunter, or a Harry Crowe periodically reminded them of their vulnerability. In the latter half of the 1960s, they were able to take advantage of the temporary shortage of qualified academics to push for and secure the entrenchment of tenure.

Conditions and attitudes changed in the 1970s. Early in the decade new appointments dwindled, and at some universities there was talk of redundancy. Interest in tenure increased, especially among junior professors. Faculty associations that had not yet secured agreements with their governing boards redoubled their efforts. Where associations transformed themselves into faculty unions, the terms under which tenure was granted and retained and the reasons for which it might be ended became parts of a collective agreement. In the process, tenure often appeared less as a safeguard for academic freedom than as a seniority system.

For this reason – and for others that will be explored more fully in the next chapter – tenure has come under vigorous attack. In recent years the historian Michael Bliss has described it as a public relations disaster,[78] the Canadian Association of University Business Officers has argued that it prevents institutional flexibility,[79] the Toronto Star has dismissed it as an unwarranted anomaly,[80] a philosophy don, Mark Kingwell, has denounced it as an impediment to academic freedom,[81] and the historians David Bercuson, Robert Bothwell, and J.L. Granatstein have deplored it as an inducement to indolence.[82] Other critics, such as Ramsay Cook, John Crispo, Peter Emberley, and, in a report prepared for the Ontario Undergraduate Student Alliance, Jane Ormrod, have stopped short of counselling the abandonment of tenure but have urged the universities to show more rigour in monitoring it.[83]

Canadian faculty associations, local, provincial, and national, have predictably defended tenure, but they have not been alone. Conrad Russell has stressed tenure's essential contribution to academic freedom in Great Britain, and an American professor of law, Matthew Finkin, has edited a selection of documents that sets out to show 'that academic tenure is good for America: that it is essential for the protection of academic freedom, that it is necessary to attract the intellectually gifted to the academic life and to create conditions that allow first-rate scholarship to flourish.' Finkin adds, 'This is not to deny its draw-backs, both for the individual and for the institution, but it is to maintain that the system is far better for society than any substitute suggested thus far.' Finkin may not have made the case for tenure persuasively enough to satisfy all scep-tics, but his book does demonstrate that the most frequently proposed alterna-tive, a system of renewable contracts, is very seriously flawed.[84]

There is also the ringing *obiter dictum* of the Supreme Court of Canada in the case of *McKinney v. University of Guelph* (1990). Ruling that the Canadian Charter of Rights and Freedoms does not apply to the universities in their employment relations, the court majority refused to end the compulsory retire-ment of professors at age sixty-five in part because this might undermine ten-ure. (Unless and until the Court overturns this ruling, those who believe that the Charter can be used to defend academic freedom are almost certainly mis-taken.) Faculty members, the Court majority held, 'must have a great measure of security of employment if they are to have the freedom necessary to the maintenance of academic excellence which is or should be the hallmark of a university. Tenure provides the necessary academic freedom to allow free and fearless search for knowledge and the propagation of ideas.' If compulsory retirement were to be ended, the Court majority argued, universities would be tempted to introduce systems of evaluation of tenured faculty that could endan-ger academic freedom.[85]

In law, university appointments can take three forms. One, in use during most of our history, provides for tenure during the pleasure of a governing board. A second provides for tenure during good behaviour, so that cause must be shown if someone is to be dismissed; this is the form of tenure now enjoyed by most Canadian professors, though often under condition that financial exigency or the termination of a program or department can serve as cause. (That this is not an empty phrase was shown at UBC in 1985 and at Carleton in 1997.)[86] The third kind of appointment consists of renewable fixed-term contracts. Used in Canada mostly for junior faculty – for probationary appointees who are eligible for tenure, as well as for sessional appointees who are not – such contracts are rarely used for more senior professors. From some perspective, each of the three forms has advantages and drawbacks. The question is which one best serves the purpose of giving professors the freedom to carry out their intellec-tual and social functions without permitting serious abuse.

We should not look for perfection. Winston Churchill is worth quoting: 'It has been said that democracy is the worst form of Government except all those other forms that have been tried from time to time.'[87] Much the same thing can be said of tenure. It may protect people whom others regard as undeserving and who may in fact be so – people who, in spite of the promise in teaching or research that they showed when they received tenure, have turned out to be mediocre or worse in accomplishment, or wanting in some important aspect of their work. But these drawbacks are the price that must be paid to protect the innovative, the outspoken, the unconventional, and the unpopular, as well as those whose fields of academic specialization have fallen into temporary disfavour – and, most of all, those who do research, sometimes very important research, that is time-consuming and for which there may be no commercial demand.

Although imperfect, tenure seems to serve the needs of the universities and of society well enough. It may be necessary, though, to monitor it more carefully in order to ensure that those who enjoy its privileges continue to deserve them. Professors should give thought to devising a system of tenure review that is neither perfunctory nor time-consuming but is fair nonetheless. This is a tall order. However, unless it can be convincingly shown that filling it is impossible, trying to fill it may be unavoidable.

12

Postscript: Academic Freedom since 1965

The professorial mood in 1965 was generally positive. Universities were expanding, salaries were rising, pension plans were improving, sabbaticals were becoming more common, and research support was increasing. Physical comfort increased as air-conditioning became standard in new buildings. By skilfully playing academic musical chairs, some academics were reaching the rank of full professor within ten years of first appointment. Materially and psychologically, academic life was better than it had been for decades.

For a few years the mood remained upbeat. The publication of the Duff-Berdahl Report on university government seemed to presage an end to autocratic presidents and boards. In 1967 the Canadian Association of University Teachers (CAUT) adopted a policy document on appointments, which stated among other things that 'academic freedom ... involves the right to criticize the university'[1] (an assertion that can be seen as a late outcome of the Crowe affair). In the later 1960s, faculty associations at a growing number of universities were able to secure governing-board agreement to guarantees of academic freedom and tenure.

But the optimism was not universal. Some professors worried about the effects of mass education on academic standards, about spreading secularism and consumerism in education, and about the growing bureaucratization of the universities. Already present were aspects of what Bill Readings has with deft irony called the University of Excellence – defined by its administrative activity rather than its scholarship and teaching.[2] As well, the rising tide of provincial funding prompted fears that governments would seek to tamper with university autonomy and academic freedom.

These fears grew when Prime Minister Lester B. Pearson announced in October 1966, without having consulted the provinces or the academic community, that federal grants to the universities would cease in 1967. Henceforth Ottawa would make tax concessions and cash grants to each province that would match its spending on higher education. (Ottawa did continue to act as the main direct funder of university research.) The change was unexpected and abrupt. For the year 1965–6 Ottawa had increased the per capita grant to five dollars. This was in line with a recommendation of a commission on university finances, appointed by the Association of Universities and Colleges of Canada (AUCC) and headed by the economist Vincent Bladen. The commission had also recommended that grants be increased annually by one dollar per capita 'until such time as ... discussions with the provinces ... lead to an appropriate revision of the amount of these grants.' Instead, the federal government, which had been facing provincial and internal criticism of its role in higher education, chose to bail out.[3]

The blow was cushioned by a guarantee that universities would receive from provincial governments an annual grant no smaller than the amount received from Ottawa in 1966–7. Nevertheless W.L. Morton, in *The Kingdom of Canada* (1969), described Pearson's announcement as 'a chill wind for the universities.' Thirty years on, inflation having robbed the 1966 guarantee of much of its value, Morton's apprehensions have been substantiated.[4]

Fears that provincial governments would attack university autonomy or academic freedom directly have proved so far to be largely groundless (though recent events in Nova Scotia suggest that change may be in the wind). In Saskatchewan, the government of Ross Thatcher tried in 1967 to gain control over the details of university spending, but public support for the move proved to be slight, and in the face of opposition from the academic community and other interested groups, the government backed off.[5]

The following year, the AUCC, the CAUT, the Canadian Union of Students, and the Union générale des étudiants du Québec jointly established a commission, consisting of René Hurtubise (Montreal) and Donald Rowat (Carleton), to study the relations between universities and governments. The commissioners reported in 1970. They acknowledged the legitimate interest that governments had in the universities while reiterating the case for a high degree of institutional autonomy.[6] Did provincial politicians take heed? So far, no premier has tried to emulate Thatcher. Instead, governments have reduced the real value of per student grants, leaving to the universities the task of apportioning the shortfalls that have developed.

Scarcely anticipated in 1965 were new challenges to the social and intellectual role of the universities that have affected academic freedom – sometimes directly, sometimes tangentially. The student movement, which disturbed many campuses in 1968–9, was the first of these challenges; it has not been the last.

The recent history of academic freedom cannot be summarized neatly. The number of Canadian universities has grown greatly during the last four decades, and many archival collections are still closed to researchers. Yet the story, though necessarily incomplete, must be carried into the present, for academic freedom is embattled today as perhaps never before.

What follows is partly chronological and partly thematic. I will deal briefly with some key events in the later 1960s and the 1970s and then discuss the two major challenges to academic freedom that have emerged since 1980 – political and economic correctness. Since the period is one during which I have been active in faculty affairs, my personal opinions will be more in evidence than in the earlier chronological chapters.

The report on university government prepared by Sir James Duff and Robert Berdahl appeared in 1966. The commissioners made suggestions for a number of changes, the most prominent being faculty membership on governing boards, but they also recommended the amendment of procedures governing appointments, tenure, and promotion. The Duff-Berdahl Report led to discussions between the CAUT and AUCC and, in 1970, to the publication of the AUCC's *Guidelines to University Organization.*[7]

Commenting on this document from the point of view of the AF & T committee was Bruce Dunlop, the committee's chairman and a law professor at Toronto. 'It was not possible to produce a commonly approved document because several fundamental differences of opinion remained ...,' he wrote. 'A body representing teachers and an organization comprised primarily of senior administrators can hardly be expected to see eye to eye on all fundamental issues.' For example, although the AUCC document affirmed tenure as 'an important guarantee of academic freedom,' it was, in Dunlop's opinion, too ready to sanction the use of nonrenewable contracts. The document also made it possible to keep people on probation indefinitely, something he thought unjustifiable.

Dunlop's other major point of criticism concerned dismissal procedures. The AUCC document adopted the recommendation of the Duff-Berdahl Report in specifying internal hearing committees on the grounds that 'members of the institution normally have a full regard for the rights of a colleague and at the same time a more acute concern for the standards and reputation of the institution than persons from outside can have.'[8] Dunlop pointed out that recent experience in several universities contradicted this: 'Major dismissal or termination disputes almost invariably polarize the campus on which they occur ... Feelings become very intense.' An outside committee was less likely to be biased, he argued.

Moreover, although the AUCC document 'assumed that the committee's decision would normally be accepted,' it did not envisage that it would be binding. If it was not, Dunlop held, a hearing might be pointless. 'It should be said,' he concluded, 'that the CAUT welcomes the AUCC's decision to seek to have its member institutions adopt appropriate procedures for protecting academic freedom and tenure. But the CAUT will continue to press for what it deems to be necessary improvements in such guidelines.'[9]

As Dunlop was writing these words, probably no institution loomed larger in his thoughts than Simon Fraser University in Burnaby, British Columbia. Founded in 1963 and opened two years later, SFU had an aura of innovation that attracted students and faculty members who were willing and even eager to break with established patterns. Some of both groups challenged the authority not only of administrators and the board of governors but also of senior professors. At the same time the university's administration, overwhelmed perhaps by rapid growth, was in disarray. Serious conflict ensued.

In October 1967 the Simon Fraser faculty association (SFUFA) asked the CAUT to investigate 'the breakdown in communications' between the faculty and the university's president, Patrick McTaggart-Cowan. Reporting in February 1968, a committee headed by James B. Milner (then chairman of the AF & T committee) identified serious procedural problems involving appointments, renewals, and the granting of tenure, and proposed several changes in academic decision-making.[10]

Three months later, another CAUT committee determined that little prospect existed of resolving SFU's problems 'in the near future.' On the advice of the AF & T committee, the CAUT's national council voted to censure SFU's board of governors for 'continued contravention of accepted principles of university governance through interference in the academic affairs of the university'; to censure President McTaggart-Cowan 'for his continued failure to carry on appropriate administration'; and to censure both for failing to deal with the problems described in the report of the Milner committee.[11]

This, the CAUT's first-ever censure, had immediate results. McTaggart-Cowan resigned on 31 May 1968, and board chairman Gordon Shrum did so in October. That month, too, the SFU board approved a document on academic freedom and tenure that had been prepared by SFUFA. Satisfied that the university was now on the right track, a new CAUT committee of inquiry reported that the censure had served its purpose in bringing about 'an energetic attack on the problems of university government' and should be lifted. In November 1968 the CAUT council agreed.[12]

Within months the CAUT censured another university. In the fall of 1968 a physicist at the University of New Brunswick, Norman Strax, objected to the introduction of identity cards for use in the library and joined several students in borrowing books without presenting cards. President Colin B. Mackay suspended Strax and ordered him to leave the campus, and when Strax ignored this order, Mackay obtained an *ex parte* injunction to remove him. Without expressing an opinion on the merits of Strax's claims, the AF & T committee found that UNB's procedures were flawed and, the president and board having declined to submit the case to arbitration, recommended censure. After the CAUT council accepted this recommendation, the UNB authorities agreed to arbitration. The censure was lifted in July 1969.[13]

In February 1969 Stanley Gray, a lecturer in political science at McGill, joined several students in disrupting meetings of the senate and the board of governors, chiefly in protest against the establishment of the Faculty of Management. Seeking to determine whether cause existed to dismiss Gray, Principal H. Rocke Robertson offered him arbitration by a committee to be named by the CAUT. Gray accepted the offer. A committee headed by Walter Tarnopolsky, dean of law at the University of Windsor, ruled in August 1969 that 'the manner and the circumstances in which Mr. Gray acted constituted gross misconduct,' justifying his dismissal.[14]

The arbitration was the CAUT's third triumph within a year. The *Vancouver Sun* commented that 'the Canadian Association of University Teachers ... seems able to snap the academic community to attention with a frown.' But the Gray case was the last victory the CAUT would savour for some time. In the spring of 1970 its national council rejected an AF & T committee recommendation to censure Montreal's Loyola College over an unresolved grievance, whereupon the AF & T chairman, Bruce Dunlop, resigned in protest. The man who succeeded him, A.E. Malloch of McGill, told me in 1996 of his continuing belief that the failure to censure Loyola had undermined the CAUT's influence everywhere. Certainly, the association's subsequent intervention in grievances was noticeably less effective than it had been in 1968 and 1969.[15]

The censure of Simon Fraser University had barely been lifted when the university entered a long period of struggle centred on the Department of Political Science, Sociology, and Anthropology (PSA). Probably the most important conflict in Canadian university history since the Crowe case, the PSA affair awaits a full account by someone who has seen all the available primary sources. On the basis of the printed sources, however, an account of sorts can be cobbled together, as follows.

In the fall of 1968 'democratization' of the university became the rallying cry of student activists at many universities. At Simon Fraser their principal focus was the PSA department. Some PSA faculty members worked with students to draft procedures that were at odds both with the SFUFA-sanctioned statement on tenure and promotion and with university policy on the selection of academic administrators. When PSA used these procedures to select a new head, Mordecai Briemberg, Dean D.H. Sullivan would not agree to the nomination.

Since the department refused to reconsider, Sullivan recommended to President Kenneth Strand that PSA be placed under trusteeship. Resentment in PSA circles grew when the university-wide tenure committee rejected ten recommendations made for the department by the dean's tenure committee. Since the negative decisions mainly affected the more radical members of PSA, they claimed this was a purge – a claim made credible by the strong academic record of several of those affected.[16]

At the beginning of the 1969–70 session most of the PSA students voted to boycott classes, and several faculty members agreed not to hold them unless Strand agreed to negotiate on the basis of four demands, whose effect would have been to give PSA near-total autonomy. The president refused, and a 'strike' began on 24 September 1969, with most students as well as eight faculty members taking part. On 3 October, ignoring SFU's statement on academic freedom and tenure, Strand invoked the British Columbia Universities Act to suspend the striking professors with pay. Two weeks later, he initiated dismissal proceedings against the eight for nonperformance of their duties. The student boycott ended amidst confusion.

Strand informed the eight that they could appeal under the university's statement on academic freedom and tenure, which entitled each to a hearing committee consisting of a president's nominee, an appellant's nominee, and a chairman chosen jointly. One of the eight, Prudence Wheeldon, asked the Supreme Court of British Columbia to rule that the statement on academic freedom and tenure was part of her contract of employment and that she had been improperly dismissed. On 18 June 1970 the court rejected her claim, ruling that it had been understood by the board and SFUFA that 'in approving the statement the Board of Governors did not intend that any legal consequences should flow from such approval.' Wheeldon then referred her file to one of two committees that had begun to hear appeals. Headed by a University of Western Ontario law professor, E.E. Palmer, this committee was dealing also with the appeals of Briemberg, Kathleen Gough Aberle, Saghir Ahmad, Louis Feldhammer, John Leggett, and David Potter.[17]

A second committee, chaired by the UBC economist Gideon Rosenbluth, adjudicated the case of Nathan Popkin. This committee reported in November 1970. Although it deplored the strike and described Popkin's part in it 'as a form of academic misconduct,' it noted that there had been serious provocation from administrators and that the offence was not 'the type of gross misconduct that furnishes cause for dismissal.'[18] Popkin was then reinstated.

Meanwhile, the other appeals were proceeding less smoothly. In July 1970 the Palmer committee had ruled unanimously that Strand's dismissive attitude to the committee's work had made 'a fair and just hearing' impossible, that he had failed to produce cause for dismissal, and that the seven faculty members should therefore be reinstated.[19] But Strand had declared this finding invalid and had asked the seven to agree to new hearings. Aberle and Potter refused and were dismissed. The charge against Leggett was dropped when his contract ended on 31 August. The other four chose new hearings.

The four appeals were at different stages when, in June 1971, the SFU board informed the committee charged with Wheeldon's appeal that it need not continue: she was being reinstated. The reason was that the committee, which was chaired by the University of Toronto law professor David L. Johnston, had ruled that not only Strand but also the university was party to the hearing, which meant that the committee could ask to see board and decanal documents as well as those emanating from the president's office. The board rejected the ruling and then suspended part of the statement on academic freedom and tenure, thereby enabling Strand to recommend that Ahmad, Briemberg, and Feldhammer be dismissed forthwith. 'This statement University has been torn by matters originating in 1969 for far too long,' Strand explained. This statement matched the dominant mood among the faculty. A motion of nonconfidence in the president and board, which had been passed by the SFUFA executive, was rejected by most of the membership.[20]

Having in November 1970 tabled a recommendation from the AF & T committee that the president and board be censured, the CAUT council finally imposed censure in May 1971. In November the censure was sharpened. Asserting that the suspension of the university's dismissal procedures and the firing of faculty members without a hearing had 'effectively destroy[ed] tenure and all protection for academic freedom at Simon Fraser University,' the council passed a resolution advising academics to avoid employment there.

Many SFU faculty took issue with this. Some believed that the PSA eight had given cause for dismissal; others simply wished to be rid of them. Either way, due process got short shrift. (It should be added that some of the eight showed no more concern for due process, except when it served their own ends.) Strand's successor, Pauline Jewett, found that faculty and administration hostility to the eight seriously hampered her attempts to end the conflict. Not until 1977, after SFU dropped the original charges against the eight and adopted 'acceptable' dismissal procedures, did the CAUT lift the censure. This was no happy ending: five grievors did not accept the deal that had been struck. But many council delegates were sick of the case and saw no point in continuing the censure.[21]

In the early 1970s the CAUT gave increased attention to protecting the academic freedom of nontenured faculty. And with good reason. Fights involving denials of tenure and nonrenewal of contracts led to the censure not only of SFU but also of Mount Allison and the Université du Québec à Montréal, as well as the president of the University of Victoria.[22]

Even good procedures could fail. The Johnston committee, which issued a report in spite of having been terminated by the SFU board, stated, 'What is really at stake ... are two fundamental issues of the modern university – can academic freedom and tenure survive and can the university govern itself internally?' Procedures that were both fair and effective were essential: 'If the dismissal mechanism does not work, critics of academic freedom and tenure may be successful in abolishing it on the argument that it is a pernicious screen to hide the incompetent or the ... undeserving. Thus, academic freedom will be destroyed indirectly. If the dismissal mechanism functions, but does not function fairly, then the mechanism itself directly destroys academic freedom.' Measured by the criteria of faculty participation and control, SFU's procedures were superior to those of most other Canadian universities, observed the committee. Yet they had proved inadequate: 'The substantive and practical challenge' was to make procedures work. If this challenge was not met, there would be 'plenty of critics who will be quick to suggest, and to implement ..., alternatives.'[23]

Administrative arbitrariness was not the only threat. Local majorities of faculty members could pose a danger to minorities. Percy Smith's successor as executive secretary of the CAUT, Alwyn Berland, in 1970 identified a growing divide 'between those we rapidly label conservative or reactionary, and those equally rapidly named progressive or radical,' with the 'so-called liberals' in between. 'However you label the parties to the dispute,' he wrote, 'the heat and anger are there, and they threaten academic freedom.'[24]

The perception that freedom was menaced from within sharpened during the next two years. The AF & T chairman, A.E. Malloch, reported to the CAUT council in May 1972 that most of the 103 appeals handled by the committee during the preceding year had resulted from nonrenewals of contracts or denials of tenure. Some professors were using budgetary cutbacks to undermine intellectual diversity: 'The time has come ... when departments, by a delicate mixture of non-renewals and new appointments, can insure that no one teaches in the department unless he shares a particular orientation toward the discipline ... defined by the voting majority of the department.' Malloch added that 'a serious commitment to academic freedom' meant 'a serious commitment to pluralism, including pluralism in academic disciplines ... When a number of faculty members who share a common perception of their discipline begin to use that perception as the touch-stone of sound learning, then we have entered a new age of orthodoxy, and for the orthodox it is notorious that error does not have the same rights of truth.'

Malloch did not minimize the demands for forebearance made on professors seeking to assess the quality of work that seemed to them wrong-headed: 'To repeat the blunt question put to me last autumn by a departmental chairman, "Yes, but how do I recognize a good radical sociologist when I see one?"' The CAUT believed that professors should have the major role in personnel decisions, he stated. However, 'if the procedures of the Policy Statement come to be used as a kind of formal orchestration of our ... intolerance or prejudices, then they will appear infinitely more mischievous than the naked authoritarianism of bad old deans and department heads.' The CAUT had to make sure that professors, as they assumed increasing control over academic appointments, did not themselves become 'enemies of academic freedom.'[25] Like Walt Kelly's Pogo, Malloch had 'met the enemy, and he is us.'

Malloch's concerns go to the heart of academic freedom as it developed in North America. The historian Joan W. Scott has noted that the ideas of discipline and competence, which are central to academic freedom, exclude some people from its protection. 'Can academic freedom,' she asks, 'protect from the tendency to orthodoxy within a discipline the critical function on which it most depends?' She answers that it should, without claiming it always will.[26]

A handful of cases that apparently involved the purging of nonconformists occurred in the 1970s. When the University of Ottawa, which had recently cut its ties with the Oblate order, did not renew the contract of Jacques Flamand, a teacher of religious studies, he charged that church authorities had pressured the university to remove him because of his anticlerical views. A CAUT committee of inquiry failed to turn up evidence of such pressure and found the likely explanation for his nonrenewal to be 'incompatibility of personality and views with the Chairman of Religious Studies.' Flamand had been 'a difficult colleague ... determined to secure reform, vocal in his criticism, not always a model of tact, and contemptuous of the incompetent.'[27] When Ottawa's governing board would not agree to arbiration, the CAUT council imposed censure in 1973.

Two controversies involved McGill. At the centre of one was the political scientist Pauline Vaillancourt, a Marxist, feminist, and Quebec nationalist. Denied a renewal of her contract in 1972, she appealed against the decision. A committee headed by the University of Toronto's David L. Johnston (later principal of McGill) identified several irregularities and inconsistencies in the department's handling of her file and recommended that she be given a further three-year contract. The board of governors accepted this recommendation, but she took a tenured appointment at the Université du Québec à Montréal instead.[28]

The sociologist Marlene Dixon was also a committed Marxist. From the moment she joined McGill, she experienced heavy weather. Believing that most of her colleagues did not wish her to have tenure, she resigned in October 1974. Two years later, she published *Things Which Are Done in Secret*, a book that expresses disdain for value-free social science and states her belief that the 'liberal university' will not protect the academic freedom of radicals such as herself.[29]

At the centre of another *cause célèbre* was a teacher of social work, Marlene Webber. A member of the Communist Party of Canada (Marxist-Leninist), she taught from 1973 to 1976 at Renison College, an Anglican institution affiliated with the University of Waterloo. During her final year at Renison, she charged that her politics had made her unacceptable to the college's principal and board, and she signalled her intention to resign. Appointed by the Memorial University of Newfoundland, she learned within months that her contract at the institution would not be renewed. A CAUT committee of inquiry chaired by C.B. Macpherson found 'that there had been a serious breach of academic freedom in that the university had based its non-renewal on the political activities of Professor Webber ... without producing admissible and cogent evidence that these ... constituted professional wrongdoing.' When Memorial would not agree to binding arbitration, the CAUT in 1978 censured the president and board of regents.[30]

Cases of personal, professional, or ideological incompatibility leading to dismissal also cropped up at other universities during the 1970s, most notably at Calgary and Windsor. 'A university is a place where difficult but competent people can be accommodated.' The words are from the report on the Flamand case. At all times, however, a good many academics have believed that difficult people, even though competent, should go and be difficult somewhere else.[31]

The student movement in Canada had its origins in the movement of protest against nuclear weapons, in support of the U.S. civil rights movement, and in opposition to the parental role assumed by university officers. Influenced by protest among U.S. students against the growing American involvement in the Vietnam War, student activism changed after 1965. Some students, seeing universities as subservient to the interests of a 'military-industrial complex,' demanded that the institutions must become a means of achieving social change. 'Our universities have become increasingly absorbed into the corporate system,' the Canadian Union of Students charged in 1968. It urged students and faculty members to 'liberate' the institutions in order to secure 'academic freedom and university autonomy.'[32]

The methods adopted in the cause of liberation sometimes ignored due process or the free speech of opponents. An attitude widespread in the student movement was that the virtuous need not respect the rights of sinners. In 1965 the philosopher Herbert Marcuse had denounced as 'repressive' the tolerance shown by the 'liberal university' for dissident views and had preached intolerance of falsehood and evil as he understood them.[33] The argument influenced many student radicals.

Probably the most cogent analysis of the relationship between the student movement and academic freedom came from the pen of Claude Bissell in 1969. He described two distinct but linked groups of 'committed students': the 'extremists,' who saw the university as the 'principal apologist' for a 'hopelessly corrupt' society and who wanted to destroy the institution and recreate it in purified form; and the 'activists,' who believed that the university should be reorganized 'to reflect the opinions and wishes of those who are most closely identified with it.'

Student freedom had traditionally focused on freedom of speech and the freedom to invite speakers to the campus, Bissell continued, but some students sought to give a more positive content to the concept, seeing it as 'the right and the power to make the decisions that shape one's environment.' Since this freedom was held to be possible only in a society of equals, the activists struggled against the superior position of the professor in the classroom, against the evaluation of students, and against the administration.

This student-centred concept clashed with the traditional faculty-centred (or 'guildist') concept of academic freedom, Bissell said. Having only recently wrested from administrators a measure of power over appointments, tenure, and promotion, professors were disinclined to share it with their students: 'This, says the faculty, would destroy the freedom of the teacher in the classroom.' Professors would owe their allegiance not to their disciplines but to fluctuating student fashions. 'I doubt,' commented Bissell, 'whether there will be any easy reconciliation between these two concepts of freedom.'

Although Bissell saw benefits in the students' willingness to experiment and in 'the awakening of an interest in the analysis of the university as an institution,' he feared the 'resolute dogmatism' of the movement as well as its 'conscious or unconscious' attachment to authoritarianism: 'Suspicious of any disinterested emphasis on things of the mind' and ready to use coercion instead of 'reasoned discussion,' the extremists threatened to undermine both the function and the autonomy of the university. 'The irony,' observed Bissell, 'is that the university, by history and inclination, will often tolerate what may ultimately destroy it.'[34]

Two incidents in early 1969 confirmed Bissell's misgivings about student activism. The more destructive one took place at Sir George Williams University, where students ended a 'sit-in' by vandalizing the computer centre. Closer to home was the disruption on 5 February 1969 of a speech by Clark Kerr, former president of the University of California in Berkeley. Student radicals took Kerr's book, *The Uses of the University* (1963), to be a defence of the 'multiversity,' the educational counterpart of bureaucratized corporations and governments. Kerr was also in bad odour because he had presided over Berkeley in 1964, when administrators had tried to suppress the 'Free Speech Movement.' Bissell used the term 'fascism' in describing the disruption of Kerr's speech at the Royal Ontario Museum on that February evening. Three weeks later he sarcastically said of the student radicals, 'Shouting down a guest speaker ... is not hooliganism or ... a denial of free speech; it is confrontation on a high spiritual plane that makes discourse (to use the liturgical word) meaningful.'[35]

Bissell's preference was for the older, faculty-centred version of academic freedom. C.B. Macpherson had a different view. The political theorist's 1969 CAUT presidential address gave considerable credence to student criticism of the liberal university. Traditional defences of the academy as 'a community of scholars' or 'a place of liberty' would prove unavailing, Macpherson said. Professors had to become 'more critically aware' of their own relationship to society and that of their disciplines to it. 'The task is to make the university not just a place for the creation of knowledge, but above all a place for the development of *critical* understanding and critical intellectual ability.' Only in this way would professors be likely to get the best students on their side, and only in this way was there 'likely to be much future for anyone worthy of the name of professor.'

Macpherson linked the future of the student movement to the response it might elicit 'from those outside the universities who feel equally impotent or threatened by ... the corporate and technological structure of power in modern society.' Yet a general revolt against a business society would be 'a very long-run affair.' In the impatience this might breed he saw grave danger to the university. Students who hoped to use their assault on the academy as a means of increasing public resistance to corporate power might intensify their attack on the university. In response to this, warned Macpherson, neither permissiveness nor calling in the police was likely to be effective. The defence of the university was 'a political matter in the broadest sense' and required a slogan. 'The slogan of liberty has served us well for a century, but it has lost its magic,' he said. Only a 'critical university' would be able to survive the radical onslaught.[36]

Were the CAUT's members impressed by Macpherson's address? Certainly, some were critical in his sense of the word, but a larger group had no inclination to be. And if any of the radical students were aware of Macpherson's speech, they probably concluded that he was more interested in preserving the university as a centre of learning than in using it to promote social change.

Macpherson's colleague, the Milton scholar Ernest Sirluck, warned late in 1969 against using the university to promote change. Institutional neutrality, he said, had become 'one of the distinguishing marks of the modern university, which was enabled thereby to develop the doctrine of academic freedom: an atmosphere tolerant of, and providing an opportunity for, variant and conflicting viewpoints and every form of intellectually responsible criticism and persuasion, all premised on the postulate that the university itself would remain permanently free from all commitment except to its own procedures.' The detachment was not always perfect, Sirluck noted; in 'times of upheaval universities often forget, or are forced to put aside, their neutrality.' But mostly they had been faithful to it. The demand was now heard that the university declare its opposition to 'the military-industrial complex,' the market economy, or Canadian complicity in the Vietnam War. This would be a mistake. Such declarations might lead governments to reduce institutional autonomy and that in turn would weaken the freedom of professors. 'University commitments to social and political positions are not consistent with academic freedom.'[37]

By the time Sirluck made his speech, the student movement was in retreat. Even where it had been strongest – at McGill, Toronto, Simon Fraser, and York University's Glendon College – it showed little staying power. There were still occasional disturbances (for instance, the disruption at McGill in 1970 of a speech by a scholar said to be implicated in the Vietnam war, and at the University of Toronto of a lecture by an allegedly racist visiting professor in 1974), but the turmoil predicted by Macpherson did not take place. Repudiated by most students, the movement rapidly subsided.[38]

For all its evanescence, the movement did end the parental role of universities and helped to give students a measure of influence in university government which they had not previously possessed. Student membership on faculty councils, senates, and their committees (and, at many institutions also on governing boards), once hard to imagine, became almost universal.

In addition, the student movement put the academic freedom of students squarely on the agenda of Canadian universities. In the nineteenth-century German university, *Lehrfreiheit*, the freedom to teach, had found its counterpart in *Lernfreiheit*, 'the absence of administrative coercions in the learning situation.' Students chose how, where, and with whom they would study, and took whatever time they needed in preparing for the *Staatsexamen*, the state-set examination. They lived in private quarters, their personal lives beyond university supervision. Walter P. Metzger writes, 'To the university student, coming from the strict and formal *Gymnasium*, *Lernfreiheit* was a precious privilege, a recognition of his arrival at man's estate.'[39]

Although *Lehrfreiheit* had influenced the North American idea of academic freedom, *Lernfreiheit* had had no significant effect on this side of the Atlantic. It was incompatible with a tradition that placed administrators *in loco parentis* over students. North American students, moreover, did not enjoy the mobility among universities enjoyed by their German counterparts. No indigenous concept of academic freedom for students had developed because students were not part of the communities of competence that were basic to the North American idea of academic freedom. The authors of the AAUP's 1915 report on academic freedom and academic tenure wrote, 'It need scarcely be pointed out that the freedom which is the object of this report is that of the teacher.' When the CAUT enunciated its statement on academic freedom, it, too, excluded students. Northrop Frye's attitude was probably shared by other Canadian professors: students had no claim to academic freedom because they lacked the knowledge necessary to make informed judgments.[40]

But if the concept of academic freedom was not thought to apply to students, they did at times seek freedom of expression, including the right to criticize professors, the curriculum, and the administration of the university. As early as 1883 the University of Toronto's *Varsity* had deplored the lack of intellectual freedom enjoyed by students and had called for reforms.[41] On occasion, too, students exerted themselves on behalf of professors who had fallen foul of presidents or governing boards, and over the years student newspapers and student clubs were sources of anxiety for more than one university president.

The reason for long denying freedom to students was twofold. One reflected the parental role assumed by universities. The other was akin to the reason for trying to limit the academic freedom of the faculty – its exercise might prompt criticism from outsiders and undermine financial support. If boards and presidents often saw professors as employees to be kept in line, they usually regarded students as adolescents who should be seen and not heard. In arguing (in 1936) that universities should not try to control student speech, or student behaviour *outside* the university, Stephen Leacock was very much in the minority.[42]

The student movement virtually ended the capacity of university authorities to control students as they had long done. By the early 1970s, campus publications and clubs enjoyed an unprecedented freedom of expression and action, and the parental role was dead. Among the results was one that had been feared: student fractiousness helped bring about a decline of public support for the universities. The movement's impact on the academic freedom of professors is more problematic than its role in securing a large measure of freedom for students. The dogmatism of many student leaders had a negative though not perhaps long-lasting effect, but their distrust of the stance of disinterestedness still casts a shadow. Political correctness has surely been influenced by it.

As well, evaluation of courses and faculty has had an effect on academic freedom. Student-run course evaluations antedated the student movement. The University of Victoria, for example, had one in 1963 (I was its editor-in-chief). However, only as students became more disposed to judge those in positions of authority – a development fostered by the student movement – did evaluations become common. The purposes varied: encouraging faculty to improve their teaching or make their courses more 'relevant' (a student-movement buzzword); guiding students towards useful or informative courses; or alerting them to entertaining or easy-grading professors.

In the 1970s the reliability and validity of evaluation became a subject of scholarly research as well as heated debate. One concern was that students might unfairly damage professors' reputations and even their careers. In 1977 the CAUT sponsored the publication of a volume of essays, *If Teaching Is Important*, whose authors were on balance supportive of course evaluations but pointed out that many questionnaires were of low quality and that, in seeking to force changes in course content, some kinds of evaluation menaced academic freedom in the classroom. Addressing the relationship between course evaluations and academic freedom, the psychologist Christopher Knapper wrote, 'It is impossible to find an easy way of reconciling [the] varying demands for teaching excellence and academic freedom.' He proposed procedural safeguards to ensure that evaluation data were not used unfairly, and he endorsed the CAUT's view that 'evaluation proceedings must have strong faculty involvement [in] planning, administration, and interpretation of results.'[43]

The widespread use of evaluations may owe less to their effectiveness in identifying and encouraging good teaching than to their appeal as a low-cost way of monitoring faculty performance. Peter Seldin wrote in 1984, 'Since student ratings are easy to administer and score, they are in popular use today for personnel decisions. Unfortunately, they are also widely abused. There can be no doubt that student ratings are an important element in evaluating teaching effectiveness. But ... [they] are only part of the whole.'

A survey carried out by John Damron indicates that many North American institutions rely on student ratings as their sole source of information about teaching. Another psychologist, Thomas E. Haskell, writes that the student-as-consumer, seeking entertainment and high grades, threatens both the quality of instruction and the academic freedom of instructors, particularly in universities that rely on student evaluations for decisions about academic careers. The threat is real, though it may have been mitigated by a recent arbitration dealing with a tenure denial at York University; in the case of Nancy Nicol, the arbitrators ruled in early 1998 that anonymous student criticism of a professor must not be part of a tenure or promotion file.[44]

Faculty unionization, scarcely thought of in 1965, was becoming commonplace ten years later. Today the majority of Canadian universities have faculty unions. The consequences for academic freedom are still under debate.

Unhappiness with low salaries and with existing forms of bargaining led faculty associations at Alberta and UBC to explore unionization in the 1940s. Neither initiative went far. Professors tended strongly to the view that unions were both unprofessional and inconsistent with the social status of the professoriate. W.L. Morton wrote in 1964 that it would be a 'tragedy' if the CAUT 'should cease to be a professional organization concerned with all matters pertinent to advanced teaching and research, and become purely an agency for collective bargaining.' That local associations might unionize seems not to have occurred to him.[45]

The Duff-Berdahl Report did not mention faculty unions. Discussing collective bargaining in 1968, an economist at York University, Albert J. Robinson, asked whether the 'loss of professional status and of the informal atmosphere of the university community' would be compensated for by 'significant gains in salaries and other material benefits.' Probably not, he answered: the demand for faculty was likely to remain strong and the outlook for salaries to remain good.[46]

Robinson's report, which appeared in the *CAUT Bulletin*, probably reinforced professors in the belief that unionization had little to recommend it. Within a few years, though, some of them were changing their minds. In the early 1970s the willingness of governments to spend money in the public sector declined. Ontario's minister of colleges and universities, John White, said in March 1971 that where postsecondary education was concerned, the government wanted 'more scholar for the dollar.'[47] Other Canadian (and American) jurisdictions adopted the same policy at much the same time. By 1972 the shortage of qualified academics had turned into a surplus as funding cuts began to bite.

In the early 1970s, too, public outrage prompted by the excesses of the student movement exposed the universities to fierce criticism. A report prepared for the Committee of Presidents of Universities of Ontario and published in 1971 cited media stories indicating that 'the attitude of the public at large to the universities of Ontario [was] entirely hostile,' and that although 'expressions of editorial outrage were for a time directed mainly against university students and university presidents,' it was now the professors who were under fire. Most people, when attacked, will defend themselves. The CAUT executive established a collective bargaining committee in 1971. That same year, the faculty of the Université du Québec opted for unionization.[48]

In 1972 university enrolments in Canada fell for the first time in two decades. This compounded the effects of financial cutbacks, so that tenure quotas and faculty redundancies suddenly appeared as possibilities. By 1973 faculty of the

Universities of Sherbrooke and Montreal were unionizing, with Laval and Manitoba, as well as Notre Dame University in Nelson, British Columbia, close behind. That year, too, the CAUT beat off a challenge from the Canadian Union of Public Employees, which some St Mary's University professors had invited to organize them into a bargaining unit. Faculty at St Thomas and Carleton universities began the process of certification in 1974, while professors at Ottawa and York followed suit a year later.[49]

Budgetary cutbacks and threats to faculty jobs were not the only reasons for unionization. Another was an autocratic administrative style, which was particularly noticeable in institutions that had until recently been under Catholic control. The example of faculty unions in the United States also played a part.[50]

By no means all professors welcomed unionization. The biologist J. Gordin Kaplan warned in his 1971 CAUT presidential address that unions might weaken university autonomy and academic freedom, might be incompatible with faculty participation in university government, might be no more effective than existing faculty associations in securing salary increases and improved benefits, and, finally, might be 'to some extent incompatible with our ideal of the liberal university.'[51] By and large, unionization had little appeal in professional faculties and not a great deal more among scientists. It was mainly professors in the humanities and social sciences, who, feeling more threatened by cutbacks, tended to the view that a collective agreement under a provincial labour relations code offered better protection than a voluntary agreement that might not have the force of law – a view influenced by the 1970 Supreme Court of British Columbia ruling in the Wheeldon case.

Grass-roots support for unionization encouraged the CAUT's officers to take a positive view of it. After all, academic freedom and tenure could be enshrined in collective agreements. Typical were the comments made in 1974 by the chairman of the CAUT collective bargaining committee, the biochemist Charles Bigelow: 'Certification is compatible with the traditional values of the academic profession ... Benefits can be gained with no undesirable restrictions in the professional freedom of the members.'[52]

That has been the received CAUT view for a quarter of a century. But not everyone agrees with it. The Dalhousie political scientist David M. Cameron has argued that although 'it cannot be said that unionization and collective bargaining are necessarily antithetical to academic freedom,' it docs seem to be the case that 'full-blown unionization, collective bargaining, and the right to strike do stand in potential conflict with the principles upon which academic freedom has come to rest.'[53]

As evidence, Cameron cites the unwillingness of faculty unions to monitor and assess the performance of their members and to make comparisons among them for the purpose of awarding salary increases based on merit. The academic freedom that he believes to be in danger from the unwillingness to draw distinctions is essentially the freedom offered within the research university. 'The scholar,' he writes, 'earns the right to academic freedom by dint of an unremitting commitment to scholarship as the surest path to truth (and conversely, the university sustains that commitment to scholarship through the institution of tenure). Abandon scholarship ... and the case for academic freedom collapses, and with it tenure.' And the results of that scholarship, of course, must be assessed by one's peers.[54]

The idea of 'communities of competence,' enunciated early in the century by the AAUP, may lose its meaning if faculty unions are unwilling to make comparisons among their members. At the same time, though, schemes intended to reward merit can be disruptive – all of us are more likely to recognize merit in ourselves and our close associates than in others – and may not produce the desired results in improved performance.[55] Beyond this, if faculty unions really are a threat to academic freedom, then the main causes of unionization – budget cuts and autocratic administrations – should be part of the discussion.

The added protection for academic freedom and tenure that came with their entrenchment in agreements between faculty associations and governing boards, and later in collective agreements, should have increased the willingness of professors to embark on bold research projects and to speak their minds freely. Doubtless it did so in some cases. On the whole, however, Canadian academics continued to be a timid crew.

The Dalhousie philosopher David Braybrooke wrote in 1972, 'The most serious complaint that the public has against professors in the matter of tenure is not that professors should not have it, but that having it they should not use their special freedom more frequently and more vigorously.' Five years later, the University of Toronto historian Desmond Morton cited the 'unpractised virtues of courage and solidarity,' adding that professors were averse to taking a stand even in self-defence. Most academics were as reluctant as ever to do or say the daring or unpopular thing, to stand out in any but conventional ways.[56] And they still are.

The professionalization of disciplines since the 1950s has reinforced the tendency to diffidence.[57] By the 1970s, many academics were writing in specialized languages and publishing in periodicals inaccessible to the general reader. For example, the *Canadian Journal of Economics and Political Science*, founded in 1935 as a quarterly whose contributors and readers included not only economists, political scientists, and historians, but also journalists, politicians, and public servants, split in two in 1967. Most of the articles in economics were already unreadable by nonspecialists; soon not a few contributions to the new *Canadian Journal of Political Science* were similarly opaque. Although some scholarly periodicals, such as *Canadian Public Policy* and *International Journal*, have continued to address the informed general reader, many academics prefer to write for their fellow specialists alone. Unread by nonacademics, they are also largely ignored by them.

Ignoring academics comes easily to the media. A few 'stars' appear as regular commentators, and Nobel Prize winners such as John Polanyi and Michael Smith can command attention, but when other professors speak, few outside academe (and not many inside) listen. The contrast with the sort of attention given in the 1930s even to junior faculty members – Eugene Forsey, Eric Havelock, and E.W.R. Steacie come to mind – is remarkable.

An explanation for the change is beyond this book's scope. Perhaps, however, the technique adopted towards Frank Scott by the *Montreal Star* in the 1940s has been copied by other editors in dealing with people of whose views they disapprove. In the 1930s the *Star* occasionally sought to controvert Scott, but a new editor abandoned this path. Instead, the newspaper ceased to refer to Scott, to cover his activities and speeches, or to print his letters.[58] This neutralized the law professor far more effectively than any number of attacks on him and his ideas. Once out of the media eye, of course, academics are apt to escape notice altogether. This may irritate some of them. It certainly annoyed Scott, who responded by publishing a rude bit of doggerel aimed at the *Star*. But obscurity increases the sense of safety felt by others.

One challenge to academic freedom that has received considerable attention in recent years and has intimidated some professors is political correctness (PC). The terms 'politically correct' and 'political correctness' had their North American origins in the radical social movements of the late 1960s, including elements of the student movement. According to the sociologist Lorna Weir, in the 1970s and 1980s the term was most often used in feminist circles, with PC coming to mean 'rigidity and self-righteousness, the humourless enforcement of an orthodoxy that results in factionalism,' while its opposite, 'political incorrectness,' came to be linked to 'diversity, art, imagination, wildness, and transgression.'[59] PC was also used more widely – generally to describe the real or alleged influence of leftists in the media and the arts.

In 1990 and 1991 a few American and Canadian writers began to identify PC with an assault on traditional values and practices in education, especially higher education. Articles describing and denouncing a new orthodoxy that was allegedly threatening academic freedom appeared in the *New York Times, Time, Newsweek, Atlantic*, the *New Republic*, and *Maclean's*.[60]

A graduate student in philosophy and former journalist, Mark Kingwell, took a more measured view of PC, describing its agenda as 'ultimately reactionary' and its politics as 'superficial'; and at the end of 1991, the playwright and newspaper columnist Rick Salutin put the matter in perspective: 'The reality of political correctness is minuscule compared to the orgy of media attention – the overkill – launched in its name.' The historian Russell Jacoby makes a similar point in *Dogmatic Wisdom* (1994), a book that exposes the excesses on both sides in the 'culture wars.'[61]

The threat that PC poses to academic freedom has been exaggerated, but this does not mean that no threat exists. The attempt to limit debate and confine teaching, research, and publication to nonthreatening topics has a history longer than academic freedom itself. In this sense, PC has always been with us. However, some radical and postmodern critics identified with PC go well beyond this, arguing that the disinterested pursuit of knowledge is a chimera, that arguments about knowledge are really struggles about power and its distribution in the academy and society, and that academic freedom lacks autonomous value and is no more than a weapon or shield to be used in power struggles.[62]

Media attention has focused less on such ideas, which may justifiably be described as subversive of academic life, than on the activities of groups that have sought to limit discussion by objecting to language and practices held to be racist, sexist, homophobic, and the like. PC has also been associated with the effort to adapt the university and the idea of academic freedom to the needs of groups that have long been powerless.

To some scholars, the traditional view of academic freedom is 'androcentric, eurocentric, and heterocentric.' In a paper first presented in 1993 and published in amended form two years later, two social scientists, Janice Drakich and Marilyn Taylor, and a law professor, Jennifer Bankier, argue that 'academic freedom *is* the inclusive university,' one that makes room for people who were for many years marginalized or even excluded altogether. The authors acknowledge that 'the principle of academic freedom is central to the highest purposes of the university and, ultimately, a democratic society,' but they see 'two major limitations in the current interpretation ...: (1) its emphasis on individual actions to the exclusion of attention to their context or social, institutional relationships; and (2) its emphasis entirely on intellect to the exclusion of other human dimensions – identities, emotions, and feelings.'

The first of these, they write, ignores the historic advantages that white, heterosexual, able-bodied men have enjoyed, fails to acknowledge imbalances of power 'in relations based on gender, race, sexuality, class, and other dimensions of difference,' and 'tends to perpetuate the exclusion of traditionally disadvantaged groups through curriculum, pedagogy, and social behaviour.' The second limitation assumes that 'reality [is] exclusively made up of ideas and ... people [are] disconnected intellects.' This 'masculinist' view fosters 'a competitive, confrontational style that seeks to establish/entrench power imbalances without regard for the "other" in the discourse.'

Bankier and her associates propose as a remedy that professors 'communicate respect, sensitivity, understanding, and tolerance ..., along with the intellectual content. These qualities, in the context of civility, are essential features of community.' But what if professors nevertheless insist on speaking freely? 'Should all "verbal behaviour," such as words in a classroom, automatically be protected by the concept of academic freedom?' The authors do not think so: 'We would argue that the answer is no. Words cease to be an expression of academic freedom when they have an effect that interferes with the academic freedom of other people, repressing, constraining, or prohibiting scholarship or inquiry.' Respect *must* be shown for the opinions and values of others.

This 'is particularly important,' they say, 'if the listeners are a captive audience, as students are.' Adopting a style 'that abuses or marginalizes others is a behavioural choice, and not a matter of intellectual right.' Academic freedom must be based on reciprocity. Difficult material should be presented 'in a way that does not disempower or demean' anyone, and with 'an explicit acknowledgment of its potential for disruption and a sound rationale for its inclusion in the course to justify its disturbing consequences.' Ideas can be presented 'in a clear and effective fashion that nevertheless [sic] reflects respect for the values and perspectives of other people involved in the discussion.'[63]

But will good faith, civility, and clarity forestall unfounded complaints or ensure that these will be rejected when registered? Not if people dislike what they hear or read, be it stated with ever so much respect for others' values, and not if the assumption is that when someone feels offended, some sort of offence has therefore been committed. Bankier and her associates tend to this view. It is more clearly present in the report by a lawyer, Joan McEwen, who was asked to investigate charges of racism and sexism made by some students against members of UBC's political science department in 1992. McEwen's report, the sociologist Patricia Marchak comments, 'made no claims to truth – indeed, she explicitly informed readers that it mattered not whether the claims were true; it was enough that the complainants believed them to be true.' Marchak writes that this stance partakes of postmodernist thought. Whether Bankier and her associates place themselves in this camp is unclear. However, insofar as they allow the effect of words to determine their meaning and intent, they do weaken academic freedom.[64]

More directly concerned with research than Drakich, Taylor, and Bankier is the psychologist Cannie Stark-Adamec, who argued in 1990 that some kinds of research should be regarded as an abuse of academic freedom, and that research perceived to be sexist or racist should be restricted or even proscribed.[65] In the absence of clear-cut, generally agreed-upon definitions of sexism and racism, conflict seems inevitable.

When PC is under discussion, a handful of controversies come easily to mind. Philippe Rushton (psychology, Western Ontario), Matin Yaqzan (mathematics, UNB), and Gordon Freeman (chemistry, Alberta) are well known examples of professors whose opinions stirred up a storm. Rushton's observations about comparative racial characteristics (which were prompted by his scholarly interests) and Yaqzan's about date rape (which were not) led to calls for their dismissal – in Rushton's case, by none other than Ontario's premier David Peterson. Freeman's allegations about the ill effects that mothers working outside the home had on their children led to a demand for the retroactive censorship of a scientific journal into which he had managed to insert an article setting forth his views. If the controversies suggested to outsiders that weird opinions are rife in the academy, some of the responses to Rushton, Yaqzan, and Freeman from within the universities may have contributed to this assessment.[66]

In fact, although the proportion of people with unusual opinions may (and should) be higher in the universities than elsewhere, it is low among academics who contribute regularly to the public discussion of social, political, and economic issues. David Bercuson, Michael Bliss, Barry Cooper, Thomas Courchene, John Crispo, and Mark Kingwell, for example, usually express opinions that, whatever else may be said of them, seem unlikely to offend many Canadians, and certainly not influential ones.

It is not always easy, of course, to predict what will offend and who will be offended. An example was provided by the 'Out of Africa' exhibition at the Royal Ontario Museum in 1989–90. Its ironic treatment of the missionaries and military men who went to Africa in the nineteenth century might have been expected to offend their descendants. Instead, some members of Ontario's Afro-Canadian communities held the exhibition to be patronizing towards Africans and racist in effect if not intent. In the fall of 1990 some people disrupted the classes of the curator, the anthropologist Jeanne Cannizzo, at Scarborough College, University of Toronto. The university's governing council, the University of Toronto Faculty Association, and the CAUT spoke out in Cannizzo's defence, but she was nevertheless driven to apply for sick leave.[67]

Whatever one may have thought of the exhibition, it is not permissible to try to settle a difference of interpretation or opinion by using the heckler's veto in the classroom. Yet some academics were apparently afraid to say so. Cannizzo's husband, the historian David Stafford, wrote in 1992: 'When several professors at U of T were asked by CBC radio to comment on Jeanne's harassment in the classroom, *not one* agreed to speak! "Too sensitive," they said.'[68] The mildew of discretion lies heavy on some professors still.

That cannot be said of the Society for Academic Freedom and Scholarship (SAFS).[69] Its executive has defended the academic freedom and free speech of academics such as Cannizzo, Rushton, and Yaqzan, and more recently of the University of Waterloo sociologist Kenneth Westhues.

Charged in 1996 with having made 'racist arguments' in class, Westhues was 'convicted' by a university ethics committee. The university's provost over-turned this decision but imposed his own punishment for a breach of confidence allegedly committed by Westhues in the course of defending himself against the original charge. He was cleared two years later, with an award for costs sustained, by an outside arbitrator who was strongly critical of Waterloo's speech code.[70]

Perhaps the foremost example of PC in Canada was a policy statement that came from Ontario's Ministry of Education and Training in 1993. Its title was *Framework regarding Harassment and Discrimination in Ontario Universities and Colleges*, but it quickly became known as the 'Zero-Tolerance document' because 'zero tolerance' was to be shown to harassment. This was defined as anything that was 'known or might reasonably be known to be offensive, hostile, and inappropriate' where gender, race, ethnic or religious origin, sexual preference, or disability was concerned. The document did not limit harassment to specific actions but held that it could be 'systemic,' creating a 'negative environment for individuals or groups.' Jokes, taunts, offensive comments and gestures, and displays of materials could create this environment; so could 'exposure to graffiti, signs, cartoons, remarks, exclusion, adverse treatment related to one or more of the prohibited grounds,' books used in class or located in the library, and exhibitions of art. Complainants did not need to feel personally targeted in order to object to what they felt to be a negative environment.[71]

Where the universities were concerned, the document was soon a dead letter, for the minister of education, Dave Cooke, denied any intention to impose it on autonomous institutions. (Lacking both autonomy and a tradition of academic freedom, the colleges of applied arts and technology quickly came to heel.) However, ideas and attitudes expressed in the document have found their way into the speech codes and harassment policies that have been adopted by a number of universities, which have acquired bureaucracies charged with preventing, monitoring, and investigating instances of alleged harassment or discrimination.[72]

Doubtless, harassment takes place on campus, and when it is identified it should be ended and, where appropriate, punished. Some of the harassment, though, is meted out by harassment officers. As civil libertarians such as Sandra Martin, Kay Stockholder, and Margaret Wente have pointed out, due process does not always rank high in the investigations that take place. A particularly egregious abuse of due process occurred in 1991–2 at the University of Western Ontario, where a student unhappy with his grade accused a Spanish professor, Marjorie Ratcliffe, of racial harassment. The evidence was of the flimsiest kind, but it took five months before an external adjudicator dismissed the charge and another nine before UWO agreed to pay Ratcliffe's legal expenses. Describing the case in his book *Moral Panic* (1994), John Fekete noted that Western's president had not yet apologized to Ratcliffe and that the university's race-relations officer was 'unrepentant.'[73]

Fekete discusses several other instances of abuse of due process by harassment officers, whose *déformation professionelle* leads some of them to assume, when a complaint reaches them, that an offence has been committed. It may seem exaggerated to describe the resulting atmosphere as 'velvet totalitarianism,' a phrase coined by the University of Toronto psychologist and former SAFS president John Furedy. But if speech and harassment codes seem unlikely to prevent all discussion of sensitive issues, they are nevertheless more than likely to discourage a good many academics from broaching such issues in the first place.[74]

What some people experience as a vigorous and bracing intellectual climate, others may find disagreeably chilly. Meanwhile, mutual forbearance and civility are often in short supply. The consequence is a certain amount of petty and not so petty sniping and an occasional full-scale battle of the kind that a few years ago came close to paralysing UBC's political science department.[75] In such an environment, academic freedom is greatly at risk.

The question remains, Whose freedom? Those who hold the traditional view argue that trying to censor and control what people say and do unacceptably restricts their academic freedom. Critics of the traditional view argue that any speech or action that offends members of historically disadvantaged groups may have the effect of silencing members of such groups and thereby undermines *their* academic freedom.

I adhere to the traditional view. Universities are not repositories of approved ideas and attitudes; they do not exist primarily to make people feel intellectually or emotionally 'at home.' And although civility is important, academics owe a loyalty to something more important yet; they must commit themselves to the search for knowledge and truth *as they see it*.

Benno Schmidt, a former president of Yale University, states, 'The university [is] not a place, first and foremost, that is about the inculcation of thought [and] habits of mind that I might agree are correct and constructive. The university ...

is a place where people have to have the right to speak the unspeakable and think the unthinkable and challenge the unchallengeable.'[76] Granted, some professors fail to do these things. But take away their right to do so, and you undermine the academic freedom and, indeed, the usefulness of all.

Universities must protect academic freedom. Occasionally this may mean putting up with ideas and opinions that seem obnoxious, foolish, or dead wrong. All students, faculty members, and other university workers have a right to be free from *personal* harassment, but this right does not extend to banning actions or censoring forms of expression that are not actionable in law.

The University of British Columbia has witnessed more than one controversy involving some form of PC. In the mid-1990s the Chair of Punjabi Language, Literature, and Sikh Studies was embroiled in serious conflict. Established in the 1980s, the chair was funded in part from the income of an endowment of $700,000, half of it donated by Sikhs and half by the federal Department of Citizenship and Multiculturalism. Unhappiness with the historian Harjot Oberoi, appointed to the chair in 1987, arose in the Sikh community early during his tenure. It grew after the publication of his book *The Construction of Religious Boundaries: Culture, Identity, and Diversity in the Sikh Tradition* (1994). The work prompted charges that Oberoi had misrepresented the history of Sikhism, and there were demands that UBC either set him straight or remove him from his post.[77]

A spokesperson for UBC insisted that the university had received the money without strings attached and could not allow the Sikh community to influence academic policy. All the same, Oberoi resigned the chair two years later and transferred to another department. His course on the history of Sikhism was dropped. 'His retreat ... may be celebrated as another victory for Sikh fundamentalists, who pushed the University of Toronto to discontinue its Sikh Studies program a few years ago,' the *Globe and Mail*'s Robert Matas commented.[78]

The belief that paying the piper entitles one to call the tune is not new. It has particular significance for funded chairs or programs. Where the belief is linked to the conviction that people have a right not to be exposed to ideas they find offensive, the threat to academic freedom is particularly potent.

No greater challenge currently faces academic freedom than the growing dominance of what the political scientist and public law teacher H.T. Wilson has called 'economic correctness.'[79] It ranges from demands that universities become more businesslike to the insistence that they become fully market-driven.

Reductions in government per-student funding have led Canadian university authorities to try to raise more money from the business community and forge closer relations with it. One result was the founding in 1983 of the Corporate–Higher Education Forum, consisting mainly of university heads and corporate CEO's. In 1984 the forum's executive committee transmitted a commissioned report to the forum's membership. Written by two private-sector economists, Judith Maxwell and Stephanie Currie, *Partnership for Growth* sought to 'provide information on the present scope of corporate-university collaboration in Canada,' to 'define the motivation for, and benefits of, that collaboration,' and to 'help to identify a relevant agenda for the Forum's ongoing work.' A covering letter from the executive committee stated that although members did not necessarily endorse all of the report's analysis and conclusions, they viewed it 'as an important contribution to public knowledge about the evolution of the corporate-academic relationship and its potential contribution to the successful adaptation of the Canadian economy to the challenges of international competition and rapid technological change.'[80]

A four-page 'executive summary' makes all the document's essential points: Corporations need 'access to leading-edge knowledge, products, processes and services to compete in the world markets of the 1990s'; they also need high-quality graduates as new employees, and 'access to continuing education to upgrade the skills of existing employees.' Universities need money for faculty renewal, for new equipment and facilities, as well as 'access to corporations' awareness of current market trends to guide research and education' so that 'the research effort and the university curriculum' may be tuned 'more closely to the needs of the marketplace.' In the past, the bonds between the corporations and the universities 'were weakened by federal and provincial support for university education and by academic antagonism to the corporate community.' More recently, the universities' financial need has meant that 'the corporate-academic relationship is becoming more extensive and intimate' in research and to a lesser extent in teaching. But barriers persist, namely, the 'cultural differences' between the two communities and 'a lack of financial or special managerial resources.'

Of these two, the cultural differences touch directly on academic freedom, though Maxwell and Currie do not use this term. They do write that the differences reflect 'the different values, expectations, and mode of operation of the two types of institutions. The university is oriented towards the extension and transmission of knowledge. Freedom of communication and publication are at the heart of the research process. The operating environment is intended to be creative and self-paced, and faculty members have some discretion over the selection and management of their research.' In other words, academic freedom is a central university value.

Corporate values are very different. Efficiency and profitability in delivering a product, process, or service are the key concerns: 'Research is oriented towards the development and commercialization of new and improved products and processes. Deadlines and reporting milestones are part of the routine, and proprietory rights are closely guarded in order to obtain a competitive edge in the marketplace.'

In *The Higher Learning in America* (1918), a book still well worth reading, Thorstein Veblen put the matter thus: The differences 'reduce themselves in the main to a question between the claims of science and scholarship on the one hand and those of business principles and pecuniary gain on the other hand.' Professors want the freedom to pursue knowledge and their vision of truth; capitalists want the freedom to acquire and accumulate productive property.[81]

Successful corporate-academic collaboration, Maxwell and Currie continue, requires the reconciliation of the cultural differences, the promotion of mutual understanding, the breaking down of institutional rigidities, and openness towards each other. Whose values will dominate? The authors do not ask this question, but we may infer an answer from the following:

The nature and scope of corporate-academic collaboration will be determined by the needs of the corporation and by the areas of expertise that a university can offer ... Universities must confront the financial squeeze head-on with a strategic plan for the 1990's. The strategic plan should define the university's mission, select areas of specialization, identify ways to build managerial flexibility and to open up to collaboration with key corporations and with local industry.

Corporations must recognize that self-interest should motivate collaboration and 'must define the need for collaboration in terms of the corporate mission.' If all this is achieved, say the authors, both corporations and universities will benefit, as will Canada as a whole.

Neither in their executive summary nor in a subsequent section on 'issues and problems' do Maxwell and Currie squarely face the fact that one set of values trumps the other, and that the corporations hold the high cards. The evasion is understandable. However eager they are to garner corporate support, university heads would not want to see it baldly stated that their institutions will get money at the cost of subverting academic freedom.

The AUCC publication *University Affairs* did not review the report, and a one-page summary written by the editor, Gloria Pierre, offered little analysis and no evaluation. The report's central and highly dubious assumption – that the differences between the two value systems 'can be reconciled without compromising each group's values' – was recorded without comment. In contrast, a review by Janice Newson and Howard Buchbinder in the *CAUT Bulletin* pointed out that academic freedom and institutional autonomy would have to be sacrificed in order to make cooperation work along the lines envisaged in *Partnership for Growth*.[82]

The Corporate–Higher Education Forum issued several further studies, on subjects such as research and development, funding the universities, and international business education. These documents, as well as proposed linkages between the corporations and the universities, received generally favourable coverage in *University Affairs*. A rare note of criticism was sounded by Robert G. Weyant, dean of general studies at the University of Calgary, who warned in 1986 that administrators were adopting 'a whole body of corporate jargon and corporate values.' It was 'disconcerting,' he wrote, to watch administrators who had quite properly resisted interference by provincial governments rush 'into relationships with private corporations, apparently with little thought being given to the loss of autonomy that these relationships may involve.'[83]

Despite the efforts of the Corporate–Higher Education Forum, doubts apparently persisted in the business community about the universities' ability to change. In 1987 a committee of the Canadian Manufacturers' Association prepared a strategy paper that assessed the negative effects of funding cuts on the role of universities in 'revitalizing the economy' and complained that 'institutional rigidities' (unspecified) did not allow them 'to respond to rapidly changing economic and competitive conditions.' The report urged CMA members to 'use their contacts and involvement with post-secondary institutions to emphasize the need for a more rationalized, efficient system of higher education.' In order to give universities 'a sharper focus and purpose,' they needed the application of 'some of the practices of business management and free enterprise.'[84]

Hampered by institutional rigidities such as collegial decision-making, tenure, and academic freedom, universities continued to respond sluggishly to the requirements of the new age. Was it this that led Douglas Auld, a public-finance economist and president of Loyalist College in Belleville, Ontario, to argue in 1996 that the universities should be deregulated? 'Reform is necessary,' he wrote, 'to inject a spirit of creativity and "paradigm shift" into universities. This can best be accomplished by removing the barriers to entry into higher education and by either returning the delivery of education and research to the private sector – that is, privatizing universities – or at least introducing a stronger measure of market economies into their management.'

With public financial support likely to decline further, said Auld, universities must 'improve productivity and lower costs.' They should eliminate weak programs that cannot be fixed without spending additional money. Ancillary services such as parking lots, residences, and athletic centres should be outsourced. Research should be privately funded. New forms of 'technologically mediated instruction' should be used to secure reductions in faculty positions and salary costs. (Auld does not mention cuts in administration.) Better performance indicators should be introduced so that teaching and research loads can be reallocated with a view to improved efficiency.[85]

More recently, the Toronto Board of Trade – believing that a government-appointed advisory panel, chaired by Queen's Principal Emeritus David C. Smith and charged with outlining future directions for higher education in Ontario, 'did not fully meet the expectations of the business community' – commissioned a random survey of 336 of its 10,000-plus members. The result was *Beyond the Status Quo* (1998), a 'business perspective on enhancing postsecondary education.'

Although the status quo is 'untenable,' the report asserts, change in the universities and colleges has been neither 'rapid nor thorough enough to respond to the other major changes in our society.' Revolutionary change is needed if Canada is to compete in a global marketplace. Having become 'critically dependent on a skilled, adaptable and creative workforce,' Canadians 'need to ensure [that] all facets of our postsecondary education system are responsive [to] and supportive of this need.[86]

Among the report's recommendations are the development of a set of performance indicators (mentioned are student satisfaction and the employment rate of graduates), the elimination of program duplication, an end to tenure, tuition-fee deregulation, the encouragement of both for-profit and non-profit private universities, and the introduction of 'leading-edge instructional technology initiatives.' The details are less important than the underlying message, which is restated in the report's conclusion: 'Postsecondary education is vital to a competitive society ... Business has a vested interest in our universities and colleges. It cannot compete globally without the skills and knowledge produced in these institutions.'[87] The reader infers that if the universities fail to meet the needs of business, they will have failed indeed.

The call for universities that collaborate with and serve business is related to but distinct from the decades-old demand that they teach useful skills. 'It's the people's money, dear Maria, and don't you forget it,' John Parlabane says in *The Rebel Angels*, 'and the people, those infallible judges of value, must have what they want, and what they think they want (because the politicians tell them so) is people who can fill useful jobs.' Although their role has rarely been and should not be limited to that task, the universities have long prepared people for the world of work. And in spite of Parlabane's sarcasm, the attitude he identifies does signal that the institutions have a part to play in serving society's wants as well as needs.

An excessive vocationalism, the pursuit of useful skills at the expense of other goals, threatens academic freedom; Second World War attitudes to the humanities and social sciences come to mind. No less dangerous, though, is the current tendency to defer to the wishes of the corporate world. This threatens a fundamental university objective, one that academic freedom is meant to protect, namely, the disinterested pursuit of knowledge.

In his 1995 Massey Lectures for the CBC, published as *The Unconscious Civilization*, John Ralston Saul identifies a courtier class that presents the 'corporatist' world view as the only one worth taking seriously. This message, he writes, is disseminated by 'the disciples of market forces, the courtiers of neo-conservatism and, of particular importance, the authoritative voices of the social science academics,' notably, economists and professors of business administration. 'The universities are in crisis and are attempting to ride out the storm by aligning themselves with various corporatist interests,' Saul continues. This is 'short-sighted and self-destructive, [and] from the point of view of their obligation to society ..., simply irresponsible.'[88]

Two points are at issue here. One is the role some academics may play in propagandizing an economic system they favour. As long as they are expressing their convictions and are not merely 'hired guns,' they can claim the right of academic free speech. Their position is analogous to that of the League for Social Reconstruction's socialists in the 1930s – though in one sense, of course, it is radically different. No powerful person challenges the right of academics to *advance* the claims of corporate capitalism.

The other point concerns the role of the university in advancing a business agenda. This is more contentious, because university heads are sensitive to charges that, in pursuing closer relations with business, they are compromising autonomy and academic freedom. Articles on university-corporate relations in *University Affairs* usually quote some administrator to the effect that an appropriate distance is being maintained. As well, the fundraising efforts of universities are accompanied by affirmations that autonomy and academic freedom are secure.[89] And in spite of considerable pressure from business and government, the universities have so far managed to maintain large parts of their traditional culture and practices.

Sceptics such as Ernie Lightman, a professor of social work at the University of Toronto, point out that strings are often attached to the donations made by corporations and individuals. Even where no strings are visible, they may operate in hidden form. A corollary of the fact that funds are often donated for specific purposes, moreover, is that some fields attract little money and have increasing difficulty in maintaining themselves. But if classics, say, or philosophy or Slavic languages are dropped from the curriculum, where will they be learned and taught? 'The university is the only accepted institution of modern culture on which the quest for knowledge unquestionably devolves,' in Veblen's words, 'and ... this [is] the only unquestioned duty incumbent on the university.'[90]

Although few if any Canadian universities will ever again be private in the way many of them were before 1950, reliance on private support will grow. Leacock's Dr Boomer, the bonhomous president of Plutoria University, will once again be haunting the Mausoleum Club in search of people with money to give away. There will be subtle and sometimes not so subtle pressure on professors to rustle up research support, to help in recruiting students and attracting donations, and to avoid saying or doing anything that may repel potential benefactors. Knowing on which side their bread is buttered, many academics will comply.

In the recent past, business interests have rarely interfered directly with academic freedom and free speech. A noteworthy exception to this rule is the recent attempt by Daishowa Inc. to silence Chris Tollefson, a professor of law at the University of Victoria.

The attempt had its roots in a dispute between the multinational pulp and paper company and the Lubicon Cree. Daishowa had obtained logging rights in an area in northern Alberta claimed by the Lubicon, who insisted that Daishowa not commence logging operations until their land claims had been settled. When Daishowa nevertheless proceeded, a group called the Friends of the Lubicon took up the natives' cause. The environmentalist Christopher Genovali writes: 'In 1991, the Friends initiated what has become a highly effective boycott of Daishowa Paper products, primarily paper bags produced by Daishowa for the Ontario retail and fast food market.' Four years later, Daishowa launched a multimillion dollar lawsuit against the Friends, seeking an injunction to end the boycott and claiming damages for defamation.[91]

The action launched by Daishowa is of a kind known in legal circles as a SLAPP suit (Strategic Lawsuits Against Public Participation) – a familiar feature of the U.S. legal landscape in particular. Tollefson, an expert on SLAPP suits, writes: 'These suits are typically brought by large corporate interests to chill lawful participation in public debate by citizens and NGOs, often in the environmental context. Such suits work by draining the resources of their targets and distracting them from the issue at hand. In my writings, I have argued that SLAPPs have become a particularly pernicious problem in B.C. due to the highly politicized nature of environmental issues in this province.'[92]

Tollefson discussed SLAPP suits in the *Canadian Bar Review* in 1994. Two years later, in another scholarly article, he described Daishowa's action against the Friends of the Lubicon as 'in many respects ... a paradigmatic SLAPP suit.'[93] This seems to have irritated executives of Daishowa's Canadian subsidiary sufficiently that in September 1996 they sought to keep him from speaking or writing about the case.

The method chosen was unusual. The defendants (Friends of the Lubicon) in the Daishowa suit applied in early September of adjourn the trial on the grounds that plaintiff had failed to disclose information pertinent to the defence. Plaintiff's legal counsel opposed the adjournment on the grounds that the damages and negative publicity suffered by Daishowa would increase during a delay. Counsel for Daishowa also argued that if the adjournment was in fact granted, it should be on condition that the Friends, their lawyer Karen Wristen, and Tollefson be barred from making public statements about the case until the trial came to an end.[94] (It ended on 14 April 1998, with judgment for plaintiff on the matter of defamation but for the defendants on the central issue of the consumer boycott.)

Tollefson was not named in person, but two of his articles and papers were introduced as evidence of the kind of adverse publicity from which Daishowa was allegedly suffering. Tollefson, who heard about the argument to be made in the adjournment motion by coincidence just before the issues were to be argued before the court, immediately appointed a lawyer to represent his interests. Madam Justice Fran Kiteley, though, would not hear Tollefson's counsel, because he had not been named. Because Judge Kiteley on 13 September banned all discussion of the case while she was considering the arguments for and against adjournment, Tollefson, though not a party to the suit, was effectively silenced until, in November 1996, Kiteley denied plaintiff's attempt to muzzle Tollefson, whom she referred to only as 'X.'

Arguing that his academic freedom was at issue, Tollefson applied to the University of Victoria faculty association for payment of his legal costs. In response, the association executive told him that they were 'unanimously' of the view 'that this issue arose out of your normal professional activities at the University and that it was therefore properly the University's responsibility to reimburse you for these expenses,' and it referred the matter to the vice-president (academic).[95]

The university administration questioned whether Tollefson's work had been affected by Kiteley's order of 13 September 1996, whether he had had an interest in the issue that required legal representation, and whether, having failed to ask the university's approval before retaining counsel, he was entitled to reimbursement at all. Tollefson pointed out that he had had less than twenty-four hours to act, that from 13 September to 1 November 1996 he had been unable to discuss the case, and that the 'no publication' order had restricted his academic freedom.

SLAPP suits were one of his main areas of scholarship, he added, he received 'almost daily requests for information [and] invitations to talk' and wrote 'at least three or four articles a year.' A ban on publication, 'no matter how narrowly one might seek to interpret it in retrospect ...,' he said, 'profoundly affected me in my academic life.' The university nevertheless declined to pay.[96]

Tollefson is once again free to speak and write about SLAPP suits in general and the Daishowa case in particular. However, the attempt to restrict his academic freedom will probably not be the last of its kind in Canada. The implications are troubling, moreover. What would be the position, for example, if a corporation were to name a university as a co-defendant in a SLAPP suit, arguing that it was liable along with an offending professor? What if a corporation were to threaten such a suit unless a university silenced a professor? These are unchartered waters, but in an age when corporations are increasingly prominent in university affairs, the waters need to be sounded in order to identify possible dangers to university autonomy and academic freedom.

Since the collapse of the Soviet empire, the capitalist countries no longer confront an explicit challenge from any state or group of states with remotely comparable military and industrial strength. Even China, though formally committed to an ideology of dialectical materialism, seems to be embracing market economics. But there is still a war of sorts going on, one waged between transnational corporations. The conditions of combat require some working people to lose their jobs and others to surrender gains in income and security wrested from their employers in collective agreements or obtained through the democratic state.

The security enjoyed by tenured professors and the freedom they enjoy in their work seem offensive in a world in which enterprises are downsized at will and employees obey orders or leave. Disliked, too, is the fact that much academic activity is not market-oriented in any recognizable way and can be made to be so only at the expense of the intellectual autonomy and academic freedom of those who do it (to say nothing of the pleasure they take in their work).[97]

For many business people, it seems, intellectual autonomy and academic freedom have no value. They are 'rigidities,' irksome barriers to making the universities useful. In any case, a society whose beat is set by corporate capitalism is bound to be impatient with institutions and people that, a good deal of the time, march to a different drummer. The attack on tenure is part of this impatience. When many working people are treated as though they were disposable utensils, it seems wrong that some academics should be largely insulated from the prevailing insecurity.

Attacks on universities as refuges from 'the real world' are not usually tempered by an appreciation of their role as the only organized (if flawed) source of independent and disinterested research, advice, and criticism in our society. Yet this role is centrally important. Society needs institutions and people who can act as independent evaluators. Robert Weyant comments: 'Few social institutions provide individuals with enough intellectual independence to play this role ... With a lack of independence, positive evaluation is rendered suspect and negative evaluation is rendered unlikely. An occasional ivory tower may not be such a bad thing.'[98]

Indeed, it may keep business and government from making bad decisions. A recent example involves the North Atlantic cod fisheries. In 1993, writes the author and educator Silver Donald Cameron, managers in the federal Department of Fisheries and Oceans (DFO), solicitous of the short-term interests of the fishing industry, suppressed internal research that showed the state of cod stocks to be worse than bureaucrats or politicians were willing to admit. A calamitous overfishing of southern cod stocks resulted. The investigative journalist Michael Harris, who has written at length about the fisheries, supports the view that the politicians need independent and disinterested research and advice. If fisheries research had been done by university scientists unbeholden to interested parties, and if the research had been published, it would have have been more difficult for DFO to recommend the course of action it did.[99]

Although universities do not conform to the 'lean and mean' image that some of their critics favour, in two aspects they have become increasingly businesslike. One is the treatment of a sizable segment of faculty members – those appointed sessionally or part time. The other is scientific research. Studies in the early 1980s indicated that (1) the use of sessional appointments was growing; (2) the term of appointment was often no more than nine months (eight was not unknown); (3) salary increments lagged behind those in the tenure stream; (4) benefits were less generous; (5) a disproportionate number of 'sessionals' were women; (6) a sizable minority were published scholars; (7) the possibility of renewal was limited; and (8) the prospects of passing into the tenure stream were dim.[100] All the same, their lot seems enviable compared with that of part-time faculty, who are employed in large numbers by universities in the major cities. In some institutions part-time teachers have unionized in an effort to secure improvements in salaries and benefits, as well as a measure of academic freedom. But they are still cheap labour.

Many administrators may believe that in an era of stagnant or declining income, they have no choice but to get 'the biggest bang for the buck.' Some freely choose to do so. 'In the businesslike view of the captains of erudition ...,' Veblen noted, 'learning and instruction are a species of skilled labour, to be hired at competitive wages and to turn out the largest merchantable output that can be obtained by shrewd bargaining.'[101] Part-time teaching scarcely existed in Veblen's day, but it is now common. And the excess of fully-qualified young academics means that the labour market favours the universities employing them.

What are the effects on academic freedom? The insecurity of sessional and part-time teachers is not conducive to boldness: the freedom of dependants is always conditional. Far more than tenured faculty, they have grounds for being cautious. Less obvious but more insidious are the effects of the use of sessional and part-time faculty on the quality of teaching. One of these academic piece-workers writes, 'Part-time teaching positions are the academic equivalent of one-night stands, or something even more unmentionable and far less lucrative: you arrive, do your job, get paid and leave, no commitments, no attachments.'[102] The message conveyed to men and women whose appointments barely outlast the teaching term is that their scholarly interests are not the university's concern. Their access to research funds is restricted; need may force them to teach all year round. As a consequence, research is apt to get short shrift. Yet a continuing commitment to scholarship is important not only to effective teaching but also to the concept of academic freedom as it has developed in North America.

Another area in which university practices are increasingly businesslike is scientific research, a matter central to the concerns of the Corporate–Higher Education Forum. The cost of scientific research was a major reason for the provincialization, from the 1940s into the 1970s, of universities that had long been private. More recently, with public funding in decline, more and more research is privatized. Links are being forged between the academy and industry as scientists seek out those who will fund their research and as corporations seek out those who can help them develop new products and processes.[103]

In the new research environment, abuses do occur. On one occasion the results were horrifying. An entrepreneurial attitude to research at Concordia University contributed in 1992 to the murder of four professors. The murderer, Valery Fabrikant, nursed grievances associated with his failure to get a tenure-track appointment and his belief that his work did not get the reward and recognition it deserved. A committee of inquiry headed by Harry W. Arthurs found serious flaws in the conduct of research at Concordia and identified as their root cause a 'production-driven research culture' that encouraged the ruthless pursuit of grants and contracts and the exploitation of junior academics.[104]

The Arthurs committee generalized from the conduct of research at Concordia to university research as a whole. Was this justified? University of Toronto President Robert Prichard denied it, but questions linger. A former president of the Canadian Graduate Council, Duncan Phillips, has identified several problems that can arise from contract research: disputes over the patenting and sale of discoveries; delays in the publication of research findings until patents are approved; discoveries kept secret in the pursuit of private gain; conflicts of interest that arise when a student or faculty member works for a company owned or controlled by a professor; and research whose direction is determined neither by intellectual interest nor by social need, but solely by the availability of funds.[105]

Contract research corrodes academic freedom most directly when it involves limitations on the right to publish the results. This right, Conrad Russell writes, 'has for a long time been taken as one of the touchstones of academic freedom ... It is also a fundamental academic value, and one in necessary conflict with commercial values, that ideas and findings must be shared with fellow scholars, and become part of our common professional stock-in-trade.' As we have seen, the corporate consumers of research are apt to insist that its findings be kept confidential.

A recent incident at the Hospital for Sick Children (a University of Toronto teaching institution) indicates the sort of problem that may result. A member of Toronto's Faculty of Medicine, Nancy Olivieri, found herself in a bind when she began to suspect in 1995 that the new drug she was testing was doing her patients more harm than good. Having agreed to confidentiality concerning her research findings when she accepted funding from the pharmaceutical firm Apotex, she found that when she wanted to warn the medical community and her patients, Apotex objected and reportedly threatened her with legal action. Although the hospital denied Olivieri's request for legal help, she nevertheless made her concerns known. When this action, described by another researcher as 'brave,' became public in the summer of 1998, it sparked a debate about the effects of corporate influence on academic freedom in pharmaceutical research. Moreover, the debate has once again raised the questions whether and how the pursuit of scientific truth and of profit can be reconciled with each other. Some Canadian scientists felt misgivings about doing secret research during the Second World War, but at that time there was at least the argument that military victory over dangerous enemies was at stake. Today the objective may be no more compelling than a corporation's wish for a competitive edge or a larger profit.[106]

The 1994 John C. Polanyi Nobel Laureates Lectures at the University of Toronto were in part a call for the freeing of science from the dictates of the marketplace. 'To profit from science,' Polanyi himself said, 'we must support individuals who have a vision, and then give them the freedom to pursue that vision.' Many of those who were interested in the applications of scientific work believed that they should redirect the efforts of scientists 'from what, to the onlooker, appear to be worthless ends' to ones that seem more promising, observed Polanyi. 'But since science is sharply directed toward making discoveries, the cost of redirection is high. It is notoriously difficult to select from among unmade discoveries those that will be the most useful. That is why it is often a bad bargain to contort the tree of knowledge so that it will grow in chosen directions.'[107]

Did many people heed this plea for academic freedom in research? A *Globe and Mail* article late in 1995 drew attention to two disputes about intellectual ownership that were agitating the University of Waterloo, some of whose faculty have been conspicuously successful in attracting research funds from the private sector. Polanyi wrote to the newspaper in comment: 'The conditions for product development are too seldom coincident with those for knowledge development to permit a serene marriage. Products are for today; knowledge is for all time.' Universities, he said, should choose knowledge, ultimately the basis of both national and international wealth. It is a choice that many researchers seem unable or unwilling to make.[108]

Insofar as non-university money is available for research in the liberal arts – and the Social Sciences and Humanities Research Council plays the major role here – incentives to turn research into more 'useful' paths also exist. A development potentially at least as damaging to academic freedom has been the attempt by the three federal research councils to adopt a code of ethics covering research on human subjects. The draft code, which seeks to protect individuals and groups from intrusive researchers, would (if rigidly applied) seriously hamper legitimate research in the social sciences. Strong objections to the draft may lead to positive changes in the final version, but at the time of writing uncertainty persists.[109]

A different threat to academic freedom in liberal arts research comes from those who argue that social scientists and humanists should spend more time in the classroom. This view gained support from the AUCC's Commission of Inquiry on Canadian University Education (1991). Prepared by Stuart L. Smith, formerly of McMaster's Faculty of Medicine and sometime leader of the Liberal Party of Ontario, the commission report concluded among other things that 'teaching is seriously undervalued at Canadian universities and nothing less than a total commitment to it is required.'[110] This implied a reduction in research, which would also allow students to be taught at reduced cost.

Desmond Morton wrote two decades ago, 'A frightening alliance of students, politicians, and taxpayers is gathering across Canada for a fresh assault on universities as centres for research and independent scholarship.' The assault may be nearing a climax. For more than two years, rumours have been circulating in Ontario that Ministry of Education bureaucrats, whose power has grown with the abolition in 1996 of the Ontario Council of University Affairs, are hoping to concentrate research in a minority of the province's universities and to reduce or end it in the others. No policy has been formally adopted, but by 1997–8 the funding formula surreptitiously favoured six universities (Guelph, McMaster, Queen's, Waterloo, Western Ontario, and Toronto, institutions in which the applied sciences are prominent) at the expense of the others in respect of research. A remark by Conrad Russell comes to mind: 'A university which does not do research is like a bicycle without wheels: one would like to know what it is for.' The comment, though apt, is unlikely to impress the universities' critics, who seem to regard a good deal of research as esoteric, impractical, or frivolous.[111]

Academic freedom faces a serious challenge not only from the business-minded but also from neoliberal economic thought, which in North America is usually called neoconservatism. (I prefer the European term 'neoliberalism' because it identifies the ideology as the offspring of nineteenth-century *laissez-faire* liberalism and social Darwinism, neither of which shares much common ground with traditional conservatism.)

Academic freedom does not fare well when the adherents of comprehensive systems of thought attain dominance. Whereas the adherents of most such ideologies and faiths have sought to control universities and curtail academic freedom by expelling critics and installing supporters, neoliberals – much like the businesspeople with whom they are often allied – seek to change the way in which the institutions function. Once these are under the discipline of the free market, the personal views of academics will matter little.

What would a market-driven university be like? An answer is not simple, since it is unclear whose consumer demands are to be met. The primary consumers are, presumably, Canadian students. But they are subsidized – some by their parents, all of them by government and the taxpayer – and the concerns of the various funders are not identical. Students want courses that interest them, that they do well in, that offer promise of employment, or all three. Parents proverbially want what is best for their children. Governments may want universities to restrict instruction to subjects that satisfy a current demand in the labour market, to cut subjects that seem unlikely to lead to jobs, and to expand into areas where qualified workers are currently in short supply.

Believing that market forces should lead students to take appropriate subjects, consistent neoliberals prefer proposals that make students the primary funders of university teaching. Research, seen as a discrete activity which the consumers of teaching should not have to subsidize, would be funded separately. Government support for universities would be supplied by means of vouchers issued to students. Even more attractive from a neoliberal perspective, though, would be to withdraw government from a funding role except possibly as a lender to students or a guarantor of their loans, and as a funder of useful kinds of research.

In May 1996 Andrew Coyne, a leading neoliberal journalist, called for a revamping of higher education along these lines. Holding that the benefits of higher education are largely private, Coyne believes that students can justifiably be charged market rates for it. They can then insist that their education be supplied on their terms, in the classroom or over the Internet, in four-month terms or all year round, without paying the costs of research that, in their judgment, is irrelevant to their courses.

'It is surprising how many changes you can think of, once you design a university around the needs of students rather than the needs of academics,' Coyne writes, describing with approval the University of Phoenix, a private, for-profit institution. 'The university designs the course, then hires professors to teach it. Most are freelancers; there is no tenure.'[112] No research either, or academic freedom.

An article in the *New Yorker* describes Phoenix, which at present enrols only students aged twenty-three and over, as 'a para-university. It has the operational core of higher education – students, teachers, classrooms, exams, degree-granting programs – without a campus life, or even an intellectual life.' President William Gibbs points out, 'Our students don't really want the education. They want what the education provides for them – better jobs, moving up in their career, the ability to speak up in meetings, that sort of thing.' Willy Loman wants to become more marketable, and in the market-driven university the customer is king. With 40,000 students, Phoenix claims to be the second-largest private university in the United States. It is flourishing. Shares in the company that controls it, Apollo Group, valued at two dollars (adjusted for a stock split) in April 1994, were trading in the low fifties only four years later.[113]

That students go to university for career-oriented reasons is nothing new. One hopes, however, that they will also get an education, that they will learn to think critically, to acquire knowledge and apply it, and, paraphrasing George Santayana, to find their place in the world and learn what things in it can truly serve them. If they graduate without having learned such things, they have been short-changed or they have short-changed themselves, no matter what credentials they may have picked up along the way. A university that accepts that its students 'don't want the education' and caters to this wish, and makes no attempt to add to the world's stock of knowledge, is a university in name only. Profitable though it may be for its owners, it is no more than a glorified degree mill.

Media critics such as Noam Chomsky, Edward S. Herman, and Robert W.

McChesney have shown that the commercial values of the marketplace have helped to coarsen and 'dumb down' much of the media and entertainment, and have seriously restricted the range of public expression and discussion. The University of Phoenix offers evidence that market values have similar effects in university life.[114]

The call for market-driven universities has disastrous implications for some of the academy's key functions: the expansion of the realm of knowledge, the development of an integrated understanding of oneself and the world, and the provision of an informed and disinterested analysis of phenomena and events. And it is not only these functions that are in danger but also the freedom of professors to determine the content of their teaching and the direction of their research.

From a business point of view, academics are employees to be managed efficiently. From a neoliberal perspective, they are suppliers of personal services who must try to 'make it' in the market. One of the fathers of neoliberalism, William F. Buckley Jr, writes in *God and Man at Yale* (1951), subtitled *The Superstitions of 'Academic Freedom'*: 'Every citizen in a free economy, no matter what wares he plies, must defer to the sovereignty of the consumer.'[115] In this brave new world, scholars and scientists are peddlers in pursuit of sales, and academic freedom is a mere superstition.

It is difficult to predict how much staying power neoliberalism will have. Its progenitors, *laissez-faire* liberalism and social Darwinism, generated strong resistance before they crumbled, discredited, amidst the social, economic, political, and military wreckage of the Depression and the Second World War. In one of the most important books published in this century, *The Great Transformation* (1944), Karl Polanyi comments, 'The true criticism of market society is not that it was based on economics – in a sense every and any society must be based on it – but that its economy was based on self-interest.'[116] Demonstrating the essential unnaturalness of the nineteenth- and early-twentieth-century market economy, Polanyi also shows that the opposition to it was entirely natural.

Neoliberalism has risen not because of its intellectual power or popular appeal – it has little of either – but because of its utility to individuals and corporations whose overriding creed is a limitless self-interest and whose delusion it is that this interest serves the interests of all. Many people are sceptical. As the gap between the rich and the rest of society widens, neoliberal dogma meets with growing criticism and resistance.[117]

For all that, attempts to impose market discipline on the universities are likely to intensify. William Thorsell of the *Globe and Mail* claimed in April 1998 that 'the universities are moving into an entrepreneurial culture in which ... excellence can be promised in a world of market accountability.' Perhaps no word is more abused today than 'excellence,' which, Bill Readings shows, has largely lost its meaning. Thorsell's use of it seems thoroughly appropriate, however. It belongs in the Newspeak world of marketing, and that is what the market requires.[118]

New Zealand has in recent years become a laboratory for neoliberal nostrums. A document prepared in 1997 by government bureaucrats proposes to turn that country's universities into market-driven, profit-making companies, to introduce a student-voucher system to pay three-quarters of the costs of higher education, with tuition fees paying the rest, and to separate the funding of teaching and research. Teaching is expected to become more sensitive to student wishes (and grading, too?). Internally funded research will be subject to institutional and government approval and supervision, ostensibly to ensure that minimum standards of quantity and quality are met. Externally funded research presumably will make its own way in the market.[119]

How far such recommendations will go, in New Zealand or elsewhere, including Canada, remains to be seen. *La lutte continue:* academic freedom will continue to be embattled.

13

Conclusion

Academic freedom in Canada has a convoluted history. In the middle of the nineteenth century neither teaching nor scholarship was safe from those who were concerned to protect religious orthodoxy. By the outbreak of the 1914–18 war, teaching and research were generally protected, but free speech outside the classroom remained insecure, and public criticism of one's institution, its head, or its governing board was very likely to lead to dismissal.

By engendering an insistence on patriotic conformity, the First World War endangered academic freedom even in the classroom but the return of peace brought a more spacious era, at least in the private institutions. In the provincial universities, professorial discussion of current political issues became a source of concern, one that prompted new attempts to restrict academic free speech. The most significant of these was Sir Robert Falconer's 1922 speech on academic freedom. During the 1930s, a decade marked by economic depression as well as the threat of renewed war in Europe, some professors claimed the 'rights' of academic freedom and free speech in order to criticize the capitalist order and the British connection. Such criticisms were unwelcome. Calls to limit the scope of academic freedom increased as a result.

The Second World War, like the first, had the effect of diminishing academic freedom even in teaching and research. Nevertheless, some academics spoke publicly to issues of social and economic change in a manner that would have been difficult thirty years earlier. In its early stages, the Cold War had the effect of reinforcing a traditional taboo, communism having never been acceptable in the academy. However, the Crowe affair inaugurated a period during which the scope of academic freedom and academic free speech expanded significantly. In the 1960s it came to include even criticism of the university and the way it was governed. Primarily responsible was the shortage of qualified academics. This prompted an improvement of their economic circumstances, made them more secure, and increased their freedom. Women and members of various ethnic minority groups were appointed in unprecedented numbers, permitting an expansion of the range of discussion and debate.

Tenure, which in law was held during the pleasure of governing boards (though by custom it was often held during good behaviour), became subject to agreements that required boards to show cause if they sought to dismiss professors. In the later 1960s and early 1970s, as a consequence, the academic freedom of tenured faculty gained an additional measure of protection. Faculty associations also sought to obtain aspects of that protection for the untenured.

If, by the mid-1960s, the future of academic freedom looked bright, within a few years the student movement, the universities' decline in public esteem, reductions in university funding, and the rise of faculty unions raised new questions about the state of academic freedom. One effect of these developments, though, was to free students from traditional controls and to make real a claim to academic freedom for students. More recently, exponents of political correctness have challenged academic freedom in its traditional sense as deleterious to the interests of various minority groups. At the same time, business values and neoliberalism now present potent challenges to university autonomy as well as to academic freedom. It would take a Dr Pangloss to contemplate with equanimity the state of academic freedom – and, indeed, of the Canadian universities.

Academics are far from united in defence of their freedom. 'For many professors in many universities,' Russell Jacoby writes, 'academic freedom meant nothing more than the freedom to be academic.' He is describing the scene in the United States, but things do not look very different north of the border. Over the years, most Canadian professors have defined their roles narrowly and have shunned controversy in any form. Some have followed this course of action because they felt vulnerable and did not want to lose their jobs, some because they simply disliked making trouble, and some because doing anything else would be unseemly, might make enemies, or might damage their careers. 'Nothing is more essential than to profess Correct Opinions,' wrote John Graves Simcoe, the first lieutenant-governor of Upper Canada, 'unless to possess a correct Acquaintance.' Over the years, this has served not a few successful academics as a guiding principle.[1]

Academic administrators and senior professors have usually been ready to remind those who needed reminding that being 'outspoken' or 'difficult' is unprofitable and even dangerous. Peer pressure has been particularly effective in fostering reticence. Like everyone else, academics want to enjoy the good opinion of their colleagues and not to be regarded as fools, cranks, or oddballs.

For decades, Canadian academics had yet another reason for taking care in stating their professional views and personal opinions. Outsiders who were unhappy about what a professor said were likely to hold his or her university responsible. This raised the possibility that the institution might suffer a reduction in its income. Since most universities lived more or less from hand to mouth, this possibility was unwelcome; some of the academics who had exercised their presumed right of academic free speech lapsed into silence when the possible ill effects on their institutions were pointed out to them. (This was even more effective when accompanied by a hint that an offender's job might be in peril.) Examples include Eric Havelock in 1937, Carlyle King in 1938, and Glen Shortliffe in 1949. A sense of care for and responsibility to the institution in which they worked probably led many others to keep their counsel even when they thought they had something to say.

This motive for exercising self-restraint began to fade during the 1950s as university funding became more automatic and impersonal. It is safer to express aberrant views today than it was fifty or a hundred years ago. A contributory reason is that the media pay less attention to what professors say than used to be the case. For many academics, however, discretion continues to be a virtue, even though the subjects about which they are discreet have changed. What religion, capitalism, and the Empire once were, gender, ethnicity, and sexual preference have become – topics best avoided unless what one has to say is unexceptional. But few academics get much attention these days unless what they say or do seems truly outlandish and offensive. And such people often get little or no support from their colleagues. Some, indeed, will join the outcry against the 'loudmouths' and 'troublemakers.' Many professors seem little interested in defending academic freedom when doing so becomes contentious.

The increased dependence of the universities on tuition fees, personal and corporate gifts, and privately sponsored research may be reinforcing this state of affairs. The advantage of public funding, particularly where a number of institutions share in the provincial subsidy, lies in its anonymity: those who vote the money do not supply it out of their own pockets. This reduces the danger that its recipients will be accused of ingratitude or waste if their work leads to unwanted conclusions or fails to produce desired results.

Private benefactors, on the other hand, may adopt a quasi-proprietorial attitude towards the programs or institutions that are the objects of their bounty; and the beneficiaries of their largesse may tacitly acknowledge an exchange relationship. For instance, what critical commentary on late-twentieth-century capitalism and the practices it fosters can one expect to emerge from schools of management that carry the names of the millionaires who have endowed them? When the *Globe and Mail*'s editorial board expresses concern about the ties between universities and business schools on the one hand, and their benefactors on the other, there is clearly cause for worry.[2]

Other restrictions on academic freedom may be in the offing. The call for market-driven universities offers an example. In such a university, course content, the classroom performance of professors, and grading will – presumably, in the interests of student satisfaction – be subject to constant monitoring and adjustment. Professors may also have to refrain from saying anything, in class or outside, that could offend any significant number of the institution's 'customers.' The implications for academic freedom are disagreeable.

Does any of this matter? Some people think it does. In 1970 C.B. Macpherson spoke of 'a sick society' and its need for 'diagnosis, at every level of its malfunctioning: ecological, physiological, economic, psychological, political, and above all (or below all), to use an old-fashioned word in little repute these days, moral.' He claimed for the university the role of diagnostician, and compared it to the medieval court jester or fool, the one person in a prince's entourage who was supposed to be outspoken and to say things no courtier was allowed to say.[3]

Desmond Morton wrote in 1977 that given the complicated problems facing society, 'we need a more effective mobilization of our organized intelligence than at any time since the Second World War.' Having lost favour with the public during the years of the student movement, the university could not expect an early return to high esteem. Yet one of its functions continued to be crucially important: 'To hold a mirror to our society, allowing neither a flattering self-portrait nor an outsider's caricature, but reality. It is the role of an honest friend.' Morton concluded: 'As both educator and analyst of its society, the university community can look forward to being more needed and less wanted than at almost any other period in its history.'[4]

More recently, the political commentator and broadcaster Dalton Camp has asked universities to challenge the 'cult of marketability' that is so strongly supported by the business community as well as by certain politicians: 'It would be a tragedy for all society to see our universities give up their most valid role at the hour of society's greatest need. This is the part of education which invites the young to be sceptical of authority and to challenge conformity and convention.'[5] Such challenges, of course, are never very welcome.

Today's universities are not well equipped to fill the roles identified by Macpherson, Morton, and Camp. The institutions are compromised by their descent into the market and burdened by large bureaucracies whose contribution to the tasks of research and teaching is (to put it gently) problematic. Some of the teaching is bad; some of what passes for research seems hardly worth the effort. The disinterested pursuit of knowledge seems far from the concern of some professors.

The failings of the institution and its faculty are only part of the picture, however. 'If England was what England seems, / An' not the England of our dreams, / But only putty, brass, an' paint. / 'Ow quick we'd drop 'er, / *But she ain't!*' Kipling's lines seem fitting. In spite of the university's shortcomings, no other institution offers its employees the opportunity to seek knowledge for its own sake and organize it into a theoretical system, or publicly to provide disinterested analysis, criticism, and advice. Academic freedom – and the tenure that secures it better than anything else yet devised – has created conditions in which scholars and scientists can teach courses, undertake research, and publish findings that challenge conventional wisdom, and in which they can publicly state their findings and opinions without fear of retaliation by their employers.

The economist and intellectual maverick Mel Watkins has recently said, 'Academics are granted a freedom of speech that is rare in our society – universities can be seen as islands of freedom in a sea of unfreedom – and it has long seemed to me that we should avail ourselves of that.' The overwhelming number of working people, including those in the media, are not free to state their views or findings if these adversely affect the private interests of their employers or their employers' customers, including (in the case of the media) major advertisers. Indeed, to advance those interests is presumed to be the duty of employees. A market economy gives people the freedom to offer their skills for sale in the market. Freedom of expression is available only to those willing and able to cope with the harmful effects its exercise may have on their marketability. 'Of course,' Watkins comments, 'one is always free to speak in support of the status quo, an activity for which my own profession of economics is well known.'[6]

If the freedom of employees is restricted by economic reality, so is that of self-employed professional men and women, many of whom cannot afford to ignore, let alone damage, the interests of current or prospective clients. Legislators and the public servants who advise them are strongly influenced by the need to seek interest-group approval and to gain election. Here, as in the private sector, the public interest will often take a back seat.

Essential to the modern university, academic freedom is a right and a privilege.[7] Its intelligent exercise is crucially important for the welfare of society, particularly at a time when multinational corporations speak so loudly and insistently and carry such big sticks. Professors owe it to themselves and their fellow citizens to use their freedom for the common good.

Notes

Abbreviations

AAUP	American Association of University Professors
AB	*Atlantic Baptist*
AUA	Acadia University Archives
AUCC	Association of Universities and Colleges of Canada
AUL	Archives de l'Université Laval
BCS	*BC Studies*
BoD	Board of Directors
BoG	Board of Governors
BoR	Board of Regents
BoT	Board of Trustees
BUA	Bishop's University Archives
CAUT	Canadian Association of University Teachers
CAUTB	*CAUT Bulletin*
CBA	Canadian Baptist Archives
CBC	Canadian Broadcasting Corporation
CCF	Co-operative Commonwealth Federation
CF	*Canadian Forum*
CH	*Calgary Herald*
CHA	Canadian Historical Association
CHR	*Canadian Historical Review*
CJEPS	*Canadian Journal of Economics and Political Science*
CPC	Communist Party of Canada
DR	*Dalhousie Review*
DUA	Dalhousie University Archives

EJ	*Edmonton Journal*
FCSO	Fellowship for a Christian Social Order
GM	*Globe and Mail*, Toronto
HH	*Halifax Herald*
IC	*Interchange*
JCS	*Journal of Canadian Studies*
KCA	King's College Archives
KWR	Kitchener-Waterloo *Record*
KWS	*Kingston Whig-Standard*
LCP	*Law and Contemporary Problems*
LD	*Le Devoir*
LFP	*London Free Press*
LPP	Labor-Progressive Party
LSR	League for Social Reconstruction
LT	*Labour/Le Travail*
ME	*Mail and Empire*, Toronto
MG	Montreal *Gazette*
MM	*Maclean's* magazine
MS	*Montreal Star*
MUA	McGill University Archives
NA	National Archives of Canada
NCCU	National Conference of Canadian Universities
NDP	New Democratic Party
NO	*New Outlook*
NYT	*New York Times*
OC	*Ottawa Citizen*
OH	*Ontario History*
OPT	*Orillia Packet and Times*
PABC	Provincial Archives of British Columbia
PAM	Provincial Archives of Manitoba
PANS	Public Archives of Nova Scotia
PAO	Provincial Archives of Ontario
PC	President's or Principal's Correspondence
PO	President's or Principal's Office
PP	President's or Principal's Papers
QCT	*Quebec Chronicle-Telegraph*
QQ	*Queen's Quarterly*
QUA	Queen's University Archives
RCMP	Royal Canadian Mounted Police

SAB	Saskatchewan Archives Board
SN	*Saturday Night*
SP	Saskatoon *(Star)-Phoenix*
TG	Toronto *Globe*
TS	*Toronto Star*
TT	Toronto *Telegram*
TCA	Trinity College Archives
UA	*University Affairs*
UAA	University of Alberta Archives
UBCA	University of British Columbia Archives
UBCSC	University of British Columbia Special Collections
UCO	*United Church Observer*
UC/VUA	United Church/Victoria University Archives
UMA	University of Manitoba Archives
UNBA	University of New Brunswick Archives
UNBSC	University of New Brunswick Special Collections
USA	University of Saskatchewan Archives
UTA	University of Toronto Archives
UTB	*University of Toronto Bulletin*
UTQ	*University of Toronto Quarterly*
UTRBL	University of Toronto Rare Book Library
UV	University of Toronto *Varsity*
UVA	University of Victoria Archives
UWaA	University of Waterloo Archives
UWiA	University of Winnipeg Archives
UWORC	University of Western Ontario, Regional Collection
VP	*Vancouver Province*
VS	*Vancouver Sun*
WFP	*Winnipeg Free Press*
WT	*Winnipeg Tribune*
YUA	York University Archives

Preface

1 Charles E. Curran, *Catholic Higher Education, Theology, and Academic Freedom* (Notre Dame, Ind. 1990), 26.
2 Paul Lacoste, 'Church and University,' in George Whalley, ed., *A Place of Liberty: Essays on the Government of Canadian Universities* (Toronto and Vancouver 1964), 137.

1: Introduction: Not a Burning Question

1 DUA, PO, Corr., MS 1-3–A398, vol. 14, NCCU 1936–39, Carleton Stanley to J.W.Dafoe, 7 Apr. 1937, copy.
2 Ibid., Lord Tweedsmuir to Stanley, 9 Apr. 1937; Stanley to W.A. Mackintosh, 4 May 1937, copy.
3 Ibid., Carleton Stanley, address to NCCU, 31 May 1937.
4 Richard Hofstadter and Walter P. Metzger, *The Development of Academic Freedom in the United States* (New York and London 1955), ix.
5 See Kenneth Hare, *On University Freedom in the Canadian Context* (Toronto 1968).
6 Hofstadter, 'The Age of the College,' in Hofstadter and Metzger, *The Development of Academic Freedom in the United States*, 3.
7 Conrad Russell, *Academic Freedom* (London and New York 1993), 24.
8 Lorna Marsden, speaking at a conference on 'Academic Freedom and the Inclusive University,' Vancouver, B.C., 12 Apr. 1997.
9 Metzger, 'The Age of the University,' in Hofstadter and Metzger, *The Development of Academic Freedom om the United States*, 387.
10 Ibid., 377; see Frederick Rudolph, *The American College and University: A History* (Athens, Ga. 1990 [1962]), 271–2.
11 Charles W. Eliot, 'Inaugural Address,' *Educational Reform* (New York 1901), 7–8.
12 Hofstadter and Metzger, *The Development of Academic Freedom in the United States*, 389; Max Weber, quoted in Konrad H. Jarausch, *Students, Society and Politics in Imperial Germany: The Rise of Academic Illiberalism* (Princeton, N.J. 1982), 171.
13 Hofstadter and Metzger, *The Development of Academic Freedom in the United States*, 405.
14 A.H. Halsey and M.A. Trow, *The British Academics* (Cambridge, Mass. 1971), 117. See also Russell, *Academic Freedom*, 43–4.
15 Robin S. Harris, *A History of Higher Education in Canada, 1663–1960* (Toronto 1976), 27; A.L. McCrimmon, *The Educational Policy of the Baptists of Ontario and Quebec* (Toronto 1920), 19.
16 Hofstadter and Metzger, *The Development of Academic Freedom in the United States*, 469–70. Into the second half of the twentieth century, those who spoke and wrote about professors invariably referred to 'men' and used the male pronoun.
17 Ibid., 476.
18 *Bulletin of the AAUP* (March 1916), quoted in Hofstadter and Metzger, *The Development of Academic Freedom in the United States*, 477.
19 'General Report of the Committee on Academic Freedom and Tenure (1915),' *LCP* 53, no. 3 (Summer 1990), 397.
20 Ibid., 403.

21 Ibid., 404–5.
22 Walter P. Metzger, 'Academic Tenure in America: A Historical Essay,' *Faculty Tenure: A Report and Recommendations by the Commission on Academic Tenure in Higher Education* (San Francisco 1973), 93–111, 122–3.
23 'General Report (1915),' 406.
24 Ellen W. Schrecker, *No Ivory Tower: McCarthyism and the Universities* (New York 1986), 18; Thomas L. Haskell, 'Justifying the Rights of Academic Freedom in the Age of "Power/Knowledge,"' in Louis Menand, ed., *The Future of Academic Freedom* (Chicago and London 1996), 54.
25 John Henry Newman, 'Discourse V: Knowledge Its Own End,' *The Idea of a University* (Oxford 1976).

2: A House Divided

 1 Hilda Neatby, *Queen's University*, vol. 1: *And Not to Yield, 1843–1917* (Montreal and Kingston 1978), 83. My account of the troubles at Queen's is drawn from this volume.
 2 Henry Roper, 'Aspects of the History of a Loyalist College: King's College, Windsor, and Nova Scotian Higher Education in the Nineteenth Century,' *Anglican and Episcopal History* 61 (1991), 450.
 3 H. Nova Scotia to W.E. Wilson, 8 Sept. 1884, reproduced in Wilson's letter to the editor, *HH*, 20 Oct. 1884.
 4 Ibid., Wilson to Binney, 20 Sept. 1884, and Wilson to the Governors, King's College, 29 Sept. 1884, copy; Roper, 'Aspects of the History,' 452.
 5 *HH*, 15 and 20 Oct. 1884.
 6 Roper, 'Aspects of the History,' 453.
 7 KCA, King's College, Windsor, Board of Governors, Minutes, vol. 6, 4 Nov. 1884.
 8 18 *Nova Scotia Reports* (1885), 196, 201.
 9 Henry Roper to the author, 4 May 1996.
10 Margaret Gillett, *We Walked Very Warily: A History of Women at McGill* (Montreal 1981), 121. Unless otherwise stated, my account of the Murray case is based on this book.
11 Stanley Brice Frost, *McGill University*, vol. 1: *1801–1895* (Kingston and Montreal 1980), 258.
12 Ibid., 259.
13 Gillett, *We Walked Very Warily*, 137, 148.
14 N. Burwash, 'The Development of the University, 1887–1904,' *The University of Toronto and Its Colleges, 1827–1906* (Toronto 1906), 58.
15 A.B. McKillop, *Matters of Mind: The University in Ontario, 1791–1951* (Toronto 1994), 154–6.

16 Robert Bothwell, *Laying the Foundation: A Century of History at University of Toronto* (Toronto 1991), 27.

17 Ibid., 29; H.S. Ferns and B. Ostry, *The Age of Mackenzie King: The Rise of the Leader* (London 1955), 23–4.

18 William Dale, 'The University,' *TG*, 9 Feb. 1895.

19 'Varsity Troubles,' *ME*, 16 Feb. 1895. See also 'Crisis at Varsity,' *TS*, 15 Feb. 1895.

20 'Mr. Dale Dismissed,' *TG*, 15 Feb. 1895; 'Professor Dale's Dismissal,' *ME*, 16 Feb. 1895.

21 'Loyalty to Varsity,' *TS*, 16 Feb. 1895; 'Misstatements Corrected,' *TS*, 18 Feb. 1895. See Ross Harkness, *J.E. Atkinson of the Star* (Toronto 1963), 32–3.

22 Quoted in Robert Choquette, *Language and Religion: A History of English-French Conflict in Ontario* (Ottawa 1975), 12.

23 Ibid., 15.

24 Ibid., 81–116, 254–7.

25 James D. Cameron, *For the People: A History of St Francis Xavier University* (Montreal and Kingston 1996), 190–1; *GM*, 7 and 8 Sept. 1984, 24 and 25 June 1988; Charles E. Curran, *Catholic Higher Education, Theology, and Academic Freedom* (Notre Dame, Ind. 1990), 26.

26 P. Roome, 'The Darwin Debate in Canada: 1860–1880,' in Louis A. Knafla et al., eds, *Science, Technology, and Culture in Historical Perspective* (Calgary 1976), 183–205; A.B. McKillop, *A Disciplined Intelligence: Critical Inquiry and Canadian Thought in the Victorian Era* (Montreal and Kingston 1979), 98–134; Ramsay Cook, *The Regenerators: Social Criticism in Late Victorian Canada* (Toronto 1985), 9–16; Michael Gauvreau, *The Evangelical Century: College and Creed in English Canada from the Great Revival to the Great Depression* (Montreal and Kingston 1991), 125–80.

27 Carl Berger, *Science, God, and Nature in Victorian Canada* (Toronto 1983), 77–8.

28 Cook, *The Regenerators*, 17–25; Marguerite Van Die, *An Evangelical Mind: Nathanael Burwash and the Methodist Tradition in Canada, 1839–1918* (Montreal and Kingston 1989), 89–113; C.B. Sissons, *A History of Victoria University* (Toronto 1952), 193.

29 George A. Boyle, 'Higher Criticism and the Struggle for Academic Freedom in Canadian Methodism,' (unpubl. PhD dissertation, Victoria University, 1965), passim.

30 Boyle, 'Higher Criticism,' 66.

31 Ibid., 77; Van Die, *An Evangelical Mind*, 103–5.

32 Boyle, 'Higher Criticism,' 78; McKillop, *Matters of Mind*, 207.

33 Boyle, 'Higher Criticism,' 261–2.

34 UC/VUA, *Journal of the Methodist General Conference*, 1910, 174.

35 Boyle reproduces the two judgments as appendices 1 and 2 to his dissertation.

36 *TG*, 26 and 27 Feb. 1909; Michael Bliss, *A Canadian Millionaire: The Life and Business Times of Sir Joseph Flavelle, Bart., 1858–1939* (Toronto 1978), 200–2.

37 *TG*, 1 Mar. 1909;

38 Quoted in Margaret Prang, *N.W. Rowell: Ontario Nationalist* (Toronto 1975), 84.

39 UC/VUA, *Journal of the Methodist General Conference, 1910*, 108; Sissons, *A History of Victoria University*, 239–40.

40 John G. Reid, *Mount Allison University*, vol. 1: *1843–1914* (Toronto 1984), 223. My account of Mount Allison is taken from this book.

41 A.G. Bedford, *The University of Winnipeg: A History of the Founding Colleges* (Toronto 1976), 129–30; James M. Pitsula, *An Act of Faith: The Early Years of Regina College* (Regina 1988), 3.

42 G.A. Rawlyk, ed., *Canadian Baptists and Christian Higher Education* (Kingston and Montreal 1988); Charles M. Johnston, *McMaster University*, vol. 1: *The Toronto Years* (Toronto 1976), 92–102.

43 CBA, file McMaster University, Matthews Controversy (MUMC), Senate, Discussion re Higher Criticism, etc., 12–13 May 1908, 1.

44 Ibid., 8, 12.

45 Ibid., 35.

46 Ibid., 42, 44; CBA, I.G. Matthews Personal, Report of the Committee Appointed by the Senate of McMaster University to Investigate Charges Made by Rev. Elmore Harris, D.D. against the Teaching of Professor I.G. Matthews [1909], 1.

47 CBA, MUMC, Correspondence, George Cross to A.C. McKay, 5 May 1909, copy; Johnston, *McMaster University*, vol. 1, 98–9.

48 CBA, MUMC, Report of the Thirteen Lectures given by Prof. Matthews in O.T. Introduction, 1907–8; MUMC, Corr., Elmore Harris to Board of Governors, 10 May 1909.

49 CBA, I.G. Matthews Personal, Report of the Committee [1909], 19; McMaster University Pamphlets, *Address by Professor Matthews of McMaster University before the Convention of the Regular Baptists of Ontario and Quebec, when in Session at Toronto, on Monday, October 24th, 1910* (Toronto [1910]), 11.

50 CBA, I.G. Matthews Personal, Report of the Senate and Board of Governors of McMaster University, presented to the Regular Baptist Convention of Ontario and Quebec, Toronto, 1910, 11.

51 Leslie Armour, 'Philosophy and Denominationalism in Ontario,' *JCS* 20, no. 1 (Spring 1985), 28.

52 Ibid.

53 P.B. Waite, *The Lives of Dalhousie University*, vol. 1: *Lord Dalhousie's College* (Montreal and Kingston 1994), 86. See also Brian Fraser, *Church, College, and Clergy: A History of Theological Education at Knox College, Toronto, 1844–1994* (Montreal and Kingston 1995).

54 Waite, *The Lives of Dalhousie University*, vol. 1, 124–52.

55 Hilda Neatby, *Queen's University*, vol. 1, 151, 164.

56 Ibid., 247–65.

57 Ibid., 273.

58 Ibid., 291–2.

59 Ibid., 265; Canada, House of Commons, *Debates*, 11 Mar. 1912, 4747, 4749.

60 Ibid., 4750, 4757, 4762, 4763, 4770.

61 Ibid., 30 March 1912, 6770.

62 Neatby, *Queen's University*, vol. 1, 265.

63 Bliss, *A Canadian Millionaire*, 203; Irving Abella, *A Coat of Many Colours: Two Centuries of Jewish Life in Canada* (Toronto 1990), 37, 45.

64 James G. Greenlee, *Sir Robert Falconer: A Biography* (Toronto 1988), 127–34; John S. Moir, *A History of Biblical Studies in Canada: A Sense of Proportion* (Chico, Calif. 1982), 29–33.

65 UTRBL, MS coll. 1, Sir Edmund Walker Papers, vol. 26B, file 6, [John Hoskin] to S.H. Blake, 14 Dec. 1908, copy.

66 UC/VUA, 92-0002/8(106), Nathanael Burwash Papers, Blake to Hoskin, 22 Dec. 1908, copy; Burwash to Blake, 9 Jan. 1909, copy.

67 Ibid., Blake to Burwash, 11 Feb. 1909; UTRBL, Walker Papers, vol. 26B, file 6, S.H. Blake, *The Teaching of Religious Knowledge in University College Ultra Vires* (Toronto 1909).

68 UTRBL, Walker Papers, vol. 26B, file 7, Proceedings of Committee (n.d.), 9, 11. See also 'Better Leave the Bible out of the Schools than Thrust it into the University,' *TT*, 17 Mar. 1909.

69 UTRBL, Walker Papers, vol. 26B, file 6, *Report of Special Committee to Board of Governors, University of Toronto* (Toronto 1909); UTA, PO (Falconer), A67-0007/6, Robert Falconer to Z.A. Lash, 22 Apr. 1909, copy.

70 Alan Karp, 'John Calvin and the Geneva Academy: Roots of the Board of Trustees,' *History of Higher Education Annual* 5 (1985), 34; John S. Brubacher and Willis Rudy, *Higher Education in Transition: A History of American Colleges and Universities, 1636–1976*, 3rd ed. (New York 1976), 30.

71 Frost, *McGill University*, vol. 1, 157.

72 Charles W. Humphries, *'Honest Enough to Be Bold': The Life and Times of Sir James Pliny Whitney* (Toronto 1985), 113–4, 126–9; Neatby, *Queen's University*, vol. 1, 109–10; QUA, coll. 2127A, J.W. Flavelle Papers, vol. 38, U of T Corr. 1900–1905, Frederick Hamilton to A.H.U. Colquhoun, 4 Oct. [1905], copy.

73 Humphries, *'Honest Enough to Be Bold'*, 127.

74 UBCSC, F.H. Soward, 'The Early History of the University of British Columbia,' (unpubl. ms, 1930), 16, 68, 74.

75 Maureen Aytenfisu, 'The University of Alberta: Objectives, Structures and Role,

1908–1928,' (unpubl. MA thesis, Univ. of Alberta 1982), 104; Michael Hayden, *Seeking a Balance: University of Saskatchewan, 1907–1982* (Vancouver 1983), 11–12; W.L. Morton, *One University: A History of the University of Manitoba, 1877–1952* (Toronto 1957), 108; University Amendment Act (7 Geo. V, 1917, ch. 96), in W.J. Spence, *University of Manitoba: Historical Notes, 1877–1917* (Winnipeg 1918), 79–80.
76 See McKillop, *A Disciplined Intelligence.*
77 Northrop Frye, 'Conclusion,' in Karl F. Klinck, ed., *Literary History of Canada* (Toronto 1965), 830.

3: The Great War

1 Carol S. Gruber, *Mars and Minerva: World War I and the Uses of the Higher Learning in America* (Baton Rouge 1975), 163.
2 A.R.M. Lower, *My First Seventy-Five Years* (Toronto 1967), 43.
3 James Greenlee, *Sir Robert Falconer* (Toronto 1988), 201–2, 206–7.
4 Ibid., 207–8.
5 UTRBL, MS col. 1, Sir Edmund Walker Papers, vol. 12, file 27, E.B. Osler to Walker, 18 Nov. 1914.
6 UTRBL, Walker Papers, vol. 26B, file 12, Walker to E.B. Osler, 19 Nov. 1914, copy.
7 Greenlee, *Falconer*, 209–10; Michael Bliss, *A Canadian Millionaire* (Toronto 1978), 244.
8 UTA, BoG, Minutes, 3 Dec. 1914.
9 UTA, BoG, Minutes, 4 Dec. 1914.
10 Greenlee, *Falconer*, 210–11; UTA, PO (Falconer) A67-0007/037, Falconer to A.B. Lowell, 7 Dec. 1914, copy; Falconer to Thomas Holgate, 16 Dec. 1914, copy; Falconer to A.P. Fitch, 2 Jan. 1915, copy, and replies.
11 UTA, PO (Falconer), A67-0007/033, I. Benzinger to Falconer, 14 May 1915, and reply.
12 Charles M. Johnston, *McMaster University*, vol. 1 (Toronto 1976), 137.
13 *TG*, 8 and 16 Dec. 1914.
14 *UV*, 11 Oct. 1914.
15 'Another Open-Minded Professor,' *ME*, 16 Oct. 1914.
16 *ME*, 19 Oct. 1914; Greenlee, *Falconer*, 203.
17 'Weakening Our Resolution,' *UV*, 21 Oct. 1914; TCA, Trinity College Corporation, Minutes, 19 Nov. 1914.
18 TCA, Office of the Provost, 986 008/005(19), 'German Professor 1914–15'; G.S. Macklem to W.D. Scott, 7 Oct. 1914, copy; Macklem to W.A. von Lubtow, 17 Oct. 1914, copy; Lubtow to Corporation of Trinity College, 17 Oct. 1914.
19 Ibid., Macklem to Lubtow, 11 Dec. 1914, copy; Osler to Macklem, 12 Dec. 1914.

20 Ibid., Macklem to Osler, 14 Dec. 1914, copy.
21 Ibid., Macklem to Lubtow, 19 Dec. 1914, copy; Lubtow to Macklem, 19 Dec. 1914; Lubtow to Chancellor, 30 Dec. 1914.
22 UTA, PO, A67-0007/034, Falconer to [B.E.] Fernow, 30 Jan. 1915, copy.
23 Ibid., Fernow to Sir Edmund Osler, 1 Feb. 1915, copy; Falconer to Fernow, 6 Feb. 1915, copy; A67-0007/033, H.R. Christie to Falconer, 4 May 1915, and reply.
24 NA, MG30, D33, O.D. Skelton Papers, vol. 1, Teaching Correspondence, G.Y. Chown to Skelton, 8 Jan. 1917 [sic].
25 Ibid., Skelton to Chown, 9 Jan. 1917 [sic], copy.
26 Ibid., R.B.T., Notes of Interview with Mr Walter Douglas, 11 Jan. 1918, copy.
27 Ibid., R. Bruce Taylor to John Macnaughton, 14 Jan. 1918, copy.
28 UBCA, PO, D IV A 7/1, vol. 8, press clippings, 'A Matter of History,' VS, 12 Jan. 1917; S. Mack Eastman Papers, D II B 6/2, vol. 1, Eastman to the Editor, Vancouver Daily Sun, 15 Jan. 1917, copy.
29 Ibid., 'A Matter of History,' VS, 17 Jan. 1917; Donald Downie, 'The Poisoning of Sacred Springs or The Neutralization of Learning,' VS, 19 Jan. 1917; UBCA, PO, D IV A 7/1, vol. 8, F.F. Wesbrook to J.D. MacLean, 16 Jan. 1917, copy.
30 UBCA, PO, D IV A 7/2, vol. 8, Ernest G. Thatcher to Wesbrook, 23 Apr. 1918.
31 UBCA, BoG, Minutes, 9 May 1918; PO, D IV A 7/2, vol. 11, S.D. Scott to Ernest Thatcher, 10 May 1918, copy; BoG, Minutes, 27 May 1918.
32 UBCA, PO, D IV A 7/2, vol. 11, Scott to J.D. MacLean, 31 May 1918, copy.
33 Michiel Horn, 'Under the Gaze of George Vancouver: The University of British Columbia and the Provincial Government, 1913–1939,' BCS 83 (Autumn 1989), 34–41.
34 H.V. Nelles, The Politics of Development: Forests, Mines and Hydro-Electric Power in Ontario, 1849–1941 (Toronto 1974), 406n.
35 UTA, PO, A67-0007/42, William Hearst to Robert Falconer, 2 Nov. 1916.
36 Ibid., A67-0007/43, James Mavor to Falconer, 9 Nov. 1916.
37 S.E.D. Shortt, The Search for an Ideal: Six Canadian Intellectuals and Their Convictions in an Age of Transition, 1890–1930 (Toronto 1976), 123.
38 UTA, PO, A67-0007/42, Hearst to Falconer, 26 and 30 Nov. 1916.
39 On Bland and the Social Gospel, see Richard Allen, The Social Passion (Toronto 1971), 54–60 and passim; A.G. Bedford, The University of Winnipeg (Toronto 1976), 127–39; Ramsay Cook, 'Ambiguous Heritage: Wesley College and the Social Gospel Re-considered,' Manitoba History 19 (Spring 1990), 4–5.
40 UWiA, Executive Committee, BoD, Wesley College, Minutes 1914–1918, 30 March 1917.
41 Bedford, University of Winnipeg, 127, 130–2.
42 UWiA, Executive Committee, BoD, Minutes 1914–1918, 25 May 1917; BoD, Minutes 1915–1938, 31 May 1917.

43 Bedford, *University of Winnipeg*, 125.

44 UWiA, Minutes, Principal Selection Committee, Wesley College, 4 June 1917; Gerald Friesen, 'Principal J.H. Riddell: The Sane and Safe Leader of Wesley College,' in Dennis L. Butcher et al., eds., *Prairie Spirit: Perspectives on the Heritage of the United Church of Canada in the West* (Winnipeg 1985), 254.

45 Bedford, *University of Winnipeg*, 126, 134–5; Allen, *Social Passion*, 56.

46 Bedford, *University of Winnipeg*, 136–8; Allen, *Social Passion*, 57–9.

47 W.J. Spence, *University of Manitoba: Historical Notes, 1877–1917* (Winnipeg 1918), 51, 53.

48 W.L. Morton, *One University* (Toronto 1957), 111.

49 University Amendment Act, 1917, ch. 96, in Spence, *Historical Notes*, 79–80; UMA, BoG, Minutes 1917–23, 28 May 1917 and 11 June 1917.

50 UMA, BoG, Minutes, 25 Apr. 1919.

51 Ibid., 5 June 1919, C. Muller to J.A. Machray, 31 May 1919; James A. MacLean to Machray, n.d.

52 Michael Hayden, *Seeking a Balance* (Vancouver 1983), 79.

53 See Derek Bok, *The Cost of Talent* (New York 1993), 26–31.

54 F.H. Leacey, ed., *Historical Statistics of Canada*, 2nd ed. (Ottawa 1983), E41–8, K1-18; Bok, *The Cost of Talent*, 31–4; UMA, BoG, Minutes 1917–23, 4 Dec. 1919, 5 Feb. and 15 Apr. 1920, and 27 Apr. 1921; UAA, BoG, Minutes, 9 Jan., 14 and 27 May, 28 Aug. 1920; UBCA, Faculty Association Records, D IV 2/4, vol. 1, Faculty Delegation on the Salary Question, 23 Apr. 1920, and file 3, Minutes, Meeting of Faculty, 29 Oct. 1920; William A. Bruneau, *A Matter of Identities: A History of the UBC Faculty Association 1920–1990* (Vancouver 1990), passim.

55 Hayden, *Seeking a Balance*, 112; USA, BoG, Minutes, 28 Feb. and 15 Aug. 1918.

56 David R. Murray and Robert A. Murray, *The Prairie Builder: Walter Murray of Saskatchewan* (Edmonton 1984), 228–39; Michael Hayden, 'The Fight that Underhill Missed: Government and Academic Freedom at the University of Saskatchewan, 1919–1920 ...,' in Michiel Horn, ed., *Academic Freedom: Harry Crowe Memorial Lectures 1986* (North York 1987), 35.

57 Hayden, *Seeking a Balance*, 78–116. See also Murray and Murray, *The Prairie Builder*, 107–28; Don Kerr and Stan Hanson, *Saskatoon: The First Half-Century* (Edmonton 1982), 218–30.

58 USA, Jean Murray Collection (JMC) E II B10, 'Copy of Notes Made by W.P. Thompson for Reminiscences at a Celebration of the 50th Anniversary of His Joining the University of Saskatchewan,' [1963].

59 USA, PP I B121/2, A.B. Macallum to W.C. Murray, 22 Apr. 1919; UTA, James Loudon Papers, B72-0031/14(46), University Council, 16 May 1900, 4, and B72-0031/14(48), 'Report of Commissioners,' 1905, 5. See also W.C. Good, *Farmer Citizen* (Toronto 1958), 48–9.

60 Hayden, 'The Fight that Underhill Missed,' 42.
61 Maureen Aytenfisu, 'The University of Alberta: Objectives, Structures and Role, 1908–1928,' (unpubl. MA thesis, University of Alberta 1982).
62 Hayden, *Seeking a Balance*, 86.
63 USA, PP I B121/1, Macallum to Murray, 22 Apr. 1919; JMC, E II B1, R.A. Falconer to Murray, 16 Apr. 1919, and A. Stanley Mackenzie to Murray, 3 May 1919.
64 USA, BoG, Minutes, 21 Apr. 1919; PP I B28, Murray to Sir Frederick Haultain, 22 Apr. 1919, copy.
65 USA BoG, Minutes, 10 July 1919.
66 Ibid., 16 June 1919.
67 Ibid., 10 July 1919.
68 USA, PP I B121/4, Ira MacKay to Board of Governors, 24 June 1919, John S. Dexter to D.P. McColl, 24 Apr. 1919; Hayden, 'The Fight that Underhill Missed,' 40. See also J. McKeen Cattell, *University Control* (New York 1977 [1913]), passim.
69 USA, PP I B121/5, Murray to Board of Governors, 25 July 1919, two letters.
70 USA, JMC, E II B1, Murray to Board of Governors, Memo re Tenure of Office, 10 July 1919.
71 USA, E II B10, W.M. Martin to Murray, 28 Aug. 1919; Charles H. Dunning to Murray, 28 Aug. 1919.
72 Murray and Murray, *The Prairie Builder*, 118–19.
73 USA, BoG, Minutes, 11 Aug. 1919; USA, PP I B121/1, Hogg, MacLaurin, and MacKay to A.R. Weir, 21 Aug. 1920.
74 Hayden, *Seeking a Balance*, 101; USA, JMC, E IV B2, Jean Bayer to Mrs Murray and Tina, 22 Nov. 1919. Moxon of the Department of Law was Murray's most active faculty ally.
75 USA, JMC, E IV B2, K.G. MacKay to James Clinkshill, 11 Dec. 1919, copy; PP I B121/6, K.G. MacKay to Clinkshill, 15 Dec. 1919, copy.
76 USA, JMC, E II B10, W.M. Martin to J.E. Allison, 19 Dec. 1919, copy.
77 *SP*, 30 Mar. 1920; USA, PP I B121/1, 'Argument on Behalf of the Board of Governors,' 24.
78 Saskatchewan, King's Bench, '*In re the University Act* ...,' *Western Weekly Reports 1920*, vol. 2, 829, 830.
79 Murray and Murray, *The Prairie Builder*, 117; Hayden, *Seeking a Balance*, 115–16.
80 Hayden, *Seeking a Balance*, 116; Hayden, 'The Fight that Underhill Missed,' 44–5.
81 UBCA, PO, mfm reel 32, file Estimates 1931–32, 'Memorandum Read by the President at the Joint Meeting of the Board of Governors and the Senate on April 10th, 1931 ...'
82 UBCSC, Lampman Report collection, Daniel Buchanan to Judge Peter Lampman, 11 May 1932; NA, MG30, D204, F.H. Underhill Papers, vol. 2, H.F. Angus to Underhill, 26 Sept. 1932.

4: The Most Treasured Privilege

1 Robert Falconer, *Academic Freedom* (Toronto 1922), 11–12.
2 P.B. Waite, *The Loner: Three Sketches of the Personal Life and Ideas of R.B. Bennett, 1870–1947* (Toronto 1992), 19.
3 MUA, RG2, PO, c.85/2202, [Dorothy McMurray], comments on a draft of the annual report [1943].
4 A.G. Bedford, *The University of Winnipeg* (Toronto 1976), 129; 'Regulations of the Board,' *Statutes of the University of Saskatchewan* (Saskatoon 1912), 53.
5 Lionel Groulx, *Mes mémoires*, vol. 3: *1926–1931* (Montreal 1972), 14 ('to preach loyalty to the Canadian constitution to my students'; 'to say or write nothing that could hurt the legitimate sensibilities of our English-Canadian compatriots').
6 Ibid., 15–17 ('The most dangerous school of thought: the heirs of the *rouge* old guard of 1850'; 'the poor rector throws up his hands; he no longer knows which way to turn'; 'A new controversy, and one on so delicate a subject as the academic freedom of professors, was not very desirable at all').
7 A.B. McKillop, *Matters of Mind* (Toronto 1994), 88; Paul Axelrod, *Making a Middle Class: Student Life in English Canada During the Thirties* (Montreal and Kingston 1990), 12–15.
8 UBCA, PO, mfm reel 6, F.F. Wesbrook to S.D. Scott, 12 Jan. 1914, copy; UWORC, University Archives, Dean of Arts, box 25, H. Michell to W. Sherwood Fox, 14 Feb. 1923, and Fox to Michell, 17 Feb. 1923, copy.
9 UWORC, Dean of Arts, box 25, W.T. Jackman to Fox, 8 Jan. 1923, and Fox to Jackman, 10 Jan. 1923, copy.
10 MUA, RG2, PO, c.61/1001, R. du Roure to A.W. Currie, 7 Apr. 1923.
11 See Margaret Gillett, *We Walked Very Warily* (Montreal 1981); Marianne Gosztonyi Ainley, ed., *Despite the Odds: Essays on Canadian Women and Science* (Montreal 1990); Alison Prentice, 'Bluestockings, Feminists, or Women Workers? A Preliminary Look at Women's Early Employment at the University of Toronto,' *Journal of the CHA*, n.s. 2 (1991); Mary Kinnear, 'Discourse by Default: Women University Teachers,' *In Subordination: Professional Women, 1870–1970* (Montreal and Kingston 1995).
12 Canada, Department of Trade and Commerce, Dominion Bureau of Statistics, Education Statistics Branch, *Higher Education in Canada, 1938–1940*, passim; Robin S. Harris, *A History of Higher Education in Canada, 1663–1960* (Toronto 1976), 212; McKillop, *Matters of Mind*, 282, 304–7.
13 R. Bruce Taylor, 'Academic Freedom,' *QQ* 27, no. 1 (Summer 1919), passim.
14 E.E. Braithwaite, 'Academic Freedom,' *TG*, 4 June 1919.
15 James G. Greenlee, *Sir Robert Falconer* (Toronto 1988), 257–64.

16 UTA, PO (Falconer), A67-0007/67, R.W. Leonard to Sir Edmund Walker, 14 Jan. 1921, copy, and Walker to Leonard, 17 Jan. 1921, copy.

17 Ibid., A67-0007/65, Falconer to Leonard, 18 Jan. 1921, copy.

18 Ibid., Leonard to Falconer, 21 Jan. 1921.

19 Ibid., Falconer to Leonard, 22 Jan. 1921, copy, and R.M. MacIver to Falconer, 27 Jan. 1921.

20 Ibid., A67-0007/72, Leonard to Falconer, 9 Dec. 1921, and Falconer to Leonard, 12 Dec. 1921, copy; Greenlee, *Sir Robert Falconer*, 278.

21 Falconer, *Academic Freedom*, passim.

22 UTA, PO, A67-0007/72, Leonard to Falconer, 24 Apr. 1922; A67-0007/81, Falconer to Board of Governors, 22 Feb. 1923, copy; A67-0007/78, Falconer to Leonard, 28 Feb. 1923, copy.

23 *ME*, 15 Feb. 1922; *TS*, 15 Feb. 1922; *TT*, 15 Feb. 1922; 'The Higher Politics,' *TG*, 16 Feb. 1922.

24 Greenlee, *Sir Robert Falconer*, 282; Lowell, quoted in Walter P. Metzger, 'The 1940 Statement of Principles on Academic Freedom and Tenure,' *LCP* 53, no. 3 (Summer 1990), 21–2.

25 UBCA, PO, mfm reel 32, E21 sp., 'Statement Made to L.S. Klinck by Mr. Hinchliffe, 5 August 1931.'

26 UTA, PO, A67-0007/83a, G.H. Ferguson to Falconer, 2 June 1924; A67-0007/83, Falconer to Ferguson, 4 June 1924, copy.

27 PAO, RG3, G. Howard Ferguson Papers, vol. 66, Ferguson to Cody, 8 Dec. 1925, copy; *TT*, 18 May 1928; *TS*, 19 May 1928.

28 UTA, PO, A67-0007/114, Ferguson to Cody, 17 Oct. 1928.

29 Ibid., Cody to Falconer, 19 Oct. 1928; F.H. Underhill to Falconer, 23 Oct. 1928; Falconer to Ferguson, 23 Oct. 1928, copy.

30 Ibid., Ferguson to Falconer, 26 Oct. 1928.

31 PAO, F980, H.J. Cody Papers, MU4964/5, Ferguson to Cody, 6 Apr. 1929.

32 Peter Oliver, *G. Howard Ferguson: Ontario Tory* (Toronto 1977), 328.

33 UBCA, PO, mfm reel 1, cl. 13, 'Memorandum of telephonic conversation with Mr. A.E. Bull ..., December 6, 1920'; L.S. Klinck, 'Socialist Club,' 17 Jan. 1921.

34 *VP*, 23 Nov. 1922.

35 *VP*, 25 Nov. 1922; *Vancouver World*, 2 Dec. 1922; UBCA, S. Mack Eastman Papers, D II B6/2, vol. 1, Eastman to J.D. MacLean, 2 Dec. 1922, copy.

36 UBCA, Eastman Papers, MacLean to Eastman, 7 Dec. 1922; S. Mack Eastman, 'Textbooks in European History,' *VP*, 7 Dec. 1922.

37 Michiel Horn, 'Under the Gaze of George Vancouver ...,' *BCS* 83 (Autumn 1989), 54–5.

38 UBCA, Faculty Association Records, D IV 2/4, vol. 1, file 3, Minutes, 26 Apr. 1923.

39 UBCA, PO, mfm reel 22, Mack Eastman to L.S. Klinck, 2 Feb. 1924.

40 Ibid., R.L. Reid to Klinck, 12 Mar. 1924.

41 Ibid., Eastman to Klinck, 14 Mar. 1924.

42 UBCA, BoG, Minutes, vol. 6, 29 Oct. 1923.

43 UAA, BoG, Minutes, 13 Oct. and 30 Nov. 1923.

44 UAA, RG19, 81–37–9, no. 19, W.H. Alexander Personal, Alexander to R.C. Wallace, 16 Oct. 1928.

45 Ibid., Wallace to Alexander, 18 Oct. 1928, copy.

46 NA, MG27 III C1, W.C. Good Papers, vol. 6, 5023–4, L.A. Wood to Good, 16 May 1923.

47 *LFP*, 17 February 1919; NA, Good Papers, 5039–45, Wood to Good, 24 May 1923; newspaper clipping, 'Arts Graduates Honor Dr. Wood' [n.p., n.d.].

48 William Sherwood Fox, *Sherwood Fox of Western: Reminiscences* (Toronto 1964), 128–9.

49 George Pedersen to the author, 8 Dec. 1992.

50 UWORC, Dean of Arts (Fox 1919–27), box 2, W.S. Fox to Wood, 13 Nov. 1919, copy; Fox to Wood, 6 Dec. 1919, copy; Wood to Fox, 9 Dec. 1919; Fox to Wood, 10 Dec. 1919 and 7 Jan. 1920, copies; Wood to Fox, 8 Jan. 1920; Fox to Wood, 26 Aug. 1920, copy.

51 Ibid., box 25, Fox to E.M. Keirstead, 28 Mar. 1921, copy; Fox to E.E. Day, 28 Mar. 1921, copy.

52 Ibid., box 4, Fox to Wood, 29 Apr. 1921, copy.

53 Norman Penner, *The Canadian Left: A Critical Analysis* (Scarborough, Ont. 1977), 178; James J. Talman to the author, 15 Jan. 1993.

54 UWORC, Dean of Arts (Fox 1919–27), box 25, Fox to R.M. MacIver, 11 Dec. 1922, copy, and Fox to H.N. Barry, 4 Jan. 1923, copy; F.H. Underhill, 'The Conception of a National Interest,' *CJEPS* 1, no. 3 (Aug. 1935), 404.

55 NA, Good Papers, vol. 8, 6250–1, Wood to Good, 5 July 1924; Foster J.K. Griezic, 'Introduction,' in Louis Aubrey Wood, *A History of Farmers' Movements in Canada* (Toronto 1975), vii.

56 John Herd Thompson with Allen Seager, *Canada 1922–1939: Decades of Discord* (Toronto 1985), 58–69; G.A. Rawlyk, 'Protestant Colleges in Canada: Past and Future,' in George M. Marsden and Bradley J. Longfield, eds., *The Secularization of the Academy* (New York and Oxford 1992), 292–8; Michael Gauvreau, 'Baptist Religion and the Social Science of Harold Innis,' *CHR* 76, no. 3 (June 1995).

57 *TS*, 16, 17, and 24 Apr. 1928; W.A. Irwin, letter in *TG*, 3 May 1928, and *TS*, 3 May 1928; John S. Moir, *A History of Biblical Studies in Canada* (Chico, Calif. 1982), 63–6.

58 UTA, PO, A67-0007/110a, W.R. Taylor to Falconer, 15 May 1928, and Falconer to Taylor, 29 May 1928, copy.

59 *UV*, 15 Jan. 1930.

60 'Faculty Must Be Supported,' *UV*, 15 Jan. 1930. On Meek, see Michiel Horn, 'Keeping Canada "Canadian": Anti-Communism and Canadianism in Toronto, 1928–29,' *Canada: An Historical Magazine* 3, no. 3 (Sept. 1975), 39–41.

61 *TS*, 15 Jan. 1930; *UV*, 16 Jan. 1930; 'A Little Learning,' *TT*, 17 Jan. 1930; 'Is Toronto University "Mildewed with Discretion"?' *ME*, 17 Jan. 1930; The Observer, 'Canada's Greatest University Must Be Free,' *TS*, 18 Jan. 1930.

62 UAA, Lewis H. Thomas Papers, 73–138–3, C.W. Lightbody to W.A. Riddell, 25 Sept. 1963, copy.

63 Moir, *A History of Biblical Studies in Canada*, 62–3.

64 Gerald Friesen, 'Principal J.H. Riddell ...,' in Dennis L. Butcher et al., eds., *Prairie Spirit* (Winnipeg 1985), 254.

65 UWiA, Wesley College, Dismissals, WC-10–1-3, J.H. Riddell to W.G. Smith, 14 Mar. 1921, copy.

66 Ibid., Smith to Riddell, 28 Mar. 1921.

67 Ibid., Riddell to Smith, 23 Apr. and 2 May 1921, copies; Friesen, 'Principal J.H. Riddell ...,' 261.

68 A.G. Bedford, *The University of Winnipeg* (Toronto 1976), 167–75.

69 UWiA, WC 10–1-3, J.H. Ashdown to Smith, 24 Mar. 1922, copy.

70 UWiA, Minutes of the Executive Committee of the Board of Directors of Wesley College, 1918–1922, 20 April, and 5 May 1922.

71 UWiA, WC 10–1-3, T.R. McNair and four others to the Principal and Governing Board of Wesley College, 6 June 1922; Joseph Wright and 32 others to the Principal and Governing Board, 6 June 1922.

72 UWiA, WC 10–1-4, Outline of an Address Given by Prof. Smith at the Sessions of the Manitoba Conference on Saturday, June 17th [1922].

73 UWiA, Minutes of the Executive Committee of the Board of Directors of Wesley College, 1918–1922, 19 June 1922; WC 10–1-4, Outline of an Address Given by the President of the College, J.H. Riddell, to the Board of Directors on the Evening of June 29th, [1922], and Synopsis of an Address Given before the Board of Wesley College by Prof. W.G. Smith [30 June 1922].

74 Bedford, *University of Winnipeg*, 175; Friesen, 'Principal J.H. Riddell ...,' 263.

75 *Smith v. Wesley College*, 3 *Western Weekly Reports* (1923), 213.

76 G.A. Rawlyk, 'A.L. McCrimmon, H.P. Whidden, T.T. Shields, Christian Education, and McMaster University,' in Rawlyk, ed., *Canadian Baptists and Christian Higher Education* (Kingston and Montreal 1988), 48.

77 Ibid., 49, 51.

78 Charles M. Johnston, *McMaster University*, vol. 1 (Toronto 1976), 169, 180; C. Allyn Russell, 'Thomas Todhunter Shields, Canadian Fundamentalist,' *OH* 70, no. 4 (Dec. 1978), passim.

79 *Gospel Witness*, 5 Nov. 1925.

80 CBA, McMaster University, Marshall Controversy, 'A Protest against the Retention of Professor L.H. Marshall,' 18 Mar. 1926; *ME*, 18 Oct. 1926. See also Frederick Griffin, 'Professor Upper-Cuts with Fighting Words,' *Star Weekly*, 23 Oct. 1926.

81 CBA, file Laurance Henry Marshall, Proceedings of the Education Session of the Baptist Convention of Ontario and Quebec, 19 May 1926, 70, 71; ibid., 'The Faith of Prof. L.H. Marshall, A Verbatim Report of an Address Delivered at the Annual Convention of Baptist Churches of Ontario and Quebec, Held in Temple Baptist Church, Toronto, Oct. 12–18, 1927.'

82 G.A. Rawlyk, 'A.L. McCrimmon ... and McMaster,' 62; Johnston, *McMaster University*, vol. 1, 203.

83 Henry Roper and James W. Clark, 'Religion and Intellectual Freedom on the Dalhousie Campus in the 1920s: The Case of Norman J. Symons,' *DR* 69, no. 2 (Spring 1989), 176, 181. Unless otherwise noted, my account is derived from this article.

84 Dalhousie *Gazette*, 22 Mar. 1929.

85 Henry Roper, 'Two Scandals in Academe,' *Royal Nova Scotia Historical Society, Collections* 43 (1991), 136–7. My account is based on this article and on P.B. Waite, *The Lives of Dalhousie University*, vol. 2: *1925–1980, The Old College Transformed* (Montreal and Kingston 1998), 39–41.

5: The Great Depression

1 Paul Axelrod, *Making a Middle Class* (Montreal and Kingston 1990), 20.

2 Michiel Horn, '"Free Speech within the Law": The Letter of the Sixty-Eight Toronto Professors, 1931,' *OH* 72, no. 1 (Mar. 1980), 27.

3 'The "Free Speech" Herring,' *TG*, 16 Jan. 1931; 'Communists Should Not Be Assisted to Become Martyrs in Cause of Free Speech,' *TT*, 16 Jan. 1931; 'University Professors and Free Speech,' *ME*, 19 Jan. 1931.

4 UTA, PO (Falconer), A67-0007/125a, Falconer to Emerson Coatsworth, 19 Jan. 1931, copy; A67-0007/126b, Falconer to R.H. Lloyd, 23 Jan. 1931, copy; A67-0007/128a, Falconer to D.J.G. Wishart, 20 Jan. 1931, copy.

5 QUA, coll. 2127a, J.W. Flavelle Papers, vol. 19, George M. Wrong to Flavelle, 18 Jan. 1931; Flavelle to Wrong, 20 Jan. 1931, copy.

6 James Greenlee, *Sir Robert Falconer* (Toronto 1988), 294; UTA, PO, A67-0007/125a, Falconer to Cody, 3 Feb. 1931, copy.

7 PAO, RG3, Prime Minister's Office, vol. 149, George S. Henry to H.J. Cody, 13 Feb. 1931, copy.

8 *TG*, 5 Feb. 1931; *ME*, 5 Feb. 1931.

9 Sir Robert Falconer, 'The Lawful Mind,' *University of Toronto Monthly* 37 (Oct. 1931), 19.
10 F.H. Underhill, 'Canada in the Great Depression,' *New Statesman and Nation*, 13 June 1931, 571; 'An Amiable Thrust from Academic Cloister,' *ME*, 26 June 1931; NA, MG30, D204, F.H. Underhill Papers, vol. 8, Robert Falconer to Underhill, 26 June 1931.
11 'Professors and Politics,' *TG*, 2 July 1931; UTA, PO, A67-0007/133, Underhill to Falconer, 24 Sept. 1931.
12 NA, Underhill Papers, vol. 16, Falconer to Underhill, 28 Sept. 1931.
13 UTA, Faculty of Forestry, A72-0025/147, W.N. Millar, Memorandum for the Dean, 14 Apr. 1924; PO, A67-0007/134, Annual News Letter of the Foresters' Club, University of Toronto, 1931.
14 Ibid., C.D. Howe, Comments on Professor Millar's Article on Self Education for Foresters in the Annual News Letter of the Foresters' Club; A67-0007/127a, W.N. Millar to Falconer, 20 June 1931.
15 Ibid., A67-0007/132a, 'Memorandum for Professor Millar,' n.d. [May–June 1932]; W.N. Millar, 'The Reforestation Plans,' *TG*, 16 Mar. 1932.
16 Greenlee, *Sir Robert Falconer*, 301; UTA, PO, A67-0007/132a, Millar to Falconer, 8 June 1932, copy; President's Secretary to Millar, 10 June 1932, copy.
17 UBCA, PO, mfm reel 39, file E2l sp., L.S. Klinck to G.M. Weir, 27 Feb. 1935, copy.
18 Michiel Horn, *The League for Social Reconstruction: Intellectual Origins of the Democratic Left in Canada, 1930–1942* (Toronto 1980), 20–2, 219.
19 NA, Underhill Papers, vol. 8, Norman Thomas to Underhill, 12 Jan. 1933, and vol. 3, S. Delbert Clark to Underhill, 13 Jan. 1933; interview with Frank H. Underhill, Ottawa, Jan. 1967.
20 G.V.F., 'C.C.F. "Brain Trust,"' *WFP*, 25 July 1933.
21 UTA, H.M. Cassidy Papers, B72-0022/17(01), Cassidy to L. Eckhardt, 18 Oct. 1933, copy, and Cassidy to D.M. LeBourdais, 18 Oct. 1933, copy; PABC, T.D. Pattullo Papers, Add. Mss. 3, vol. 67, file 6, Provincial Secretary, Conference with Premier, 29 May 1934.
22 A.B. McKillop, *Matters of Mind* (Toronto 1994), 393; *TG*, 20 Dec. 1933.
23 McKillop, *Matters of Mind*, 390–3; D.C. Masters, *Henry John Cody: An Outstanding Life* (Toronto 1995), 204; UTA, Cassidy Papers, A72-0022/17(01), Cassidy to Cody, 22 June 1934, copy.
24 University of Toronto, *President's Report, 1934–35* (Toronto 1936), 23.
25 NA, Underhill Papers, vol. 2, Underhill to W.H. Alexander, 25 Jan. 1936, copy.
26 NA, MG28 IV I, CCF Records, vol. 109, J.F. Parkinson to J.S. Woodsworth, 20 Dec. 1935.
27 NA, Underhill Papers, vol. 4, R.G. Dingman to Underhill, 1 Dec. 1933.

28 Ibid., vol. 9, G.M. Wrong to Underhill, 7 and 11 Dec. 1933.

29 Frank H. Underhill, 'Introduction,' *In Search of Canadian Liberalism* (Toronto 1961), x.

30 UTA, PO (Cody), A68-0006/012(03), clipping from *OPT*, 9 Nov. 1933.

31 Ibid., 'Professor Underhill's Ramp at Orillia,' *ME*, undated clipping.

32 PAO, RG3, PO, Henry General Correspondence, vol. 169, file 03-08-0–429, R. Kershaw to [R.B. Bennett], 6 Dec. 1933, with undated clipping from the Victoria *Daily Colonist*; Andrew D. MacLean to C.J. Foster, 12 Dec. 1933; Foster to MacLean, 13 Dec. 1933, copy.

33 UTA, PO, A68-0006/012(03), C.W. Tobey to Cody, 17 Nov. 1933; Cody to Tobey, 23 Nov. 1933, copy.

34 NA, Underhill Papers, vol. 18, Writings 1934; 'A Prophetic Professor,' *TG*, 20 Oct. 1934.

35 R. Douglas Francis, *Frank H. Underhill: Intellectual Provocateur* (Toronto 1986), 97; Underhill, 'Keep Canada Out of War,' *Maclean's*, 15 May 1937.

36 Francis, *Frank H. Underhill*, 97; Underhill, 'Beatty and the University Reds,' *CF* 15 (Dec. 1935), 385; MUA, RG2, PO, c.54/729, E.W. Beatty to A.E. Morgan, 6 Dec. 1935.

37 Donald Creighton, *Harold Adams Innis: Portrait of a Scholar* (Toronto 1957), 91–4; Underhill, 'The Conception of a National Interest,' *CJEPS* 1, no. 3 (Aug. 1935), 407.

38 H.A. Innis, 'For the People,' *UTQ* 5 (Jan. 1936), 285ff.; Underhill, 'On Professors and Politics,' *CF* 15 (Mar. 1936), 7.

39 NA, Underhill Papers, vol. 18, Writings 1937, 'Freedom of the Press'; Brian J. Young, 'C. George McCullagh and the Leadership League,' *CHR* 47, no. 3 (Sept. 1966), 202.

40 'Professor Underhill "Educates,"' *GM*, 1 June 1937.

41 NA, Underhill Papers, vol. 3, Underhill to Steven Cartwright, 4 June 1937, copy; QUA, coll. 5072, A.R.M. Lower Papers, vol. 2, file A10, Underhill to Lower, 10 Feb. 1938.

42 'Comment That Isn't So Emanates from University,' *TT*, 19 Nov. 1938.

43 UTA, PO A68-0006/039(03), Cody to Underhill, 25 Nov. 1938, copy; Notes on Meeting between H.J. Cody and F.H. Underhill.

44 UAA, BoG, Executive Committee, Minutes, 25 June 1930.

45 UAA, RG19, W.H. Alexander Personal, 81-37–9, R.C. Wallace to Fred White, 3 Jan. 1933, copy.

46 Ibid., Wallace to Alexander, 7 Dec. 1934, copy; UAA, BoG, Minutes, 4 Jan. 1935.

47 UAA, RG19, W.H. Alexander Personal, Alexander to Wallace, 31 Dec. 1934.

48 UAA, BoG, Minutes, 4 Jan. 1935.

49 NA, Underhill Papers, vol. 2, Alexander to Underhill, 26 Jan. 1935.

50 *CH*, 16 and 19 Jan. 1935.

51 *CH*, 13 Mar. and 4 Apr. 1935.

52 UAA, BoG, Minutes, 10 Apr. 1935; NA, Underhill Papers, vol. 2, Alexander to Underhill, 18 Oct. 1935; *CH*, 20 Apr. 1935.

53 W. Peter Ward, *White Canada Forever: Popular Attitudes and Public Policy toward Orientals in British Columbia* (Montreal 1978), 141; UBCA, BoG, Minutes, vol. 13, 30 Apr. 1934.

54 UBCA, BoG, Minutes, vol. 15, 30 Mar. and 27 Apr. 1936; Robin Fisher, *Duff Pattullo of British Columbia* (Toronto 1991), 273–6, 294–5, 308–9.

55 UBCA, BoG, Minutes, vol. 12, 29 May and 26 June 1933.

56 Ibid., 10 August 1933.

57 UBCA, PO, mfm reel 83A, file George M. Weir, Memorandum on the Interview with the Honourable Premier, 7 Dec. 1933; BoG, Minutes, vol. 12, 18 Dec. 1933.

58 PABC, T.D. Pattullo Papers, Add. Mss. 3, vol. 73, file 7, J.N. Ellis to Pattullo, 3 Sept. 1935.

59 Ibid., Pattullo to Ellis, 4 Sept. 1935, copy.

60 UBCA, BoG, Minutes, vol. 14, 4 and 28 Oct., 20 Nov. 1935; PABC, GR1222, British Columbia, Premier, vol. 137, file 2, T.D. Pattullo to Klinck, 22 Oct. 1935; UBCA, PO, mfm reel 43, E21 sp., G.M. Weir to Klinck, 23 Nov. 1935.

61 Michiel Horn, 'Under the Gaze of George Vancouver,' *BCS* 83 (Autumn 1989), 65–6.

62 Interview with Carlyle King, Regina, Sask., Aug. 1986; USA, PP II B22(1), unidentified newspaper clipping, 30 Mar. 1938.

63 Ibid., James Balfour to J.S. Thomson, 31 Mar. 1938; Thomson to Balfour, 1 and 11 Apr. 1938, copies; Thomson to P.E. MacKenzie, n.d., copy.

64 USA, PP II B63, J.W. Estey to Thomson, 2 and 11 Aug. 1938; A29, Wilfred Heffernan to Thomson, 23 Sept. 1938; R.J. Gibson to the Editor, Regina *Leader Post*, 26 Sept. 1938, copy.

65 Ibid., Thomson to the Editor, *SP*, 1 Oct. 1938, copy.

66 NA, Underhill Papers, vol. 5, King to Underhill, 6 Oct. 1938; [Helen Orpwood], 'Free Speech in Saskatchewan,' *CF* 18 (Dec. 1938); King interview, Aug. 1986.

67 UNBA, RG136, PC, D-1940, John B. McNair to C.C. Jones, 14 Mar. 1938. See also PC, 1951–3, L-R, file 9, A.W. Trueman to McNair, 8 Apr. 1952, copy; UNBSC, Oral History Program, Francis James Toole, taped interview 1973, 11, 17.

68 UNBSC, Oral history program, A.G. Bailey, taped interview 1973–4, 13.

69 UNBSC, Minutes of the University Senate, 15 Feb. 1938.

70 J.L. Granatstein, *The Ottawa Men: The Civil Service Mandarins 1935–1957* (Toronto 1982), 239.

71 DUA, MS 1–3, 299, R.A. MacKay Personal, Stanley to J.S. Thomson, 23 Dec. 1937, copy.

72 Ibid., Thomson to Stanley, 17 Dec. 1937.

73 UMA, UA20, PP, vol. 2, S.E. Smith to Mr. Justice Dysart, 11 Jan. 1935, copy, and J.W. Dafoe to Smith, 2 Feb. 1935; ibid., vol. 21, W.Y. Elliott to Smith, 29 Jan. 1938; NA, MG31, E46, Escott Reid Papers, vol. 36, Reid to Underhill, 25 Mar. 1938, copy.

74 Interview with R.E.K. Pemberton, London, Mar. 1967; Charles M. Johnston, *McMaster University*, vol. 2: *The Early Years in Hamilton, 1930–1957* (Toronto 1981), 78.

75 Interviews with Gregory Vlastos, Princeton, N.J., Apr. 1967, and Toronto, Nov. 1978; H. Martyn Estall to the author, 1 Dec. 1977.

76 Quoted in McKillop, *Matters of Mind*, 644.

77 QUA, Flavelle Papers, J.M. Macdonnell to Flavelle, 21 Jan. 1931; coll. 1125, F.W. Gibson Papers, vol. 3, file Academic Freedom, Macdonnell to R.C. Wallace 10 Dec. 1937, copy.

78 R.A. MacKay, 'After Beauharnois – What?' *Maclean's*, 15 Oct. 1931.

79 See P.B. Waite, *The Lives of Dalhousie University*, vol. 2 (Montreal and Kingston 1998), 54–6.

80 UNBA, R.B. Bennett Papers, vol. 908, 568994–6, G. Fred Pearson to R.B. Bennett, 6 Apr. 1932, and 568998, Bennett to Pearson, 12 Apr. 1932, copy; DUA, PO, Correspondence, MS1-3, A167, vol. 3, Bennett to W.E. Thompson, 28 Sept. 1932. See also PANS, MG17, Dalhousie University, vol. 20, Carleton Stanley Dispute, Minutes, Board of Governors, 28 Nov. 1944, 15.

81 UNBA, Bennett Papers, vol. 908, 569069–70, Hector McInnes to Bennett, 12 Jan. 1933; DUA, PO, A174, vol. 3, *Statements relating to the Incumbency of Carleton W. Stanley, President of Dalhousie University ...* (Halifax 1932).

82 DUA, Carleton Stanley Papers, B17, Stanley to W.D. Herridge, 18 Jan. 1932, copy; NA, Underhill Papers, vol. 5, H.L. Keenleyside to Underhill, 9 Nov. 1933; R.A. MacKay to the author, 4 Oct. 1972.

83 DUA, PO, Correspondence, MS1-3–A299, R.A. MacKay Personal, MacKay to Stanley, 25 Nov. 1935.

84 QUA, Lower Papers, vol. 1, file A8, Lower to MacKay, 14 Nov. 1936, copy; MacKay to Lower, 22 Nov. 1936.

85 Ibid., Lower to MacKay, 15 Dec. 1936, copy.

86 Ibid., file A6, Lower to 'Howard,' 23 Nov. 1934, copy.

87 Ibid., file A8, Lower to Andrew [Brown], 17 Apr. 1936, copy; file A10, Lower to Jack [Pickersgill], 16 Feb. 1938, copy.

88 Ibid., G.M.A. Grube to Lower, 2 Apr. 1938; Lower to Grube, 6 Apr. 1938, copy; Lower to W.H. Alexander, 6 June 1938, copy.

89 Roger Hutchinson, 'The Canadian Social Gospel in the Context of Christian Social Ethics,' in Richard Allen, ed., *The Social Gospel in Canada* (Ottawa 1975), 294; *NO*, 9 May 1934; MUA, RG2, PO, c.54/729, Beatty to A.E. Morgan, 13 Apr. 1937.

90 UC/VUA, PP, 89–130V, vol. 53–4, George S. Henry to J.R.L. Starr, 22 July 1932, copy; *TS*, 27 Oct. 1932; UC/VUA, PP, 89–130V, vol. 53–4, Henry to E.W. Wallace, 28 Oct. 1932.

91 Ibid., Henry to Wallace, 6 Feb. 1933; Wallace to Henry, 8 Feb. 1933, copy.

92 Ibid., Henry to Wallace, 13 Feb. 1933.

93 Ibid., Wallace to Henry, 10 Mar. 1933, copy.

94 Ibid., Henry to W.T. Brown, 9 Jan. 1934; Brown to Henry, 16 Jan. 1934, copy.

95 *TG*, 31 Mar. 1936.

96 Interview with E.A. Havelock, New Haven, Conn., April 1967; *GM*, 17 Apr. 1937.

97 UC/VUA, PP, 89–130V, 53–4, W.J. Little to E.W. Wallace, 17 Apr. 1937.

98 Ibid., H.C. Nixon to Wallace, 21 Apr. 1937; George McCullagh to Wallace, 29 Apr. 1937.

99 Havelock interview, Apr. 1967; UC/VUA, PP, 89–130V, 53–4, Havelock to Mitchell F. Hepburn, 24 Apr. 1937, copy; Havelock to Wallace, 1 and 2 May 1937.

100 Ibid., Wallace to Hepburn, 8 May 1937, copy; Wallace to Gregory Vlastos, 18 May 1937, copy.

101 Irving Martin Abella, *Nationalism, Communism, and Canadian Labour: The CIO, the Communist Party, and the Canadian Congress of Labour, 1935–56* (Toronto 1973), 19.

102 J. King Gordon, 'A Christian Socialist in the 1930s,' in Allen, ed., *The Social Gospel in Canada*, 140–1.

103 BUA, United Church of Canada, Montreal and Ottawa Conference, 1/2/1, Report of the Dean to the Board of Governors, 1931–2; Report of the Dean to the Board of Governors 1932–3.

104 BUA, 2/10/2, United Theological College, Senate Minutes, 25 Oct. 1932; MUA, RG2, PO, c.43/301, W.M. Birks to A.W. Currie, 22 Mar. 1933.

105 'The Front Page,' *SN*, 8 Apr. 1933.

106 *MG*, 31 Mar. 1933; NA, MG30, C241, J. King Gordon Papers, vol. 11, UTC, Montreal; BUA, UTC, Senate Minutes, 27 Apr. 1933; NA, Gordon Papers, vol. 11, file 17, R.H. Barron to Gordon, 24 Mar. 1934; NA, MG30, D211, F.R. Scott Papers, mfm reel M3733, 63, 'Charge J. King Gordon "Sacrificed" for Stand on Economic Questions,' unidentified undated clipping; NA, Gordon Papers, vol. 11, file 19, W.D. Lighthall to Gordon, 18 Apr. 1934.

107 NA, Gordon Papers, vol. 10, Corr. 1933–4, G.V. Ferguson to Gordon, 5 Apr. 1934, and J.S. Woodsworth to Gordon, 26 Apr. 1934; Corr. 1934, Terry MacDermot to Gordon, 22 Sept. 1934; vol. 7, file 32, Harry F. Ward to Gordon, 25 Oct. 1934; file 34, Gregory Vlastos to the Editor, *The Christian Century*, 7 Oct. 1934, copy; 'The Front Page,' *SN*, 12 May 1934; 'The Case of the Montreal College,' *NO*, 11 Apr. 1934.

108 *MS*, 20 Sept. and 13 Oct. 1934; Graham Spry, 'The Case of King Gordon,' *New Commonwealth*, 27 Oct. 1934.

109 'United Theological College, Montreal, Chair of Ethics,' and 'Editorial: The King Gordon Case,' *NO*, 6 Dec. 1934.

110 King Gordon to the author, 2 Oct. 1972.

111 'What's the Matter with Old McGill?' *QCT*, 11 Jan. 1939.

112 MUA, RG2, PO, c.43/303, Lewis Douglas to J.W. McConnell, 4 Jan. 1939, copy.

113 Ibid., Beatty to Douglas, 12 and 20 Jan. 1939.

114 Ibid., Arthur G. Penny to Beatty, 21 Jan. 1939, copy; 'A Teacher Should Enlighten, Not Guide,' *QCT*, 21 Jan. 1939.

115 Ibid., Beatty to Penny, 15 Feb. 1939, copy.

116 Ibid., Douglas to Beatty, 20 Feb. 1939, copy; Penny to Beatty, 17 Feb. 1939, copy.

117 *MG*, 13 Apr. 1939; MUA, RG2, PP, c.43/303, A.G. Morphy to Beatty, 14 Apr. 1939, and L.A. McL[illegible] to Douglas, 13 Apr. 1939.

118 *GM*, 8 Apr. 1939.

119 *GM*, 13 and 14 Apr. 1939.

120 Underhill, quoted in R.A. MacKay and E.B. Rogers, *Canada Looks Abroad* (Toronto 1938), 269.

121 *GM*, 14 Apr. 1939; Humphrey Carver, 'Premier Hepburn and the Professors,' *CF* 19 (May 1939), 41.

122 'Free Speech or Wise Speech,' *GM*, 15 Apr. 1939; 'Premier Entitled to Demand Disciplining of Professors,' *TT*, 15 Apr. 1939; 'Universities and Professors,' *MG*, 15 Apr. 1939.

123 'New Prexy for Varsity,' *SN*, 22 Apr. 1939; NA, Scott Papers, vol. 1, file Academic Freedom, A.B. Plaunt to Scott, 26 Apr. 1939.

124 'University Professors and Free Speech,' *Ottawa Journal*, 19 Apr. 1939.

125 UTA, PO, A72-0033/001(03), Chester Martin to Cody, 19 Apr. 1939.

126 NA, Underhill Papers, vol. 4, Underhill to George Ferguson, 21 Apr. 1939, copy; QUA, Lower Papers, vol. 1, file A13, Underhill to Lower, 1 May 1939.

127 UTA, A72-0033/001(03), Underhill to Cody, 18 Apr. 1939.

128 NA, Underhill Papers, vol. 5, B.S. Keirstead to Underhill, 15 Apr. 1939; vol. 6, R.A. MacKay to Underhill, 17 Apr. 1939; vol. 7, Escott Reid to Underhill, 4 May 1939.

129 UTA, PO, A72-0033/001(03), H.J. Beveridge to Cody, 19 Apr. 1939, and petitions; J.R. Mutchmor to Cody, 17 Apr. 1939; C.E. Silcox to Cody, 17 Apr. 1939, and 'Statement on Academic Freedom and the Rights of the Citizen'; A72-0033/001(04), Olga Johnson to Cody, 18 Apr. 1939.

130 Peter Oliver, *G. Howard Ferguson* (Toronto 1977), 438. See also Francis, *Frank H. Underhill*, 110; McKillop, *Matters of Mind*, 397–8; Neil McKenty, *Mitch Hepburn* (Toronto 1967), 190.

131 UTA, PO, A72-0033/001(03), Balmer Neilly to C.E. Higginbottom, 8 May 1939, copy; 'Statement Regarding Professor Frank Underhill' [June 1939].

132 Conversation with G.M.A. Grube, Toronto, Apr. 1966; TCA, Grube Provostial file
     987-0003, G.M.A. Grube to the Provost, 12 Apr. 1939.
133 Ibid., Grube to the Provost, 17 Apr. 1939.
134 Ibid., Memorandum Submitted to Professor Grube as Approved by Executive Com-
     mittee, April 1939.
135 Ibid., Grube to the Provost, 27 Apr. 1939.
136 'Free Speech in Toronto,' *CF* 19 (June 1939), 72; QUA, Lower Papers, vol. 1, file
     A13, Gerald Riddell to Lower, 29 Apr. 1939.
137 QUA, Lower Papers, vol. 1, file A12, Lower to Grube, 17 Apr. 1939, copy; UBCA,
     Alan B. Plaunt Papers, vol. 2–4, Plaunt to George A. Drew, 17 Apr. 1939, copy.
138 UBCA, Plaunt Papers, George Drew to Plaunt, 18 Apr. 1939.
139 But see Charles E. Lindblom, *Politics and Markets* (New York 1977), 199.
140 Interview with Stanley B. Ryerson, Montreal, Jan. 1990; conversation with Earle
     Birney, Toronto, Apr. 1967; Elspeth Cameron, *Earle Birney: A Life* (Toronto 1994),
     169–77.
141 W.H. Alexander, 'Will Radical Leadership Emerge from Canadian Universities?'
     Saskatchewan CCF Research 1 (July 1934), 15.
142 W.H. Alexander, '"Noli Episcopari": Letter to a Young Man Contemplating an
     Academic Career,' *CF* 19 (Oct. 1939), 220–3.
143 QUA, Lower Papers, vol. 1, file A10, Alexander to Lower, 28 Feb. 1938.
144 DUA, PO, MS1-3–A398, Correspondence, vol. 14, various letters from and to
     Carleton Stanley.

6: Socialism and Academic Freedom at McGill

1 MUA, RG2, PO, c.43/301, AWC, Re Professors Forsey and Scott, 26 Oct. 1933.
2 *MG*, 3 Feb. 1931; Sandra Djwa, *The Politics of the Imagination: A Life of F.R. Scott*
   (Toronto 1987), 113–14.
3 *MG*, 4 Feb. 1931; 'Police and Seditionists,' 5 Feb. 1931; 'Not Free Speech, but
   Licence,' *MG*, 7 Feb. 1931; 'Communists Need to Be Curbed,' *MG*, 11 Feb. 1931;
   conversations with Frank R. Scott, Montreal, Dec. 1966 and later.
4 MUA, RG2, PO, c.43/301, A.W. Currie to John W. Ross, 23 Nov. 1932, copy.
5 Eugene Forsey, *A Life on the Fringe: Memoirs* (Toronto 1990), 52.
6 MUA, PO, RG2, c.43/301, A.J. Nesbitt to Currie, 21 Nov. 1932; J.H. MacBrien to
   Wilfrid Bovey, 13 Dec. 1932.
7 Ibid., Bovey to MacBrien, 20 Dec. 1932, copy; Currie to A.J. Nesbitt, 22 Nov.
   1932, copy; Currie to John W. Ross, 23 Nov. 1932, copy.
8 Ibid., MacBrien to Currie, 13 Feb. 1933; Currie to Herbert Molson, 15 Feb. 1933,
   copy.
9 Ibid., Stephen Leacock to Currie, 13 May 1933.

10 Ibid., Currie to J.B. Maclean, 10 July 1933, copy.

11 Ibid., W.L. Grant to Currie, 13 Oct. 1933; Currie to Grant, 16 Oct. 1933, copy.

12 *MS*, 18 Oct. 1933; 'Socialism in Our Universities,' *QCT*, 19 Oct. 1933; 'Socialism in Universities,' *TG*, 26 Oct. 1933.

13 'A Professor Asks a Very Proper Question,' *TS*, 25 Oct. 1933; NA, MG 30, D211, F.R. Scott Papers, mfm M3733, Scrapbooks, 78, clipping from *OC*, 31 Oct. 1933.

14 MUA, RG2, PO, c.43/301, Arthur Purvis to Currie, 28 Oct. 1933.

15 Ibid., Currie to Forsey, 26 Oct. 1933, copy; Forsey to Currie, 26 Oct. 1933; Currie to Cyril H. Adair, 4 Nov. 1933, copy; Currie to S.P. Rose, 25 Oct. 1933, copy. See also Paul Axelrod, 'McGill University on the Landscape of Canadian Higher Education: Historical Reflections,' *Higher Education Perspectives* 1 (1996–7), 128.

16 MUA, RG2, PO, c.43/301, Currie to L.-A. Taschereau, 21 Oct. 1933, copy; Currie to A.B. Purvis, 24 Oct. 1933, copy.

17 Ibid., Currie to Lorne C. Webster, 24 Oct. 1933, copy.

18 Ibid., AWC, Re Professors Forsey and Scott, 26 Oct. 1933.

19 *Report of the Committee Appointed by the Government to Investigate the Finances of British Columbia ... with Appendix Containing Comments by the Government of British Columbia* (Victoria 1932), 36, 69.

20 UBCSC, Kidd Report clippings file; Robin Fisher, *Duff Pattullo of British Columbia* (Toronto 1991), 222.

21 UBCA, BoG, Minutes, vol. 11, 8 Feb. 1932; Stanley Brice Frost *McGill University*, vol. 2: *1895–1971* (Kingston and Montreal 1984), 189, 196.

22 *MG*, 26 Oct. 1935.

23 MUA, RG2, PO, c.54/729, E.W. Beatty to A.E. Morgan, 18 Feb. 1936.

24 Ibid., Morgan to Beatty, 20 Feb. 1936, copy; Beatty to Morgan, 28 Dec. 1936; Morgan to Beatty, 30 Dec. 1936, copy.

25 Ibid., Beatty to Morgan, 5 Jan. 1937.

26 *MG*, 24 Feb. 1937.

27 Edward Beatty, 'Freedom and the Universities,' *QQ* 44, no. 4 (Winter 1937–8), 470.

28 'One of Our Teachers,' *MG*, 15 Aug. 1938.

29 MUA, RG2, PO, c.47/442, Francis H. Clergue to Beatty, 15 Aug. 1938, copy.

30 Ibid., Beatty to Clergue, 18 Aug. 1938, copy; Beatty to Lewis Douglas, 18 Aug. 1938.

31 MUA, Scrapbooks, vol. 9, 326, *MG*, 3 Dec. 1935.

32 Frost, *McGill University*, vol. 2, 128, 137n19; MUA, RG2, PO, c.687/2028, F. Cyril James to W.M. Birks, 28 Sept. 1940, copy.

33 MUA, RG2, PO, c.47/443, Ira MacKay to Currie, 21 July 1933.

34 Ibid., c.47/442, memorandum for Principal Douglas, 7 July 1938.

35 Ibid., T.H. Matthews to Douglas, 24 Jan. 1939; Douglas to Matthews, 26 Jan. 1939, copy; Matthews to Douglas, 27 Jan. 1939.

36 Frost, *McGill University*, vol. 2, 192–6.

37 Ibid., 198–200.

38 Marlene Shore, *The Science of Social Redemption: McGill, the Chicago School, and the Origins of Social Research in Canada* (Toronto 1987), 12; Leonard C. Marsh, 'Foreword,' *Employment Research: An Introduction to the McGill Programme of Research in the Social Sciences* (Toronto 1935), vii.

39 MUA, RG2, PO, c.62/1053, Leacock to Currie, 6 June 1931; Shore, *The Science of Social Redemption*, 14; Allan Irving, 'Leonard Marsh and the McGill Social Science Research Project,' *JCS* 21, no. 2 (Summer 1986).

40 MUA, RG2, PO, c.62/1055 [Dorothy McMurray], 'Social Science Research' [1938].

41 Ibid., c.56/837, 'Founder's Day Dinner,' *McGill News* (Winter 1938), 24.

42 Ibid., c.54/730, Douglas to Beatty, 3 Feb. 1939, copy. On salaries, see Vincent Bladen, *Bladen on Bladen: Memoirs of a Political Economist* (Toronto 1977), 216–8. On Lionel Robbins, see Robert Skidelsky, *John Maynard Keynes*, vol. 2: *The Economist as Saviour, 1920–1937* (London 1992), 341, 368–9, 455, 596–7.

43 See MUA, RG2, PO, c.90/2550, especially Dorothy McMurray, 'Tenure of Appointment: Summary of Information in Principal's Files Obtained in 1920 When Tenure of Appointment Was under Consideration,' n.d.; Frost, *McGill University*, vol. 2, 206.

44 MUA, RG2, PO, c.54/730, Douglas to Beatty, 23 Nov. 1939, copy; c.90/2550, Statement of Policy Governing Tenure of Appointment for All Grades under the Rank of Professor, 25 Feb. 1939.

45 Frost, *McGill University*, vol. 2, 202; MUA, RG2, PO, c.62/1055, Marsh to W.H. Brittain, 12 Oct. 1937; Brittain to Marsh, 14 Oct. 1937, copy; 'L.C. Marsh' [1938].

46 MUA, RG2, PO, c.62/1055, Douglas to Marsh, 21 Dec. 1938, copy; J.J. O'Neill to Douglas, 23 Feb. 1939; BoG, Minute Book, mfm reel 5, 28 Nov. 1939.

47 MUA, RG2, PO, c.62/1055, memo LWD/DM, 30 Nov. 1939.

48 Ibid., J.C. Hemmeon to W.H. Brittain, 14 Oct. 1937; F.C. James to L.H. Douglas, Dec. 1939; DM, memorandum, 1 Dec. 1939.

49 Ibid., W. Bentley to Marsh, 2 Dec. 1939, copy, and c.62/1053, Memorandum for the Principal, re Social Science Research, 1 Oct. 1930; interview with Leonard Marsh, Montreal, June 1967.

50 MUA, MG1038, Eugene Forsey Papers, vol. 2, James to Forsey, 17 June 1940. See also Frost, *McGill University*, vol. 2, 202.

51 Forsey, *A Life on the Fringe*, 33; MUA, Forsey Papers, vol. 2, J.C. Hemmeon to Forsey, 12 July 1940.

52 MUA, Forsey Papers, James to Forsey, 16 Dec. 1940; Forsey to James, 18 Dec. 1940, copy; James to Forsey, 4 Jan. 1941.

53 NA, MG30, D204, F.H. Underhill Papers, vol. 4, Forsey to Underhill, 2 May 1941.

54 NA, MG27 III B1, C.H. Cahan Papers, vol. 2, E.W. Beatty to Cahan, 14 Mar. 1941.

55 Telephone conversation with Helen Forsey, November 1997. The closed file is MUA, RG2, PO, c.92/2598.

56 MUA, MG1052, David C. Munroe Papers, F.C. James file, James to Munroe, 4 Mar. 1969. On Stanley Gray, see Frost, *McGill University*, vol. 2, 460, 472.

57 Michael Bliss, 'Preface,' *Report on Social Security for Canada 1943* (Toronto 1975), ix.

58 Frost, *McGill University*, vol. 2, 202; Shore, *The Science of Social Redemption*, 266–7.

7: The Second World War

1 MUA, RG2, PO, c.61/1010, Thomas J. Coonan to A.E. Morgan, 10 Feb. 1937, and Morgan to Coonan, 17 Feb. 1937, copy; *MG*, 12 Oct. 1938; F.R.F., letter to the editor, *MG*, 16 Oct, 1938; *MG*, 15 Nov. 1939; *MS*, 14 Nov. 1939.

2 'A Graceless Exhibition,' *MS*, 15 Nov. 1939; 'A Misrepresentation of Fact,' *MS*, 20 Nov. 1939.

3 'Nazis Capitalize Adair Speech,' *MG*, 22 Nov. 1939.

4 Letter from the Law Undergraduate Society, *McGill Daily*, 17 Nov. 1939.

5 MUA, Michael Perceval-Maxwell, 'The History of History at McGill,' James McGill Society, 2 Apr. 1981, 31.

6 DUA, MS2–163, B48, Stanley Papers, Corr., Edward Beatty to Carleton Stanley, 27 Nov. 1939.

7 Ibid., Stanley to Beatty, 29 Nov. 1939, copy.

8 NA, MG30, D211, F.R. Scott Papers, vol. 1, Academic Freedom file, C.O. Knowles, 'Academic Freedom,' typescript of broadcast, 18 Dec. 1938, over the national network of the CBC, passim.

9 Carlton McNaught, *Canada Gets the News* (Toronto 1940), 19–21.

10 Ramsay Cook, 'Canadian Freedom in Wartime, 1939–1945,' in W.H. Heick and Roger Graham, eds., *His Own Man: Essays in Honour of Arthur Reginald Marsden Lower* (Montreal and London 1974), 38–41, 44–5; Norman Penner, *Canadian Communism: The Stalin Years and Beyond* (Toronto 1988), 170–1.

11 P.B. Waite, *The Lives of Dalhousie University*, vol. 2: *1925–1980* (Montreal and Kingston 1998), 106.

12 UTA, PO (Cody), A68-0006/046(02), Hamilton Cassels to C.E. Higginbottom, 25 Oct. and 22 Nov. 1940, copies; Memorandum for the Bursar re Dr. Samuel Levine, 26 Nov. 1940; A68-0006/050(04), E.F. Burton, Memorandum regarding Dr. Levine, 8 Dec. 1941. See also Leopold Infeld, 'The Story of Samuel Levine,' *CF*, 21 (Nov. 1941); Burton, 'The Case of Dr. S. Levine,' *Science* 95 (23 Jan. 1942).

13 UTA, A68-0006/046(03), Cody to Ph. Thibault, 10 Mar. 1941, copy; A68-0006/ 050(04), F.A. Brewin to Cody, 4, 14, and 28 July 1941; Samuel Levine to Cody, 14 Oct. 1941.

14 Harry Grundfest, 'War Hysteria in Canada,' *Science* 94 (14 Nov. 1941), 461–2; UTA, A68-0006/050(03), Cody to Israel Halperin, 17 Dec. 1941, copy; A68-0006/ 050(04), Cody to Norman Levinson, 6 Jan. 1942, copy, and Levine to Cody, 9 Apr. 1942.

15 Penner, *Canadian Communism*, 183, 185–93; Reg Whitaker, 'Official Repression of Communism during World War II,' *LT* 17 (Spring 1986).

16 Watson Kirkconnell, *Seven Pillars of Freedom* (Toronto 1944), ix.

17 Kirkconnell, *A Slice of Canada: Memoirs* (Toronto 1967), 321.

18 'The Nazi "Line,"' *TS*, 29 May 1945; 'Soviet Russia and the Jews,' *TS*, 14 June 1945; 'The Front Page,' *SN*, 26 May 1945. On Atkinson and the Soviet Union, see Ross Harkness, *J.E. Atkinson of the Star* (Toronto 1963), 325.

19 See Michiel Horn, 'Academic Freedom and the Dismissal of George Hunter,' *DR* 69, no. 3 (Fall 1989).

20 Interview with Margaret Hunter, Montreal, Oct. 1988; Margaret Hunter to the author, 19 Aug. 1990; UAA, RG19, Personnel files, 73–112, George Hunter personal file (GHF), [unsigned], 'George Hunter,' n.d.

21 Gregory S. Kealey and Reg Whitaker, eds., *R.C.M.P. Security Bulletins: The War Series, 1939–1941* (St John's 1989), 140; Paul Axelrod, 'Spying on the Young in Depression and War: Students, Youth Groups and the RCMP, 1935–1942,' *LT* 35 (Spring 1995), 44–5.

22 UAA, GHF, 'Re: Prof. G. Hunter, University of Alberta, Edmonton, Alta,' 12 Apr. 1940.

23 UAA, BoG, Executive Committee Minutes, 16 Apr. 1940.

24 UAA, GHF, 'Dr. George Hunter, April 19th, 1940'; Hunter to Kerr, 22 Apr. 1940.

25 UAA, BoG, Minutes, 14 May 1940, 11–12.

26 UAA, GHF, Kerr to Hunter, 18 May 1940, unsigned original.

27 Ibid., note attached to unsent letter, 20 May 1940

28 UAA, Senate, Minutes, vol. 5, 12 May 1941.

29 UAA, PO, 3/3/12–13, W.A.R. Kerr to the Cabinet, 20 May 1941, and attachment; Kerr to J.H. Blackmore, 31 May 1941, copy.

30 BoG, Minutes, Executive Committee, 9 Sept. 1941, copy of Order-in-Council 1117/ 41.

31 University of Alberta, Survey Committee, *Interim Report*, Alberta, Sessional Paper no. 50, 1942, 24.

32 UAA, Robert Newton, 'I Passed This Way,' 298–301, 338.

33 University of Alberta, Survey Committee, *Interim Report*, 31.

34 BoG, Minutes, 29 June and 12 Dec. 1942.

35 J.L. Granatstein, *Canada's War: The Politics of the Mackenzie King Government, 1939–1945* (Toronto 1975), 128.
36 NA, MG30, D204, Frank H. Underhill Papers, vol. 19, Writings 1940, 'A United American Front.'
37 UTA, PO, A72-0033/001(03), clippings file, *TT*, 24 Aug. 1940; 'Professor Underhill Again Misinterprets Canada's Attitude to Great Britain,' *OPT*, 29 Aug. 1940; 'Charge of Persecution Does Not Fit in This Case,' *TT*, 24 Sept. 1940; Roger Graham, *Arthur Meighen*, vol. 3: *No Surrender* (Toronto and Vancouver 1965), 123.
38 UTA, PO, A72-0033/001(03), J.S. Hart to Cody, 30 Aug. 1940; William J. Deadman to Cody, 1 Sept. 1940.
39 'An Ill-Timed Address,' *TS*, 31 Aug. 1940.
40 UTA, PO, A72-0033/001(03), Underhill to Cody, 1 Sept. 1940, with Underhill to the editor, *Toronto Daily Star*, 1 Sept. 1940, copy.
41 Ibid., Neilly to Cody, 28 Aug. 1940; Mulock to Cody, 31 Aug. 1940; Underhill to Cody, 4 Sept. 1940.
42 R. Douglas Francis, *Frank H. Underhill* (Toronto 1986), 117; UTA, A70-0024, BoG, Minutes, 12 September 1940.
43 UTA, PO, A72-0033/001(03), C.E. Silcox to Cody, 15 Sept. 1940; E.J. Tarr to Cody, 4 Sept. 1940; B.K. Sandwell to Cody, 16 Sept. 1940.
44 Ibid., Malcolm Wallace to Cody, 15 Sept. 1940; DUA, MS 2–163, B56, Carleton Stanley Papers, Corr., Underhill to Stanley, 18 Sept. 1940.
45 UTA, PO, A72-0033/001(03), Hamilton Cassels to the Chairman of the Board of Governors, 16 Sept. 1940, copy.
46 UTA, PO, A70-0024, BoG, Minutes, 16 Sept. 1940; *TS*, 17 Sept. 1940.
47 UBCA, N.A.M. MacKenzie Papers, Main Correspondence, vol. 21, file 2, Underhill to MacKenzie, 18 Sept. 1940.
48 DUA, Stanley Papers, Stanley to Underhill, 23 Sept. 1940, copy.
49 'University Governors Present a Sorry Spectacle,' *TT*, 18 Sept. 1940; 'Playing Politics with Principles,' *GM*, 25 Sept. 1940; UTA, PO, A72-0033/001(03), W.R. Yendall to Cody, 1 Oct. 1940.
50 UTA, BoG, Minutes, 26 Sept. 1940; PO, A72-0033/001(03), attachment to Balmer Neilly to Cody, 6 Dec. 1940, italics in the document.
51 UTA, BoG, Minutes, 10 Oct. 1940; PO, A72-0033/001(03), Neilly to Cody, 6 Dec. 1940; also Neilly to Cody, 12[?] Dec. 1940.
52 See D.C. Masters, *Henry John Cody* (Toronto 1995), 262–3.
53 UTA, PO, A72-0033/001(03), H.J. Cody, Confidential statement, n.d.; A70-0024, BoG, Minutes, 19 Dec. 1940.
54 UTA, BoG, Minutes, 27 Dec. 1940; Francis, *Frank H. Underhill*, 121. Andrei Vishinsky was prosecutor in Stalin's show trials of the later 1930s.

55 NA, Underhill Papers, vol. 8, Universities file, 'Statement by Professor F.H. Underhill as to an Interview between him and a Committee of the Board of Governors on January 2, 1941.'
56 NA, Underhill Papers, vol. 6, Leopold Macaulay to Underhill, 6 Jan. 1941; NA, Scott Papers, vol. 29, Underhill to Scott, 4 Jan. 1941.
57 NA, Underhill Papers, vol. 8, Herbert Davis to Underhill, 9 Jan. 1941; UTA, PO, A72-0033/001(01), Chester Martin to Cody, 3 Jan. 1941.
58 NA, Scott Papers, vol. 29, Underhill to Scott, 4 Jan. 1941; Underhill Papers, vol. 8, 'Statement ... January 2, 1941.'
59 Many of the letters that reached Cody are in UTA, PO, A72-0033/001.
60 UTA, PO, A72-0033/001(01), [H.J. Cody], untitled four-page document, 7 Jan. 1941.
61 Ibid.
62 Ibid., Underhill to D. Bruce Macdonald, 8 Jan. 1941; Underhill to Cody, 9 Jan. 1941.
63 UTA, PO, A72-0033/001(02), 36 students to Cody; Harold I. Nelson and John F. Gray to Cody, 9 Jan. 1941, and attachment; Clifford Sifton to Cody, 10 and 20 Jan. 1941; A72-0033/001(01), V. Evan Gray to Cody, 8 Jan. 1941; O.M. Biggar to Cody, 10 and 15 Jan. 1941.
64 UTA, PO, A72-0033/001(02), H.L. Keenleyside to Cody, 8 Jan. 1941.
65 UTA, PO, A72-0033/001(01), J. Bartlet Brebner to H.A. Innis, 10 Jan. 1941.
66 Ibid., Cody to Gray, 15 Jan. 1941, copy; Cody to Biggar, 13 Jan. 1941, copy.
67 UTA, PO, A72-0033/001(02), Cody to Sifton, 13 Jan. 1941, copy.
68 Ibid., Cody to Keenleyside, 13 Jan. 1941, copy.
69 Ibid., Keenleyside to Cody, 15 Jan. 1941.
70 Hugh L. Keenleyside, Memoirs, vol. 1: Hammer the Golden Day (Toronto 1981), 189; vol. 2: On the Bridge of Time (Toronto 1982), 109.
71 NA, MG26, J13, W.L.M. King Papers, vol. 336, Keenleyside to W.L.M. King, 7 Jan. 1941; Keenleyside, Memoirs, vol. 2, 108.
72 J.W. Pickersgill, 'The Decisive Battle for Academic Freedom in Canada,' unpublished paper, n.d., 15.
73 UTA, A70-0024, BoG, Minutes, 9 Jan. 1941; UTA, PO, A72-0033/001(01), Cody to Gray, 15 Jan. 1941, copy; Francis, Frank H. Underhill, 125.
74 UTA, BoG, Minutes, 26 June 1941.
75 Francis, Frank H. Underhill, 127.
76 NA, Scott Papers, vol. 29, F.H. Underhill, Some Account of Recent Strange Happenings in the University of Toronto, 14 Jan. 1941.
77 NA, MG30, D45, J.W. Dafoe Papers, vol. 12, Clifford Sifton to J.W. Dafoe, 22 Jan. 1941.
78 Pickersgill, 'The Decisive Battle for Academic Freedom in Canada,' 15; Donald

Creighton, 'The Ogdensburg Agreement and F.H. Underhill,' *The Passionate Observer: Selected Writings* (Toronto: 1980), 139.

79 NA, Underhill Papers, vol. 5, Underhill to Murray G. Lawson, 20 Aug. 1941, copy; Scott Papers, vol. 29, Louise Parkin to Scott, 9 Jan. 1941.

80 Francis, *Frank H. Underhill*, 128–57.

81 UTA, PO, A68-0006/046(03), W.P.M. Kennedy to Cody, 21 Sept. 1940; italics in the original.

82 Irving Abella, 'The Making of a Chief Justice: Bora Laskin, The Early Years,' *Upper Canada Law Society Gazette* 24, no. 3 (Sept. 1990), 191; C. Ian Kyer and Jerome E. Bickenbach, *The Fiercest Debate: Cecil A. Wright, the Benchers, and Legal Education in Ontario, 1923–1957* (Toronto 1987), 165, 310n19; Robert Bothwell, *Laying the Foundation* (Toronto 1991), 68, 110; F.W. Gibson, *Queen's University*, vol. 2 (Kingston and Montreal 1983), 199–202; Stanley Brice Frost, *McGill University*, vol. 2 (Kingston and Montreal 1984), 128, 137n19; A.B. McKillop, *Matters of Mind* (Toronto 1994), 359–61.

83 NA, Underhill Papers, vol. 4, Marvin Gelber to Underhill, 27 July 1936; telephone conversation with Sydney Eisen, Aug. 1995; interview with Ernest Sirluck, Toronto, Sept. 1995.

84 Herbert A. Strauss and Werner Röder, eds., *International Biographical Dictionary of Central European Emigrés, 1933–1945*, vol 2: *The Arts, Sciences, and Literature* (Munich 1983), passim; Lawrence D. Stokes, 'Canada and an Academic Refugee from Nazi Germany: The Case of Gerhard Herzberg,' *CHR* 57, no. 2 (June 1976); Irving Abella and Harold Troper, 'Canada and the Refugee Intellectual, 1933–1939,' in Jarrell C. Jackman and Carole S. Borden, eds., *The Muses Flee Hitler: Cultural Transfer and Adaptation, 1930–1945* (Washington, D.C. 1983), 260.

85 NA, Scott Papers, vol. 24, James to C.S. LeMesurier, 14 Aug. 1942.

86 Ibid., vol. 1, Academic Freedom Corr. 1938–1950, Wilfrid Bovey to Scott, 25 Mar. 1942, 12 July, 6 Aug., and 16 Sept. 1943.

87 Frank R. Scott, 'What Did "No" Mean?' *CF* 22 (June 1942).

88 Eugene Forsey, letter to *CF* 22 (Aug. 1942), 141; 'Those Who Render Disservice,' *WFP* (2 July 1942); 'The Front Page,' *SN*, 10 Oct. 1942; Sandra Djwa, *The Politics of the Imagination* (Toronto 1987), 202, 204.

89 MUA, RG2, PO, c.85/2202, 'Academic Freedom of Speech.'

90 Ibid., [Dorothy McMurray], comments on 'Academic Freedom of Speech,' n.d. [1943];

91 TCA, G.M.A. Grube Papers, MS 98, vol. 18, illegible [Bursar] to Grube, 15 Feb. 1940.

92 Ibid., series II, vol. 2, 'The Intellectual in Politics,' n.d. [1944], 13, 15, 16.

93 TCA, Grube Provostial File, 987-0003, Memorandum re Interview between the Provost and Professor Grube, 1 June 1943; *TS*, 9 Dec. 1943; Grube Provostial File, Memorandum, 14 Dec. 1943.

94 Ibid., Grube to Provost, 22 Dec. 1943.

95 Most of my information about J. Stanley Allen I owe to Richard Allen, who has written about his uncle in a history of the Allen family, publication forthcoming.

96 MUA, RG2, PO, c.85/2202, W.H. Howard to R.E. Powell, 22 Nov. 1943, copy.

97 Ibid., F. Cyril James to W.M. Birks, 29 Nov. 1943, copy.

98 Gerald L. Caplan, *The Dilemma of Canadian Socialism: The CCF in Ontario* (Toronto 1973), 110–29.

99 UC/VUA, PO, 89-130V, 52–18, Walter T. Brown, 'The Staff and Politics,' 18 Apr. 1945.

100 Ibid., 49–11, E.A. Havelock to Brown, 10 May 1945; interview with Eric Havelock, New Haven, Conn., Apr. 1967.

101 UC/VUA, PO, 89-130V, 30-344, Brown to Havelock, 12 June 1945, copy; Havelock interview, Apr. 1967.

102 SAB, R61-3, W.S. Lloyd Papers, vol. 39, E25, file 1, J.S. Thomson to Lloyd, 27 Dec. 1944.

103 SAB, R33-1, T.C. Douglas Papers, vol. 224 (5–3), Raphael Tuck to Douglas, 10 Mar. 1945.

104 Michael Hayden, *Seeking a Balance* (Vancouver 1983), 209, 214ff; SAB, Lloyd Papers, vol. 39, E25, file 2, Lloyd to the Committee of Enquiry into the University Act and University Practices, 6 Oct. 1945.

105 SAB, Douglas Papers, vol. 224 (5–3), file 1, 'The Report of the University of Saskatchewan Survey Committee,' 14 Dec. 1945, attached to Lloyd to Douglas, 3 Jan. 1946; USA, Regulations of the Board of Governors, [1948], 11.

106 USA, BoG, Minutes, 10 Jan. 1950; Michael Hayden to the author, 15 July 1994.

107 Stanley Brice Frost, *McGill University*, vol. 2, 242; John Bryden, *Deadly Allies: Canada's Secret War, 1937–1947* (Toronto 1990), viii–ix.

108 UAA, Robert Newton, 'I Passed This Way' (unpublished typescript [n.d.]), 347; E.A. Corbett, *Sidney Earle Smith* (Toronto 1961), 52; conversation with Donald Avery, Toronto, Nov. 1997.

109 UTA, PO, A68/0006/050(04), 'Conviction re War,' attached to J.D. Ketchum to Cody, 17 Nov. 1941; emphasis in the original.

110 Ibid., Cody to Ketchum, 19 Nov. 1941, copy; also Ketchum to Cody, 20 Nov. 1941.

111 Ibid., Ketchum to Cody, 20 Jan. 1942.

112 NA, Underhill Papers, vol. 2, George E. Britnell to Underhill, 26 Jan. 1941.

113 UNBA, Dominick S. Graham, 'A Fly-by-Night President' (unpublished typescript, 1982), 2.

114 UAA, BoG, Executive Committee, Minutes, 13 Sept. 1940 and 28 Aug. 1942.

115 Waite, *The Lives of Dalhousie University*, vol. 2, 62–4; R.C. Wallace, 'The University Carries On,' *Queen's Review* 16 (June 1942), 165; McKillop, *Matters of Mind*, 167–80. 532.

116 Ibid., 677n; 'Arts Courses in Wartime,' *GM*, 24 Dec. 1942; Gwendoline Evans Pilkington, *Speaking with One Voice: Universities in Dialogue with Government* (Montreal 1983), 29.

117 McKillop, *Matters of Mind*, 532. See Nancy Kiefer and Ruth Roach Pierson, 'The War Effort and Women Students at the University of Toronto, 1939–45,' in Paul Axelrod and John G. Reid, eds., *Youth, University and Canadian Society* (Kingston and Montreal 1989).

118 Donald Creighton, *Harold Adams Innis* (Toronto 1957), 116; UTA, PO, A68/0006/ 055(04), Kirkconnell to Cody, 8 Dec. 1942; Memorial on Studies in the Humanities in Canada, attached to Kirkconnell to Cody, 31 Dec. 1942.

119 Frederick W. Gibson, *Queen's University*, vol. 2, 211; Pilkington, *Speaking with One Voice*, 30–1; Stanley Brice Frost, *The Man in the Ivory Tower* (Montreal and Kingston 1991), 111.

120 Gibson, *Queen's University*, vol. 2, 212.

121 Charles M. Johnston, *McMaster University*, vol. 2 (Toronto 1981), 84; CBA, McMaster University, Fine Arts Department, Professor Stanley Hart (1936–43), G.P. Gilmour to Hart, 15 Apr. 1942, copy.

122 CBA, McMaster University, BoG Executive, 'Memorandum on Continuance of Fine Arts Department, for discussion April 15, 1942.'

123 Ibid., W.B. Hurd to Whidden, [Jan. 1940].

124 Ibid., Whidden to Hart, 9 Mar. 1940, copy.

125 DUA, PO, Corr., MS1-3-A540, vol. 18, Modern Languages 1911–56, Carleton Stanley to H.E. Macdonald, 7 Feb. 1936, copy, in reply to Macdonald to Stanley, 5 Feb. 1936; UTA, PO, A72-0033/001(01), Stanley to Cody, 26 Feb. 1941.

126 On Stanley's dismissal, see Waite, *The Lives of Dalhousie University*, vol. 2, 129–38.

127 DUA, PO, MS1-3-A175, Corr., vol. 3, W.E. McNeill to Stanley, 2 Sept. 1944, and Sherwood Fox to Stanley, 6 Sept. 1944.

128 P.B. Waite to the author, 2 Aug. 1995.

129 DUA, MS1-1-A10, BoG, Minutes, 15 Sept. 1944.

130 Ibid., 28 Nov. 1944.

131 DUA, MS2-163, Stanley Papers, Corr., B77, J.C. Webster to K.C. Laurie, 2[?] and 17 Nov. 1944, copies.

132 DUA, BoG, Minutes, 28 Nov. 1944; Waite, *The Lives of Dalhousie University*, vol. 2, 134.

133 Ibid., 19; DUA, MS2-163, Stanley Papers, Corr., B64, Robert P. Ludlum to K.C. Laurie, 15 Jan. 1945, copy.

134 DUA, Stanley Papers, B84, BoG, stenographic report, meeting, 23 Jan. 1945.

135 Ibid.

136 DUA, Stanley Papers, B84, Stanley to C.F. Mackenzie, 6 Feb. 1945, copy; B65, Stanley to Leonard Brockington, 7 Feb. 1945, copy.

137 Ibid., B76, Macdonald, McInnes, Macquarrie & Pattillo to J.B. Walker, Feb. 1945, copy; A.G. Bedford, *The University of Winnipeg* (Toronto 1975), 282.

138 'Carleton Stanley Resigns,' *WFP*, 16 Feb. 1945; 'Dr. Stanley Retires,' *SN*, 24 Feb. 1945; J.V. McAree, 'Dalhousie to Lose Its Famous President,' *GM*, 26 Feb. 1945.

139 Judith Robinson, 'Dalhousie Drops a President,' *Nation*, 10 Mar. 1945, 275.

140 PANS, MG17, vol. 20, Universities and Colleges, Dalhousie University, Stanley dispute, John Doull to Bennett, 26 Jan. 1945, copy; Laurie to Bennett, 31 May 1945, copy.

141 In a letter to the author dated 2 August 1995, P.B. Waite states that this assessment occurs in a memoir, 'Memories of My Father' (1991), by Laura Stanley Woolmer.

142 DUA, Stanley Papers, B64, Roy Fraser to Stanley, 14 Feb. 1945; B68, W.H. Alexander to Stanley, 8 Apr. 1945.

143 Ibid., B75, Underhill to Stanley, 13 Feb. 1945.

144 Ibid., Stanley to Underhill [n.d.], copy.

8: The Coming of the Cold War

1 *MS*, 15 Mar. 1946; *MG*, 23 Mar. 1946; Reg Whitaker and Gary Marcuse, *Cold War Canada: The Making of a National Insecurity State, 1945–1957* (Toronto 1994), 72–4, 161; Stanley Brice Frost, *McGill University*, vol. 2 (Kingston and Montreal 1984), 242.

2 'The Mind of Mr. Low,' *MS*, 20 Mar. 1946; Paul Dufour, '"Eggheads" and Espionage: The Gouzenko Affair in Canada,' *JCS* 16, nos. 3 and 4 (Fall-Winter 1981), 194.

3 Frost, *McGill University*, vol. 2, 242.

4 Frederick W. Gibson, *Queen's University*, vol. 2 (Kingston and Montreal 1983), 277–80.

5 QUA, coll. 1125, F.W. Gibson Papers, vol. 4, Israel Halperin file, D.A. Gillies to R.C. Wallace, 30 May 1947; Wallace to Gillies, 18 Aug. 1947; Francis King to Wallace, 24 Sept. 1947. All documents in the Gibson Papers are photocopies of originals located mainly in the records of the principal's office.

6 Gibson, *Queen's University*, vol. 2, 284; QUA, Gibson Papers, vol. 4, BoT, Minutes, 15 May 1948.

7 QUA, Gibson Papers, vol. 4, Glen Shortliffe file, Margaret McEnaney to Glen Shortliffe, 19 Nov. 1945; Shortliffe to the Editor, *Queen's Journal*, 22 Nov. 1947.

8 Ibid., Shortliffe to R.C. Wallace, 26 Feb. 1948.

9 Ibid., Shortliffe to Marjorie McEnaney, 7 Oct. 1948.

10 QUA, coll. 1061, Glen Shortliffe Papers, vol. 5, Shortliffe to the editor, *KWS*, 6 Nov. 1948, copy; 'Prof. Shortliffe's Facts Are Scanty,' *KWS*, 6 Nov. 1948.

11 'Shattering Reflections over CBC,' *MG*, 23 Dec. 1948; QUA, Gibson Papers, vol. 4,

J.B. Stirling to R.C. Wallace, n.d.; *Radio Broadcasting Report*, Dec. 30, 1948 – Jan. 6, 1949; M.N. Hay to Wallace, 1 Feb. 1949; J.C. Macfarlane to Wallace, n.d.

12 QUA, Gibson Papers, vol. 4, 'Week-end Review,' 13 Feb. 1949, and J.C. Walsh to R.C. Wallace, 14 Feb. 1949; Gibson, *Queen's University*, vol. 2, 289.

13 QUA, Gibson Papers, vol. 4, Shortliffe to Wallace, 15 Feb. 1949, and Wallace to Shortliffe, 17 Feb. 1949.

14 Gibson, *Queen's University*, vol. 2, 291, 292; QUA, Gibson Papers, vol. 4, Shortliffe to Wallace, 23 Feb. 1949.

15 Glen Shortliffe, 'Class Conflict and International Politics,' *International Journal* 4, no. 2 (Spring 1949); 'Correspondence,' *International Journal* 4, no. 3 (Summer 1949); 'News Letter,' Department of Economic Development, Canadian Chamber of Commerce, no. 85 (May 1949), passim.

16 QUA, Gibson Papers, vol. 4, J.B. Stirling to Wallace, 17 May 1949.

17 Gibson, *Queen's University*, vol. 2, 293; QUA, Gibson Papers, vol. 4, Ralph Campney to Shortliffe, 13 Dec. 1954.

18 QUA, Gibson Papers, vol. 4, Shortliffe to Monroe Scott, 18 Feb. 1961.

19 Whitaker and Marcuse, *Cold War Canada*, 108–10.

20 H.S. Ferns, *Reading from Left to Right: One Man's Political History* (Toronto 1988), 228–49, 288.

21 Ibid., 285.

22 Ibid., 293, 295.

23 NA, MG30, D211, F.R. Scott Papers, vol. 1, Academic Freedom Corr. 1938–1950, F. Cyril James to LeMesurier, 10 Oct. 1947, copy.

24 Ibid., Scott to George Pope Shannon, 13 Nov. 1947, copy; Shannon to Scott, 4 Dec. 1947; Scott to Shannon, 11 Dec. 1947, copy.

25 MUA, BoG, Minutes, 14 Jan. 1948; NA, Scott Papers, vol. 1, William Bentley to distribution, 21 Jan. 1948, copy.

26 NA, Scott Papers, vol. 1, Harold Laski to Scott, 27 Jan. 1948, and 'Universities and Political Activity,' attached to Scott to O.S. Tyndale, 10 Feb. 1948, copy; MUA, BoG, Minutes, 10 Mar. 1948.

27 Scott to the author, 11 Sept. 1968; Sandra Djwa, *The Politics of the Imagination* (Toronto 1987), 359–70.

28 Djwa, *The Politics of the Imagination*, 240. Concerning the *Roncarelli* and *Switzman* cases, see Djwa, 297–317.

29 Roderick A. Macdonald, 'The National Law Programme at McGill: Origins, Establishment, Prospects,' *Dalhousie Law Journal* 13, no. 1 (May 1990), 283; Stanley Brice Frost, *The Man in the Ivory Tower* (Montreal and Kingston 1991), 185–90, 225–9. This account is more complete than the one in Frost's history of McGill.

30 Frank R. Scott, 'Author's Preface,' in Michiel Horn, ed., *A New Endeavour: Selected Political Essays, Letters, and Addresses* (Toronto 1986), x.

31 Michael Behiels, 'Father Georges-Henri Lévesque and the Introduction of Social
Sciences at Laval, 1938–55,' in Paul Axelrod and John G. Reid, eds., *Youth, University and Canadian Society* (Kingston and Montreal 1989), 330–2; Ray Ellenwood,
'Introduction,' *Total Refusal: The Complete 1948 Manifesto of the Montreal Automatists* (Toronto 1985), 12. See also F.-M. Gagnon, *Paul-Émile Borduas: Biographie
critique et analyse de l'oeuvre* (Montreal 1978), 256ff.

32 Stephen Clarkson and Christina McCall, *Trudeau and Our Times*, vol. 1: *The Magnificent Obsession* (Toronto 1990), 66.

33 AUL, Fonds Gérard Dion, P117, D1/6.37, BP3630, 1, *Ad usum sacerdotum* 11, nos.
9–10 (June–July 1956); a draft of the document is in the same location.

34 'La politique provinciale: Une vue d'ensemble,' *LD*, 7 Aug. 1956; Robert Duffy,
'Priests Charge Corrupt Methods in Quebec Voting,' *GM*, 7 Aug. 1956.

35 Robert Duffy, 'Election Study Work of Priests on Laval Faculty,' *GM*, 8 Aug. 1956;
Cyrille Felteau, 'La déclaration Dion-O'Neil [*sic*] avait été acceptée par la censure
ecclésiastique,' *LD*, 11 Aug. 1956 ('All in all, what have we said that everybody did
not already know? Is it not disturbing to see that in our province the plain and simple
truth cannot be expressed publicly without provoking what could be called a scandal
among the weak minded?').

36 AUL, Fonds Dion, BP3630, 20, *Chronique sociale de France* 64 (1 Nov. 1956);
Évangeliser 11, no. 63 (Nov.–Dec. 1956).

37 *LD*, 11 et 18 Aug. 1956 ('avant de faire un pas sur ce terrain ultra-glissant').

38 AUL, Fonds Dion, BP3630, 7, Alphonse-Marie Parent to Gérard Dion, 9 Aug. 1956
('Monsignor the archbishop has asked me if there is a censor available to "Ad Usum
Sacerdotum"').

39 Ibid., Dion to Parent, 10 Aug. 1956, copy ('The censor who was assigned to me
by the diocesan authorities is the former dean of the Faculty of Theology ...,
Monsignor Ernest Lemieux'); William F. Kelly to Dion, 13 Sept. 1956; Dion to
Kelly, 15 Sept. 1956, copy.

40 René Lagace, 'Il n'y a pas au monde de population plus honnête,' *LS*, 5 Sept. 1956
('Nowhere else on earth is there a more honest population than that of our province.
And there is not a clergy more noble than that of the province of Quebec'). See also
LD, 6 Sept. 1956.

41 Robert Rumilly, *A propos d'un mémoire 'confidentiel': Réponse à MM. les abbés
Dion et O'Neill* (Montreal [1956]), 3, 11–12 ('an anti-Quebec memorandum'; 'the
headquarters of the left-wing movement in the province of Quebec'); AUL, Fonds
Dion, BP3629, 3, unidentified newspaper clipping, 29 Oct. 1956, 'M. Duplessis n'a
pas lu la déclaration Dion-O'Neill.'

42 AUL, Fonds Dion, BP3630, 15, photocopy of a typed report, 25 Sept. 1956. ('We
plan to work with an ultrasensitive microphone and tape indoor conversations. We
have the recording equipment').

43 Ibid.

44 'No Curb on Reformers,' *TS*, 16 Oct. 1956; Gérard Filion, 'De la liberté
    académique,' *LD*, 17 Oct. 1956 ('without which intellectual work is impossible').

45 Blair Fraser, 'The "Religious Crisis" in Quebec Politics,' *MM*, 10 Nov. 1956, 15;
    conversation with Raymond Houde, Montreal, Mar. 1986.

46 UAA, RG19, 73–112, George Hunter personal file (GHF), Walter H. Johns, 'Memo-
    randum on Remarks Alleged to Have Been Made by Dr. George Hunter during
    the Final Lecture in Biochemistry 11 and 50 on April 7, 1949'; see Michiel
    Horn, 'Academic Freedom and the Dismissal of George Hunter,' *DR*, 69, no. 3 (Fall
    1989).

47 UAA, GHF, two documents dated 25 April 1949; Robert Newton to Hunter, 26 May,
    1949, copy; Hunter to Newton, 31 May 1949; Newton to Hunter, 25 June 1949,
    copy; G. Hunter, 'Memo to the Board of Governors in Reply to Statement Signed by
    17 Students concerning My Lecture on April 7 and Others [*sic*] Lectures, 28 June
    ·1949.

48 UAA, BoG, Minutes, 29 June 1949; interview with Margaret Hunter, Montreal, Oct.
    1988.

49 UAA, GHF, Newton to Hardolph Wasteneys, 13 Sept. 1949, copy; *GM*, 6 July 1949;
    UAA, AASUA Papers, Faculty Relations Committee (FRC), 68–1, vol. 31, Newton
    to J.W. Gilles, 12 Sept. 1949, copy.

50 UAA, AASUA Papers, FRC, 68–1, vol. 31, 'Report of the Subcommittee appointed
    July 14, 1949 ...,' 28 July 1949.

51 UAA, AASUA Papers, 73-162, AASUA/2, file 12, Minutes of the Regular Meeting
    of the ATSUA, 28 Oct. 1949; UAA, William Rowan Papers, 69-16, vol. 13, Rowan to
    Leopold Infeld, 16 Oct. 1949, copy.

52 UAA, GHF, Minutes, Ad Hoc Committee, 24 Apr. 1946; AASUA files, 73-162-137,
    FRC, Minute Book, 3 May 1946.

53 UAA, GHF, Hunter to Newton, 13 Aug. 1943, and Newton to Hunter, 16 Aug. 1943,
    copy; AASUA Papers, 73-162, AASUA/2, file 12, Association of the Teaching Staff
    of the University of Alberta, Minutes of the annual meeting, 29 Mar. 1945; RG 19,
    81-37-1167, Robert Newton, 'John Reymes-King,' 24; F.M. Salter, 'Robert Newton,
    President,' *The New Trail* 8 (Fall 1950), 147; Rowan Papers, 69-16, vol. 13, Rowan
    to Richard J. Needham, 21 July 1949, copy.

54 UAA, GHF, Minutes of Proceedings of Board Meeting, 4 May 1946; BoG, Minutes,
    27 Sept. 1946.

55 UAA, BoG, Minutes, 19 Sept. 1947.

56 MUA, RG2, PO, c.118/3209, Newton to F. Cyril James, 3 Sept. 1947; James to New-
    ton, 10 Sept. 1947, copy.

57 UTA, PO (Smith), A68-0007/30(01), Newton to Sidney E. Smith, 3 Sept. 1947;
    Smith to Newton, 5 Sept. 1947, copy.

58 UAA, GHF, Confidential Memo, Dr Hunter, 25 Nov. 1946; Dr Hunter, 2 Apr. 1947; ref. Dr Hunter, 7 Apr. 1947.

59 *EJ*, 2 and 6 July 1949; *CH*, 8 July 1949; *GM*, 6 July 1949; *TS*, 6 July 1949; 'Wrong Lecture,' *Time*, 18 July 1949.

60 'Academic Freedom Again,' *SN*, 19 July 1949; L. Freeman, 'Dr. Hunter's Dismissal,' *CF* 29 (Oct. 1949).

61 NA, Scott Papers, vol. 1, Academic Freedom Correspondence 1938–50, A.R.M. Lower to Scott, 5 Oct. 1949.

62 Ibid., W.F. Bowker to Scott, 18 Oct. 1949, and Elmer E. Roper to Scott, 24 Oct. 1949.

63 Ibid., Scott to Lower, 27 Oct. 1949, copy.

64 UAA, GHF, Hardolph Wasteneys to Ralph Shaner, 20 Feb. 1950, copy.

65 Ibid., Hunter to A.C. Chibnall, 14 July 1949, copy; Newton to Chibnall, 8 Aug. 1949, copy: Chibnall to Newton, 26 Aug. 1949.

66 UTA, PO, A72-0033/001(03), Chester Martin to H.J. Cody, 19 Apr. 1939.

67 'Academic Freedom Again,' *SN*, 19 July 1949.

68 UAA, Rowan Papers, 69–16, vol. 13, Rowan to Leopold Infeld, 16 Oct. 1949, copy; NA, Scott Papers, vol. 1, Academic Freedom Correspondence 1938–50, W.F. Bowker to Scott, 18 Oct. 1949.

69 Walter H. Johns, *A History of the University of Alberta* (Edmonton 1981), 240; UAA, Robert Newton, 'I Passed This Way,' 305.

70 UAA, PO, 68-1-1158, Andrew Stewart to E.C. Manning, 17 Nov. 1952, copy.

71 Banesh Hoffmann and Helen Dukas, *Albert Einstein: Creator and Rebel* (New York 1972), 233; UTA, PO (Cody), A68/037/04, A.L. Jolliffe to Cody, 8 Aug. 1939.

72 Leopold Infeld, *Quest: The Evolution of a Scientist* (Garden City, N.Y. 1941), 324.

73 Leopold Infeld, *Why I Left Canada: Reflections on Science and Politics*, trans. Helen Infeld, ed. Lewis Pyenson (Montreal and London 1978), 29.

74 UTA, PO (Smith), A68-0007/033(10), Smith to Infeld, 11 June 1948, copy; A68-0007/049(01), Beatty to Smith, 15 Mar. 1949.

75 Ibid., A68-0007/062(18), S. Beatty to Eugene P. Wignor, 3 Nov. 1949, copy; Infeld to Smith, 7 Nov. 1949; S. Beatty to Smith, 8 and 17 Nov. 1949.

76 Ibid., Smith to Beatty, 19 Nov. 1949, copy; Beatty to Smith, 28 Nov. 1949, with annotation by Smith.

77 Leopold Infeld, 'Visit to Poland,' *Scientific American* 181, no. 6 (December 1949); UTA, PO, A68-0007/062(18), Jack Thompson to Smith, 7 Mar. 1950; undated memorandum, marked 'Approved by the President,' containing the text of a proposed telegram from Infeld to the editor, *Ensign*, n.d. See also K.S. Edey to Smith, n.d., rec. 7 Mar. 1950.

78 Canada, House of Commons, *Debates*, 16 Mar. 1950, 793.

79 *GM*, 17 Mar. 1950.

80 *GM*, 18 Mar. 1950.

81 Ibid.
82 UTA, PO, A68-0007/062(18), Edey to Smith, 21 Mar. 1950.
83 Ibid., Beatty to Smith, 4 Apr. 1950.
84 Ibid., [S.E. Smith], 'Memorandum of Meeting with Dean Beatty and Professor Infeld on Thursday, April 13th, in My Office.'
85 Ibid., Smith to G.P. Glazebrook, 13 Apr. 1950, copy.
86 Ibid., handwritten notes, 'Geo Glazebrook Noon April 19th.'
87 Ibid., handwritten notes, 'SB, LI, April 20th 11 a.m. My Office.'
88 Ibid., Beatty to Smith, 20 May 1950.
89 Ibid., Beatty to Smith, 29 May 1950; Smith to Beatty, 30 May 1950, copy.
90 UTA, PO, A68-0007/062(15), Chester Martin to Smith, 25 Feb. 1950.
91 UTA, PO, A68-0007/062(18), Beatty to Smith, 15 June 1950; Infeld fyle [sic], 20 June 1950; Smith to the Bursar, 20 June 1950, copy.
92 Ibid., Infeld to Beatty, 10 August 1950, copy, italics in the original; Smith to Beatty, 22 Aug. 1950, copy.
93 Ibid., Infeld to Beatty, 13 Sept. 1950, copy.
94 Ibid., Smith to W.E. Phillips, 22 Sept. 1950, copy.
95 TS, 21 Sept. 1950; TT, 21 Sept. 1950; Lex Schrag, 'Prof. Infeld Stays in Poland but Doubt He Took A-Secrets,' GM, 22 Sept. 1950; UV, 22 Sept. 1950; 'No Loss,' GM, 25 Sept. 1950.
96 Conversation with Eric Infeld, phoning from Warsaw, Oct. 1995.
97 Interview with Claude T. Bissell, Toronto, Dec. 1989.
98 Infeld, Why I Left Canada, 67–9; GM, 14 Oct. 1995.
99 Eric Infeld conversation, Oct. 1995.
100 Conversations with Louise Starkman, Jack Dimond, and Michael Marrus, Toronto, Oct.-Nov. 1995; Susan Bloch-Nevitte, 'Closing the Circle,' UTB, 29 May 1995.
101 Ernest Sirluck, First Generation: An Autobiography (Toronto 1996), 30–98 passim; interview with Ernest Sirluck, Toronto, Sept. 1995; telephone conversation with Albert Rose, Nov. 1995.
102 Sirluck interview, Toronto, Sept. 1995; Sirluck, First Generation, 154–5; Rose conversation, Nov. 1995.
103 Judith Fingard, 'Gender and Inequality at Dalhousie: Faculty Women before 1950,' DR 64, no. 4 (Winter 1984–5); also P.B. Waite, The Lives of Dalhousie University, vol. 2 (Montreal and Kingston 1998), 186–7; DUA, MS1-3-A544, PO, Corr., vol. 19, Political Science 1922–47, R.A. MacKay to A.E. Kerr, 9 Sept. 1946, and Kerr to MacKay, 13 Sept. 1946, copy.
104 DUA, MS1-1-A11, BoG, Minutes, 10 May 1946; BoG, Executive Committee, 12 Feb. 1946.; BoG, Minutes, 6 Dec. 1949; Executive Committee, 13 Jan. 1950; BoG, Minutes, 1950–3, Executive Committee, 6 Feb. and 18 June 1953; BoG, Minutes, Executive Committee, 13 Jan. 1950.

105 PANS, MG17/108/32, Dalhousie Faculty Association Papers, Dalhousie University, Regulations concerning Academic Appointments and Tenure (1956), 7; DUA, BoG, Minutes, 28 Feb. 1953.

106 DUA, M1-3-A545, PO, Corr., vol. 19, Psychology Department, Kerr to K.C. Laurie, 2 July 1953, copy.

107 Fingard, 'Gender and Inequality at Dalhousie,' 699.

108 Lee Stewart, *'It's Up to You': Women at UBC in the Early Years* (Vancouver 1990), 77; UBCA, BoG, Minutes, vol. 21, 21 Dec. 1942, and vol. 24, 30 Apr. and 30 July 1945.

109 John Norris, 'Margaret Ormsby,' *BCS* 32 (Winter 1976–7).

110 Interview with Robert M. Clark, Vancouver, April 1987; P.B. Waite, *Lord of Point Grey: Larry MacKenzie of UBC* (Vancouver 1987), 142.

111 Jean Burnet, 'Minorities I Have Belonged To,' *Canadian Ethnic Studies* 13, no. 1 (1981), 30, 32.

112 Jean Burnet to the author, 9 Jan. 1996.

113 UNBA, RG136, PC, 1945–7, file 18, F.J. Toole, 'Condition of Department of Modern Languages,' 11 May 1946.

114 Ibid., Milton F. Gregg to Marcel de Merten, 16 June 1946, copy; UNBSC, Senate, Minutes, 8 Oct. 1946; UNBA, RG136, PC, 1948–50 A–E, file 36, A. McAndrew to A.W. Trueman, 10 Apr. 1950, and attachment, 'A Department of Modern Languages'; UNBSC, Senate, Minutes, 17 May 1950.

115 UNBA, RG 136, PC, 1948–50 A-E, file 38, Trueman to De Merten, 23 May 1950, copy, and De Merten to Trueman, 12 June 1950; UBCA, PO, mfm reel 120, file D18 Misc, De Merten to N.A.M. MacKenzie, 25 May 1950.

116 UNBA, RG 136, PC, file 38, Trueman to De Merten, 17 June 1950, copy.

117 Ibid., De Merten to Trueman, 23 June 1950; UBCA, PO, mfm reel 120, file D18 Misc, De Merten to MacKenzie, 19 Aug. 1950.

118 John G. Reid, *Mount Allison University*, vol. 2 (Toronto 1984), 152.

119 UNBA, RG136, PC, file 38, Trueman to Franz Stoessl, 26 June 1950, copy; 1951–3 D-K, file 19, Modern Languages, Trueman to Jean Hubener, 5 Feb. 1951, copy.

120 UNBA, RG136, PC, 1951–53 D-K, file 24, Allan McAndrew, 'Annual Report of the Department of Modern Languages,' and file 19 [A.W. Trueman], 'Consideration of Making German Separate Department,' n.d.; UNBSC, Senate, Minutes, 2 Sept. 1952.

121 Max Foran, ed., *Grant MacEwan's Journals* (Edmonton 1986), 105–6.

122 UMA, UA/14, vol. 46, BoG, Minutes, 12 Apr. and 1 May 1951.

123 UMA, PP, UA20, vol. 149, file 7, W.G. Stobie to Members of the Board of Governors, 16 June 1952.

124 Ibid., file 6, Stobie to Members, Board of Governors, 5 Feb. 1953.

125 Ibid., attachment to Stobie to Members, Board of Governors, 5 Feb. 1953.

126 Ibid., J. Hoogstraten, 'Chairman's Report,' 30 Mar. 1954.

127 UTA, BoG, Minutes, vol. 26, 26 Oct. 1950.

128 Most of what follows was suggested to me by reading Richard Hofstadter, *Anti-Intellectualism in American Life* (New York 1966 [1963]), and Philo Hutcheson, 'McCarthyism and the Professoriate: A Historiographic Nightmare?' in John Smart, ed., *Higher Education: Handbook of Theory and Research* 12 (New York 1997).

129 Whitaker and Marcuse, *Cold War Canada*, 227–58.

130 Gerald L. Caplan, *The Dilemma of Canadian Socialism* (Toronto 1973), 110–29 passim.

131 Ellen W. Schrecker, *No Ivory Tower* (New York 1986), 290–1.

132 P.B. Waite to the author, 12 May 1993.

133 David Kimmel, 'The People vs. Margaret and Barker Fairley,' *UTB*, 23 March 1998.

9: The Crowe Caws

1 NA, MG30, D204, Frank Underhill Papers, vol. 6, Underhill to W.A. Mackintosh, 6 Dec. 1958, copy.

2 Ibid., Mackintosh to Underhill, 8 Dec. 1958. The St James's Club is in Montreal.

3 Paul Litt, *The Muses, the Masses, and the Massey Commission* (Toronto 1992), 166.

4 UAA, 73–162, AASUA Papers, AASUA/2, file 12, ATSUA General, special meeting, 4 Nov. 1949; ATSUA meeting, 31 Mar. 1950.

5 UNBA, RG136, PC 1948–50, A-E, file 11, A.W. Trueman to W.S. MacNutt, 11 Dec. 1950, copy; UMA, UA20, PP, vol. 149, folder 7, N.A.M. MacKenzie to A.H.S. Gillson, 29 Jan. 1952; Gwendoline Evans Pilkington, *Speaking with One Voice* (Montreal 1983), 97–8.

6 NA, RG28 I 208, CAUT Papers, vol. 123, Minutes of the Executive Council, 9–10 June 1958. See also Frank Abbott, 'The Crowe Affair: The Academic Profession and Academic Freedom,' *QQ* 98, no. 4 (Winter 1991).

7 NA, CAUT Papers, vol. 123, Clarence Barber to R.W. Torrens, 22 July 1958, copy; Torrens to Barber, 12 Sept. 1958.

8 Interviews with Kenneth W. McNaught, Toronto, May 1987, and E.D. Eagle, Winnipeg, July 1987.

9 UWiA, United College, Personal Records, Dr Graham 1946–51, file 3, W.C. Graham to H.A. Innis, 7 Apr. 1949, copy; McNaught interview, May 1987.

10 NA, Underhill Papers, vol. 7, Stewart Reid to Underhill, 10 May 1955.

11 McNaught interview, May 1987; Eagle interview, July 1987; interview with William Packer, Toronto, Dec. 1995.

12 A.G. Bedford, *The University of Winnipeg (UoW)* (Toronto 1976), 275–7, 302.

13 YUA, F297, Harry S. Crowe Papers, vol. 1, Corr. 1957, Crowe to McNaught, 7 Oct. 1957, copy.
14 Ibid., Corr. 1958, Harry to Viljo, 14 Mar. 1958. This is the original letter, returned to Crowe by Packer in April 1958 (Packer interview, Dec. 1995).
15 Interview with W.C. Lockhart, Toronto, Oct. 1985.
16 Bedford, UoW, 305; Lockhart interview, Oct. 1985.
17 YUA, Crowe Papers, vol. 1, Corr. 1958, Packer to Crowe, 22 Apr. 1958; Packer interview, Dec. 1995.
18 YUA, Crowe Papers, Lockhart to Crowe, 23 Apr. 1958; Crowe to Lockhart, 23 May 1958 (copy).
19 Lockhart interview, Oct. 1985; YUA, Crowe Papers, vol. 1, Corr. 1958, McNaught to Crowe, 20 and 26 Apr. 1958.
20 YUA, Crowe Papers, vol. 2, United College, James Wilson to Crowe, 5 May 1958.
21 Ibid., vol. 1, Corr. 1958, Crowe to Wilson, 23 May 1958, copy.
22 Interview with Frederick W. Gibson, Kingston, Ont., Aug. 1991; YUA, Crowe Papers, vol. 1, Corr. 1958, H.S. Ferns to Harry and Jean Crowe, 3 June 1958.
23 YUA, Crowe Papers, McNaught to Crowe, 11 May 1958; Donald C. Savage and Christopher Holmes, 'The CAUT, the Crowe Case, and the Development of the Idea of Academic Freedom in Canada,' CAUTB 24, no. 3 (Dec. 1975), 23; Bedford, UoW, 306; YUA, Crowe Papers, vol. 1, Corr. 1959, Pierre Berton to Crowe, 2 Feb. 1959. For a passionately felt personal account of the affair, see Kenneth McNaught's memoirs, to be published posthumously in 1999.
24 University of Winnipeg (UoW), Registrar's Office, United College, BoR, Minutes, 8 May 1958; YUA, Crowe Papers, vol. 1, Corr. 1958, Crowe to Allan H. Watson, 8 May 1958, copy.
25 YUA, Crowe Papers, Crowe to Lockhart, 23 May 1958, copy; Lockhart to Crowe, 28 May 1958; UoW, BoR, Minutes, 27 May 1958.
26 YUA, Crowe Papers, vol. 1, Corr. 1958, Crowe to Watson, 10 June 1958, copy; Watson to Crowe, 20 June 1958.
27 Ibid., Crowe to Watson, 26 June 1958, copy.
28 Lockhart interview, Oct. 1985; UoW, BoR, Minutes, 2 July 1958.
29 Lockhart interview, Oct. 1985; YUA, Crowe Papers, vol. 1, Corr. 1958, Watson to Crowe, 4 July 1958.
30 Bedford, UoW, 309; McNaught interview, May 1987; conversation with Jean Crowe, Toronto, Oct. 1991.
31 YUA, Crowe Papers, vol. 2, United College, Reid to Crowe, [11 July 1958].
32 PAM, MG14, B35, Ralph Maybank Papers, file 40, Mildred McMurray, 12 Dec. 1958.
33 YUA, Crowe Papers, vol. 1, Corr. 1958, Mac Ross to Crowe, 16 July 1958; Bill Morton to Crowe, 15 July 1958; Michael Oliver to Crowe, 4 Aug. 1958.

34 Ibid., Crowe to Watson, 15 July 1958, copy; Watson to Crowe, 21 July 1958; Crowe to Watson, 25 July 1958, copy; Watson to Crowe, 7 Aug. 1958; Crowe to Watson, 14 Aug. 1958, copy.

35 Ibid., McNaught to Crowe, 12 June 1958; NA, CAUT Papers, vol. 129, McNaught to Clarence Barber, 9 July 1958.

36 NA, CAUT Papers, vol. 129, B.N. Kropp to Barber, 18 July 1958; Barber to Vernon C. Fowke, 31 July 1958, copy.

37 Ibid., Bert McCready to Barber, 26 July 1958.

38 Bedford, *UoW*, 302; YUA, Crowe Papers, vol. 1, Corr. 1958, Packer to Crowe, 23 Jan. 1958; Eagle interview, July 1987; Interview with Kenneth McNaught, Toronto, Nov. 1995; McNaught, Nov. 1995; Packer interview, Dec. 1995.

39 YUA, Crowe Papers, vol. 1, Corr. 1958, Gordon Blake to Crowe, 15 July 1958; UWiA, UC 8–1, Crowe Collection, file 4, Blake to Alfred D. Longman, 21 July 1958.

40 UWiA, Crowe Collection, McNaught to Longman, 31 July 1958; V. Leathers, W.A. Packer and G. Taylor to Longman, 3 Aug. 1958; Longman to Packer, 4 Aug. 1958, copy; Packer interview, Dec. 1995; NA, CAUT Papers, vol. 129, McNaught to George Boyes, 6 Aug. 1958.

41 UWiA, Crowe Collection, file 3 [A.D. Longman], undated pencil-written note.

42 NA, CAUT Papers, vol. 129, Blake to McNaught, 6 Aug. 1958, copy; Blake to Barber, 7 Aug. 1958.

43 UWiA, Crowe Collection, file 4, Richard Stingle to Blake, 5 Aug. 1958, copy; NA, CAUT Papers, vol. 129, McNaught to Blake, 11 Aug. 1958, copy.

44 NA, CAUT Papers, vol. 129, Barber to McCready, 8 Aug. 1958, copy; vol. 163, Fowke to Ralph Fuchs, 10 Aug. 1958, copy; Bertram H. Davis to Fowke, 15 Aug. 1958.

45 YUA, Crowe Papers, vol. 1, Corr. 1958, Watson to Crowe, 25 Aug. 1958; UWiA, Crowe Collection, file 4, Watson to the faculty, United College, 26 Aug. 1958, copy.

46 NA, CAUT Papers, vol. 163, Crowe to Fowke, 4 Sept. 1958; YUA, Crowe Papers, vol. 1, Corr. 1958, Sydney Wise to Crowe, 9 Sept. 1958.

47 Bedford, *UoW*, 311; UoW, BoR, Minutes, 9 Sept. 1958; YUA, Crowe Papers, vol. 1, Corr. 1958, Watson to Crowe, 15 Sept. 1958; Fillmore, Riley et al. to Aikins, MacAulay & Co., 22 Sept. 1958, copy.

48 *WFP*, 20 and 22 Sept. 1958; NA, CAUT Papers, vol. 162, Crowe, press release, 22 Sept. 1958, reproduced as document no. 49 in 'Report of the Investigation by the Committee of the Canadian Association of University Teachers into the Dismissal of Professor H.S. Crowe by United College, Winnipeg, Manitoba' (Fowke-Laskin Report), *CAUTB* 7, no. 3 (Jan. 1959), 74; YUA, Crowe Papers, vol. 1, Herta Hartmanshenn to Crowe, 22 Sept. 1958.

49 NA, CAUT Papers, vol. 163, 'Provisional Statement of Facts Respecting the Dismissal of Harry Crowe by United College, Winnipeg, Manitoba,' 31 July 1958; Watson to Barber, 20 and 27 Aug. 1958; vol. 129, David Slater to Barber, 11 Aug. 1958, and Martin W. Johns to Barber, 10 Oct. 1958.

50 Ibid., Watson to Barber, Fowke and Laskin, 6 and 7 Oct. 1958.

51 See Fowke-Laskin Report, appendix C, 88; also, in CAUT Papers, vol. 129, Blake to Barber, 26 Oct. and 15 Nov. 1958; Bedford, *UoW*, 317; A.G. Bedford to the author, 4 Mar. 1996.

52 YUA Crowe Papers, vol. 1, Corr. 1958, Gibson to Crowe, 21 Oct. 1958.

53 Fowke-Laskin Report, 25.

54 Ibid., 45, 46.

55 Ibid., 38.

56 Ibid., 38, 40.

57 NA, CAUT Papers, vol. 162, Fowke to Laskin, 7 Nov. 1958; Fowke-Laskin Report, appendix D, 90.

58 Interview with A.G. Bedford, Winnipeg, Aug. 1986; Bedford to the author, 4 Mar. 1996; J.E.G. Dixon, 'The Crowe Case and Academic Freedom,' in Michiel Horn, ed., *Academic Freedom* (North York 1987), 104; conversation with John Warkentin, Toronto, March 1998.

59 Fowke-Laskin Report, 49.

60 A.R.M. Lower, letter to the editor, *WT*, 4 Dec. 1958; Fowke-Laskin Report, 49.

61 T.B. McDormand, 'Time Bomb to Destroy Freedom,' *UCO*, 1 Oct. 1959.

62 Fowke-Laskin Report, 39.

63 Ibid., appendix D, 90; YUA, Crowe Papers, vol. 2, United College, W.C. Graham to Crowe, 9 May 1950.

64 NA, CAUT Papers, vol. 163, Slater to Fowke, 5 Nov. 1958; George P. Grant to Fowke, 26 Nov. 1958; Jim Aitchison to Fowke, 28 Nov. 1958; Vincent Bladen to Fowke, 19 Feb. 1959; Underhill to Fowke, 8 Apr. 1959; Bertram H. Davis to Fowke 10 Feb. 1959.

65 *WFP*, 25 Nov. 1958; 'Hope for Winnipeg Solution,' *UCO*, 15 Dec. 1958.

66 'Peace in Winnipeg' *UCO*, 1 Jan. 1959.

67 NA, CAUT Papers, vol. 129, R.N. Hallstead to Barber, 1 Nov. 1958; Bedford, *UoW*, 311.

68 'Unite the College,' *WFP*, 25 Nov. 1958; UoW, BoR, Minutes, 27 Oct. 1958.

69 YUA, Crowe Papers, vol. 1, Corr. 1958, Crowe to Fred Gibson, 29 and 31 Oct. 1958, copies; ibid., J.H. Howes, M.J. Howes, and Joan Ross, 'Statement Reporting a Meeting with Dr. Graham Pincock on 14 Oct. 1958,' 22 Oct. 1958; McNaught interview, Nov. 1995; *WFP*, 27 Nov. 1958.

70 *WFP*, 27 Nov. 1958.

71 Savage and Holmes, 'The CAUT, the Crowe Case and the Development of the Idea

of Academic Freedom in Canada,' 25, 27; Bedford, *UoW*, 326–7; UoW, BoR, Minutes, 6 Dec. 1958; Lockhart interview, Oct. 1985.

72 UoW, BoR, Minutes, 1, 6, and 8 Dec. 1958; Bedford, *UoW*, 323; 'United College,' *WFP*, 10 Dec. 1958; 'Arbitrate the Dispute,' *WT*, 11 Dec. 1958.

73 Bedford, *UoW*, 325; YUA, Crowe Papers, vol. 1, envelope, handwritten statement [13 Dec. 1958].

74 UoW, BoR, Minutes, 14 Dec. 1958.

75 'Freedom the Victor at United College,' *TS*, 16 Dec. 1958; YUA, Crowe Papers, vol. 1, Corr. 1958, Ramsay Cook to Crowe, 15 Dec. 1958.

76 UWiA, Crowe Collection, file 4, T.A. Crerar to Longman, 10 Jan. 1959; AUA, Watson Kirkconnell Papers, vol. 44, file P14/12, Kirkconnell to Longman, 20 Jan. 1959, copy.

77 UoW, BoR, Minutes, 26 Jan. 1959, appendix A, 'Statement by the Sub-Executive of the General Council of the United Church of Canada, 17 Dec. 1958.'

78 Ibid., appendix C, Angus J. MacQueen, 'View on Winnipeg Situation, 7 Jan. 1959.'

79 UoW, BoR, Minutes, 29 Dec. 1958 and 26 Jan. 1959.

80 NA, CAUT Papers, vol. 163, McNaught to Fowke, n.d. [12 Dec. 1958?]; McNaught interview, Nov. 1995; UoW, BoR, Minutes, 26 Apr. 1959.

81 YUA, Crowe Papers, vol. 1, Corr. 1959, Crowe to Watson, 22 Mar. 1959, copy, and Crowe to Churchill, 24 Mar. 1959, copy; Kenneth W. McNaught, 'History and Conscience' (ms, tbp 1999), 10: 24.

82 Savage and Holmes, 'The CAUT, the Crowe Case, and the Development of the Idea of Academic Freedom in Canada,' 27.

83 Bedford, *UoW*, 330; Lockhart interview, Oct. 1985.

84 Pierre Berton, 'The Crowe-Lockhart Drama: A Tragedy as Ancient as Oedipus,' *TS*, 17 Dec. 1958.

85 AUA, Kirkconnell Papers, vol. 44, file P14/12, Longman to Kirkconnell, 13 Dec. 1959; Cornelius Jaenen to the author, 14 July 1996.

86 UoW, BoR, Minutes, 26 May 1959; Bedford, *UoW*, 324.

87 Bedford interview, Aug. 1986.

88 Savage and Holmes, 'The CAUT, the Crowe Case, and the Development of the Idea of Academic Freedom in Canada,' 25; UoW, BoR, Minutes, 30 Mar. 1959, containing Watson to Barber, 23 Feb. 1959, and Barber to Watson, 11 Mar. 1959; Clarence L. Barber, 'President's Report,' *CAUTB* 8, no. 1 (Oct. 1959), 17.

89 'Distribution of the Special (Crowe Case) Bulletin' and 'Report of the Scott Committee on the United College Dispute,' *CAUTB*, 8, no. 1 (Oct. 1959), 14, 17, 19–20, 26; interview with John Clake, Winnipeg, Aug. 1986; conversations with Clarence L. Barber, Victoria, and J. Percy Smith, Toronto, both in May 1996.

90 'Report of the Scott Committee,' *CAUTB* 8, no. 1 (Oct. 1959), 20, 21.

91 'Collection of Primary Documents ...' and 'Business Arising Out of the Minutes: An Editorial,' *CAUTB* 8, no. 4 (Apr. 1960), 6.
92 Clarence L. Barber, 'President's Report ..., June 7, 1959,' *CAUTB* 8, no. 1 (Oct. 1959), 11, 12.
93 Ibid., 11; Barber conversation, May 1996.

10: A Place of Liberty

1 Claude Bissell, *Halfway Up Parnassus: A Personal Account of the University of Toronto, 1932–1971* (Toronto 1974), esp. 44–57; Murray G. Ross, *The Way Must Be Tried: Memoirs of a University Man* (Toronto 1992), esp. 35–56. For a sceptical view, see F.H. Underhill, 'How Good Are Our Universities?' *CAUTB* 11, no. 1 (Sept. 1962).
2 E.F. Sheffield, 'Canadian University and College Enrolment Projected to 1965,' *National Conference of Canadian Universities, Proceedings 1955*, 39–46; Sheffield, 'The Post-War Surge in Post-Secondary Education,' in J. Donald Wilson, Robert M. Stamp, and Louis-Philippe Audet, eds., *Canadian Education: A History* (Scarborough, Ont. 1970), 420.
3 Economic Council of Canada, *Second Annual Review: Towards Sustained and Balanced Growth* (Ottawa 1965), 75.
4 David A.A. Stager, 'Federal Government Grants to Canadian Universities, 1951–66,' *CHR* 54, no. 3 (Sept. 1973), 297.
5 NA, RG28 I 208, CAUT Papers, vol. 123, 'Interim Report of the Ad Hoc Committee on Academic Freedom and Tenure of the Faculty Association, University of Western Ontario,' 10 Nov. 1958.
6 Ibid., T.H. Matthews to Clarence Barber, 9 Feb. 1959.
7 Ibid., 'Notes on a Meeting of the NCCU "Academic Freedom" Committee ...,' 3 Feb. 1959; QUA, coll. 3655, Queen's University Faculty Association, vol. 1, Barber to H.M. Estall, 18 Feb. 1959.
8 NA, CAUT Papers, vol. 123, A.T. Elder to Barber, 28 Feb. 1959; Pauline Jewett to Barber, 23 Feb. 1959; Keith Callard to Barber, 10 Apr. 1959; R.J. Douglas to Barber, 10 Mar. 1959; K.A.H. Buckley to Barber, 27 Mar. 1959; A.W.R. Carrothers to Barber, 9 Apr. 1959.
9 Ibid., Turner to Barber, 25 Mar. 1959; NA, CAUT Papers, vol. 1, Ad Hoc Committee on Academic Freedom and Tenure, 'Report to the Executive Council ...,' May 1959, 3–5.
10 NA, CAUT Papers, vol. 1, Ad Hoc Committee on Academic Freedom and Tenure, 'Report to the Executive Council,' May 1959, 2–3.
11 Ibid., AF & T Committee, J.H.S. Reid to J.E.L. Graham, 1 July 1959, copy; Bora Laskin to Reid, 2 Sept. 1959; James B. Milner to Reid, 11 Nov. 1959.

12 Ibid., Reid to Turner, 3 Dec. 1959, copy; Gaston Laurion to Harold Good, 21 July 1959.
13 G.H. Turner, 'Academic Freedom and Tenure: Notes on Investigational Procedures,' *CAUTB* 12, no. 3 (Feb. 1964), passim.
14 J.B.M., 'Report of the A.F. & T. Committee,' *CAUTB* 14, no. 2 (Dec. 1965), 44, 45.
15 NA, CAUT Papers, vol. 73, Minutes, National Council, 14–15 Nov. 1959, 'Summary of Discussion on Report of ad hoc Committee on Academic Freedom and Tenure.'
16 'Principles of Academic Freedom and Tenure,' *CAUTB* 8, no. 3 (Feb. 1960), 16.
17 UBCA, PO, mfm reel 229, Faculty Association, 'Report of the Personnel Services Committee ...,' 14 Mar. 1960; NA, CAUT Papers, vol. 1, Turner to Reid, 14 Dec. 1959 and 4 May 1960, and vol. 126, Turner to Professors Dansereau, Graham, Milner, Read and Smith, 16 May 1960, copy.
18 NA, CAUT Papers, vol. 161, 'Principles of Academic Freedom and Tenure (As Revised and Adopted by Council, June 1960)'; Donald C. Savage and Christopher Holmes, 'The CAUT, the Crowe Case, and the Development of the Idea of Academic Freedom in Canada,' *CAUTB* 24, no. 3 (Dec. 1975), 26.
19 UVA, Victoria College, PO, vol. 1, file 14, Appointments, Promotions and Tenure, Oct. 1960, 7, 8.
20 Ibid., vol. 3, file 7(b), R.J. Bishop to W.H. Hickman, 18 Jan. 1962.
21 Ibid., F.E. Deloume to Hickman, 18 Jan. 1963.
22 NA, CAUT Papers, vol. 161, Dorothy Allen to W.T.R. Flemington, 16 Jan. 1962, copy.
23 Ibid., Allen to Reid, 7 Feb. 1962.
24 John G. Reid, *Mount Allison University*, vol. 2 (Toronto 1984), 302–9.
25 NA, CAUT Papers, vol. 161, Mount Allison University, Report of the Committee on Art and Music [1959], 9, and Report of Faculty of Conservatory of Music, 9 Dec. 1959.
26 Ibid., Flemington to Allen, 26 June 1962, copy.
27 Ibid., Turner and Reid to members of the Standing Committee on Academic Freedom and Tenure, 25 Aug. 1962, copy.
28 Ibid., Turner to Allen, 4 Sept. 1962, copy; Allen to Turner, 13 Nov. 1962.
29 Ibid., Turner to N.T. Avard, 2 Jan. 1963, copy.
30 Ibid., Smith to Turner, 28 Aug. 1962, copy.
31 QUA, coll. 1042, F.A. Knox Papers, vol. 17, George Grant to Knox, Jan. 1951; V.C. Fowke and Bora Laskin, 'Report of the Investigation ... into the Dismissal of Professor H.S. Crowe by United College, Winnipeg, Manitoba,' *CAUTB* 7, no. 3 (Jan. 1959), 12–13.
32 NA, CAUT Papers, vol. 163, Norman Ward to Fowke, 16 Feb. 1959.
33 V.C. Fowke, 'Who Should Determine University Policy?' *CAUTB* 7, no. 4 (Apr. 1959); J. Percy Smith, 'University Government,' *CAUTB* 8, no. 3 (Feb. 1960), 6.

34 'The Reform of University Government: A Statement by the Committee on University Government Presented to the Executive Council of the Canadian Association of University Teachers as a Basis for Discussion, June 12, 1960,' *CAUTB* 9, no. 1 (Nov. 1960), passim.

35 'The Reform of University Government: An Editorial,' *CAUTB* 9, no. 1 (Nov. 1960), 4; PANS, MG17/109/13, Dalhousie Faculty Association, Minutes, 1 Nov. 1960.

36 W.P. Thompson, 'University Government,' *CAUTB* 9, no. 2 (Dec. 1960), passim.

37 W.L. Morton, 'University Government: The Alienation of the Administration,' *CAUTB* 9, no. 3 (Feb. 1961), passim.

38 N.A.M. MacKenzie, 'Faculty Participation in University Administration'; 'A Debate in the Dark: An Editorial,' *CAUTB* 9, no. 4 (Apr. 1961).

39 QUA, coll. 1032A, George Whalley Papers, vol. 1, file 17, Reid to Whalley, 20 Dec. 1961.

40 Ibid., Whalley to All Possible Contributors, 11 Mar. 1962, copy; 'Community of Scholars,' Ottawa, 21 July 1962.

41 George Whalley, 'Preface,' *A Place of Liberty: Essays on the Government of Canadian Universities* (Toronto and Vancouver 1964), vii–ix passim.

42 F.R. Scott, 'The Law of the University Constitution,' in Whalley, ed., *A Place of Liberty*, 34.

43 Frank H. Underhill, 'The Scholar: Man Thinking,' in Whalley, ed., *A Place of Liberty*, 61–71 passim; C. Northcote Parkinson, *Parkinson's Law and Other Studies in Administration* (Boston 1957), 2, 12.

44 'Interim Report of the CAUT Committee to Study the Extent of Discrimination against Women University Teachers,' *CAUTB* 15, no. 1 (Oct. 1966).

45 Michael Hayden to the author, 21 Aug. 1995.

46 A.W.R. Carrothers, 'Report of the President ...,' *CAUTB* 11, no. 1 (Sept. 1962), 6; 'Academics in Politics,' *CAUTB* 11, no. 2 (Nov. 1962), 2.

47 NA, CAUT Papers, vol. 2, AF & T, J.H. Aitchison to Reid, 3 Apr. 1962.

48 Ibid., Aitchison to Reid, 1 May 1962.

49 Ibid., Pauline Jewett to Reid, 23 May 1963.

50 William H. Nelson, *The Search for Faculty Power: The History of the University of Toronto Faculty Association, 1942–1992* (Toronto 1993), 14–31 passim; conversation with W.H. Nelson, Toronto, May 1994.

51 UTA, PO (Bissell), A71-0011/96, 'Arrangements for Political Candidacy,' attached to Bissell, Memorandum to the Teaching Staff, 7 June 1966.

52 'The Academic in Politics,' *GM*, 7 July 1966; Claude Bissell and K.G. McNeill, letters, *GM*, 7 July 1966. For a copy of Macpherson's letter, see UTA, PO, A71-0011/96.

53 NA, CAUT Papers, vol. 2, 'Inquiry into RCMP Activities: Chronology of Events.'

54 Ibid., Reid to E. Davie Fulton, 16 Feb. 1962, copy; Fulton to Reid, 16 Mar. 1962; Reid to Fulton, 27 Apr. 1962, copy.

55 Ibid., 'Memorandum: Telephone Call from Mr Michael Beery of Mr Fulton's office: May 22, 1962.'

56 Ibid., 'Inquiry into RCMP Activities: Interview with Mr Davie Fulton, 21 Aug. 1962.'

57 Ibid., 'Proposed Resolution concerning RCMP Activity on the Campus'; J.H.S. Reid, 'The November Council Meeting: A Report by the Executive Secretary,' *CAUTB* 11, no. 3 (Dec. 1962), 5.

58 'Resolution on CAUT Policy regarding RCMP Activity on University Campuses,' *CAUTB* 12, no. 1 (Oct. 1963), 19.

59 NA, CAUT Papers, vol. 164, Laskin to Members of the Executive Committee, 17 Jan. 1964.

60 Ibid., Pearson to Laskin, 10 Apr. 1964; Laskin and Reid, 'Memorandum Concerning RCMP Activities on University Campuses,' *CAUTB* 12, no. 4 (Apr. 1964), 36.

61 Conversation with Marc Ferro, Calgary, Aug. 1966.

62 Paul Lacoste, 'Church and University,' in Whalley, ed., *A Place of Liberty*, 129–30.

63 Paul-André Laberge, *L'Université Laval, 1952–1977: Vers l'autonomie* (Québec 1978), 41 ('All were deceived, the former in their hopes, the latter in their fears').

64 NA, CAUT Papers, vol. 97, Disputes: Waterloo Lutheran, 1959–60, James Stone to Stewart Reid, 11 Jan. 1960; James Senter, 'A University Rises, a College Sinks,' *GM*, 8 June 1960; UWaA, Kenneth McLaughlin, 'Introduction,' University of Waterloo Arts Lecture, 24 Nov. 1992, 10–14.

65 McLaughlin, 'Introduction,' 16–17, 20; UWaA, James Stone Papers, H.M. Axford, 'An Independent Waterloo Lutheran University,' 12 May 1960; *KWR*, 13 May 1960; *GM*, 15 and 16 May 1960.

66 NA, CAUT Papers, vol. 97, Waterloo College Faculty Association, 'Academic Freedom and Tenure,' 11 Nov. 1959.

67 Ibid., Faculty Brief, 14 Dec. 1959.

68 Ibid., James Stone to Reid, 24 Dec. 1959.

69 Ibid., Stone to Reid, 11 Jan. 1960.

70 Ibid., 'Meeting with President Axford to ascertain Mr. Sandison's Future Status at Waterloo University College' [2 Feb. 1960].

71 Ibid., J.M. Sandison, statement, 11 Feb. 1960; Donald C. Savage and twenty-one others, 'A Petition to the Board,' attached to a letter to Axford, 1 Mar. 1960, copy.

72 UWaA, Stone Papers, Report of Committee on Academic Freedom and Tenure; H.M. Axford to 'Dear Colleagues,' 9 May 1960, copy, with attachment.

73 Ibid., L.H. Schaus to Stone, 17 May 1960; NA, CAUT Papers, vol. 97, Stone to Reid, 18 May 1960.

74 NA, CAUT Papers, Stone to Reid, 18 May and 2 June 1960; *KWR*, 27 May 1960; *GM*, 28 May 1960.

75 NA, CAUT Papers, vol. 97, H.W. McCready to J.H. Aitchison, 14 July 1960, copy, and Reid to Aitchison, 15 July 1960, copy; CAUT Papers, vol. 1, Reid to Gordon Turner, 27 Dec. 1960, copy.

76 NA, CAUT Papers, vol. 97, 'Situation at Waterloo University College, March 1962'; Waterloo Lutheran University, Committee on University Philosophy and Policy, 'Statement of University Philosophy,' [Jan. 1962], 4–5.

77 Ibid., Waterloo Lutheran University, 'Revision of the Statement on Academic Freedom and Tenure, 6 Feb. 1962'; 'Statement on University Philosophy,' 3.

78 Ibid., Ralph Krueger to Reid, 4 May 1962.

79 Ibid., Reid to Turner, 8 May 1962, copy; Turner to Reid, 15 May 1962.

80 Ibid., H.G. Thorburn to Reid, 8 May 1962; Reid to Thorburn, 16 May 1962, copy.

81 J. Percy Smith to George Haggar, 12 Feb. 1968, copy, insert in 'Association News,' *CAUTB* 16, no. 3 (Feb. 1968).

82 Watson Kirkconnell, *A Slice of Canada* (Toronto 1967), 168; AUA, United Baptist Convention of the Atlantic Provinces (UBCAP) Papers, Convention files, Higher Education Committee, 'Supplementary Statement of the Executive of Convention,' n.d.

83 AUA, UBCAP Papers, Convention Committee on Higher Education, Minutes, 12 Nov. 1964.

84 Ibid., Fred W. Gordon to H.A. Renfree, 20 Nov. 1964. See also 'Acadia: Size and Mission,' *AB*, 15 Jan. 1965.

85 Robert Fancy, 'Religion Questioned,' *Athenaeum*, 15 Jan. 1965.

86 AUA, UBCAP Papers, Convention files, Renfree to Members of the Higher Education Committee, 26 Jan. 1965 and attachment; Notes on Acadia, Jan. 1965; Committee on Higher Education, Minutes, 2 Feb. 1965.

87 'The Professor Is the Key,' *AB*, 15 Feb. 1965; 'Christian Professors,' *AB*, 15 May 1965.

88 'Professors: Christian and Non-Christian,' *AB*, 15 Apr. 1965, italics in the original.

89 'Alumni Face Significant Decision,' *AB*, 1 May 1965; 'A Secularized Acadia?' *AB*, 1 June 1965.

90 A.H. MacLean, 'If Freedom Be Established ... Truth Will Prevail'; Evan M. Whidden, 'What of Academic Freedom?' *AB*, 1 July 1965.

91 AUA, UBCAP Papers, Higher Education Committee, Convention Committee on Higher Education with Board of Governors' Committee on Interrelationships, Wolfville, N.S., 11 Aug. 1965; Report of the Committee on Higher Education, Aug. 1965.

92 Ibid., Report of the Committee on Higher Education.

93 AUA, J.M.R. Beveridge Papers, vol. 10, file 6.3.8, Watson Kirkconnell, 'A Philosophy of Higher Education as Functioning in a Christian University,' [1965], 3.

94 AUA, UBCAP Papers, Higher Education Committee, Draft Submission to Executive

of the Associated Faculty of Acadia University re Report on Higher Education to the United Baptist Convention of the Atlantic Provinces; AUA, Beveridge Papers, vol. 10, file 6.3.8, Shirley Chuter for Executive, AUFA, to J.M.R. Beveridge, 15 Oct. 1965; 'Disestablishment,' *Athenaeum*, 24 Sept. 1965; AAAU and Beveridge quoted in ibid.

95 AUA, Beveridge Papers, vol. 10, file 6.3.8, K.E. Spencer and H.A. Renfree to Pastors and People, 15 Sept. 1965, copy; Spencer and Renfree to Members of the Associated Alumni of Acadia University, 5 Oct. 1965, copy.
96 AUA, Beveridge Papers, vol. 10, Beveridge to Bruce Wallace, 6 Nov. 1965, copy; Kirkconnell to G.I. Smith, 21 Feb. 1966, copy; Beveridge to Lawrence E. Toombs, 1 Dec. 1965, copy; R.H. McNeill to Beveridge, 22 Nov. 1965.
97 Ibid., Acadia University, Board of Governors, Resolution [Nov. 1965].
98 Kirkconnell, *A Slice of Canada*, 169; AUA, Kirkconnell Papers, vol. 40, file P12/25.
99 AUA, Beveridge Papers, vol. 10, Kirkconnell to G.I. Smith, 21 Feb. 1966, copy.
100 Nova Scotia, *Statutes* (1966), ch. 112.
101 'Press Release, 19 Oct. 1965,' *CAUTB* 14, no. 2 (Jan. 1966), 2.
102 Simon Cardew, 'UBC Professor Says: "If There's a God, Prove It,"' *VS*, 20 Nov. 1962.
103 'God and Dr. Remnant,' *VS*, 27 Nov. 1962.
104 UBCA, BoG, Minutes, 27 Nov. 1962.
105 Ibid.
106 Interview with W.E. Mann, Toronto, Apr. 1994.
107 Ibid.
108 Jon Ruddy, 'What Happened to Canada's Kinsey?' *MM*, 1 Oct. 1966, 22.
109 Murray G. Ross, *The Way Must Be Tried*, 22–34.
110 William Christian, *George Grant: A Biography* (Toronto 1993), 122–7, 155; George P. Grant, 'Philosophy,' in *Royal Commission Studies: A Selection of Essays Prepared for the Royal Commission on National Development in the Arts, Letters and Sciences* (Ottawa 1951), 132.
111 Christian, *George Grant*, 203–4. In his memoirs, Murray Ross does not mention Grant.
112 Christian, *George Grant*, 206, 207, 209–10, 323ff.
113 Charles M. Johnston, *McMaster University*, vol. 2 (Toronto 1981), 172–99, 240–67.
114 Christian, *George Grant*, 223.

11: Freedom and Security: The Matter of Tenure

1 John Ralston Saul, *The Doubter's Companion: A Dictionary of Aggressive Common Sense* (Toronto 1994), 283.

2 Walter P. Metzger, 'Academic Tenure in America: A Historical Essay,' in *Faculty Tenure* (San Francisco 1973), 94. Unless noted otherwise, the material and quotations in the next few pages are from this source.

3 Gibbon, quoted in Robert Falconer, *Academic Freedom* (Toronto 1922), 4; Adam Smith, *An Inquiry into the Nature and Causes of the Wealth of Nations* [5th edn, 1789], ed. Edwin Cannan (New York 1937), 718.

4 'General Report of the Committee on Academic Freedom and Academic Tenure (1915),' *LCP* 53, no. 3 (Summer 1990), 405–6.

5 *Re Wilson*, 18 *Nova Scotia Reports* (Apr. 1885), 196.

6 UNBSC, Senate, Minutes, 10 Sept. 1860, 1 and 27 Mar. 1861.

7 *Ex Parte Jacob*, 10 *New Brunswick Reports* (1861), 162–3.

8 *Weir v. Mathieson*, 11 *Grant's Chancery Reports* (1865), 385–6, 387.

9 Ibid., 404–5.

10 *Weir v. Mathieson*, 3 *Grant's Error and Appeal Reports* (1866), 123.

11 Ibid., 152, 162, 163.

12 Hilda Neatby, *Queen's University*, vol. 1 (Montreal 1978), 178; MUA, RG2, PO, c.90/2550, R. Bruce Taylor to Frank Adams, 31 May 1920.

13 *Re Wilson*, 18 *Nova Scotia Reports* (Apr. 1885), 189, 196.

14 KCA, King's College, BoG, Minutes, vol. 6, 23 Apr. and 9 July 1885; Henry Roper to the author, 4 May 1996.

15 *In re The University Act*, 2 *Western Weekly Reports* (1920), 824, 826, 829, 831.

16 Daniel A. Soberman, 'Tenure in Canadian Universities,' *CAUTB* 13, no. 3 (Mar. 1965), 19.

17 *Smith v. Wesley College*, 3 *Western Weekly Reports* (1923), 213, 201, 202.

18 Soberman, 'Tenure in Canadian Universities,' 6; 'General Report of the Committee on Academic Freedom and Academic Tenure (1915),' in *LCP* 53, no. 3 (Summer 1990), 396, 405; USA, PP I B121/5, clipping from *SP*, 18 Aug. 1919.

19 G.H.L. Fridman, 'Judicial Intervention into University Affairs,' *Chitty's Law Journal* 21, no. 6 (June 1973), 186.

20 Conrad Russell, *Academic Freedom* (London and New York 1993), 26; Michael S. McPherson and Gordon C. Winston, 'The Economics of Academic Tenure: A Relational Prespective,' in Matthew W. Finkin, ed., *The Case for Tenure* (Ithaca, N.Y. and London 1996), 101, 104.

21 UTA, PO (Falconer), A72-0033/001, Falconer to J. Craig, 11 Mar. 1915, copy.

22 Ibid., A67-0007/59A, Falconer to J.D. MacLean, 2 Jan. 1919, copy.

23 Ibid., A72-0033/001, Falconer to Craig, 26 June 1920, copy; Craig to Falconer, 28 June 1920; Falconer to Craig, 30 June 1920, copy.

24 Ibid., Craig to Falconer, 14 Oct. 1920.

25 Ibid., The Carnegie Foundation for the Advancement of Teaching, *Rules for the Admission of Institutions and for the Granting of Retiring Allowances*, 1918.

26 Ibid., Falconer to employees, 1 Feb. 1919, copy attached to Falconer to Craig, 30 Oct. 1920, copy; Craig to Falconer, 4 Nov. 1920; F.A. Mouré to Craig, 26 Mar. 1921, copy.

27 Ibid., Craig to Falconer, 1 Feb. 1922, copy; A70-0024/11, BoG, Minutes, 9 Feb. 1922, 11 May, 13 July 1922; PO, A72-0033/001, Mouré to Craig, 10 Feb. 1922, copy; Craig to Falconer, 22 Feb. 1922; E. Bayly to Chairman, Board of Governors, 24 June 1922, copy; Statement of Claim, 1 Sept. 1922.

28 UTA, PO A72-0033/001, Statement of Defence, 23 Sept. 1922; *Craig v. Governors of the University of Toronto*, 53 *Ontario Law Reports* (1923), 319–22 passim. On the doctrine of mutuality, see Metzger, 'Academic Tenure in America,' 134; Clark Byse and Louis Joughin, *Tenure in American Higher Education* (New York 1959), 93.

29 NA, MG30, D204, F.H. Underhill Papers, vol. 6, Leopold Macaulay to Underhill, 6 Jan. 1941.

30 UBCA, PO, mfm reel 33, Gen. Corr., file Re 57 Special, R.L. Reid to L.S. Klinck, 23 Feb. 1932.

31 UBCA, BoG, Minutes, vol. 11, 25 July 1932; PO, mfm reel 33, Gen. Corr., file Ow 52 Special, Eivion Owen to Klinck, 6 Aug. 1932.

32 PABC, GR1222, British Columbia, Premier, vol. 120, H.M. Cassidy to S.F. Tolmie, 24 Feb. 1932.

33 UBCA, BoG, Minutes, vol. 1, 15 Dec. 1913; vol. 5, 4 Feb. 1920; vol. 13, 24 Sept. 1934; vol. 19, 26 Feb. 1940. Also interview with Robert M. Clark, Vancouver, Apr. 1987.

34 UBCA, Faculty Association Records, D IV 2/4, vol. 1, folders 4–7; folder 9, Finance Committee, Minutes, 4 Feb. 1948; Executive Committee, Minutes, 8 Mar. 1948. See also William A. Bruneau, *A Matter of Identities* (Vancouver 1990), passim; UBCA, PO, mfm reel 108, file C14 sp., N.A.M. MacKenzie to Board of Governors and Senate, 4 Jan. 1949, copy.

35 UBCA, BoG, Minutes, vol. 28, 28 Feb. 1949; Faculty Association Records, D IV 2/4, vol. 2, folder 11, Executive Committee, Minutes, 23 Mar. 1950. See also University of British Columbia, *The Faculty Handbook* (Vancouver 1960), 3, 5.

36 University of British Columbia, *Faculty Handbook* (Vancouver 1962), 16–20 passim.

37 British Columbia, *Statutes, An Act Respecting Universities*, 11–12 Elizabeth II, 1963, ch. 52, ss. 46(d) and 57(a).

38 AUA, BoG Executive Committee, Minutes, 30 July 1930, undated [1933] and 15 Feb. 1934; W.L. Morton, *One University* (Toronto 1957), 148–51, 153–4; UMA, BoG, Minutes, 25 Aug. 1932, 30 May and 10 Aug. 1933.

39 UMA, BoG, Minutes, 30 Jan. 1934.

40 Ibid., 15 Mar. 1934.

41 Ibid., 10 Oct. 1934; UMA, UA/20, PP, vol. 8, *The University of Manitoba Act, R.S.M.*, 1940, ch. 224; Morton, *One University*, 164.

42 UMA, UA/14, Office of the Comptroller, vol. 43, Minutes, Staff Committee, 18 Apr. and 9 May 1952.

43 UMA, UA/20, PP, vol. 167, file 9, Hugh H. Saunderson, 'Academic Tenure,' 20 Jan. 1959.

44 UAA, BoG, Executive Committee, Minutes, 7 Jan. 1942; RG19, Personnel files, 81-37-1167, Robert Newton, 'John Reymes-King,' 17 Jan. 1948, 24.

45 McGill University, 'Statutes, ch. VI,' *Extracts from the Will of the Founder; Royal Charters; Acts of Parliament; Statutes* (Montreal 1883).

46 MUA, RG2, PO, c.90/2550, R. Bruce Taylor to Frank Adams, 31 May 1920.

47 Regulations, 1920, reprinted in McGill University, *Annual Report, 1932–33* (Montreal 1933), 23.

48 MUA, BoG, Minutes, 3 Oct. 1921.

49 MUA, RG2, PO, c.61/1007, Charles M. Cotton to Currie, 30 Mar. 1922; Currie to Gordon J. Laing, 31 Mar. 1922, copy; Hermann Walter to Currie, 4 Apr. 1922; Currie, 'Memorandum for Finance Committee, 5 Apr. 1922.'

50 MUA, BoG, Minutes, 1 May 1922 and 29 Jan. 1923; PO, RG2, c.61/1007, Currie to Gregor Barclay, 3 Jan. 1923 (copy). See also Andrew Collard, ed., *The McGill You Knew: An Anthology of Memories, 1920–1960* (Toronto 1975), 68–9.

51 MUA, RG2, PO, c.55/779, Currie to W.J. Spence, 1 Aug. 1933, copy.

52 Ibid., Currie to Joseph S. Ames, 25 Apr. 1933, copy; McGill University, *Annual Report, 1932–33* (Montreal 1933), 22.

53 MUA, RG2, PO, c.43/301, Stephen Leacock to Currie, 13 May 1933.

54 Ibid., c.55/779, Dorothy McMurray to E.W. Beatty, 7 June 1934, copy.

55 MUA, BoG, Minutes, 7 June 1935; 'Changes at Old McGill,' *Montreal Herald*, 19 Dec. 1935.

56 Robertson Davies, 'Stephen Leacock,' in C.T. Bissell, ed., *Our Living Tradition: Seven Canadians* (Toronto 1957), 131; Stephen Leacock, 'Academic Freedom,' *MM*, 1 Feb. 1936, 38–9.

57 MUA, RG2, PO, c.90/2550, 'Summary of Replies from Deans re Tenure of Appointment' [1938], and attached letters; 'Statement of Policy Governing Tenure of Appointment for All Grades Under the Rank of Professor,' 25 Feb. 1939; c.54/730, Douglas to Beatty, 3 Feb. and 23 Nov. 1939, copies.

58 P.B. Waite to the author, 13 Apr. 1996.

59 DUA, MS1-1-A10, BoG, Minutes 1941–45, Executive Committee, 22 Aug. 1944. See also meeting of 21 Mar. 1944.

60 Ibid., MS1-1-A12, Minutes 1950–53, 15 Apr. 1952.

61 DUA, PO, MS1-3-A485, vol. 16, K.C. Laurie to the Board Members of the Board-Senate Committee, 9 July 1952, copy, and attachment.

62 Ibid., MS1-3-53-B4, Report of the Committee on Appointments, Promotion and Tenure, 15 Mar. 1954, passim.
63 Ibid., MS1-3-53-B4, untitled, undated statement, 8 pages; MS1-1-A13, BoG, Minutes 1953–56, Executive Committee, 14 Mar. 1955; PANS, Dalhousie Faculty Association Papers, MG17/108/32, Regulations Concerning Academic Appointments and Tenure, 1956.
64 DUA, Senate, Minute Book 1943–1968, 6 Dec. 1955; P.B. Waite, *The Lives of Dalhousie University*, vol. 2 (Montreal and Kingston 1998), 199.
65 Fowke-Laskin Report, *CAUTB* 7, no. 3 (Jan. 1959), 40.
66 'Principles of Academic Freedom and Tenure,' *CAUTB* 8, no. 3 (Feb. 1960), 16.
67 'Tenure and Tenacity: An Editorial,' *CAUTB* 11, no. 3 (Dec. 1962), 2. The book was W.H.C. Eddy's *Orr*.
68 Bora Laskin, 'Some Cases at Law,' in George Whalley, ed., *A Place of Liberty* Toronto and Vancouver 1964), 177.
69 Bora Laskin and J. Percy Smith, 'The CAUT and Tenure: Two Editorials,' *CAUTB* 13, no. 3 (Mar. 1965), 2–3 passim.
70 Quoted in Daniel Soberman, 'Tenure in Canadian Universities,' *CAUTB* 13, no. 3 (Mar. 1965), 6.
71 Soberman, passim.
72 Daniel Soberman to the author, 9 Apr. 1997.
73 H.W. Arthurs, 'Standards, Size, and Security of Tenure,' *CAUTB* 13, no. 3 (Mar. 1965), 84–7 passim.
74 J.B. Milner, untitled essay, *CAUTB* 13, no. 3 (Mar. 1965), 87–90 passim; David J. Mullan to the author, 28 May 1996.
75 'La stabilité d'emploi des professeurs d'universités de la province de Québec,' *CAUTB* 14, no. 3 (Feb. 1966), 4, 6 ('In short, their contracts would seem to be for an indeterminate period ..., but they would seem to be entitled to three months' notice should the employer wish to terminate their contracts, since their appointment is normally for a year').
76 James Duff and Robert O. Berdahl, *University Government in Canada* (Toronto 1966), 36.
77 William H. Nelson, *The Search for Faculty Power* (Toronto 1993), 33.
78 Michael Bliss, 'Anachronistic University Tenure Should Be Abolished,' *TS*, 28 July 1995.
79 'University Funds CAUBO's War on Faculty,' *CAUTB* 42, no. 8 (Oct. 1995).
80 'Questioning Tenure,' *TS*, 19 Aug. 1996.
81 Mark Kingwell, 'Absent Minded,' *THIS Magazine* 30, no. 4 (Jan.-Feb. 1997), 10.
82 David Bercuson, Robert Bothwell, and J.L. Granatstein, *Petrified Campus: The Crisis in Canada's Universities* (Toronto 1997), 125–52 passim. For yet another criticism of the drawbacks of tenure, see Christopher J. Lucas, *Crisis in*

the Academy: Rethinking Higher Education in America (New York 1996), 173–89.

83 Ramsay Cook, 'A Peace Proposal for the War of the Sexes,' *GM*, 10 May 1990; John Crispo, 'Tenure Vital to Academic Freedom,' *TS*, 2 Sept. 1996; Peter C.Emberley, *Zero Tolerance: Hot Button Politics in Canada's Universities* (Toronto 1996), 260; Jane Ormrod, *Tenure, Teaching Quality and Accountability*, prepared for the Ontario Undergraduate Student Alliance, Oct. 1996, 19–22.

84 Russell, *Academic Freedom*, 23–7; Matthew W. Finkin, 'Introduction,' *The Case for Tenure*, 1.

85 *McKinney v. University of Guelph* 3 *Supreme Court Reports* (1990), 229.

86 Cynthia Hardy, *The Politics of Collegiality: Retrenchment Strategies in Canadian Universities* (Montreal and Kingston 1996), 91–4; E. Peter Fitzgerald, 'A Cautionary Tale from Carleton University,' *CAUTB* 45, no. 1 (Jan. 1998).

87 Quoted in *The Oxford Dictionary of Quotations*, 4th edn (Oxford and New York 1992), 202.

12: Postscript: Academic Freedom since 1965

1 'Policy Statement on Academic Appointments and Tenure,' *CAUTB*, 16, no. 3 (Feb. 1968), 7.

2 Bill Readings, *The University in Ruins* (Cambridge, Mass. and London 1996).

3 *Financing Higher Education in Canada: Being the Report of a Commission to the Association of Universities and Colleges of Canada* (Toronto 1965), 68; Richard Simeon, *Federal-Provincial Diplomacy: The Making of Recent Policy in Canada* (Toronto 1972), 71–85, 281–2.

4 W.L. Morton, *The Kingdom of Canada: A General History from Earliest Times*, 2nd edn (Toronto 1969), 551.

5 'Is a University a Government Spending Department?' *UA* 9, no. 2 (Dec. 1967); Michael Hayden, *Seeking a Balance* (Vancouver 1983), 254–6; Paul Axelrod, *Scholars and Dollars: Politics, Economics, and the Universities of Ontario, 1945–1980* (Toronto 1982), 141–213; 'The Nova Scotia Experience: How Not to Rationalize the Universities,' *CAUTB* 44, no. 8 (Oct. 1997).

6 René Hurtubise and Donald C. Rowat, *The University, Society and Government: The Report of the Commission on the Relations Between Universities and Governments* (Ottawa 1970), passim.

7 'Guidelines on University Organization,' *UA* 11, no. 3 (Apr. 1970).

8 Ibid., [18].

9 Bruce Dunlop, 'Guidelines on Appointments and Tenure: The C.A.U.T.'s or the A.U.C.C.'s,' *CAUTB* 19 no. 4 (Summer 1971), passim.

10 'Report on Simon Fraser University ...,' *CAUTB* 16, no. 4 (Apr. 1968).

11 J. Percy Smith, 'Faculty Power and Simon Fraser,' *CF* 48 (Sept. 1968); 'Developments at Simon Fraser University,' *CAUTB* 17, no. 1 (Oct. 1968), 24.

12 'Removal of Censure of Simon Fraser University,' *CAUTB* 17, no. 2 (Dec. 1968). See Gordon Shrum, *An Autobiography*, with Peter Stursberg, ed. Clive Cocking (Vancouver 1986), 119 and passim.

13 J.B. Milner, 'The Strax Affair,' *CAUTB* 17, no. 3 (Feb. 1969), 38 and passim; Alwyn Berland, 'The Strax Case at U.N.B.,' *CAUTB* 17, no. 4 (Apr. 1969); E.J. Monahan, 'The Strax Case,' *CAUTB* 18, no. 1 (Oct. 1969).

14 Stanley Brice Frost, *McGill University*, vol. 2 (Kingston and Montreal 1984), 452–62; Ronald Lebel, 'Board Dismisses McGill Lecturer, Recommends Year's Compensation,' *GM*, 19 Aug. 1969.

15 'Fair Warning,' *VS*, 26 Sept. 1969; J.B. Dunlop, 'Academic Freedom and Tenure Committee Chairman's Report,' *CAUTB* 18, no. 4 (Summer 1970); telephone conversation with A.E. Malloch, July 1996.

16 Douglas Sagi, 'Committee Takes Over SFU Department,' *GM*, 19 July 1969; Alwyn Berland, 'Report on the Simon Fraser University Dispute,' *CAUTB* 18, no. 2 (Winter 1970); Douglas L. Cole to the author, 13 Aug. 1996; Martin Loney to the author, 5 Nov. 1997.

17 *Wheeldon v. Simon Fraser University*, 15 *Dominion Law Reports* (3rd), 645; 'Simon Fraser University,' *CAUTB* 19, no. 1 (Autumn 1970), 60.

18 'Arbitration at SFU: The Popkin Case,' *CAUTB* 19, no. 2 (Winter 1971), 28.

19 'The Palmer Committee Report,' *CAUTB* 19, no. 1 (Autumn 1970), 73–4. See also David Braybrooke, 'The Logical Character of Verdicts: A Case Study,' *University of Toronto Law Journal* 22 (1972).

20 'C.A.U.T. Motion concerning Simon Fraser University,' *CAUTB* 19, no. 4 (Summer 1971), 60; 'Simon Fraser University: Professor Prudence Wheeldon Dismissal Hearing Report,' *CAUTB* 20, no. 1 (Autumn 1971), 63, 68–9; *VS*, 19 June 1971.

21 'Simon Fraser Motion,' *CAUTB* 20, no. 2 (Winter 1972), 63; Douglas L. Cole to the author, 13 Aug. 1996; 'Simon Fraser, Mount Allison, Ottawa Censures Lifted,' *CAUTB* 25, no. 4 (Sept. 1977). The assessment of the mood at the 1977 meeting, which I attended, is mine.

22 'CAUT Policy Statement on Probationary Appointments,' *CAUTB* 18, no. 4 (Summer 1970), 66; Edward J. Monahan, 'Academic Freedom and Tenure and the CAUT: The First Twenty Years,' ibid., 90; 'Censure of Mount Allison University' and 'Censure de l'Université du Québec,' *CAUTB* 19, no. 2 (Winter 1971); 'CAUT Censure of the President of the University of Victoria' and 'Three Cases at the University of Victoria,' *CAUTB* 19, no. 4 (Summer 1971).

23 'Report on Simon Fraser University, III,' *CAUTB* 20, no. 2 (Winter 1972), 96–7.

24 Alwyn Berland, 'On the Present State of Academic Freedom,' *CAUTB* 18, no. 2 (Winter 1970), 5–11 passim.

25 A.E. Malloch, 'Committee on Academic Freedom and Tenure: Annual Report,' *CAUTB* 21, no. 1 (Oct. 1972), passim. See also Malloch, 'Academic Freedom and the Canadian Professor: Part II,' *CAUTB* 30, no. 1 (Feb. 1983); Malloch, 'Academic Freedom and Its Limits,' in Michiel Horn, ed., *Academic Freedom* (North York, Ont. 1987), 12–16.
26 Joan W. Scott, 'Academic Freedom as an Ethical Practice,' in Louis Menand, ed., *The Future of Academic Freedom* (Chicago 1996), 175.
27 Israel Cinman, 'CAUT Council Censures U of Ottawa,' *CAUTB* 21, no. 6 (June 1973).
28 'Committee of Enquiry Settles Dispute at McGill,' *CAUTB* 22, no. 2 (Nov. 1973).
29 Marlene Dixon, *Things Which Are Done in Secret* (Montreal 1976), 273–81.
30 Marlene Webber, 'Comment,' *Chevron* (21 Nov. 1975); Helen Baxter, 'CAUT Board Votes to Censure Memorial,' *CAUTB* 25, no. 11 (Dec. 1978); Baxter, 'The Webber Case at Memorial University,' *CAUTB* 26, no. 4 (Sept. 1979).
31 'The Abounda [*sic*] Case at the University of Calgary' and 'The McClelland Case at the University of Windsor,' *CAUTB* 26, no. 4 (Sept. 1979); Cinman, 'CAUT Council Censures U of Ottawa,' *CAUTB* 21, no. 6 (June 1973).
32 'Canadian Union of Students Condemns "Corporate" Universities,' *UA* 10, no. 2 (Oct. 1968), 16; Tim and Julyan Reid, *Student Power and the Canadian Campus* (Toronto 1969), esp. 1–27. See also Jack Quarter, *The Student Movement of the 60's: A Social-Psychological Analysis* (Toronto 1972).
33 Herbert Marcuse, 'Repressive Tolerance,' in Robert Paul Wolff, Barrington Moore, Jr, and Marcuse, *A Critique of Pure Tolerance* (Boston 1965).
34 Claude Bissell, 'Academic Freedom: The Student Version,' *QQ* 76, no. 2 (Summer 1969), passim.
35 Claude Bissell, *Halfway up Parnassus* (Toronto 1974), 141–3; Bissell, 'Academic Freedom: The Student Version,' 183.
36 C.B. Macpherson, 'The Violent Society and the Liberal,' *CAUTB* 18, no. 1 (Oct. 1969), passim.
37 'If Detachment Goes Freedom Goes Too – Sirluck,' *UA* 11, no. 1 (Jan. 1970), 6.
38 Alvin Finkel, article in the *Manitoban*, 28 Oct. 1969, reprinted in *UA* 11, no. 2 (Feb. 1970), 21–2; Frost, *McGill University*, vol. 2, 463; Bissell, *Halfway up Parnassus*, 147; Cyril Levitt, *Children of Privilege: Student Revolt in the Sixties* (Toronto 1984), 50–3.
39 Richard Hofstadter and Walter P. Metzger, *The Development of Academic Freedom in the United States* (New York 1955), 386, 387.
40 'General Report of the Committee on Academic Freedom and Tenure (1915),' *LCP* 53, no. 3 (Summer 1990), 393; Howard Woodhouse, 'Northrop Frye on Academic Freedom: A Critique,' *IC* 23, nos. 1–2 (1992). See also Sidney Hook, *Academic Freedom and Academic Anarchy* (New York 1970), 44–5.

41 'Undergraduate Freedom,' *UV*, 3 Mar. 1883.

42 Stephen Leacock, 'Academic Freedom,' *MM*, 1 Feb. 1936, 14–15.

43 Christopher K. Knapper, 'Teaching Evaluation and Academic Freedom,' in Knapper, George L. Geis, Charles E. Pascal, and Bruce M. Shore, eds., *If Teaching Is Important: The Evaluation of Instruction in Higher Education* (Toronto and Vancouver 1977), 200, 201.

44 Peter Seldin, *Changing Practices in Faculty Evaluation: A Critical Assessment and Recommendations for Improvement* (San Francisco 1984), 134; John Damron, 'Instructor Personality and the Politics of the Classroom,' ftp://ftp.csd.uwm.edu/pub/Psychology ... -of-instructor-evaluation-damron, 1996; Robert E. Haskell, 'Academic Freedom, Tenure, and Student Evaluation of Faculty: Galloping Polls in the 21st Century,' *Education Policy Analysis Archives* 5, no. 6 (Feb. 1997), http://olam.ed.asu.edu/epaa/v5n6.html; telephone conversation with Walter Whiteley (York University Faculty Association), Apr. 1998.

45 UAA, AASUA Papers, 73–162, AASUA/2, file 12, ATSUA Minutes, 29 Mar. and 11 May 1945; QUA, c.1042, F.A. Knox Papers, vol. 17, R.M. Clark to W.J. Waines, 20 Apr. 1951, copy, attached to Clark to F.A. Knox, 27 Apr. 1951; W.L. Morton, 'Scholar and Administrator,' in George Whalley, ed., *A Place of Liberty* (Toronto and Vancouver 1964), 99.

46 Albert J. Robinson, 'Would Collective Bargaining Increase Academic Salaries?' *CAUTB* 16, no 4. (Apr. 1968), 74.

47 Quoted in Axelrod, *Scholars and Dollars*, 147.

48 Ibid., 147–50; Committee of Presidents of Universities of Ontario, Subcommittee on Research and Planning, *Towards 2000: The Future of Post-Secondary Education in Ontario* (Toronto 1971), 25.

49 Donald C. Savage, 'Report from the Executive Secretary,' *CAUTB* 22, no. 6 (June 1974); 'Collective Bargaining: Special Report,' *CAUTB*, 23 no. 1 (Sept. 1974).

50 D.C. Savage, 'How and Why the CAUT Became Involved in Collective Bargaining, *IC* 25, no. 1 (Jan. 1994), 57–8.

51 J. Gordin Kaplan, 'Faculty Power and Some of Its Consequences,' *CAUTB* 19, no. 4 (Summer 1971), 27–9.

52 Charles Bigelow, 'Report on Behalf of the Collective Bargaining Committee,' *CAUTB* 22 no. 6 (June 1974), 38.

53 David M. Cameron, 'Academic Freedom and the Canadian University,' *AUCC Research File* 1, no. 3 (Mar. 1996), 7–8.

54 David M. Cameron to the author, 23 Sept. 1996. See also Cameron, *More Than an Academic Question: Universities, Government, and Public Policy in Canada* (Halifax 1991), 380–2.

55 Peter Larson, 'Reward Systems Don't Work,' *OC*, 19 July 1997; Michael Skolnik, 'Merit by Numbers,' *UTB*, 5 Jan. 1998.

56 David Braybrooke, 'Tenure: Illusion and Reality,' quoted in Janet Scarfe and Edward Sheffield, 'Notes on the Canadian Professoriate,' *Higher Education* 6 (1977), 345; Desmond Morton, 'Canadian Universities and Colleges: After the Power Trip, Priorities,' in Hugh A. Stevenson and J. Donald Wilson, eds., *Precepts, Policy and Process: Perspectives on Contemporary Canadian Education* (London, Ont. 1977), 190.

57 See Burton R. Clark, 'The Fragmentation of Research, Teaching, and Study: An Explorative Essay,' in Martin Trow and Thorsten Nybom, eds., *University and Society: Essays on the Social Role of Research and Higher Education* (London 1991).

58 Sandra Djwa, *The Politics of the Imagination* (Toronto 1987), 222.

59 Lorna Weir, 'PC Then and Now: Resignifying Political Correctness,' in Stephen Richer and Lorna Weir, eds., *Beyond Political Correctness: Toward the Inclusive University* (Toronto 1995), 58.

60 For samples of the attack on PC, see Richard Bernstein, 'The Rising Hegemony of the Politically Correct,' *NYT,* 28 Oct. 1990; Dinesh D'Souza, *Illiberal Education: The Politics of Race and Sex on Campus* (New York 1991); Kevin Doyle, 'The Evil of the Nons,' and Tom Fennell, 'The Silencers,' *MM,* 27 May 1991.

61 Mark Kingwell, 'Enter the Campus Thought Police,' *GM,* 15 (April 1991; Rick Salutin, 'Loose Canons,' *SN* (Dec. 1991), 20; Russell Jacoby, *Dogmatic Wisdom: How the Culture Wars Divert Education and Distract America* (New York 1994), esp. 1–28, 51–7.

62 Thomas L. Haskell, 'Justifying the Rights of Academic Freedom in the Era of "Power/Knowledge,"' in Menand, ed., *The Future of Academic Freedom* , 72–83. See also Stanley Fish, *There's No Such Thing as Free Speech and It's a Good Thing, Too* (New York 1994).

63 Janice Drakich, Marilyn Taylor, and Jennifer Bankier, 'Academic Freedom *Is* the Inclusive University,' in Richer and Weir, eds., *Beyond Political Correctness*, 120–7 passim.

64 M. Patricia Marchak, *Racism, Sexism, and the University: The Political Science Affair at the University of British Columbia* (Montreal and Kingston 1996), 146.

65 Cannie Stark-Adamec, 'Sexism in Research: The Limits of Academic Freedom,' Gender, Science and Medicine Conference, Toronto, 2 Nov. 1990.

66 On Freeman, see Peter C. Emberley, *Zero Tolerance* (Toronto 1996), 76–7; on Rushton and Yaqzan, see John Fekete, *Moral Panic: Biopolitics Rising* (Montreal and Toronto 1994), 214–16, 248–54.

67 Fekete, *Moral Panic*, 210–11.

68 David Stafford to the author, 22 July 1992; italicized words underlined in the original.

69 Thomas Walkom, 'A Life Preserver for Academics in Hot Water,' *TS*, 25 Oct. 1997.

70 See articles by John Furedy and Jeffrey Shallit in *SAFS Newsletter* 19 (April 1998), 4.

71 Ontario, Ministry of Education and Training, *Framework regarding Harassment and Discrimination in Ontario Universities and Colleges* (Toronto 1993), 3.

72 Emberley, *Zero Tolerance*, 240.

73 Sandra Martin, 'Why Can't our Universities Make Their Sexual-Harassment Policies Work?' *GM*, 21 June 1997; Kay Stockholder, 'Trouble on the Harassment Watch,' *GM*, 18 July 1997; Margaret Wente, 'Campus Life in the Nineties,' *GM*, 22 Nov. 1997; Fekete, *Moral Panic*, 231.

74 John Furedy, 'Academic Freedom versus the Velvet Totalitarian Culture of Comfort on Current Canadian Campuses: Some Fundamental Terms and Distinctions,' *IC* 28, no. 4 (1997). For a contrary opinion, see Fred Wilson, 'In Defence of Speech Codes,' *IC* 27, no. 2 (1996).

75 Marchak, *Racism, Sexism, and the University*, esp. 34–72.

76 Quoted in Nat Hentoff, *Free Speech for Me – But Not for Thee: How the American Left and Right Relentlessly Censor Each Other* (New York 1992), 152.

77 J. Mark Langdon, 'UBC's Chair of Sikh Studies Stands Firm for Academic Freedom,' *CAUTB* 41, no. 7 (Sept. 1994).

78 Robert Matas, 'Under Fire, Sikh Retreats from UBC Post,' *GM*, 18 July 1996.

79 H.T. Wilson, *No Ivory Tower: Neoconservatism and the Impending Transformation of Higher Education in Canada* (Toronto 1998), passim. I am grateful to Prof. Wilson for lending me a pre-publication copy of his ms.

80 Judith Maxwell and Stephanie Currie, *Partnership for Growth: Corporate-University Cooperation in Canada* (Montreal 1984), v, vi. Unless otherwise noted, quotations in the next few paragraps are from pp. 1–4 of this document.

81 Thorstein Veblen, *The Higher Learning in America: A Memorandum on the Conduct of Universities by Business Men* (New York 1965 [1918]), 48.

82 Gloria Pierre, 'Partnership for Growth,' *UA* 25, no. 6 (June–July 1984), 5; Janice Newson and Howard Buchbinder, 'Corporation, Cooperation, Co-optation,' *CAUTB* 32, no. 2 (Apr. 1985).

83 Robert G. Weyant, 'Corporate-University Interaction ...,' *UA* 27, no. 1 (Jan. 1986).

84 Canadian Manufacturers' Association, *The Importance of Post-Secondary Education: Keeping Canada Competitive*, Strategy Paper, April 1987, passim.

85 Douglas Auld, *Expanding Horizons: Privatizing Universities* (Toronto 1996), 42 and passim.

86 Toronto Board of Trade, *Beyond the Status Quo: A Business Perspective on Enhancing Postsecondary Education* (Toronto, Feb. 1998), 7.

87 Ibid., 30. See also Jennifer Lewington, 'Johnson Encourages Colleges to Specialize,' *GM*, 15 Apr. 1998.

88 John Ralston Saul, *The Unconscious Civilization* (Concord, Ont. 1995), 27, 173.

89 See, for example, Bruce Rolston, 'Commitment to Academic Freedom Reaffirmed,' *UTB*, 8 Dec. 1997; Rolston, 'Gift Guidelines Brought Forward,' *UTB*, 6 Apr. 1998.

90 Tanya Talaga, 'A New Degree of Raising Funds,' *TS*, 5 Apr. 1998; Veblen, *The Higher Learning in America*, 15.

91 An account of the historical background and course of the dispute may be found in the judgment by Mr Justice J.C. Macpherson in *Daishowa Inc. v. Friends of the Lubicon et al.*, 14 Apr. 1998, Court File no. 95-CQ-59707, Ontario Court of Justice (General Division); Christopher Genovali, 'Daishowa Tries to Gag Critics,' *Alternatives Journal* 23, no. 2 (Spring 1997), 12. See also 'Logger Bows to Band, Lubicon Lift Boycott,' *GM*, 13 June 1998.

92 Chris Tollefson to Rod Symington and the UVic Local CAUT Executive [*sic*], 13 Sept. 1996, copy. This and other documents referred to were supplied to me by Professor Tollefson.

93 Chris Tollefson, 'Strategic Lawsuits against Public Participation: Developing a Canadian Response,' *Canadian Bar Review* 73 no. 2 (June 1994); Tollefson, 'Strategic Lawsuits and Environmental Policies: Daishowa Inc. v Friends of the Lubicon,' *JCS* 31, no. 1 (Spring 1996), 121.

94 Ibid.

95 Tollefson to Symington and Executive, 28 Jan. 1997, copy; Symington to Tollefson, 18 Feb. 1997, copy; Symington to P. Codding, 18 Feb. 1997, copy.

96 Tollefson to Lyman Robinson, 6 June 1997, copy; Tollefson to the author, 4 June 1998.

97 See Shirley Neuman, 'Redesigning the Ruins,' *UTQ* 66, no. 4 (Fall 1997).

98 Robert G. Weyant, 'Corporate-University Interaction ...,' *UA* 27, no. 1 (Jan. 1986), 15.

99 Silver Donald Cameron, 'Why Aren't Heads Rolling?' *GM*, 20 Jan. 1998; Michael Harris, *Lament for an Ocean: The Collapse of the Atlantic Cod Fishery* (Toronto 1998), 289–313.

100 Tim Barton, 'Sessionals Treated as "Second-Class Citizens" Studies Show,' *CAUTB* 30, no. 1 (Feb. 1983).

101 Veblen, *The Higher Learning in America*, 116.

102 F.X. Charet, 'A Journey through Higher Education,' *UA*, 39, no. 3, Mar. 1998, 13.

103 See Howard Buchbinder and Janice Newson, *The University Means Business: Universities, Corporations and Academic Work* (Toronto 1988). For an issue that has arisen at the university at which Buchbinder and Newson work, see Naomi Klein, 'York Adventure with Private Firms Raises Questions,' *TS*, 23 June 1997.

104 H.W. Arthurs, Roger Blais, and Jon Thompson, 'Integrity in Scholarship: A Report to Concordia University,' 1994. See also 'Crisis at Concordia: Research Ethics,' *CAUTB* 41, no. 7 (Sept. 1994).

105 Doug Saunders, 'Sophisticated Rules Needed for Protection of Ideas,' *GM*, 4 Dec. 1995. See also Alan Cassels, 'Epidemics for Rich and Poor,' *GM*, 21 Feb. 1998.

106 Russell, *Academic Freedom*, 79–80; Paul Taylor, 'A Doctor Takes On a Drug Com-

pany,' *GM*,13 Aug. 1998; 'Investigator's Disclosure Fuels Ethics Debate,' *CAUTB* 45, no. 7 (Sept. 1998); Michael Valpy, 'Salvage Group Tackles Sick Kids' Image Disaster,' *GM*, 2 Nov. 1998.

107 John C. Polanyi, 'Understanding Discovery,' in Martin Moskovits, ed., *Science and Society* (Concord, Ont. 1995), 7–8.

108 Doug Saunders, 'Fruits of Academe Are Golden for Some,' *GM*, 4 Dec. 1995; John C. Polanyi, letter to the editor, *GM*, 7 Dec. 1995.

109 *Striking the Balance: A Five-Year Strategy for the Social Sciences and Humanities Research Council of Canada, 1996–2001*, (Ottawa 1996); 'CAUT Objects to New Research Code,' *CAUTB* 43, no. 7 (Sept. 1996); Board of Directors of the Society for Academic Freedom and Scholarship to the Presidents of the Medical Research Council, Natural Sciences and Engineering Research Council, and Social Sciences and Humanities Research Council, 6 June 1997, copy; *SAFS Newsletter*, no. 18, Feb. 1998; Rhoda Howard to Nina Stipich, 20 Feb. 1998, copy; Patrick O'Neill, 'Problematic Expansion of Ethical Concerns in Research,' Academic Issues Conference, Toronto, June 1998.

110 Quoted in Emberley, *Zero Tolerance*, 79.

111 Morton, 'Canadian Universities and Colleges ...,' in Stevenson and Wilson, eds., *Precepts, Policy and Process*, 189; Jennifer Lewington, 'Massive Overhaul in Store for Postsecondary Schools,' *GM*, 10 Feb. 1996; conversation with Lorna Marsden, Toronto, May 1998; Russell, *Academic Freedom*, 106.

112 Andrew Coyne, 'The Case for Blowing Up Our Ivory Towers,' *GM*, 4 May 1996.

113 James Traub, 'Drive-Thru U.,' *New Yorker*, 20 and 27 Oct. 1997.

114 See Edward S. Herman and Noam Chomsky, *Manufacturing Consent: The Political Economy of the Mass Media* (New York 1988); Robert W. McChesney, *Corporate Media and the Threat to Democracy* (New York 1997); Herman and McChesney, *The Global Media: The New Missionaries of Corporate Capitalism* (Washington, D.C., and London 1997), esp. 138–45. See also Brent Staples, 'Why Colleges Shower Their Students with A's,' *NYT*, 8 Mar. 1998.

115 William F. Buckley Jr, *God and Man at Yale: The Superstitions of 'Academic Freedom'* (Chicago 1951), 185.

116 Karl Polanyi, *The Great Transformation: The Political and Economic Origins of Our Time* (Boston 1957 [1944]), 249.

117 See, for example, George Soros, 'The Capitalist Threat,' *Atlantic Monthly* 279, no. 2 (Feb. 1997); Thomas Walkom, 'Canadians Begin Turning against Cuts,' *TS*, 5 Apr. 1997; David E. Sanger, 'Look Who's Carping Most about Capitalism,' *NYT*, 6 Apr. 1997; Dalton Camp, 'Opening a Dialogue on Today's Conservatism,' *TS*, 5 Nov. 1997; Bob Goudzwaard and Harry de Lange, *Beyond Poverty and Affluence: Towards a Canadian Economy of Care* (Toronto 1995), esp. 47–50; Hugh Segal,

Beyond Greed: A Traditional Conservative Confronts Neoconservative Excess (Toronto 1997), esp. 25–38.

118 William Thorsell, 'How to Encourage Universities to Play to Their Strengths,' *GM*, 25 Apr. 1998. On 'excellence,' see Bill Readings, *The University in Ruins*, 21–43 passim; Michiel Horn, 'Comments,' *UTQ* 66, no. 4 (Fall 1997), 634.

119 'New Zealand's Universities: Radical Reforms,' *CAUTB* 44, no. 7 (Sept 1997), 3. See 'World Bank Promotes Its Agenda in Paris,' *CAUTB* 45, no. 9 (Nov. 1998).

13: Conclusion

1 Russell Jacoby, *The Last Intellectuals: American Culture in the Age of Academe* (New York 1987), 119; Simcoe, quoted in S.R. Mealing, 'The Enthusiasms of John Graves Simcoe,' *CHA: Historical Papers* (1958), 61.

2 'The Business of Universities,' *GM*, 21 Nov. 1997.

3 C.B. Macpherson, 'The University as Multiple Fool,' *CAUTB* 19, no. 1 (Autumn 1970), 4.

4 Desmond Morton, 'Canadian Universities and Colleges ...,' in Hugh A. Stevenson and J. Donald Wilson, eds., *Precepts, Policy and Process* (London, Ont. 1977), 190.

5 Dalton Camp, 'Universities' Job Is to Challenge Cult of Marketability,' *TS*, 30 Nov. 1997.

6 Mel Watkins, 'Reflections in Retirement,' *UTB*, 4 May 1998, 12.

7 See also Richard T. De George, *Academic Freedom and Tenure: Ethical Issues* (Lanham, Md 1997).

Index